Die Orchideen von Zypern

The Orchids of Cyprus

Beschreibung, Lebensweise, Verbreitung, Gefährdung, Schutz und Ikonographie

Description, Pattern of Life, Distribution, Threat, Conservation and Iconography

C.A.J. Kreutz

Impressum

Kreutz C.A.J.

Die Orchideen von Zypern
(Beschreibung, Lebensweise, Verbreitung, Gefährdung, Schutz
und Ikonographie)

The Orchids of Cyprus
(Description, Pattern of Life, Distribution, Threat, Conservation and Iconography)

Mit Farbaufnahmen vom Autor und von / With colour pictures
from the author and from:
H. Arbirk (s. 362, 366 l.o.), Dr. Y. Christofides (s. 312 l.o.,
342 l.o.), N.A. van der Cingel (s. 80 l.u.), R. Constantinides
(s. 342, 343, 400, 402 l.o., 403), P. Delforge (s. 406 r.b.,
406 l.u., 406 r.u., 407 l.o., 407 r.u.), W. Errulat (s. 366
r.b.), J. Hubbard (s. 66 r., 67), C. Koch (s. 366 l.u.), Dr. H.
Kretzschmar (s. 176, 178 l.o., 178 l.u., 310, 312 l.u., 312 r.u.)
und Prof. Dr. H.F. Paulus (s. 58, 60, 415).

C.A.J. Kreutz, Landgraaf 2004

ISBN: 90-806626-3-1   NUGI: 824

Orchideen: Zypern
Orchids: Cyprus

Autor/Author: C.A.J. Kreutz, Landgraaf
Grafische Gestaltung/Layout: C.A.J. Kreutz, Landgraaf
Lithografien/Scans: ImageStudio, Nuth
Computersatz/Typeset: ImageStudio, Nuth
Druck/Printed: Spektra Druk b.v., Valkenburg aan de Geul

Printed in the Netherlands, Oktober 2004

© C.A.J. Kreutz, Landgraaf, NL
Website: http://www.kreutz.info

Umschlagbild / Front Cover
Ophrys kotschyi, Alethriko, 6.3.2002

Titelbild / Title Page:
Ophrys flavomarginata, Souni, 13.3.2002

Rückumschlagbild / Back Cover
Orchis xtochniana (*Orchis italica* x *Orchis punctulata*),
Tochni, 13.3.2002
Verbreitungskarte von *Ophrys kotschyi* (UTM-2 km Raster) /
Distribution map of *Ophrys kotschyi* (UTM-2 km Grid)

INHALTSVERZEICHNIS

CONTENTS

Epipactis veratrifolia, Pano Amiantos, 22.6.2002

Vorwort

Seit vielen Jahren beschäftigt sich der Autor mit den Orchideen Europas und des Vorderen Orients. Er hat in diesen Jahren auf zahlreichen Reisen fast alle Arten, Unterarten und Varietäten dieser schönen Pflanzenfamilie mit ihren wunderschönen und zum Teil geheimnisvollen Blüten an den natürlichen Fundorten aufgesucht, sie untersucht und fotografiert. Die Ergebnisse dieser Studien wurden in zahlreichen Artikeln in niederländischen und in deutschen botanischen Zeitschriften und in verschiedenen Büchern veröffentlicht. Dieses Buch befasst sich mit den Orchideen Zyperns, einer wunderschönen Insel mit vielen ostmediterranen und orientalischen Orchideenarten, von denen einige endemisch sind.

Zypern wurde wegen des Vorkommens vieler Orchideenarten auf engstem Raum und wegen der einfachen Erreichbarkeit schon immer gern von Botanikern und Orchideenliebhabern besucht. Ausserdem sind im Vergleich mit der nahe gelegenen Türkei die Fundorte auf Zypern fast immer individuenreich und sehr leicht zu erreichen. Vor allem im Süden der Insel gibt es noch immer recht individuenreiche Fundorte. Im Norden der Insel ist der Orchideenreichtum weniger ausgeprägt als im Süden. Die Orchideen sind hier seltener und schwächer verbreitet, weil es im Norden (mit Ausnahme der Pinienwälder im Pentadactylos-Gebirge und der Karpasia-Halbinsel) viele intensiv genutzte landwirtschaftliche Flächen und zahlreiche Militäranlagen gibt.

Wurden auf Zypern in früheren Jahren die meisten Fundorte im Norden der Insel, der heute türkisch ist, besucht, so hat sich in den letzten Jahren die Suche vor allem auf den griechische Teil im Süden der Insel verschoben. Dort sind aber in den letzten Jahren leider viele Fundorte als Folge verkehrstechnischer Erschliessung, Ausdehnung der Siedlungen, sowie Bau von großflächigen Hotelanlagen verschwunden.

Seit etwa 1975 wird Zypern verstärkt durch viele Orchideenfreunde und Botaniker besucht und intensiv kartiert. Darüber hinaus wohnen auf Zypern mehrere Orchideologen, wie YIANNIS CHRISTOFIDES, ROLANDOS CONSTANTINIDES, CHRISTOS GEORGIADES, JOAN HUBBARD, YURIY KULYEV und PAMELA SCRATON, die ganzjährig die Orchideen auf Zypern studieren und kartieren. Wie erwartet sind die Orchideen Zyperns dann auch besonders gut erforscht, aber trotzdem ist noch immer mit neuen Arten oder interessanten Funden zu rechnen, wie zum Beispiel die Beiträge von KREUTZ, SEGERS & WALRAVEN, 2002 (Neubeschreibung von *Ophrys alasiatica*) oder SCRATON, 2001 und KREUTZ & SCRATON, 2002 (Neufund von *Orchis caspia*) zeigen.

Zypern hat dem Orchideenliebhaber viel zu bieten, weil auf der Insel neben Macchien, Phrygana und Pinienwäldern mit ihrer typischen Mittelmeerflora, zwei andere wichtige floristische Gebiete vorhanden sind: einerseits die tief gelegenen, Salz beeinflussten Küstenareale mit vielen (z.T. endemischen) Orchideenarten und an-

Preface

For many years, the orchids of Europe and the Near East have been the author's special interest. On his many trips during these years he has been able to find, examine and photograph in their natural habitat most of the species, subspecies and varieties of this beautiful plant family with their exquisite and somewhat mysterious flowers. The results of these studies have been published in numerous articles in Dutch and German botanical journals. This book deals with the orchids of Cyprus, a beautiful island with many Eastern Mediterranean and oriental orchid species, some of which are endemic.

Because of the occurrence of many orchid species in a small area and their easy accessibility, Cyprus has always been a favourite destination of botanists and orchid enthusiasts. The Cyprus habitats are almost always very rich in individuals, in contrast to neighbouring Turkey. In the south of the island in particular, one can still find large individual-rich habitats. The numbers of orchids in the north of the island are less striking than in the south. There, the orchids are rarer, and more sparsely distributed, as there are many intensively used agricultural plains and numerous military complexes (except in the pine forests of the Pentadactylos Mountains and on the Karpasia peninsula).

While most visits to the habitats of Cyprus in the early years were to the north (the Turkish-occupied part), more recently the search area has been focused mainly on the southern (Greek) part of the island. In the last few years unfortunately, many habitats have been lost because of the development of roads, the growth of towns, and the construction of large-scale hotel complexes.

Since about 1975, Cyprus is being more frequently visited and intensively charted by many orchidophiles and botanists. Moreover, several orchidologists whose home is in Cyprus (by birth or adoption), such as YIANNIS CHRISTOFIDES, ROLANDOS CONSTANTINIDES, CHRISTOS GEORGIADES, JOAN HUBBARD, YURIY KULYEV and PAMELA SCRATON, study and chart orchids all year round. As might be expected therefore, the orchids of Cyprus have been thoroughly researched, but one can still discover new species or make interesting findings, as for example the following contributions show: KREUTZ, SEGERS & WALRAVEN, 2002 (Description of *Ophrys alasiatica*) or SCRATON, 2001 and KREUTZ & SCRATON, 2002 (new site of *Orchis caspia*).

Cyprus has much to offer to the orchidophile, because in addition to the maquis, phrygana and pine forests characterized by typical Mediterranean flora which exist on this island, two other important floral areas are also found here. We have on the one hand the low-lying saline-influenced coastal regions, with many (including en-

dererseits das höher gelegene Troodos-Gebirge und seine Randgebiete mit ihren mächtigen Schwarzkiefern (*Pinus nigra* subsp. *pallasiana*) und Zypern-Zedern (*Cedrus brevifolia*). Hier kommen seltene und überwiegend mitteleuropäische, beziehungsweise mediterrane Orchideenarten wie *Cephalanthera rubra, Dactylorhiza iberica, Epipactis condensata, Epipactis microphylla, Epipactis troodi, Epipactis veratrifolia, Limodorum abortivum* und *Platanthera holmboei* vor. Im Gegensatz zu Rhodos oder der Türkei ist die Bestimmung der meisten Arten auf Zypern unproblematisch, ja sogar einfach. Nur bei der Abgrenzung der Arten des *Ophrys sphegodes-mammosa* Formenkreises gibt es manchmal Bestimmungsprobleme. Mitglieder dieses Formenkreises waren bis vor 2002 meist schwierig zu bestimmen und wurden im Laufe der Zeit zu den verschiedensten Arten gestellt. Durch den Beitrag von Kreutz, Segers & Walraven (2002) wurden die Arten des *Ophrys sphegodes-mammosa* Formenkreises auf Zypern neu gegliedert und mit der Beschreibung von *Ophrys alasiatica* und der Neubeschreibung von *Ophrys morio* H.F. Paulus & Kreutz in diesem Buch weitgehend gelöst. Auf Zypern kommen 5 Arten aus dem *Ophrys sphegodes-mammosa* Komplex vor: *Ophrys alasiatica* (eine früh blühende Art mit großen, *Ophrys aesculapii*-ähnlichen Blüten), *Ophrys herae* (sieht auf Zypern wie eine mitteleuropäische *Ophrys sphegodes* aus, hat aber etwas größere Blüten, blüht schon ab Mitte Februar), *Ophrys hystera* (eine spät blühende und besonders hochwüchsige Art, mit großen, *Ophrys mammosa*-ähnlichen Blüten), *Ophrys mammosa* (auf Zypern meist mit schlankem Habitus) und *Ophrys morio* (bisher in Zypern als *Ophrys transhyrcana* bezeichnet). Die Pflanzen von Zypern sind nicht identisch mit der typischen *Ophrys transhyrcana*, beschrieben aus Turkmenistan (Kopeth Dagh). Die Pflanzen Zyperns gehören zu einer neuen eigenständigen Art und wurden deswegen als *Ophrys morio* in diesem Buch neu beschrieben.

Manchmal können auch einige *Serapias*-Arten für Bestimmungsprobleme sorgen, aber mit der Beschreibung von *Serapias aphroditae* (Delforge, 1990) wurde die Problematik dieses Formenkreises weitgehend behoben.

Von einigen Arten auf Zypern (*Aceras anthropophorum, Cephalanthera damasonium, Cephalanthera longifolia, Epipactis helleborine, Ophrys ciliata, Ophrys sintenisii, Ophrys spruneri, Serapias orientalis* und *Serapias vomeracea*) ist der Nachweis zweifelhaft, weil keine Herbar- oder fotografischen Belege existieren. Von drei Arten (*Ophrys aegaea, Ophrys omegaifera* und *Ophrys straussii*) konnte die Existenz bisher nicht mit Sicherheit festgestellt werden. All diese Arten wurden in ein separates Kapitel aufgenommen.

Seit 1985 besuchte der Verfasser Zypern mehrmals, um speziell die dortige Orchideenflora zu studieren, wobei besonders Material über die Verbreitung und Ökologie der Arten zusammengetragen wurde. Dabei wurden viele neue Fundorte entdeckt und auch einige bis dahin

demic) orchid species, and on the other hand the high Troodos mountain range and its fringe areas with mighty Black Pines (*Pinus nigra* subsp. *pallasiana*) and Cyprus Cedars (*Cedrus brevifolia*). Rare and primarily Central European and Mediterranean orchid species such as *Cephalanthera rubra, Dactylorhiza iberica, Epipactis condensata, Epipactis microphylla, Epipactis troodi, Epipactis veratrifolia, Limodorum abortivum* and *Platanthera holmboei* can be found here.

In contrast to Rhodes or Turkey, the identification of most species in Cyprus is straightforward, and even easy. Only the species in the *Ophrys sphegodes-mammosa* group can sometimes give rise to identificaton errors. Members of this group have been classified under a wide variety of taxa over the years and remained very difficult to determine until 2002. The contribution of Kreutz, Segers & Walraven (2002) reclassified the species of the *Ophrys sphegodes-mammosa* group found in Cyprus, and the description of *Ophrys alasiatica* and from *Ophrys morio* H.F. Paulus & Kreutz in this book helped to solve these problems. In Cyprus 5 species of the *Ophrys sphegodes-mammosa* group occur: *Ophrys alasiatica* (an early flowering species with large *Ophrys aesculapii*-like flowers), *Ophrys herae* (looking like a Central European *Ophrys sphegodes* on Cyprus, but with slightly bigger flowers, and flowering from mid-February), *Ophrys hystera* (a late flowering and exceptionally tall species, with large *Ophrys mammosa*-like flowers), *Ophrys mammosa* (mostly with a slender growth on Cyprus) and *Ophrys morio* (in the past known as *Ophrys transhyrcana* from Cyprus). The plants on Cyprus are not identical to typical *Ophrys transhyrcana*, described from Turkmenistan (Kopeth Dagh). The plants on Cyprus belong to an independent taxon and were described in this book as *Ophrys morio*.

Some *Serapias* species can also cause indentification problems, but with the description of *Serapias aphroditae* (Delforge, 1990) the problems of this species group were largely solved.

Of some species (*Aceras anthropophorum, Cephalanthera damasonium, Cephalanthera longifolia, Epipactis helleborine, Ophrys ciliata, Ophrys sintenisii, Ophrys spruneri, Serapias orientalis* and *Serapias vomeracea*) the evidence of their existence is doubtful as there is no botanical or photographic proof. Equally, the existence of *Ophrys aegaea, Ophrys omegaifera* and *Ophrys straussii* could not be verified with certainty. Additionally, all these species have been incorporated into a separate chapter.

Since 1985, the author has visited Cyprus many times, primarily to study the local orchid flora, of which, in particular, information on distribution and ecology of the species was gathered. In the course of this work, many new habitats were discovered and taxa until then

unbekannte Sippen gefunden und neu beschrieben. Im vorliegenden Buch werden alle Orchideen, die auf Zypern vorkommen, behandelt. Auch die neuesten Arten wurden in diesem Buch berücksichtigt. Spezielle Aufmerksamkeit wurde dem schwierigen Formenkreis von *Ophrys sphegodes-mammosa* gewidmet, dessen Vertreter auf Zypern weit verbreitet sind.

Mit Hilfe eines Bestimmungsschlüssels zu den Gattungen, Blütenzeichnungen und einer kurzen aber prägnanten Beschreibung der einzelnen Arten, die auf den wissenschaftlichen Erkenntnissen bis einschließlich 2004 basieren, ist es möglich, alle Taxa sicher zu bestimmen. Weiterhin geben 485 Farbbilder die charakteristischen Merkmale der einzelnen Sippen wieder, wobei von fast jeder Art auch eine Abbildung ihres natürlichen Standortes/Biotops auf Zypern gezeigt wird. Ausserdem werden von jedem Taxon Standort/Biotop, Blütezeit, Höhenverbreitung, Gesamtverbreitung, Verbreitung auf Zypern, Bemerkungen und Gefährdung behandelt und alle derzeit bekannten Hybriden der Sippe aufgelistet. Um die Arten innerhalb eines Formenkreises schnell und leicht zu bestimmen, wurde von der alphabetischen Reihenfolge der wissenschaftlichen Namen der Arten abgewichen und die Arten innerhalb ihrer Verwandtschaftsgruppen zusammengestellt. Innerhalb dieser Verwandtschaftsgruppen wurden dann die zugehörigen Arten wieder alphabetisch aufgelistet. Durch die Zusammenstellung in Gruppen ist es einfacher, auf den Abbildungen die Unterschiede bzw. Ähnlichkeiten der nahe verwandten Arten zu erkennen. Weitere Kapitel des Buches informieren über Zypern im Allgemeinen, die Landschaften mit ihren Orchideen, das Klima, die Vegetation, Flora und Orchideen von Zypern, Gefährdung und Schutz und die botanische Erforschung der Orchideen Zyperns.

In diesem Buch wird weder näher auf die taxonomische und nomenklatorische Einteilung von BATEMAN, PRIDGEON & CHASE (1997), BATEMAN (2001) und PRIDGEON, BATEMAN, COX, HAPEMAN & CHASE (1997) eingegangen, noch wird sie übernommen. Bei einigen Arten wie *Aceras anthropophorum* oder *Neotinea maculata* kann man sich zwar vorstellen, dass sie möglicherweise in die Gattung *Orchis* gehören, aber bei *Anacamptis pyramidalis* hat der Verfasser doch grundsätzliche Bedenken, dies zu übernehmen. Umgekehrt wurden viele Arten der Gattung *Orchis* (z.B. alle Arten des *Orchis palustris* und *Orchis papilionacea*-Formenkreises sowie *Orchis tridentata*) nach Meinung des Verfassers zu Unrecht in die Gattung *Anacamptis* eingestuft, beziehungsweise umkombiniert. In den neueren Ausgaben nationaler Floren sowie in den meisten aktuellen Orchideenbüchern wurden die taxonomischen Überlegungen von BATEMAN, PRIDGEON & CHASE (1997), BATEMAN (2001) und PRIDGEON, BATEMAN, COX, HAPEMAN & CHASE (1997) ohnehin auch nicht übernommen.

In Übereinstimmung mit mehreren Autoren (zum Beispiel P. DELFORGE, J. DEVILLERS-TERSCHUREN & P. DEVILLERS, H.F. PAULUS, H.F. PAULUS & C. GACK) wurden in diesem Buch fast alle Taxa im Artrang aufgenommen. In frühe-

unknown were also found and described for the first time. In this book all orchid species which occur on Cyprus are documented, including the most recently discovered and described. Special attention is paid to the difficult species group of *Ophrys sphegodes-mammosa*, the representatives of which are widely distributed on Cyprus.

With the help of an indentification chart of genera, flower markings, and a short concise description of all individual taxa, which are based on scientific results up to and including 2004, it is possible to identify all species reliably. In this book 485 colour photographs show the typical characteristics of all individual taxa, and almost for each species a picture is also included to show the natural habitat on Cyprus. For each taxa, the habitat, flowering time, altitude distribution, overall distribution, distribution within Cyprus, remarks and threats are covered and all currently known hybrids of each taxon are listed. In order to facilitate the quick and easy determination of species within a species group, the scientific names have not been arranged in alphabetical order, but rather arranged according to their relational groups. Within these relational groups however, the respective species have been arranged in alphabetical order. By arranging the species into groups, it is made easier to recognize the similarities and differences of closely related species in the pictures. Further chapters in this book give information about Cyprus in general, the landscapes and their orchids, the climate, the vegetation, the flora and orchids of Cyprus, threats and conservation, and the botanical research of orchids on Cyprus.

In this book, the taxonomic and terminological classification of BATEMAN, PRIDGEON & CHASE (1997), BATEMAN (2001) und PRIDGEON, BATEMAN, COX, HAPEMAN & CHASE (1997) has not been followed, nor has it been adopted. With some species, such as *Aceras anthropophorum* or *Neotinea maculata*, one can imagine that they might possibly belong to the *Orchis* genera, but with *Anacamptis pyramidalis*, for instance, the author has fundamental doubts about the classification. Many species of the *Orchis* genera (e.g. all species of the *Orchis palustris*, the *Orchis papilionacea* group and *Orchis tridentata*) were, in the opinion of the author, wrongly classified or rather recombined under *Anacamptis*. Both in newer editions of national flora and in most of the current orchid books, the taxonomic suggestions made BATEMAN, PRIDGEON & CHASE (1997), BATEMAN (2001) und PRIDGEON, BATEMAN, COX, HAPEMAN & CHASE (1997) have also not in any case been adopted.

In accordance with several authors (such as P. DELFORGE, J. DEVILLERS-TERSCHUREN & P. DEVILLERS, H.F. PAULUS, H.F. PAULUS & C. GACK) almost all taxa have been recorded at species rank in this book. In early years however,

8   *Orchis punctulata*, Kato Drys, 6.3.2002

ren Jahren aber wurden von den meisten Autoren überwiegend Unterarten beschrieben, wobei klar blieb, zu welcher Art diese gehörten. In den letzten zwanzig Jahren wurde dieses Konzept verlassen, und viele Autoren beschrieben neue Taxa fast ausschliesslich im Artrang, oder sie erhoben Unterarten in den Artrang. Durch diese Vorgehensweise wurden viele Taxa zu hoch bewertet, und der Zusammenhang der verwandten Taxa war nicht mehr erkennbar. Als Vorarbeit zum Buch 'Die Orchideen von Europa' habe ich mich schon längere Zeit mit einer taxonomischen und nomenklatorischen Liste der europäischen Orchideen beschäftigt. In dieser Vorarbeit (Kompendium der Europäischen Orchideen – in Vorbereitung) wird ein taxonomisches Konzept präsentiert, in dem die zuerst beschriebene Art als Nominatspezies auftritt, und alle später beschriebenen, verwandten Taxa wieder als Unterart geführt oder in den Unterartrang umkombiniert wurden. Diese Eingliederung hat den Vorteil, dass (nahe) verwandte Arten schnell und zuverlässig zu bestimmen sind. Dieses Vorgehen wird auch in meinem neuen Buch über die Orchideen von Europa, Nordafrika und dem Nahen Osten übernommen. Dieses Buch, in deutscher und englischer Sprache, soll alle Arten, Unterarten und wichtigsten Varietäten und Formen der Orchideen von Europa, Nordafrika und dem Nahen Osten umfassen. Ausserdem werden Verbreitungskarten im UTM 50-km Raster aufgenommen, und von allen Taxa werden Farbaufnahmen vom Biotop, Habitus, Blütenstand und Einzelblüte abgebildet. In diesem Werk wird natürlich auch detaillierter auf die vorgestellte taxonomische Gliederung eingegangen. Im vorliegenden Buch wurde das neue taxonomische Konzept nicht eingesetzt, weil der Zusammenhang zu den übrigen europäischen Arten fehlt, es ausserdem nur wenige Taxa betrifft, und es nicht das geeignete Medium ist, eingehende taxonomische und nomenklatorische Änderungen vor zu nehmen.

Dieses Buch wäre ohne die Mitwirkung vieler Orchideenfreunde nicht möglich gewesen. Besonderen Dank schulde ich Dr. Chr. F. Gembardt (Weinheim, D) für die kritische Durchsicht des Manuskripts, P. Scraton (Akrounta, Cy) für die Korrekturlesung des englischen Textes, Dr. H. Kretzschmar (Bad Hersfeld, D) für die Unterstützung durch sein EDV-Kartierungsprogramm INKA und allen in der Danksagung aufgeführten Orchideenfreunden für die Überlassung kompletter Fundort- und Artenangaben von Zypern, sowie für Fotomaterial und viele wertvolle Anregungen.

Das vorliegende Buch soll nicht nur dem Orchideen-Spezialisten eine umfassende Darstellung der Arten von Zypern bieten, sondern es soll dem interessierten Laien auch ermöglichen, die Orchideenflora der Insel kennen zu lernen. Der Autor glaubt damit einen wesentlichen Beitrag zur Kenntnis und Verbreitung der Orchideen von Zypern geliefert zu haben und würde sich über weitere Fundortangaben besonders freuen.

Landgraaf, im September 2004.

---

most authors primarily described subspecies, and it was clear to which species these belonged. In the last twenty years this concept has been abandoned, and now many authors describe new taxa almost entirely at species rank, or raise subspecies to species rank. By so doing, many taxa have been too highly classified and the correlation of related taxa can no longer be recognized. For a long time now I have been occupied with a taxonomic and nomenclatural list of European orchids as a preparatory work to the book 'The Orchids of Europe'. In this preparatory work (Catalogue of European Orchids – in prep.) a new taxonomic concept has been created in which the species that was described first is regarded as the nominate species, and subsequently described and related taxa are classified as subspecies or lowered to subspecies rank. This classification has the advantage that (closely) related species can easily and reliably be classified. This approach will also be used in my new book about the orchids of Europe, North Africa and the Near East. This book, in English and German, will include all species, subspecies and the most important varieties and forms of European orchids. Distribution maps on a UTM 50-km grid will also be included, and colour photographs of all taxa in their biotope, with general appearance, inflorescence and individual flower. More detailed information on taxonomic classification mentioned above will of course also be found in the book. The new taxonomic concept was not adopted in this book, as the relationship between the other European species is lacking; also it concerns only a few taxa and is not an appropriate means of undertaking extensive taxonomic and nomenclatural changes.

This book would not have been possible without the cooperation of many orchidophiles. Special thanks go to Dr. Chr. F. Gembardt (Weinheim, D) for his critical review of the manuscript, P. Scraton (Akrounta, Cy) for correcting the proofs of the English text, Dr. H. Kretzschmar (Bad Hersfeld, D) for his assistance by means of his EDV-charting programme INKA and to orchidophiles mentioned in the acknowledgements for giving access to complete reports on habitats and species of Cyprus and also for photographic material and many valuable suggestions.

This book should not only offer a comprehensive representation of the species of Cyprus to orchid specialists, but should also give the interested layman the opportunity to acquaint himself with the orchid flora of the island. The author feels he has contributed significantly to the promotion of the orchids of Cyprus and would be very pleased to receive further reports on orchid locations.

Landgraaf, September 2004.

Allgemeiner Teil

Einleitung

Die Insel Zypern liegt im östlichen Mittelmeer zwischen Orient und Okzident im Schnittpunkt von drei Kontinenten (Europa, Asien und Afrika). Sie liegt etwa 100 km westlich von Syrien, 65 km südlich der Türkei und 380 km nördlich von Ägypten. Die Insel ist mit etwa 230 km Ost-West-Ausdehnung etwa 100 Kilometer breit und mit einer Gesamtfläche von etwa 9.251 km² nach Sizilien und Sardinien die drittgrößte Insel im Mittelmeerraum. Sie ist ausserdem auch die am weitesten östlich gelegene Insel des Mittelmeeres. Ihre Küstenlinie hat eine Länge von etwa 780 Kilometern. Im südlichen Teil liegt das Troodos-Gebirge, dessen höchste Erhebung mit 1.951 m der Olympus (Khionistra) ist. Der Name Zypern leitet sich vom griechischen Wort 'Kypros' ab, was sich auf das Metall Kupfer bezieht, das schon vor 4000 Jahren auf der Insel abgebaut wurde. Zypern wird geografisch zu Asien gerechnet, obwohl es durch ihre Geschichte und Kultur eng mit dem europäischen Kontinent verbunden ist.

Zypern hat etwa 760.000 Einwohner, davon gehören etwa 84% der griechischen und 12% der türkischen Volksgruppe an. Die restlichen 4% sind Ausländer, vor allem Engländer. Nicht mitgezählt sind die vom Festland stammenden Türken, die nach 1974 im Norden der Insel angesiedelt wurden, ferner die in den britischen Militärstützpunkten bei Akrotiri und Dekeleia stationierten 17.000 Soldaten und die ca. 1.200 UN-Soldaten. Im türkisch besetzten Norden der Insel leben zur Zeit schätzungsweise 180.000 Menschen (BAEDEKER, 2001). Die meisten Einwohner leben in den größeren Städten der Insel, nämlich in Famagusta (Ammochostos), Kyrenia (Keryneia), Larnaka (Larnaca), Lefkosia (Nicosia), Lemesos (Limassol) und Pafos (Paphos).

Zypern ist durch Straßen sehr gut erschlossen. Es gibt gut ausgebaute Autobahnen zwischen den Städten Pafos, Lemesos, Larnaka und Lefkosia. In den letzten Jahren wurden auch viele kleinere Straßen ausgebaut, und heute ist auch das Innere der Insel durch viele asphaltierte Straßen gut erschlossen. Viele interessante Fundorte befinden sich jedoch entlang unbefestigter Straßen.

Zypern gehört schon seit vielen Jahrzehnten zu einem der beliebtesten Reiseziele im Mittelmeerraum. Wegen ihres Sonnenreichtums gehört die Insel zu den begehrtesten und viel besuchten Urlaubsgebieten. Mit zunehmendem Tourismus wird Zypern ab 1970 auch von Berufs- und Hobbybotanikern aus vielen Ländern Europas verstärkt besucht, und fast jeder Orchideenfreund hat Zypern wegen seiner Vielfalt an Arten (mehrmals) besucht. Zumindest in den letzten drei Jahrzehnten wurde die Insel sehr häufig von Orchideologen besucht und intensiv kartiert. Zypern gehört deshalb zu den am besten kartierten Gebieten im Mittelmeerraum und zeigt einen hohen Bekanntheitsgrad der möglichen Orchideenvorkommen.

Die bisher einzige Verbreitungsübersicht über die Orchi-

General part

Introduction

The island of Cyprus is situated in the Eastern Mediterranean, between Orient and Occident, at the intersection of three continents (Europe, Asia and Africa). Cyprus is situated about 100 km west of Syria, 65 km south of Turkey and 380 km north of Egypt. The island is nearly 230 km from east to west, about 100 km from north to south, and with a total surface area of about 9,251 km² it is the third largest island in the Mediterranean, after Sicily and Sardinia. It lies the furthest east of all the Mediterranean islands. Its coastline has a length of about 780 kilometres. In the south are the Troodos Mountains, of which the highest point is Olympus (Khionistra) at 1,951 metres. The name Cyprus comes from the Greek word 'Kypros', which refers to the metal copper, which has been mined here for 4,000 years. Cyprus is geographically part of Asia, although it is closely connected to the European continent through its history and culture.

Cyprus has about 760,000 inhabitants, of which about 84% belong to the Greek community and 12% to the Turkish. The other 4% are foreigners, mainly British people. The population figure does not include Turkish people from the mainland, who settled in the northern part of the island after 1974, and it also does not include 17,000 soldiers stationed at British military installations at Akrotiri and Dekeleia and about 1,200 UN soldiers. Approximately 180,000 people live in the Turkish occupied northern part of the island (BAEDEKER, 2001). Most of the inhabitants live in the larger towns of the island, namely Famagusta (Ammochostos), Kyrenia (Keryneia), Larnaka (Larnaca), Lefkosia (Nicosia), Lemesos (Limassol) and Pafos (Paphos).

Cyprus is well served by roads. There are well developed motorways between the towns of Pafos, Lemesos, Larnaka and Lefkosia. In recent years, many smaller roads have also been constructed, and now the interior of the island is easily accessible by asphalted roads. However many interesting habitats are found along unsurfaced roads.

For decades, Cyprus has been one of the most popular travel destinations in the Mediterranean. Because of its many hours of sunshine, the island is one of the most favoured and frequently visited holiday areas. Alongside this ever-growing tourism, Cyprus has increasingly been visited by professional and amateur botanists from many European countries, and almost every orchidophile has (often more than once) visited Cyprus because of its diversity in species. At least in the last three decades, the island has been both frequently visited and intensively charted by orchidologists. Cyprus therefore belongs to one of the best-investigated regions in the Mediterranean and has a high rate of possible orchid occurrences because of this.

deen der Insel Zypern wurde 1990 von Hansen, Kreutz & U. & D. Rückbrodt veröffentlicht. Danach erschienen mehrere Bücher (G. & K. Morschek, 1996; Georgiades, 1998ab, Christofides, 2001 und J. Hubbard & P. Scraton, 2001), viele Beiträge und zusätzliche Kartierungsergebnisse in verschiedenen botanischen Zeitschriften. Eine aktuelle Übersicht blieb aber bis heute aus, und dieses Buch soll dazu beitragen, diese Lücke zu schliessen. In diesem Buch werden neben allen bereits bekannten und veröffentlichten Angaben auch alle unveröffentlichten Fundortlisten, die im Besitz des Verfassers sind, berücksichtigt und in die Verbreitungskarten eingearbeitet.

Bedingt durch die geographische Lage, die klimatischen Unterschiede in Temperatur, ausgiebige Regenfälle im Winter und die montanen Lagen im Troodes-Gebirge haben sich auf Zypern eine Fülle von Biotopen (unter anderem Haselnusspflanzungen, Kiefern- und Pinienwälder, Kalkquellsümpfe, Fluss- und Bachufer, Nass- und Feuchtwiesen, Macchien, Phrygana, ungedüngte (montane) Magerrasen, Weideareale und die hochgelegenen Schwarzkiefern- und Zedernwälder) entwickelt, mit fruchtbaren Gebieten im Landesinneren, rauhen, kalkhaltigen Bergen im Pentadactylos-Gebirge, lavahaltigem Gestein an den südlichen Abhängen und auf den Hochebenen des Troodes-Gebirges, sandigen und felsigen Küstenstreifen sowie Feuchtgebieten, Sanddünen und Salzseen bei Larnaka und auf der Akrotiri-Halbinsel. Durch diese große Anzahl verschiedener Biotope hat sich auf Zypern eine überaus reichhaltige und interessante Flora entwickelt, in der viele ostmediterrane und orientalische Pflanzenarten wachsen. Bedingt durch die Insellage und die schon seit langer Zeit bestehende Trennung vom Festland haben sich unter den auf Zypern vorkommenden 1.800 Pflanzenarten fast 140 Endemiten entwickelt (Georgiades, 1998ab), die nur hier vorkommen. Unter diesen Endemiten finden sich mit *Epipactis troodi*, *Ophrys alasiatica*, *Ophrys elegans*, *Ophrys kotschyi*, *Orchis troodi* und *Serapias aphroditae* auch 6 endemische Orchideentaxa. Vermutlich ist auch *Ophrys morio* endemisch, weil noch nicht mit Sicherheit nachgewiesen konnte ob diese Art auch in der Südtürkei vorkommt. Nach heutigem Kenntnisstand kommen auf Zypern 52 Arten vor. Sie wachsen in allen Höhenlagen, von Meereshöhe bis in die höchsten Lagen des Troodes-Gebirges, wo in den weitläufigen Schwarzkiefernwäldern dieses Gebirges unter anderem die sehr seltene Orchideen *Dactylorhiza iberica*, *Epipactis condensata*, *Epipactis troodi*, *Epipactis veratrifolia* und *Platanthera holmboei* vorkommen.

Zypern stellt für den Orchideenfreund ein wahres Paradies dar, da sowohl zahlreiche Arten in großen Mengen vorkommen, als auch diese leicht zu erreichen sind, und mit etwas Glück findet man auf Zypern zu allen Jahreszeiten Orchideen. Die Saison beginnt bereits im Januar, wenn *Orchis collina* nach den Winterniederschlägen zu blühen anfängt. Sie überschneidet sich dabei manchmal gerade noch mit *Spiranthes spiralis*, die als letzte Orchidee zwischen Mitte Oktober und Mitte Dezember vor dem Einsetzen der Winterniederschläge erblüht.

The first and only distribution overview of the orchids of Cyprus was published by Hansen, Kreutz & U. & D. Rückbrodt in 1990. Later, several books (G. & K. Morschek, 1996; Georgiades, 1998ab; Christofides, 2001 and J. Hubbard & P. Scraton, 2001) were published, and many articles and additional charting results appeared in various botanical journals. An actual overview was absent until now, and this book will help toward filling this gap. In this work, not only are all already known and published statements documented and incorporated into the distribution maps, but also all unpublished habitat lists which are in the possession of the author.

Because of its geographical location, the climatic variations in temperature, the sometimes copious rainfall in winter and the mountainous reaches of the Troodos massif, varied biotopes have been able to develop (such as hazelnut plantations, pine forests, chalk bogs, riversides and streams, wetlands and marshes, maquis, phrygana, barren (mountainous) grasslands, pastures and high-altitude Black Pine and Cedar forests), with fertile areas in the interior; calcareous formations in the Pentadactylos Range; igneous formations in the southern slopes and high altitudes of the Troodos Range; both sandy and rocky coastlines as well as marshes, sand dunes and salt lakes near Larnaka and on the Akrotiri peninsula. Due to the large variety of biotopes on Cyprus, an exceptionally rich and interesting flora has therefore been able to develop, in which many Eastern Mediterranean and oriental plant species thrive. Because of the position of the island and its millennia-long separation from the mainland, almost 140 endemic species (Georgiades, 1998ab) that only occur here have evolved amongst the 1,800 plant species which occur on Cyprus. Amongst these endemic species are 6 endemic orchid taxa: *Epipactis troodi*, *Ophrys alasiatica*, *Ophrys elegans*, *Ophrys kotschyi*, *Orchis troodi* and *Serapias aphroditae*. *Ophrys morio* probably also belongs to the endemic Cypriot species, because it has not yet been varified if this species occurs in southern Turkey. According to the current state of knowledge, 52 species occur on Cyprus. They grow at all altitudes, from sea level up to the highest elevations of the Troodos Range, where in the vast Black Pine forests of these mountains occur among others the very rare orchids *Dactylorhiza iberica*, *Epipactis condensata*, *Epipactis troodi*, *Epipactis veratrifolia* and *Platanthera holmboei*.

Cyprus is to the orchidophile a true paradise, as it harbours numerous species in large numbers, which can easily be reached, and with luck one can find orchids on Cyprus all the year round. The orchid season starts in January when *Orchis collina* starts flowering after the early winter rains. It narrowly overlaps with *Spiranthes spiralis*, which is the last orchid to flower, between mid-October and mid-December, with flowers before the first winter rainfall.

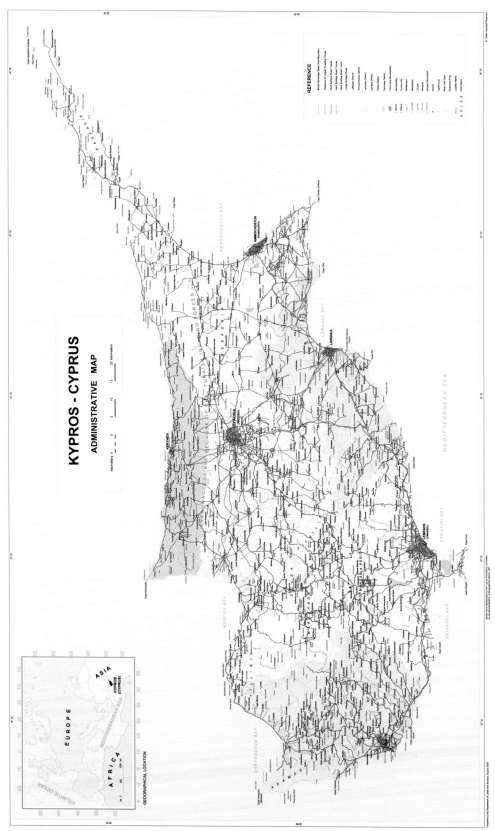

KYPROS - CYPRUS

ADMINISTRATIVE MAP

Kurze Geschichte Zyperns

Durch seine geographisch exponierte Lage als Tor nach Kleinasien und in den Fernen Osten blieb Zypern, mit Ausnahme einer kurzen Epoche in der Zeit des Niederganges des altpersischen Reiches, immer im Besitz von Fremdmächten, wodurch Zypern seit prähistorischen Zeiten bis heute Schauplatz machtpolitischer Auseinandersetzungen ist. Griechen, Phönizier, Ägypter, Perser, Byzantiner, Kreuzfahrer und Venezianer wechselten sich in der Herrschaft ab. Nach ihrem Sieg über die Venezianer 1571 waren es die Osmanen, die die Insel für mehr als 300 Jahre regierten. In dieser Zeit siedelten sie mehr als 30.000 türkische Soldaten an, um ihren Machtanspruch zu festigen.

Von 1878 an stand das Land unter englischer Verwaltung, bis es 1914 annektiert und dem Britischen Commonwealth eingegliedert wurde. 1960 erhielt Zypern seine Unabhängigkeit. Die Engländer sicherten sich jedoch einige Militärbasen, über die sie auch heute noch verfügen. Eine von Ihnen, Episkopi, ist wegen des Vorkommens der früh blühenden, immer Laub tragenden *Epipactis veratrifolia* das Ziel vieler Orchideensucher. Nach bürgerkriegsähnlichen Unruhen zwischen den griechisch und den türkisch sprechenden Bewohnern und Annektionsbestrebungen der griechischen Militärregierung besetzten Mitte August 1974 türkische Truppen 38% der Fläche der Insel und zwar den gesamten Norden bis zu einer gedachten Linie Morphou-Lefkosia-Famagusta. Der türkisch sprechende Teil der Bevölkerung flüchtete in den Norden, während die griechisch sprechende Nordzyprioten im Süden eine neue Heimat fanden.

Die Teilung Zyperns wurde durch die einseitige Ausrufung der 'Türkischen Republik von Nordzypern' 1983 zementiert, von den Vereinten Nationen aber nie anerkannt. Nur die Türkei unterhält diplomatische Beziehungen zur 'Republik Nordzypern', und hier gilt weitgehend türkisches Recht. Zwischen dem Norden und Süden verläuft eine 217 km lange und 10 bis 7000 m breite Pufferzone, die etwa 3% der zypriotischen Grundfläche ausmacht, und an der seit 1964 UN-Friedenstruppen mit einem hohen Kostenaufwand stationiert sind (BAUMANN & KÜNKELE, 1994). Die Einreise vom griechischen Süden in den türkischen Norden und umgekehrt ist generell nicht möglich. In Lefkosia sind jedoch Ausnahmen zugelassen. Hier erhält man Passierscheine für einen eintägigen Besuch von Nordzypern. Allerdings kann man nur ohne Auto einreisen, muss bis 17:00 Uhr wieder zurück in Lefkosia sein, und die Regelung gilt nicht für Bewohner Nordzyperns, die nicht nach Südzypern einreisen dürfen. Die Infrastruktur der 'Republik Nordzypern' ähnelt sehr stark der der Türkei. Wenn man die Grenze in Lefkosia passiert hat, wähnt man sich in der Türkei. Der Rumpfstaat im Süden passte dagegen seine Infrastruktur sehr schnell den neuen Gegebenheiten an. Straßen und Häfen wurden ausgebaut beziehungsweise neu angelegt, moderne Ferienzentren in Ayia Napa und an der Südwestküste bei Pafos und im Süden

Short history of Cyprus

Due to its geographical position as a gateway to Asia Minor and the Far East, Cyprus has always been in the possession of foreign powers, with the exception of a short period during the downfall of the ancient Persian Empire. This has turned Cyprus into an arena for political conflicts from prehistoric times to the present day. Greeks, Phoenicians, Egyptians, Persians, Byzantines, the Crusaders, and Venetians successively replaced each other as owners of the island. After defeating the Venetians in 1571, the Ottomans controlled the island for more than 300 years. During this period, more than 30,000 Turkish soldiers settled here to enforce their claim.

From 1878 onward, the country was under British administration until it was annexed in 1914 and integrated into the British Commonwealth. In 1960 Cyprus was given independence. The British however ensured that some military bases would remain, to which they still have access to the present day. One of these, Episkopi, is the destination of many orchid seekers as the only early-flowering example of the evergreen *Epipactis veratrifolia* occurs here.

After civil-war-like unrest between the Greek and Turkish speaking inhabitants, and after attempts at annexation by the Greek military government, Turkish troops once more occupied more than 38% of the island, consisting of the whole northern part of the island down to the line Morphou-Lefkosia-Famagusta, in mid-August 1974. The Turkish speaking part of the population fled to the north, while Greek-speaking northern Cypriots found a new home in the south.

The division of Cyprus was finalized by the unilateral proclamation of the 'Turkish Republic of Northern Cyprus' in 1983, but never recognized by the United Nations. Only Turkey maintains diplomatic relations with the 'Republic of Northern Cyprus' and Turkish law is applied there to a large extent. A 217 km long and 10 to 7,000 m wide area (3% of the surface area of Cyprus) forms a buffer zone between the north and the south, along which the UN peace corps has been stationed since 1964 at high cost (BAUMANN & KÜNKELE, 1994). Entry from the Greek south into the Turkish north and viceversa was until recently generally impossible. However, exceptions were made at Lefkosia. Permits could be obtained for a one-day visit to northern Cyprus here, but one could only enter without a car, and had to be back in Lefkosia by 17:00 o'clock. The arrangement did not apply to inhabitants of northern Cyprus, who were not permitted to enter southern Cyprus. The infrastructure of the 'Republic of Northern Cyprus' strongly resembles that of Turkey. After crossing the border, one has the illusion of being in Turkey. In contrast, the government in the south quickly adapted its infrastructure to the new conditions. Roads and harbours were expanded or newly erected, modern holiday centres in Ayia Napa and along the southwestern coast near Pafos and in the south near Lemesos replaced the northern holiday areas

bei Lemesos traten an die Stelle der im Norden liegenden Urlaubsgebiete von Famagusta und Kyrenia. Während der Tourismus im Süden schon bald wieder zur Haupteinnahmequelle wurde, geriet der Norden fast in Vergessenheit und wirtschaftlich in die totale Abhängigkeit der Türkei. Türkisches Militär ist auch heute noch allgegenwärtig, einige Gebiete sind nicht zugängliche militärische Sperrgebiete, und einige Straßen sind nur mit Erlaubnisschein passierbar. Die Wirtschaft beschränkte sich lange Zeit nur auf Schaf- und Ziegenzucht. Fast alle Dinge des täglichen Bedarfs, einschließlich des frischen Gemüses, kamen und kommen auch heute noch vom türkischen Festland. Auch der Norden bemüht sich wieder um den Touristen. Viele Hotels stammen zwar überwiegend aus der Zeit vor der Teilung, Gastfreundschaft und eine grandiose Landschaft aber lassen die vorhandenen Unzulänglichkeiten leicht verschmerzen (HANSEN, KREUTZ & U. & D. RÜCKBRODT, 1990).

1990 hat die Republik Zypern die Vollmitgliedschaft in der Europäischen Union beantragt. Die EU würde es begrüßen, die Republik Zypern als Mitglied aufzunehmen, wenn der Konflikt zwischen Griechen und Türken um die Teilung der Insel geklärt ist. Die EU hat die Mitgliedschaft aber nicht von einer Lösung des Teilungsproblems abhängig gemacht. Seit dem Jahre 2000 bemüht sich auch die Türkei um einen EU-Beitritt, wodurch günstige Voraussetzungen für eine Lösung des Teilungsproblems vorhanden sind. In letzter Zeit fanden wiederholt Demonstrationen statt, bei denen sich auch die türkische Bevölkerung im Norden der Insel für eine Wiedervereinigung der beiden Inselteile ausgesprochen hat. Die Parlamentswahl im türkischen Nord-Zypern im Dezember 2003 hat aber ein Patt zwischen der bisherigen Regierung und der Opposition ergeben. Mit fast 50 Prozent erhielten die Oppositionsparteien zwar die meisten Stimmen, ins Parlament entsenden sie jedoch die gleiche Anzahl von Abgeordneten wie die bisher regierenden Parteien, die gegen eine Wiedervereinigung mit Süd-Zypern sind. Eines haben die Wahlen überraschend deutlich gemacht: Der Gegensatz zwischen Türken und Griechen ist nicht der einzige auf Zypern. Die türkische Gemeinschaft selbst ist tief gespalten. Denn die Abstimmung war zugleich Referendum über eine nationale Schicksalsfrage: die Wiedervereinigung der Insel nach dem Modell des Friedensplans von UNO-Generalsekretär Kofi Annan, verbunden mit der Aussicht auf eine EU-Mitgliedschaft, auch des türkischen Teils. Es fällt schwer, das Ergebnis des Referendums einzuordnen. Einerseits haben die Europa- und Wiedervereinigungsorientierten Kräfte auf Nord-Zypern ihr bisher bestes Wahlresultat eingefahren, andererseits jedoch hatten bei Demonstrationen noch zwei Drittel der Bevölkerung für weitere Verhandlungen und gegen die Blockadepolitik von Präsident Rauf Denktash demonstriert. So gesehen hätte der Stimmenzuwachs für die Oppositionskräfte in der nur von Ankara anerkannten 'Türkischen Republik Nord-Zypern' auch deutlicher ausfallen können. Mit dem jetzigen Ergebnis können sie jedenfalls nicht voll zufrieden sein. Ebenso wenig die EU, die

of Famagusta and Kyrenia. While tourism rapidly became the main source of income in the south, the north sank into obscurity and became economically dependent on Turkey. The Turkish armed forces are still omnipresent, some areas are restricted military areas, and some roads are only accessible with a permit. The economy was limited for a long time to sheep and goat farming. Almost all daily needs, including fresh vegetables, came from the Turkish mainland, and still do. Also the north has been trying to attract tourists again. Many hotels however date from the time before the division, though with the hospitality and the beautiful landscape one easily forgets their shortcomings (HANSEN, KREUTZ & U. & D. RÜCKBRODT, 1990).

In 1990 the Republic of Cyprus filed an application for membership of the European Union, in response to which the EU has made it clear that, while the entry of Cyprus will not depend on a solution of the problem of division, a re-unified Cyprus would be very much preferred. Turkey is also trying to become a member of the EU, which creates a favorable basis for a solution to the division problem. Recently, repeated demonstrations have taken place, in which the ethnic Turkish population in the northern part of the island have also voiced their desire for reunification of the island. The parliamentary elections in Turkish northern Cyprus in December 2003 have however resulted in a stalemate between the existing government and the opposition. With almost 50 percent of the votes, the opposition parties in fact gathered a majority of votes, but in parliament this results in their having exactly the same number of representatives as the previously governing parties who oppose reunification with southern Cyprus. One thing has however been made surprisingly clear by the elections: antagonism between Turks and Greeks is not the only rift in Cyprus. The Turkish community is itself deeply divided. As the parliamentary election was at the same time a referendum about a question of national importance – the reunification of the island according to the peace plan set out by UN Secretary General Kofi Annan, linked with the prospect of EU-membership including the Turkish part – it is difficult to comprehend the result. It is true that the powers in northern Cyprus focused on Europe and reunification have achieved their best election results yet. At the same time, two thirds of the population demonstrated for further negotiations and against the blockade politics of President Rauf Denktash. Taking this into consideration, the increase in votes for the opposition parties in the 'Turkish Republic of Northern Cyprus', which is only recognized by Ankara, might have been more pronounced and they can not be satisfied with the current result. And even less so the EU, which openly supported Denktash's opponent during the elections. Whoever is charged with the formation of a government in northern Cyprus, President Denktash's

14

bei dieser Abstimmung recht unverhohlen Denktashs Gegner unterstützt hatte. Wer immer nun auf Nord-Zypern mit der Regierungsbildung beauftragt wird: Präsident Denktash ist keineswegs so geschwächt, dass eine Zypern-Lösung einfach an ihm vorbei verhandelt werden könnte. Er dürfte vor allem die zahlreichen zugewanderten Türken aus Anatolien hinter sich haben, Menschen, die von der nordzypriotischen Führung einst gezielt nach Zypern gelockt wurden, um das türkische Lager zu stärken. Nun befürchten sie, bei einer Wiedervereinigung ihre Häuser an die ursprünglichen griechischen Besitzer zurückgeben zu müssen oder gar in ihre alte Heimat zurückgeschickt zu werden. Das Denktash-Lager hat genau diese Befürchtungen erfolgreich im Wahlkampf instrumentalisiert und sich so Stimmen für einen Fortbestand der Teilung erkämpft. Die Opposition hingegen hat es versäumt, die verständlichen Ängste dieser Menschen zu zerstreuen. Dabei würden gerade die Bürger im isolierten und wirtschaftlich rückständigen Nord-Zypern von einem EU-Beitritt profitieren. Doch angesichts des Wahlausgangs dürfte es mehr als schwer werden, wie erhofft noch vor Ende April 2004 zu einer Lösung zu kommen. Ende April 2004 aber tritt die griechisch dominierte südliche Republik Zypern der EU bei. Weil diese Inselhälfte völkerrechtlich trotz der Teilung noch immer als Vertreterin des ganzen Landes gilt, würde somit die Türkei mit ihren über 30.000 Soldaten auf Nord-Zypern schlagartig zur Besatzungsmacht in einem Mitgliedsland der Europäischen Union. Keine gute Voraussetzung für die EU-Beitrittswünsche der Türkei. Brüssel hat oft genug deutlich gemacht, dass die ungelöste Zypern-Frage ein ernst zu nehmendes Hindernis ist. Andererseits jedoch dürfte Ankara auch weiterhin versucht sein, Zypern umgekehrt als Trumpfkarte für die eigenen Interessen zu instrumentalisieren. Die Rechnung ist denkbar einfach und lautet in Worte gefasst: Wenn Ihr Europäer uns Türken einen verlässlichen Weg in die EU aufzeigt, dann sorgen wir unsererseits für eine Lösung des Zypern-Problems. Die Macht dazu hat Ankara noch immer. Auch deshalb, weil drei Jahrzehnte internationale Isolation dazu geführt haben, dass Nord-Zypern politisch, wirtschaftlich und militärisch von Ankara abhängig ist (SOLLICH, Deutsche Welle, 2003).

Ab 2004 strebt die Republik Zypern einen alleinigen Beitritt in die EU ohne Wiedervereinigung mit dem Norden an. Als Lösung böte sich aber ein Beitritt der Republik Zypern in Form einer Föderation aus zwei weitgehend autonomen Bundesstaaten an. Zum Zeitpunkt der Drucklegung dieses Buches war Zypern immer noch nicht wiedervereinigt. Während der türkisch-zypriotische Norden mehrheitlich dem Annan-Plan zur Wiedervereinigung zustimmte, lehnten die griechischen Zyprioten diesen ab und traten am 1. Mai 2004 allein der Europäischen Gemeinschaft bei. Die Verhandlungen werden zwar fortgesetzt, aber ob und wann es zu einer Wiedervereinigung der Insel kommt, wird erst die Zukunft zeigen.

position is by no means weakened to the point that a solution for Cyprus can be negotiated without him. He could particularly have the support of numerous Turks brought in from Anatolia-people who were specifically lured to Cyprus by the northern Cypriot leadership, in order to strengthen the Turkish camp. Now they fear that reunification would mean they will have to return their homes to the original Greek owners and may even be sent back to their homeland. The Denktash camp successfully played on these fears in their election campaign and thus won votes for a continuity of the division. The opposition on the other hand neglected to calm the understandable fears of these people. In fact the citizens of isolated and economically underdeveloped northern Cyprus would profit greatly from an EU membership. But in the light of these election results, it is going to be very difficult to come to a solution by the hoped for deadline of the end of April 2004. At the end of April 2004, the Greek dominated southern Republic of Cyprus will become a member of the EU. As this half of the island would count as a representative for the whole country, according to international law, Turkey and its 30,000 soldiers in northern Cyprus would suddenly become an occupation force in a member state of the EU; not a good pre-requisite for Turkey's wish to become an EU member. Brussels has stated clearly and often enough that an unresolved Cyprus problem will be an unwelcome complication. On the other hand however Ankara might be tempted to use Cyprus as a trump card to further its own interests. One could imagine the offer: "When you Europeans show us Turkish people a reliable road to the EU, then we will see to it on our side that there will be a solution to the Cyprus problem". Ankara still has the power to achieve this, because three decades of international isolation have led to political, economic and military dependence on Ankara (SOLLICH, Deutsche Welle, 2003).

From 2004 the Republic of Cyprus is working towards unilateral entrance into the EU without reunification with the north. One solution would be to admit the Republic of Cyprus as a federation of two largely autonomous states. At the time of going to press, there is still no unified Cyprus. Although the Turkish-Cypriot north of the island voted to accept the Annan Plan for reunification, the Greek-Cypriot south gave it a resounding thumbs down, and went alone into the European Union on May 1st 2004. Negotiations continue, but the future of the island will only become apparent in the fullness of time.

16   *Dactylorhiza iberica* und/and *Epipactis veratrifolia*, Kato Amiantos, 23.6.2002

Die Landschaften Zyperns mit ihren Orchideen

Die Insel lässt sich in vier größere landschaftliche Einheiten gliedern:
- der Norden mit dem Pentadactylos-Gebirge und der Karpasia-Halbinsel
- das südliche Hügelland
- die Mesaoria-Ebene im Osten
- das Troodos-Massiv.

Der Norden mit dem Pentadactylos-Gebirge und der Karpasia-Halbinsel

Der Norden Zyperns wird geprägt von einem parallel zur Küste verlaufenden, scharfgratigen Gebirgszug, der Kyrenia (Girne)-Gebirgskette, besser unter dem Namen Pentadactylos-Gebirge bekannt. Es erhebt sich im Westen bei Vasilia (Kariyaka) steil aus der Ebene, ist etwa 6 bis 8 km breit und verläuft ungefähr 80 km in West-Ost-Richtung, um in einem langen 'Finger' – der landschaftlich sehr reizvollen und immer schmaler werdenden Karpasia (Karpas)-Halbinsel – bei Epthakomi (Yedikonuk) auszulaufen. Seine höchste Erhebung, der Kyparissovouno, misst 1.024 m. Das Gebirge besteht zum größten Teil aus kalkhaltigen Gesteinsformationen, wie unter anderem Mergel, Dolomit, rekristallisiertem Kalk sowie Marmor. Eingesprengt sind Flecken aus Basalt und Rhyolith.

Die Höhen sind überwiegend mit Aleppokiefern (*Pinus halepensis*) und Mittelmeerzypressen (*Cupressus sempervirens*) bewaldet. An den Nordhängen, die sehr steil zum schmalen, aus Kalken und Schwemmland bestehenden Küstenstreifen abfallen, findet man einen zum Teil sehr dichten, macchie- und phryganaartigen Bewuchs. Charakteristische Pflanzen sind hier z.B. die Kleinblütige, die Salbeiblättrige und die Kretische Zistrose *(Cistus parviflorus, Cistus salviifolius* und *Cistus creticus)*. Häufig findet man auch die Dornigen Bibernelle *(Sarcopoterium spinosum)*, sowie Arten der Gattung *Pistacia, Salvia, Styrax* und den durch seine rote Rinde markanten Östlichen Erdbeerbaum (*Arbutus andrachne*), der in Baum- und Buschform auftritt. Die Südhänge in Richtung Mesaoria-Ebene sind weniger steil. Sie sind aber botanisch weit weniger ergiebig, da sie sehr viel trockener als der Nordabfall sind. Im Gegensatz zur Küstenregion, die zum großen Teil landwirtschaftlich genutzt wird, ist der Höhenzug naturbelassen, und nur wenige Picknick- und Freizeitanlagen stören den Gesamteindruck an einigen Stellen (Hansen, Kreutz & U. & D. Rückbrodt, 1990).

Früher war dieser Teil Zyperns ein Eldorado für Botaniker, speziell für Orchideologen. In den letzten Jahren aber ist die Anzahl der blühenden Pflanzen stark zurückgegangen, hauptsächlich durch die sich immer noch ausdehnenden Schaf- und Ziegenherden. Außerdem werden die fruchtbaren Ebenen landwirtschaftlich intensiver genutzt, wobei vor allem die Orchideen, die an feuchten Stellen und an Bachufern

The landscapes of Cyprus and their orchids

The island can be divided into four geological zones:
- the north with the Pentadactylos Range and the Karpasia peninsula
- the southern uplands
- the Mesaoria plains in the east
- the Troodos massif

The north with the Pentadactylos Range and the Karpasia peninsula

Northern Cyprus is characterized by a craggy mountain range that runs parallel to the coast, the Kyrenia (Girne) Range, better known as the Pentadactylos Range. It rises sharply from the plains in the west near Vasilia (Kariyaka), is about 6 to 8 km wide and runs from west to east for about 80 km, tapering off into the long 'finger' of the scenic and narrowing Karpasia (Karpas) peninsula near Epthakomi (Yedikonuk). Its highest elevation, the Kyparissovouno, is 1,024 m. The mountains mainly consist of calcareous formations, such as marl, dolomite, recrystallized limestone and marble. Mixed in are areas of basalt and ryolite.

The higher altitudes are wooded with Aleppo Pines (*Pinus halepensis*) and Italian Cypresses (*Cupressus sempervirens*). On the northern slopes, which fall away into chalky and alluvial coasts, one can find sometimes very dense maquis and phrygana-like growth. Characteristic plants include the Pink, the White and the Cretan Rockrose (*Cistus parviflorus, Cistus salviifolius* and *Cistus creticus*). One can very often also find Thorny Burnet (*Sarcopoterium spinosum*), as well as species of the taxa *Pistacia, Salvia, Styrax* and the Strawberry Tree with its striking red bark, which occurs in bush and tree forms. The southern slopes towards the Mesaoria plains are less steep. They are also botanically less productive, as they are much more arid than the northern slopes. In contrast to the coastal region, which is mainly used for agriculture, the mountain range is left to nature, and only a very few picnic and holiday facilities in places disturb the overall impression (Hansen, Kreutz & U. & D. Rückbrodt, 1990).

In the past, this part of Cyprus was an eldorado for botanists, especially for orchidologists. In recent years however the number of flowering plants has decreased considerably, primarily due to ever-expanding sheep and goat herds. The fertile plains are also being used more intensively, with consequent negative effects, especially on the orchids growing in wet places and by the side of streams. Above all, the habitats are general-

wachsen, besonders nachteilig betroffen sind. Darüber hinaus sind die Standorte im Durchschnitt weniger reich besetzt als im Süden, was vermutlich unter anderem auch durch das Ausgraben der Knollen verursacht wird.

Die Gebirgskette im Norden erreicht bei weitem nicht die Höhe des Troodos-Massivs, weshalb hier alle montane Arten fehlen. Dadurch ist die Artenvielfalt im Norden geringer als im Südteil der Insel. So fehlen im Norden die montanen Arten *Cephalanthera rubra*, *Dactylorhiza iberica*, *Epipactis condensata*, *Epipactis microphylla*, *Epipactis troodi*, *Epipactis veratrifolia* und *Platanthera holmboei*, und in den niedrigeren Lagen *Ophrys alasiatica*, *Ophrys tenthredinifera*, *Orchis caspia*, *Orchis laxiflora*, *Orchis palustris* und *Orchis troodi*. Vorkommen von *Barlia robertiana*, *Ophrys apifera*, *Ophrys herae*, *Ophrys hystera*, *Ophrys rhodia*, *Orchis punctulata*, *Orchis sezikiana*, *Serapias aphroditae* und *Serapias parviflora* wurden im Norden bis heute nur sehr wenig beobachtet. Andererseits sind viele Arten im Norden relativ häufig und weit verbreitet. Dazu gehören *Neotinea maculata*, *Ophrys bornmuelleri*, *Ophrys cinereophila*, *Ophrys elegans*, *Ophrys flavomarginata*, *Ophrys israelitica*, *Ophrys kotschyi*, *Ophrys lapethica*, *Ophrys sicula*, *Ophrys umbilicata*, *Orchis anatolica*, *Orchis fragrans*, *Orchis italica*, *Orchis syriaca* und *Serapias levantina*. Auffallend ist das häufige vorkommen von *Ophrys kotschyi* im Norden. Diese endemische und besonders attraktive Art, kommt im Norden häufig vor, wogegen sie im Süden relativ selten ist. Sehr häufig und weit verbreitet sind im Norden auch *Neotinea maculata* und *Orchis anatolica*. Während *Orchis anatolica* im Süden überwiegend von *Orchis sezikiana* und *Orchis troodi* vertreten wird (mit Ausnahme im Gebiet vom Makheras Kloster), ist sie im Norden (vor allem im Pentadactylos-Gebirge) in ihrer typischen Erscheinungsform stellenweise häufig.

Barlia robertiana, *Dactylorhiza romana*, *Ophrys apifera*, *Ophrys attica*, *Orchis sezikiana*, *Orchis punctulata* und *Orchis simia* sind im Norden viel seltener als im Süden. So wurde *Orchis punctulata* erst 1989 für den Norden nachgewiesen, und aktuell ist sie nur bei Hirsanköy in nennenswerter Anzahl vorhanden.

Die Anzahl von Fundorten von *Ophrys lapethica* im Norden dürfte sich in Zukunft stark erhöhen, da viele Funde dieser Art in der Vergangenheit irrtümlich unter *Ophrys attica* oder unter *Ophrys umbilicata* aufgelistet worden sind.

Ophrys alasiatica wurde bisher noch nicht mit Sicherheit für den Norden nachgewiesen. Diese Art wird hier vermutlich auch vorkommen, obwohl ihr Verbreitungsgebiet nach dem heutigen Kenntnisstand nur im mittleren Süden gelegen ist.

Zu erwähnen wäre noch der Fund von *Ophrys ciliata*. Von mehreren Orchideologen und Botanikern wird diese Unterart für den Norden angegeben (HANSEN, KREUTZ & U. & D. RÜCKBRODT, 1990; GEORGIADES, 1998b;

ly less populated than in the south, mainly because the plants are frequently dug up.

The northern mountain range nowhere near reaches the heights of the Troodos massif, which means that mountainous species are absent. The range of species is therefore smaller in the northern part of the island than in the south. Species that are absent from the north are the mountainous taxa *Cephalanthera rubra*, *Dactylorhiza iberica*, *Epipactis condensata*, *Epipactis microphylla*, *Epipactis troodi*, *Epipactis veratrifolia* and *Platanthera holmboei*, and at lower altitudes *Ophrys alasiatica*, *Ophrys tenthredinifera*, *Orchis caspia*, *Orchis laxiflora*, *Orchis palustris* and *Orchis troodi* are not found. Sites of *Barlia robertiana*, *Ophrys apifera*, *Ophrys herae*, *Ophrys hystera*, *Ophrys rhodia*, *Orchis punctulata*, *Orchis sezikiana*, *Serapias aphroditae* and *Serapias parviflora* are extremely rare in the north. Many species are however relatively abundant and widespread. These include *Neotinea maculata*, *Ophrys bornmuelleri*, *Ophrys cinereophila*, *Ophrys elegans*, *Ophrys flavomarginata*, *Ophrys israelitica*, *Ophrys kotschyi*, *Ophrys lapethica*, *Ophrys sicula*, *Ophrys umbilicata*, *Orchis anatolica*, *Orchis fragrans*, *Orchis italica*, *Orchis syriaca* and *Serapias levantina*. Quite exceptional is the prolific occurrence of *Ophrys kotschyi* in the north. This endemic and especially attractive species occurs abundantly in the north, but is relatively rare in the south. *Orchis anatolica* is particularly interesting; while this species is mainly represented by *Orchis sezikiana* and *Orchis troodi* in the south (with the exception of the area around Makheras monastery), it is abundant in some places in its typical form in the north (especially in the Pentadactylos Range).

Barlia robertiana, *Dactylorhiza romana*, *Ophrys apifera*, *Ophrys attica*, *Orchis sezikiana*, *Orchis punctulata* and *Orchis simia* are all much rarer in the north than in the south. Evidence for *Orchis punctulata* for example was first provided from the north in 1989, and at the moment it is only present in noteworthy numbers near Hirsanköy.

The number of habitats of *Ophrys lapethica* in the north may increase strongly in the future, as many earlier findings of this species were listed erroneously under *Ophrys attica* or *Ophrys umbilicata* in the past.

Evidence for *Ophrys alasiatica* has not yet been provided with certainty for the north. This species may occur here also, although its distribution area is situated in the central south according to the current state of knowledge.

Noteworthy is the finding of *Ophrys ciliata*. Several orchidologists and botanists have listed this subspecies for the north (HANSEN, KREUTZ & U. & D. RÜCKBRODT, 1990; GEORGIADES, 1998b, CHRISTOFIDES, 2001). There is

CHRISTOFIDIS, 2001). Von all diesen Fundmeldungen gibt es jedoch keine Fotos oder Herbarbelege.

Von allen genannten Arten liegt die Blütezeit in den niedrigen Lagen in der ersten Märzhälfte, in den Gebirgslagen bis zu 14 Tage später. *Ophrys bornmuelleri* blüht etwa ab Mitte März, zwei Wochen später als *Ophrys levantina*. Zwei bis drei Wochen später folgen dann unter anderem *Anacamptis pyramidalis*, *Orchis fragrans* und *Orchis sancta*, die beiden letzteren in grösseren Beständen in küstennahen Gebieten und auf der Karpasia-Halbinsel.

Limodorum abortivum blüht auf Zypern fast nur in höheren Lagen und bedingt dadurch spät. Seine Blütezeit kann bis in den Juni hinein reichen, im Süden, im Troodos-Gebirge sogar bis Mitte Juli. Die späte Blütezeit ist sicherlich auch der Grund dafür, dass nur wenige aktuelle Daten dieser Art vorliegen. Im Norden ist *Limodorum abortivum* auch selten und wurde unter anderem von HANSEN, KREUTZ & U. & D. RÜCKBRODT (1990) entweder austreibend oder knospig, beziehungsweise als Fruchtstand des Vorjahres gefunden.

Wie im Süden endet auch im Norden Zyperns die Orchideensaison im Dezember mit der Blüte von *Spiranthes spiralis* und fängt im Januar wieder mit der Blüte von *Orchis collina* an.

Das südliche Hügelland

Von der Umgebung um Larnaka bis zur im äussersten Westen gelegenen Akamas-Halbinsel erstreckt sich ein Areal, das durch sehr differenzierte geologische Verhältnisse gekennzeichnet ist. Äusseres Zeichen dafür ist das Vorkommen von basophilen Orchideenarten in direkter Nachbarschaft von acidophilen Arten. Neben den Orchideen erfreuen den Wanderer auf der Akamas-Halbinsel ab Mitte März Tausende von *Cyclamen persicum*, die Stammpflanze des gezüchteten Alpenveilchens. Vereinzelt findet sich hier auch die endemische Tulpe *Tulipa cypria*. Die Akamas-Halbinsel ist ausserdem besonders reich an Orchideen. In den weitläufigen Phryganaflächen und an Waldlichtungen ist in diesem Gebiet vor allem die seltene und gefährdete *Orchis punctulata* zu finden, weiterhin *Serapias aphroditae* und viele Exemplare von *Orchis troodi*. Ausserdem hat *Ophrys tenthredinifera* hier ihren einzigen Fundort. Weitere Orchideenarten, die hier häufig vorkommen, sind *Barlia robertiana*, *Neotinea maculata*, *Ophrys bornmuelleri*, *Ophrys elegans*, *Ophrys flavomarginata*, *Ophrys israelitica*, *Ophrys sicula* und *Serapias bergonii*. Leider wird dieses Gebiet sehr stark beweidet. Besonders nachteilig ist davon *Orchis punctulata* betroffen, von der nur noch wenige Fundstellen mit einzelnen Pflanzen vorhanden sind. Aspektbildend in diesem Gebiet ist *Dactylorhiza romana*, die hier in Tausenden Exemplaren vorkommt.

Der schmale Streifen Schwemmland, der den Küstenbereich bildet, besteht hauptsächlich aus Kies, Sand und Schlamm. Dabei stellen die beiden Salzseen auf der Halbinsel Akrotiri und bei Larnaka eine grosse

however no photographic evidence or plant material of these findings.

The flowering time of all the species named starts in the first half of March on the lower altitudes, 14 days later in mountainous altitudes. *Ophrys bornmuelleri* flowers from about mid-March, two weeks later than *Ophrys levantina*. *Anacamptis pyramidalis*, *Orchis fragrans* and *Orchis sancta* for example follow two to three weeks later, the last two in large stands in coastal areas and on the Karpasia peninsula.

Limodorum abortivum flowers on Cyprus only in the higher altitudes and is late because of this. Its flowering period can extend into June, and in the south, in the Troodos Range, even into mid-July. The late flowering period is certainly the reason for the small amount of recent data on this species. *Limodorum abortivum* is very rare in the north and such as HANSEN, KREUTZ & U. & D. RÜCKBRODT (1990) found it only with buds or shoots, or with spring fruits.

Just as in the south, the orchid season ends in December in the north with *Spiranthes spiralis* and starts again in January when *Orchis collina* starts to flower.

The southern uplands

An area characterized by very varied geological conditions stretches from in the area of Larnaka to the far western Akamas peninsula. Visual evidence is provided by the occurrence of basophile orchid species right next to acidophile species. Next to these orchids, from mid-March hikers on the Akamas peninsula may enjoy thousands of *Cyclamen persicum*, the stem plant of the cultured cyclamen. One can also find solitary specimens of the endemic tulip *Tulipa cypria*. The Akamas peninsula is exceptionally rich in orchids. The rare and endangered *Orchis punctulata* can be found in the vast phrygana plains and in wood clearings in this area, as well as *Serapias aphroditae* and many specimens of *Orchis troodi*. *Ophrys tenthredinifera* has its only habitat here. Other orchid species which occur here abundantly are *Barlia robertiana*, *Neotinea maculata*, *Ophrys bornmuelleri*, *Ophrys elegans*, *Ophrys flavomarginata*, *Ophrys israelitica*, *Ophrys sicula* and *Serapias bergonii*. This area is unfortunately heavily grazed, with adverse effect on *Orchis punctulata*, of which only a few sites with some plants remain. Outstanding in this area is the abundant *Dactylorhiza romana*, with thousands of individuals.

The narrow band of alluvial deposits which form the coastal area primarily consists of gravel, sand and silt. The two salt lakes on the Akrotiri peninsula and near Larnaka are special features. The lake near Larnaka in

Pentadactylos Range, 18.3.2002

Gerasa-Apsiou (mit/with *Orchis italica*), 7.3.2002

Pano Amiantos, 23.6.2002

Besonderheit dar. Vor allem letzterer beherbergt während der Wintermonate große Schwärme von Flamingos. An seinem Rand liegt eines der größten moslemischen Heiligtümer, die Hala Sultan Tekke mit dem Grab der Pflegemutter des Propheten Mohammed. Die Orchideenblüte in diesem Gebiet beginnt schon sehr früh. *Orchis collina* macht ab Januar den Anfang, gefolgt von *Barlia robertiana* und *Orchis syriaca* und im Februar und März von vielen *Ophrys*-Arten. An mäßig feuchten Stellen im Grasland und in den Waldlichtungen in Pinien- und Kiefernwäldern blühen viele Pflanzen von *Ophrys attica, Ophrys cinereophila, Ophrys flavomarginata, Ophrys israelitica, Ophrys melena, Ophrys rhodia, Ophrys sicula, Ophrys umbilicata* und *Orchis italica* und in der Umgebung des Salzsees auf der Akrotiri-Halbinsel dazu viele *Ophrys kotschyi*. Hier gibt es sehr selten auch *Serapias parviflora*, die auf Zypern aber weniger typisch ist als im restlichen Mittelmeerraum, weil die Pflanzen meist niederwüchsiger sind, weniger Blüten und eine größere Lippe haben. Am Salzsee bei Larnaka kommt ausserdem die seltene *Serapias levantina* vor.

Später, ab Ende März, beginnen *Anacamptis pyramidalis, Ophrys apifera, Ophrys hystera* und *Orchis fragrans* zu blühen, zwei bis drei Wochen später gefolgt von *Orchis sancta*, die vor allem auf der Akrotiri-Halbinsel in großen Beständen vorkommt und dort nicht selten Hybriden mit *Orchis fragrans* bildet. Vor allem *Ophrys apifera* hat auf der Akrotiri-Halbinsel reich besetzte Standorte. Inmitten ausgedehnter Felder, die von Feuchtwiesen, Binsen bewachsenen Wiesenflächen, Buschwerk und Pinienwäldern unterbrochen werden, blühen ab Mitte bis Ende März viele hundert Pflanzen dieser Art. Ausserdem kommen hier nicht selten zwei Varietäten von *Ophrys apifera* vor, nämlich *Ophrys apifera* var. *bicolor* und *Ophrys apifera* var. *chlorantha*.

Auf der Akrotiri-Halbinsel kommt ausserdem die sehr seltene *Orchis palustris* vor. Sie wächst auf Zypern nur in diesem Gebiet und nur noch in sehr wenigen Exemplare in den weitläufigen Schilfbeständen. Durch Trockenlegung, verursacht 1985 durch den Bau des Kouris Staudammes nördlich von Lemesos, ist *Orchis palustris* an vielen Stellen verschwunden, und der einzig aktuelle Standort zeigt nur noch einen kleinen Restbestand. Die letzten Pflanzen, weniger als zehn, wachsen dort in einem trockenen Bachbett und sind zur Blütezeit im Mai von einer Ruderalflora völlig überwuchert. An der anderen Fundstelle, ein ebenfalls ausgetrocknetes Bachbett etwa ein Kilometer von der erstgenannten Stelle entfernt, wurde *Orchis palustris* in den letzten Jahren nicht mehr gefunden. Ergiebige Regenfälle im Jahre 2004 haben dazu geführt, dass der Kouris Staudamm geflutet wurde, wodurch die (ehemaligen) Sumpfgebiete nach 20 Jahre wieder reichlich mit Wasser versorgt wurden. Es ist zu hoffen, dass sich der Restbestand von *Orchis palustris* hierdurch wieder etwas erholen kann.

particular harbours large flocks of flamingoes during the winter months. One of the most important Islamic shrines, the Hala Sultan Tekke with the grave of the foster mother of the prophet Mohammed, is situated at its edge. The flowering period of the orchids in this area starts very early. *Orchis collina* has already started in January, followed by *Barlia robertiana* and *Orchis syriaca*, and in February and March by many *Ophrys* species. In moderately moist places in the grasslands and in the clearings of coniferous forests, many plants of *Ophrys attica, Ophrys cinereophila, Ophrys flavomarginata, Ophrys israelitica, Ophrys melena, Ophrys rhodia, Ophrys sicula, Ophrys umbilicata* and *Orchis italica* flower, and in the vicinity of the salt lake on the Akrotiri peninsula many plants of *Ophrys kotschyi* also. Very rarely, *Serapias parviflora* may also be found, in not quite the typical form of the rest of the Mediterranean, as the plants are of a short build, have fewer flowers and larger labella. At the Larnaka salt lake, the rare *Serapias levantina* also occurs.

Later, from the end of March, *Anacamptis pyramidalis, Ophrys apifera, Ophrys hystera* and *Orchis fragrans* start to flower, followed two to three weeks later by *Orchis sancta*, which mainly grows in large populations on the Akrotiri peninsula, where it commonly forms hybrids with *Orchis fragrans*. *Ophrys apifera* especially has densely populated habitats on the Akrotiri peninsula. From mid until late March many hundreds of plants of this species flower in vast fields, interspersed by marshes, rushy meadows, scrubs and pine woodland. Furthermore, two varieties of *Ophrys apifera* are common here, namely *Ophrys apifera* var. *bicolor* and *Ophrys apifera* var. *chlorantha*.

The very rare *Orchis palustris* also occurs on the Akrotiri peninsula. It grows on Cyprus only in this area and only as a very few specimens in the vast reed stands. Due to drying out, because of the building in 1985 of the Kouris dam, the huge water reservoir north of Lemesos, *Orchis palustris* has disappeared from most habitats and the current habitat has only a small remaining population. These last remaining plants, fewer than ten, are growing in a dry stream bed, completely overgrown by weeds during the flowering period. At the other site, also a dry ditch about a kilometre from the first site, *Orchis palustris* has not been seen in recent years. Because of extreme rainfalls in 2004 the Kouris dam overflowed. This means that for the first time in 20 years there was a lot of water in the marshlands around Akrotiri and hopefully this will benefit the remaining population of *Orchis palustris* and reestablish the decent population.

Besonders viele Orchideen wachsen in der Umgebung von Choulou, sowohl arten- als zahlenmäßig. Hier findet man Fundorte mit Massenbeständen von *Ophrys morio, Ophrys levantina* und *Orchis italica*. Auch kommt in diesem Gebiet die seltene *Ophrys mammosa* vor, hauptsächlich aber in den höheren Lagen. Weiter südlich in den Niederungen kommt auch die sehr seltene und gefährdete *Orchis laxiflora* vor. Die Art wächst hier noch in einigen Feuchtgebieten und entlang von Bachläufen, meist mit *Serapias bergonii* vergesellschaftet. Beide Arten sind hier aber durch Trockenlegung und Mahd stark bedroht.

Eine besonders stattliche und attraktive Art ist *Orchis punctulata*, die ihre Hauptverbreitung nördlich und nordöstlich von Lemesos hat. Vor allem in der Umgebung von Kato Drys und südlich von Moni in der Umgebung von Agios Georgios ist die Art stellenweise noch reichlich in der dornigen Phrygana zu finden. Besonders bei Kato Drys ist diese sehr schöne Art durch Überweidung, Verbuschung und Bebauung ihrer Standorte stark bedroht.

Im Süden der Mesaoria-Ebene, in den kalkreichen Hügeln zwischen Lemesos und Larnaka und in den feuchten küstennahen Gebieten auf der Akrotiri-Halbinsel wächst die besonders attraktive und endemische *Ophrys kotschyi*. Vor allem auf der Akrotiri-Halbinsel bildet diese Art größere Bestände. Sie wächst hier in der direkten Umgebung des Salzsees, bevorzugt in feuchten, manchmal überschwemmten und spärlich bewachsenen Gebieten.

Ophrys alasiatica, die erst 2002 beschrieben wurde (KREUTZ, SEGERS & WALRAVEN, 2002) und die davor mit vielen (Arbeits) Namen versehen bzw. vielen verschiedenen Arten zugeordnet wurde, ist hauptsächlich im mittleren Süden verbreitet. Bevorzugt wächst sie in aufgelassenen Oliven- und Weinhainen, dort meist von *Ophrys iricolor* und *Ophrys lapethica* begleitet.

Relativ selten ist *Ophrys herae*. Aktuelle Fundorte finden sich unter anderem südlich von Lefkosia und in der Umgebung von Kato Drys. Wegen ihrer frühen Blütezeit wurde sie bis heute nur wenig beobachtet.

Auf Zypern ist *Orchis sezikiana* weit verbreitet und häufig. Typische Exemplare der sehr nahe verwandten *Orchis anatolica* sind dagegen selten. Diese Art wächst eigentlich nur im Norden der Insel im Pentadactylos-Gebirge und im Wald von Makheras, sowie in der weiteren Umgebung des Makheras Klosters im Südosten Zyperns. Die nahe verwandte *Orchis troodi* findet man hauptsächlich in höheren Lagen, vor allem an den Südhängen des Troodos-Gebirges.

Sehr reich an Orchideen ist das Gebiet nördlich von Souni und bei Gerasa im mittleren Westen der Insel. Neben *Ophrys bornmuelleri, Ophrys levantina* und *Orchis sezikiana* kommt hier ausserdem die seltene und etwas später blühende mittel- und südeuropäische *Orchis simia* vor. Sie bildet hier mitten in der dornigen Phrygana an mehreren Stellen sehr schöne Bestände mit stattlichen Exemplaren.

An exceptional number of orchids in both populations and species grow in the vicinity of Choulou. Sites with huge populations of *Ophrys morio, Ophrys levantina* and *Orchis italica* can be found here. The rare *Ophrys mammosa* also occurs in this area, though primarily at higher altitudes. Further to the south in the lowlands, the very rare and endangered *Orchis laxiflora* can be found. The species still grows here in some wetlands and along streams, mostly together with *Serapias bergonii*. But both species are strongly endangered by drainage and mowing here.

A particularly stately and attractive species is *Orchis punctulata*, which has a main distribution area to the north and northeast of Lemesos. In the area around Kato Drys especially, and south of Moni in the vicinity of Agios Georgios, the species can still be found in abundance in places amongst the thorny phrygana. In particular near Kato Drys, this very beautiful species is gravely threatened by overgrazing, shrub encroachment and new housing at its habitats.

The attractive and endemic *Ophrys kotschyi* grows in the south of the Mesaoria plains, in the calcareous hills between Lemesos and Larnaka and in the moist coastal areas of the Akrotiri peninsula. Especially on the Akrotiri peninsula, this species grows in large populations. It grows here right next to the salt lake, preferring moist, often inundated and sparsely covered areas.

Ophrys alasiatica, first described in 2002 (KREUTZ, SEGERS & WALRAVEN, 2002) and prior to that provided with many (preliminary) names and classified under various species, is mainly distributed in the central south. It prefers abandoned olive groves and vineyards, and is often accompanied by *Ophrys iricolor* and *Ophrys lapethica*.

Relatively rare is *Ophrys herae*. Recent findings have been made for instance south of Lefkosia and in the vicinity of Kato Drys. Due to its early flowering time it has rarely been noticed until now.

Orchis sezikiana is widespread and abundant on Cyprus. Typical specimens of the closely related *Orchis anatolica* are however rare. This species actually only grows in the north of the island in the Pentadactylos Range, in the woods of Makheras, and in the area around the Makheras monastery in the south-east of Cyprus. The closely related *Orchis troodi* is primarily found in the higher altitudes, especially on the southern slopes of the Troodos Range.

The area north of Souni and near Gerasa in the central west of the island is very rich in orchids. Besides *Ophrys bornmuelleri, Ophrys levantina* and *Orchis sezikiana*, the rare and slightly later flowering Central and Southern European *Orchis simia* also occurs here. It forms very beautiful stands with stately specimens sporadically in the midst of the thorny phrygana.

WOOD berichtet erstmals über einen Einzelfund von *Orchis caspia* auf Zypern, gefunden 1960 von SPARROW (WOOD, 1985) auf der Halbinsel Akrotiri (nördlich vom Salzsee). 2001 wurde diese Art dann erneut zwischen Lemesos und Larnaka nahe Choirokoitia gefunden (SCRATON 2001), zusammen mit einigen Hybriden mit *Orchis syriaca*. *Orchis caspia* wächst hier in einem ehemals landwirtschaftlich genutzten Gebiet nahe eines großen Stausees (Kalavasos dam). Der Standort weist eine typische Phrygana-Vegetation mit Arten wie *Thymus capitatus, Sarcopoterium spinosum, Asphodelus aestivus* und vielen anderen Pflanzen- und Orchideenarten auf.

Die Mesaoria-Ebene im Osten

Südlich der Pentadactylos-Gebirgskette und östlich vom Troodos-Massiv erstreckt sich über einen großen Teil der Insellänge die in weiten Teilen baumlose, fruchtbare Mesaoria-Ebene, die heute überwiegend im türkisch besetzten Norden liegt. Sowohl im Ost- als auch im Westteil besteht der Boden aus Schwemmland (Schlamm, Sand und Kies), im mittleren Teil primär aus Mergel, Sand und Kies mit eingestreuten Kalk- und Gipsformationen. Die Getreidemonokultur vor der Teilung (die Mesaoria galt als die Kornkammer Zyperns) und der Einsatz von Herbiziden hatte dieses Gebiet gründlich von 'Unkräutern' befreit. Da große Teile der Ebene aber seit 1974 brach liegen, beziehungsweise nur als Weideflächen genutzt wurden, hat sich die Flora ein wenig erholt. Im ufernahen Gelände der wenigen, sommertrockenen Bachläufe steht Mitte Februar *Orchis collina* in Hochblüte, gefolgt von *Ophrys umbilicata* und *Orchis italica*. Diese Standorte sind jedoch schon wieder gefährdet, da die brachliegenden Äcker zunehmend als Anbaufläche genutzt werden und sich die Schafherden in den letzten Jahren um ein Vielfaches vermehrt haben (HANSEN, KREUTZ & U. & D. RÜCKBRODT, 1990).

Das Troodos-Massiv

Ein besonderes Refugium stellt das Troodos-Gebirge mit seinen majestätisch wirkenden Mittelmeerzypressen (*Cupressus sempervirens*), seinen gewaltigen Schwarzkiefern (*Pinus nigra* subsp. *pallasiana*) und Zypern-Zedern (*Cedrus brevifolia*) dar. Es ist vulkanischen Ursprungs und meist über 1.000 m hoch. Die höchste Erhebung Zyperns, der Olympus (Khionistra), erreicht 1.951 m. Harzburgit, Gabbro und Serpentin bilden die Hochlagen des Gebirges. Südlich und westlich des Troodos wechseln sich dunkle Gesteine vulkanischen Ursprungs mit hellen, kalkigen Meeresablagerungen ab. Sie bilden eine hügelige Landschaft mit Hochebenen und tiefen Tälern. Das Gestein der tieferen Lagen besteht primär aus Grünstein. Sehr unterschiedlich stellt sich, der Bodenbeschaffenheit entsprechend, das Orchideenvorkommen dar. Relativ wenige Arten im Vulkangestein, wie *Dactylorhiza romana, Neotinea maculata* und *Orchis troodi* stehen im Gegensatz zur Artenvielfalt auf den

WOOD was the first person who refered to a solitary finding of *Orchis caspia* on Cyprus, found in 1960 by SPARROW (WOOD, 1985) on the Akrotiri peninsula (north of the salt lake). In 2001, this species was found again between Lemesos and Larnaka, near Choirokoitia (SCRATON 2001), together with some hybrids with *Orchis syriaca*. *Orchis caspia* grows here in a former agricultural area near a large reservoir (Kalavasos dam). The habitat harbours phrygana vegetation with species such as *Thymus capitatus, Sarcopoterium spinosum, Asphodelus aestivus* and many other plant and orchid species.

The Mesaoria plain in the east

The primarily treeless, fertile Mesaoria plain, largely situated in the Turkish occupied north, stretches over a large part of the length of the island, southwards from the Pentadactylos Range to east of the Troodos massif. Both in the east and in the west, the terrain consists of alluvial deposits (silt, sand and gravel); in the central part it primarily consists of marl, sand and gravel with formations of chalk and gypsum interspersed. The monoculture of grain before the division (Mesaoria used to be the granary of Cyprus) and the use of herbicides has thoroughly rid the region of 'weeds'. Since large parts of the plains have lain fallow, or have only been used as meadows since 1974, the flora has been able to recover slightly. On the watersides of the few (dry in summer) streams, *Orchis collina* can be found in mid-February in full bloom, followed by *Ophrys umbilicata* and *Orchis italica*. These habitats are however threatened anew, as the barren fields are increasingly being used as cultivable land and sheep herds have multiplied considerably in recent years (HANSEN, KREUTZ & U. & D. RÜCKBRODT, 1990).

The Troodos massif

A special sanctuary is the Troodos mountain range, with majestic Italian Cypresses (*Cupressus sempervirens*), mighty Black Pines (*Pinus nigra* subsp. *pallasiana*) and Cyprus Cedars (*Cedrus brevifolia*). It is of volcanic origin and mostly over 1,000 m high. The highest point of Cyprus, Olympus (Khionistra), reaches 1,951 m. Harzburgite, gabbro and serpentine form the higher reaches of the mountains. Southwards and westwards of the Troodos range, dark rocks of volcanic origin alternate with calcereous marine sedimentations. They form a hilly landscape with elevated plains and deep valleys. The lower altitudes consist primarily of igneous rocks. According to the composition of the soil, occurrences of orchids vary greatly. Relatively few species on volcanic rock, such as *Dactylorhiza romana, Neotinea maculata* and *Orchis troodi* are in contrast to the species diversity on calcareous soil. The occurrence of *Barlia robertiana*, which can grow up to 1,200 m in the middle altitudes of the Troodos mountains, is wor-

Akrotiri (Salt lake), (mit/with *Ophrys kotschyi*), 8.3.2002

Larnaka (Salt lake), (mit/with *Orchis italica*), 9.3.2002

Troodos-Gebirge/Troodos mountains, 26.6.2002

Troodos-Gebirge/Troodos mountains, 26.6.2002

kalkhaltigen Böden. Bemerkenswert ist das Vorkommen von *Barlia robertiana*, die in den mittleren Höhenlagen des Troodos-Gebirges noch bis 1.200 m Höhe vorkommt. In den montanen Lagen des Troodos-Gebirges, die hauptsächlich mit Schwarzkiefern (*Pinus nigra* subsp. *pallasiana*) locker bewaldet sind, wachsen mehrere und für Zypern und das Mittelmeergebiet sehr seltene, Orchideenarten wie *Dactylorhiza iberica, Epipactis condensata, Epipactis microphylla, Epipactis troodi, Epipactis veratrifolia* und *Platanthera holmboei*, von denen *Epipactis troodi* endemisch ist. Am Rande des schmelzenden Schnees erscheint hier im Frühjahr der ebenfalls endemische Zypriotische Krokus (*Crocus cyprius*). Der dichtere Wald der tieferen Lagen besteht hauptsächlich aus der Kalabrischen Kiefer (*Pinus brutia*). Auch der zypressenähnliche Wacholder (*Juniperus foetidissimus*), sowie der Östliche Erdbeerbaum *(Arbutus andrachne)* bilden größere, zusammenhängende Bestände. Besonders in der Umgebung von Makheras und Prodromos ist die endemische Goldeiche *(Quercus alnifolia)* nicht selten. Am Westende des Massivs, im berühmten Zederntal (Cedar Valley), befinden sich noch Restbestände des ehemals ausgedehnten Zypern-Zedernwaldes (*Cedrus brevifolia*). Auch diese Zedernart gehört zur Gruppe der Endemiten Zyperns. Einige wenige Bachläufe im Troodos-Gebirge führen das ganze Jahr über Wasser. An geeigneten Stellen blüht hier von Mitte Juni bis Anfang August *Epipactis veratrifolia*, an wenigen Stellen zusammen mit *Dactylorhiza iberica*. Vor allem in der Umgebung von Kakopetria und Agios Nikolaos wachsen Gruppen aus mehreren Dutzend Pflanzen von *Epipactis veratrifolia*, die manchmal über einen Meter hoch werden. Besonders interessant ist ein Hangmoor in der Umgebung von Pano Amiantos. Dort blühen an einem ständig überrieselten Quellhang Ende Juni mehrere hundert Pflanzen. *Epipactis veratrifolia* kommt auf Zypern übrigens in zwei sehr unterschiedlichen Ausprägungsformen vor. Im Süden, westlich von Lemesos, wo die Art schon ab Mitte März zur Blüte gelangt, wächst sie an einem steilen, völlig durchnässten und ständig überrieselten Quellhang. Je nach Witterung wachsen hier jährlich mehrere Dutzend sehr kräftige Pflanzen. Das Laub dieser Pflanzen ist das ganze Jahr über grün, während die oberirdische Teile der Pflanzen im Troodos-Gebirge im Winter absterben.

Dactylorhiza iberica, neben *Dactylorhiza romana* die einzige auf der Insel vorkommende *Dactylorhiza*-Art, erscheint an einigen Feuchtstellen am Unterlauf der Bäche, jedoch nirgendwo in größeren Beständen (zwischen fünf und bis etwa zwanzig blühende Pflanzen höchstens). Die Art ist zwar besonders selten, sie ist jedoch an mehreren Feuchtstellen im Troodos-Gebirge nachgewiesen worden. Auch im Zederntal ist *Dactylorhiza iberica* an einigen Stellen zu finden. *Cephalanthera rubra, Limodorum abortivum* und *Platanthera holmboei* wachsen oft zusammen in den weitläufigen, lockeren und imposanten Schwarzkiefer-

thy of note. In the mountainous reaches of the Troodos mountains, which are primarily wooded by Black Pines (*Pinus nigra* subsp. *pallasiana*), several orchid species that are very rare on Cyprus and in the Mediterranean can be found, such as *Dactylorhiza iberica, Epipactis condensata, Epipactis microphylla, Epipactis troodi, Epipactis veratrifolia* and *Platanthera holmboei*, of which *Epipactis troodi* is endemic. The endemic Cyprus crocus (*Crocus cyprius*) also appears here in spring at the edges of the melting snow. The dense forests of the lower reaches consist primarily of Calabrian Pine (*Pinus brutia*). Both the cypress-like Juniper *(Juniperus foetidissimus)* and the Strawberry Tree *(Arbutus andrachne)* form large consistent stands. Notably in the vicinity of Makheras and Prodromos, the endemic Golden Oak *(Quercus alnifolia)* is not uncommon. At the western end of the massif, in the famous Cedar Valley, one can find remaining stands of the original vast Cyprus Cedar forests (*Cedrus brevifolia*). This Cedar species also belongs to the group of Cyprus endemic species.

Some streams in the Troodos mountains have water all the year round. In suitable places, *Epipactis veratrifolia* flowers here from mid-June until the beginning of August, sometimes together with *Dactylorhiza iberica*. In the vicinity of Kakopetria and Agios Nikolaos especially, groups of several thousand plants of *Epipactis veratrifolia* grow, sometimes reaching a height of one metre. Particularly interesting is a wet bank in the vicinity of Pano Amiantos, where several hundred plants flower towards the end of June on a slope with perpetually trickling water. *Epipactis veratrifolia* incidentally occurs on Cyprus in two very differing appearances. In the south, west of Lemesos, where the species succeeds in flowering from mid-March, it grows on a steep, fully saturated slope with constant seepage. Weather permitting, thousands of very robust plants may grow here. The foliage of these plants is green the whole year through, while in the Troodos mountains the above-ground part of the plants dies back in winter.

Dactylorhiza iberica, besides *Dactylorhiza romana* the only *Dactylorhiza* species on the island, is found in some wet places and by streams, but nowhere in large stands (from five to twenty flowering plants at most). This species is very rare, but it has been found at several wet places in the Troodos mountains. *Dactylorhiza iberica* is also found at some places in the Cedar Valley.

Cephalanthera rubra, Limodorum abortivum and *Platanthera holmboei* often grow together in the vast, open and imposing Black Pine forests. With the excep-

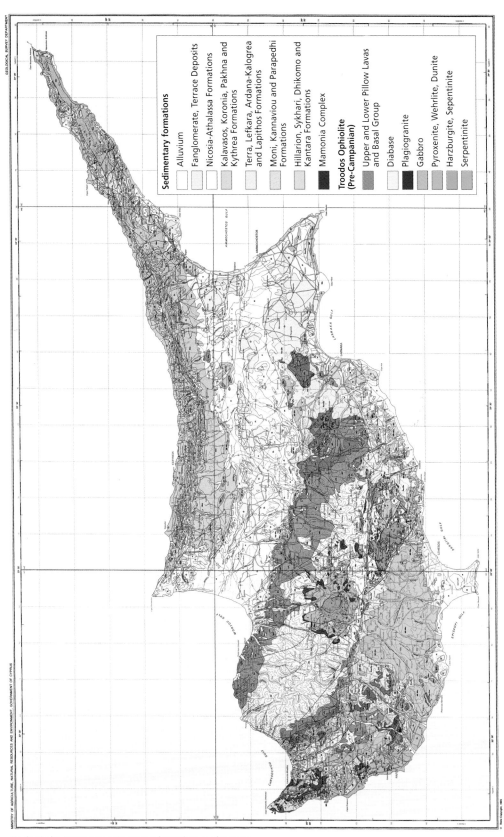

Sedimentary formations

- Alluvium
- Fanglomerate, Terrace Deposits
- Nicosia-Athalassa Formations
- Kalavasos, Koronia, Pakhna and Kythrea Formations
- Terra, Lefkara, Ardana-Kalogrea and Lapithos Formations
- Moni, Kannaviou and Parapedhi Formations
- Hillarion, Sykhari, Dhikomo and Kantara Formations
- Mamonia Complex

Troodos Ophiolite (Pre-Campanian)

- Upper and Lower Pillow Lavas and Basal Group
- Diabase
- Plagiogranite
- Gabbro
- Pyroxenite, Wehrlite, Dunite
- Harzburgite, Sepentinite
- Serpentinite

Geologische Karte von Zypern/Geological map of Cyprus

The Geological Survey Department, Cyprus (1995)

wäldern. Mit Ausnahme von *Cephalanthera rubra* sind diese Arten an vielen Stellen zu finden, besonders auf Waldlichtungen und an Straßenböschungen. Manchmal sind sie mit *Epipactis troodi* vergesellschaftet, einer endemischen *Epipactis*-Art von Zypern, die im Gegensatz zu *Epipactis condensata* und *Epipactis microphylla* im Troodos-Gebirge recht viele Fundorte hat, aber dort fast immer nur in wenigen Exemplaren vorkommt. Eine weitere sehr bemerkenswerte Art ist *Epipactis condensata*, die nur von wenigen Fundorten in den höheren Lagen des Troodos-Massivs bekannt ist. Auf Lichtungen und im Halbschatten der Schwarzkiefern treibt sie kräftige und reichblütige Blütenstände aus, die manchmal sehr dicht beieinander stehen. *Epipactis condensata* gehört mit ihren großen, grünlich bis rot gefärbten Blüten zu den schönsten *Epipactis*-Arten. In den mittleren Lagen, an nordexponierten Hängen, in der Umgebung von Pitsilia wächst ausserdem noch eine andere *Epipactis*-Art, nämlich *Epipactis microphylla*, die nur an wenigen, schattigen und feuchten Stellen in Haselnusskulturen vorkommt. Im Troodos-Gebirge schmarotzt auf *Pterocephalus strictus* und auf *Salvia acetabulosa* die endemische Zypriotische Orobanche (*Orobanche cypria*), eine wunderschöne Sommerwurzart mit feuerroten Blüten.

Das Klima Zyperns

Das mediterrane Klima Zyperns ist gekennzeichnet durch einen kurzen, relativ kühlen und feuchten Winter und einen langen, heissen und extrem trockenen Sommer. Die Temperaturen differieren beträchtlich. Während die Mesaoria-Ebene so gut wie keinen Frost kennt, und in der Gegend von Pafos sogar Bananen angebaut werden, liegt in den Hochlagen des Troodos-Gebirges etwa drei Monate lang Schnee. Der Frühling fängt auf Zypern schon im Februar an und die Temperatur steigt dann schon auf 15 bis 20 Grad an. Im März und vor allem im April wird es deutlich wärmer, manchmal schon bis um die 25 Grad. Der Sommer beginnt auf Zypern bereits Ende April bis Anfang Mai, und er dauert bis zum Oktober. In dieser Zeit ist es auf Zypern meist trocken, und vor allem später im Sommer herrscht in den Tiefebenen ausgesprochene Dürre und Hitze. Die Sommertemperaturen erreichen im Flachland nicht selten über 35°C. Schon ab Mai sehen große Teile der Insel, besonders die Südhänge, braun und verbrannt aus (HANSEN, KREUTZ & U. & D. RÜCKBRODT, 1990). An der Küste sorgt jedoch der Seewind an heissen Tage für etwas Kühlung. Dieser Wind reicht aber nicht weit ins Landesinnere. Er führt in den höheren Lagen des Troodos-Massivs meist zu Wolkenbildung. Im Troodos-Gebirge herrschen bis in den Juli hinein angenehme Temperaturen, und es wird deswegen im Sommer von der einheimischen Bevölkerung als kühles Ausflugsziel genutzt. Vor allem an den Wochenenden werden die Picknickplätze dort gerne

tion of *Cephalanthera rubra*, these species can be found at many places, especially in forest clearings and among roadside bushes. They are often accompanied by *Epipactis troodi*, an endemic species of Cyprus, which, in contrast to *Epipactis condensata* and *Epipactis microphylla*, has many habitats in the Troodos mountains, but almost always occurs as just a few specimens there. Another very remarkable species is *Epipactis condensata*, which is only known from a few habitats in the higher reaches of the Troodos massif. In the clearings and half shade of the Black Pines it creates vigorous and densely flowered stands, often clustering close together. With its large, greenish to red coloured flowers, *Epipactis condensata* belongs to one of the most beautiful *Epipactis* species. Another *Epipactis* species, *Epipactis microphylla*, also grows at medium-high altitudes on slopes exposed to the north in the vicinity of Pitsilia, and only occurs at a few shady and moist places in hazelnut plantations. In the Troodos mountains, the endemic Cyprus orobanche (*Orobanche cypria*), a gorgeous broomrape species with deep red flowers, parasitises *Pterocephalus strictus* and *Salvia acetabulosa*.

The climate of Cyprus

The Mediterranean climate of Cyprus is characterized by a short, relatively cool and wet winter and a long, hot and extremely dry summer. Temperatures differ considerably. The Mesaoria plains almost never knows any frost, while even bananas grow near Pafos, but at the higher altitudes of the Troodos mountains snow falls during three of the winter months. Spring in Cyprus starts in February and the temperature begins to rise then to about 15 to 20 degrees. In March and especially in April it gets obviously warmer, sometimes even up to 25 degrees. Summer starts at the end of April or early May and lasts until about October. It is usually dry during this period, and especially later in summer, pronounced drought and heat reign at the low altitudes. Summer temperatures often reach above 35 degrees in the lowlands. As early as May, large parts of the island, especially the southern slopes, appear brown and burnt (HANSEN, KREUTZ & U. & D. RÜCKBRODT, 1990). At the coast however the sea breeze provides some cooling even during the hottest days, but it does not reach into the interior. At the higher altitudes of the Troodos massif clouds form, and in the mountains as a whole agreeable temperatures reign right into July, forming a cool sanctuary for the inhabitants during summer. At weekends especially, they like to visit the picnic areas in the Troodos mountains for recreational purposes. Then temperatures start to fall gradually from October. At the same time, precipitation starts to increase slowly. November to February are the coolest months, and the

als Erholungsziele angefahren. Ab Oktober nehmen die Temperaturen allmählich ab. Gleichzeitig nehmen die Niederschläge langsam wieder zu. Von November bis Februar ist es meist kühl, wobei die niedrigsten Temperaturen im Januar und Februar erreicht werden. Bis in den Spätherbst hinein bewirkt das noch relativ warme Mittelmeerwasser vergleichsweise angenehme Temperaturen.

Zwischen November und März fällt der meiste Regen, durchschnittlich ca. 500 mm, wobei im Dezember und Januar die höchsten Niederschläge des ganzen Jahres zu verzeichnen sind. Allerdings ist dieser Wert nicht sehr aussagekräftig, weil sich die Regenmengen zu unterschiedlich über die Insel verteilen. Am regenreichsten sind die Höhen des Troodos-Gebirges (durchschnittlich 1.200 mm jährlich) und der Pentadactylos-Gebirgskette, während in der Mesaoria-Ebene die mittlere Niederschlagsmenge kaum mehr als 300 mm erreicht. Allgemein kann gesagt werden, dass die Menge des Regens mit der Höhe zunimmt. Vor allem auf der Luvseite des Gebirges kommt es durch Aufsteigen und Abkühlen der Luftmassen zu Wolkenbildung und im Extremfall zu Niederschlag, während sich auf der windabgewandte Seite die Wolken wieder auflösen, und es insgesamt weniger regnet. Im Troodos-Gebirge fallen im Januar sogar 225 mm Niederschlag, der bis auf etwa 1.000 m hinab als Schnee fällt, und über 1.500 m ermöglichen Schneehöhen von zwei bis drei Metern sogar Wintersport, nicht selten bis Ende März. Von Februar bis März nehmen die Niederschläge quantitativ kontinuierlich ab, während die Temperaturen ansteigen. Im Juli und August fallen auf der ganzen Insel keine Niederschläge mit Ausnahme vom Troodos-Gebirge, wo in jedem Monat ein Niederschlagstag durchschnittlich 5 mm Regen bringt. Auch das Pentadactylos-Gebirge empfängt in den Wintermonaten reiche Niederschläge. So verwundert es nicht, dass an der kahlen Südseite des Gebirgszuges eine der ergiebigsten Quellen der Insel austritt. Das ganze Jahr über gibt es hier genug Wasser für Oliven und Johannisbrotbäume. Die Nordseite ist bewaldet und ähnelt mit jähen, zum Klettern animierenden Felsgraten und -zinnen ein wenig den Kalkalpen.

In den regenreichen Wintermonaten führen die meisten Bäche und Flüsse Wasser. Während der längsten Zeit des Jahres fallen sie aber trocken. Lediglich im Spätherbst, Winter und Frühling fließen die Niederschläge beziehungsweise Schmelzwässer von den Höhen des Troodos und des Pentadactylos-Gebirges hinunter in die Mesaoria-Ebene und zur Küste. Recht wild gebärdet sich zur Zeit der Schneeschmelze auf dem Troodos der Fluss Karyotis, der gelegentlich zu einem reissenden Gebirgsfluss anschwellen kann (Baedeker, 2001). An einigen Orten wurden kleine Stauseen für Bewässerungszwecke angelegt. Dank des Wasserreichtums ist Zypern vor allem im Frühjahr eine grüne Insel.

lowest temperatures of all are in January and February. The relatively warm Mediterranean sea ensures comparatively pleasant temperatures until late autumn.

Most precipitation falls between November and March, on average about 500 mm, of which the largest amounts of the whole year fall in December and January. The total amount however does not signify, as rainfall is distributed very unequally over the island. The areas of highest rainfall are the heights of the Troodos mountains (on average 1,200 mm per year) and the Pentadactylos Range, but the average amount of precipitation in the Mesaoria plain hardly reaches 300 mm. Generally speaking, the higher the altitude the more the amount of rain increases. Especially on the windward side of the mountains, clouds are formed by the rising and cooling of the air masses and in some cases this leads to rainfall, while on the leeward side the clouds dissipate, and on average less rain falls. In January 225 mm of rain falls in the Troodos mountains, turning to snow above 1,000m, and above 1,500m a layer of snow two to three metres thick makes winter sports possible, often until the end of March. From February to March precipitation decreases steadily, while temperatures increase. In July and August no precipitation falls throughout the island, with the exception of the Troodos mountains, where each month averages one day of precipitation, bringing 5 mm of rain. The Pentadactylos range also receives copious amounts of rain during the winter months. So it is not surprising that on the bare southern side of the mountain range, one of the most productive springs of the island emerges. Throughout the year, enough water is available for the olive and carob groves. The northern slopes are wooded and slightly resemble the limestone alps, with steep ridges and pinnacles enticing to rock climbers.

In the wet winter months, most rivers and streams flow, but during the greater part of the year they are dry. Not until late autumn, winter and spring does the water from rainfall and melting snow stream down from the Troodos and Pentadactylos ranges into the Mesaoria plains and finally to the coast. The river Karyotis becomes greatly swollen as the snow melts on the Troodos mountains, and can occasionally even grow into a mountain torrent (Baedeker, 2001). At some places small dams have been erected for irrigation purposes. Due to this wealth of water on Cyprus, it is a green island especially during spring.

Vegetation, Flora und Orchideen Zyperns

Zypern bietet dank seines milden und ausgeglichenen Mittelmeerklimas einer Vielfalt an Pflanzen Lebensraum. Insgesamt 1.800 verschiedene Pflanzenarten wachsen auf dieser Insel, von denen rund 140 Arten als endemisch gelten und nur auf Zypern zu finden sind.

Ihren ganzen Reiz bietet die Flora in den Monaten März und April, in denen Zypern von einem vielfarbigen Blütenmeer überzogen ist. Neben mehr als fünfzig verschiedenen Orchideenarten, die auf der ganzen Insel vorkommen, entfalten Tulpen, Gladiolen, Schwertlilien, wilder Mohn und große Felder intensiv riechenden Rapses, sowie Obst- und Zierbäume ihre volle Blütenpracht.

Da die Wasserläufe nach der Schneeschmelze und der kurzen Regenzeit im Frühjahr bald versiegen, wirkt die Insel im Hochsommer eher karg und ausgedörrt. Das Landesinnere mit den großen Ebenen und die Küstenstreifen sind sonnenverbrannt, das Goldgelb des Getreides geht in verschiedene Brauntöne über. Lediglich die blühenden Oleandersträuche setzen kleine Farbtupfer. Die Nadel- und Laubbäume im Bergland sind jedoch auch im Sommer grün.

Fast der ganzen Baumbestand wird durch die Aleppo-Kiefer (*Pinus halepensis*), die in tieferen Regionen wächst, abgedeckt. In Höhen von über 1.200 m wachsen im Troodos fast ausschließlich Schwarzkiefern (*Pinus nigra* subsp. *pallasiana*), Mittelmeerzypressen (*Cupressus sempervirens*), Zypriotische Goldeichen (*Quercus alnifolia*) und sehr selten die Zypernzeder (*Cedrus brevifolia*). In den Ausläufern des Troodos-Gebirges wachsen Eukalyptus- und Olivenbäume. In den Ebenen werden in Obstplantagen Äpfel, Kirschen und Birnen sowie Mandeln und Haselnüsse angebaut. Hier gedeihen neben den auch im Vorgebirge wachsenden Bäumen ausserdem Johannisbrotbaum, Lorbeerbaum, Weinreben, Zitrusfrüchte und Bananenstauden. Getreide und Gemüse werden in der Mesaoria-Ebene und in den Küstengebieten angebaut.

Große Teile der Insel bestehen aus Phrygana und Macchie, die vor allem auf der Akamas-Halbinsel mit Kermes-Eichen (*Quercus coccifera*) durchsetzt sind. In diesen Gebieten sind die meisten Orchideen zu finden. Die vier für Orchideen wichtigen Biotope, nämlich Phrygana und Macchien, Olivenhaine und Weinbergterrassen, Umgebung der Salzseen bei Larnaka und der Akrotiri-Halbinsel, sowie die Pinien- und Kiefernwälder werden nachfolgend separat behandelt.

Phrygana und Macchien

Die Phrygana ist eine der kärgsten und botanisch doch so reichen Lebensräume am Mittelmeer. Sie ist ein Gestrüpp aus stacheligen Büschen und Sträuchern, die große Teile der Insel mit einem dunklen Grün überzieht. Sie ist aus der Schaf- und Ziegenbeweidung hervorgegangen, vergleichbar den mitteleuropäischen Wacholderheiden. Die dort siedelnden Pflanzen sind voll

Vegetation, flora and orchids of Cyprus

Cyprus offers living space to a multitude of plants thanks to its mild and balanced Mediterranean climate. A total of 1,800 different plant species grow on this island, of which about 140 species are endemic and can only be found on Cyprus.

Flowering plants show their full allure in the months of March and April, when Cyprus is covered with a multicoloured carpet of flowers. Beside the more than 50 different orchid species which occur on the island, other plants such as tulips, gladioli, sword lilies, wild poppies and large fields of rapeseed, fruit trees and ornamental trees display the full beauty of their flowers.

As the streams begin to run dry after the snowmelt and the brief period of rain in spring, the island becomes barren and parched. The interior with its great plains and the coastal areas are scorched by the sun, and the golden yellow tones of the crops shade into varied browns. Only the flowering oleander bushes display small patches of colour. The coniferous and deciduous trees on the highlands however remain green through the summer.

Almost the whole tree population in low-lying regions is accounted for by Aleppo Pine (*Pinus halepensis*). In the heights of above 1,200 m, little but Black Pines (*Pinus nigra* subsp. *pallasiana*), Italian Cypresses (*Cupressus sempervirens*), Cyprus Golden Oaks (*Quercus alnifolia*) and the very rare Cyprus Cedars (*Cedrus brevifolia*) grow. Eucalyptus and Olive trees grow in the foothills of the Troodos mountains. Orchards of apple, cherry and pear trees, as well as almonds and hazels are cultivated in the plains. In addition to these trees that also grow in the foothills, carob and laurel trees, grape vines, citrus fruits and banana plants also thrive here. Corn and vegetables are cultivated in the Mesaoria plains and in the coastal areas.

Large parts of the island consist of phrygana and maquis, which are interspersed with Kermes Oaks (*Quercus coccifera*), especially on the Akamas peninsula. In these areas, most of the orchids can be found. The four biotopes that are important for orchids, namely phrygana and maquis, olive groves and vineyard terraces, the area around the salt lakes near Larnaka and on the Akrotiri peninsula, as well as the pine forests are treated separately from here on.

Phrygana and maquis

Although it is one of the poorest habitats of the Mediterranean, it is botanically very rich. It is scrubland consisting of thorny bushes and shrubs, that forms a dark green carpet covering large parts of the island. Phrygana has been created by the grazing of sheep and goats, similar to the Central European juniper heath land. The plants that grow here are exposed to the sun

Alethriko (Standort von/site of *Ophrys kotschyi*), 6.3.2002

Choirokoitia (Standort von/site of *Orchis caspia*), 10.3.2002

Tsada-Pitargou (Standort von/site of *Orchis italica*), 17.3.2002

der Sonne und dem Wind ausgesetzt und müssen mit einem Minimum an Boden auskommen. In der Küstenphrygana dominieren niedrige, fast immer unter einem Meter hohe, oft kugelförmige und mit scharfen Dornen und spitzen Stacheln bewehrte Pflanzen aus vielen Familien, unter ihnen Wolfsmilchgewächse, Seidelbastverwandte, Rauhblattgewächse, Leguminosen, Lippenblütler, wie zum Beispiel Kopfiger Thymian (*Thymus capitatus*), Dornige Bibernelle (*Sarcopoterium spinosum*) und niedrig bleibende weiss, rosa und rot blühende Zistrosen. Diese Dornsträucher und die noch niedrigeren Polsterpflanzen setzen die Eigenverdunstung durch die Reduzierung der Blätter und starke Behaarung auf ein Minimum herab. Die teilweise mit Flechten überzogenen Felspartien, von denen die Küstenphrygana durchzogen wird, verleihen ihr über weite Strecken den Charakter eines bizarren Steingartens, an dessen Schönheit und Vielgestaltigkeit jedoch keiner unserer bewusst gestalteten Steingärten heranreicht. Zwischen den robusten Dornbüschen spriessen und blühen zarte, einjährige Pflanzen und Geophyten (Zwiebel- und Knollengewächse), darunter viele Orchideen. Oft schieben sie sich aufs beste geschützt durch einen Dornbusch nach oben, nicht selten aber wachsen sie auch aus den Löchern der Felspartien hervor.

Die Phrygana prägt auch große Teile der verkarsteten Berglagen der Insel. Dabei handelt es sich um mehr oder weniger offene mediterrane und bis zu zwei Meter hohe Gebüschformationen, in denen Kermes-Eichen, Aleppokiefern, Granatäpfel, Myrte, Mastix sowie diverse andere Hartlaubzwergsträucher, Erdbeerbäume und Wolfsmilchgewächse vergesellschaftet sind, wie zum Beispiel Mastixstrauch (*Pistacia lentiscus*), Johannisbrotbaum (*Ceratonia siliqua*), Ginster (*Genista sphacelata*), Behaarter Dornginster (*Calicotome villosa*) und Olivenbaum (*Olea europea*). Auch Feigenkakteen und Agaven trifft man an. In diese Vegetation gehören auch Oregano, Majoran, Lavendel, Rosmarin, Thymian und Salbei sowie verschiedene Orchideen- und Irisarten (Baedeker, 1999).

Olivenhaine und Weinbergterrassen

Andere wichtige Standorte bilden die Olivenhaine, deren Boden in den Frühlingsmonaten von bunt blühenden Kräutern bedeckt ist. Die Blütenfülle dieser wiesenartigen Gesellschaften zwischen den alten knorrigen Bäumen ist unübersehbar. Den Ton geben dabei Roter Mohn (*Papaver rhoeas*) und die gelbweisse Kronen-Wucherblume (*Chrysanthemum coronarium*) an. Doch in Wirklichkeit ist dieser vom Menschen geschaffene Biotop trotz des auffallenden Vorherrschens einiger Pflanzen sehr viel artenreicher. Er umfasst auf sehr kleinem Raum eine Vielzahl von Wiesenpflanzen, Ackerwildkräutern, Mauerfugenpflanzen und dort, wo Gebüsch die in Stufen angelegten Ölbaumhaine begrenzt, garigueähnliche Gesellschaften mit Zistrosen und anderen bedornten Sträuchern, sowie Reste von Laub- und Nadelwald (Bechtel, 1980).

and wind and have to manage with a minimum of soil. They are short, almost always below one metre tall, often rounded and prickly plants with sharp thorns, belonging to various families. Relatives for instance of the spurge, the daphne, the borage, the legume and the labiate family, such as Headed Savory (*Thymus capitatus*) and Thorny Burnet (*Sarcopoterium spinosum*) as well as always short, white-, pink- and red-flowered rock roses dominate the coastal phrygana. These thorn bushes and the even shorter cushion plants lower the amount of evaporation by reducing the size of their leaves and by covering them with dense hairs. The partially lichen-covered rocks, which permeate the coastal phrygana, give the phrygana the character of a bizarre rock garden of vast area, though its beauty and diversity do not in any way resemble our artificially created rock gardens. Delicate annuals and geophytes (bulbous and tuberous plants) including many orchids, manage to shoot and flower between the robust thorn bushes. They often grow upwards supported by a thorn bush, but they also grow from crevices between the rocks.

Phrygana also dominates large areas of the rocky mountains on the island. This involves more or less open Mediterranean, shrub formations up to two metres in height, in which Kermes Oaks, Aleppo Pines, Pomegranates, Myrtle and Mastic trees, as well as coniferous dwarf shrubs, Strawberry Trees and spurges commonly occur, such as the Evergreen Pistache (*Pistacia lentiscus*), Carob (*Ceratonia siliqua*), Thorny Gorse (*Genista sphacelata*), Spiny Broom (*Calicotome villosa*) and Olive (*Olea europea*). Fig Cacti and Agave can also be found here. Other species which also belong in this vegetation are, for instance Oregano, Marjoram, Lavender, Rosemary, Thyme and Sage, as well as various orchid and iris species (Baedeker, 1999).

Olive groves and vineyard terraces

Other important habitats are the olive groves, where the soil is covered with brightly coloured herbs in the months of spring. The wealth of flowers in these grassland communities between the gnarled old trees are not to be missed. Red Poppies (*Papaver rhoeas*) and yellow-white Crown Daisies (*Chrysanthemum coronarium*) predominate. But in reality, these biotopes created by man are much richer in species than the definite predominance of a few species would suggest. At very close quarters, they include a multitude of grassland plants, field herbs, and stonecrops, and where bushes border the olive groves, garrigue-like communities of rock roses and other thorny bushes can be found, as well as the remnants of deciduous and coniferous woods (Bechtel, 1980).

Potamiou (Standort von/site of *Orchis italica*), 15.3.2002   Trimiklini, 17.3.2002

Akrotiri (Standort von/site of *Ophrys kotschyi* und/and *Serapias parviflora*), 22.3.2002

Die Umgebung der Salzseen bei Larnaka und der Akrotiri-Halbinsel

Eine Besonderheit stellen die beiden Salzseen auf der Halbinsel Akrotiri und südlich Larnaka dar. Nahe dem Dorf Akrotiri, südwestlich von Lemesos, breitet sich ein etwa 9 km² großer Salzsee aus, der im Sommer stets austrocknet, aber nach den winterlichen Regenfällen ein beliebter Rastplatz für Flamingos ist. Auch am Salzsee bei Larnaka sind bis in den Frühling große Gruppen Flamingos zu beobachten. In der Umgebung der beiden Salzseen kommen viele seltene Orchideenarten vor.

Auf der Halbinsel Akrotiri wächst *Ophrys kotschyi* in Tausenden von Exemplaren in den weitläufigen, sandigen, mehr oder weniger Salz beeinflussten Wiesenarealen. Sie ist dort meist vergesellschaftet mit *Ophrys attica* und *Ophrys umbilicata*, mit der sie oft Hybriden bildet. Unweit der englischen Militärbasis hat *Ophrys apifera* besonders reich besetzte Fundorte. Inmitten der küstennahen, ausgedehnten und landwirtschaftlich genutzten Flächen und Olivenhaine sowie den spärlich bewachsenen, Salz beeinflussten Wiesenarealen blühen ab Ende März viele hunderte Pflanzen dieser Art in Feuchtwiesen, binsenbewachsenen Wiesenflächen und Buschwerk. Sehr häufig wird *Ophrys apifera* hier von *Ophrys cinereophila* und *Ophrys kotschyi* begleitet. Ausserdem wachsen hier viele Pflanzen der Varietäten *bicolor* und *chlorantha*. In den weitläufigen Schilfbeständen blüht im Mai die besonders seltene *Orchis palustris*. In den letzten Jahren ist die Art aber durch Trockenlegung an den meisten Standorten verschwunden, und der letzte aktuelle Standort zeigt nur noch einen kleinen Restbestand. Die letzten Pflanzen, weniger als zehn, wachsen dort in einem bereits trockenen Bachbett und sind zur Blütezeit von einer Ruderalflora völlig überwuchert. An der anderen Fundstelle, ebenfalls in einem ausgetrockneten Bachbett etwa ein Kilometer von der erstgenannten Stelle entfernt, wurde *Orchis palustris* in den letzten Jahren nicht mehr gefunden.

Die Umgebung des Salzsees südlich von Larnaka stellt ein besonderes Refugium für Orchideen dar. In diesem Gebiet kommen nicht nur eine ganze Reihe von Orchideentaxa vor, hier wachsen auch viele seltene Arten, wie zum Beispiel *Ophrys melena* und *Ophrys rhodia*, sowie *Serapias levantina*. Dieses Gebiet ist bei Orchideenfreunden sehr bekannt und wurde im Laufe der Zeit sehr gut untersucht und kartiert. Mitte April 1995 wurde nahe der Hala Sultan Tekke ein Fund von *Ophrys straussii*-ähnliche Pflanzen gemacht (Van der Cingel, 1997). Weiterhin kommen hier besonders typische Exemplare der seltenen *Ophrys hystera* vor. Bereits Mitte bis Ende März öffnen sich die ersten Blüten dieser Art.

Das Gebiet um den Salzsee ist sehr weitläufig, und *Ophrys hystera* wächst in diesem Gebiet sehr vereinzelt und zerstreut im Schatten und am Rande der Gebüschzonen. Wegen der relativ späten Blütezeit wurde *Ophrys hystera* auf Zypern bisher nur wenig beobachtet, vermutlich aber auch verwechselt mit anderen Arten aus

The area around the salt lakes near Larnaka and the Akrotiri peninsula

The two salt lakes on the Akrotiri peninsula and south of Larnaka are a special feature. A 9 km² large salt lake spreads out near the village of Akrotiri, southwest of Lemesos, which is always dry in summer, but after the winter rainfall turns into a favourite resting place for Flamingoes. Large groups of Flamingoes can also be seen at the salt lake near Larnaka, until spring. Many rare orchid species occur near both salt lakes.

On the Akrotiri peninsula thousands of specimens of *Ophrys kotschyi* grow in the vast, sandy, more or less salty meadows. This species is usually accompanied there by *Ophrys umbilicata* and *Ophrys attica*, with which it forms many hybrids. Around the British military bases, *Ophrys apifera* has densely populated habitats. Between the large coastal areas of agriculture and olive groves, and the sparsely vegetated salt meadows, many hundreds of plants of this species flower from the end of March in grasslands, reedy meadows and light woodland. *Ophrys apifera* is very often accompanied by *Ophrys cinereophila* and *Ophrys kotschyi*. Many plants of the variety *bicolor* and *chlorantha* also grow here. The exceptionally rare *Orchis palustris* flowers in May in the vast reed stands. In recent years however the species has disappeared from most sites as they have dried out, and the remaining habitat only show small residual stands. The last plants, fewer than ten of them, grow in a dry drainage ditch and during their flowering time are completely overgrown by weeds. At the only other site, also a dry ditch about one kilometre from the first site, *Orchis palustris* has not been found at all in recent years.

The area around the salt lake south of Larnaka represents a special refuge for orchids. Not only does a whole array of orchid species occur in this area, but many rare species also, such as *Ophrys melena* and *Ophrys rhodia*, as well as *Serapias levantina*. This area is well known among orchid lovers and has been thoroughly researched and charted in the course of time. In the middle of April 1995 a finding of possible plants of *Ophrys straussii* was made near the Hala Sultan Tekke (Van der Cingel, 1997). Furthermore, really typical specimens of the rare *Ophrys hystera* occur here. From mid till the end of March the first flowers of this species are already in bloom.

The area around the salt lake is vast, and *Ophrys hystera* is dispersed sporadically in shady places at the edge of bushy zones in the area. Its relativ late flowering time has meant that *Ophrys hystera* has been recorded only rarely until now. And probably due to wrong identification and confusing with other members from the

34   *Orobanche cypria* (endemische Sommerwurzart Zyperns/Cypriot endemic broomrape), Prodromos-Platania, 21.6.2002

dem *Ophrys sphegodes-mammosa* Komplex oder falsch bestimmt. Wegen der Flamingos und der Hala Sultan Tekke wurden am Salzsee mehrere Picknickplätze eingerichtet. Sie stellen für die Einheimischen und Touristen ein beliebtes Ausflugsziel dar. Die Pflanzen am Salzsee und dessen weiterer Umgebung sind stark gefährdet und zeigen starken Rückgang, hauptsächlich durch Pflücken, Waldrodung, intensivere Bewirtschaftung und Bebauung.

Pinien- und Kiefernwälder

Schon in der Antike begann man die reichen Waldbestände der Insel abzuholzen. Damals verwendeten die Seemächte des östlichen Mittelmeers das Holz für den Bau ihrer Flotten. Über Jahrhunderte wurde unkontrolliert Holz gefällt. Überweidung durch Ziegen, Waldbrände und das Abwerfen türkischer Brandbomben im Jahre 1974 taten ein übriges, um den Baumbestand dieser einst so grünen Mittelmeerinsel drastisch auf knapp 20% zu reduzieren.

Der Großteil der Wälder ist in staatlicher Hand und wächst hauptsächlich an den Hängen des Troodos, wo seit dem Jahre 1982 intensive Wiederaufforstung betrieben wird. Mögliche Waldbrände versucht man durch Forsttelefone für Notrufe frühzeitig zu erkennen und durch spezielle Feuerbekämpfungstruppen einzudämmen. Waldreservate und Nationalparks wie etwa bei Kyrenia tragen ebenfalls zum Schutz des Waldes bei.

Fast 90% des Baumbestandes wird durch die Aleppo-Kiefer (*Pinus halepensis*) abgedeckt, die in tieferen Regionen wächst. Ausserdem finden sich in den lichten Waldformationen Mittelmeerzypressen (*Cupressus sempervirens*), Styraxbaum (*Styrax officinalis*), Mastixstrauch (*Pistacia lentiscus*) und Östlicher Erdbeerbaum (*Arbutus andrachne*) (BAUMANN & KÜNKELE, 1994). An den tiefer gelegenen Berghängen des Troodos-Massivs wachsen hauptsächlich die Kalabrische Kiefer (*Pinus brutia*), die Goldeiche (*Quercus alnifolia*) und der Östliche Erdbeerbaum (*Arbutus andrachne*), und in Höhen über 1.200 m stehen dazwischen auch noch die zuweilen bizarr wirkenden Schwarzkiefern (*Pinus nigra* subsp. *pallasiana*). Es ist in diesem Gebiet, wo die seltenen, montanen, zypriotischen Orchideen wachsen, wie *Cephalanthera rubra, Dactylorhiza iberica, Epipactis condensata, Epipactis microphylla, Epipactis troodi, Epipactis veratrifolia, Limodorum abortivum* und *Platanthera holmboei*, sowie die endemische zypriotische *Orobanche cypria*. Doch prägen auch Mittelmeerzypressen (*Cupressus sempervirens*), Goldeichen (*Quercus alnifolia*) und Zypern-Zedern (*Cedrus brevifolia*) das urwüchsige Landschaftsbild des Troodos-Gebirges. In seinem Ausläufern ist das Troodos-Gebirge mit Eukalyptus- und Olivenbäumen bewachsen. Apfel-, Kirsch- und Birnbäume können aufgrund des milden Klimas bis zu einer Höhe von 1.200 m ebenso in Plantagen angebaut werden wie Mandel- und Nussbäume (teils nach BAEDEKER, 2001).

Ophrys sphegodes-mammosa species group *Ophrys hystera* was also recorded rarely. Several picnic areas were set up near the salt lake, because of the Flamingoes and the Hala Sultan Tekke, and they are a popular excursion destination for tourists and local people alike. The plants at the salt lake and its environs face a number of threats and are showing a sharp decline, primarily caused by culling, clearing of woods, more intensive cultivation and building development.

Pine forests

The destruction of the dense forests on the island started way back in antiquity. The naval powers of the Eastern Mediterranean used the timber in the construction of their fleets. In the course of hundreds of years, uncontrolled wood cutting took place. Overgrazing by goats, forest fires and Turkish incendiary bombs in 1974 all helped to reduce the tree population of this once lush Mediterranean island to 20% of what it once was.

Most of the woodland is state-controlled and is mainly found on the slopes of the Troodos mountains, where intensive reforestation has been undertaken since 1982. Attempts are made to spot possible forest fires in advance by use of forest telephones, and special fire fighting troops confine the fires. Forest reserves and national parks, such as that near Kyrenia, also contribute to the protection of the forests.

Almost 90% of the tree population is accounted for by the Aleppo Pine (*Pinus halepensis*), which grows at lower altitudes. Italian Cypresses (*Cupressus sempervirens*), Snowbells (*Styrax officinalis*), Mastic Trees (*Pistacia lentiscus*) and Strawberry Trees (*Arbutus andrachne*) also grow in the open forest formations (BAUMANN & KÜNKELE, 1994). Calabrian Pines (*Pinus brutia*), Golden Oaks (*Quercus alnifolia*) and Strawberry Trees (*Arbutus andrachne*) primarily grow on the lower slopes of the Troodos massif, and in between these trees at heights above 1,200 m the occasionally bizarre-looking Black Pines (*Pinus nigra* subsp. *palasiana*) grow. But Italian Cypresses (*Cupressus sempervirens*), Golden Oaks (*Quercus alnifolia*) and Cyprus Cedars (*Cedrus brevifolia*) are also part of the original natural landscape of the Troodos mountains. It is in this area where the rare, mountainous Cypriot orchids grow, like *Cephalanthera rubra, Dactylorhiza iberica, Epipactis condensata, Epipactis microphylla, Epipactis troodi, Epipactis veratrifolia, Limodorum abortivum* and *Platanthera holmboei*, as well as the endemic Cypriot *Orobanche cypria*. The foothills of the Troodos mountains are overgrown by Eucalyptus and Olive trees. Apple, Cherry and Pear trees can grow at altitudes of up to 1,200 m due to the mild climate, as well as plantations of, for example, nut trees (partly after BAEDEKER, 2001).

36   Kato Drys-Vavla (abgebrannter Weinberg mit *Orchis italica*/burned vineyard with *Orchis italica*), 21.3.2002

Gefährdung und Schutz
der Orchideen Zyperns

In den Jahren nach der Teilung Zyperns hat sich der Naturschutz weitgehend auf die Bemühungen einiger weniger Privatpersonen beschränkt, zum größten Teil Ausländer. Dies gilt auch heute noch für den Nordteil der Insel, wo Natur- und Artenschutz noch immer wenig Priorität haben. Anders ist es im Süden. Dort gab es glücklicherweise Zyprioten, die erkannt hatten, welchen Wert eine halbwegs intakte Natur für den Tourismus besitzt. Durch Medienarbeit, Gespräche mit der Regierung und jährliche Ausstellungen schufen sie die Basis für ein, wenn auch bescheidenes, Umweltbewusstsein. Hinzu kommt, dass es einem Großteil der Bevölkerung in der Zwischenzeit wirtschaftlich so gut geht, dass man vielleicht glaubt, sich den 'Luxus' eines Umweltschutzgedankens leisten zu können. Die Schäden, die in der Zeit des stürmischen Neuaufbaus verursacht wurden, lassen sich jedoch nicht mehr reparieren (HANSEN, KREUTZ & U. & D. RÜCKBRODT, 1990).
Aber in letzter Zeit scheinen sich die offiziellen Stellen in Zypern des Wertes der einheimischen Flora und Fauna bewusst geworden zu sein. Im Norden wurden in den touristischen Prospekten mehrere Male einheimische Orchideen abgebildet. Im Norden, im Alevkaya Forsthaus, befindet sich das Nationale Herbar Nordzyperns. Die Einrichtung dieses Herbariums geht auf Anregungen des Botanikers VINEY zurück. VINEY, der Autor des grundlegenden zweibändigen Werkes 'An Illustrated Flora of North Cyprus' (1994, 1996), konnte mit Unterstützung des staatlichen Forstamtes eine umfangreiche Pflanzensammlung zusammentragen, die zum Zeitpunkt der Eröffnung des Herbariums 1989 zunächst 450 Arten umfaßte und im Sommer 1990 schon auf 800 angewachsen war, darunter viele endemische Pflanzen. Das Ziel des Herbariums ist, den Bestand der einheimischen Flora zum Nutzen der Forschung und zur Unterrichtung der interessierten Öffentlichkeit zuverlässig zu dokumentieren. Nach Erkenntnissen des Botanikers MEIKLE (1977, 1985) kann ein Richtwert von etwa 1.100 Arten für das Territorium Nordzyperns angenommen werden. Die Pflanzenwelt Nordzyperns wird dem Besucher des Herbariums in unterschiedlicher Weise präsentiert, nämlich einmal als gepresste und getrocknete Pflanzen oder ausserdem als Pflanzen, die in Glasgefäßen in einem Alkohol-Glyzerin-Gemisch aufbewahrt werden. Die zweite Form wurde für die Orchideen angewendet, die ihre Formenvielfalt und Farbe durch Pressen und Trocknen sonst verlören. An einer Wand sind die meisten heimischen Orchideen Zyperns von HANSEN fotografisch abgebildet. Ausserdem liegen im Herbarium zahlreiche Federzeichnungen von VINEY, die mit ihren wissenschaftlichen Namen bezeichnet sind (verändert nach INTERNET-REISEMAGAZIN SCHWARZAUFWEISS, GBR).
1981 wurde eine Serie von vier Briefmarken herausgegeben, die *Epipactis veratrifolia, Ophrys elegans,*

Conservation of the orchids
of Cyprus and main threats

In the years following the division of Cyprus, nature conservation was limited on the whole to efforts made by a few private people, mainly foreigners. This still applies today to the northern part of the island, where nature and species conservation has less priority. It is different however for the south. Fortunately, there are Cypriots who recognized the value which relatively untouched nature represents for tourism. By using press coverage, and arranging talks with the government and annual exhibitions they created the beginnings of environmental awareness, albeit modest. At the same time, much of the population has achieved economic prosperity, to the extent that they now believe they can afford the 'luxury' of environmental friendliness. The damage caused in the period of turbulent rebuilding is however irreparable (HANSEN, KREUTZ & U. & D. RÜCKBRODT, 1990).

More recently the authorities throughout Cyprus seem to have become aware of the value of their endemic flora and fauna. Pictures of endemic orchids are now repeatedly shown in tourist prospectuses in the north. The National Herbarium of Northern Cyprus is situated in the Alevkaya forester's lodge. This herbarium was laid out according to the suggestions made by the botanist VINEY. VINEY, the author of the fundamental two-volume work 'An Illustrated Flora of North Cyprus' (1994, 1996), was able to bring together a large plant collection with the support of the state-run forestry department, which at the opening of the herbarium in 1989 consisted of almost 450 species and by the summer of 1990 had grown to 800, including many endemic species. The aim of the herbarium is to document the population of the endemic flora with accuracy, in order to aid in research and the education of the interested public. According to the botanist MEIKLE (1977, 1985) an indicatory value of about 1,100 species for the territory of northern Cyprus can be assumed. The flora of northern Cyprus is presented to the visitor of the herbarium in different ways, namely as pressed and dried plants or as whole plants in an alcohol-glycerine preservative in glass containers. The latter was chosen for the orchids, which otherwise lose their shape and colour during pressing and drying. On one wall, pictures by HANSEN of most of the endemic orchids of Cyprus are displayed. Numerous pen-and-ink drawings made by VINEY, labelled with their scientific name, are in the possession of the herbarium (text originating and altered from INTERNET-REISEMAGAZIN SCHWARZAUFWEISS, GBR).

In 1981 a series of four stamps was issued, which depict *Epipactis veratrifolia, Ophrys elegans, Ophrys*

Ophrys kotschyi und Orchis punctulata zeigen. Auch wurde 1982 ein großformatiger Kalender der Bank of Cyprus mit dem Titel 'Wild Flowers of Cyprus' herausgegeben, in dem sehr ansprechende Fotografien von *Epipactis veratrifolia, Ophrys kotschyi und Orchis punctulata* von DAVIES & DAVIES abgebildet sind (F. & I. MOYSICH, 1984).

Aber trotz dieses Bewusstseins sind die Orchideen auf Zypern nach wie vor stark bedroht. Im Norden sind die zunehmende Tendenz des massenhaften Aushakkens der Orchideenknollen und eine zunehmende Überweidung der Biotope Vorzeichen einer bevorstehenden Ausrottung. Hinzu kommt auf der ganzen Insel der ungeregelte Landschaftsverbrauch (starke Zersiedelung, Straßenbau), ohne dass eine Prüfung der Umweltverträglichkeit stattfindet. Eine Arealschrumpfung ist bereits feststellbar, insbesondere in der Umgebung von Lefkosia und an der Nordost- und Südküste. In den intensiv landwirtschaftlich genutzten Räumen fehlen ökologische Ausgleichsflächen fast vollständig. Zu den Gefährdungsursachen gehört ferner ein fehlendes Management der naturnahen Halbkulturbiotope; zu vermeiden wäre insbesondere eine zu starke Beschattung. Der Rückstand Zyperns gegenüber dem Stand des Naturschutzrechts der Europäische Union beträgt praktisch 100% (BAUMANN & KÜNKELE, 1994). Vor allem im Küstenbereich zeigen die Pflanzen einen alarmierenden Rückgang. Hauptsächlich im Süden der Insel hat der Massentourismus stark dazu beigetragen, dass viele neue Straßen, Siedlungen und neue, großflächige Hotelanlagen entstanden sind. Besonders betroffen ist die Südküste östlich von Lemesos mit ihren küstennahen Kalkböden. Hotels und Ferienanlagen haben hier ehemals reiche Orchideenvorkommen vernichtet. Auch die Umgebung der Großstädte Lemesos, Larnaka und Pafos werden zunehmend verbaut, und dadurch sind viele Standorte verloren gegangen. Ausserdem wurden viele Hotels an vielen Stellen mitten in die Küstenphrygana, in alte Ölbaumhaine oder anderes Kulturland gebaut. So sind die Standorte von *Orchis punctulata* auf Zypern besonders stark rückgängig. Vor allem sind die Standorte in der Umgebung von Moni, wo früher sehr große Bestände von *Orchis punctulata* vorkamen, heute fast alle verschwunden. Auch bei Kato Drys, *wo Orchis punctulata* früher weit verbreitet war, ist sie heute durch Neubauten fast erloschen. Das gleiche gilt für die Akamas-Halbinsel. Auch dort ist *Orchis punctulata* stark gefährdet, hier vor allem verursacht durch übermäßige Beweidung von Schafen und Ziegen. *Orchis punctulata* gehört damit zu den am meisten gefährdeten Orchideen von Zypern. F. & I. MOYSICH berichteten schon 1984, dass *Orchis punctulata* am Fundort westlich von Ayia Napa bald durch Bebauung verloren ginge, da westlich und östlich davon bereits Hotelkomplexe an der Küste entstanden seien, beziehungsweise entstünden. An einigen Stellen wird das Brachland in zunehmendem Maße als Müllhalde benutzt. Das führt zur Belas-

kotschyi and Orchis punctulata. In 1982 a large calender was published by the Bank of Cyprus with the title 'Wild Flowers of Cyprus', in which very attractive photographs of *Epipactis veratrifolia, Ophrys kotschyi* and *Orchis punctulata* by DAVIES & DAVIES were displayed (F. & I. MOYSICH, 1984).

Despite this awareness however, the orchids of Cyprus are just as heavily threatened as in the past. In the north, the ever-increasing trend towards large-scale removal of orchid bulbs and overgrazing of the biotopes are omens of looming extinction; and no less menacing is the unregulated use of the landscape over the whole island for uncontrolled development and road construction, without proper assessment of the environmental impact. Marked contraction of undeveloped areas is already noticeable, especially in the vicinity of Lefkosia and along the northeast and south coasts. In the intensively used agricultural areas, ecological buffer zones are totally absent. Another threat is caused by the absence of management in the seminatural, semi-cultivated biotopes; in particular, too much shading needs to be avoided. The decline of Cyprus compared to the status of the environmental protection laws of the European Union is a difference as of night and day (BAUMANN & KÜNKELE, 1994). Especially in the coastal areas, plants are showing an alarming decline. Mainly in the south of the island, mass tourism has contributed greatly to the construction of many new streets, residential areas and large new hotel complexes. Hard hit is the south coast east of Lemesos, with its coastal chalky soils. Hotels and holiday complexes have also destroyed formerly rich orchid habitats. The areas around towns like Lemesos, Larnaka and Pafos are being increasingly built upon, causing many habitats to disappear. Furthermore, hotels are being built at many places in the middle of the coastal phrygana, in old olive groves or other cultivated land. The number of habitats of *Orchis punctulata* on Cyprus for instance is really plummeting. Habitats in the vicinity of Moni, for example, where once large populations of *Orchis punctulata* stood, have nowadays almost disappeared. Again, near Kato Drys *Orchis punctulata* used to be widespread, but is now almost extinct due to the construction of new buildings. The same applies to the Akamas peninsula; *Orchis punctulata* is heavily threatened here, particularly due to the excessive overgrazing by sheep and goats. *Orchis punctulata* is therefore one of the most threatened orchids of Cyprus. F. & I. MOYSICH reported as early as 1984 that *Orchis punctulata* would be lost at its site west of Ayia Napa due to construction, as both westwards and eastwards from this site hotel complexes had risen or were being erected.

In some places fallow land is increasingly being used as a rubbish tip. This affects the soil through the

tung des Bodens mit Schadstoffen oder zur Eutrophierung und damit zu Beeinträchtigung des Wachstums von Orchideen und anderen Pflanzen. Weiterhin geht immer mehr Brachland, worin meist viele seltene Orchideen wachsen, durch immer intensivere Bewirtschaftung (besonders Umwandlung in Olivenhaine) verloren. Vor allem im Norden der Insel sind dadurch in den letzten zwanzig Jahren sehr viele Standorte verloren gegangen. Aber auch im Süden geht immer mehr Brachland verloren, und dadurch verschwinden in raschem Tempo schöne Orchideenstandorte.

Extrem gefährdet sind die wenigen Feuchtgebiete wie zum Beispiel auf der Akrotiri-Halbinsel, bei der Hala Sultan Tekke südlich Larnaka, entlang des Flusses Xeros Potamos im Südwesten Zyperns und im Troodos-Gebirge. Vor allem *Orchis laxiflora* und *Orchis palustris* sind davon stark betroffen. In den letzten Jahren sind beide Arten durch Trockenlegung bereits an den meisten Standorten verschwunden und die aktuellen Standorte zeigen nur noch kleine Restbestände. Besonders gefährdet ist die schon ohnehin sehr seltene *Orchis palustris*, die auf Zypern nur in den weitläufigen Schilfbeständen der Halbinsel Akrotiri vorkommt. Die letzten Pflanzen, weniger als zehn, wachsen in einem ausgetrockneten Bachbett und sind dort zur Blütezeit im Mai von einer Ruderalflora völlig überwuchert. An der andere Fundstelle, ebenfalls in einem ausgetrockneten Bachbett, etwa ein Kilometer von der ersten Stelle entfernt, wurde die Art in den letzten Jahren nicht mehr gefunden. Sie ist daher besonders stark gefährdet und akut vom Aussterben bedroht. Auch die seltene *Orchis laxiflora* hat aktuell nur noch sehr wenige Fundorte auf Zypern. Durch Trockenlegung und Düngung sind bereits viele ihrer Fundorte verschwunden. Aktuell wächst sie nur noch in größerer Anzahl bei Nata, nordöstlich von Pafos, und bei Drouseia, südwestlich von Polis im Akamas, ist aber an beide Standorte durch Trockenlegung schon stark gefährdet.

Besonders gefährdet ist auch *Orchis caspia*. Diese Art ist auf Zypern nur von einer Fundstelle bei Choirokoitia im Osten der Insel bekannt. Der Fundort grenzt unmittelbar an einen Acker, und es besteht die Möglichkeit, dass er durch Ausdehnung des Ackerlandes ganz verschwindet. Damit ist sie als besonders gefährdet einzustufen.

Auch *Dactylorhiza iberica* und *Epipactis veratrifolia*, die beide in Ufernähe von Gebirgsbächen vorkommen, könnten bei eventueller Nutzung dieser Bäche zur Bewässerung oder Kanalisierung sehr schnell vom Aussterben bedroht sein. Vor allem *Epipactis veratrifolia* wäre hiervon sofort betroffen, weil diese Art sehr hohe Ansprüche an ihre Standorte stellt.

Weitgehend geschützt sind die Orchideen im Troodos-Gebirge und seiner weiteren Umgebung. Hier sind noch großräumige Kiefernwälder vorhanden, die weitgehend geschützt sind, wodurch die Orchideen hier ohne Probleme überleben können. Auch in der nähe-

dumping of harmful substances upsetting the natural balance and so causing damage to the growth of orchids and other plants. Additionally, more and more fallow land, where most of the rare orchids grow, is being lost to intensifying cultivation (especially as olive groves). In the last twenty years, many habitats have been lost because of this, especially in the north. But in the south also, more and more fallow land is being lost, and thus beautiful orchid habitats are disappearing at an alarming rate.

Threatened in the extreme are the few wetlands, such as on the Akrotiri peninsula, near the Hala Sultan Tekke south of Larnaka, along the Xeros Potamos river in the southwest of Cyprus and in the Troodos mountains. In particular *Orchis laxiflora* and *Orchis palustris* are adversely affected. In recent years, both species have disappeared from most habitats and current habitats only have small remaining populations. Particularly threatened is the already rare *Orchis palustris*, which only occurs on Cyprus in the vast reed stands on the Akrotiri peninsula. The last plants, fewer than ten, grow in a dry drainage ditch and are completely overgrown by weeds during their flowering period in May. At the other site, also a dry drainage ditch, almost one kilometre from the first site, the species has not been found in recent years. It is therefore acutely endangered and imminently threatened with extinction. The rare *Orchis laxiflora* also has only very few sites on Cyprus. Due to drainage and fertilisation, many of its sites have disappeared. At the moment it only grows in large numbers near Nata, northeast of Pafos, and by Drouseia, southwest of Polis in Akamas, but is on both places heavily threatened by loss of water.

Threatened also is *Orchis caspia*. This species is only known at one site near Choirokoitia in the east of the island. The site borders directly on to a cultivated field, so it is possible that it will completely disappear if the field is enlarged. For this reason this species should be classified as heavily threatened.

Dactylorhiza iberica and *Epipactis veratrifolia*, which both occur near the banks of mountain rivers, could also rapidly become threatened with extinction with the eventual use of these rivers for watering or canalisation. *Epipactis veratrifolia* especially could be affected by this, as this species has very specific requirements for its habitat.

The orchids in the Troodos mountains and the immediate environs are to a large extent protected. Vast pine forests can still be found here, which are widely protected, which means that the orchids are able to survive without any problems. A decline of the orchids

ren Zukunft ist im Troodos-Massiv nicht mit einem Rückgang der Orchideen zu rechnen. So wurde östlich von Platres der Kaledonia-Naturlehrpfad angelegt, der zu den gleichnamigen Wasserfällen führt. Entlang dieses Naturlehrpfades wachsen auch mehrere, meist sehr seltene Orchideenarten, die einfach und bequem zu erreichen sind (*Cephalanthera rubra, Dactylorhiza iberica, Epipactis veratrifolia, Epipactis troodi* und *Limodorum abortivum*).

Viele Standorte sind in den letzten Jahren durch Waldbrände verloren gegangen. Vor allem im mittleren Teil der Insel wurden großräumige Flächen in Asche gelegt. Die Regenerierung wird sicherlich mehrere Jahrzehnte dauern. Diese Waldbrände werden manchmal von Bauern gelegt, um so ihre Agrarflächen zu vergrößern, aber manchmal sind sie auch aus Unachtsamkeit entstanden. Durch diese Waldbrände hat die Erosion Zugriff auf große Landflächen bekommen und hat sowohl Ackerland als auch Orchideenbiotope vernichtet.

Wie in der Türkei werden die Orchideen im Norden Zyperns auch ausgegraben, aber weniger stark als in der Türkei selbst. VINEY (1994) schreibt, dass *Orchis italica* und *Serapias vomeracea* subsp. *orientalis* (also *Serapias levantina*) zu den am meisten gefährdeten Orchideenarten Nordzyperns gehören, weil die Knollen dieser beiden Taxa zur Bereitung von Salep getrocknet und gemahlen werden, der hauptsächlich als (verdickende) Grundlage von Medikamenten dient. Als Eigenschaft des Salep wird eine reizmildernde Wirkung bei Reizhusten oder auch als Schleimhautschutz bei Einläufen beschrieben. Der in den Knollen in großen Mengen enthaltene Schleim spaltet sich hydrolytisch in Mannose und Glukose, die Knollen sind also sehr nahrhaft. Ausserdem werden die Orchideenknollen in Nordzypern, wie auch in der Türkei, als Aphrodisiakum und als allgemeines Stärkungsmittel verwendet. In Mitteleuropa spielt dieser Volksglauben keine Rolle mehr, und in der medizinischen Verwendung wurde die Schleimdroge durch synthetische Produkte ersetzt. Weiterhin werden die Knollen der genannten Orchideenarten auch für die Zubereitung von Kaffee und Tee gebraucht. Eine weitere Verwendung für Salep-Pulver ist sein Zusatz zum Speiseeis.

Die Beweidung durch Schaf- und Ziegenherden ist noch nicht so intensiv wie in der Türkei. Wahrscheinlich ist auch in Zukunft nicht mit einer intensiveren Beweidung als bisher zu rechnen, weil die meisten Einwohner weitgehend vom Tourismus leben. Ausserdem wachsen viele Orchideen in den Waldgebieten im Troodos- und im Pentadactylos-Gebirge. Diese Waldgebiete werden kaum beweidet und sind daher nicht gefährdet.

in the Troodos massif is not expected in the immediate future. For example, the Caledonia Trail has been laid out east of Platres, which leads to the waterfalls of the same name. Various, mostly very rare orchid species (*Cephalanthera rubra, Dactylorhiza iberica, Epipactis veratrifolia, Epipactis troodi* and *Limodorum abortivum*), grow alongside this nature trail, which can easily and comfortably be reached.

Many habitats have been lost to forest fires in recent years. Particularly in the central region of the island huge areas have been reduced to ashes. Regeneration will certainly take many decades. These forest fires are often started by farmers, in order to enlarge their acreage, but they are often also started by negligence. Because of these forest fires erosion has gained a hold on large areas and has destroyed both fields and orchid biotopes.

As in Turkey, orchids are dug up in the north of Cyprus, though less often than in Turkey itself. VINEY (1994) writes that *Orchis italica* and *Serapias vomeracea* subsp. *orientalis* (thus *Serapias levantina*) belong to the most threatened orchid species of northern Cyprus, as the bulbs of both species are dried and ground up during the manufacture of salep, which is primarily used as a (thickening) base for medications. Properties that are attributed to salep include the alleviation of dry coughs and protection for the mucous membranes during the application of enemas. The large quantities of mucilage contained within the orchid bulbs can be split into mannose and glucose; the bulbs are therefore also very nutritious. Orchid bulbs are also used in northern Cyprus, just as in Turkey, as an aphrodisiac and as a universal tonic. This popular belief has declined in Central Europe, and the mucilage has been replaced by synthetic products in medicinal use. The bulbs of certain orchid species are used in the preparation of coffee and tea. And salep powder is also used as a topping for ice-cream.

Grazing by sheep and goat herds is not yet as intensive as in Turkey. In all likelihood, more intensive grazing will not occur in future as most of the inhabitants now live on tourism. Moreover, many orchids grow in the wooded areas of the Troodos and Pentadactylos mountains. These wooded areas are hardly grazed at all and are therefore not threatened.

Botanische Erforschung der Orchideen Zyperns

Zypern wurde touristisch schon früh erschlossen und wegen des Vorkommens von vielen ostmediterranen und einigen orientalischen Orchideenarten häufig von Orchideenkartierern besucht. In den früheren Jahren wurde vor allem der nördliche Teil besucht, später, nach der Teilung im Jahre 1974, fast nur noch der südliche Teil. Durch die verkehrstechnische Erschließung der Insel sind heute alle Arten einfach zu erreichen.

Die geologische und botanische Erforschung Zyperns hat schon sehr früh begonnen. Eine erste Übersicht erschien von UNGER & KOTSCHY. Sie unternahmen zwischen 1859 und 1862 drei Reisen nach Zypern. Ihre 1865 erschienene Veröffentlichung 'Die Insel Cypern' (UNGER & KOTSCHY, 1865) enthält ausführliche Fund- und Pflanzenlisten, wobei 24 Orchideenarten erwähnt wurden. Fast zwanzig Jahre später, im Zeitraum 1881 bis 1882, erfolgte dann eine wissenschaftliche Bearbeitung von SINTENIS und dem Italiener RIGO (SINTENIS, 1881-1882), gefolgt von THOMPSON (1906), der eine Liste der zypriotischen Orchideen herausgab. Im Jahre 1914 berichtet HOLMBOE in den 'Studies on the vegetations of Cyprus' über seine von ihm im Frühjahr und Sommer 1905 vorgenommenen Untersuchungen. In diesem Bericht gibt er für Zypern 34 Orchideenarten an. Die Veröffentlichungen von RENZ (1928) und SOÓ (1929), die Zypern über mehrere Jahren bereisten, beinhalten nicht nur weitere, sehr präzise Fundlisten, sondern fassen auch bisherige Erkenntnisse zusammen. Bei RENZ (1929) werden einige neue Arten von Zypern veröffentlicht, so auch *Ophrys cypria* RENZ, die schon 1926 von H. FLEISCHMANN & SOÓ als *Ophrys kotschyi* beschrieben worden war. 1939 besuchte H. LINDBERG Zypern und sammelte unter anderem Pflanzen von *Epipactis troodi*, die sein Sohn 1942 (LINDBERG, 1942) als neue Art beschrieb. Später besuchte auch E. NELSON Zypern, um Zeichnungen für seine Orchideenmonographien anzufertigen. 1980 erschien von J. WOOD in 'Die Orchidee' eine umfassende Arbeit über die Unterarten von *Ophrys sphegodes* im östlichen Mittelmeerraum und auf Zypern. 1985 bearbeitete J. WOOD in MEIKLE (1985) die Orchideen von Zypern, die seinerzeit mit 51 Arten und Unterarten vertreten waren. In diesem wichtigen Werk wurden alle Orchideen Zyperns ausführlich beschrieben, und von einigen wurden Federzeichnungen abgebildet. Ausserdem wurden alle Arten, die möglicherweise falsch für Zypern angegeben wurden, aufgelistet.

Von R.-B. HANSEN, C.A.J. KREUTZ & U. & D. RÜCKBRODT (1990) wurde dann erstmals eine umfassende Verbreitungsübersicht über die Orchideen von Zypern veröffentlicht. In diesem Artikel wurden 43 Arten, beziehungsweise Unterarten im UTM-5 km Raster erfasst. Dabei wurden von einigen besonderen und schwer zu identifizierenden Orchideenarten wichtige Erkenntnisse (unter anderem Standortansprüche, Bestimmungsprobleme und Verbreitungsangaben) beschrieben.

Botanical exploration of the orchids of Cyprus

Cyprus was opened up early on to tourism and due to the occurrence of many Eastern Mediterranean and some oriental orchid species, it has been visited regularly by orchid observers. In the early years mainly the northern part of the island was visited, but later, after the division in 1974, the southern part was almost only visited. Because of the infrastructural coverage of the whole island, all species can easily be reached nowadays.

The geological and botanical exploration of Cyprus started very early. A first overview was published by UNGER & KOTSCHY. Between 1859 and 1862 they undertook three trips to Cyprus. Their publication 'Die Insel Cypern' (UNGER & KOTSCHY, 1865) contains extensive findings and plant lists, in which 24 orchid species are put on record. Almost twenty years later, in the period 1881 to 1882, a scientific adaptation by SINTENIS and the Italian RIGO (SINTENIS, 1881-1882) appeared, later followed by THOMPSON (1906), who published a list of Cypriot species. In 1914 HOLMBOE referred to the explorations he undertook in the spring and summer of 1905. In this account he listed 34 orchid species for Cyprus. The publications by RENZ (1928) und SOÓ (1929), who travelled to Cyprus many times, not only include more, and very precise lists of findings, but also summarize previous insights. RENZ (1929) announced some new species for Cyprus, of course including *Ophrys cypria* RENZ, which was first described by H. FLEISCHMANN & SOÓ in 1926 as *Ophrys kotschyi*. In 1939 H. LINDBERG visited Cyprus and collected such plants as *Epipactis troodi*, which was described by his son in 1942 (LINDBERG, 1942) as a new species. Later E. NELSON visited Cyprus, in order to create drawings for his orchid monographs. In 1980 J. WOOD published in 'Die Orchidee' a comprehensive work on the subspecies of *Ophrys sphegodes* in the Eastern Mediterranean and on Cyprus. In 1985 J. WOOD covered the orchids of Cyprus in MEIKLE (1985), which at that time were represented by 51 species. In this important work all orchids of Cyprus were described extensively, and of some, pen-and-ink drawings were shown. All species that had been possibly erroneously specified for Cyprus were also listed.

R.-B. HANSEN, C.A.J. KREUTZ & U. & D. RÜCKBRODT (1990) published the first comprehensive distribution overview of the orchids of Cyprus. In this article 43 species and subspecies were brought together on a UTM-5 km grid. Important results (such as habitat claims, identification problems and distribution specifications) on some special and difficult to identify orchid species were also described.

Pentadactylos Range, 18.3.2002

Kato Drys-Vavla, 21.3.2002

Eine weitere umfassende und wichtige Arbeit stammt von DELFORGE (1990). In seinem Beitrag gibt er eine Übersicht aller seinerzeit bekannten *Ophrys*- und *Serapias*-Arten von Südzypern und behandelt deren taxonomische Stellung. Er beschreibt *Serapias aphroditae*, eine neue *Serapias* Art, sowie einige *Ophrys*- und *Serapias*-Hybriden.

Später erschienen mehrere Bücher, die sich speziell mit den Orchideen Zyperns beschäftigten. Das erste Buch verfassten G. & K. MORSCHEK (1996). Von jeder Art, beziehungsweise Unterart wurden eine oder zwei Aufnahmen abgebildet, und einige Besonderheiten wurden kurz besprochen. In diesem Buch wurde die taxonomische Stellung von einigen Arten und Unterarten geändert. Wie G. & K. MORSCHEK (1996) in ihrem Vorwort angeben, ist ihr Buch in erste Linie für den Orchideenliebhaber gedacht und nicht für den Orchideenspezialisten. Sie haben *Orchis quadripunctata* CYRILLO ex TENORE in ihr Werk aufgenommen, eine Art, die auf Zypern und in der Türkei in ihrer typischen Form nicht vorkommt, sondern dort durch *Orchis sezikiana* vertreten wird, ausserdem *Orchis coriophora* statt *Orchis fragrans* und *Serapias orientalis*, eine Art, die auf Zypern nicht vorkommt. Auch wurde *Ophrys fusca* statt *Ophrys cinereophila* aufgenommen, allerdings war diese Art 1996 noch nicht beschrieben.

Im Jahre 1998 erschienen von GEORGIADES zwei weitere Übersichten der Orchideen Zyperns in Buchform. Das erste Buch stellt einen Feldführer dar, worin alle ihm bekannten Arten und Unterarten Zyperns aufgelistet wurden. Ausserdem wurde jede Art und Unterart durch eine oder mehrere Farbaufnahmen abgebildet. Das zweite Buch ist ein großformatiges Werk, mit schönen, ganzseitigen Aquarellen aller Orchideenarten Zyperns. In beiden Büchern wurde der gleiche Text abgedruckt. In diesen beiden Büchern wurden allerdings einige abgebildeten Pflanzen mit falschen Namen versehen und zwar mit Namen von Arten, die in Zypern nicht vorkommen. Es handelt sich hierbei um *Ophrys cinereophila*, die als *Ophrys funerea* VIVIANI abgebildet wird, eine Art, die auf Korsika, Sardinien und am Mt. Argentario (Italien) vorkommt und um *Orchis sezikiana*, die unter dem Namen *Orchis quadripunctata* abgebildet ist. Darüber hinaus wurde auch *Ophrys sintenisii* in beiden Büchern behandelt, eine Art, die ihr Verbreitungsgebiet unter anderem im Iran, Israel und der Osttürkei hat und nicht auf Zypern vorkommt. Mittlerweile wurden die zypriotischen *Ophrys sintenisii*-ähnlichen Pflanzen von KREUTZ, SEGERS & WALRAVEN (2002) als *Ophrys alasiatica* neu beschrieben. Ausserdem wurden in die Bücher von GEORGIADES *Serapias orientalis* und *Serapias vomeracea* aufgenommen, zwei *Serapias*-Arten, die nach dem heutigen Kenntnisstand nicht auf Zypern vorkommen.

2001 erschien von CHRISTOFIDES eine weitere vollständige Übersicht der Orchideen Zyperns. In diesem Buch werden alle Arten und Unterarten aufgelistet

Another extensive and important work was written by DELFORGE (1990). In his article he gives an overview of all the then-known *Ophrys* and *Serapias* species of southern Cyprus and discusses their taxonomic rank. With *Serapias aphroditae* he describes a new *Serapias* species, as well as some *Ophrys* and *Serapias* hybrids.

Later on several books were published, especially concerned with the orchids of Cyprus. The first book was compiled by G. & K. MORSCHEK (1996). Of each species and subspecies, one or two pictures were given, and some details were briefly discussed. In this book the taxonomic rank of some species and subspecies had been changed. As G. & K. MORSCHEK (1996) declare in their preface, their book is primarily intended for orchid enthusiasts and not for orchid specialists. They included *Orchis quadripunctata* CYRILLO ex TENORE in their work, a species that does not occur on Cyprus or in Turkey in its typical shape, but is represented there by *Orchis sezikiana*, and they also included *Orchis coriophora* instead of *Orchis fragrans* and *Serapias orientalis*, a species that does not occur on Cyprus. *Ophrys fusca* was included instead of *Ophrys cinereophila*, a species that was not to be described until 1996.

In 1998 two further overviews of the orchids of Cyprus in book-form were published by GEORGIADES. The first book comprises a field guide, in which all species and subspecies on Cyprus that he knew of, were listed. The second book is a large-size work with beautiful, full-page watercolours of all orchid species on Cyprus. The same text was printed in both books. In both of these books some species were listed with wrong names, because these species do not occur on Cyprus. These species are *Ophrys cinereophila*, which is depicted as *Ophrys funerea* VIVIANI, a species that occurs on Corsica, Sardinia and at Mt. Argentario (Italy), and *Orchis sezikiana*, which is depicted under the name *Orchis quadripunctata*. Moreover, *Ophrys sintenisii* is treated in both books, a species that has a distribution area for example in Iran, Israel and eastern Turkey and does not occur on Cyprus. Since then, the Cypriot *Ophrys sintenisii*-like plants were redescribed by KREUTZ, SEGERS & WALRAVEN (2002) as *Ophrys alasiatica*. In GEORGIADES's books *Serapias orientalis* and *Serapias vomeracea* were also included, two *Serapias* species that do not occur on Cyprus according to the current state of knowledge.

In 2001, CHRISTOFIDES published another complete overview of the orchids of Cyprus. In this book all species and subspecies are listed and briefly com-

und kurz erläutert. Von jeder Sippe wurden eine oder mehrere Farbaufnahmen abgebildet. In dieses Buch wurden *Ophrys funerea* statt *Ophrys cinereophila*, *Ophrys sintenisii* statt *Ophrys alasiatica*, *Ophrys sphegodes* statt *Ophrys herae* und *Orchis quadripunctata* statt *Orchis sezikiana* aufgenommen. Ausserdem wurden die Arten *Serapias orientalis* und *Serapias vomeracea* behandelt, die eine mehr westliche Verbreitung haben und auf Zypern nicht vorkommen.

Die bisher letzte Übersicht stammt von HUBBARD & SCRATON (2001). Ihr Werk zeigt alle Arten Zyperns auf einen Videoband, ergänzt durch einen Textband mit Farbaufnahmen der einzelnen Arten. Auch in diesem Buch wurden *Orchis quadripunctata* als *Orchis sezikiana*, *Ophrys sintenisii* an Stelle von *Ophrys alasiatica* und *Ophrys funerea* als *Ophrys cinereophila* abgehandelt. Ausserdem wurden die Arten *Ophrys omegaifera*, *Serapias orientalis* und *Serapias vomeracea* behandelt und abgebildet, Arten die nach dem heutigen Kenntnisstand nicht auf Zypern vorkommen.

Weitere wichtige Veröffentlichungen gibt es von H. BAUMANN (1991), H. BAUMANN & KÜNKELE (1981b, 1994), E. & R. BREINER (1979a, 1982, 1989), DAVIES (1965), DAVIS (1951, 1959), DE LANGHE & D'HOSE (1982), DOSTMANN & STERN (1996), GÖLZ & REINHARD (1985, 1989, 1994), GUMPRECHT (1964), HERMJAKOB (1969, 1974), HERTEL (1984), KAJAN (1984), KREUTZ (1985ab), KREUTZ, SEGERS & WALRAVEN (2002), KREUTZ & SCRATON (2002, 2003), LIEBISCH, PIEPER, RYSY & ZAISS (1984), MILLOT & MILLOT (1984), F. & I. MOYSICH (1984), PAULUS & GACK (1990a), ROBATSCH (1980), SCRATON (2001), B. & E. WILLING (1975, 1976) und WOOD (1980, 1981, 1985). Wichtige, mehr allgemeinere Arbeiten über die ostmediterranen Orchideen gibt es von H. BAUMANN & KÜNKELE (1981ab, 1982ab, 1983, 1986, 1988b, 1989), BOISSIER (1884), BORNMÜLLER (1898), GÖLZ & REINHARD (1993), RECHINGER (1929), SUNDERMANN (1969b) und YOUNG (1970).

Allgemeine Orchideenwerke, in denen auch die Orchideen Zyperns abgehandelt werden, stammen von H. BAUMANN & KÜNKELE (1982a, 1988a), BUTTLER (1986), DELFORGE (1994, 2001), LANDWEHR (1977), NELSON (1962, 1968, 1976, 2001) und SUNDERMANN (1975, 1980).

Werke über die gesamte Flora von Zypern unter Einschluss der Orchideen wurden von MEGAW & MEIKLE (1973), MEIKLE (1977, 1985), OSORIO-TAFALL & SERAPHIM (1973) und VINEY (1994, 1996) publiziert.

mented on. One or more photographs of each taxon are given. *Ophrys funerea* instead of *Ophrys cinereophila*, *Ophrys sintenisii* instead of *Ophrys alasiatica*, *Ophrys sphegodes* instead of *Ophrys herae* and *Orchis quadripunctata* instead of *Orchis sezikiana* were included in this book. The species *Serapias orientalis* and *Serapias vomeracea* are also mentioned, which have a more westerly distribution and do not occur on Cyprus.

The last overview was published by HUBBARD & SCRATON (2001). Their work shows all species of Cyprus on a video tape, complemented with a book with colour photographs of each species. *Orchis quadripunctata* instead of *Orchis sezikiana*, *Ophrys sintenisii* instead of *Ophrys alasiatica* and *Ophrys funerea* instead of *Ophrys cinereophila* are also listed in this book. Moreover, the species *Ophrys omegaifera*, *Serapias orientalis* and *Serapias vomeracea* are also mentioned and depicted, species that do not occur on Cyprus according to the state of knowledge now.

Other important publications have been made by H. BAUMANN (1991), H. BAUMANN & KÜNKELE (1981b, 1994), E. & R. BREINER (1979a, 1982, 1989), DAVIES (1965), DAVIS (1951, 1959), DE LANGHE & D'HOSE (1982), DOSTMANN & STERN (1996), GÖLZ & REINHARD (1985, 1989, 1994), GUMPRECHT (1964), HERMJAKOB (1969, 1974), HERTEL (1984), KAJAN (1984), KREUTZ (1985ab), KREUTZ, SEGERS & WALRAVEN (2002), KREUTZ & SCRATON (2002, 2003), LIEBISCH, PIEPER, RYSY & ZAISS (1984), MILLOT & MILLOT (1984), F. & I. MOYSICH (1984), PAULUS & GACK (1990a), ROBATSCH (1980), SCRATON (2001), B. & E. WILLING (1975, 1976) and WOOD (1980, 1981, 1985).

Important but more general works about the Eastern Mediterranean orchids have been made by H. BAUMANN & KÜNKELE (1981ab, 1982ab, 1983, 1986, 1988b, 1989), BOISSIER (1884), BORNMÜLLER (1898), GÖLZ & REINHARD (1993), RECHINGER (1929), SUNDERMANN (1969b) and YOUNG (1970).

General orchid books, in which the orchids of Cyprus are also treated, have been produced by H. BAUMANN & KÜNKELE (1982a, 1988a), BUTTLER (1986), DELFORGE (1994, 2001), LANDWEHR (1977), NELSON (1962, 1968, 1976, 2001) and SUNDERMANN (1975, 1980).

Works about the whole flora of Cyprus, including orchids were published by MEGAW & MEIKLE (1973), MEIKLE (1977, 1985), OSORIO-TAFALL & SERAPHIM (1973) and VINEY (1994, 1996).

Einführung zum Buch

Im vorliegenden Buch werden alle Arten, Unterarten und die wichtigsten Varietäten, sowie einige Hybriden Zyperns behandelt und ihre Verbreitung bis einschließlich 2004 im UTM-2 km Raster gezeigt. In diesem Raster entspricht jeder Punkt einer Fläche von 4 km² (ein blauer Punkt bezieht sich auf Angaben bis 1990, ein roter Punkt gibt Funde ab 1990 wieder).

Von jeder Sippe werden mehrere Farbfotografien abgebildet, die Habitus, Blütenstand, Teile des Blütenstandes und meistens auch Einzelblüten der Pflanze und ihr Biotop zeigen. Die Orchideenarten werden in diesem Buch in alphabetischer Reihenfolge behandelt, mit Ausnahme von nahe verwandten Arten (vor allem bei der Gattung *Ophrys* und *Orchis*). Diese werden als Formenkreis behandelt. Mit Hilfe des Inhaltsverzeichnisses ist aber ein alphabetischer Zugriff auf jede Art leicht möglich.

Von den Arten *Aceras anthropophorum*, *Cephalanthera damasonium*, *Cephalanthera longifolia*, *Epipactis helleborine*, *Ophrys aegaea*, *Ophrys ciliata*, *Ophrys omegaifera*, *Ophrys sintenisii*, *Ophrys spruneri*, *Ophrys straussii*, *Serapias orientalis* und *Serapias vomeracea* ist der Nachweis auf Zypern zweifelhaft, weil keine Herbar- oder eindeutige fotografischen Belege existieren. Diese Arten wurden in ein separates Kapitel aufgenommen, und es wurde auf eine Verbreitungskarte verzichtet.

Die Taxonomie und Nomenklatur richtet sich in erster Linie nach BUTTLER (1986), berücksichtigt aber auch H. BAUMANN & KÜNKELE (1988a) und DELFORGE (1994, 2001). Bei Taxa, die von diesen Autoren in ihren Werken nicht berücksichtigt wurden, wurden die Arten nach dem heutigen Stand der Taxonomie und Nomenklatur übernommen.

Die Beschreibung der Sippen ist in folgende Rubriken unterteilt: Beschreibung der Sippe, Standort/Biotop, Blütezeit, Höhenverbreitung, Gesamtverbreitung (bezieht sich nur auf Europa und Vorderasien), Verbreitung auf Zypern, Bemerkungen, Gefährdung, Hybriden und, wenn erforderlich, Bemerkungen zu der Verbreitungskarte. In der Rubrik Bemerkungen werden gegebenenfalls zusätzliche, wichtige Erkenntnisse erwähnt, beziehungsweise erläutert. In dieser Rubrik werden auch bei den nahe verwandten Arten (wie zum Beispiel bei den Arten aus dem *Ophrys sphegodes-mammosa*- und *Serapias*-Formenkreis) die Unterschiede zwischen den Sippen kurz erklärt. Die Beschreibung der Arten ist meist kurz gehalten, da diese bereits in vielen anderen Bestimmungsbüchern (BAUMANN & KÜNKELE, 1982a, 1988a; BUTTLER, 1986 und DELFORGE, 1994, 2001) ausführlich dargestellt wurden. Eine umfassende Beschreibung wurde lediglich für jene Arten vorgenommen, die leicht mit anderen Arten verwechselt werden können oder die besondere Merkmale aufweisen, wie zum Beispiel bei einigen *Ophrys*- und *Serapias*-Sippen. Um auch Laien das Lesen zu erleichtern, wurden im Sinne einer Verein-

Introduction to the book

In this book, all species, subspecies and the most important varieties and some hybrids of Cyprus are treated and their distribution up to and including 2004 is shown on a UTM-2 km grid. In this grid, each dot represents an area of 4 km² (a blue dot involves reports up to 1990, a red dot shows locations from 1990 onwards).

For each taxon, several colour photographs are included, which show the whole plant, inflorescence, parts of the inflorescence and often also single flowers and biotope. The orchid species are treated in alphabetical order with the exception of closely related species (especially in the genera of *Ophrys* and *Orchis*). These are treated as a species group. The contents page however greatly facilitates easy alphabetical reference to each species.

Of some species *Aceras anthropophorum*, *Cephalanthera damasonium*, *Cephalanthera longifolia*, *Epipactis helleborine*, *Ophrys aegaea*, *Ophrys ciliata*, *Ophrys omegaifera*, *Ophrys sintenisii*, *Ophrys spruneri*, *Ophrys straussii*, *Serapias orientalis* and *Serapias vomeracea* the evidence of their existence in Cyprus is doubtful as there is no botanical or real photographic proof. Additionally, all these species have been incorporated into a separate chapter and a distribution map has been omitted.

The taxonomy and nomenclature are in accordance first with BUTTLER (1986), then largely to BAUMANN & KÜNKELE (1988a) and DELFORGE (1994, 2001). In the case of taxa which have not been documented by these authors in their works, the species were treated according to the current state of taxonomy and nomenclature.

The description of each taxon is divided into the following sections: description of the taxon, habitat, flowering time, altitude distribution, overall distribution (only for Europe and the Near East), distribution in Cyprus, remarks, threats, hybrids and when necessary remarks concerning the distribution maps. In the section 'remarks', essential additional and significant insights are mentioned and illustrated respectively. In the same section, the differences between closely related species of two taxa (for example, species from the *Ophrys sphegodes-mammosa* and *Serapias* groups) are explained in brief. The description of species is mostly kept short, as these have already been extensively documented in many other identification books (BAUMANN & KÜNKELE, 1982a, 1988a; BUTTLER, 1986 and DELFORGE, 1994, 2001). Comprehensive descriptions of those species that can easily be confused with other species or that have special characteristics, for example some *Ophrys* and *Serapias* taxa have been included. To make this book easier for the layman to understand, some technical terms used in the description of species have been taken from books by BAUMANN & KÜNKELE (1982a,

Blick auf das Troodos-Gebirge bei Trimiklini/View on the Troodos mountains near Trimiklini, 17.3.2002

heitlichung einige Fachausdrücke zu den Artenbe-schreibungen den Büchern von BAUMANN & KÜNKELE (1982a, 1988a) und BUTTLER (1986) entnommen. Die Angaben über die Höhenverbreitung wurden aus den Fundlisten vieler Orchideenfreunde und durch eigene Beobachtungen ermittelt. Die Rubrik Gesamtverbreitung gibt eine vollständige Übersicht vom Verbreitungsgebiet der Art. Weiter wurde die Rubrik Gefährdung aufgenommen, die den Status (Vorkommen und Schutz) der einzelne Sippen kurz erläutert. Andere Rubriken wie Standort, Blütezeit und Verbreitung auf Zypern berücksichtigen neben den eigenen Aufzeichnungen unter anderem die Angaben von HANSEN, KREUTZ & U. & D. RÜCKBRODT (1990), alle bekannten Literaturquellen (siehe Kapitel Botanische Erforschung der Orchideen von Zypern und Literaturliste), sowie alle bisher unveröffentlichten Fundortlisten (siehe Danksagung), die mir zur Verfügung gestellt wurden. In der Rubrik Hybriden wurden nur die Hybriden aufgelistet, die der Autor selbst nachweisen konnte oder von denen ihm fotografische Belege der Finder von Material aus Zypern vorlagen. Zweifelhafte Bastarde zwischen nahe verwandten *Ophrys*- oder *Serapias*-Arten wurden nicht berücksichtigt.

1988a) and BUTTLER (1986), for purposes of simplification. The reports on altitude distribution were taken from location lists from many orchidophiles and from personal observations. The section overall distribution gives a complete overview of the distribution area of a species. A section on threats has also been included, which briefly illustrates the status (occurrence and conservation) of individual taxa. Other sections, such as habitat, flowering time, and distribution on Cyprus include, besides personal notes, reports from, for instance HANSEN, KREUTZ & D. & U. RÜCKBRODT (1990), all known literary sources (see chapter Botanical exploration of the orchids of Cyprus and the literature list), as well as until now unpublished habitat lists (see Acknowledgements), which were placed at my disposal. In the section hybrids, only hybrids which the author could identify himself or of which photographic evidence from Cyprus was provided by the finder, have been listed. Doubtful hybrids between close related *Ophrys* and *Serapias* species were left out.

Verbreitungskarten und statistische Auswertungen

Von jeder Orchideenart gibt es in diesem Buch eine Verbreitungskarte. Als Grundlage dieser Verbreitungskarten wurde eine Reliefkarte verwendet. Alle bekannten Fundpunkte werden in einem UTM-2 km Raster dargestellt, wodurch jeder Punkt eine Fläche von 4 km² repräsentiert. Durch diese Größenordnung bleiben die Verbreitungsangaben übersichtlich und ausreichend detailliert. Bedingt durch eine relative Ungenauigkeit der Fundortangaben und die Übertragung dieser Angaben in die Verbreitungskarten können Fehler nicht ausgeschlossen werden, da schon eine Abweichung von wenigen hundert Metern über die Zugehörigkeit zum einen oder zum anderen Feld entscheidet. Die Übersichtskarte mit den Artenzahlen gibt an, wie viele Arten in den entsprechenden Feldern gefunden wurden.

In den Verbreitungskarten werden zwei Zeitzonen angegeben, nämlich vor und nach 1990. Bei Angaben vor 1990 wurde ein blauer Punkt verwendet, ein roter Punkt steht für Angaben ab 1990.

Beim Eintragen der Fundorte, die nicht mit GPS-Peilern gemessen wurden, bedarf es bei der Zuordnung äusserster Genauigkeit. Da die Lage einiger Fundorte mit einem geringen Ungenauigkeitsfaktor behaftet ist, kann es passieren, dass sie nicht im korrekten UTM-2 km Rasterfeld eingetragen sind, sondern in einem benachbarten. Aber eigentlich spielen diese Abweichungen sowie mögliche Fehler beim Übertragen der Fundorte in die Verbreitungskarten eine untergeord-

Distribution maps and statistical evaluations

A distribution map for each orchid species has been included in this book. A relief map was used as the basis for these distribution maps. All known locations are depicted in a UTM-2 km grid, which means that each point represents a surface area of 4 km². With these dimensions, the indications of distribution are clear and sufficiently detailed. Of course, due to some lack of precision in the habitat reports and the transfer of these reports into the distribution maps, mistakes can not be excluded, as even a variance of a few hundred metres can alter the grouping between one division or another. The overview map with species numbers indicates how many species were found in the appropriate division.

Two time zones are specified on the distribution maps, one for reports from before 1990 and one for after 1990. Reports from before 1990 are indicated with a blue dot, reports after 1990 with a red dot.

The transfer from the locations on the maps, which were not measured with GPS sensors, extreme precision was needed. As the specifications of the sites are affected by slight imprecision, it is possible that some locations were transferred into the adjacent UTM-2 km grid. These variations, as well as possible errors during the transfer of the locations into the distribution maps are however of only marginal importance in the light of the fact that a clear perspective on the

Zederntal/Cedar Valley, 16.3.2002

Zederntal/Cedar Valley, 16.3.2002

Karaman (Pentadactylos Range), 18.3.2002

nete Rolle angesichts der Absicht, mit der Erstellung der Verbreitungskarten ein möglichst aussagekräftiges Verbreitungsbild der Orchideen auf Zypern zu erstellen.

Schon seit längerer Zeit ist die Kartierung wesentlich einfacher geworden. Durch die Verfügbarkeit von GPS-Peilern (GPS = Global Positioning System) kann der Fundort bis auf 25 Meter genau ermittelt werden. Diese Angaben sind sehr genau und wurden korrekt in die Verbreitungskarten übertragen.

Zypern liegt in der UTM-Zone 36S, innerhalb dieser in den 100 km-Quadranten VD, VE, WD, WE und XE. Für Zypern gibt es auf UTM-10 km Basis 127 Rasterfelder. Den vorliegenden Verbreitungskarten liegt das UTM-1 km Raster zugrunde, aber der Übersichtlichkeit und des Abbildungsmaßstabes wegen wurden die Verbreitungskarten im UTM-2 km Raster wiedergegeben. Da eine Verbreitungskarte im UTM-1 km Raster die Verbreitung noch genauer wiedergibt, wurde von 4 Arten (*Ophrys kotschyi, Ophrys umbilicata, Orchis punctulata* und *Platanthera holmboei*) eine Verbreitungskarte im UTM-1 km Raster erstellt. Grundlage für diese Verbreitungskarten ist die Jet Navigation Chart 1:2.000.000 (JNC, Blatt 22), auf die das UTM-Raster von der Tactical Pilotage Chart 1:500.000 (TPC, Blatt G-4D) übertragen wurde. Weiter wurde die vom RV-Verlag herausgegebene Straßenkarte Zyperns (1:200.000) verwendet, in die das UTM-10 km Raster übertragen wurde. Mit Hilfe dieses Rasters wurden die Funde ohne GPS-Koordinaten ermittelt.

Als Grundlage für die Verbreitungskarten dienten unter anderem die Fundortangaben und Verbreitungskarten aus den Arbeiten von Hansen, Kreutz & U. & D. Rückbrodt (1990), Delforge (1990), Baumann & Künkele (1994) und Kreutz, Segers & Walraven (2002), ferner alle Fundortangaben aus der Literatur, alle Fundorte, die in irgendeiner Form in der Literaturübersicht aufgelistet wurden, sowie alle Fundortangaben von Orchideenforschern und Botanikern, die mir zur Verfügung gestellt wurden (siehe Danksagung) und alle Funde des Verfassers, die er während seiner Reisen ermittelt hat.

Mit Ausnahme der Mesaoria-Ebene, wo bedingt durch die intensive landwirtschaftliche Nutzung weniger Orchideen vorkommen und abgesehen von militärischen Sperrgebieten, sowie der näheren Umgebung der Großstädte Famagusta, Kyrenia, Larnaka, Lefkosia, Lemesos und Pafos wurde durch die große Anzahl ermittelter Daten eine sehr hohe Flächendeckung erreicht. Weiter zeigt sich, dass die Artenzahl auf Zypern mit 29 Arten in einem UTM-2 km Feld und mit 29 Arten in mehreren UTM-5 km Feldern sehr hoch ist. Aus den Übersichtskarten geht deutlich hervor, wie der Kenntnisstand über die Verbreitung der Orchideen auf Zypern nach 1990 vertieft wurde. Aber auf den Verbreitungskarten (Funde ab 1990) ist auch zu sehen, dass vor allem im Süden Zyperns ein beträchtlicher Artenrückgang zu erkennen ist, der durch anthropogene Einflüsse wie Tourismus und die schnell wachsende Bevölkerung verursacht wurde.

distribution of orchids on Cyprus will have been made possible by drawing up the distribution maps.

In recent times, charting has become much easier. With the availability of GPS (Global Positioning System) sensors, the location of a habitat can be measured within 25 metres. These measurements with GPS-systems, are very precise and they were transferred correctly on to the distribution maps.

Cyprus is situated in the UTM zone 36S, within the 100 km quadrants VD, VE, WD, WE and XE. 127 grids on a 10 km UTM basis are available for Cyprus. The basis of the distribution maps in this book is the UTM-1 km Grid, but for reasons of clarity and reproduction scale, the distribution maps are shown on a UTM-2 km grid. A UTM-1 km grid distribution map depicts an even more precise distribution, thus 4 species (*Ophrys kotschyi, Ophrys umbilicata, Orchis punctulata* and *Platanthera holmboei*) are shown on a distribution map with a UTM-1 km grid. The maps which were used as basis for the distribution maps are Jet Navigation Charts 1:2,000,000 (JNC, page 22), on to which the UTM grid of the Tactical Pilotage Chart 1:500,000 (TPC, pages G-4D) were transferred. The road map of Cyprus (1:200,000), published by RV-Publisher was also used, on which the 10 km UTM grid was superimposed. Those locations without GPS coordinates were determined with the help of this grid.

The distribution maps were based on the habitat specifications and distribution maps in the following works by Hansen, Kreutz & D. & U. Rückbrodt (1990), Delforge (1990), Baumann & Künkele (1994) and Kreutz, Segers & Walraven (2002). Other sources are all habitat specifications from literature, all habitat locations which were listed in any way possible in sources in the literature overview, as well as all habitat specifications from orchid researchers and botanists, which were placed at my disposal (see Acknowledgements), and all findings made by the author during his travels.

With the exception of the Mesaoria plains, where admittedly fewer orchids occur due to intensive agricultural use and apart from the military restricted areas, as well as the direct vicinity of the towns, Famagusta, Kyrenia, Larnaka, Lefkosia, Lemesos and Pafos, a very wide surface coverage has been achieved. Furthermore, it has been established that the number of species on Cyprus is very high, with up to 29 species in a UTM-2 km square and up to 29 species in several UTM-5 km squares. One can see from the overview maps how much the state of knowledge on the distribution of orchids on Cyprus has progressed since 1990. But one can also see on the distribution maps (findings made after 1990), that a considerable decline in the number of species is taking place, mainly in the south of Cyprus, and mainly caused by human influences, such as tourism and a rapidly growing population.

Choulou (*Orchis italica*), 12.3.2002

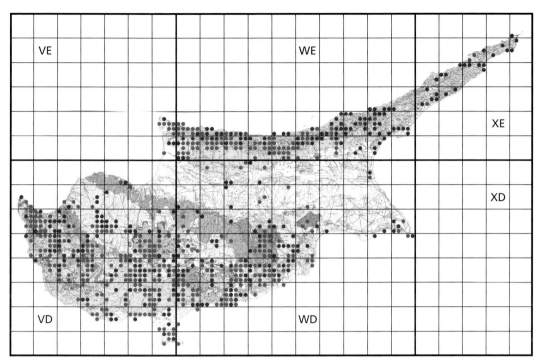

Verbreitungsübersicht im UTM-2 km Rasterfeld im Zeitraum 1900-2004, 10.246 Meldungen/Angaben
(blaue Punkte: Angaben vor 1990; rote Punkte: Angaben ab 1990)

Distribution overview in UTM-2 km grid over the period 1900-2004, 10,246 reports
(blue dots: reports before 1990; red dots: reports after 1990)

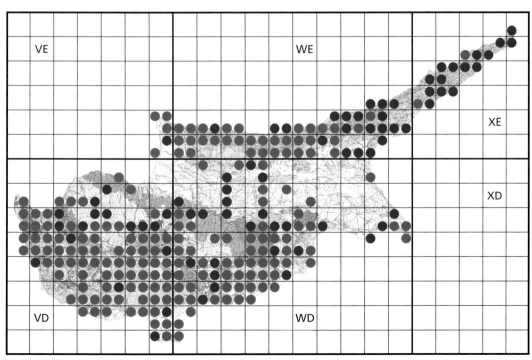

Verbreitungsübersicht im UTM-5 km Rasterfeld im Zeitraum 1900-2004, 10.246 Meldungen/Angaben
(blaue Punkte: Angaben vor 1990; rote Punkte: Angaben ab 1990)

Distribution overview in UTM-5 km grid over the period 1900-2004, 10,246 reports
(blue dots: reports before 1990; red dots: reports after 1990)

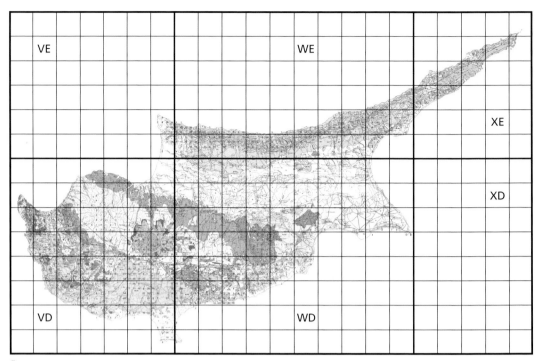

Übersichtskarte mit den Artenzahlen im UTM-2 km Rasterfeld im Zeitraum 1900-2004

Overview map with species numbers in UTM-2 km grid over the period 1900-2004

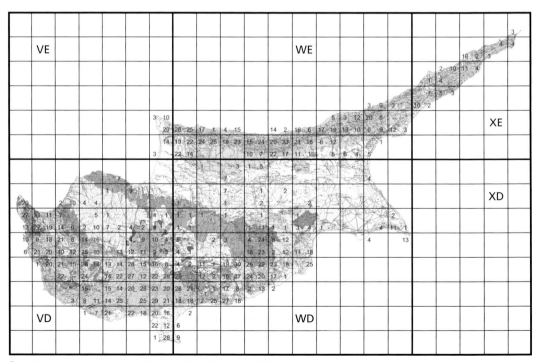

Übersichtskarte mit den Artenzahlen im UTM-5 km Rasterfeld im Zeitraum 1900-2004

Overview map with species numbers in UTM-5 km grid over the period 1900-2004

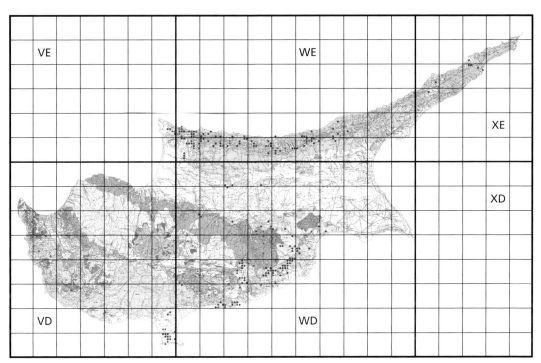

Verbreitungsübersicht im UTM-1 km Rasterfeld im Zeitraum 1900-2004 von *Ophrys kotschyi*, 311 Meldungen/Angaben
(blaue Punkte: Angaben vor 1990; rote Punkte: Angaben ab 1990)

Distribution overview in UTM-1 km grid over the period 1900-2004 from *Ophrys kotschyi*, 311 reports
(blue dots: reports before 1990; red dots: reports after 1990)

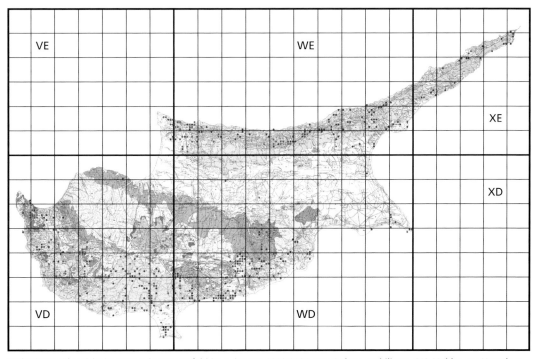

Verbreitungsübersicht im UTM-1 km Rasterfeld im Zeitraum 1900-2004 von *Ophrys umbilicata*, 643 Meldungen/Angaben
(blaue Punkte: Angaben vor 1990; rote Punkte: Angaben ab 1990)

Distribution overview in UTM-1 km grid over the period 1900-2004 from *Ophrys umbilicata*, 643 reports
(blue dots: reports before 1990; red dots: reports after 1990)

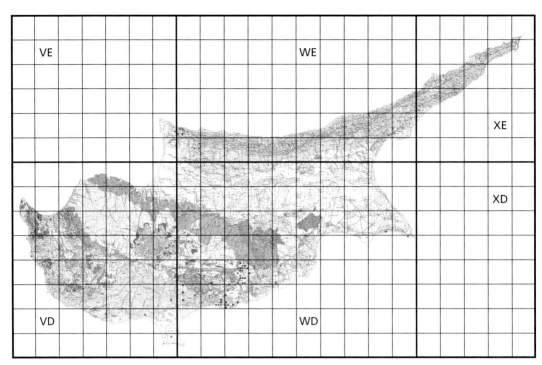

Verbreitungsübersicht im UTM-1 km Rasterfeld im Zeitraum 1900-2004 von *Orchis punctulata*, **96 Meldungen/Angaben**
(blaue Punkte: Angaben vor 1990; rote Punkte: Angaben ab 1990)

Distribution overview in UTM-1 km grid over the period 1900-2004 from *Orchis punctulata*, **96 reports**
(blue dots: reports before 1990; red dots: reports after 1990)

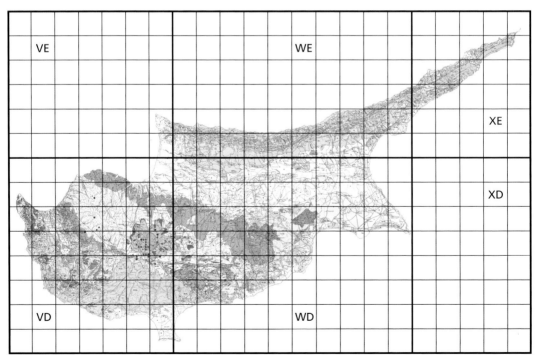

Verbreitungsübersicht im UTM-1 km Rasterfeld im Zeitraum 1900-2004 von *Platanthera holmboei*, **64 Meldungen/Angaben**
(blaue Punkte: Angaben vor 1990; rote Punkte: Angaben ab 1990)

Distribution overview in UTM-1 km grid over the period 1900-2004 from *Platanthera holmboei*, **64 reports**
(blue dots: reports before 1990; red dots: reports after 1990)

Spezieller Teil

Taxonomie und Nomenklatur

Taxonomische Gliederung

Aufgrund genetischer Untersuchungen der sogenannten ITS-Segmente der DNA wurden Verwandtschaftsbeziehungen der europäischen Orchideen festgestellt und in einer rechnerisch ermittelten Darstellung veröffentlicht (Bateman, Pridgeon & Chase (1997), Bateman (2001) und Pridgeon, Bateman, Cox, Hapeman & Chase (1997). Die Ergebnisse hatten zufolge, dass die taxonomische Gliederung der europäischen Orchideen stark geändert wurde. So wurden vor allem Änderungen in den Gattungen *Aceras, Anacamptis, Coeloglossum, Neotinea* und *Orchis* vorgenommen. Bei einigen Arten wie *Aceras anthropophorum* oder *Neotinea maculata* kann man sich vorstellen, dass sie möglicherweise in die Gattung *Orchis* gehören, aber bei *Anacamptis pyramidalis* habe ich grundsätzliche Bedenken, dies zu übernehmen. Umgekehrt wurden viele Arten der Gattung *Orchis* (zum Beispiel alle Arten und Unterarten von *Orchis palustris* und *Orchis papilionacea*) nach meiner Meinung zu Unrecht in die Gattung *Anacamptis* überführt, beziehungsweise umkombiniert. Andere Arten, wie zum Beispiel *Orchis ustulata* wurden der Gattung *Neotinea* zugeteilt, und *Coeloglossum viride* wurde in die Gattung *Dactylorhiza* eingegliedert. Ebenso habe ich grundsätzliche Probleme damit, dass die Gattung *Nigritella* in der Gattung *Gymnadenia* aufgegangen ist. Ohne hier näher auf die morphologischen Übereinstimmungen und Unterschiede von *Nigritella* und *Gymnadenia* einzugehen, hat *Nigritella* ein so eigenständiges Erscheinungsbild, dass sie meines Erachtens als separate Gattung unbedingt erhalten bleiben muss. In den neueren Ausgaben nationaler Floren sowie in den meisten aktuellen Orchideenbücher (u.a. Bournérias *et al.*, 2002; Baumann, Künkele & Lorenz, 2002 und Ströhle, 2003) wurden die taxonomischen Überlegungen von Bateman, Pridgeon & Chase (1997), Bateman (2001) und Pridgeon, Bateman, Cox, Hapeman & Chase (1997) ohnehin nicht übernommen. Während der Drucklegung dieser Arbeit erschienen vier weitere Orchideenbüchern (Jouandoudet, 2004; Perko, 2004; Souche, 2004 und H. & G. Kretzschmar & Eccarius, 2004). Auch in diesen Büchern wurde die klassische Taxonomie und Nomenklatur ebenso beibehalten wie in der Checklist of the Iberian and Balearic Orchids (Galan Cela & Gamarra, 2002). Auch in diesem Buch wird weder näher auf die taxonomische und nomenklatorische Einteilung der Arbeitsgruppe um Bateman *et al.* eingegangen, noch wurde sie übernommen. In meinem geplanten Buch 'Die Orchideen von Europa, Nordafrika und dem Nahen Osten' werde ich zwar auf die taxonomischen Vorstellungen der genannten Autoren eingehen, an eine Übernahme ihrer Auslassungen ist aber zur Zeit nicht gedacht.

Specific part

Taxonomy and Nomenclature

Taxonomic grouping

Based on genetic research of so-called ITS segments in DNA, relational connections of European orchids have been established and have been published in a calculated diagram (Bateman, Pridgeon & Chase (1997), Bateman (2001) and Pridgeon, Bateman, Cox, Hapeman & Chase (1997). The findings resulted in a substantial modification of the taxonomic classification of European orchids. In particular modifications in the generas *Aceras, Anacamptis, Coeloglossum, Neotinea* and *Orchis* have been made. One can imagine that some species such as *Aceras anthropophorum* or *Neotinea maculata* possibly belong to the *Orchis* genera, however, I do have considerable doubts whether this applies to *Anacamptis pyramidalis*. On the other hand, I am of the opinion that many species of the *Orchis* genera (e.g. all species and subspecies of *Orchis palustris* and *Orchis papilionacea*) were wrongly classified or wrongly rearranged into the *Anacamptis* genera. As a result, other species, such as *Orchis ustulata* were placed in the *Neotinea* genera and *Coeloglossum viride* in the *Dactylorhiza* genera. I also have fundamental problems with the fact that the *Nigritella* genera has been merged into the *Gymnadenia* genera. Without going into the morphological similarities and differences of *Nigritella* and *Gymnadenia, Nigritella* has such an independent appearance, that in my opinion it should be maintained as a separate genera. In the newer editions of national flora and in most of the recent orchid books (such as Bournérias *et al.*, 2002; Baumann, Künkele & Lorenz, 2002 and Ströhle 2003) the taxonomic considerations of Bateman, Pridgeon & Chase (1997), Bateman (2001) and Pridgeon, Bateman, Cox, Hapeman & Chase (1997) were not adopted anyway. Four other orchid books (Jouandoudet, 2004; Perko, 2004; Souche, 2004 and H. & G. Kretzschmar & Eccarius, 2004) were published while this book is going to press. Classic taxonomy and nomenclature were also maintained in these books, also in the Checklist of the Iberian and Balearic Orchids (Galan Cela & Gamarra, 2002). In this book also, the taxonomic and nomenclatoric grouping of Bateman *et al.* will not be dealt with or adopted. In my planned book 'The Orchids of Europe, North Africa and the Near-East' I will be going into the taxonomic ideas of before-mentioned authors, there are however no plans to adopt their suggestions.

Epipactis condensata, Troodos (British Camp), 26.6.2002

Epipactis microphylla, Lagoudera, 21.6.2002

Epipactis troodi, Prodromos-Platania, 21.6.2002

Epipactis veratrifolia, Pano Amiantos, 22.6.2002

Artabgrenzung

Wie alle mediterranen Gebiete ist auch Zypern durch das Vorkommen vieler *Ophrys*-Arten gekennzeichnet. Aber im Gegensatz etwa zu Rhodos oder der Türkei ist die Bestimmung der meisten Arten auf Zypern unproblematisch, ja sogar einfach. Nur bei den Arten des *Ophrys sphegodes-mammosa* Formenkreises gibt es manchmal Bestimmungsprobleme. Mitglieder dieses Formenkreises waren vor 2002 meist schwierig zu bestimmen und wurden davor zu den verschiedensten Arten gestellt. Durch den Beitrag von KREUTZ, SEGERS & WALRAVEN (2002) wurden die Arten des *Ophrys sphegodes-mammosa* Formenkreises auf Zypern neu gegliedert und die bestehenden Bestimmungsprobleme durch die Beschreibung von *Ophrys alasiatica* und *Ophrys morio* H.F. PAULUS & KREUTZ in diesem Buch weitgehend gelöst. Darüber hinaus kommen auf Zypern keine Vertreter der schwierigen Formenkreise von *Ophrys holoserica* oder *Ophrys oestrifera* vor.

Die drei Taxa aus dem *Ophrys fusca*-Komplex (*Ophrys cinereophila, Ophrys iricolor* und *Ophrys israelitica*) sind ohne Schwierigkeiten zu unterscheiden.

Machmal konnten die *Serapias*-Arten Bestimmungsprobleme bereiten, aber mit der Beschreibung von *Serapias aphroditae* durch DELFORGE (1990) wurden die Probleme dieses Formenkreises ebenfalls weitgehend behoben.

Zusammenfassend kann daher gesagt werden, dass auf Zypern die Arten dieser drei Formenkreise (die *Ophrys sphegodes-mammosa*- und die *Ophrys fusca*-Gruppe sowie die *Serapias*-Arten) meist ohne Schwierigkeiten zu bestimmen sind. Hierauf wird bei den oben genannten drei Formenkreisen noch näher eingegangen. Alle andere Orchideensippen, die auf Zypern vorkommen, sind deutlich von einander abgegrenzt und problemlos zu bestimmen. Ausserdem werden neue Erkentnisse über *Ophrys levantina* und *Ophrys holoserica* subsp. *grandiflora* besprochen.

Der *Ophrys sphegodes-mammosa* Formenkreis

Die Systematik der *Ophrys*-Arten der *Ophrys sphegodes-mammosa* Gruppe auf Zypern war bis zum Jahre 2002 nur mangelhaft abgeklärt. Mitglieder dieses Formenkreises waren vor 2002 meist schwierig zu bestimmen und wurden davor den verschiedensten Arten zugeordnet. B. & E. WILLING (1976) versuchten erstmals mit einem ausführlichen Beitrag die Probleme dieses Formenkreises zu klären. WOOD (1980) beschrieb in einer umfassenden Arbeit die Unterarten von *Ophrys sphegodes* in Zypern und dem östlichen Mittelmeerraum. Durch den Beitrag von KREUTZ, SEGERS & WALRAVEN (2002) wurden die Arten des *Ophrys sphegodes-mammosa* Formenkreises auf Zypern neu gegliedert und die bis dahin bestehenden Bestimmungsprobleme mit der Beschreibung von *Ophrys alasiatica*, sowie der Neubeschreibung von *Ophrys morio* H.F. PAULUS & KREUTZ in diesem Buch, weitgehend gelöst.

Species distinction

Like all other Mediterranean areas Cyprus is characterized by the occurrence of many *Ophrys* species. But in contrast with, for example Rhodes or Turkey, the identification of most of the species on Cyprus is straightforward, even easy. Identification problems only really occur with species of the *Ophrys sphegodes-mammosa* group. Members of this complex were difficult to identify before 2002 and were classified under the most widely varying species over time. Following the contribution made by KREUTZ, SEGERS & WALRAVEN (2002), the species of the *Ophrys sphegodes-mammosa* group in Cyprus were redefined and the existing identification problems were largely solved by the description of *Ophrys alasiatica* and by *Ophrys morio* H.F. PAULUS & KREUTZ in this book. Furthermore, no representatives of the difficult species group of *Ophrys holoserica* or *Ophrys oestrifera* occur on Cyprus.

The three taxa of the *Ophrys fusca* complex (*Ophrys cinereophila, Ophrys iricolor* and *Ophrys israelitica*) can also easily be identified.

Sometimes, the *Serapias* species can give rise to identification problems, but with the description of *Serapias aphroditae* by DELFORGE (1990) the problems of this species group also were largely solved.

To recapitulate, the species of these three groups (the *Ophrys sphegodes-mammosa* and *Ophrys fusca* group as well as the *Serapias* species) are mostly easy to identify. The three species groups mentioned above will be dealt with in detail. All other orchid genera that occur on Cyprus can clearly be distinguished from one another and are easy to identify. Moreover new investigations about *Ophrys levantina* and *Ophrys holoserica* subsp. *grandiflora* are written down.

The *Ophrys sphegodes-mammosa* species group

The systematics of the *Ophrys* species in the *Ophrys sphegodes-mammosa* group on Cyprus were unclear until 2002. Members of this complex were mostly difficult to identify and had been classified under widely varying taxa in the course of time. B. & E. WILLING (1976) were the first to try to solve the problems of this species group with a detailed contribution. WOOD (1980) described the subspecies of *Ophrys sphegodes* in Cyprus and the Eastern Mediterranean in a comprehensive work. With the contribution of KREUTZ, SEGERS & WALRAVEN (2002), a new differentiation of the species of the *Ophrys sphegodes-mammosa* group on Cyprus was made and the existing identification problems were solved with the description of *Ophrys alasiatica* and *Ophrys morio* H.F. PAULUS & KREUTZ in this book.

Melecta tuberculata auf/on *Ophrys kotschyi*,
Agios Georgios (Moni), 4.3.1986

Melecta tuberculata auf/on *Ophrys kotschyi*,
Agios Georgios (Moni), 4.3.1986

Andrena bimaculata auf/on *Ophrys alasiatica*,
Para Pedi-Mandria (Troodos), 11.3.1986

Andrena bimaculata auf/on *Ophrys alasiatica*,
Para Pedi-Mandria (Troodos), 11.3.1986

Die *Ophrys sphegodes-mammosa* Gruppe ist auf Zypern mit 5 Taxa vertreten, nämlich *Ophrys alasiatica*, *Ophrys herae*, *Ophrys hystera*, *Ophrys mammosa* und *Ophrys morio*. Die Arten dieser Gruppe sind sehr variabel, so dass die Abgrenzungen nicht immer leicht sind. Wenn man aber die Blütezeiten und die Streuung der Merkmale in den Populationen beachtet, kommt man in der Regel zu eindeutigen Zuordnungen.

Ophrys alasiatica ist eine früh blühende Art mit mittelgroßen Blüten. Die Pflanzen sind meist hochwüchsig, kräftig und vielblütig. Die Blüten gleichen denen von *Ophrys aesculapii* RENZ, da die Lippe fast immer einen deutlichen, ziemlich breiten gelben Rand hat und die Malzeichnung ähnlich *Ophrys aesculapii* aussieht. Pflanzen mit einem braunen Rand kommen auch vor. Vor allem die Malzeichnung ist sehr typisch. Diese besteht aus zwei parallelen, meistens bläulichen bis purpurnen Streifen, die mit einem weissen Rand versehen sind, oder sie ist in der Form einer H-Zeichnung ausgebildet. Diese Art wurde früher oft als *Ophrys sintenisii* (PAULUS & GACK, 1990a), *Ophrys aesculapii* (WOOD, 1980; DE LANGHE & D'HOSE, 1982) oder als Hybride zwischen *Ophrys mammosa* und *Ophrys transhyrcana* (*Ophrys morio*) (WOOD, 1985) angesprochen. *Ophrys alasiatica* hat *Andrena bimaculata* als Bestäuber (PAULUS & GACK, 1990a).

Ophrys herae hat viele gemeinsame Merkmale mit unserer mitteleuropäischen *Ophrys sphegodes*, unterscheidet sich aber von dieser unter anderem durch etwas größere Blüten und einen zierlicheren und höheren Wuchs. Auf Zypern blüht sie schon ab Anfang Februar als erster Vertreter des *Ophrys sphegodes*-Komplexes. Sie vermittelt zwischen *Ophrys mammosa* und der mitteleuropäischen *Ophrys sphegodes*, weshalb sie früher wohl meist als *Ophrys sphegodes* subsp. *sphegodes* angesprochen wurde (GUMPRECHT, 1964; WOOD, 1985).

Ophrys herae wurde 1992 von HIRTH & SPAETH von Samos als eine endemische Art mit vermutlich hybridogenem Ursprung zwischen *Ophrys sphegodes* s.l. und *Ophrys mammosa* beschrieben. Diese Art ist wahrscheinlich identisch mit *Ophrys pseudomammosa*, die von RENZ (1928) als vermutliche Hybride zwischen *Ophrys mammosa* und *Ophrys sphegodes* s.l. von der Insel Korfu beschrieben wurde: "Tracht einer *mammosa*. Lippe breit, flach, etwas blasser und bräunlicher bis bräunlich-violett als bei *Ophrys mammosa*, etwas stärker behaart, ohne Höcker oder mit ganz kleinen rundlichen. Unter den Eltern in der Flora von Korfu (südlich Benitze, Ende März)". DELFORGE (1992) ergänzte darauf die Originalbeschreibung von *Ophrys herae* und erweiterte das Verbreitungsgebiet dieser Art mit Korfu, den anderen Ionischen Inseln, dem griechischen Festland, einigen weiteren Ostägäischen Inseln, Kreta und Zypern, wobei er *Ophrys pseudomammosa* als Hybride zwischen *Ophrys herae* und *Ophrys cephalonica* bewertete. Weil nicht mehr mit Sicherheit festgestellt werden kann, was RENZ damals unter *Ophrys pseudomammosa* gemeint und beschrie-

The *Ophrys sphegodes-mammosa* group is represented by five taxa on Cyprus, namely *Ophrys alasiatica*, *Ophrys herae*, *Ophrys hystera*, *Ophrys mammosa* and *Ophrys morio*. The species of this group are very variable, making it difficult to draw clear distinctions. However, if flowering times and the diversification of characteristics in the populations are compared, distinct classifications can usually be made.

Ophrys alasiatica is an early flowering species with medium-sized flowers. The plants are mostly tall, vigorous and many-flowered. The flowers are similar to those of *Ophrys aesculapii* RENZ, as the labella almost always have a clear, fairly wide yellow edge and a typical speculum like *Ophrys aesculapii*. Plants with a brown edge also occur. The speculum marking in particular is very typical. It consists of two parallel, mostly bluish to purple stripes, accentuated by a white edge, or it takes the form of an H-shape. This species was often called *Ophrys sintenisii* (PAULUS & GACK, 1990a), or *Ophrys aesculapii* (WOOD, 1980; DE LANGHE & D'HOSE, 1982) or seen as a hybrid between *Ophrys mammosa* and *Ophrys transhyrcana* (*Ophrys morio*) (WOOD, 1985). *Ophrys alasiatica* is pollinated by *Andrena bimaculata* (PAULUS & GACK, 1990a).

Ophrys herae has many characteristics in common with the Central European *Ophrys sphegodes*, but can be distinguished by slightly bigger flowers and an elegant, taller growth. On Cyprus it is already in flower in early February as the first representative of the *Ophrys sphegodes-mammosa* complex. It differs between *Ophrys mammosa* and the Central European *Ophrys sphegodes*, and in the past was mostly identified as *Ophrys sphegodes* subsp. *sphegodes* (GUMPRECHT, 1964; WOOD, 1985).

HIRTH & SPAETH described *Ophrys herae* for Samos in 1992, as an endemic species of possible hybridogenic origin between *Ophrys sphegodes* s.l. and *Ophrys mammosa*. This species is probably identical with *Ophrys pseudomammosa* a species that was described by RENZ (1928) as a possible hybrid between *Ophrys mammosa* and *Ophrys sphegodes* s.l. on the island of Corfu: "Appearance as that of *mammosa*. Labellum wide, flat, somewhat paler and more brownish to brownish-violet than *Ophrys mammosa*, somewhat more pubescent, without protuberances or with very small round ones. Under the parents in the flora of Corfu (Southern Benitze, late March)". DELFORGE (1992) complemented the original description and enlarged the distribution area of this species to include Corfu, the other Ionian islands, the Greek mainland, some other Eastern Aegean islands, Crete and Cyprus, and he also rated *Ophrys pseudomammosa* as a hybrid between *Ophrys herae* and *Ophrys cephalonica*. As it is no longer possible to establish with certainty what RENZ meant and described as *Ophrys pseudomammosa*, the name of *Ophrys herae* (although descibed much later)

Andrena morio auf/on *Ophrys morio*,
Malia, 9.3.1986

Anthophora erschowi auf/on *Ophrys elegans*,
Akrotiri, 3.3.1986

Eucera dimidiata auf/on *Ophrys flavomarginata*,
Akrotiri, 1.3.1986

Andrena cinereophila auf/on *Ophrys cinereophila*,
Vavla, 8.3.1986

ben hat, wurde der Name *Ophrys herae* (obwohl viel später beschrieben) für diese Art beibehalten. Das Verbreitungsgebiet von *Ophrys herae* umfasst nach dem heutigen Kenntnisstand also Kreta, die Ionischen und Ostägäischen Inseln, Samos, das griechische Festland und Zypern.

Ophrys hystera ist vor allem an ihrer späten Blütezeit (ab Ende März), ihrem hohen Wuchs und ihren sehr großen, weit auseinander stehenden Blüten deutlich zu erkennen. Ausserdem ist der Mittellappen der Blüte meist relativ spitz nach vorne ausgezogen, bisweilen verlängert. Eine Verwechslung mit *Ophrys mammosa* ist praktisch nicht möglich, da diese etwa einen Monat früher blüht und einen viel gedrungeneren Wuchs und kleinere Blüten hat.

Ophrys mammosa zeigt starke Verwandtschaft mit *Ophrys hystera*. Sie unterscheidet sich jedoch von dieser Art durch kleinere, mehr rundliche Blüten, eine eiförmige bis ovale, ungeteilte, stark gewölbte Lippe, die im oberen Teil stark gehöckert ist (Höcker innen kahl, aussen stark behaart), durch den viel kürzeren Konnektivfortsatz, eine frühere Blütezeit (Mitte Februar bis Ende März) und niedrigeren Wuchs.

Die in diesem Buch neu beschriebene *Ophrys morio* H.F. Paulus & Kreutz (vorher in Zypern als *Ophrys transhyrcana* bezeichnet) erreicht auf Zypern ihre westliche Verbreitungsgrenze. *Ophrys morio* wurde in diesem Buch neu beschrieben, weil die bisher von Zypern unter dem Namen *Ophrys transhyrcana* beschriebenen Pflanzen morphologisch nicht mit dieser Art übereinstimmen und mit *Andrena morio* auch einen anderen Bestäuber haben. In einem Artikel (in Vorbereitung) wird näher auf die morphologischen Unterschiede und die Gegenüberstellung mit den anderen Vertretern des *Ophrys sphegodes-mammosa* Komplexes näher und ausführlich eingegangen. Die neue Art kommt wahrscheinlich auch in der Südtürkei vor (Kreutz, 1988). Bestäubernachweise in Süd-Zypern mit der Biene *Andrena morio* auf *Ophrys morio* sind zahlreich (Paulus & Gack 1990ab). Dieselbe Bienenart ist in Zypern Bestäuber von *Ophrys iricolor*, so dass man männliche Bienen mit Kopf- und gleichzeitig am Abdomen anhaftende Pollinien finden kann. Im westlichen Mittelmeergebiet bestäubt *Andrena morio Ophrys incubacea*. Der Bestäuber von *Ophrys alasiatica* ist die braune *Andrena bimaculata* (Paulus & Gack 1990ab). Auch hier wurden zahlreiche Pseudokopulationen gesehen. Der Bestäuber der israelischen *Ophrys transhyrcana* ist die ebenfalls schwarze *Andrena fuscosa*, eine Biene, die im östlichen Mittelmeergebiet *Ophrys mammosa* besucht (Paulus & Gack 1986). In Zypern war keine Gelegenheit vorhanden, die dortige *Ophrys mammosa* auf Attraktion für *Andrena fuscosa* zu überprüfen, wohl aber für *Ophrys morio* und *Ophrys alasiatica*. Beide Arten wurden von den Insekten nicht beachtet (schriftl. Mittlg. Paulus 2004).

was therefore for this species maintained. Based on this, the distribution area of *Ophrys herae* covers, according to the current state of knowledge, Crete, the Ionian and Eastern Aegean islands, Samos, the Greek mainland and Cyprus.

Ophrys hystera can mainly be recognized by its late flowering time (from late March on), its tall growth and its very large, very laxly arranged flowers. The middle lobe of its flowers is usually relatively emarginate, and sometimes elongated. It is virtually impossible to confuse it with *Ophrys mammosa*, which blooms about one month earlier and has a much more compact growth and smaller flowers.

Ophrys mammosa shows a strong relationship with *Ophrys hystera*. It can however be distinguished from the latter species by its smaller, more rounded flowers, an ovate to oval, undivided, strongly convex labellum, which has large protuberances on the upper part (interior glabrous, exterior strongly pubescent), by the much shorter connective extension, earlier flowering period (mid-February to late March) and compact growth.

Ophrys morio H.F. Paulus & Kreutz, a new species described in this book (formerly described as *Ophrys transhyrcana* from Cyprus), reaches the westernmost boundary of its distribution on Cyprus. This species was redescribed as the plants on Cyprus are not identical to the plants commonly described as *Ophrys transhyrcana* and moreover they have a different pollinator, namely *Andrena morio*. The morphologically differences and the comparison with the other representatives of the *Ophrys sphegodes-mammosa* species group will be discussed in an separate article (in prep.). This new species probably also occurs in southern Turkey (Kreutz, 1988). Evidence for the pollinator in Southern Cyprus concerning the bee *Andrena morio* for *Ophrys morio* is numerous (Paulus & Gack 1990ab). The same bee species is the pollinator of *Ophrys iricolor* in Cyprus, so one can find male bees with both head and abdomen pollinia. In the western Mediterranean region *Andrena morio* pollinates *Ophrys incubacea*. The pollinator of *Ophrys alasiatica* is the brown *Andrena bimaculata* (Paulus & Gack 1990ab). Numerous pseudo-copulations were also observed here. The pollinator of the Israeli *Ophrys transhyrcana* is the equally black *Andrena fuscosa*, a bee which visits *Ophrys mammosa* in the eastern Mediterranean region (Paulus & Gack 1986). On Cyprus there was no opportunity to verify the attraction of *Ophrys mammosa* for *Andrena fuscosa*. This was however also the case by *Ophrys morio* and *Ophrys alasiatica*; neither species was considered by the insects (written correspondence Paulus 2004).

Während *Ophrys morio* außer auf Zypern offenbar auch in der Südtürkei vorkommt, ist die nahe verwandte *Ophrys transhyrcana* von Nordisrael, über Libanon, Westjordanien, Westsyrien und die Süd- und Südosttürkei verbreitet und weiter ostwärts von den nördlichen Zagrosbergen (Iran) bis zu den Ufern des Kaspischen Meeres (Nordiran) und in Süd-Turkmenistan (Kopeth-Dagh: locus typicus). *Ophrys morio* unterscheidet sich von den anderen Vertretern des *Ophrys sphegodes-mammosa* Komplexes auf Zypern vor allem durch eine ziemlich lange, breit-eiförmige, konvex gewölbte, leicht gehöckerte und gelegentlich nach vorne allmählich schmaler werdende Lippe. Solche Blüten sind dann extrem dreilappig. Ausserdem hat *Ophrys morio* in der Regel ein hellbraunes Basalfeld, das sich farblich von der dunklen Lippe absetzt. Die seitlichen Sepalen sind fast immer sehr kräftig zweifarbig. Ihre Blüten sind etwa so groß wie die von *Ophrys alasiatica* und *Ophrys mammosa*, aber kleiner als von *Ophrys hystera*. *Ophrys morio* ist im Februar/März in Zypern neben *Ophrys alasiatica* die dominierende und am weitesten verbreitete Art der *Ophrys sphegodes-mammosa* Gruppe und fällt vor allem durch ihre oft sehr hochwüchsige und kräftige Gestalt auf.

Mehrmals wurde das Vorkommen von *Ophrys sintenisii* H. FLEISCHMANN & BORNMÜLLER für Zypern angegeben (B. & E. WILLING, 1976; PAULUS & GACK, 1990; DELFORGE, 1990; GEORGIADES, 1998ab; CHRISTOFIDES, 2001; HUBBARD & SCRATON, 2001). 2002 wurden diese *Ophrys sintenisii*-ähnlichen Pflanzen aus Zypern von KREUTZ, SEGERS & WALRAVEN als *Ophrys alasiatica* neu beschrieben.

Der *Ophrys fusca*-Formenkreis

Auf Zypern ist der *Ophrys fusca*-Komplex problemlos, und die einzelnen Arten sind einfach zu bestimmen. Zwar kommen an einigen Stellen schwierig einzuordnende Einzelpflanzen vor, aber das sind so wenige Exemplare, dass sie eigentlich wenig Beachtung verdienen. Vermutlich stellen diese Pflanzen Hybriden mit den anderen Vertretern des *Ophrys fusca*-Formenkreises dar.

Auf Zypern gibt es bislang nur (!!) drei Taxa aus dem *Ophrys fusca*-Formenkreis, nämlich *Ophrys cinereophila*, *Ophrys iricolor* und *Ophrys israelitica*. Diese drei Arten sind sehr leicht und ohne Schwierigkeiten zu unterscheiden.

Die charakteristischen Merkmale von *Ophrys cinereophila* sind vor allem ihre kleinen und meist stark gebogenen und waagerecht vom Stängel abstehenden Blüten. Ausserdem sind ihre Blüten mit einem kleinen gelblichen Rand umgeben.

Ophrys iricolor gehört als großblütige Art mit leuchtend blauem Mal und intensiv roter bis rotbrauner Lippenrückseite im Mittelmeerraum zu den schönsten und großblütigsten *Ophrys*-Arten. Sie ist mit den beiden anderen Arten aus dem *Ophrys fusca*-Formenkreis auf Zypern nicht zu verwechseln. Ein sicheres

Whereas *Ophrys morio* only occurs on Cyprus and apparently also in southern Turkey, the closely related *Ophrys transhyrcana* is distributed from northern Israel, through Lebanon, western Jordan, western Syria and south and south-east Turkey, and more eastwards from the northern Zagros mountains (Iran) as far as the shores of the Caspian Sea (northern Iran) and southern Turkmenistan (Kopeth-Dagh: locus typicus). *Ophrys morio* can be distinguished from other representatives of the *Ophrys sphegodes-mammosa* species group on Cyprus primarily by a fairly long, wide-ovate, convexly rounded, slightly humped and occasionally gradually narrowing labellum. Such flowers are strongly three-lobed. *Ophrys morio* generally also has a light brown basal field, which contrasts in colour with the dark labellum and the lateral sepals are almost always very vigorously bi-coloured. Its flowers are almost as large as those of *Ophrys alasiatica* and *Ophrys mammosa*, but smaller than those of *Ophrys hystera*. Besides *Ophrys alasiatica*, *Ophrys morio* is the dominant and most wide-spread species of the *Ophrys sphegodes-mammosa* group in February/March on Cyprus and usually stand out due to their often tall and vigorous form.

The occurrence of *Ophrys sintenisii* H. FLEISCHMANN & BORNMÜLLER on Cyprus has been indicated often (B. & E. WILLING, 1976; PAULUS & GACK, 1990; DELFORGE, 1990; GEORGIADES, 1998ab; CHRISTOFIDES, 2001; HUBBARD & SCRATON, 2001). In 2002, the Cypriot *Ophrys sintenisii*-like plants were described by KREUTZ, SEGERS & WALRAVEN as *Ophrys alasiatica*.

The *Ophrys fusca* species group

The *Ophrys fusca* species group on Cyprus is straightforward and the individual species are easy to identify. In some places, individual plants that are difficult to identify do however occur, but in such small numbers, as to make them not worthy of note. These plants are probably hybrids with other representatives of the *Ophrys fusca* group.

In Cyprus there are so far only (!!) three taxa of the *Ophrys fusca* group, namely *Ophrys cinereophila*, *Ophrys iricolor* and *Ophrys israelitica*. These three species can very easily be identified without any problems.

The main distinguishing characteristics of *Ophrys cinereophila* are its small and usually strongly bent flowers, horizontal to the stem. The flowers are also surrounded by a small yellowish edge.

A large-flowered species with a bright blue marking and intense red to red-brown labellum on the ventral side, *Ophrys iricolor* is one of the most beautiful and largest flowered of the *Ophrys* species in the Mediterranean. It can not be confused with the other two species of the *Ophrys fusca* species group on Cyprus.

Merkmal für die Bestimmung von *Ophrys iricolor* ist die Farbe der Lippenrückseite, die immer rot bis rotbraun gefärbt ist.

Ophrys israelitica ist auf Zypern auch ohne Probleme von den beiden anderen Vertretern des *Ophrys fusca*-Formenkreises zu unterscheiden. Sie ähnelt vor allem *Ophrys omegaifera*, die aber auf Zypern nicht vorkommt, obwohl mehrere Autoren sie für Zypern angegeben haben (unter anderem HANSEN, KREUTZ & U. & D. RÜCKBRODT, 1990; GEORGIADES, 1998ab; HUBBARD & SCRATON, 2001). *Ophrys israelitica* unterscheidet sich von *Ophrys omegaifera* und von *Ophrys iricolor* durch ihre flache Lippe, die im unteren Teil meist dunkelbraun bis violettbraun und im basalen Teil violettbläulich gefärbt ist. Ausserdem hat *Ophrys israelitica* kein markantes stahlblaues Mal und ihre Lippe ist nicht durch eine bleigraue bis weissliche 'Omega'-förmige Linie begrenzt. Von *Ophrys iricolor* und *Ophrys cinereophila* unterscheidet sich *Ophrys israelitica* ausserdem durch das Fehlen der Kerbe an der Lippenbasis.

Der *Serapias*-Komplex

Die Arten der Gattung *Serapias* zählen zu den am schwierigsten gegeneinander abzugrenzenden Orchideenarten Europas, wobei vor allem im östlichen Mittelmeer die Abgrenzung der Arten und ihrer Konglomerate von Übergangsformen Probleme aufwirft. G. & K. MORSCHEK (1996) machen darauf aufmerksam, dass bei der Bestimmung von Orchideen kaum berücksichtigt wird, dass kleine, zierliche Pflanzen meist keine eigene Art repräsentieren, sondern Jungpflanzen sind, die erst in einigen Jahren ihre normale Größe erreichen. Deshalb bilden individuenreiche Populationen immer wieder ein buntes Bild großer und kleiner, robusterer und zierlicherer Pflanzen. Dies trifft im besonderen Maße für die Gattung *Serapias* zu. SUNDERMANN & TAUBENHEIM (1981a) schreiben: "So klar die Gattung selbst zu definieren ist, so schwierig und unscharf sind die artlichen Grenzen zu ziehen". NELSON (1968) hat erstmals versucht die östlichen *Serapias*-Sippen zu gliedern. Weitere wichtige taxonomische und nomenklatorische Arbeiten stammen von BAUMANN & KÜNKELE (1989), GÖLZ & REINHARD (1977, 1980, 1993) und SUNDERMANN & TAUBENHEIM (1981ab). Auf Zypern sind die wichtigsten Arbeiten zur Gattung *Serapias* von GÖLZ & REINHARD (1994); HANSEN, KREUTZ & U. & D. RÜCKBRODT (1990) und DELFORGE (1990). Auch WOOD (in MEIKLE, 1985) lieferte einen Beitrag zu dieser Gattung auf Zypern. Aber vor allem mit der Beschreibung von *Serapias aphroditae* durch DELFORGE (1990) wurde die Problematik dieses Formenkreises auf Zypern weitgehend behoben. Davor wurden die Pflanzen zu den verschiedensten *Serapias*-Arten gestellt.

Auf Zypern kommen nach dem heutigen Kenntnisstand vier *Serapias*-Arten vor, nämlich *Serapias aphroditae*, *Serapias bergonii*, *Serapias levantina* und *Serapias parviflora*.

A positive marker for the identification of *Ophrys iricolor* is the colour of the ventral side of the labellum, which is always red to red-brown.

Ophrys israelitica can also easily be distinguished from both of the other representatives of the *Ophrys fusca* species group on Cyprus. It particularly resembles *Ophrys omegaifera*, which does not occur on Cyprus, although several authors have indicated it for Cyprus (such as HANSEN, KREUTZ & U. & D. RÜCKBRODT, 1990; GEORGIADES, 1998ab; HUBBARD & SCRATON, 2001). *Ophrys israelitica* can be distinguished from *Ophrys omegaifera* and from *Ophrys iricolor* by its flat labellum, which is mostly dark brown to violet brown in the lower part and violet bluish in the basal part. Furthermore, *Ophrys israelitica* has no striking steel-blue marking and its labellum is not bordered by a lead-grey to whitish 'omega'-shaped line. *Ophrys israelitica* can also be distinguished from *Ophrys iricolor* and from *Ophrys cinereophila* by the absence of a notch at the base of the labellum.

The *Serapias* complex

The species of the genus *Serapias* are among the most difficult of the European orchids to distinguish from one another where the differentiation of the species and the multitude of transitional forms give rise to problems, especially in the Eastern Mediterranean. G. & K. MORSCHEK (1996) point out that when identifying orchids, hardly anyone takes into account that small, delicate plants do not in most cases represent a separate species, but are simply seedlings that will reach their normal size in a few years. Therefore, individual-rich populations always form colourful stands of large and small, robust and delicate plants. This also applies to some degree to the genus *Serapias*. SUNDERMANN & TAUBENHEIM (1981a) write: "The genus itself is so easy to define, but how difficult it is to draw the fuzzy species-lines". NELSON (1968) tried for the first time to organize the eastern *Serapias* taxa. Other important taxonomic and nomenclatural works originate from BAUMANN & KÜNKELE (1989), GÖLZ & REINHARD (1977, 1980, 1993) and SUNDERMANN & TAUBENHEIM (1981ab). The most important works on the genus *Serapias* on Cyprus are those by GÖLZ & REINHARD (1994), HANSEN, KREUTZ & U. & D. RÜCKBRODT (1990) and DELFORGE (1990). WOOD (in MEIKLE, 1985) also made a contribution to this genus on Cyprus. The problems surrounding this species group on Cyprus were largely solved with the description of *Serapias aphroditae* by DELFORGE (1990), the plants of which had previously been classified under widely varying *Serapias* taxa.

According to the current state of knowledge, four *Serapias* species occur on Cyprus, namely *Serapias aphroditae*, *Serapias bergonii*, *Serapias levantina* and *Serapias parviflora*.

Serapias aphroditae sieht auf den ersten Blick wie eine Hybride zwischen *Serapias bergonii* und *Serapias parviflora* aus. *Serapias aphroditae* ist aber durch einen viel zierlicheren und schlankeren Wuchs, einen sehr lockerblütigen und gestreckten Blütenstand, viel kleinere Blüten und ein sehr spitzes, verlängertes, schmal-lanzettliches und zurückgebogenes, beziehungsweise vertikal abwärts gerichtetes Epichil deutlich von *Serapias bergonii* zu unterscheiden. Von *Serapias parviflora* unterscheidet sich *Serapias aphroditae* vor allen Dingen durch die Allogamie von *Serapias aphroditae*. Wichtigstes Erkennungsmerkmal von *Serapias parviflora* ist nämlich die Autogamie der Art, denn bereits im Knospenstadium ist der Fruchtknoten von *Serapias parviflora* deutlich angeschwollen. *Serapias aphroditae* ist im Gelände also ohne Schwierigkeiten als eigene Art anzusprechen.

Serapias bergonii ist eine im ostmediterranen Raum häufige und weit verbreitete Sippe. Die Art wurde in ältere Publikationen mehrmals unter *Serapias laxiflora* geführt. Von Baumann & Künkele (1989) wurde aber begründet, warum *Serapias bergonii* vor *Serapias laxiflora* prioritätsberechtigt ist. Zuweilen kann die Bestimmung Schwierigkeiten bereiten, da *Serapias bergonii* zahlreiche Hybriden mit anderen *Serapias*-Arten bildet. In typischer Ausprägung ist die im östlichen Mittelmeer weit verbreitete *Serapias bergonii* kaum verwechselbar. Es sind relativ kräftigen Pflanzen und sie sind meistens am lockerblütigen und sehr langen Blütenstand zu erkennen. Die Pflanzen sind schlank, die Vorderlippe schmal-lanzettlich und herabgebogen. *Serapias bergonii* ist in allen Merkmalen deutlich kräftiger entwickelt als *Serapias aphroditae*.

Serapias levantina erinnert an eine Übergangsform zwischen *Serapias vomeracea* subsp. *vomeracea* (N. L. Burman) Briquet und *Serapias orientalis* subsp. *carica* H. Baumann & Künkele. Auch nach Delforge (1994) ist *Serapias levantina* wahrscheinlich eine intermediäre Sippe zwischen *Serapias orientalis* s.l. und *Serapias vomeracea* s.l. Sie wurde 1989 von Baumann & Künkele von *Serapias orientalis* abgetrennt. Auf Zypern ist *Serapias levantina* deutlich von den drei anderen *Serapias*-Arten zu unterscheiden, nämlich durch die größere Blattzahl, breitere Grundblätter, ein längeres oberstes Stängelblatt, das den Beginn des Blütenstandes deutlich überragt, einen kürzeren, armblütigeren Blütenstand, breitere Sepalen und Petalen und eine kürzere und viel breitere Vorderlippe. *Serapias levantina* ist ausserdem durch ihren gedrungenen Wuchs und ihre relativ wenigen und sehr großen Blüten gut von den anderen *Serapias*-Arten zu unterscheiden.

Serapias parviflora ist an ihrer kurzen und lockerblütigen Infloreszenz zu erkennen, wobei die Blüten sehr klein sind, dem Stängel mehr oder weniger eng anliegen und steil aufwärts gerichtet sind. Weitere typische Merkmale sind die sehr kurze, stark zurückgeschlagene Vorderlippe, die der Hinterlippe anliegt und die purpurne Strichelung des Stängelgrundes.

At first glance, *Serapias aphroditae* looks like a hybrid between *Serapias bergonii* and *Serapias parviflora*. *Serapias aphroditae* can however be easily distinguished from *Serapias bergonii* by a much more delicate and slender growth, a very lax-flowered and extended inflorescence, much smaller flowers and a sharply acuminate, elongated, narrowly lanceolate and reflexed or vertical, downward pointing epichile. And it can also be easily distinguished from *Serapias parviflora* by the allogamy of *Serapias aphroditae*. The most important distinguishing characteristic of *Serapias parviflora* is the autogamy of the species, which is already obvious at the bud stage, when the ovaries of *Serapias parviflora* are clearly swollen. *Serapias aphroditae* can therefore easily be recognized as a separate species in the field.

Serapias bergonii is an abundant and widespread taxon in the Eastern Mediterranean region. The species regularly used to be classified under *Serapias laxiflora* in older publications. Baumann & Künkele (1989) however justified the reasons for *Serapias bergonii* taking priority over *Serapias laxiflora*. The identification can be problematical at times as *Serapias bergonii* forms many hybrids with other *Serapias* species. In its typical occurrence *Serapias bergonii*, widespread in the Eastern Mediterranean, is unmistakable. Its plants are relatively vigorous and are mostly recognizable by their lax-flowered and very long inflorescence. The plants are slender and the forepart of the labellum is narrowly lanceolate and bent downwards. *Serapias bergonii* is more strongly developed in all its features than *Serapias aphroditae*.

Serapias levantina resembles a transitional form between *Serapias vomeracea* subsp. *vomeracea* (N.L. Burman) Briquet and *Serapias orientalis* subsp. *carica* H. Baumann & Künkele. According to Delforge (1994) also, *Serapias levantina* is probably an intermediate taxon between *Serapias orientalis* s.l. and *Serapias vomeracea* s.l. It was separated from *Serapias orientalis* by Baumann & Künkele in 1989. On Cyprus, *Serapias levantina* can clearly be distinguished from the three other *Serapias* species, namely by the larger number of leaves, wider ground foliage, longer upper stem leaves, which clearly extend past the beginning of the inflorescence, a shorter sparsely flowered inflorescence, wider sepals and petals, and a shorter and much wider labellum fore-part. *Serapias levantina* can also easily be distinguished from the other *Serapias* species by its compact growth and its relatively few and very large flowers.

Serapias parviflora can be recognized by its short and lax-flowered inflorescence, in which the flowers are very small, more or less close to the stem, and pointing directly upwards. Other typical characteristics are its short epichile, which is strongly reflexed towards the rear part of the labellum, and the purple spotted stem. The most important distinguishing char-

Wichtigstes Erkennungsmerkmal von *Serapias parviflora* ist ihre Autogamie, wodurch der Fruchtknoten bereits im Knospenstadium deutlich angeschwollen ist.

Ophrys levantina Gölz & Reinhard versus *Ophrys holoserica* subsp. *grandiflora* (H. Fleischmann & Soó) Faurholdt

Von H. Fleischmann & Soó wurde 1927 *Ophrys bornmuelleri* forma *grandiflora* (Repert. Spec. Nov. Regni Veg. 24: 26, 1927) aus Syrien beschrieben [(Beschreibung: *Ophrys bornmülleri* Schulze forma *grandiflora* Fleischmann et Soó (var. *grandiflora* Fleischmann in sched. sine descr.!) floribus maioribus, labello minimum 10 mm longo, 15 mm lato. Cum typo in Syria, sic Svedia (Kotschy) Jerusalem (Dinsmore)]. Diese Pflanzen wurden dann später von verschiedenen Autoren den unterschiedlichsten Arten beziehungsweise Unterarten zugeordnet (*Ophrys fuciflora* subsp. *bornmuelleri* var. *grandiflora* (H. Fleischmann & Soó) B. & E. Willing, 1975; *Ophrys holoserica* subsp. *bornmuelleri* var. *grandiflora* (H. Fleischmann & Soó) Landwehr, 1977 (nom. nud.); *Ophrys bornmuelleri* subsp. *grandiflora* (H. Fleischmann & Soó) Renz & Taubenheim, 1983; *Ophrys pseudolevantina* M. & H. Schönfelder, 2001 (nom. prov.) und *Ophrys holoserica* subsp. *grandiflora* (H. Fleischmann & Soó) Faurholdt, 2003). Mit Ausnahme von M. & H. Schönfelder sind alle Autoren zu Unrecht davon ausgegangen, dass H. Fleischmann & Soó die groß- und frühblühende Hummelragwurz von Zypern gemeint haben, die von Gölz & Reinhard 1985 als *Ophrys levantina* beschrieben wurde. Funde von *Ophrys levantina* wurden auch aus der Süd- und Südosttürkei gemeldet (Renz & Taubenheim, 1984; Kreutz, 1988). Meines Erachtens nach stimmen die Pflanzen aus der Südosttürkei jedoch nicht mit denen von Zypern überein. Während es sich bei *Ophrys levantina* aus Zypern um Pflanzen handelt, deren mittelgroße Blüten vertikal abwärts gerichtet sind und eine rundliche, stark gehöckerte Lippe haben, sind die Lippen der türkischen Pflanzen mehr rechteckig bis trapezförmig und fast doppelt so groß wie die von *Ophrys levantina*. Ausserdem sind die zypriotischen Pflanzen viel niedriger und kräftiger als die südtürkischen Pflanzen, die manchmal eine Höhe von 80 cm erreichen. Die Pflanzen aus der Südosttürkei werden daher aus morphologischer Sicht als großblütige Exemplare von *Ophrys holoserica* bewertet, die jedoch nicht mit *Ophrys holoserica* subsp. *episcopalis* oder *Ophrys holoserica* subsp. *maxima* identisch sind aber *Ophrys bornmuelleri* forma *grandiflora* H. Fleischmann & Soó entsprechen. M. & H. Schönfelder (2001) haben in einem ausführlichen Beitrag diesen Pflanzen, die sie auch in Nordwest Syrien gefunden haben, den vorläufigen Arbeitsnamen *Ophrys pseudolevantina* gegeben, wahrscheinlich ohne zu wissen, dass derartige Pflanzen bereits von Fleischmann & Soó (1927) als *Ophrys bornmuelleri* forma *grandiflora* beschrieben worden waren. Schliess-

acteristic of *Serapias parviflora* is the autogamy of the species, which is already obvious at the bud stage, when the ovaries of *Serapias parviflora* are clearly swollen.

Ophrys levantina Gölz & Reinhard versus *Ophrys holoserica* subsp. *grandiflora* (H. Fleischmann & Soó) Faurholdt

H. Fleischmann & Soó described *Ophrys bornmuelleri* forma *grandiflora* (Repert. Spec. Nov. Regni Veg. 24: 26, 1927) for Syria in 1927 [(Description: *Ophrys bornmülleri* Schulze forma *grandiflora* Fleischmann et Soó (var. *grandiflora* Fleischmann in sched. sine descr.!) floribus maioribus, labello minimum 10 mm longo, 15 mm lato. Cum typo in Syria, sic Svedia (Kotschy) Jerusalem (Dinsmore)]. Later on these plants were classified under various species or subspecies by several authors (*Ophrys fuciflora* subsp. *bornmuelleri* var. *grandiflora* (H. Fleischmann & Soó) B. & E. Willing, 1975; *Ophrys holoserica* subsp. *bornmuelleri* var. *grandiflora* (H. Fleischmann & Soó) Landwehr, 1977 (nom. nud.); *Ophrys bornmuelleri* subsp. *grandiflora* (H. Fleischmann & Soó) Renz & Taubenheim, 1983; *Ophrys pseudolevantina* M. & H. Schönfelder, 2001 (nom. prov.) and *Ophrys holoserica* subsp. *grandiflora* (H. Fleischmann & Soó) Faurholdt, 2003). With the exception of M. & H. Schönfelder, all authors faultly assumed that H. Fleischmann & Soó meant the large and early flowering Late Spider Ophrys of Cyprus, which was described by Gölz & Reinhard as *Ophrys levantina* in 1985. Findings of *Ophrys levantina* were also reported from Southern Turkey (Renz & Taubenheim, 1984; Kreutz, 1988). In my opinion especially the plants from southeastern Turkey however do not correspond with those of Cyprus. Whereas *Ophrys levantina* of Cyprus has medium-sized flowers which are directed vertically downwards and its labellum is roundish and with many protuberances, those of the Turkish plants are more rectangular to trapezoid and almost twice as large as those of *Ophrys levantina*. The Cypriotic plants are also much lower and more vigorous than the Turkish plants, which often reach a height of 80 cm. The plants of southeastern Turkey are therefore valued as large-flowered specimens of *Ophrys holoserica* for morphological purposes, but are however not identical to *Ophrys holoserica* subsp. *episcopalis* or *Ophrys holoserica* subsp. *maxima*, but they are identical with *Ophrys bornmuelleri* forma *grandiflora* H. Fleischmann & Soó. M. & H. Schönfelder (2001) have given these plants, they found also in northwestern Syria, in an extensive article the preliminary name of *Ophrys pseudolevantina*, probably without knowing that such plants were already described by Fleischmann & Soó (1927) as *Ophrys bornmuelleri* forma *grandiflora*. Finally Faurholdt (2003) rearranged these plants as a large-flowered subspecies of *Ophrys holoserica* (*Ophrys holoserica* subsp. *grandiflora* (H. Fleischmann & Soó) Faurholdt), of which he cer-

Epipactis condensata, Troodos (Jubilee Hotel), 8.7.2001

lich hat FAURHOLDT (2003) derartige Pflanzen als groß-blütige Unterart von *Ophrys holoserica* umkombiniert (*Ophrys holoserica* subsp. *grandiflora* (H. FLEISCH-MANN & SOÓ) FAURHOLDT), wobei er aber mit Sicherheit *Ophrys levantina* von Zypern gemeint hat und nicht die Pflanzen aus der Südosttürkei. Die Umkombina-tion der zypriotischen *Ophrys levantina* als Unterart von *Ophrys holoserica* ist meiner Meinung nach unzutreffend, weil *Ophrys levantina* ein gut definier-tes Taxon auf Artrang darstellt, das sich deutlich von *Ophrys holoserica* unterscheidet. *Ophrys levantina* gehört auch nicht in der Verwandtschaftskreis von *Ophrys bornmuelleri*, wo sie oft von vielen Autoren als Unterart oder Varietät bewertet wurde. DELFORGE (2001) bildet auf Seite 430 beide Taxa ab, oben eine typische *Ophrys levantina* von Zypern und auf der gleichen Seite unten eine Pflanze aus der Südtürkei (*Ophrys bornmuelleri* forma *grandiflora*). Aus den beiden Bildern geht klar hervor, dass es sich klar um zwei verschiedene Taxa handelt, oben *Ophrys levan-tina*, unten *Ophrys bornmuelleri* forma *grandiflora* (= *Ophrys holoserica* subsp. *grandiflora*).

tainly must have meant *Ophrys levantina* of Cyprus and not those of southeastern Turkey. Rearrangement of the Cypriotic *Ophrys levantina* into a subspecies of *Ophrys holoserica* is, in my opinion unfounded, as *Ophrys levantina* very clearly differs from *Ophrys holoserica* and represents a taxon at species rank. *Ophrys levantina* belongs also not to the relational group of *Ophrys bornmuelleri*, as she was many times classified by serveral authors as subspecies or variety of this species. DELFORGE (2001) clearly shows at the top of page 430 a typical *Ophrys levantina* from Cyprus and at the bottom of the same page a plant from Southern Turkey (*Ophrys bornmuelleri* forma *grandiflora*). Both pictures clearly show two different taxa, on the top of page 430 *Ophrys levan-tina* and on the bottom *Ophrys bornmuelleri* for-ma *grandiflora* (= *Ophrys holoserica* subsp. *grandi-flora*).

Dactylorhiza iberica, Pano Platres (Caledonia Trail), 18.6.2001

Dactylorhiza iberica, Pano Platres (Caledonia Trail), 23.6.2002   67

Aceras anthropophorum

(L.) W.T. Aiton

Ohnsporn

Man Orchid

Beschreibung

Ziemlich kräftige Pflanze, 20 bis 45 cm hoch. Stängel aufrecht, hellgrün, kahl. Untere Laubblätter lanzettlich, rinnig gefaltet, rosettig gehäuft, die oberen in scheidige Stängelblätter übergehend, stets ungefleckt, hellgrün bis gelblichgrün (bereits im Herbst austreibend). Blütenstand locker- bis dichtblütig, meist langgestreckt, mit zahlreichen Blüten. Tragblätter lanzettlich, kürzer als der Fruchtknoten. Blüten ziemlich klein, gelb bis grünlichgelb und an den Rändern meist rötlich überlaufen. Perigonblätter einen geschlossenen Helm bildend. Sepalen eiförmig-lanzettlich, an den Rändern rötlichbraun getönt. Petalen etwas kürzer als die Sepalen. Lippe lang und schmal, tief dreilappig, der Mittellappen im unteren Teil in zwei Zipfel gespalten, diese etwa gleich lang wie die Seitenlappen, grünlich- bis ockergelb, oft rotbraun oder rötlich überlaufen. Sporn fehlt. Die Art ist mit Ausnahme der Blütenfarbe wenig variabel.

Standort

Lockere Kiefernwälder, lichte Gebüsche, Macchien und Phrygana, rasige Weideflächen und trockene Magerwiesen; bevorzugt basische und kalkreiche Böden.

Blütezeit

Ende März bis Ende April.

Gesamtverbreitung

Vor allem im westlichen Teil Mitteleuropas (nördlich bis Südengland, die Niederlande und Mitteldeutschland) und im ganzen Mittelmeergebiet (östlich bis Kleinasien und Rhodos). Auch in Nordafrika.

Bemerkungen

Mehrmals wurde über Funde von *Aceras anthropophorum* berichtet. So wurde die Art bei Wood (1985) von einem Fundort bei Agios Therapon zwischen Omodos und Lemesos angegeben, wo die Art von Kotschy 1859 gefunden wurde (Unger & Kotschy, 1865). Dieser Bereich wurde später häufig aufgesucht, aber die Art konnte dort nicht mehr nachgewiesen werden (Hansen, Kreutz & U. & D. Rückbrodt, 1990).

Ein weiterer Nachweis stammt von Smitak (Fundortangaben 1999). Er fand Ende März 1999 einige austreibende Pflanzen in einem Kiefernwald in der Umgebung von Trimiklini unweit von Platres (im Troodos-Gebirge). Weil die Pflanzen noch weit von der Blütezeit entfernt waren, hat Smitak eine Pflanze ausgegraben und mitgenommen. Diese Pflanze blühte dann später in seinem Haus als *Aceras anthropo-*

Description

Fairly vigorous plant, 20 to 45 cm tall. Stem erect, light green, bare. Lower foliage leaves lanceolate, grooved, rosette-like, upper leaves merging into sheathing stem leaves, always unspotted, light green to yellowish-green (already emerging in autumn). Inflorescence lax to densely flowered, mostly elongate, with numerous flowers. Bracts lanceolate, shorter than ovary. Flowers fairly small, yellow to greenish-yellow, mostly tinged reddish at margins. Perianth segments form a closed hood. Sepals ovate-lanceolate, tinged reddish-brown at margins. Petals slightly shorter than sepals. Labellum long and narrow, deeply three-lobed, lower half of middle lobe bipartite, but both parts as long as lateral lobes, greenish to ochre-yellow, often tinged red-brown or reddish. No spur. With the exception of flower colour, the species is hardly variable.

Habitat

Open coniferous woods, light scrub, maquis and phrygana, grassy pastures and arid meadows; prefers basic and calcareous soils.

Flowering time

From late March to late April.

Overall distribution

Mainly in the western parts of Central Europe (northwards as far as southern England, the Netherlands and central Germany) and in the whole of the Mediterranean region (eastwards as far as Asia Minor and Rhodes). Also in North Africa.

Remarks

There have repeatedly been reports of findings of *Aceras anthropophorum*. The species has for example been reported by Wood (1985) at a site near Agios Therapon between Omodos and Lemesos, where the species had also been found by Kotschy in 1859 (Unger & Kotschy, 1865). This area has been visited often in later years, but the species could not be verified again (Hansen, Kreutz & U. & D. Rückbrodt, 1990).

Other evidence originates from Smitak (location list 1999). In late March 1999, he found some emerging plants in a coniferous forest near Trimiklini, not very far from Platres (in the Troodos mountains). As the plants still had a while to go before flowering, Smitak dug up a plant and took it with him. This plant then flowered in his house as *Aceras anthropophorum*. Unfortunately there is no photo-

phorum auf. Leider existieren von dieser Pflanze weder fotografische noch Herbarbelege. Auch konnten die Pflanzen an diesem Fundort und in der weiteren Umgebung später nicht mehr bestätigt werden.

Fazit

Aceras anthropophorum erreicht in der mittleren Südtürkei die östliche Verbreitungsgrenze. Ein Fund auf Zypern ist damit durchaus möglich. Es liegen aber keine fotografischen oder Herbarbelege vor, die eine einwandfreie Existenz für Zypern bestätigen könnten. *Aceras anthropophorum* wird daher für Zypern als fraglich angesehen.

graphic or botanical evidence of these plants. Also later, these plants could not be found at the aforementioned site or anywhere in the vicinity.

Conclusions

Aceras anthropophorum reaches its easternmost distribution boundary in central Southern Turkey. A finding on Cyprus therefore must be considered a possibility. There is no photographic or botanical evidence to verify the existence of this species on Cyprus without doubt. The occurence of *Aceras anthropophorum* in Cyprus is therefore doubtful.

Cephalanthera damasonium
(MILLER) DRUCE

Weisses Waldvögelein

Large White Helleborine

Beschreibung

Schlanke Pflanze, 30 bis 50 cm hoch. Stängel ziemlich kräftig, kahl, leicht hin und her gebogen, blassgrün. Laubblätter eiförmig-lanzettlich bis länglich-oval, waagerecht abstehend bis schwach aufwärts gerichtet, zumeist flach ausgebreitet, oder rinnig gefaltet, im Bereich des Blütenstandes in Tragblätter übergehend. Blütenstand ziemlich locker, gestreckt, mit bis zu 20 Blüten. Tragblätter lanzettlich bis schmallanzettlich, bei den unteren Blüten länger als bei den oberen. Blüten mittelgroß, dem Stängel anliegend, weiss bis gelblich, meist geschlossen bleibend oder nur wenig geöffnet. Sepalen eiförmig-lanzettlich bis lanzettlich, stumpf. Petalen in Form und Farbe fast gleich den Sepalen aber etwas kürzer als diese. Lippe zweigliedrig. Hypochil mit abgerundeten Seitenlappen, weiss und am Grunde mit einem gelben Fleck. Epichil herzförmig mit schwach hochgebogenen Rändern, weiss, mit 3 bis 5 orangegelben Längsleisten. Sporn fehlt.

Description

Slender plant, 30 to 50 cm tall. Stem fairly vigorous, bare, slightly flexuose, pale green. Foliage leaves ovate-lanceolate to oblong-oval, spreading horizontally to slightly directed upwards, mostly flat, or grooved, merging into bracts near the inflorescence. Inflorescence fairly lax, elongated, with up to 20 flowers. Bracts lanceolate to narrowly lanceolate, near the lower flowers as long as the upper. Flowers medium-sized, close to stem, white to yellowish, mostly closed or just slightly opened. Sepals ovate-lanceolate to lanceolate, obtuse. Petals almost the same as sepals in shape and colour, but slightly shorter. Labellum bipartite. Hypochile with rounded lateral lobes, white and a yellow spot at base. Epichile cordate with slightly convoluted edges, white, with 3 to 5 orange-yellow longitudinal ridges. No spur.

Standort

Trockene bis mäßig feuchte Stellen in lichten Kiefern- und Pinienwäldern, selten an offenen, ungeschützten Stellen; auf frischen, basischen bis kalkhaltigen Böden.

Habitat

Arid to moderately moist places in light coniferous woods, rarely in open unprotected places; on fresh, basic to calcareous soils.

Blütezeit

Anfang bis Ende Juni.

Flowering time

Early to late June.

Gesamtverbreitung

Europa; nördlich bis Südengland, Dänemark, Gotland; östlich bis Vorderasien (Kaukasus bis Nordiran). Im Mittelmeergebiet selten und in einigen Gebieten ganz fehlend (wie im westlichen Teil der Iberischen Halbinsel und Süditalien).

Overall distribution

Europe; northwards as far as southern England, Denmark, Gotland; eastwards as far as the Near East (Caucasia to Northern Iran). Rare in the Mediterranean area and totally absent in some areas (such as the western part of the Iberian peninsula and southern Italy).

Bemerkungen

KOTSCHY (in UNGER & KOTSCHY, 1865) gibt diese Art für Zypern an: "Selten in Wäldern der Schwarzföhren 22. Mai in Blättern bei Prodromo". Hieraus geht hervor, dass KOTSCHY mit Sicherheit keine blühenden Pflanzen gesehen hat. Im Jahre 1994 wurde *Cephalanthera damasonium* von WAKEFIELD in der Um-

Remarks

KOTSCHY (in UNGER & KOTSCHY, 1865) indicates this species for Cyprus: "Rare in Black Pine forests 22nd May in leaves near Prodromo". This means that KOTSCHY certainly did not see flowering plants. In 1994 *Cephalanthera damasonium* was found by WAKEFIELD in the vicinity of Smigies. It was however never

Troodos-Olympos (Khionistra), 26.6.2002

Troodos-Olympos (Khionistra), 26.6.2002

Troodos-Olympos (Khionistra), 26.6.2002

Troodos (Standort von/site of *Epipactis condensata*), 26.6.2002

gebung von Smigies gefunden. Sie wurde aber später an dieser Fundstelle nicht mehr beobachtet (Hubbard & Scraton, 2001). Auch von dieser Art existieren keine Fotos oder Herbarbelege (mündl. Mittlg., Scraton, 2003). Weitere Funde zu dieser Art sind nicht bekannt geworden.

Fazit

Zypern gehört zu den am besten kartierten Gebieten Europas. *Cephalanthera damasonium wurde* niemals mit Sicherheit für Zypern nachgewiesen, obwohl sie in der nahe gelegenen Türkei vorkommt. Auch von Wakefields Fund existieren keine Herbaroder Fotobelege. Bei dem Fund von Kotschy hat es sich vermutlich um Laubblätter einer *Epipactis*-Art gehandelt, bei Wakefield vermutlich um eine abweichende *Cephalanthera rubra*.

seen again at this location (Hubbard & Scraton, 2001). There are no photos or botanical evidence of this species either (oral correspondence, Scraton, 2003). Other findings of this species are not known.

Conclusions

Cyprus belongs to the best charted regions of Europe. *Cephalanthera damasonium* has never been verified without doubt for Cyprus, although it occurs in neighbouring Turkey. There is no photographic or botanical evidence of Wakefield's find either. The find made by Kotschy probably concerns foliage leaves of an *Epipactis* species, Wakefield's probably concerns an aberrant *Cephalanthera rubra*.

Cephalanthera longifolia
(L.) Fritsch

Schwertblättriges Waldvögelein

Sword-Leaved Helleborine

Beschreibung

Schlanke bis kräftige Pflanze, 30 bis 50 cm hoch. Stängel relativ kräftig, schwach hin und her gebogen, dicht beblättert, rinnig, hell- bis blassgrün. Laubblätter zweizeilig angeordnet, schmal-lanzettlich bis lanzettlich, überwiegend schräg aufwärts gerichtet bis überhängend, meist rinnig gefaltet und am Ende zugespitzt. Blütenstand locker und langgestreckt, selten ziemlich dicht, meist mit zahlreichen (20-30) Blüten. Tragblätter schmal-lanzettlich, bei den unteren Blüten länger, bei den oberen sehr kurz. Blüten mittelgroß, schräg aufwärts gerichtet, rein weiss und meist halb geöffnet. Sepalen lanzettlich, zusammenneigend und spitz. Petalen oval bis schmal-lanzettlich, etwas kürzer als die Sepalen. Lippe zweigliedrig. Hypochil mit aufgerichteten Seitenlappen, weiss, am Grunde mit einem goldgelben Fleck versehen. Epichil herzförmig, weiss, mit 4 bis 7 orangegelben Längsleisten und goldgelber Spitze. Sporn fehlt.

Standort

Lichte Kiefernwälder, Waldränder und Gebüschformationen; auf trockenen bis mäßig feuchten, basenreichen Böden.

Blütezeit

Anfang bis Ende April.

Gesamtverbreitung

Fast ganz Europa, mit Ausnahme vom mittleren und nördlichen Teil Skandinaviens; klingt im kontinentalen Osteuropa aus. Östlich bis Vorderasien (Levante, Kaukasus), Iran bis zum West Himalaya. Auch in Nordafrika.

Bemerkungen

Cephalanthera longifolia wurde von Kotschy (Unger & Kotschy, 1865) für Zypern angegeben. Leider fehlen Herbar- oder fotografische Belege dieser Art. Weitere Funde sind später nicht mehr nachgewiesen.

Description

Slender to vigorous plant, 30 to 50 cm tall. Stem relatively vigorous, slightly flexuose, densely sheathed with leaves grooved, light to pale green. Foliage leaves alternate, narrowly lanceolate to lanceolate, primarily oblique to pendant, mostly grooved and pointed at the end. Inflorescence lax and elongate, rarely fairly dense, mostly with numerous (20-30) flowers. Bracts narrowly lanceolate, longer near lower flowers, upper ones very short. Flowers medium-sized, obliquely directed upwards, pure white and mostly half-open. Sepals lanceolate, connivent and acuminate. Petals oval to narrowly lanceolate, slightly shorter than sepals. Labellum bipartite. Hypochile with erect lateral lobes, white, with a golden yellow mark at base. Epichile cordate, white with 4 to 7 orange-yellow longitudinal ridges and golden yellow point. No spur.

Habitat

Light coniferous woods, forest edges and bushes; on arid to moderately moist, base-rich soils.

Flowering time

From early to late April.

Overall distribution

Almost all of Europe, except the central and northern parts of Scandinavia, tailing off into continental Eastern Europe. Eastwards as far as the Near East (Levant, Caucasus), Iran and up to the western Himalayas. Also in North Africa.

Remarks

Cephalanthera longifolia was specified for Cyprus by Kotschy (Unger & Kotschy, 1865). Unfortunately there is no photographic or botanical evidence of this species. Other findings have not been verified thereafter.

Funde von *Cephalanthera longifolia* sind auf Zypern möglich. Die Biotope in den höheren Lagen im Troodos sind für diese Art durchaus geeignet, ausserdem kommt sie auch in der benachbarten Türkei (KREUTZ, 1998), auf Lesbos und auf Rhodos vor. Darüber hinaus war KOTSCHY ein guter Botaniker, so dass eine Verwechslung mit *Cephalanthera rubra* unwahrscheinlich ist. *Cephalanthera longifolia* wird daher für Zypern als verschollen angesehen.

Findings of *Cephalanthera longifolia* on Cyprus are possible. The biotopes in the higher altitudes of the Troodos are perfectly suitable for this species, and it also occurs in neighbouring Turkey (KREUTZ, 1998), on Lesbos and on Rhodes. Above all, KOTSCHY was a good botanist, and confusions with *Cephalanthera rubra* are unlikely. *Cephalanthera longifolia* is therefore regarded as extinct on Cyprus.

Epipactis helleborine

(L.) CRANTZ

Breitblättrige Stendelwurz

Broad-Leaved Helleborine

Beschreibung

Schlanke und meist hochwüchsige Pflanze, 25 bis 70 cm hoch. Stängel relativ dünn, im unteren Teil reich beblättert. Laubblätter zahlreich, waagerecht ausgebreitet, grün bis dunkelgrün, abstehend. Untere Laubblätter breit-eiförmig bis lanzettlich und groß, die oberen lanzettlich und in Tragblätter übergehend. Blütenstand lang, locker- bis dichtblütig. Tragblätter schmal-lanzettlich, hell- bis dunkelgrün, die unteren die Blüten überragend, meist waagerecht abstehend. Blüten mittelgroß, weit geöffnet, abstehend bis leicht herabhängend. Perigonblätter glockenförmig zusammenneigend, später weit abstehend. Sepalen eiförmig-lanzettlich, zugespitzt, hellgrün bis grün, meist violett überlaufen. Petalen kürzer als die Sepalen, hellgrün oder violett. Lippe zweigliedrig. Hypochil halbkugelig, innen oliv- bis dunkelbraun, nektarführend. Epichil breit dreieckig bis herzförmig, an der Basis kräftig violett, mit zwei Höckern. Rostellum gut entwickelt und funktionstüchtig (allogam).

Standort

Laub- und Kiefernwälder; auf nährstoffreichen, kalkreichen und basischen Böden.

Blütezeit

Mitte Juni bis Ende Juli.

Gesamtverbreitung

Fast ganz Europa, mit Ausnahme des nördlichen Teils Skandinaviens und Kretas. Auch in Nordafrika, Kleinasien, den Kaukasusländern und Kanada.

Bemerkungen

WOOD (1985) gibt einen Fund von *Epipactis helleborine* bei Kryos Potamos an. Auch existiert ein Herbarbeleg von Zypern in Kew. Leider fehlen hier Ort, Datum und Angabe des Finders. Typische Exemplare von *Epipactis helleborine* sind im Mittelmeerraum sehr selten, und Fundangaben dieser Art haben sich sehr oft als falsch erwiesen.

Fazit:

Funde von *Epipactis helleborine* sind auf Zypern sehr fraglich, weil die Art in der benachbarten Südtürkei sehr selten ist und dort meist von *Epipactis turcica* KREUTZ (KREUTZ, 1998) oder *Epipactis densi-*

Description

Slender and mostly tall plant, 25 to 70 cm tall. Stem relatively thin, lower part densely leaved. Foliage leaves numerous, fanning out horizontally, green to dark green, spreading. Lower foliage leaves widely ovate to lanceolate and large, upper leaves lanceolate and merging into bracts. Inflorescence long, lax- to dense-flowered. Bracts narrowly lanceolate, bright to dark green, lower leaves longer than flowers, mostly spreading horizontally. Flower medium-sized, wide-open, spreading to slightly pendant. Perianth segments connivent to forming a bell shape, later widely separated. Sepals ovate-lanceolate, acuminate, light green to green, mostly tinged violet. Petals shorter than sepals, light green or violet. Labellum bipartite. Hypochile hemispherical, interior olive to dark brown, nectiferous. Epichile widely triangular to cordate, vividly violet at base, with two protuberances. Rostellum well-developed and functional (allogamous).

Habitat

Deciduous and coniferous forests; on fertile, calcareous and basic soils.

Flowering time

Mid-June to late July.

Overall distribution

Almost all of Europe, except the northern part of Scandinavia and Crete. Also in northern Africa, Asia Minor, Caucasus and Canada.

Remarks

WOOD (1985) specifies a find of *Epipactis helleborine* near Kryos Potamos. Botanical evidence from Cyprus also exists in Kew. Unfortunately, location, date and indication of the finder are absent. Typical specimens of *Epipactis helleborine* are very rare in the Mediterranean region, and findings of this species have often turned out to be false.

Conclusions

Findings of *Epipactis helleborine* on Cyprus are very doubtful, because this species is very rare in neighbouring Turkey where it is almost always replaced by *Epipactis turcica* KREUTZ (KREUTZ, 1998)

folia W. Hahn, J. Passin & R. Wegener ersetzt wird. Bei dem Harbarbeleg von Kew und die Angabe von Wood (1985) handelt es sich höchstwahrscheinlich um eine abweichende Pflanze von *Epipactis troodi*.

oder *Epipactis densifolia* W. Hahn, J. Passin & R. Wegener. The botanical evidence from Kew and the finding from Wood (1985) probably concerns an aberrant *Epipactis troodi*.

Ophrys aegaea

Kalteisen & H.R. Reinhard

Ägäische Ragwurz

Aegean Ophrys

Beschreibung

Ziemlich kräftige, mittelgroße Pflanze, 10 bis 30 cm hoch. Stängel aufrecht, hell- bis gelblichgrün. Blütenstand locker, mit durchschnittlich 3 bis 5 Blüten. Blüten groß. Sepalen länglich-eiförmig, weisslich, rosa, hellviolett, mit ausgeprägten grünen oder grünlichbraunen Adern. Petalen länglich-lanzettlich bis dreieckig, gelegentlich stumpf endend, intensiv purpurbraun oder olivbraun gefärbt, behaart, Rand oft schwach gewellt, dieser seitwärts bis rückwärts gebogen. Lippe groß, breit elliptisch bis rundlich, ungelappt, selten schwach gehöckert, Rand flach ausgebreitet, dunkel kastanienbraun mit auffällig hellerem, orangebraunem, basalem Zentrum, mehr oder weniger dicht bräunlich behaart. Mal von der Lippenbasis abgelöst und im mittleren Lippendrittel plaziert, aus zwei isolierten, sich manchmal berührenden, oft auch durch einen Steg verbundenen Flecken bestehend, grau bis graublau. Anhängsel klein, spitz, gelblich, abwärts bis vorwärts gerichtet.

Standort

Grasige (Zistrosen)phrygana, Affodill- und Felsfluren, Straßenböschungen, Olivenhaine, lichte Pinienwälder; auf basischen bis leicht sauren Böden.

Blütezeit

(Anfang) Mitte März bis Anfang April.

Gesamtverbreitung

Endemische Art der griechischen Inseln Karpathos und Kasos.

Bemerkungen

Ophrys aegaea wurde von Kalteisen & Reinhard (1987) aus dem Ägäischen Archipel beschrieben. Diese Art gehört in den Verwandtschaftskreis von *Ophrys argolica, Ophrys biscutella, Ophrys crabonifera, Ophrys elegans, Ophrys lesbis, Ophrys lucis* und *Ophrys pollinensis*. Sie wurde deswegen von Pedersen & Faurholdt (2002) als Unterart von *Ophrys argolica* bewertet.

Im Straßengraben an den bekannten Fundort von *Ophrys elegans* zwischen Kofinou und Lefkosia wurde 2001 von Hansson und Lidberg (Hansson, 2001) ein Exemplar von *Ophrys aegaea* gefunden. Der Fund wurde dann später anhand von Bildern von Kalteisen bestätigt. Nach dem Studium der Beschreibung der Pflanze (Hansson, 2001) und der fotografischen Belege sieht die in Frage stehende Pflanze *Ophrys aegaea* tatsächlich ähnlich. Funde dieser Pflanze konnten später nicht mehr bestätigt werden (mündl. Mittlg. Sischka, 2004).

Description

Fairly vigorous, medium-sized plant, 10 to 30 cm tall. Stem erect, light to yellowish green. Inflorescence lax with an average of 3 to 5 flowers. Flowers large. Sepals oblong-ovate, whitish, pink, bright violet, with green or greenish-brown distinct veins. Petals oblong-lanceolate to triangular, at times obtuse, intense purple- or olive-brown, pubescent, margins often slightly wavy, bent to the side or backwards. Labellum large, widely elliptical to roundish, unlobed, rarely with small protuberances, margins spread out flat, dark chestnut-brown with distinct light orange-brown basal centre, more or less covered with dense brownish hairs. Speculum separated from base of labellum and situated in middle third of labellum, consisting of two isolated, sometimes touching spots, but which are often also connected by a wedge, grey to grey-blue. Appendage small, acuminate, directed downwards to forwards.

Habitat

Grassy (rock rose) phrygana, in asphodel and rocky fields, roadside banks, olive groves, light pine woods; on basic to lightly acidic soils.

Flowering time

From (early-) mid-March to early April.

Overall distribution

Endemic species of the Greek islands Karpathos and Kasos.

Remarks

Ophrys aegaea was described by Kalteisen & Reinhard in 1987 from the Aegean archipelago. This species belongs to the relational group of *Ophrys argolica, Ophrys biscutella, Ophrys crabonifera, Ophrys elegans, Ophrys lesbis, Ophrys lucis* and *Ophrys pollinensis*. Therefore this species was recombined as a subspecies of *Ophrys argolica* (Pedersen & Faurholdt, 2002).

In a roadside ditch at the well-known location of *Ophrys elegans* between Kofinou and Lefkosia, Hansson and Lidberg (Hansson, 2001) found one specimen of *Ophrys aegaea* in 2001. Later, the find was verified by pictures through Kalteisen. After studying the description of the plant (Hansson, 2001) and the photographic evidence, the plant in question does indeed resemble *Ophrys aegaea*. Recent findings of this plant could not been varified (oral correspondence, Sischka, 2004).

Ophrys aegaea kommt in ihrer typischen Ausprägung nur auf Karpathos und Kasos vor. Auch von Rhodos, das nördlich von Karpathos liegt, wurden immer wieder Funde von *Ophrys aegaea* gemeldet, die aber nach kritischer Überprüfung ausnahmslos als *Ophrys lucis* identifiziert wurden. Daher ist die auf Zypern inmitten von vielen *Ophrys elegans*, ihrer nächstverwandten Art, gefundene Pflanze vermutlich eine Pflanze hybridogenen Ursprungs oder eine untypische *Ophrys elegans*.

Ophrys aegaea only occurs in its typical form on Karpathos and Kasos. Findings of *Ophrys aegaea* have also repeatedly been reported from Rhodes (north of Karpathos), but all were however identified as *Ophrys lucis* after close inspection. The plant found on Cyprus in the midst of many *Ophrys elegans*, its closest related species, is presumably a plant of hybridogenic origin or an atypical *Ophrys elegans*.

Ophrys ciliata

BIVONA-BERNARDI

Spiegel-Ragwurz

Mirror Ophrys

Beschreibung

Gedrungene bis schlanke Pflanze, 10 bis 30 cm hoch. Laubblätter bläulich- bis dunkelgrün, die unteren lanzettlich, rosettig gehäuft, die oberen länglich-lanzettlich, aufgerichtet bis abstehend, bisweilen mit wenigen stängelumfassenden Hochblättern. Blütenstand locker mit 2 bis 9 Blüten. Blüten mittelgroß, schräg abstehend. Sepalen länglich-eiförmig, hellgrün gefärbt, in der Mitte und in der unteren Hälfte braun gestreift oder violett bis braunviolett überlaufen, manchmal zusätzlich mit violetten Punkten, die seitlichen Sepalen leicht nach vorne gebogen, das mittlere stark nach vorne gekrümmt. Petalen klein, eiförmig, nach vorne gebogen und dunkelbraun. Lippe eiförmig, im oberen Teil stark dreilappig, schwach gewölbt und am Rande stark rotbraun oder dunkelbraun behaart; Seitenlappen breit lanzettlich bis eiförmig; Mittellappen nur leicht gewölbt, auf der Fläche kahl. Lippenfarbe leuchtend dunkelblau, glänzend, ohne oder meist nur mit einem schmalen gelblichen Farbsaum vor dem Haarsaum, Labellum-Haarkranz auffällig dunkelrotbraun, Innenflächen der Seitenlappen geschwärzt. Anhängsel fehlt.

Description

Compact to slender plant, 10 to 30 cm tall. Foliage leaves bluish to dark green, lower leaves lanceolate, arranged in a rosette, upper leaves oblong-lanceolate, erect to spreading, sometimes with a few upper stem-sheathing leaves. Inflorescence lax with 2 to 9 flowers. Flowers medium-sized, spreading obliquely. Sepals oblong-ovate, light green, striped brown or tinged with violet to brown-violet (often also with violet dots) in the centre and lower half, lateral sepals slightly bent forwards, dorsal sepal strongly curved forwards. Petals small, ovate, bent forwards and dark brown. Labellum ovate, deeply three-lobed in the upper part, weakly domed and covered in dense dark brown or red-brown hairs at margins; lateral lobes broadly lanceolate to ovate; middle lobe only slightly domed, glabrous on the surface. Colour of labellum bright deep blue, shining, without, or more often with only a narrow, yellow border in front of hair line, labellum hairs distinctly dark red-brown, interior of lateral lobes blackened. Appendage absent.

Standort

Gerne in Trockenarealen und an Schottersäumen, in Affodillfluren, aufgelassenen Oliventerrassen, in offenen Macchien, Phrygana, Wiesenflächen, lichten Kiefernwäldern, Ödland und im Gebüsch; auf trockenen bis mäßig feuchten, basenreichen Böden.

Habitat

Prefers arid habitats and gravel roadsides, asphodel fields, abandoned olive terraces, open maquis, phrygana, meadows, light coniferous woods, wasteland and scrub; on arid to moderately moist, base-rich soils.

Blütezeit

(Mitte Februar) Anfang März bis Anfang April.

Flowering time

From (mid-February) early March to early April.

Gesamtverbreitung

Ophrys ciliata ist von Portugal, Spanien, Südfrankreich, Italien über Griechenland über die gesamte Ägäis bis in die West- und Südtürkei verbreitet.

Overall distribution

Ophrys ciliata occurs from Portugal, Spain, southern France, Italy through Greece and throughout the whole of the Aegean, to as far as western and southern Turkey.

Bemerkungen

Diese Art wurde mehrmals von Zypern gemeldet. So gibt es bei HANSEN, KREUTZ & U. & D. RÜCKBRODT (1990) eine Angabe dieser Art aus dem Jahre 1988, wo sie an der Straße zwischen Tepebaşi und Akdeniz im Nordwesten Zyperns gefunden wurde. Nach CHRIS-

Remarks

The species has been reported repeatedly from Cyprus. There is for example a report from 1988 of this species from HANSEN, KREUTZ & U. & D. RÜCKBRODT (1990), where it was found along the road between Tepebaşi and Akdeniz in northwestern Cyprus. Ac-

TOFIDIS (mündl. Mittlg., 2002) gibt es ein Aquarell von *Ophrys ciliata*. Diese Zeichnung soll von einer Frau aus der Umgebung von Polis stammen, also auch aus der Umgebung zwischen Tepebaŝi und Akdeniz.

GEORGIADES (1998b) berichtet in seinem großformatigen Buch, dass *Ophrys speculum* (= *Ophrys ciliata*) in den angrenzenden Ländern allgemein vorkommt, aber auf Zypern besonders selten war. Er schreibt weiter, dass die Art nur von zwei Fundstellen an der Nordküste bekannt war, und zwar von einem grasigen Fundort zwischen Pachyammos and Pyrgos und von einem weiteren Fundort in Phryganaflächen bei Nea Demata. An beiden Fundorten, die auf etwa 250 m Höhe liegen, soll sie nicht selten gewesen sein und dort in größeren Populationen vorgekommen sein. Aus dem Text geht aber nicht hervor, woher das abgebildete Exemplar stammt. Bei allen anderen größeren Werken über Zypern (zum Beispiel bei G. & K. MORSCHEK, 1996, bei CHRISTOFIDES, 2001 und HUBBARD & SCRATON, 2001) wird diese Art nicht aufgeführt.

Fazit

Obwohl die Biotope auf Zypern durchaus für *Ophrys ciliata* geeignet sind, konnte sie trotz intensiver Suche mehrerer Orchideenkartierer, auf denen gezielt und ausgiebig nach dieser Art gesucht wurde, nicht aktuell bestätigt werden (BOG, 2002). Ein Vorkommen von *Ophrys ciliata* kann auf Zypern nicht ausgeschlossen werden. Ihr Verbreitungsgebiet umfasst fast das ganze Mittelmeergebiet, wobei sie ihre östliche Verbreitungsgrenze in der mittleren Südwesttürkei erreicht. *Ophrys ciliata* wird daher für Zypern als verschollen angesehen.

cording to CHRISTOFIDES (oral correspondence, 2002) there is a water-colouring of *Ophrys ciliata*. This drawing is supposed to have been made by a lady from the Polis area, from a plant again found in the area between Tepebaŝi and Akdeniz.

GEORGIADES (1998b) reports in his large-format book that *Ophrys speculum* (= *Ophrys ciliata*) occurs commonly in neighbouring countries, but is rather rare on Cyprus. He also writes that the species is only known at two sites on the north coast, namely a grassy location between Pachyammos and Pyrgos and from another location in phrygana plains near Nea Demata. At both locations, situated at about 250 m altitude, the subspecies was reportedly not really rare and occurred in large populations. It is not however clear from the text where the depicted specimen comes from. In all other large works about Cyprus (e.g. G. & K. MORSCHEK, 1996; CHRISTOFIDES, 2001 and HUBBARD & SCRATON, 2001) the species is not listed as present.

Conclusions

Although the biotopes on Cyprus are thoroughly appropriate for *Ophrys ciliata*, it has not recently been verified despite targeted and thorough research by several orchid observers (BOG, 2002). An occurrence of *Ophrys ciliata* can not be discounted for Cyprus. Its distribution area covers almost the whole Mediterranean region, where it reaches its easternmost distribution boundary in central southwestern Turkey. *Ophrys ciliata* is extinct on Cyprus.

Ophrys omegaifera   H. FLEISCHMANN

Omega-Ragwurz

Omega Ophrys

Beschreibung

Schlanke und gedrungene Pflanze, 10 bis 20 cm hoch. Untere Laubblätter am Grunde rosettig angeordnet, eiförmig bis oval, hell- bis gelblichgrün. Nach oben in mehrere stängelumfassende Hochblätter übergehend. Blütenstand ziemlich locker, mit nur wenigen Blüten, meist nicht mehr als 3, aber Pflanzen mit nur einer Blüte sind keine Ausnahme. Blüten mittelgroß bis groß, fast horizontal vom Blütenstängel abstehend. Sepalen eiförmig bis eiförmig-lanzettlich, grünlichgelb bis grün, die beiden seitlichen abstehend, das mittlere stark vornübergebeugt. Petalen lanzettlich, meist etwas dunkler als die Sepalen gefärbt, gewellt und purpurn überlaufen. Lippe stark knieförmig gebogen, stark gewölbt, in der Mitte dreilappig, hellbraun bis kastanienbraun, Mittellappen am Grunde meist schwach gekerbt, die beiden Seitenlappen flach, stark zurückgeschlagen und an den Aussenseiten dicht pelzig

Description

Slender and compact plant, 10 to 20 cm tall. Lower foliage leaves arranged in a rosette at the base, ovate to oval, light to yellowish-green, merging into several sheathing stem leaves towards the top. Inflorescence fairly lax, bearing only a few flowers, mostly not exceeding 3, but plants with only one flower are no exception. Flowers medium-sized to large, spreading almost horizontally from the axis. Sepals ovate to ovate-lanceolate, greenish-yellow to green, both laterals spreading, dorsal sepal curved over forwards. Petals lanceolate, mostly slightly darker than sepals, wavy and tinged purple. Labellum strongly geniculate, strongly domed, three-lobed in the centre, light brown to chestnut-brown, middle lobe slightly grooved at the base, both lateral lobes flat, strongly reflexed and exterior heavily pubescent. Speculum marking has 'omega'-shaped border and is bluish. Appendage absent.

behaart. Die Malzeichnung stellt eine 'Omega'-förmige Umrandung dar und ist bläulich gefärbt. Anhängsel fehlt.

Standort

Typische Art lichter Kiefernwälder; seltener in Ödland, Olivenhainen, Macchien, Phrygana, Feuchtwiesen und in Gebüschen; hauptsächlich auf trockenen, kalkhaltigen Böden.

Blütezeit

Von Mitte Februar bis Mitte April.

Gesamtverbreitung

Östliches Mittelmeergebiet: Ägäische Inseln (Kos, Paros, Naxos, Skyros, Andros, Kreta, Rhodos und Karpathos) und Südwesttürkei. Auf Kreta und Rhodos ist *Ophrys omegaifera* weit verbreitet und nicht selten.

Bemerkungen

Auf Zypern wurden Pflanzen gefunden, die mit der kretischen *Ophrys omegaifera* identisch sein sollen (zitiert nach HANSEN, KREUTZ & U. & D. RÜCKBRODT, 1990). Diese Pflanzen, die bereits im Februar zur Blüte gelangten, wurden zwischen Pafos und Polis gemeldet. Leider gibt es von diesen Funden keine Fotos oder Herbarbelege.

Auch KOHLMÜLLER (1990) berichtet von Pflanzen, die *Ophrys omegaifera* ähnlich sahen. Die in seinem Artikel abgebildete Pflanze sieht zwar wie *Ophrys omegaifera* aus (unter anderem Omega-Mal), aber die Lippe ist nicht stark knieförmig gebogen und auch nicht stark gewölbt. Bei diesen Funden handelt es sich mit Sicherheit um abweichende Pflanzen von *Ophrys israelitica*. Weitere Meldungen dieser Art gibt es nicht. *Ophrys israelitica* weist gewisse Ähnlichkeit mit *Ophrys omegaifera* auf, Fehlbestimmungen sind dadurch nicht ausgeschlossen und dadurch ist eine einwandfreie Bestimmung manchmal schwer.

Ophrys omegaifera erreicht ihre östliche Verbreitungsgrenze in der Südwesttürkei und auf Rhodos. Mit einem Fund auf Zypern ist also normalerweise nicht zu rechnen. Auch WOOD (1985) schreibt, dass Angaben von *Ophrys omegaifera* Verwechslungen mit *Ophrys fleischmannii* darstellen (damals war *Ophrys israelitica* noch nicht von *Ophrys fleischmannii* abgetrennt).

KRETZSCHMAR (1995) hat Zypern in der zweiten Februarwoche besucht. Dabei konnte er die früheren Angaben der frühblühenden *Ophrys omegaifera* nicht bestätigen.

Fazit

Weil die Funde von *Ophrys omegaifera* nicht eindeutig durch Fotos und Herbarmaterial belegt werden konnten und Zypern ausserhalb des Verbreitungsgebietes dieser Art liegt, wurde sie in diesem Kapitel aufgelistet. Die Art wird als nicht auf Zypern vorkommend eingestuft.

Habitat

Typical species of light coniferous woods; rarer in wasteland, olive groves, maquis, phrygana, wet meadows and in scrub; mainly on arid, calcareous soils.

Flowering time

From mid-February to mid-April.

Overall distribution

Eastern Mediterranean region: Aegean islands (Kos, Paros, Naxos, Skyros, Andros, Crete, Rhodes and Karpathos) and southwestern Turkey. *Ophrys omegaifera* is widely distributed on Crete and Rhodes and not rare.

Remarks

Plants that are presumably identical to the Cretan *Ophrys omegaifera* were found on Cyprus (cited in HANSEN, KREUTZ & U. & D. RÜCKBRODT, 1990). These plants, already in bloom in February, were reported between Pafos and Polis. Unfortunately there is however no photographic or botanical evidence of these findings.

KOHLMÜLLER (1990) also reported on plants that resembled *Ophrys omegaifera*. The plant depicted in his article does indeed have some resemblances to *Ophrys omegaifera* (such as the omega speculum), but the labellum is not strongly geniculate and also not strongly domed. These findings are surely aberrant plants of *Ophrys israelitica*. Other reports of this species are non-existent. *Ophrys israelitica* does show some likeness to *Ophrys omegaifera*, which gives rise to faulty identifications and a certain identification is therefore often difficult.

Ophrys omegaifera reaches its easternmost distribution boundary in southwestern Turkey and on Rhodes. A find on Cyprus is therefore highly unlikely. WOOD (1985) also writes that reports of *Ophrys omegaifera* are misidentified *Ophrys fleischmannii* (*Ophrys israelitica* had not been separated from *Ophrys fleischmannii* at the time).

KRETZSCHMAR (1995) visited Cyprus in the second week of February, and he could not verify the earlier reports of the early-flowering *Ophrys omegaifera*.

Conclusions

As the find of *Ophrys omegaifera* could not be verified with photographic or botanical evidence and because it is situated outside of the distribution area of this species, it is listed in this chapter. The species is classified as non-existent on Cyprus.

Ophrys sintenisii

H. Fleischmann & Bornmüller

Sintenis Ragwurz

Beschreibung

Kräftige, schlanke, hochwüchsige Pflanze mit einem lockeren, langgestreckten, reichblütigen Blütenstand, dieser mit etwa 8 bis 12 (25) Blüten. Blüten groß, über die mittlere und obere Stängelhälfte verteilt. Sepalen länglich-eiförmig, abstehend, (hell)grün bis gelblichgrün oder rosa, manchmal in der Mitte rötlich überlaufen, die seitlichen meist leicht zurückgeschlagen oder schwach nach vorne gekrümmt, das mittlere etwas nach vorne gebogen. Petalen lanzettlich bis eiförmig-lanzettlich, am Rande gewellt, gelblichgrün (an der Basis oft schwach rötlich überlaufen) oder rosa. Lippe rundlich bis eiförmig, ungeteilt bis schwach dreilappig, schwach gehöckert, gewölbt, an den Rändern stark behaart, braun bis rötlichbraun. Mal H-förmig, stahlblau bis purpurviolett gefärbt, manchmal von einem hellen, weißlichen Rand umgeben. Anhängsel gelblich und sehr schwach entwickelt.

Standort

Gebüschränder, Phrygana, Olivenhaine, Straßenböschungen; auf frischen bis mäßig trockenen, kalkhaltigen Böden.

Blütezeit

Ende April bis Mitte Mai.

Gesamtverbreitung

Osttürkei, Libanon, Israel, Syrien und Iran. Ihr Verbreitungsgebiet ist unklar, weil sie oft mit anderen Arten aus ihrem Formenkreis verwechselt wird.

Bemerkungen

Mehrmals wurde das Vorkommen von *Ophrys sintenisii* für Zypern angegeben (B. & E. Willing, 1976; Paulus & Gack, 1990a; Delforge, 1990; Georgiades, 1998ab; Christofides, 2001; Hubbard & Scraton, 2001). Die Angaben von *Ophrys sintenisii*-ähnlichen Pflanzen aus Zypern beziehen sich wahrscheinlich alle auf die 2002 von Kreutz, Segers & Walraven neu beschriebene Art *Ophrys alasiatica*.

Fazit

Die Arbeit von Kreutz, Segers & Walraven (2002) hat belegt, dass *Ophrys sintenisii* nicht auf Zypern vorkommt und dass die Angaben dieser Art zu der von ihnen neu beschriebene *Ophrys alasiatica* gehören. Die Art wird als nicht auf Zypern vorkommend eingestuft.

Sintenis Ophrys

Description

Vigorous, slender, tall plant with a lax, elongated, densely-flowered inflorescence, bearing about 8 to 12 (25) flowers. Flowers large, divided over central and upper part of stem. Sepals oblong-ovate, spreading, (light) green to yellowish-green or pink, often tinged reddish in the middle, laterals mostly slightly reflexed or slightly bent forwards, dorsal sepal slightly bent forwards. Petals lanceolate to ovate-lanceolate, wavy at margins, yellowish-green (faintly tinged reddish at base) or pink. Labellum roundish to ovate, undivided to slightly three-lobed, slight protuberances, domed, densely pubescent at the edges, brown to reddish brown. Speculum H-shaped, steel blue to purple violet, often surrounded by a bright, whitish edge. Appendage yellowish and very underdeveloped.

Habitat

Bush edges, phrygana, olive groves, roadside embankments; on fresh to moderately arid, calcareous soils.

Flowering time

Late April to mid-May.

Overall distribution

Eastern Turkey, Lebanon, Israel, Syria and Iran. Its distribution area is unclear, as it has often been confused with other species of its species group.

Remarks

The occurrence of *Ophrys sintenisii* on Cyprus has been reported many times (B. & E. Willing, 1976; Paulus & Gack, 1990a; Delforge, 1990; Georgiades, 1998ab; Christofides, 2001; Hubbard & Scraton, 2001). These reports of Cypriot *Ophrys sintenisii*-like plants probably all concern *Ophrys alasiatica*, described as a new species in 2002 by Kreutz, Segers & Walraven.

Conclusions

The work of Kreutz, Segers & Walraven (2002) has established that *Ophrys sintenisii* does not occur on Cyprus and that the reports of this species concern the newly described species *Ophrys alasiatica*. The species is classified as non-existent on Cyprus.

Ophrys spruneri

Nyman

Spruners Ragwurz

Beschreibung

Schlanke, meist kräftige und hochwüchsige Pflanze, 20 bis 40 cm hoch. Untere Laubblätter lanzettlich bis schmal-lanzettlich, am Grunde rosettig gehäuft,

Spruner's Ophrys

Description

Slender, mostly vigorous and tall plant, 20 to 40 cm tall. Lower foliage leaves lanceolate to narrowly lanceolate, rosette-like at the base, upper leaves oblong-

die oberen länglich-lanzettlich, locker am Stängel verteilt, stängelumfassend. Blütenstand meist langgestreckt, mit 2 bis 10 großen und locker angeordneten Blüten. Sepalen lanzettlich bis eiförmig-lanzettlich, die seitlichen abstehend, bisweilen schräg abwärts gerichtet, das mittlere meist schmaler, schwach nach vorne gebogen oder aufgerichtet, rosa oder purpurn, selten grünlichweiss oder grün mit grünem Mittelnerv, die untere Hälfte der seitlichen Sepalen meist dunkler gefärbt. Petalen dreieckig-lanzettlich, stumpf, rötlich, an den Rändern meist purpurn überlaufen. Lippe sehr groß und langgestreckt, im oberen Teil tief dreilappig, ungehöckert, dunkelbraun bis dunkelpurpurbraun; Seitenlappen seitlich abstehend bis abwärts gerichtet, stark weisslichbraun behaart; Mittellappen ziemlich schmal, stark gewölbt, mit einer blauvioletten, weiss umrahmten Zeichnung (Mal meist aus zwei parallelen Streifen bestehend oder H-förmig). Anhängsel gelblich bis grünlichgelb, sehr klein, nach vorne gerichtet.

Standort
Lockere Kiefernwälder, Phrygana, Macchien, Ödland und Olivenhaine. Gerne an frischen, mäßig feuchten und schattigen Stellen; auf basenreichen oder kalkhaltigen Böden.

Blütezeit
Anfang bis Ende April.

Gesamtverbreitung
Festland von Griechenland, Ägäische Inseln und Kreta.

Bemerkungen
Ophrys spruneri wurde mehrmals für Zypern angegeben (unter anderem von NELSON, 1962; OSORIO-TAFALL & SERAPHIM, 1973; MEGAW & MEIKLE, 1973; SUNDERMANN, 1980; WOOD, 1980, 1981), früher zum Teil als *Ophrys hiulca* SPRUNER ex REICHENBACH (POST, 1900; THOMPSON, 1906; HOLMBOE, 1914). Die Pflanzen, die POST (1900) mit der kurzen Angabe 'Plaines de Chypre, mars 1894' beschriftet hat, stellen nach WOOD (1985) sicherlich keine *Ophrys spruneri* dar, sind aber vermutlich identisch mit *Ophrys hystera* oder *Ophrys mammosa*, zwei Arten die gewisse Ähnlichkeiten mit *Ophrys spruneri* aufweisen. Von V.S. SUMMERHAYES wurde das zypriotische Material im Kew Herbarium als *Ophrys elegans* identifiziert (WOOD, 1981, 1985). Die Pflanze die von MEGAW (1973) im Buch 'Wild Flowers of Cyprus' abgebildet und mit *Ophrys sphecodes* subsp. *spruneri* beschriftet wurde, stellt wegen der ungeteilte Lippe keine *Ophrys elegans* dar (WOOD, 1981, 1985). Auch B. & E. WILLING (1976) konnten die Art nicht bestätigen und vermuteten, dass es sich um untypische Exemplare von *Ophrys sphegodes*, *Ophrys mammosa* bzw. *Ophrys sintenisii* handelte oder um Übergänge zwischen diesen drei Arten.

Fazit
Ophrys spruneri kommt auf Zypern nicht vor. Alle Funde stellen Verwechslungen mit *Ophrys hystera*

lanceolate, laxly distributed along, and sheathing the stem. Inflorescence mostly elongated with 2 to 10 large and laxly arranged flowers. Sepals lanceolate to ovate-lanceolate, laterals spreading to sometimes slightly directed downwards, dorsal sepal mostly narrower, slightly bent forwards or erect, pink to purple, rarely greenish-white or green with green central vein, lower half of lateral sepals mostly darker. Petals triangular-lanceolate, obtuse, reddish, tinged purple at edges. Labellum very large and elongated, deeply three-lobed in the upper part, no protuberances, dark brown to dark purple brown; lateral lobes spreading laterally to directed downwards, covered in dense whitish-brown hairs; central lobes fairly narrow, strongly domed, with a blue-violet, white-edged marking (speculum mostly consisting of two parallel stripes, or H-shaped). Appendage yellowish to greenish-yellow, very small, directed forwards.

Habitat
Light coniferous forests, phrygana, maquis, wasteland and olive groves. Prefers fresh, moderately moist and shady places; on base-rich or calcareous soils.

Flowering time
Early to late April.

Overall distribution
Mainland of Greece, Aegean Islands and Crete.

Remarks
Ophrys spruneri has been reported for Cyprus many times (for example by NELSON, 1962; OSORIO-TAFALL & SERAPHIM, 1973; MEGAW & MEIKLE, 1973; SUNDERMANN, 1980; WOOD, 1980, 1981), first partly as *Ophrys hiulca* SPRUNER ex REICHENBACH (POST, 1900; THOMPSON, 1906; HOLMBOE, 1914). The plants that POST (1900) described with the short report 'Plaines de Chypre, mars 1894', are according to WOOD (1985) definitely not *Ophrys spruneri*, but are probably identical to *Ophrys hystera* or *Ophrys mammosa*, two species that show certain similarities to *Ophrys spruneri*. The Cypriot material in the herbarium at Kew was identified by V.S. SUMMERHAYES as *Ophrys elegans* (WOOD, 1981, 1985). The plants depicted by MEGAW (1973) in the book 'Wild Flowers of Cyprus', which were described as *Ophrys sphecodes* subsp. *spruneri*, could not possibly be *Ophrys elegans* because of the undivided labellum (WOOD, 1981, 1985). B. & E. WILLING (1976) could not verify the species either and suspected that they were atypical specimens of *Ophrys sphegodes*, *Ophrys mammosa*, *Ophrys sintenisii* or transitional forms between these three species.

Conclusions
Ophrys spruneri does not occur on Cyprus. All findings are confusions with *Ophrys hystera* or *Ophrys*

oder *Ophrys mammosa* dar. Ausserdem endet das Verbreitungsgebiet weit westlich von Zypern, und die Art kommt auch im Süden der Türkei nicht vor.

mammosa. Furthermore, the distribution area ends far to the west of Cyprus, and the species does not occur either in the south of Turkey.

Ophrys straussii

H. Fleischmann & Bornmüller

Strauss-Ragwurz

Strauss Ophrys

Beschreibung

Schlanke und hochwüchsige Pflanze, 30 bis 50 cm hoch. Untere Laubblätter eiförmig-lanzettlich, rosettig gehäuft, die oberen länglich-lanzettlich, locker am Stängel verteilt, stängelumfassend. Blütenstand lang, mit 3 bis 10 kleinen, locker angeordneten Blüten. Sepalen eiförmig-lanzettlich bis lanzettlich, abstehend oder zurückgeschlagen, das mittlere manchmal schwach nach vorne gebogen, rosa oder purpurn, selten grünlichweiss oder grün mit grünem Mittelnerv. Petalen klein, dreieckig-lanzettlich, stumpf, rötlich, dunkelbraun oder violett gefärbt. Lippe im oberen Teil tief dreilappig, dunkelbraun bis dunkelpurpurbraun; Seitenlappen ziemlich lang, weisslichgrau oder weisslichbraun behaart; Mittellappen oft stark gewölbt mit variabler Zeichnung, diese meist aus zwei tropfenförmigen Flecken bestehend, die oft miteinander verbunden sind, rein weiss oder mehrfarbig. Anhängsel sehr klein, gelblich bis grünlichgelb, nach vorne gerichtet.

Description

Tall slender plant, 30 to 50 cm tall. Lower foliage leaves ovate-lanceolate, arranged in a rosette, upper leaves oblong-lanceolate, laxly divided along, and sheathing the stem. Inflorescence long and bearing 3 to 10 small laxly arranged flowers. Sepals ovate-lanceolate to lanceolate, spreading or reflexed, dorsal sometimes faintly bent forwards, pink or purple, rarely greenish-white or green with green mid-vein. Petals small, triangular-lanceolate, obtuse, reddish, dark brown or violet. Labellum deeply three-lobed in upper part, dark brown to dark purple brown; lateral lobes fairly long with whitish-green or whitish brown hairs; central lobe often strongly domed with variable marking, mostly consisting of two drop-shaped spots, often connected with one another; pure white or multi-coloured. Appendage very small, yellowish to greenish yellow, directed forwards.

Standort

Lockere Kiefernwälder mit sparsamem Unterwuchs. Bevorzugt frische und schattige Stellen; auf basenreichen oder kalkhaltigen Böden.

Habitat

Light coniferous forests with sparse undergrowth. Prefers cool and shady places; on base-rich or calcareous soils.

Blütezeit

Mitte bis Ende April.

Flowering time

Mid- to late-April.

Gesamtverbreitung

Endemische Art der Türkei, dort im mittleren Süden des Landes (Antalya bis Kahramanmaraş) und in Ostanatolien verbreitet. Ausserdem sehr selten in der südostanatolischen Region.

Overall distribution

Endemic species of Turkey, distributed from the central south of the country (between Antalya and Kahramanmaraş) to eastern Anatolia. Very rare in the southeastern Anatolian region.

Bemerkungen

Mitte April 1995 wurde einen Fund dieser Art von Van der Cingel (1997) aus der Umgebung des Salzsees nahe der Hala Sultan Tekke bei Larnaka nachgewiesen. Dieser Fundort ist bei Orchideenfreunden sehr bekannt, weil hier viele und seltene Orchideenarten wachsen. Bei diesem Fund handelte es sich um zwei Pflanzen. Im Artikel von Van der Cingel (1997) wurde auch die Möglichkeit untersucht, ob die gefundenen Pflanzen nicht zu *Ophrys reinholdii* gehören, eine nahe verwandte Art, die eine mehr westliche Verbreitung hat (von Griechenland bis Antalya in der mittleren Südtürkei). Zypern liegt also genau auf der Arealgrenze der beide Arten. Aber wie Van der Cingel (1997) schon angibt, gehören beide Pflanzen vermutlich *Ophrys straussii* an. Die beiden Pflanzen wurden Mitte April in Hochblüte gefunden, was auch mit der Blütezeit von *Ophrys straussii* in der benachbarten Südtürkei überein

Remarks

In mid-April 1995, a find of this species was verified by Van der Cingel (1997) in the vicinity of the salt lake near the Hala Sultan Tekke of Larnaka. This location is well-known to orchidophiles, as many and rare orchid species grow there. This find involved two plants. In the article by Van der Cingel (1997), the possibilty was discussed that the plants found possibly belonged to *Ophrys reinholdii*, a closely related species, which has a more western distribution (from Greece to Antalya in central southern Turkey). Cyprus is therefore situated at the boundary of both species. However, as Van der Cingel (1997) had already indicated, both plants probably belong to *Ophrys straussii*. Both plants were found in full bloom, which coincides with the flowering time of *Ophrys straussii* in neighbouring southern Turkey. After studying the photographic evidence, it can be concluded that these plants indeed resemble

Troodos-Omodos, 26.6.2002

Tochni (Standort von/site of *Orchis punctulata*), 13.3.2002

Ophrys straussii, Larnaka (Salt lake), 19.4.1995

stimmt. Nach dem Studium der Fotobelege hat sich herausgestellt, dass diese Pflanzen tatsächlich *Ophrys straussii* sehr ähnlich sehen. Aber leider konnte die Art später nicht mehr nachgewiesen werden. Bei diesen Fund handelt es sich vermutlich um einen transienten Anflieger, dessen Etablierung in Zypern bisher jedoch nicht erfolgte.

Fazit

Bisher wurden nur zwei Exemplare von *Ophrys straussii*-ähnliche Pflanzen an einem Fundort auf Zypern gefunden, und später nicht mehr aktuell für Zypern bestätigt. *Ophrys straussii*, insofern die beiden Pflanzen diese Art tatsächlich darstellten, muss als verschollen angesehen werden.

Ophrys straussii. The species could however unfortunately not be verified later. This find probably involves a transient 'immigrant', as its establishment in Cyprus has not succeeded so far.

Conclusions

The two plants on Cyprus do strongly resembles *Ophrys straussii*. They have so far been found at only one location on Cyprus, and they could not later be verified for Cyprus. *Ophrys straussii*, as the two plants really represent this species, is therefore extinct on Cyprus.

Serapias orientalis

(Greuter) H. Baumann & Künkele

Orientalischer Zungenständel

Oriental Serapias

Beschreibung

Kräftige, 15 bis 40 cm hohe Pflanze. Stängel relativ kräftig und dick, hellgrün bis grün, im oberen Teil rötlichviolett überlaufen. Laubblätter breit-lanzettlich, aufrecht bis abstehend, die unteren oft zurückgebogen, (hell)grün bis gelblichgrün gefärbt, schräg aufrecht bis abstehend; die oberen Laubblätter tragblattartig und den Beginn des Blütenstandes deutlich erreichend oder überragend, rotviolett bis braunrot überlaufen. Blütenstand dicht, kurz, verlängert oder eiförmig, gedrängt, arm- bis ziemlich reichblütig, gewöhnlich bis zu 10 cm lang, mit 3 bis 6 ziemlich dicht angeordneten Blüten; diese groß, hellbraun bis rosaviolett. Brakteen breit-eiförmig, zugespitzt, kürzer als die Blüten, vielnervig, rötlichbraun, die unteren Tragblätter meist die Blüten überragend. Perigonblätter lanzettlich, zugespitzt, genervt, helmförmig zusammenneigend, außen hellviolett, entlang der Nerven dunkelrotviolett gefärbt, waagrecht oder steil bis schräg aufwärts gerichtet. Lippe zweigliedrig, am Grunde mit zwei parallelen Schwielen. Hypochil deutlich aus dem Sepalhelm hervortretend, dunkelrotbraun, an den Rändern dunkelviolett. Epichil breit-lanzettlich bis eiförmig, zurückgekrümmt, dunkelviolettrot, im Zentrum hell behaart.

Description

Vigorous, 15 to 40 cm tall plant. Stem relatively sturdy and thick, light green to green, tinged reddish violet in upper part. Foliage leaves broadly lanceolate, erect to spreading; lower leaves often reflexed, (light) green to yellowish green, obliquely erect to spreading; upper foliage leaves resemble bracts and clearly extend to or past the inflorescence, tinged red-violet to brown-red. Inflorescence dense, short, elongate to ovate, compact, few to fairly densely flowered, normally up to 10 cm long with 3 to 6 fairly densely arranged flowers; these large, light brown to pink-violet. Bracts broadly lanceolate, acuminate, shorter than flowers, many-veined, reddish-brown, lower bracts mostly extend past flowers. Perianth segments lanceolate, acuminate, veined, connivent to forming a hood, exterior light violet, dark red violet along veins, directed horizontally or erectly to slightly upwards. Labellum bipartite, two parallel ridges at base. Hypochile clearly extending from sepal hood, dark red brown, dark violet at edges. Epichile broadly-lanceolate to ovate, reflexed, dark violet red, covered in light hairs at centre.

Standort

Macchien, Phrygana, Wiesenflächen, aufgelassene Weinbergterrassen, Steinfluren, grasiges Ödland, selten in feuchten Wiesen; auf basischen oder kalkhaltigen Böden.

Habitat

Maquis, phrygana, grasslands, abandoned vineyard terraces, rocky meadows, grassy wasteland, rarely in wet meadows; on basic or calcareous soils.

Blütezeit

Ende März bis Mitte (Ende) April.

Flowering time

Late March to mid- (late-) April.

Gesamtverbreitung

Die Art hat eine ostmediterrane Verbreitung (von Südgriechenland bis Kreta und Karpathos).

Overall distribution

The species has an Eastern Mediterranean distribution (from southern Greece to Crete and Karpathos).

Bemerkungen

Bei *Serapias orientalis* s.l. handelt es sich um einen polymorphen Formenkreis, der sich infolge einer geographischen Isolierung in räumlich völlig ge-

Remarks

Serapias orientalis s.l. involves a polymorphic species group, which can reasonably be divided into widely separated subspecies because of their geo-

81

trenne Unterarten sinnvoll aufgliedern lässt (BAU-MANN & KÜNKELE, 1989). So wurde *Serapias orientalis* s.l. von BAUMANN & KÜNKELE (1989) in drei Unterarten aufgegliedert, nämlich in *Serapias orientalis* subsp. *orientalis*, *Serapias orientalis* subsp. *carica* H. BAUMANN & KÜNKELE und *Serapias orientalis* subsp. *apulica* H. BAUMANN & KÜNKELE.

Serapias orientalis subsp. *orientalis* hat ihre Verbreitung von Südgriechenland bis Kreta und Karpathos. Weiter nach Osten wird sie von *Serapias orientalis* subsp. *carica* abgelöst.

Serapias orientalis subsp. *carica* besiedelt nur ein kleines Areal in der Südwesttürkei (Bodrum bis Fethiye), sowie die der türkischen Küste vorgelagerten Inseln Rhodos, Samos, Lesbos und die Kykladen. Das Areal von *Serapias orientalis* subsp. *apulica* erstreckt sich in Italien vom Monte Gargano im Norden bis an die Südspitze der Salentina (Tricase).

Serapias orientalis subsp. *carica* und *Serapias orientalis* subsp. *orientalis* sind nur schwierig zu unterscheiden. An gemeinsamen Merkmalen sind hervorzuheben: frühe Blütezeit, große, bauchige Tragblätter und große Blütendimensionen mit breiten Petalen. Unterschiede bestehen jedoch in der Blütenfarbe, die bei *Serapias orientalis* subsp. *carica* dunkelrot ist, wogegen sie bei *Serapias orientalis* subsp. *orientalis* durchwegs heller rot ist. Ausserdem ist die Breite der Kronblätter bei *Serapias orientalis* subsp. *carica* geringer, und die Vorderlippe ist deutlich breiter als bei *Serapias orientalis* subsp. *orientalis* (BAUMANN & KÜNKELE, 1989).

Von mehreren Autoren (zum Beispiel WOOD, 1985; DELFORGE, 1990; GEORGIADES, 1998ab, CHRISTOFIDES, 2001 und VINEY, 1994) wurde *Serapias orientalis* subsp. *orientalis* für Zypern angegeben. Diese Art, sowie die nahe verwandte *Serapias orientalis* subsp. *carica* kommen aber auf Zypern nicht vor. Die Funde gehören ausnahmslos zu *Serapias levantina*.

Fazit

Serapias orientalis erreicht ihre östliche Verbreitungsgrenze auf Kreta und Karpathos. Weiter nach Osten wird sie von *Serapias orientalis* subsp. *carica* abgelöst. Auch im Süden der Türkei kommt die Art nicht vor. *Serapias orientalis* kommt auf Zypern nicht vor. Alle Funde stellen Verwechslungen mit *Serapias levantina* dar.

graphical isolation (BAUMANN & KÜNKELE, 1989). *Serapias orientalis* s.l. for example was divided into three subspecies by BAUMANN & KÜNKELE (1989), namely *Serapias orientalis* subsp. *orientalis*, *Serapias orientalis* subsp. *carica* H. BAUMANN & KÜNKELE and *Serapias orientalis* subsp. *apulica* H. BAUMANN & KÜNKELE.

Serapias orientalis subsp. *orientalis* is distributed from southern Greece to Crete and Karpathos. Further to the east it is replaced by *Serapias orientalis* subsp. *carica*.

Serapias orientalis subsp. *carica* populates just a small area in southwestern Turkey (Bodrum to Fethiye), and the islands situated along the Turkish coast: Rhodes, Samos, Lesbos and the Cyclades. The distribution area of *Serapias orientalis* subsp. *apulica* stretches from Monte Gargano in northern Italy to the southern tip of Salentina (Tricase).

Serapias orientalis subsp. *carica* and *Serapias orientalis* subsp. *orientalis* are very difficult to distinguish from each other. Common characteristics are: early flowering time, large, domed bracts and large floral dimensions with wide petals. Differences can however be found in flower colour, which is dark red in the case of *Serapias orientalis* subsp. *carica*, and a lighter red in the case of *Serapias orientalis* subsp. *orientalis*. Moreover, the width of the crown leaves of *Serapias orientalis* subsp. *carica* is smaller and the labellum fore-part is clearly wider than *Serapias orientalis* subsp. *orientalis* (BAUMANN & KÜNKELE, 1989).

Several authors (e.g. WOOD, 1985; DELFORGE, 1990; GEORGIADES, 1998ab, CHRISTOFIDES, 2001 and VINEY, 1994) reported *Serapias orientalis* subsp. *orientalis* for Cyprus. This species, and the closely related *Serapias orientalis* subsp. *carica* however do not occur on Cyprus. Without exception, these findings all belong to *Serapias levantina*.

Conclusions

Serapias orientalis reaches its easternmost distribution boundary on Crete and Karpathos. Further to the east it is replaced by *Serapias orientalis* subsp. *carica*. The species does not occur in southern Turkey. *Serapias orientalis* does not occur on Cyprus. All findings are confusions with *Serapias levantina*.

Serapias vomeracea

(N.L. BURMAN) BRIQUET

Pflugschar-Zungenständel

Long-Lipped Serapias

Beschreibung

Schlanke, hochwüchsige, 30 bis 60 cm hohe Pflanze. Stängel relativ kräftig, hellgrün bis grün, im oberen Teil meist rötlich überlaufen. Laubblätter schmal-lanzettlich, die unteren aufrecht bis abstehend, bläulich gefärbt, bisweilen rötlich punktiert;

Description

Slender, tall, 30 to 60 cm tall plant. Stem relatively vigorous, light green to green, tinged reddish in upper part. Foliage leaves narrowly lanceolate, lower leaves erect to spreading, tinged bluish at times with reddish dots; upper leaves resemble

die oberen Laubblätter tragblattartig, schräg aufrecht bis abstehend und den Beginn des Blütenstandes erreichend, rotviolett bis braunrot überlaufen. Blütenstand locker, verlängert oder eiförmig, ziemlich reichblütig, mit 3 bis 8 locker angeordneten Blüten; diese groß, hellbraun bis rötlichbraun. Tragblätter eiförmig, zugespitzt, länger als die Blüten, vielnervig, rötlichbraun, die unteren Tragblätter meist die Blüten überragend. Perigonblätter lanzettlich, zugespitzt, genervt, helmförmig zusammenneigend, graublauviolett, meist steil aufwärts gerichtet. Lippe zweigliedrig, am Grunde mit zwei parallelen Schwielen. Hypochil herzförmig, die Seitenlappen kaum aus dem Sepalhelm hervortretend, braunrot gefärbt. Epichil schmal-lanzettlich, herabhängend bis zurückgekrümmt, dunkelrotbraun bis bräunlichviolett, am Ansatz des Epichils dicht und ziemlich lang behaart.

Standort
Macchien, Phrygana, aufgelassene Weinbergterrassen, Wiesenflächen und in feuchten Wiesen; auf basischen oder kalkhaltigen Böden.

Blütezeit
Mitte bis Ende April.

Gesamtverbreitung
Serapias vomeracea besitzt eine westliche und mittlere mediterrane Verbreitung (von Portugal bis Griechenland).

Bemerkungen
Von Wood, 1985; Georgiades, 1998ab, Delforge, 1990; Christofides, 2001 und Viney, 1994 wurden immer wieder Einzelfunde von *Serapias vomerac*ea für Zypern angegeben, eine *Serapias*-Art , die aber eine westliche und mittlere mediterrane Verbreitung hat (Portugal bis Griechenland). Auf Bestimmungsprobleme im östlichen Mittelmeerraum haben bereits Sundermann & Taubenheim (1981ab) und Kreutz (1998) hingewiesen, wobei es Sundermann & Taubenheim (1981ab) oftmals völlig unmöglich erschien, eine befriedigende Zuordnung in den Merkmalskomplexen *bergonii/vomeracea* und *vomeracea/ orientalis* zu erreichen. Auch Delforge (1990) gibt *Serapias vomeracea* für Zypern an.

Fazit
Auf den südostägäischen Inseln sowie auf Zypern wurden nie einheitlich ausgeprägte, größere Populationen nachgewiesen, die sich zweifelsfrei als *Serapias vomeracea* identifizieren liessen. Die gefundenen Pflanzen auf Zypern stellen mit Sicherheit Hybridschwärme zwischen *Serapias levantina* mit *Serapias bergonii* dar. Ausserdem endet das Verbreitungsgebiet weit westlich von Zypern. Die Art wird als nicht auf Zypern vorkommend eingestuft.

bracts, obliquely erect to spreading and reaching the beginning of the inflorescence, red-violet to brown with red tinges. Inflorescence lax, elongate to ovoid, fairly dense-flowered with 3 to 8 laxly arranged flowers; these large, light brown to reddish brown. Bracts ovate, acuminate, longer than flowers, many-veined, reddish brown, lower bracts extending past flowers. Perianth segments lanceolate, acuminate, veined, connivent to forming a hood, grey blue-violet, mostly directed straight upwards. Labellum bipartite, with two parallel ridges at base. Hypochile cordate, lateral lobes scarcely extending from hood, brown-red. Epichile narrowly lanceolate, pendant to reflexed, dark red-brown to brownish violet, dense and fairly long hairs at base of epichile.

Habitat
Maquis, phrygana, abandoned vineyard terraces, grassy plains and wet meadows; on basic or calcareous soils.

Flowering time
Mid- to late April.

Overall distribution
Serapias vomeracea has a Western and Central Mediterranean distribution (from Portugal to Greece).

Remarks
Wood, 1985; Georgiades, 1998ab, Delforge, 1990; Christofides, 2001 and Viney, 1994 repeatedly reported solitary findings of *Serapias vomeracea* for Cyprus, a *Serapias* species which however has a Western and Central Mediterranean distribution (Portugal to Greece). Sundermann & Taubenheim (1981ab) and Kreutz (1998) had already addressed identification problems for the Eastern Mediterranean, where it often seemed totally impossible to Sundermann & Taubenheim (1981ab) to achieve a satisfying classification into one of the characteristic complexes of *bergonii/ vomeracea* and *vomeracea/ orientalis*. Delforge (1990) also specifies *Serapias vomeracea* for Cyprus.

Conclusions
Uniformly pronounced, larger populations which could doubtlessly be identified as *Serapias vomeracea* have never been found on the southeastern Aegean islands or on Cyprus. The plants found on Cyprus are certainly transitional stages between *Serapias levantina* and *Serapias bergonii*. The distribution area also ends far to the west of Cyprus. The species is categorized as non-existent on Cyprus.

Bestimmung und Blütenbau der Orchideen

Schlüssel zu den auf Zypern vorkommenden Orchideengattungen

1a. Pflanze ohne grüne Laubblätter. Stängel violett; Blüten groß, violett oder rot ....***Limodorum***

1b Pflanze mit grünen Laubblättern **2**

2a Lippe in zwei ungleiche Abschnitte (Hypochil [basaler Teil] und Epichil [endständiger Teil]) gegliedert..**3**

2b Lippe nicht quer gegliedert (aber manchmal mit Lappen und Zipfeln) **5**

3a Hypochil mit aufgerichteten Seitenlappen, größtenteils im geschlossenen Perigonhelm verborgen; Epichil herabhängend, zungenförmig; Tragblätter auffällig geädert ....***Serapias***

3b Blüten anders **4**

4a Blüten abstehend bis hängend; Sepalen grünlich bis trüb rotbraun; Hypochil schüsselförmig, innen dunkler, glänzend durch Nektar ....***Epipactis***

4b Blüten sehr groß, aufgerichtet; Sepalen weiß oder hellrot; Epichil mit Längsleisten ...***Cephalanthera***

5a Lippe samtartig behaart, meistens mit auffälliger Malzeichnung, meist stark gewölbt und insektenähnlich..***Ophrys***

5b Lippe anders, kahl, ohne Malzeichnung................**6**

6a Blüten (gelb)grünlich; Lippe ungeteilt, zungenförmig; Blüte lang gespornt ....***Platanthera***

6b Lippe nicht zungenförmig **7**

7a Lippe an der Basis mit 2 senkrechten Längsleisten; Blütenstand pyramiden- bis eiförmig...***Anacamptis***

7b Lippe an der Basis ohne Längsleisten **8**

8a Blüten klein, weißlich, spiralig angeordnet; Blütezeit Spätsommer bis Herbst.......................***Spiranthes***

8b Blüten nicht spiralig angeordnet, Blütezeit Frühling und Frühsommer **9**

9a Sepalen und Petalen helmförmig zusammenneigend **10**

9b Sepalen und Petalen abstehend **11**

10a Blütenlippe breit, Mittellappen geteilt; Pflanze sehr kräftig ....***Barlia***

10b Blütenlippe schlank. 3-lappig, insgesamt 4-zipflig ('menschenförmig') ....***Aceras***

11a Pflanze klein, meist unauffällig; Laubblätter meist violett überlaufen, bisweilen gefleckt; Blütenstand sehr dicht; Blüten sehr klein, weiss bis rosa, ohne Zeichnung, kurz gespornt......................***Neotinea***

11b Pflanzen und Blüten anders, meist sehr auffällig...**12**

12a Laubblätter oft in einer Rosette angeordnet; Blütenstand bis zum Aufblühen durch die Laubblätter umhüllt; Tragblätter kaum länger als der Fruchtknoten; Lippe oft 'menschenförmig'...........***Orchis***

12b Laubblätter meistens am Stängel verteilt; junger Blütenstand nicht durch Laubblätter umhüllt; Tragblätter krautig, im unteren Teil des Blütenstandes meist beträchtlich länger als der Fruchtknoten und öfters violett überlaufen ....***Dactylorhiza***

Identification of orchids and structure of orchid flowers

Key to orchid genera on Cyprus

1a. Plant without green foliage leaves. Stem violet; flowers large, violet or red.....................***Limodorum***

1b Plant with green foliage leaves **2**

2a Labellum divided into two uneven segments (hypochile [basal part] and epichile [apical part].......**3**

2b Labellum not tranversely divided (but sometimes with lobes and swellings).....................................**5**

3a Hypochile with erect lateral lobes, largely hidden in closed perianth hood; epichile pendant, tongue shaped; bracts distinctly veined ....***Serapias***

3b Flowers different **4**

4a Flowers spreading to pendant; sepals greenish to dull red brown; hypochile cupped, interior dark, gleaming with nectar ....***Epipactis***

4b Flowers very large, erect, sepals white to bright red; epichile with longitudinal ridges ..***Cephalanthera***

5a Labellum covered in velvety hairs, mostly with distinct speculum, mostly strongly domed and insect shaped...***Ophrys***

5b Labellum different, glabrous, no speculum **6**

6a Flowers (yellow)greenish; labellum undivided, tongue shaped; flowers with long spur.........***Platanthera***

6b Labellum not tongue shaped **7**

7a Labellum with 2 vertical longitudinal ridges; inflorescence pyramidal to ovate ....***Anacamptis***

7b Labellum with no longitudinal ridges at base **8**

8a Flowers small, whitish, arranged spirally; flowering time late summer to autumn...............***Spiranthes***

8b Flowers not arranged spirally, flowering time spring to early summer..**9**

9a Sepals and petals connivent to forming a hood...**10**

9b Sepals and petals spreading................................**11**

10a Flower labellum wide, median lobe divided; plant very vigorous ....***Barlia***

10b Flower labellum narrow. Three-lobed, total of four segments (man shaped) ....***Aceras***

11a Plant small, mostly inconspicuous; foliage leaves mostly tinged violet, at times spotted; inflorescence very dense; flowers very small, white to pink, no marking, short spur....................................***Neotinea***

11b Plants and flowers different, mostly very conspicuous **12**

12a Foliage leaves often arranged in a rosette; inflorescence sheathed with foliage leaves up to flowering time; bracts hardly longer than ovary; labellum often 'man shaped' ....***Orchis***

12b Foliage leaves divided along stem; young inflorescence not sheathed by foliage leaves; bracts leafy, at lower part of inflorescence mostly considerably longer than ovary and often tinged violet ....***Dactylorhiza***

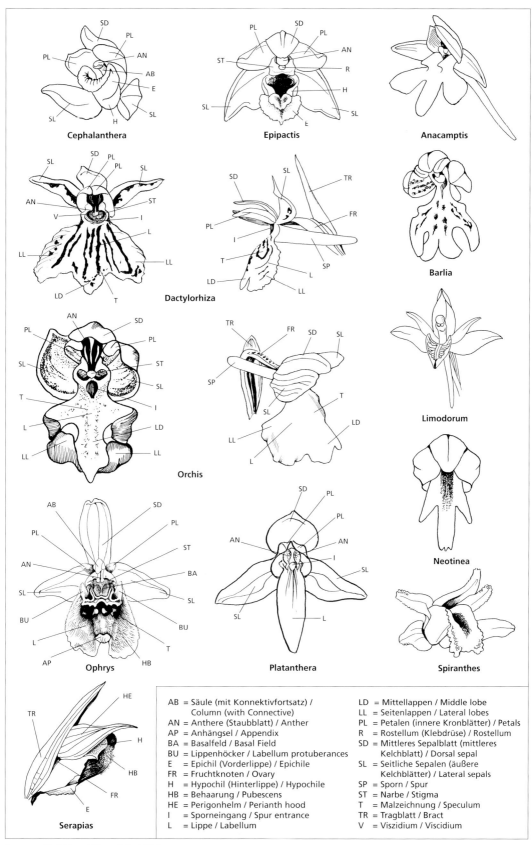

Cephalanthera

Epipactis

Anacamptis

Dactylorhiza

Barlia

Orchis

Limodorum

Neotinea

Ophrys

Platanthera

Spiranthes

Serapias

AB = Säule (mit Konnektivfortsatz) / Column (with Connective)	LD = Mittellappen / Middle lobe
AN = Anthere (Staubblatt) / Anther	LL = Seitenlappen / Lateral lobes
AP = Anhängsel / Appendix	PL = Petalen (innere Kronblätter) / Petals
BA = Basalfeld / Basal Field	R = Rostellum (Klebdrüse) / Rostellum
BU = Lippenhöcker / Labellum protuberances	SD = Mittleres Sepalblatt (mittleres Kelchblatt) / Dorsal sepal
E = Epichil (Vorderlippe) / Epichile	SL = Seitliche Sepalen (äußere Kelchblätter) / Lateral sepals
FR = Fruchtknoten / Ovary	SP = Sporn / Spur
H = Hypochil (Hinterlippe) / Hypochile	ST = Narbe / Stigma
HB = Behaarung / Pubescens	T = Malzeichnung / Speculum
HE = Perigonhelm / Perianth hood	TR = Tragblatt / Bract
I = Sporneingang / Spur entrance	V = Viszidium / Viscidium
L = Lippe / Labellum	

Bau von Orchideenblüten / Orchid flower structure

Prodromos-Platania (Standort von/site of *Epipactis troodi* und/and *Orobanche cypria*), 21.6.2002

Die Taxa

Die Autorennamen richten sich weitgehend nach BRUMMITT & POWELL (1992). In der Nomenklatur wurde weitgehend DELFORGE (1994, 2001) gefolgt, soweit die Taxa dort schon beschrieben sind. Spätere Neubeschreibungen wurden unter deren Namen übernommen. Bei Arten, die zu einem Formenkreis gehören und daher meist schwierig zuzuordnen sind, wurde von der alphabetischen Reihenfolge der wissenschaftlichen Namen abgewichen. Sie wurden innerhalb der Verwandtschaftsgruppen zusammengefasst. Innerhalb dieser Verwandtschaftsgruppen wurden die zugehörigen Arten dann wieder alphabetisch aufgelistet. Durch die Zusammenstellung solcher Arten in Gruppen ist es einfacher, die Ähnlichkeiten und Unterschiede der einzelnen Arten zu erkennen.

Nicht selten existieren für eine Art mehrere deutschsprachige Namen (siehe unter anderem BUTTLER, 1986). Im vorliegenden Buch wurde immer nur ein deutscher Name verwendet. Dieses Verfahren wurde auch von BAUMANN & KÜNKELE (1982a, 1988a) angewandt. Deutschsprachige Namen, die bisher noch nicht existierten, wurden neu gewählt. Die englischen Namen wurden, sofern bekannt, aus dem Buch von DAVIES, DAVIES & HUXLEY (1983) und aus BUTTLER (1991) übernommen. Englische Namen, die dort nicht aufgelistet waren, wurden neu ausgewählt.

The taxa

Authors' names have primarily been adopted from BRUMMITT & POWELL (1992). For nomenclature, DELFORGE (1994, 2001) was largely followed, as far as the taxa were already described there. Subsequent new descriptions were adopted under the names given. In the case of species which belong to species groups and which may therefore be difficult to identify, their scientific names have not been arranged in alphabetical order, but arranged according to relational groups. Within these relational groups the respective species have been arranged in alphabetical order. Arranging the species into groups, makes it is easier to recognize similarities and differences of closely related species.

There are often several German names for one species (see for example BUTTLER, 1986). In this book only one German name is used. This method was also used by BAUMANN & KÜNKELE (1982a, 1988a). German names which did not exist until now, have been chosen for the first time. English names were taken from books by DAVIES, DAVIES & HUXLEY (1983) and BUTTLER (1991). English names which are not used there have been chosen for the first time.

Alevkaya (Standort von/site of *Neotinea maculata* und/and *Orchis anatolica*), 18.3.2002

Verzeichnis der wissenschaftlichen Orchideennamen (in alphabetischer Reihenfolge) / Index of scientific orchid names (in alphabetical order)

Die Orchideenarten werden in diesem Buch in alphabetischer Reihenfolge behandelt, mit Ausnahme von nahe verwandten Arten (vor allem bei der Gattung *Ophrys* und *Orchis*). Diese werden als Formenkreis behandelt. Mit Hilfe dieses Inhaltsverzeichnisses ist aber ein alphabetischer Zugriff zum Nachschlagen leicht möglich.

The orchid species are dealt with in alphabetical order in this book, with the exception of closely related species (especially in the genera of *Ophrys* and *Orchis*). These are treated as a species group. This index however greatly facilitates easy alphabetical reference to the species.

Verzeichnis der wissenschaftlichen Orchideennamen (in taxonomischer Reihenfolge) / Index of scientific orchid names (in taxonomical order)

Die Orchideenarten werden in diesem Buch in alphabetischer Reihenfolge behandelt, mit Ausnahme von nahe verwandten Arten (vor allem bei der Gattung *Ophrys* und *Orchis*). Diese werden als Formenkreis behandelt. Mit Hilfe dieses Inhaltsverzeichnisses ist aber ein alphabetischer Zugriff zum Nachschlagen leicht möglich.

The orchid species are dealt with in alphabetical order in this book, with the exception of closely related species (especially in the genera of *Ophrys* and *Orchis*). These are treated as a species group. This index however greatly facilitates easy alphabetical reference to the species.

1 Anacamptis pyramidalis (L.) L.C.M. Richard

Pyramidenorchis

De Orchid. Eur.: 33 (1817)

Basionym

Orchis pyramidalis L., Sp. Pl. 2: 940 (1753).

Synonym

Aceras pyramidalis (L.) Reichenbach fil., Icon. Fl. Germ. Helv. 13/14: 6, no. 6, tab 9, fig. I (1851).

Beschreibung

Zierliche, hochwüchsige und schlanke Pflanze, 20 bis 40 cm hoch. Stängel aufrecht, ziemlich dünn, gelblichgrün. Untere Laubblätter schmal-lanzettlich bis lanzettlich, hellgrün bis gelblichgrün, rosettig gehäuft, schräg abstehend, die oberen schmal-lanzettlich, den Stängel scheidig umfassend. Blütenstand anfangs pyramidenförmig, später, in voll aufgeblühtem Zustand, kegel- bis eiförmig. Tragblätter linealisch-lanzettlich, meist purpurn überlaufen, länger als der Fruchtknoten. Blüten ziemlich klein bis mittelgroß, (hell)-rosa, rot bis dunkelrot, sehr selten weisslich. Sepalen lanzettlich, waagerecht abstehend, das mittlere leicht nach vorne gebogen. Petalen eiförmig-lanzettlich, mit dem mittleren Sepal helmförmig zusammenneigend. Lippe tief dreilappig mit zwei Längsleisten an der Basis, die beiden Seitenlappen etwa so lang wie oder etwas kürzer als der Mittellappen. Sporn abwärts gerichtet, lang und sehr dünn.

Standort

Gebüsch, Ödland, Straßenböschungen, Macchien, Phrygana, aufgelassene Kulturterrassen und Olivenhaine, selten an offenen Stellen in lockeren Kiefernwäldern; auf trockenen, selten feuchten, kalkhaltigen Böden.

Blütezeit

Von (Mitte) Ende März im Süden bis Ende April (Anfang Mai) im Norden. Stellenweise blüht die Art im Süden bei Larnaka und auf der Halbinsel Akrotiri schon ab Mitte März.

Höhenverbreitung

Von der Küste bis 900 m.

Gesamtverbreitung

Anacamptis pyramidalis besiedelt fast ganz Europa; nördlich geht sie bis Öland und Gotland, östlich bis in den Kaukasus, Iran und Irak.

Verbreitung auf Zypern

Anacamptis pyramidalis ist im Gegensatz zu anderen Inseln im Mittelmeergebiet auf Zypern eher selten. Verbreitet ist sie vor allem im Süden und im Pentadactylos-Gebirge. Mehrere Fundorte hat die Art auf der Halbinsel Akrotiri im Süden und beim St. Barnabas Kloster im Norden.

Bemerkungen

Anacamptis pyramidalis wächst von Meereshöhe in den weitläufigen und sandigen Küstenstreifen in der direkten Umgebung der beiden Salzseen bei Akrotiri und Larnaka bis in den trockenen und lockeren Kiefernwäldern der mittleren montanen Lagen im Troodos- und Pentadactylos-Gebirge.

Form und Blütenfarbe der Art sind auf Zypern vielgestaltig. Mann findet Pflanzen mit rein weissen, hell- oder dunkelrosa Blüten. Darüber hinaus gibt es kleine und gedrungene Pflanzen, wobei die Blüten einen ziemlich breiten Mittellappen haben und schlanke und relativ hochwüchsige Exemplare mit schmalem Mittellappen.

Von der Nominatrasse werden die im Mittelmeerraum (so auch auf Zypern) vorkommenden Pflanzen oft als *Anacamptis pyramidalis* var. *brachystachys* (D'Urville) Boissier oder als *Anacamptis pyramidalis* var. *urvilleana* (Sommier et Gatto) Schlechter abgetrennt. Beide Varietäten *Anacamptis pyramidalis* var. *brachystachys* und *Anacamptis pyramidalis* var. *urvilleana* unterscheiden sich von der Nominatform hauptsächlich durch einen gedrungeneren Habitus, blassere und kleinere Blüten und einen lockereren Blütenstand. *Anacamptis pyramidalis* var. *urvilleana* wurde von Malta beschrieben, und sie ist wahrscheinlich identisch mit der Varietät *brachystachys*. Bemerkenswerterweise kommt auf Malta auch die Nominatform vor, die dort aber etwa 3 Wochen später als die Varietät *urvilleana* blüht. Aus den anderen südlichen Mittelmeerländern oder Gebieten, so auch auf Zypern, ist das Vorkommen von zwei *Anacamptis pyramidalis* Sippen, die ausserdem in Habitus, Blütenform und Blütezeit so verschieden sind, bisher nicht bekannt.

Gefährdung

Eine aktuelle Gefährdung besteht nicht. Vor allem im Süden Zyperns bildet die Art mehrere Populationen, wobei die Pflanzen meist zerstreut im Gelände und vereinzelt an den Straßenrändern wachsen.

Hybriden

Mit *Orchis fragrans*.

Akrotiri (Moni Agios Nikolaos), 22.3.2002   Neo Chorio (Akamas), 21.3.2002

Anacamptis pyramidalis
Pyramidal Orchid

(L.) L.C.M. Richard

De Orchid. Eur.: 33 (1817)

Basionym

Orchis pyramidalis L., Sp. Pl. 2: 940 (1753).

Synonym

Aceras pyramidalis (L.) Reichenbach fil., Icon. Fl. Germ. Helv. 13/14: 6, no. 6, tab 9, fig. I (1851).

Description

Elegant, tall and slender plant, 20 to 40 cm tall. Stem erect, fairly thin, yellowish green. Lower foliage leaves narrowly lanceolate to lanceolate, light green to yellowish green, arranged in a rosette, spreading obliquely, upper leaves narrowly lanceolate, sheathing stem. Inflorescence first pyramidal, later, in full bloom, conical to ovoidal. Bracts linear-lanceolate, usually tinged purple, longer than ovary. Flowers fairly small to medium-sized, (light) pink, red to deep red, very rarely whitish. Sepals lanceolate, spreading horizontally, dorsal sepal slightly bent forwards. Petals ovate-lanceolate, connivent to forming a hood with dorsal sepal. Labellum deeply three-lobed with two longitudinal ridges at base, both lateral lobes as long as, or slightly shorter than, middle lobe. Spur long and very thin, directed downwards.

Habitat

Scrub, wasteland, roadside embankments, maquis, phrygana, abandoned terraces and olive groves, rarely in open places in light coniferous woods; on arid, rarely moist, calcareous soils.

Flowering time

From (mid-) late March in the south to late April (early May) in the north. In places the species starts flowering from mid-March in the south, near Larnaka and on the Akrotiri peninsula.

Altitude distribution

From sea-level up to 900 m.

Overall distribution

Anacamptis pyramidalis populates almost the whole of Europe; northwards as far as Öland and Gotland, eastwards as far as the Caucasian region, Iran and Iraq.

Distribution on Cyprus

Anacamptis pyramidalis is rarer on Cyprus than on the other islands in the Mediterranean region. It is mainly distributed in the south and in the Pentadactylos mountains. The species has several habitats on the Akrotiri peninsula in the south and near the St. Barnabas monastery in the north.

Remarks

Anacamptis pyramidalis grows from sea level, in the vast and sandy coastal strips in the direct vicinity of the two salt lakes near Akrotiri and Larnaka, up to the arid and open coniferous forests of medium-high altitudes in the Troodos mountains and Pentadactylos Range.

Shape and flower colour of the species are variable on Cyprus. One can find plants with pure white, light or deep pink flowers. There are also small and compact plants, where the flowers have fairly wide middle lobes, and slender, relatively tall specimens with narrower middle lobes.

The plants in the Mediterranean region (thus also on Cyprus) are often separated from the nominate species as *Anacamptis pyramidalis* var. *brachystachys* (D'Urville) Boissier or as *Anacamptis pyramidalis* var. *urvilleana* (Sommier et Gatto) Schlechter. Both varieties, *Anacamptis pyramidalis* var. *brachystachys* and *Anacamptis pyramidalis* var. *urvilleana*, differ from the nominate form by a more compact appearance, paler and smaller flowers and a lax inflorescence. *Anacamptis pyramidalis* var. *urvilleana* was described from Malta, and is probably identical to the variety *brachystachys*. Remarkably, the nominate form also occurs on Malta, but flowers 3 weeks later than the variety *urvilleana*.

The occurrence of two *Anacamptis pyramidalis* taxa, which are so dissimilar in appearance, flower shape and flowering time, is so far unknown elsewhere in the southern Mediterranean.

Threats

Actual threats are non-existent. The species has a number of populations, mainly in southern Cyprus, with plants growing scattered through fields and sporadically by the road-side.

Hybrids

With *Orchis fragrans*.

Neo Chorio (Akamas), 21.3.2002

Neo Chorio (Akamas), 21.3.2002

Akrotiri (Moni Agios Nikolaos), 22.3.2002

Akrotiri (Moni Agios Nikolaos), 22.3.2002

Akrotiri (Moni Agios Nikolaos), 22.3.2002

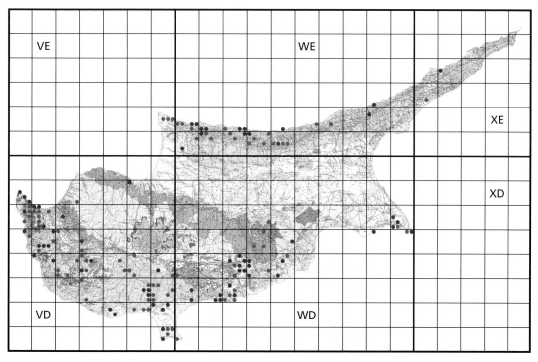

237 Meldungen / Reports

Anacamptis pyramidalis

2 Barlia robertiana

Roberts Mastorchis

(LOISELEUR) GREUTER

Boissiera 13: 192 (1967)

Basionym

Orchis robertiana LOISELEUR, Fl. Gall. ed. 1: 606 (1806).

Synonyme

Orchis longibracteata BIVONA-BERNARDI, Sicul. Pl. Cent. 1: 57 (1809), nom. illeg.; *Aceras longibracteatum* (BIVONA-BERNARDI) REICHENBACH fil., Icon. Fl. Germ. Helv. 13/14: 3 (1851), nom. illeg.; *Barlia longibracteata* (BIVONA-BERNARDI) PARLATORE, Nouv. Gen. Sp. Monocot. 6 (1858), nom. illeg.; *Loroglossum longibracteatum* MORIS ex ARDOINO, Flora Alpes-Marit.: 351 (1867); *Himantoglossum longibracteatum* (BIVONA-BERNARDI) SCHLECHTER, Repert. Spec. Nov. Regni Veg. 15: 288 (1918), nom. illeg.; *Himantoglossum robertianum* (LOISELEUR) P. DELFORGE, Natural. Belges 80 (Special Orchidées 12): 401 (1999).

Beschreibung

Sehr kräftige und hochwüchsige Pflanze, 20 bis 50 cm hoch. Laubblätter am Grunde rosettig gehäuft, breitlanzettlich bis eiförmig, glänzend, ungefleckt, die oberen meist den Stängel umfassend. Blütenstand zylindrisch, dicht- und reichblütig. Tragblätter etwas länger als der Fruchtknoten. Blüten groß, von schmutzig weisser Grundfarbe, oft mit braunroter, grüner und brauner Tönung. Perigonblätter einen lockeren Helm bildend, innen rötlich punktiert. Sepalen eiförmig bis oval; Petalen eiförmig-lanzettlich, deutlich kürzer als die Sepalen. Lippe stark dreilappig, Mittellappen fast doppelt so lang wie die beiden Seitenlappen, im unteren Teil nochmals zweigeteilt; Seitenlappen am Rande wellig. Sporn kegelförmig, kurz und abwärts gerichtet. Die Art variiert in der Blütenfarbe von grünlichweiss bis dunkelpurpurn. Die Laubblätter zeigen wegen der sehr frühen Blütezeit oft Frostschäden.

Standort

Lockere Kiefernwälder, grasiges Ödland, Straßenböschungen, Affodillfluren, Macchien, Phrygana, Olivenhaine, beweidetes Ödland, ehemalige Weinbergterrassen und Magerrasen; auf trockenen bis mäßig feuchten, basenreichen Böden.

Blütezeit

Eine sehr früh blühende Art. Von (Mitte) Ende Februar bis Mitte (Ende) März, stellenweise schon ab Mitte Januar. In den höheren Lagen manchmal noch bis Anfang April.

Höhenverbreitung

Von der Küste bis 1.200 m.

Gesamtverbreitung

Im ganzen Mittelmeergebiet verbreitet, von Portugal bis Kleinasien, auch in Nordafrika.

Verbreitung auf Zypern

Die Art besiedelt hauptsächlich den süd- und südwestlichen Teil der Insel. Im Norden ist sie seltener und wurde dort in den letzten Jahren nur wenig beobachtet.

Bemerkungen

Individuenreiche Populationen gibt es nördlich von Pafos in der Umgebung von Tsada, dort meist vergesellschaftet mit *Ophrys cinereophila*. Sie wächst dort an offenen Stellen zwischen dichter Phrygana auf dem spärlich bewachsen, kalkreichen Boden. Es ist eine bemerkenswerte Erscheinung, dass hier so viele kräftige Pflanzen von *Barlia robertiana* vergesellschaftet sind mit vielen zierlichen Exemplaren von *Ophrys cinereophila*.

An den Südhängen des Troodos-Gebirges ist *Barlia robertiana* selten und kommt dort meist nur in Einzelexemplaren vor, die dann aber oft von *Orchis italica* begleitet werden. Überraschend ist das Vorkommen dieser Art bis in mittlere Höhenlagen, wo sie noch bis 1.200 m an verschiedenen Fundorten wächst.

Im Pentadactylos-Gebirge ist die Art besonders selten. Sie wächst hier meist in kleineren Gruppen, bevorzugt an Straßenböschungen, in lockeren Pinienwäldern und auf trockenen, grasigen Stellen in Waldhängen, wie zum Beispiel im Pentadactylos-Gebirge östlich von Gönyeli und in lockeren Pinienwäldern und unter Östlichen Erdbeerbäumen *(Arbutus andrachne)* zwischen Alevkaya und Besparmak (VINEY, 1994).

Barlia robertiana treibt auf Zypern schon im November ihre Rosetten aus. Die Art ist unverwechselbar, und sie stellt mit ihren großen Laubblätter, dem langgestreckten Blütenstand und ihren großen Blüten eine stattliche Erscheinung dar.

Die Art variiert auf Zypern ziemlich stark in der Blütenfarbe, nämlich von dunkelrosa bis grünlichweiss.

Gefährdung

Barlia robertiana ist auf Zypern im Süden weit verbreitet und allgemein, im Norden aber sehr selten. Die Art ist nicht besonders gefährdet.

Hybriden

Nicht bekannt.

Mathikoloni-Apsiou, 5.3.2002

Barlia robertiana
Giant Orchid

(Loiseleur) Greuter

Boissiera 13: 192 (1967)

Basionym

Orchis robertiana Loiseleur, Fl. Gall. ed. 1: 606 (1806).

Synonyms

Orchis longibracteata Bivona-Bernardi, Sicul. Pl. Cent. 1: 57 (1809), nom. illeg.; *Aceras longibracteatum* (Bivona-Bernardi) Reichenbach fil., Icon. Fl. Germ. Helv. 13/14: 3 (1851), nom. illeg.; *Barlia longibracteata* (Bivona-Bernardi) Parlatore, Nouv. Gen. Sp. Monocot. 6 (1858), nom. illeg.; *Loroglossum longibracteatum* Moris ex Ardoino, Flora Alpes-Marit.: 351 (1867); *Himantoglossum longibracteatum* (Bivona-Bernardi) Schlechter, Repert. Spec. Nov. Regni Veg. 15: 288 (1918), nom. illeg.; *Himantoglossum robertianum* (Loiseleur) P. Delforge, Natural. Belges 80 (Special Orchidées 12): 401 (1999).

Description

Very vigorous tall plant, 20-50 cm tall. Foliage leaves in a basal rosette, broadly lanceolate to ovate, shiny, unspotted; upper leaves sheathing stem. Inflorescence cylindrical, dense and many-flowered. Bracts slightly longer than ovary. Flowers large, background colour off-white, often with brownish red, green and brown tints. Perianth segments form a loose hood, the interior with reddish dots. Sepals ovate to oval; petals ovate-lanceolate, clearly shorter than sepals. Labellum deeply three-lobed, middle lobe almost twice as long as lateral lobes, divided in lower half; lateral lobes wavy at margins. Spur conical, short and directed downwards. Flower colouration ranges from greenish white to dark purple. Foliage leaves often display frost damage due to very early flowering time.

Habitat

Light coniferous woods, grassy wasteland, roadside embankments, asphodel fields, maquis, phrygana, olive groves, cultivation edges, former vineyard terraces and neglected grasslands; on arid to moderately moist, base-rich soils.

Flowering time

A very early flowering species. From (mid-) late February to mid- (late) March, in places as early as mid-January. At higher altitudes often until early April.

Altitude distribution

From sea-level up to 1,200 m.

Overall distribution

Distributed throughout the entire Mediterranean region, from Portugal to Asia Minor; also in North Africa.

Distribution on Cyprus

The species primarily populates the southern and southwestern parts of the island. Very rare in the north, in recent years only seen a few times.

Remarks

Individual-rich populations occur north of Pafos in the vicinity of Tsada, there often accompanied by *Ophrys cinereophila*. It grows in open places between the phrygana, on sparsely covered calcareous soils, and the sight of so many vigorous plants of *Barlia robertiana* accompanied by numerous elegant specimens of *Ophrys cinereophila* is quite remarkable.

On the southern slopes of the Troodos mountains, *Barlia robertiana* is rare and occurs there mostly as solitary specimens, often accompanied by *Orchis italica*. The occurrence of this species is surprising at medium-range altitudes, where it grows at various locations up to 1,200 m.

The species is extremely rare in the Pentadactylos Range. It grows there in small groups, preferring roadside embankments, open pine forests and arid grassy spots in forested slopes, e.g. in the Pentadactylos Range eastwards of Gönyeli, in the open pine forests and under strawberry trees *(Arbutus andrachne)* between Alevkaya and Besparmak (Viney, 1994).

Barlia robertiana's rosettes appear as early as November on Cyprus. The species is unmistakable, and its green foliage leaves, elongated inflorescence and large flowers give it a stately appearance.

The species varies widely in flower colour on Cyprus, from deep pink to greenish white.

Threats

Barlia robertiana is in the south of Cyprus widespread and not rare, in the north extremely rare. The species is not particularly threatened.

Hybrids

Unknown.

Neo Chorio-Agios Minas (Akamas), 3.3.2002

Pano Kivides, 20.3.2002

Alevkaya (Pentadactylos Range), 18.3.2002

Drouseia (Akamas), 3.3.2002

Neo Chorio (Akamas), 10.3.2002

Mathikoloni, 5.3.2002

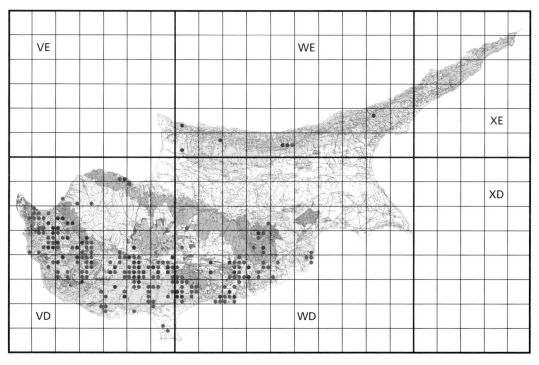

VE

WE

XE

XD

VD

WD

Barlia robertiana

3 Cephalanthera rubra

(L.) L.C.M. Richard

Rotes Waldvögelein

De Orchid. Eur.: 38 (1817)

Basionym

Serapias rubra L., Syst. Nat. ed. 12, 2: 594 (1767).

Synonyme

Epipactis rubra (L.) Allioni, Fl. Pedem. 2: 153 (1785); *Epipactis purpurea* (L.) Crantz, Stirp. Austr. Fasc. ed. 2, 2: 457 (1769).

Beschreibung

Schlanke und zierliche Pflanze, 30 bis 50 cm hoch. Stängel schwach hin und her gebogen, im oberen Teil dicht drüsig behaart und manchmal purpurn überlaufen, am Grunde mit mehreren Schuppenblättern. Laubblätter meist zweizeilig angeordnet, lanzettlich bis lineal-lanzettlich, rinnig gefaltet, bläulich- bis dunkelgrün, waagerecht abstehend bis aufwärts gerichtet. Blütenstand sehr locker und langgestreckt mit 3-15 Blüten. Tragblätter dunkelgrün und stark behaart, die unteren viel länger als der Fruchtknoten, die oberen kürzer. Blüten mittelgroß bis groß, weit geöffnet, hellrosa bis kräftig rotlila. Sepalen eiförmig-lanzettlich bis länglich-lanzettlich, zugespitzt, die beiden seitlichen abstehend, das mittlere vornübergeneigt. Petalen in Form und Farbe wie die Sepalen aber etwas kürzer als diese. Lippe zweigliedrig. Hypochil mit aufgerichteten Seitenlappen. Epichil eiförmig-lanzettlich, zugespitzt, weisslich mit mehreren gelbbraunen Längsleisten. Sporn fehlt.

Standort

In Nadel- und Kiefernwäldern, auf Lichtungen und an Gebüschrändern; auf kalkreichem Boden.

Blütezeit

Mitte Juni bis Mitte Juli.

Höhenverbreitung

Von 1.400 bis 1.600 m.

Gesamtverbreitung

Europa mit Ausnahme des westlichen Teils der Iberischen Halbinsel, Mittel- und Nordenglands, Irlands und des nördlichen Teils von Skandinavien. Östlich bis Zentralsibirien, die Kaukasusländer, Zypern und den Iran. Auch in Nordafrika.

Verbreitung auf Zypern

Die Art ist auf ein kleines Areal im Troodos-Gebirge beschränkt. Nach Georgiades (1998ab) ist *Cephalanthera rubra* stellenweise in der Umgebung des Naturlehrpfades bei Kryos Potamos verbreitet, weiterhin bei Khionistra, auf der Troodos-Hochebene, in der Umgebung des Forestry College und am Prodromos Stausee. Nach Wood (1985) ist die Art in den höheren Lagen bei Khionistra nicht selten.

Bemerkungen

Die attraktive und schattenliebende Art bildet in den lichten Kiefernwäldern (gerne in Waldlichtungen unter *Pinus nigra*) im Troodos-Gebirge mehrere kleinere Populationen, durchschnittlich bis zu zehn Pflanzen. Ein schöner Bestand wächst in der Umgebung der Kaledonia Wasserfälle. In den Lichtungen des Kiefernwaldes finden sich dort mehrere Gruppen zierlicher Pflanzen.

An vielen Fundorten kommt *Cephalanthera rubra* zusammen mit *Epipactis troodi* und *Limodorum abortivum* vor. Diese beiden Arten blühen etwa gleichzeitig mit *Cephalanthera rubra*, wobei die späte Blütezeit von *Limodorum abortivum* bemerkenswert ist, weil diese Art im Mittelmeerraum normalerweise viel früher blüht.

Im Gegensatz zu den westeuropäischen Pflanzen sind die Blüten von *Cephalanthera rubra* auf Zypern hellrosa, manchmal sogar ganz weiss.

Gefährdung

Obwohl die Art nur wenige Standorte im Troodos-Gebirge hat und obwohl die Anzahl der Pflanzen dort sehr klein ist, besteht keine aktuelle Gefährdung, weil die Art in den weitläufigen Kiefernwäldern im Troodos-Gebirge genügend geschützt ist. Sicherlich besitzt *Cephalanthera rubra* noch weitere Vorkommen in den ausgedehnten, bisher zur Blütezeit dieser Art nur wenig untersuchten Kiefernwäldern im Troodos-Gebirge.

Hybriden

Nicht bekannt.

Pano Platres (Caledonia Trail), 22.6.2002   Troodos (Troodos), 21.6.2002

Cephalanthera rubra

(L.) L.C.M. Richard

Red Helleborine

De Orchid. Eur.: 38 (1817)

Basionym

Serapias rubra L., Syst. Nat. ed. 12, 2: 594 (1767).

Synonyms

Epipactis rubra (L.) Allioni, Fl. Pedem. 2: 153 (1785); *Epipactis purpurea* (L.) Crantz, Stirp. Austr. Fasc. ed. 2, 2: 457 (1769).

Description

Slender and elegant plant, 30 to 50 cm tall. Stem slightly flexuose, upper part covered in velvety hairs and sometimes tinged purple, several scale leaves at base. Foliage leaves mostly alternate, lanceolate to linear-lanceolate, grooved, dark to bluish green, spreading horizontally to directed upwards. Inflorescence very lax and elongated with 3-15 flowers. Bracts dark green and covered in dense hairs, lower ones much longer than ovary, upper ones shorter. Flowers medium-sized to large, wide-open, bright pink to vibrant lilac-red. Sepals ovate-lanceolate to oblong-lanceolate, acuminate, both laterals spreading, middle lobe directed forwards. Petals same as sepals in shape and colour but slightly shorter. Labellum bipartite. Hypochile with erect lateral lobes. Epichile ovate-lanceolate, acuminate, whitish with several yellow-brown longitudinal ridges. No spur.

Habitat

Coniferous forests, in open places and woodland margins, on calcareous soil.

Flowering time

Mid-June to mid-July.

Altitude distribution

From 1,400 to 1,600 m.

Overall distribution

Europe, except western parts of the Iberian peninsula, central and northern England, Ireland and the northern part of Scandinavia. Eastwards as far as central Siberia, Caucasian countries, Cyprus and Iran. Also in North Africa.

Distribution on Cyprus

The species is limited to a small area in the Troodos mountains. According to Georgiades (1998ab), *Cephalanthera rubra* is sporadically distributed along the nature trail near Kryos Potamos, also near Khionistra, on the Troodos plateau, around the Forestry College and at the Prodromos reservoir. According to Wood (1985), the species is not rare at higher altitudes near Khionistra.

Remarks

This attractive and shade-loving species forms a number of smaller populations, on average up to ten plants, in the open coniferous woods of the Troodos mountains, preferring clearings under *Pinus nigra*. A beautiful population grows in the vicinity of the Caledonian Falls. In clearings in the coniferous woodland there, several groups of elegant plants grow.

At many locations, *Cephalanthera rubra* occurs together with *Epipactis troodi* and *Limodorum abortivum*. Both species bloom almost at the same time as *Cephalanthera rubra*, but the late flowering time of *Limodorum abortivum* is remarkable as it normally flowers much earlier in the Mediterranean region.

In contrast to western European plants, the flowers of *Cephalanthera rubra* on Cyprus are bright pink, at times even totally white.

Threats

Although the species has few habitats in the Troodos mountains and the number of plants is very small, there is no actual threat, as the species is sufficiently protected in the vast coniferous forests of the Troodos mountains. *Cephalanthera rubra* could most certainly be found at other sites in the extensive and, during its flowering time, little researched coniferous forests of the Troodos mountains.

Hybrids

Unknown.

Troodos (Troodos), 21.6.2002

Troodos (Troodos), 21.6.2002

Pano Platres (Caledonia Trail), 22.6.2002

Troodos (Troodos), 24.6.2002

Pano Platres (Caledonia Trail), 22.6.2002

Pano Platres (Caledonia Trail), 22.6.2002

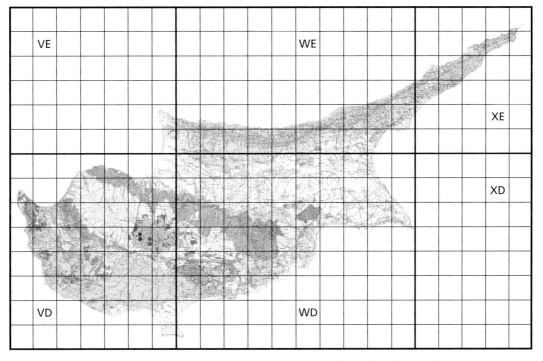

Cephalanthera rubra

4 Dactylorhiza iberica
Krim-Knabenkraut

(F.A.M. VON BIEBERSTEIN
ex WILLDENOW) SOÓ

Nom. Nova Gen. Dactylorhizae: 3 (1962)

Basionym

Orchis iberica F.A.M. VON BIEBERSTEIN ex WILLDENOW, Sp. Pl. ed. 4, 4 (1): 25 (1805).

Synonyme

Dactylorchis iberica (F.A.M. VON BIEBERSTEIN ex WILLDENOW) VERMEULEN, Stud. Dactylorchis: 65 (1947); *Orchis angustifolia* F.A.M. VON BIEBERSTEIN, Fl. Taur.-Caucas. 2: 368 (1808); *Orchis leptophylla* K. KOCH, Linnaea 22 (3): 282 (1849); *Orchis natolica* FISCHER & MEYER, Ann. Sci. Nat. Bot., ser. 4, 1: 30 (1854).

Beschreibung

Zierliche, schlanke Pflanze, 30 bis 50 cm hoch. Stängel markig, aufrecht, hell- bis gelblichgrün. Laubblätter lineal-lanzettlich, überwiegend gleichmäßig am Stängel verteilt, schräg aufgerichtet, ungefleckt, zugespitzt, die oberen in tragblattartige Laubblätter übergehend. Blütenstand zylindrisch, locker- und vielblütig. Tragblätter hellgrün bis gelblichgrün, schmallanzettlich, etwa so lang wie der Fruchtknoten. Blüten klein bis mittelgroß, hellrosa bis dunkelrosa gefärbt. Perigonblätter einen lockeren, nur selten geschlossenen Helm bildend. Sepalen eiförmig-lanzettlich bis breit-lanzettlich, stumpf. Petalen eiförmig-lanzettlich. Lippe breit-eiförmig bis rundlich, flach ausgebreitet, im unteren Teil dreilappig mit zahnförmigem Mittellappen, rosa bis weisslich, an den Rändern purpurn gefärbt. Lippenzeichnung aus rosafarbenen bis purpurnen Punkten oder Strichen bestehend. Sporn dünn, zylindrisch, abwärts gerichtet, halb bis dreiviertel so lang wie der Fruchtknoten.

Standort

Kalkquellsümpfe, entlang von Fluss- und Bachufern, Nasswiesen, feuchte Straßenböschungen; auf kalkreichen Böden.

Blütezeit

Von Mitte Juni bis Mitte Juli.

Höhenverbreitung

Von 1.200 bis 1.600 m.

Gesamtverbreitung

Von Südosteuropa (Griechenland, Bulgarien) über Vorderasien (Türkei, Zypern, Nordirak, Libanon, Syrien, Israel), die Krim und die Kaukasusländer bis nach Nord- und Westiran.

Verbreitung auf Zypern

Die seltene Art wächst nur in den höheren Lagen des Troodos-Gebirges und in der Umgebung der Zedernschlucht. WOOD (1985) berichtet ausserdem von Fundorten im Pafos Forest.

Bemerkungen

Dactylorhiza iberica gehört im Mittelmeerraum zu den spätblühenden *Dactylorhiza*-Arten. Auch auf Zypern blüht sie spät und in Jahren mit normaler Witterung erst ab Mitte Juni. Wegen ihrer vegetativen Vermehrung ist die Art besonders einheitlich in der Form und Farbe. Die zierliche Art bildet auf Zypern in Kalkquellsümpfen und an Flussufern immer nur kleinere Populationen von bis zu zehn blühenden Pflanzen.

Nach WOOD (1985) ist *Dactylorhiza iberica* auf Zypern nicht selten und im zentralen Teil des Troodos-Gebirges weit verbreitet. So allgemein wie WOOD (l.s.) sie angibt ist die Art auf Zypern aber sicherlich nicht mehr. Sie ist eher als selten bis sehr selten einzustufen. An den wenigen bekannten Fundorten entlang von Flussufern oder in Kalkquellsümpfen bestehen die Populationen meist nur aus einzelnen Exemplaren oder kleineren Gruppen von bis zu zehn Pflanzen. Nur in den höheren Lagen des Troodos-Gebirges, in der Nähe der alten Asbestminen südlich von Kato Amiantos, hat die Art grössere Vorkommen. Sie wächst hier entlang eines Wanderweges im 'Old Juniperus Valley' an einem Bachrand zusammen mit dicht stehenden Büscheln *von Epipactis veratrifolia*, die zur Blütezeit von *Dactylorhiza iberica* aber noch weitgehend knospig sind.

ROBATSCH (1980) fand *Dactylorhiza iberica* im Troodos-Gebirge in einer größeren Population von etwa 50 Exemplaren in einer mit Minze bestandenen ufernahen Wiese entlang eines Waldbaches. ROBATSCH (l.s.) merkte ausserdem an, dass alle Pflanzen dieser Population unauffällig waren, bzw. nicht vom Typus abwichen, bis auf eine, die eine intensive Rotfärbung aufwies.

Gefährdung

Eine aktuelle Gefährdung besteht nicht, aber es sind nur wenige Biotope vorhanden, wo die Art wächst, und einige Standorte sind durch eine starke Wald- und Buschentwicklung bei gleichzeitigem Wasserentzug gefährdet.

Hybriden

Nicht bekannt.

Pano Platres (Caledonia Trail), 21.6.2002

Dactylorhiza iberica
Crimean Orchid

(F.A.M. VON BIEBERSTEIN ex WILLDENOW) SOÓ

Nom. Nova Gen. Dactylorhizae: 3 (1962)

Basionym

Orchis iberica F.A.M. VON BIEBERSTEIN ex WILLDENOW, Sp. Pl. ed. 4, 4 (1): 25 (1805).

Synonyms

Dactylorchis iberica (F.A.M. VON BIEBERSTEIN ex WILLDENOW) VERMEULEN, Stud. Dactylorchis: 65 (1947); *Orchis angustifolia* F.A.M. VON BIEBERSTEIN, Fl. Taur.-Caucas. 2: 368 (1808); *Orchis leptophylla* K. KOCH, Linnaea 22 (3): 282 (1849); *Orchis natolica* FISCHER & MEYER, Ann. Sci. Nat. Bot., ser. 4, 1: 30 (1854).

Description

Elegant, slender plant, 30 to 50 cm tall. Stem thick, erect, light to yellowish green. Foliage leaves linear-lanceolate, usually evenly distributed along stem, obliquely erect, unspotted, acuminate, upper leaves merging into bract-like foliage leaves. Inflorescence cylindrical, lax and many-flowered. Bracts light green to yellowish green, narrowly lanceolate, about as long as ovary. Flowers small to medium-sized, light pink to deep pink. Perianth segments form a loose, rarely closed, hood. Sepals ovate-lanceolate to broadly lanceolate, obtuse. Petals ovate-lanceolate. Labellum broadly ovate to roundish, spread out flat, three-lobed in lower part with tooth-like middle lobe, pink to whitish, purple at edges. Labellum marking consisting of pink to purple dots or dashes. Spur thin, cylindrical, reflexed, half-to-three-quarters as long as ovary.

Habitat

Chalk bogs, along the edges of rivers and streams, wet pastures, damp roadside embankments; on calcareous soils.

Flowering time

From mid-June to mid-July.

Altitude distribution

From 1,200 m to 1,600 m.

Overall distribution

From southern Europe (Greece, Bulgaria) through the Near East (Turkey, Cyprus, northern Iraq, Lebanon, Syria, Israel), Crimea and the Caucasian countries to northern and western Iran.

Distribution on Cyprus

This rare species only grows at higher altitudes in the Troodos mountains and in the vicinity of the Cedar Valley. WOOD (1985) also reports locations in the Pafos forest.

Remarks

In the Mediterranean region, *Dactylorhiza iberica* belongs to the late flowering *Dactylorhiza* species. On Cyprus also, it flowers late, in years with normal weather conditions, from mid-June. Because it reproduces vegetatively, the species is exceptionally uniform in shape and colour. On Cyprus this elegant species creates only small populations of up to ten flowering plants in chalk bogs and along riverbanks. According to WOOD (1985), *Dactylorhiza iberica* is not rare on Cyprus and widespread in the central part of the Troodos mountains. However the species is certainly no longer as common on Cyprus as WOOD (l.s.) indicates. It can more accurately be categorized as rare to very rare. At the few known locations along riverbanks or in chalk bogs, the populations mostly consist of only a few specimens or small groups of up to ten plants. The species only has larger populations at higher altitudes in the Troodos mountains, near the old asbestos mines, south of Kato Amiantos.

It grows at the side of a stream along the nature trail in the 'Old Juniperus Valley', accompanied by dense stands of *Epipactis veratrifolia*, which are still at the bud stage during the flowering time of *Dactylorhiza iberica*.

ROBATSCH (1980) found *Dactylorhiza iberica* in the Troodos Range as a large population of about 50 specimens, in a meadow overgrown with mint along a forest stream. ROBATSCH (l.s.) also remarks that all plants of this population were uniform, not different from the normal type, except for one, which had an intense red colour.

Threats

There is no actual threat, but there are few biotopes present where the species can grow, and some locations are threatened by intensive forest and shrub development with concurrent drainage.

Hybrids

Unknown.

Kato Amiantos (Troodos), 23.6.2002

Kato Amiantos (Troodos), 23.6.2002

Pano Platres (Caledonia Trail), 21.6.2002

Kato Amiantos (Troodos), 23.6.2002

Kato Amiantos (Troodos), mit/with
Epipactis veratrifolia, 23.6.2002

Trooditissa (Troodos), 23.6.2002

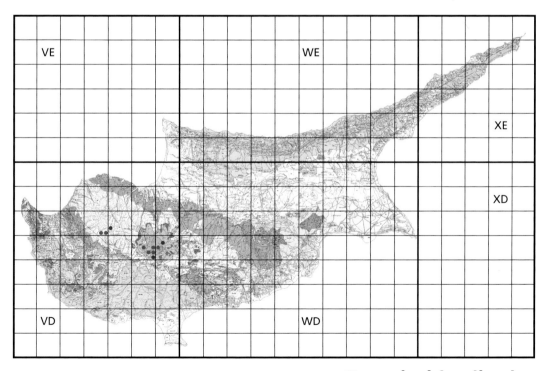

Dactylorhiza iberica

5 Dactylorhiza romana
(SEBASTIANI) SOÓ

Römisches Knabenkraut

Nom. Nova Gen. Dactylorhizae: 3 (1962)

Basionym

Orchis romana SEBASTIANI, Roman. Pl. Fasc. Prim.: 12 (1813).

Synonyme

Orchis pseudosambucina subsp. *romana* (SEBASTIANI) GANDOGER, Nov. Consp. Fl. Eur.: 462 (1910), nom. illeg.; *Dactylorchis romana* (SEBASTIANI) VERMEULEN, Stud. Dactylorchis: 65 (1947); *Orchis pseudosambucina* TENORE, Fl. Napol. 1: 72 (1811-1815). ('*pseudosambucina*'); *Orchis mediterranea* subsp. *pseudosambucina* (TENORE) KLINGE, Acta Horti Petrop. 17 (1): 151, 164 (1898), comb. illeg.; *Dactylorhiza sulphurea* subsp. *pseudosambucina* (TENORE) FRANCO, Bot. J. Linn. Soc. 76 (4): 366 (1978), nom. inval.; *Dactylorhiza sambucina* subsp. *pseudosambucina* (TENORE) SUNDERMANN, Eur. Medit. Orch. ed. 3: 40 (1980); *Orchis mediterranea* KLINGE, Acta Horti Petrop. 17 (1): 151 & 163 (1898), nom. illeg.; *Orchis romana* subsp. *libanotica* MOUTERDE, Nouv. Fl. Liban Syrie 1: 342 (1966); *Dactylorhiza libanotica* (MOUTERDE) AVERYANOV, Bot. Zhurn. 69 (6): 876 (1984).

Beschreibung

Schlanke Pflanze, bis 30 cm hoch. Stängel markig, hell- bis gelblichgrün. Laubblätter schmal-lanzettlich, die unteren am Grunde rosettig gehäuft, die oberen schräg aufwärts gerichtet. Blütenstand eiförmig bis kurz zylindrisch, arm- bis reichblütig, selten dichtblütig. Tragblätter grün bis violettgrün, schmal-lanzettlich, die unteren den Blütenstand etwas überragend, die oberen etwa so lang wie die Blüten. Blüten mittelgroß, (hell)gelb bis schwefelgelb, weisslich, rosa oder rötlich (nicht auf Zypern) bis violett gefärbt. Sepalen breit-eiförmig bis eiförmig-lanzettlich, die seitlichen zurückgeschlagen bis aufwärts gerichtet, das mittlere mit den Petalen helmförmig zusammenneigend. Petalen schmal- bis breit-eiförmig. Lippe breit, rundlich, flach ausgebreitet oder die beiden Seitenlappen zurückgeschlagen, im unteren Teil dreilappig, ohne Malzeichnung. Sporn zylindrisch, steil aufwärts gerichtet, länger als der Fruchtknoten.

Standort

Trockene bis mäßig feuchte Kiefernwälder, Macchien; auf schwach sauren bis basischen Böden.

Blütezeit

Ende Februar bis Ende März.

Höhenverbreitung

Von 150 bis 900 m.

Gesamtverbreitung

Mittleres und östliches Mittelmeergebiet, südlich bis Sizilien, Kreta, Zypern, Türkei und Israel. In Italien bildet sie stellenweise Massenpopulationen und in einigen Gebieten, wie auf Zypern, findet man nur die gelb blühende Form.

Verbreitung auf Zypern

Dactylorhiza romana ist auf Zypern nur im Süden ziemlich weit verbreitet. Sie kommt vor allem in den Südlagen des Troodos-Gebirges und auf der Akamas-Halbinsel vor; sie ist besonders selten im Pentadactylos-Gebirge. Die Art wächst gerne in *Pinus brutia* Wäldern und in *Cistus* Vegetationen mit *Thymus integer* (GEORGIADES, 1998ab).

Bemerkungen

Auf Zypern ist die Gattung *Dactylorhiza* nur mit zwei Arten vertreten, nämlich ausser *Dactylorhiza romana* noch *Dactylorhiza iberica*. Aber hier bildet Zypern keine Ausnahme. Sieht man einmal von *Dactylorhiza romana* ab, dann sind Vertreter der Gattung *Dactylorhiza* auf den meisten Inseln im Mittelmeerraum sehr selten.

Dactylorhiza romana, die in ihrem gesamten Verbreitungsgebiet fast immer in zwei Farbvarianten vorkommt (hell- bis schwefelgelb oder rosa, rötlich bis violett), ist auf Zypern nur in gelblicher Farbe vertreten. Das ist in so weit bemerkenswert, als sie in der benachbarten Südtürkei in beiden Farbvarianten vorkommt, wobei die rote Variante an manchen Fundorten reichlich vertreten ist und dort teilweise sogar häufiger als die gelbliche Farbvariante ist.

Dactylorhiza romana kommt hauptsächlich im südlichen Teil Zyperns vor. Die Art wächst hier bevorzugt auf den bewaldeten Südhängen des Troodos-Gebirges und meist in größeren Gruppen. An einigen Fundorten bildet sie oft mehrere Gruppen dicht stehender Pflanzen. Sie ist in diesem Gebiet meist mit *Neotinea maculata*, seltener mit *Orchis troodi* vergesellschaftet.

Lange Zeit waren Vorkommen von *Dactylorhiza romana* nur aus dem Süden Zyperns bekannt bis die Art in den siebziger Jahren von HANSEN & HANSEN (VINEY, 1994) erstmals in den Waldhängen zwischen Hilarion und Kar?iyaka gefunden wurde. Es ist bemerkenswert, dass diese Art im Norden Zyperns so selten ist, und trotz ihrer auffallend großen und gelben Blüten nicht früher im botanisch gut erforschten Norden gefunden wurde.

Auf Kreta und in Israel kommt *Dactylorhiza romana* auch ausserhalb von Wäldern vor; sie wächst dort auch in der offener Macchie und in der Phrygana.

Gefährdung

Die Art ist auf Zypern nicht gefährdet. In den weitläufigen Kiefernwäldern ist sie hinreichend geschützt und nur durch Waldbrände gefährdet.

Hybriden

Nicht bekannt.

Gerasa-Agios Paraskevi, 5.3.2002

Dactylorhiza romana

(Sebastiani) Soó

Roman Orchid

Nom. Nova Gen. Dactylorhizae: 3 (1962)

Basionym

Orchis romana Sebastiani, Roman. Pl. Fasc. Prim.: 12 (1813).

Synonyms

Orchis pseudosambucina subsp. *romana* (Sebastiani) Gandoger, Nov. Consp. Fl. Eur.: 462 (1910), nom. illeg.; *Dactylorchis romana* (Sebastiani) Vermeulen, Stud. Dactylorchis: 65 (1947); *Orchis pseudosambucina* Tenore, Fl. Napol. 1: 72 (1811-1815). ('*pseudo-sambucina*'); *Orchis mediterranea* subsp. *pseudosambucina* (Tenore) Klinge, Acta Horti Petrop. 17 (1): 151, 164 (1898), comb. illeg.; *Dactylorhiza sulphurea* subsp. *pseudosambucina* (Tenore) Franco, Bot. J. Linn. Soc. 76 (4): 366 (1978), nom. inval.; *Dactylorhiza sambucina* subsp. *pseudosambucina* (Tenore) Sundermann, Eur. Medit. Orch. ed. 3: 40 (1980); *Orchis mediterranea* Klinge, Acta Horti Petrop. 17 (1): 151 & 163 (1898), nom. illeg.; *Orchis romana* subsp. *libanotica* Mouterde, Nouv. Fl. Liban Syrie 1: 342 (1966); *Dactylorhiza libanotica* (Mouterde) Averyanov, Bot. Zhurn. 69 (6): 876 (1984).

Description

Slender plant, up to 30 cm tall. Stem sturdy, light to yellowish green. Foliage leaves narrowly lanceolate, lower leaves in a basal rosette, upper leaves obliquely erect. Inflorescence ovoid to short cylindrical, few to many-flowered, rarely densely flowered. Bracts green to violet green, narrowly lanceolate, lower bracts slightly exceed inflorescence, upper bracts about as long as the flowers. Flowers medium-sized, (light) yellow to sulphur yellow, whitish, pink or reddish to violet (absent in Cyprus). Sepals broadly ovate to ovate-lanceolate, lateral sepals reflexed to erect, dorsal sepal connivent to forming a hood with petals. Petals narrowly to broadly ovate. Labellum wide, rounded, spread out flat or both laterals reflexed, three-lobed in lower half, no markings. Spur cylindrical, erect, longer than ovary.

Habitat

Arid to moderately moist coniferous woods, maquis; on weakly acidic to basic soils.

Flowering time

Late February to late March.

Altitude distribution

From 150 to 900 m.

Overall distribution

Central and Eastern Mediterranean region, southwards as far as Sicily, Crete, Cyprus, Turkey and Israel. In some places in Italy, it forms large populations and in some areas, e.g. on Cyprus, one can only find the yellow flowering variety.

Distribution on Cyprus

Dactylorhiza romana is fairly widespread in the south on Cyprus. It mainly occurs on the southern slopes of the Troodos mountains and on the Akamas peninsula; it is extremely rare in the Pentadactylos mountains. The species prefers *Pinus brutia* woods and *Cistus* vegetations with *Thymus integer* (Georgiades, 1998ab).

Remarks

The genus *Dactylorhiza* is only represented by two species on Cyprus, namely *Dactylorhiza romana* and *Dactylorhiza iberica*. But Cyprus is no exception in this respect. Excluding *Dactylorhiza romana*, representatives of the genus *Dactylorhiza* are very rare on most of the Mediterranean islands.

Dactylorhiza romana, which in its main distribution area almost always occurs in two colourations (light yellow to sulphur yellow, or pink, reddish to violet) only occurs in the yellow colour form on Cyprus. This is remarkable, as the species occurs in both colourations in neighbouring southern Turkey, where the red-coloured type is abundantly represented at many locations and sometimes even more abundantly than the yellow-coloured form.

Dactylorhiza romana primarily occurs in the southern part of Cyprus. The species prefers the wooded southern slopes of the Troodos mountains and mostly occurs in large groups. At some locations, it forms a number of densely-packed groups. In this area, it is often accompanied by *Neotinea maculata*, and more rarely by *Orchis troodi*.

For a long time the occurrence of *Dactylorhiza romana* on Cyprus was only known from the south, until the species was found for the first time in the seventies by Hansen & Hansen (Viney, 1994) on the wooded slopes between Hilarion and Karsiyaka. It is remarkable that this species is so extremely rare in the north and that it had not been found earlier in the botanically well researched north, despite its strikingly large yellow flowers.

On Crete and in Israel, *Dactylorhiza romana* occurs not only in forests, but also in open maquis and in phrygana.

Threats

The species is not threatened on Cyprus. In the vast coniferous forests it is thoroughly protected and only threatened by forest fires.

Hybrids

Unknown.

Gerasa-Agios Paraskevi, 5.3.2002

Neo Chorio-Agios Minas (Akamas), 10.3.2002

Gerasa-Agios Paraskevi, 5.3.2002

Gerasa-Agios Paraskevi, 5.3.2002

Neo Chorio-Agios Minas (Akamas), 10.3.2002

Gerasa-Agios Paraskevi, 5.3.2002

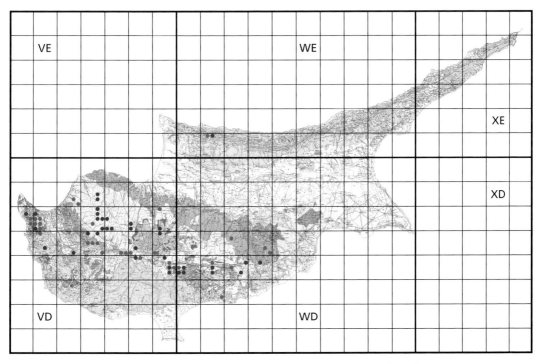

Dactylorhiza romana

6 Epipactis condensata

Dichtblütige Stendelwurz

Boissier ex D.P. Young

Jahresber. Naturwiss. Vereins
Wuppertal 23: 106 (1970)

Synonym

Epipactis helleborine subsp. *condensata* (Boissier ex D.P. Young) Sundermann, Eur. Medit. Orch. ed. 3: 41 (1980).

Beschreibung

Kräftige und meist hochwüchsige Pflanze, 20 bis 50 cm hoch, oft mit mehreren dicht beieinander stehenden Blütentrieben (büschelweise). Stängel dick, ziemlich reich beblättert, hellgrün gefärbt. Untere Laubblätter eiförmig, kurz und klein, die oberen lanzettlich, hell- bis gelblichgrün oder bräunlichgelbgrün, gelegentlich purpurn überlaufen. Blütenstand dicht- und reichblütig, manchmal auch lockerblütig mit überwiegend einseitswendigen und sehr weit geöffneten, meist rötlich gefärbten Blüten. Blüten weit geöffnet, abstehend bis leicht herabhängend. Perigonblätter glockenförmig zusammenneigend. Sepalen eiförmig-lanzettlich, zugespitzt, hellgrün, mit grünen Nerven, das mittlere vornübergeneigt. Petalen kürzer als die Sepalen, hellgrün oder zart rosa, in der Mitte weisslich, an der Spitze gelblich. Lippe zweigliedrig. Hypochil halbkugelig, aussen grünlichweiss, innen tiefschwarz, nektarführend. Epichil breit dreieckig bis herzförmig, weisslich, an der Basis kräftig rötlich mit zwei großen, rosa bis roten, gefurchten Höckern. Rostellum gut entwickelt und funktionstüchtig (allogam).

Standort

Nur in den höheren Lagen des Troodos-Gebirges, dort bevorzugt in lichten Kiefernwäldern, und seltener an offenen, besonnten, felsigen Stellen und Straßenrändern; auf kalkreichen bis mergeligen Böden.

Blütezeit

Mitte Juni bis Mitte Juli.

Höhenverbreitung

Von 1.500 bis 1.900 m.

Gesamtverbreitung

Orientalische Art (Türkei, Westsyrien, Libanon und Zypern), auch im Kaukasus. Wahrscheinlich auch auf Samos.

Verbreitung auf Zypern

Epipactis condensata ist auf Zypern ausgesprochen selten. Ihre Standorte liegen ohne Ausnahme in den höchsten Teilen (oberhalb von 1.500 m) des Troodos-Gebirges, wo das Vorkommen dieser Art nur auf ein kleines Gebiet beschränkt ist. Die Art kommt hier hauptsächlich an steinigen und felsigen Standorten vor und bevorzugt warme, südlich exponierte Hänge auf lavahaltigem Gestein. Die meisten Exemplare wachsen im Halbschatten unter sehr großen und kräftigen Kiefern (*Pinus nigra* subsp. *pallasiana*), meist in Begleitung von *Pteridium aquilinum, Viola sieaneana* und *Berberis cretica* (Georgiades, 1998ab).

Bemerkungen

Die recht stattliche *Epipactis condensata* wächst in der Umgebung von Khionistra (Mt. Olympus) fast ausschließlich unter oder in der Nähe von *Pinus nigra* subsp. *pallasiana* und bildet dort an einigen Fundorten Horste aus mehreren, dicht beieinander stehenden Pflanzen. Die Gesamtzahl blühender Pflanzen liegt bei nicht mehr als etwa dreißig pro Jahr. In trockenen Jahren blühen deutlich weniger Pflanzen, in Jahren mit viel Niederschlag, wie etwa 2002, waren es etwa fünfzig Exemplare. Die meisten Pflanzen wachsen in der englischen Militärbasis nahe Troodos, beziehungsweise um sie herum. Dort stehen etliche Pflanzen hinter dem Zaun oder direkt ausserhalb der Basis am Straßenrand, wo sie meistens von Autos beschädigt werden. Weitere Standorte gibt es in der Umgebung von Khionistra, in der Nähe des Prodromos Stausees und bei Kryos Potamos (Wood, 1985; Georgiades, 1998ab), ausserdem in der Umgebung des Jubilee Hotels entlang der Straße zum Gipfel des Mt. Olympos.

Epipactis condensata ist eine gut definierte Art und auf Zypern problemlos von den anderen *Epipactis*-Arten zu unterscheiden. Charakteristische Merkmale sind ihre großen, eiförmigen bis lanzettlichen, hellgrünen Laubblätter, der dicke, hellgrüne Stängel und ein sehr dichter, überwiegend einseitswendiger Blütenstand mit sehr weit geöffneten, meist rötlich gefärbten Blüten.

Gefährdung

Trotz ihres kleinen Verbreitungsgebietes ist *Epipactis condensata* auf Zypern nicht sonderlich gefährdet.

Hybriden

Nicht nachgewiesen.

Troodos (Troodos), 26.6.2002   Jubilee Hotel (Troodos), 25.6.2002

Epipactis condensata
Dense-Flowered Helleborine

Boissier ex D.P. Young

Jahresber. Naturwiss. Vereins
Wuppertal 23: 106 (1970)

Synonym

Epipactis helleborine subsp. *condensata* (Boissier ex D.P. Young) Sundermann, Eur. Medit. Orch. ed. 3: 41 (1980).

Description

Vigorous and usually tall plant, 20 to 50 cm tall, often with several flower-stems together in a cluster. Stem thick, fairly densely leafy, light green. Lower foliage leaves ovate, short and small, upper leaves lanceolate, light to yellowish green or brownish yellow-green, occasionally purple tinged. Inflorescence dense and many-flowered, also sometimes lax-flowered, with wide open, mostly reddish flowers, mostly facing one way. Flowers wide open, spreading to slightly pendant. Perianth segments connivent to forming a bell shape. Sepals ovate-lanceolate, acuminate, light green with green veins, dorsal sepal directed forwards. Petals shorter than sepals, light green or subtle pink, whitish in the centre, yellowish at the point. Labellum bipartite. Hypochile hemispherical, exterior greenish white, interior deep black, nectiferous. Epichile broadly triangular to cordate, whitish, strong red at the base with two large, pink to red, crenate protuberances. Rostellum well-developed and functional (allogamous).

Habitat

Only at higher altitudes in the Troodos mountains, where it prefers light coniferous woods, and more rarely in open, sunny and rocky places and roadside edges; on calcareous to marly soils.

Flowering time

Mid-June to mid-July.

Altitude distribution

From 1.500 up to 1.900 m.

Overall distribution

Oriental species (Turkey, western Syria, Lebanon and Cyprus), also in the Caucasus. Probably also on Samos.

Distribution on Cyprus

Epipactis condensata is extremely rare on Cyprus. All its habitats are situated at the highest altitudes (above 1,500 m) in the Troodos mountains, where the occurrence of this species is limited to a small area. The species mainly occurs there on igneous rocks in rocky and stony habitats and prefers warm slopes exposed to the south. Most specimens grow in the semi-shade of very large and robust conifers (*Pinus nigra* subsp. *pallasiana*), and mostly accompanied by *Pteridium aquilinum*, *Viola siecheana* and *Berberis cretica* (Georgiades, 1998ab).

Remarks

The quite stately *Epipactis condensata* grows near Khionistra (Mt. Olympus) almost exclusively beneath or near *Pinus nigra* subsp. *pallasiana* and forms several dense clusters of plants there in several locations. The total number of flowering plants is about thirty each year. There are noticably fewer plants flowering in years with dry weather, and in a year with plenty of rainfall, such as 2002, there may be up to fifty plants. Many plants grow at and around the English military base near Troodos. Many plants grow there behind the fence or right next to the base along the road, where they are often damaged by cars. Other locations are in the vicinity of Khionistra, near the reservoir of Prodromos and near Kryos Potamos (Wood, 1985; Georgiades, 1998ab), and also around the Jubilee Hotel, along the road leading to the summit of Mt. Olympos.

Epipactis condensata is a well-defined species and can easily be distinguished from other *Epipactis* species. Distinguishing characteristics are its large, ovate to lanceolate, light green foliage leaves, its thick, light green stem and a very dense inflorescence with predominantly secund and very wide open, mostly reddish coloured flowers.

Threats

Epipactis condensata is not particularly threatened on Cyprus despite its small distribution area.

Hybrids

Not proven.

Troodos (Troodos), 26.6.2002

Troodos (Troodos), 26.6.2002

Troodos (Troodos), 26.6.2002

Troodos (Troodos), 26.6.2002

Troodos (Troodos), 26.6.2002   Troodos (Troodos), 26.6.2002

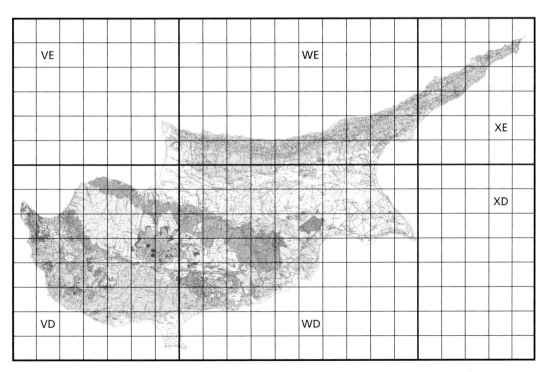

9 Meldungen / Reports

Epipactis condensata

7 Epipactis microphylla (Ehrhardt) Swartz
Kleinblättrige Stendelwurz

Kongl. Vetensk. Acad. Nya Handl. 21: 232 (1800)

Basionym

Serapias microphylla Ehrhardt, Beitr. Naturk. 4: 42 (1791).

Synonyme

Epipactis helleborine var. *microphylla* (Ehrhardt) Reichenbach fil., Icon. Fl. Germ. Helv. 13/14: 141 (1851); *Helleborine microphylla* (Ehrhardt) Schinz & Thellung, Vierteljahresschr. Nat. Ges. Zürich: 589 (1909); *Epipactis latifolia* var. *microphylla* (Ehrhardt) De Candolle in Lamarck & De Candolle Fl. Franc., ed. 3, 6: 334 (1815); *Epipactis latifolia* subsp. *microphylla* (Ehrhardt) Bonnier & Layens, Tabl. Syn. Pl. Vasc. France 1: 309 (1894); *Epipactis latifolia* subsp. *microphylla* (Ehrhardt) Rivas Goday & Borga, Anales Inst. Bot. Cavanilles 19: 537 (1961), nom. inval.; *Epipactis helleborine* subsp. *microphylla* (Ehrhardt) Rivas Goday & Borga, Anales Inst. Bot. Cavanilles 19: 537 (1961), nom. inval.; *Epipactis latiflora* subsp. *parviflora* (Persoon) K. Richter, Pl. Eur. 1: 284 (1890).

Beschreibung

Schlanke, zierliche Pflanze, 15 bis 40 cm hoch. Stängel dünn, dicht graufilzig behaart. Laubblätter sehr klein, graugrün, oft stark violett überlaufen. Untere Laubblätter eiförmig bis lanzettlich, die oberen schmal-lanzettlich und in Tragblätter übergehend. Blütenstand locker- und relativ armblütig, oft einseitswendig. Tragblätter lineal-lanzettlich, meist violett überlaufen, waagerecht abstehend. Blüten grünlich, bisweilen rötlich überlaufen, klein, wenig geöffnet, abstehend bis leicht herabhängend, nach Vanille duftend. Perigonblätter glockenförmig zusammenneigend, hell- bis dunkelgrün, meist braunrot überlaufen. Sepalen eiförmig-lanzettlich, zugespitzt. Petalen lanzettlich. Lippe zweigliedrig. Hypochil halbkugelig bis eiförmig, innen schwach rosa. Epichil dreieckig bis herzförmig, grünlich bis rötlichweiss, selten violett überlaufen mit zwei stark gekrausten Höckern und einer länglichen Mittelleiste. Rostellum zwar vorhanden, aber kaum funktionstüchtig (allogam und autogam).

Standort

In lichten, kraut- und unterholzarmen, schattigen Laubwäldern und Haselnusspflanzungen; auf frischen, kalkreichen Böden.

Blütezeit

Mitte bis Ende Juni.

Höhenverbreitung

Zwischen 800 und 1.100 m Höhe.

Gesamtverbreitung

Hauptsächlich Mittel- und Südeuropa, westlich bis Mittelspanien und östlich bis Kleinasien und Zypern.

Ausserdem in Transkaukasien, der Krim und im Nordiran.

Verbreitung auf Zypern

Die Art ist auf Zypern äusserst selten und nur von sehr wenigen Fundstellen bekannt.

Bemerkungen

Epipactis microphylla gehört auf Zypern zu den seltensten Orchideenarten. Sie wächst in den niedrigen und mittleren Lagen des Troodos-Gebirges (Pitsylia) an feuchten und schattigen Standorten in der Umgebung von Polystypos, Alona, Platanistasa und Lagoudera und in wenigen Exemplaren auch bei Fini und Perapedi (Wood, 1985; Georgiades, 1998ab).

Bei Lagoudera wächst *Epipactis microphylla* in einer kleinen Haselnusspflanzung. An dieser Fundstelle gelangen je nach Witterung jährlich zwischen fünf und zehn Pflanzen zur Blüte. Wegen der hohen Temperaturen während der Blütezeit im Juni ist die Blütezeit meist sehr kurz, und in etwa einer Woche sind die Pflanzen abgeblüht. Bei einigen Pflanzen öffnen sich die Blüten nicht, sie bleiben kleistogam. In der gleichen Haselnusspflanzung wachsen in der direkten Umgebung von *Epipactis microphylla* auch einige Exemplare von *Epipactis troodi*, die während der Hauptblüte von *Epipactis microphylla* ihre ersten Blüten öffnen. Hybriden zwischen beiden Arten wurden noch nicht festgestellt.

Von Gügel (Standortangaben 1990) wurden zwischen Kampos und Stavros (Zederntal) an einer feuchten Stelle im Wald mehrere cleistogame Pflanzen von *Epipactis microphylla* gefunden. Die Art wurde dort in Begleitung von *Dactylorhiza iberica, Epipactis troodi* und *Platanthera holmboei* gefunden. Aktuelle Angaben aus dem Zederntal sind zur Zeit nicht bekannt.

Gefährdung

Epipactis microphylla ist auf Zypern schon wegen des Vorkommens an nur sehr wenigen Fundorten stark gefährdet. Nach G. & K. Morschek (1996) bzw. Scraton (mündl. Mittlg., 2002) kommt die Art aktuell nur noch bei Lagoudera vor! Und tatsächlich konnte die Art trotz langjähriger und intensiver Suche in der Umgebung von Lagoudera an keinem anderen Fundort nachgewiesen werden. Würde die Haselnussplantage bei Lagoudera gedüngt oder sogar abgeholzt, dann ginge die Art für Zypern verloren. Schutzmaßnahmen, in die der Eigentümer der Haselnussplantage einbezogen werden muss, wären daher zur Erhaltung der Art auf Zypern dringend angezeigt.

Hybriden

Nicht bekannt.

Lagoudera (Pitsylia), 21.6.2002

Lagoudera (Pitsylia), 21.6.2002

Epipactis microphylla (Ehrhardt) Swartz
Small-Leaved Helleborine

Kongl. Vetensk. Acad. Nya Handl. 21: 232 (1800)

Basionym

Serapias microphylla Ehrhardt, Beitr. Naturk. 4: 42 (1791).

Synonyms

Epipactis helleborine var. *microphylla* (Ehrhardt) Reichenbach fil., Icon. Fl. Germ. Helv. 13/14: 141 (1851); *Helleborine microphylla* (Ehrhardt) Schinz & Thellung, Vierteljahresschr. Nat. Ges. Zürich: 589 (1909); *Epipactis latifolia* var. *microphylla* (Ehrhardt) De Candolle in Lamarck & De Candolle Fl. Franc., ed. 3, 6: 334 (1815); *Epipactis latifolia* subsp. *microphylla* (Ehrhardt) Bonnier & Layens, Tabl. Syn. Pl. Vasc. France 1: 309 (1894); *Epipactis latifolia* subsp. *microphylla* (Ehrhardt) Rivas Goday & Borga, Anales Inst. Bot. Cavanilles 19: 537 (1961), nom. inval.; *Epipactis helleborine* subsp. *microphylla* (Ehrhardt) Rivas Goday & Borga, Anales Inst. Bot. Cavanilles 19: 537 (1961), nom. inval.; *Epipactis latiflora* subsp. *parviflora* (Persoon) K. Richter, Pl. Eur. 1: 284 (1890).

Description

Slender, elegant plant, 15 to 40 cm tall. Stem thin, covered in a dense mat of short fine grey hairs. Foliage leaves very small, grey-green, often strongly tinged violet. Lower foliage leaves ovate to lanceolate, upper leaves narrowly lanceolate and merging into bracts. Inflorescence lax- and relatively few-flowered, often secund. Bracts linear-lanceolate, mostly with a violet tinge, spreading horizontally. Flowers greenish, sometimes tinged reddish, small, slightly open, spreading to slightly pendant, with a vanilla scent. Perianth segments connivent to forming a bell shape, light to dark green, mostly with a brown-red tinge. Sepals ovate-lanceolate, acuminate. Petals lanceolate. Labellum bipartite. Hypochile hemispherical to ovate, interior faintly pink. Epichile triangular to cordate, greenish to reddish white, rarely tinged violet with two very irregular protuberances and a longitudinal central ridge. Rostellum present, but scarcely functional (allogamous and autogamous).

Habitat

In light deciduous woods with sparse undergrowth and in hazelnut plantations; on fresh, calcareous soils.

Flowering time

Mid- to late June.

Altitude distribution

Between 800 and 1,100 m.

Overall distribution

Primarily in central and southern Europe, westwards as far as central Spain and eastwards as far as Asia Minor and Cyprus. Also in Transcaucasia, the Crimea and in northern Iran.

Distribution on Cyprus

The species is extremely rare on Cyprus and known at only a few sites.

Remarks

Epipactis microphylla is one of the rarest orchid species on Cyprus. It grows at low and medium-high altitudes in the Troodos mountains (Pitsylia) in moist and shady places in the vicinity of Polystypos, Alona, Platanistasa and Lagoudera, and some specimens grow near Fini and Perapedi (Wood, 1985; Georgiades, 1998ab).

Near Lagoudera, *Epipactis microphylla* grows in a small hazelnut plantation. Each year, depending on the weather, about five to ten plants are successful in blooming at this site. Its flowering time is mostly very short due to the high temperatures during its flowering period in June, and within about one week most plants will have finished flowering. The flowers of some of the plants do not even open, but remain cleistogamous. Some specimens of *Epipactis troodi* grow at the same hazelnut plantation right next to *Epipactis microphylla*, which open their first flowers during the peak flowering time of *Epipactis microphylla*. Hybrids between the two species have not yet been identified.

Gügel (habitat reports 1990) found several cleistogamous plants of *Epipactis microphylla* between Kampos and Stavros (Cedar Valley) in a wet spot in some woods. The species was accompanied there by *Dactylorhiza iberica*, *Epipactis troodi* and *Platanthera holmboei*. Recent reports from the Cedar Valley are unknown at this moment.

Threats

Due to the occurrence of this species at so few locations, *Epipactis microphylla* is heavily threatened on Cyprus. According to G. & K. Morschek (1996) and Scraton (oral correspondence, 2002), the species only still occurs near Lagoudera! And indeed, despite continuous and intensive field-work of many years in the vicinity of Lagoudera, it has not been possible to find it at other locations. If the hazelnut plantation near Lagoudera were to be fertilized or even cleared, then the species would disappear from Cyprus. Protectionary measures, in which the owners of the hazelnut plantation would need to be involved, are urgently needed for the conservation of this species on Cyprus.

Hybrids

Unknown.

Lagoudera (Pitsylia), 21.6.2002

Lagoudera (Pitsylia), 21.6.2002

Lagoudera (Pitsylia), 21.6.2002

Lagoudera (Pitsylia), 21.6.2002

Lagoudera (Pitsylia), 21.6.2002

Lagoudera (Pitsylia), 21.6.2002

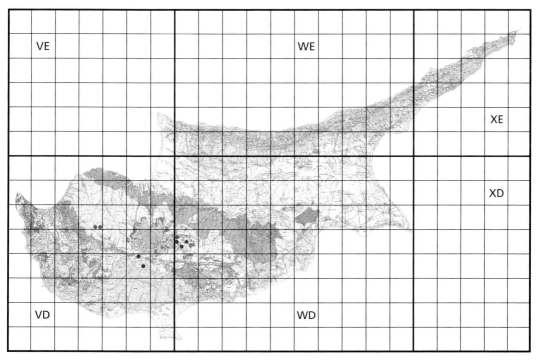

Epipactis microphylla

8 Epipactis troodi
Zypriotische Stendelwurz

H. LINDBERG

Arsbok-Vuosik. Soc. Sci. Fenn. 20B, Nr. 7: 4 (1942)

Synonyme

Epipactis persica subsp. *troodi* (H. LINDBERG) TAUBENHEIM in J. LANDWEHR, Wilde Orch. Eur. 2: 510 (1977), nom. nud.; *Epipactis helleborine* subsp. *troodi* (H. LINDBERG) SUNDERMANN, Eur. Medit. Orch. ed. 3: 41 (1980).

Beschreibung

Schlanke, mittelgroße, zierliche Pflanze, 30 bis 45 cm hoch. Stängel dünn, fast kahl, meist dunkelgrün. Laubblätter klein bis mittelgroß, dunkelgrün, purpurviolett überlaufen und spiralig am Stängel verteilt. Untere Laubblätter eiförmig bis oval-lanzettlich, die oberen schmal-lanzettlich und in Tragblätter übergehend. Blütenstand locker- und relativ armblütig. Tragblätter lanzettlich bis lineal-lanzettlich, meist violett überlaufen, fast waagerecht abstehend bis leicht schräg nach oben gerichtet. Blüten hell bis dunkelgrün, mittelgroß, weit geöffnet, abstehend bis leicht herabhängend. Perigonblätter zusammenneigend, bisweilen leicht abstehend, gelblichgrün bis olivgrün. Sepalen eiförmig-lanzettlich, zugespitzt. Petalen breit-lanzettlich, spitz, weisslichgrün. Lippe zweigliedrig. Hypochil schüsselförmig, innen rötlich, aussen hellgrün. Epichil dreieckig bis eiförmig, rötlich an den Aussenseiten und grünlich in der Mitte oder mit grünem Mittelstreifen und mit zwei kleinen, glatten Höckern. Rostellum vorhanden und funktionstüchtig (allogam und autogam).

Standort

Gebüschränder, Straßengräben und lichte Kiefern-, und Mischwälder, sowie in Haselnusspflanzungen; über feuchtem, humosem, basenreichem, kalkhaltigem oder vulkanischem Gestein.

Blütezeit

Von Mitte Juni bis Mitte Juli.

Höhenverbreitung

Von 800 bis 1.800 m.

Gesamtverbreitung

Endemische Art von Zypern.

Verbreitung auf Zypern

Die Art ist zwar auf Zypern (sehr) selten, sie ist aber dennoch ziemlich weit verbreitet. Mann findet sie im Troodos-Gebirge, aber auch im Zederntal, sowie in der Haselnusspflanzung am Fundort von *Epipactis microphylla* bei Lagoudera. An ihren Fundstellen sind meist nur wenige Pflanzen vorhanden, die zudem schwer zu finden sind. Nur manchmal bildet *Epipactis troodi* in den mittleren und oberen Lagen des Troodos-Gebirges auch kleinere Gruppen blühender Pflanzen. In diesem Gebiet wächst sie fast ausschließlich in vulkanischem Gestein an feuchten, schattigen und kühlen Stellen in der Krautschicht lichter Misch- und Nadelwälder (hauptsächlich unter

Pinus brutia und *Pinus nigra* subsp. *pallasiana*), aber auch entlang kleineren Bächen unter *Platanus orientalis* zwischen Adlerfarn (*Pteridium aquilinum*). Sie ist hier oft mit *Cephalanthera rubra, Neotinea maculata, Limodorum abortivum* und seltener mit *Epipactis condensata* und *Platanthera holmboei* vergesellschaftet.

Nach GEORGIADES (1998ab) kommt *Epipactis troodi* in der weiteren Umgebung des Prodromos Stausees und am Kaledonia Wasserfall vor, weiter bei Kryos Potamos, Mesa Potamos, Platania, auf der Troodos-Hochebene und bei Khionistra, ausserdem bei Kakopetria und Prodromos.

Bemerkungen

Epipactis troodi ist wenig variabel und ohne Schwierigkeiten zu bestimmen. Sie ist eine gut definierte Art und klar von den ihr am nächsten verwandten Arten *Epipactis cretica, Epipactis gracilis* und *Epipactis persica* zu unterscheiden. Nach Untersuchungen von YOUNG (1970) tritt wahrscheinlich sowohl Fremd- als Selbstbestäubung auf (allogam und autogam), was die Art in die Verwandtschaft von *Epipactis microphylla* rückt. Nach TAUBENHEIM (in WOOD, 1985) zeigt das Typusmaterial von *Epipactis troodi* gewisse Ähnlichkeiten mit *Epipactis persica* (SOÓ) NANNFELDT, eine Art, die in der Nordtürkei und im Iran vorkommt. *Epipactis troodi* unterscheidet sich jedoch von *Epipactis persica* unter anderem durch ihre 2 bis 3 oval-lanzettlichen Laubblätter, die violett überlaufen sind, die größeren Dimensionen der Laubblätter und Brakteen, die weit geöffneten Blüten und ihre mehr oder weniger rückwärts gebogenen Petalen. Ausserdem ist das Hypochil von *Epipactis troodi* aussen rötlich und das Epichil länglich-dreieckig, rot, mit einem grünen Mittelstreifen und mit zwei kleinen, glatten Höckern versehen (ROBATSCH, 1980; RENZ & TAUBENHEIM, 1984).

Epipactis troodi ist nach dem derzeitigen Kenntnisstand nur von Zypern bekannt. Angaben von der Türkei aus der Provinz Antalya (TAUBENHEIM in ROBATSCH 1980, WOOD, 1985) und aus den Provinzen Içel und Hatay (WOOD, 1985) sind falsch und beziehen sich auf andere *Epipactis*-Arten (KREUTZ, 1998).

Gefährdung

Die Art ist nicht besonders gefährdet. Im Gegensatz zu *Epipactis condensata* und *Epipactis microphylla* besiedelt *Epipactis troodi* ein viel größeres Areal, und im Troodos-Gebirge sind genügend Fundorte vorhanden, wo die Art vorkommt oder sich noch weiter ausbreiten kann.

Hybriden

Nicht bekannt.

134　　Prodromos-Platania (Troodos), 21.6.2002

Pano Amiantos (Troodos), 23.6.2002

Epipactis troodi
Cyprus Helleborine

H. LINDBERG

Arsbok-Vuosik. Soc. Sci. Fenn. 20B, Nr. 7: 4 (1942)

Synonyms

Epipactis persica subsp. *troodi* (H. LINDBERG) TAUBEN-HEIM in J. LANDWEHR, Wilde Orch. Eur. 2: 510 (1977), nom. nud.; *Epipactis helleborine* subsp. *troodi* (H. LINDBERG) SUNDERMANN, Eur. Medit. Orch. ed. 3: 41 (1980).

Description

Slender, medium-sized, elegant plant, 30 to 45 cm tall. Stem thin, almost glabrous, mostly dark green. Foliage leaves small to medium-sized, dark green, purple-violet tinged and spirally distributed along the stem. Lower foliage leaves ovate to oval-lanceolate, upper leaves narrowly lanceolate and merging into bracts. Inflorescence lax- and relatively few-flowered. Bracts lanceolate to linear-lanceolate, mostly tinged violet, almost spreading horizontally to slightly directed obliquely upwards. Flowers light to dark green, medium-sized, wide open, spreading to slightly pendant. Perianth segments connivent, at times slightly spreading, yellowish green to olive-green. Sepals ovate-lanceolate, acuminate. Petals broadly lanceolate, acuminate, whitish green. Labellum bipartite. Hypochile cupped, interior reddish, exterior light green. Epichile triangular to ovate, reddish at the edges and greenish in the centre or with a green central stripe and two small glabrous protuberances. Rostellum present and functional (allogamous and autogamous).

Habitat

Copse edges, roadside ditches, light coniferous and mixed woods, in hazelnut plantations; on moist, humous, base-rich, calcareous or volcanic rock.

Flowering time

From mid-June to mid-July.

Altitude dsitribution

From 800 up to 1,800 m.

Overall distribution

Endemic species of Cyprus.

Distribution on Cyprus

Although the species is (very) rare on Cyprus, it is fairly widespread. It can be found in the Troodos mountains, but also in the Cedar Valley, and in the hazelnut plantation of the *Epipactis microphylla* site near Lagoudera. There are mostly only a few plants present at its locations, which are also difficult to find. Only once in a while does *Epipactis troodi* form a small group of flowering plants at medium-high and high altitudes in the Troodos mountains. In this area, it almost exclusively grows on volcanic rocks in moist, shady and cool places in the vegetation layer consisting of light mixed and coniferous woods (primarily under *Pinus brutia* and *Pinus nigra* subsp. *pallasiana*), but also along-side small streams under *Platanus orientalis* between Western Brackenfern (*Pteridium aquilinum*). It is often accompanied there by *Cephalanthera rubra*, *Neotinea maculata*, *Limodorum abortivum* and more rarely by *Epipactis condensata* and *Platanthera holmboei*.

According to GEORGIADES (1998ab), *Epipactis troodi* occurs in the area around Prodromos reservoir, by the Caledonian Falls, and also near Kryos Potamos, Mesa Potamos, Platania, on the Troodos plateau and near Khionistra, as well as near Kakopetria and Prodromos.

Remarks

Epipactis troodi is hardly variable and easy to identify. It is a well-defined species and easy to distinguish from the closely related species of *Epipactis cretica*, *Epipactis gracilis* and *Epipactis persica*. According to research done by YOUNG (1970), cross-pollination and self-pollination (allogamy and autogamy) probably occur, which means that relationally it belongs to *Epipactis microphylla*. According to TAUBENHEIM (in WOOD, 1985), the type-material of *Epipactis troodi* hints at certain similarities with *Epipactis persica* (SOÓ) NANNFELDT, a species which occurs in northern Turkey and in Iran. *Epipactis troodi* can however be distinguished from *Epipactis persica* by, among other things, its 2 to 3 oval-lanceolate foliage leaves, which have purple tinges, the larger dimensions of the foliage leaves and bracts, the widely opened flowers and its more or less reflexed petals. Moreover, the hypochile of *Epipactis troodi* is reddish on the exterior and the epichile is oblong-triangular, red with a green central stripe and with two small glabrous protuberances (ROBATSCH, 1980; RENZ & TAUBENHEIM, 1984).

According to the state of knowledge at this time, *Epipactis troodi* is only known from Cyprus. Reports from the province Antalya (TAUBENHEIM in ROBATSCH 1980, WOOD, 1985) and from the provinces of Içel and Hatay (WOOD, 1985) are false and involve other *Epipactis* species (KREUTZ, 1998).

Threats

The species is not particularly threatened. In contrast with *Epipactis condensata* and *Epipactis microphylla*, *Epipactis troodi* covers a much larger area, and there are sufficient locations present in the Troodos mountains, where the species occurs or where it can expand.

Hybrids

Unknown.

Pano Platres (Myllomeris Falls), 23.6.2002

Prodromos-Platania (Troodos), 21.6.2002

Prodromos-Platania (Troodos), 21.6.2002

Trooditissa-Prodromos (Troodos), 24.6.2002

Trypylos (Cedar Valley), 25.6.2002

Trooditissa (Troodos), 24.6.2002

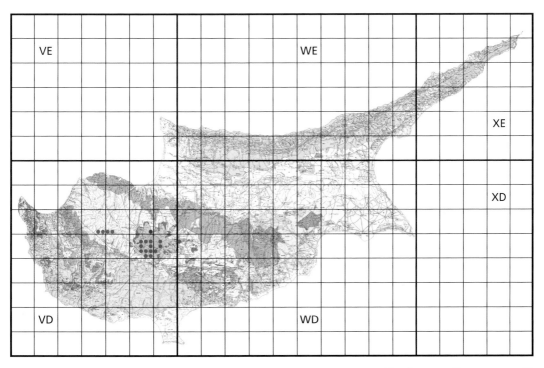

49 Meldungen / Reports

Epipactis troodi

9 Epipactis veratrifolia BOISSIER & HOHENACKER

Germerblättrige Stendelwurz

P.E. Boissier, Diagn. Pl. Orient., 13: 11 (1854)

Synonyme

Epipactis consimilis WALLICH ex HOOKER fil., Fl. Brit. Ind. 6: 126 (1890); *Epipactis somaliensis* ROLFE in THIESELTON-DYER, Fl. Trop. Afr. 7: 189 (1897); *Epipactis abyssinica* PAX, Engl. Jahrb. 39: 612 (1907).

Beschreibung

Robuste, hochwüchsige, bis zu 70 cm hohe Pflanze, im unteren Teil reich beblättert. Laubblätter grün bis dunkelgrün gefärbt, aufrecht bis abstehend, die unteren breitoval bis lanzettlich, groß und lang zugespitzt, die oberen schmal lanzettlich, lang zugespitzt und nach oben in Tragblätter übergehend. Blütenstand ziemlich locker- und meist reichblütig, oft einseitswendig. Blüten weit geöffnet, groß, abstehend bis nickend. Perigonblätter anfangs glockenförmig zusammenneigend, später abstehend. Sepalen eiförmig-lanzettlich, zugespitzt, grünlichgelb und an den Rändern stark rötlich bis braunrot überlaufen, das mittlere vornübergeneigt. Petalen kürzer als die Sepalen, eiförmig, grünlichgelb und wie die Sepalen an den Rändern stark rötlich bis braunrot überlaufen. Lippe zweigliedrig. Hypochil länglich kahnförmig, an der Basis mit zwei aufgerichteten Seitenlappen, rötlich bis purpurn gefärbt. Epichil lanzettlich (am Grunde eiförmig) mit aufgerichteten Seitenlappen, weiss bis rötlich gefärbt mit rötlichgelbem Querband und weisser Spitze. Rostellum gut entwickelt und funktionstüchtig (allogam).

Standort

Völlig durchnässte, ständig überrieselte Quell- und Felshänge mit starker Kalkaussinterung; an schattigen Stellen an Flussufern und Quellfluren oder an Ufersäumen kleiner Bergbäche und Nasswiesen; auf Quellhängen auf extrem kalkhaltigem Substrat. Sie bevorzugt steile bis überhängende Lagen, wo sie infolge vegetativer Vermehrung große Horste bildet. Durch ihre Spezialisierung sind ihre Standorte beschränkt.

Blütezeit

Mitte März bei Episkopi und von (Mitte) Ende Juni bis Ende Juli im Troodos-Gebirge.

Höhenverbreitung

Bei Episkopi um 150 m, im Troodos von 800 bis 1.900 m.

Gesamtverbreitung

Orientalische und kaukasische Art. Vorderasien: von Zypern über die Türkei entlang der Levante bis zur Sinai-Halbinsel. Ausserdem ostwärts über die Kaukasusländer durch Irak, Iran, Afghanistan und Pakistan bis Nepal; isolierte Vorkommen in Ostafrika (Somalia). Sie erreicht auf Zypern ihre Westgrenze.

Verbreitung auf Zypern

Bei Episkopi, westlich von Lemesos und in den höheren Lagen im zentralen Teil des Troodos-Gebirges.

Bemerkungen

Epipactis veratrifolia gehört zu den schönsten und seltensten Orchideen Vorderasiens. Auf Zypern kommt die Art in zwei sehr unterschiedlichen Biotopen vor. Im Süden, westlich von Lemesos bei Episkopi, wo die Art schon ab Mitte März zur Blüte gelangt, wächst *Epipactis veratrifolia* an einem steilen, völlig durchnässten und ständig überrieselten Quellhang, oft zusammen mit *Adiantum capillus-veneris*, *Inula* spec und mit der filigranen *Pinguicula christallina*. Je nach Witterung wachsen hier jährlich mehrere Dutzend sehr kräftige Pflanzen.

Weiter hat die Art mehrere Vorkommen im Troodos-Gebirge, wo *Epipactis veratrifolia* an Flussufern, Quellfluren und an Ufersäumen kleiner Bergbäche in vollem Sonnenschein vorkommt, dort meist vergesellschaftet von *Dactylorhiza iberica*. Der schönste und individuenreichste Fundort dort liegt unweit von Pano Amiantos. Dort blühen an einem steilen Quellhang Ende Juni mehrere Hundert Pflanzen. Weitere Fundorte befinden sich in den höheren Lagen des Troodos-Gebirges in der weiteren Umgebung von Prodromos (unter anderem bei Khrysovrysi), Agios Nikolaos tis Stegis bei Kakopetria, Platania und Spilia. In der Nähe der Asbestminen von Kato Amiantos gibt es einige Stellen, an denen *Epipactis veratrifolia* auch auf durchfeuchteten Sekundärstandorten, die durch den Minenabbau entstanden sind, vorkommt und einen wundervollen Anblick bietet. Leider werden die fließenden Gewässer in Brunnenstuben abgeleitet, wodurch sie zeitweilig völlig austrocknen (ROBATSCH, 1980).

Die Art kommt auf Zypern wie in Israel in zwei unterschiedlichen Vegetationsformen vor. Bei Episkopi auf Zypern wie bei En Gedi im Sinai ist das Laub der Pflanzen das ganze Jahr über grün, während die oberirdischen Teile der Pflanzen im Troodos-Gebirge im Winter absterben. In den höheren Lagen des Troodos-Gebirges, sowie im Nationalpark Horshat Tal im Norden Israels wachsen die Pflanzen direkt aus den nackten Boden und sterben im Herbst ab. Im Frühling bilden sich dann wieder neue Triebe, die etwa zwei Monate später blühen.

Gefährdung

Die Art ist im Troodos-Gebirge durch Entwässerung ihrer Standorte gefährdet. Besonders gefährdet ist sie an dem Fundort westlich von Lemesos. Durch Entwässerung oder Verlegung der Straße könnten die Pflanzen dort verschwinden. Positiv zu vermerken ist aber, dass der Fundort im britischen Militärlager liegt, und die Briten über diese seltene Art informiert sind.

Hybriden

Nicht bekannt.

Episkopi (British Base), 22.3.2002

Epipactis veratrifolia

BOISSIER & HOHENACKER

Eastern Marsh Helleborine

P.E. Boissier, Diagn. Pl. Orient., 13: 11 (1854)

Synonyms

Epipactis consimilis WALLICH EX HOOKER fil., Fl. Brit. Ind. 6: 126 (1890); *Epipactis somaliensis* ROLFE in THISELTON-DYER, Fl. Trop. Afr. 7: 189 (1897); *Epipactis abyssinica* PAX, Engl. Jahrb. 39: 612 (1907).

Description

Robust, up to 70 cm tall plant, densely leaved in lower part. Foliage leaves green to dark green, erect to spreading, lower leaves broadly ovate to lanceolate, large and drawn out into a long point, upper leaves narrowly lanceolate, also drawn out into a long point and merging into bracts towards the top. Inflorescence fairly lax-, and usually many-flowered, often secund. Flowers wide open, large, spreading to pendant. Perianth segments first connivent to forming a bell shape, later spreading. Sepals ovate-lanceolate, acuminate, greenish yellow with vivid reddish to brown-red tinges at the edges, dorsal sepal directed forwards. Petals shorter than sepals, ovate, greenish yellow with vivid reddish to brown-red tinges at the edges like the sepals. Labellum bipartite. Hypochile oblong boat shape, with two erect lateral lobes at the base, reddish to purple. Epichile lanceolate (ovate at the base) with erect lateral lobes, white to reddish with reddish yellow transverse stripe and white tip. Rostellum well-developed and functional (allogamous).

Habitat

Fully saturated, rocky slopes with perpetually trickling water, which deposits large amounts of calcium; in shady places along rivers and springs or at the sides of small mountain streams and wetlands; on wet slopes consisting of extremely calcareous substrate. It favours steep slopes to overhanging rocks, where it forms large clusters by vegetative propagation. Its specialization has limited its habitats.

Flowering time

Mid-March near Episkopi and from (mid-) late June to late July in the Troodos Range.

Altitude distribution

Near Episkopi at about 150 m, in the Troodos mountains from 800 m to 1,900 m.

Overall distribution

Oriental and Caucasian species. Near East: from Cyprus throughout Turkey, along the Levant as far as the Sinai peninsula. Also eastwards through the Caucasian countries to Iraq, Iran, Afghanistan and Pakistan as far as Nepal; isolated occurrences in eastern Africa (Somalia). It reaches its westernmost boundary in Cyprus.

Distribution on Cyprus

Near Episkopi, west of Lemesos and at higher altitudes in the central part of the Troodos mountains.

Remarks

Epipactis veratrifolia is one of the rarest and most beautiful orchids of the Near East. On Cyprus it occurs in two strongly varying biotopes. In the south, west of Lemesos near Episkopi, where the species is already in flower from mid-March, *Epipactis veratrifolia* grows on a steep slope with perpetually trickling water, often together with *Adiantum capillus-veneris*, *Inula* sp. and with the filigree *Pinguicula christallina*, an endemic Cypriot species. Depending on the weather, several dozen very vigorous plants grow there each year.

The species occurs at several other sites in the Troodos mountains, where *Epipactis veratrifolia* occurs along rivers and springs and along the banks of mountain streams in the direct sun, often accompanied by *Dactylorhiza iberica*. The most beautiful and most individual-rich site is situated near Pano Amiantos. Several hundred plants grow there in late June on a steep wet slope. Other sites can be found at higher altitudes in the Troodos mountains in the area around Prodromos (such as near Khrysovrysi), Agios Nikolaos tis Stegis near Kakopetria, Platania and Spilia. In the vicinity of the asbestos mines of Kato Amiantos, there are some spots where *Epipactis veratrifolia* also occurs in wet secondary habitats created by mining, where it is a spectacular sight. Unfortunately all the flowing water is being drained into cisterns, which causes the orchids to dry out (ROBATSCH, 1980).

The species occurs in two different forms of vegetation as in Israel. Near Episkopi as near En Gedi in the Sinai, the foliage of the plants is green all the year round, while the above-ground parts of the plants die off in winter in the Troodos mountains. At higher altitudes in the Troodos mountains, and in the Horshat Valley National Park in northern Israel, the plants grow up from ground level and die off in autumn. New shoots are formed again in spring, which come into bloom two months later.

Threats

The species is relatively heavily threatened by drainage of its habitats in the Troodos mountains. It is particularly threatened at its site west of Lemesos. Drainage, or alterations to the road could cause the plants to disappear. One fact in its favour is that this site is situated inside a British military base, and the British forces have been notified of the existence of this rare species.

Hybrids

Unknown.

Pano Amiantos (Troodos), 22.6.2002

Pano Amiantos (Troodos), 22.6.2002

Episkopi (British Base), 7.3.2002

Kato Amiantos (Troodos), 23.6.2002

Kato Amiantos (Troodos), 23.6.2002　　　　　　Episkopi (British Base), 7.3.2002

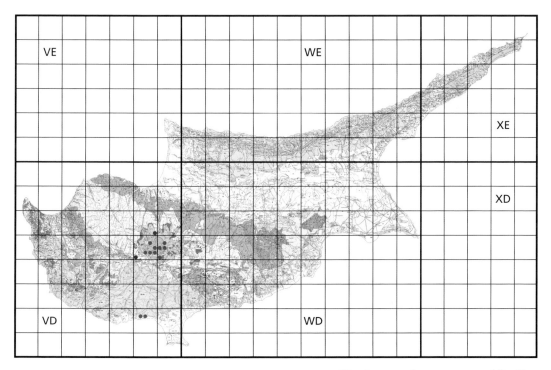

Epipactis veratrifolia

Basionym

Orchis abortiva L., Sp. Pl. 2: 943 (1753).

Synonyme

Centrosis abortiva (L.) SWARTZ, Summa Veg. Scand.: 32 (1814); *Ionorchis abortiva* (L.) BECK, Fl. Nieder-Österreich 1: 215 (1890).

Beschreibung

Robuste und hochwüchsige Pflanze, 20 bis 70 cm hoch. Stängel kräftig und dick, stahlblau bis blau-violett. Pflanze ohne Laubblätter aber mit zahlrei-chen, kurzen, scheidenförmigen, genervten, bläu-lichen bis violetten Blattschuppen. Blütenstand meist sehr lang gestreckt, meist reichblütig. Tragblätter ei-förmig-lanzettlich, lang-zugespitzt, bläulich bis vio-lett überlaufen, schräg aufwärts gerichtet, länger als der Fruchtknoten. Blüten groß, weit geöffnet, pur-pur- bis blassviolett. Sepalen länglich-eiförmig, die seitlichen waagerecht abstehend bis zurückgeschla-gen, das mittlere stark nach vorne gebogen. Petalen schmal-lanzettlich, abstehend bis zurückgeschlagen und kürzer als die Sepalen. Lippe aus zwei Teilen bestehend. Hypochil schmal mit hochstehenden Rän-dern, hellviolett. Epichil oval mit nach oben gekrümm-ten Rändern, weisslich bis hellviolett, mit dunkel-violetten Längslinien. Sporn abwärts gerichtet, blau-violett, etwa so lang wie der Fruchtknoten.

Standort

Lichte Kiefernwälder, Lichtungen und deren Ränder, Phrygana; auf basenreichen oder kalkhaltigen Böden.

Blütezeit

Anfang Juni bis Mitte Juli.

Höhenverbreitung

Überwiegend von 1.200 m bis 1.900 m im Troodos-Gebirge. Im Norden im Pentadactylos-Gebirge auch ab 200 m und sehr selten in der Koymandaria Region im Süden ab 500 m Höhe.

Gesamtverbreitung

Mitteleuropa und Mittelmeergebiet; nördlich bis Süd-belgien und Luxemburg, Süddeutschland, Österreich und Rumänien; östlich bis in die Kaukasusländer und den Nordiran, südlich bis Kreta, Zypern und Israel, auch in Nordafrika.

Verbreitung auf Zypern

Allgemein in den höheren Lagen des Troodos-Ge-birges verbreitet (unter anderem bei Prodromos, Troodos, Platania, Kykko Kloster, Khrysorroyiatissa Kloster, Stavros tis Psokas, Cedar Valley und Platres; WOOD, 1985). Sehr selten in der Koymandaria Region nördlich von Lemesos. Selten im Pentadactylos-Gebirge (Kantara Schloss und bei Alevkaya), wo er gerne an offenen, aber schattigen Stellen unter *Pinus brutia*, *Pinus nigra* subsp. *pallasiana* und *Juni-perus foetidissima* vorkommt, sowie an Straßen-rändern und Böschungen.

Es ist bemerkenswert, dass *Limodorum abortivum* auf Zypern hauptsächlich in den höheren Berglagen ab 1.200 m vorkommt, wogegen die Art im übrigen Mittelmeerraum meistens in viel niedrigeren Lagen wächst.

Bemerkungen

Neben der Nominatform sind zwei auffällige Farbva-rianten von *Limodorum abortivum* bekannt, näm-lich eine mit roten und eine mit dunkelpurpurnen Blüten. Die rot blühende Farbvariante (*Limodorum abortivum* var. *rubrum* SUNDERMANN ex KREUTZ), die auch in der Türkei (KREUTZ, 1998) und auf Lesbos (BIEL, 1998) vorkommt, wurde auf Zypern nur von WOOD (1985) erwähnt. Aus seiner Bemerkung "Forms from Cyprus and S. Turkey with rose-pink flowers have been named var. *rubrum* RÜCKBRODT" geht aber nicht hervor, ob er diese rot blühende Variante auch tatsächlich auf Zypern gesehen hat. Jedenfalls sind keine Nachweise dieser Varietät von Zypern bekannt. Auf Zypern kommen dagegen Pflanzen mit sehr dunk-len, purpurnen Blüten vor. Diese Farbvariante wurde an mehreren Stellen im Troodos-Gebirge, sowie auf Rhodos (KREUTZ, 2002) gefunden.

Vor allem in den lichten Kiefernwäldern unweit der englischen Basis am Troodos Gipfel und in der wei-teren Umgebung der Kaledonia Wasserfälle bei Pla-tres bildet *Limodorum abortivum* größere Popula-tionen blühender Pflanzen, überwiegend in dunkel-violetter Farbe.

Von ERHARDT, HILLER & KALTEISEN (Standortangaben 2002) wurde *Limodorum abortivum* auch an zwei relativ niedrig gelegenen Standorte in etwa 540 m Höhe in einem Kiefernwald in der Koymandaria Region zwischen Agios Mamas und Kalo Chorio (15 km nördlich von Lemesos) gefunden.

An vielen Fundorten im Troodos-Gebirge ist *Limodo-rum abortivum* mit *Cephalanthera rubra*, *Epipac-tis condensata*, *Epipactis troodi* und *Platanthera holmboei* vergesellschaftet. Diese Arten blühen auf Zypern etwa gleichzeitig mit *Limodorum abortivum*. Die späte Blütezeit von *Limodorum abortivum* ist bemerkenswert, weil sie im Mittelmeerraum norma-lerweise früher als diese Arten blüht

Gefährdung

Limodorum abortivum ist hauptsächlich im Troodos-Gebirge verbreitet, dort stellenweise häufig und ziem-lich weit verbreitet. Die Art ist als nicht gefährdet einzustufen.

Hybriden

Nicht bekannt.

Limodorum abortivum

Violet Limodore

(L.) Swartz

Nova Acta Reg. Soc. Sci. ser. 6: 80 (1799)

Basionym

Orchis abortiva L., Sp. Pl. 2: 943 (1753).

Synonyms

Centrosis abortiva (L.) Swartz, Summa Veg. Scand.: 32 (1814); *Ionorchis abortiva* (L.) Beck, Fl. Nieder-Österreich 1: 215 (1890).

Description

Tall robust plant, 20 to 70 cm tall. Stem vigorous and thick, steel-blue to blue-violet. Plant without foliage leaves, but with numerous short, sheathing, veined, bluish to violet scale leaves. Inflorescence very elongated, mostly densely flowered. Bracts ovate-lanceolate, long and acuminate, tinged bluish to violet, directed obliquely upwards, longer than ovary. Flowers large, wide open, purple to pale violet. Sepals oblong-ovate, lateral sepals spreading horizontally to reflexed, dorsal sepal strongly curved forwards. Petals narrowly lanceolate, spreading to reflexed and shorter than sepals. Labellum bipartite. Hypochile narrow with erect edges, light violet. Epichile oval, with edges curving upwards, whitish to light violet with dark violet longitudinal ridges. Spur directed downwards, blue-violet, about as long as ovary.

Habitat

Light coniferous woods, in clearings and edges, phrygana; on base-rich or calcareous soils.

Flowering time

Early June to mid-July.

Altitude distribution

Predominantly from 1,200 up to 1,900 m in the Troodos mountains. In the Pentadactylos Range in the north also from 200 m, and very rare in the Koymandaria Region in the south from 500 m.

Overall distribution

Central Europe and Mediterranean region; northwards as far as southern Belgium and Luxemburg, southern Germany, Austria and Romania, eastwards as far as the Caucasian countries and northern Iran, southwards as far as Crete, Cyprus and Israel. Also in northern Africa.

Distribution on Cyprus

Mainly distributed at higher altitudes throughout the Troodos range (such as near Prodromos, Troodos, Platania, Kykko monastery, Khrysorroyiatissa monastery, Stavros tis Psokas, the Cedar Valley and Platres; Wood, 1985). Very rare in the Koymandaria Region north of Lemesos. Rare in the Pentadactylos mountains (Kantara castle and near Alevkaya), where it prefers open, but shady places under *Pinus brutia, Pinus nigra* subsp. *pallasiana* and *Juniperus foetidissima*, and roadside edges and banks. It is remarkable that *Limodorum abortivum* mainly occurs at higher altitudes from 1,200 m upwards, whereas the species mostly grows at lower altitudes in the rest of the Mediterranean region.

Remarks

Alongside the nominate form, there are two noteworthy colour variations of *Limodorum abortivum*, namely one with red and one with dark purple flowers. The red colouration (*Limodorum abortivum* var. *rubrum* Sundermann ex Kreutz), which also occurs in Turkey (Kreutz, 1998) and on Lesbos (Biel, 1998) has only been recorded by Wood (1985) on Cyprus. It is however not clear from his comment "Forms from Cyprus and S. Turkey with rose-pink flowers have been named var. *rubrum* Rückbrodt" whether he actually saw this red colouration on Cyprus. In any case, there is no evidence available for the existence of this variety on Cyprus. Plants with very deep purple flowers however do occur on Cyprus. This colouration has been found at several sites in the Troodos mountains and on Rhodes (Kreutz, 2002).

Particularly in the light coniferous woods near the British base at the summit of the Troodos mountains and in the area around the Caledonian Falls near Platres, *Limodorum abortivum* forms larger populations of flowering plants, predominantly in the deep purple variation.

Limodorum abortivum was also found in 2002 in a pine forest by Erhardt, Hiller & Kalteisen (site descriptions 2002) at two places in lower altitudes (540 m), namely in the Koymandaria region between Agios Mamas and Kalo Chorio (15 km north of Lemesos).

Limodorum abortivum is accompanied by *Cephalanthera rubra, Epipactis condensata, Epipactis troodi* and *Platanthera holmboei* at many of its sites in the Troodos mountains. These species bloom at around the same time as *Limodorum abortivum*. The late flowering time of *Limodorum abortivum* is remarkable as it does not normally flower at the same time as these species in the Mediterranean region.

Threats

Limodorum abortivum is mainly distributed in the Troodos mountains, and is at times abundant, and fairly widespread. The species can be categorized as not threatened.

Hybrids

Unknown.

Pano Platres (Caledonia Trail), 22.6.2002

Troodos (Troodos), 26.6.2002

Troodos (Troodos), 21.6.2002

Troodos (Troodos), 21.6.2002

Troodos (Troodos), 21.6.2002

Pano Platres (Caledonia Trail), 22.6.2002

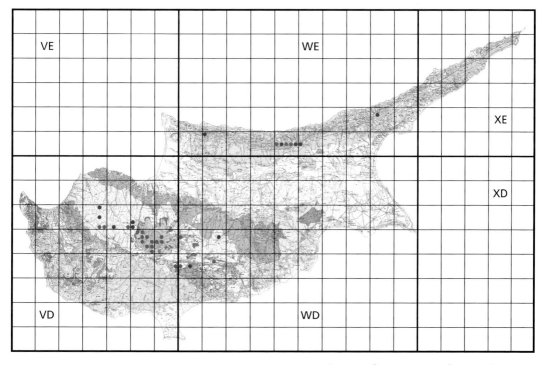

Limodorum abortivum

Basionym

Satyrium maculatum DESFONTAINES, Fl. Atlant. 2 (8): 319 & 320 (1799).

Synonyme

Peristylus maculatus (DESFONTAINES) REICHENBACH fil., Icon. Fl. Germ. Helv. 13/14: 2 (1851), nom. inval.; *Aceras maculata* (DESFONTAINES) GRENIER in GRENIER & GODRON, Fl. France 3 (1): 282 (1855), nom. inval.; *Neotinea maculata* var. *stricta* LANDWEHR, Wilde Orch. Eur. 2: 556 (1977); *Orchis intacta* LINK in J. Bot. (SCHRADER) 2 (2): 322 (1800, publ. 1799); *Neotinea intacta* (LINK) REICHENBACH fil., De Pollin. Orchid.: 18, 29 (1852); *Aceras intacta* REICHENBACH fil., Icon. Fl. Germ. Helv. 13/14: 2 (1851); *Habenaria intacta* (LINK) LINDLEY ex BENTHAM, Proc. Linn. Soc. Lond. 18: 354 (1881); *Tineo intacta* (LINK) BOISSIER, Fl. Orient. 5 (1): 58 (1882); *Satyrium densiflorum* BROTERO, Fl. Lusit. (1): 22 (1804); *Peristylus densiflorus* (BROTERO) LINDLEY, Gen. Sp. Orchid. Pl. (7): 298 (1835); *Aceras densiflorum* (BROTERO) BOISSIER, Voy. Bot. Espagne 2 (19): 595 (1842); *Aceras densiflora* BOISSIER, Voy. Midi Espagne 2: 595 (1845); *Coeloglossum densiflorum* (BROTERO) HARTMAN ex WILLKOMM & LANGE, Prodr. Fl. Hispan. 1 (1): 64 (1861), nom. inval.; *Orchis secundiflora* BERTOLONI, Rar. Ital. Pl. 2: 42, no. 8 (1806); *Himantoglossum secundiflorum* (BERTOLONI) REICHENBACH, Fl. Germ. Excurs. 1: 120, no. 815 (1831-1832); *Aceras secundiflora* (BERTOLONI) LINDLEY in S.T. EDWARDS, Bot. Reg. 18: ad t. 1525 (1833).

Beschreibung

Zarte und schlanke Pflanze, bis 20 cm hoch. Untere Laubblätter rosettig gehäuft, blaugrün, meistens schwarzbraun gefleckt oder rötlich-bräunlich überlaufen, die oberen stängelumfassend. Blütenstand zylindrisch, dicht und vielblütig. Tragblätter lanzettlich, etwa halb so lang wie der Fruchtknoten. Blüten sehr klein, von (grün)weisslicher Grundfarbe, oft rosa bis purpurn überlaufen. Perigonblätter helmförmig zusammenneigend, grün, weisslich bis hellgelb oder rötlich bis purpurn. Sepalen lanzettlich bis eiförmig-lanzettlich. Petalen lanzettlich bis schmallanzettlich. Lippe stark dreilappig, die beiden Seitenlappen kürzer als der Mittellappen; Mittellappen an der Spitze meist dreizähnig, schräg nach unten gerichtet. Sporn konisch, abwärts gerichtet. Die Art variiert in der Blütenfarbe von grünlichweiss bis rein weiss und von zart rosa bis dunkelviolett.

Standort

Lichte, unterwuchsarme Kiefernwälder und Gebüschränder; sehr selten in Macchien und Phrygana; auf trockenen bis frischen, mäßig feuchten Böden. Die Art wächst mit Vorliebe an nordexponierten, feuchten Berghängen unter Kiefern (*Pinus brutia*) oder Mittelmeerzypressen (*Cupressus sempervirens*).

Blütezeit

Von Anfang März in niederen Lagen bis Mitte April in höheren Lagen des Troodos- und Pentadactylos-Gebirges.

Höhenverbreitung

Von der Küste bis 1.500 m.

Gesamtverbreitung

Von den Kanarischen Inseln, Madeira bis Vorderasien (Türkei, Libanon, Israel und Zypern). Auch in Südwestirland, Westfrankreich und auf der Isle of Man (England).

Verbreitung auf Zypern

Auf der ganzen Insel verbreitet. Vor allem in den mittleren Gebirgslagen ist die Art stellenweise häufig.

Bemerkungen

Neotinea maculata ist eine kleine, zarte Pflanze, die wegen ihres unauffälligen Erscheinungsbildes häufig übersehen wird. Sie bildet öfters größere Populationen blühender Pflanzen. *Neotinea maculata* ist auf Zypern sehr variabel. Es kommen sowohl Pflanzen mit stark gefleckten Laubblättern vor als auch solche mit wenig gefleckten oder ungefleckten Blättern. Ausserdem existieren auf Zypern mehrere Farbvarianten. Es gibt Pflanzen mit weissen, gelben, rosa oder rot gefärbten Blüten, wobei die rot blühende Form am häufigsten verbreitet ist. Auch in der Blütenform gibt es Unterschiede, wobei vor allem der Mittellappen variabel ist. RENZ (1929) hat *Neotinea intacta* lusus *luteola* vom Troodos-Gebirge beschrieben, eine Variante mit hellgelben bis grünlichen Brakteen und Blüten.

In den Pinienwäldern auf der Akamas-Halbinsel im Westen Zyperns sowie im Makheras Wald in der Nähe des Makheras Klosters ist *Neotinea maculata* nicht selten, stellenweise sogar besonders häufig. In diesen Gebieten bildet sie in den weitläufigen Pinienwäldern an mehreren Stellen individuenreiche Populationen von Pflanzen mit kräftig purpurn gefärbten Blüten.

Im Pentadactylos-Gebirge und in den montanen Lagen der Karpasia-Halbinsel hat *Neotinea maculata* weitere individuenreiche Vorkommen, und sie kommt auch in diesem Gebiet in verschieden Blütenfarben vor. Ausserhalb der Waldgebiete ist die Art selten und nur von wenigen Fundorten bekannt.

Gefährdung

Neotinea maculata ist in Kiefernwäldern der mittleren montanen Lage weit verbreitet und dort kaum gefährdet. Starken Rückgang zeigt sie aber vor allem in den weitläufigen Phrygana-Gebieten.

Hybriden

Nicht nachgewiesen.

152   Gerasa, 20.3.2002

Neotinea maculata

Dense-Flowered Orchid

(Desfontaines) Stearn

Ann. Mus. Goulandris 2: 79 (1974, publ. 1975)

Basionym

Satyrium maculatum Desfontaines, Fl. Atlant. 2 (8): 319 & 320 (1799).

Synonyms

Peristylus maculatus (Desfontaines) Reichenbach fil., Icon. Fl. Germ. Helv. 13/14: 2 (1851), nom. inval.; *Aceras maculata* (Desfontaines) Grenier in Grenier & Godron, Fl. France 3 (1): 282 (1855), nom. inval.; *Neotinea maculata* var. *stricta* Landwehr, Wilde Orch. Eur. 2: 556 (1977); *Orchis intacta* Link in J. Bot. (Schrader) 2 (2): 322 (1800, publ. 1799); *Neotinea intacta* (Link) Reichenbach fil., De Pollin. Orchid.: 18, 29 (1852); *Aceras intacta* Reichenbach fil., Icon. Fl. Germ. Helv. 13/14: 2 (1851); *Habenaria intacta* (Link) Lindley ex Bentham, Proc. Linn. Soc. Lond. 18: 354 (1881); *Tineo intacta* (Link) Boissier, Fl. Orient. 5 (1): 58 (1882); *Satyrium densiflorum* Brotero, Fl. Lusit. (1): 22 (1804); *Peristylus densiflorus* (Brotero) Lindley, Gen. Sp. Orchid. Pl. (7): 298 (1835); *Aceras densiflorum* (Brotero) Boissier, Voy. Bot. Espagne 2 (19): 595 (1842); *Aceras densiflora* Boissier, Voy. Midi Espagne 2: 595 (1845); *Coeloglossum densiflorum* (Brotero) Hartman ex Willkomm & Lange, Prodr. Fl. Hispan. 1 (1): 64 (1861), nom. inval.; *Orchis secundiflora* Bertoloni, Rar. Ital. Pl. 2: 42, no. 8 (1806); *Himantoglossum secundiflorum* (Bertoloni) Reichenbach, Fl. Germ. Excurs. 1: 120, no. 815 (1831-1832); *Aceras secundiflora* (Bertoloni) Lindley in S.T. Edwards, Bot. Reg. 18: ad t. 1525 (1833).

Description

Delicate and slender plant, up to 20 cm tall. Lower foliage leaves forming a rosette, blue-green, usually with black-brown spots or reddish-brownish tinges, upper leaves stem-sheathing. Inflorescence cylindrical, dense- and many-flowered. Bracts lanceolate, about half as long as ovary. Flowers very small, with (green) whitish background colour, often with pink to purple tinges. Perianth segments connivent to forming a hood, green, whitish to pale yellow or reddish to purple. Sepals lanceolate to ovate-lanceolate. Petals lanceolate to narrowly lanceolate. Labellum deeply three-lobed, both lateral lobes shorter than middle lobe; middle lobe mostly three-toothed at apex, pointing downwards at an angle. Spur conical, pointing downwards. This species varies in flower colouration from greenish white to pure white and from delicate pink to deep purple.

Habitat

Light coniferous woods and shrubland edges with sparse undergrowth; very rarely in maquis and phrygana; on arid to fresh, more or less moist soils. *Neotinea maculata* especially favours moist mountain slopes with a northern exposure, under Pines (*Pinus brutia*) or Italian Cypresses (*Cupressus sempervirens*).

Flowering time

From early March at lower altitudes to mid-April at the higher altitudes of the Troodos and Pentadactylos mountains.

Altitude distribution

From sea level up to 1,500 m.

Overall distribution

From the Canary Islands and Madeira as far as the Near East (Turkey, Lebanon, Israel and Cyprus). Also in southwestern Ireland, western France and on the Isle of Man (UK).

Distribution on Cyprus

Widely distributed throughout the whole island. The species is abundant in some places, especially in the mountains at medium-high altitudes.

Remarks

Neotinea maculata is a small, delicate plant, which is often overlooked due to its lack of prominence. It often forms large populations of flowering plants. *Neotinea maculata* is very variable on Cyprus. There are plants with heavily spotted foliage leaves, and plants with sparsely spotted or unspotted leaves. There are also several colour varieties on Cyprus. Plants can be found with white, yellow, pink and red flowers, of which the red-coloured variety is the most abundant. There are also differences in flower shape, in which the middle lobe is the most variable. Renz (1929) has described *Neotinea intacta* lusus *luteola* for the Troodos mountains, a variety with bright yellow to greenish bracts and flowers.

Neotinea maculata is not rare, at some places even very abundant in the pine forests of the Akamas peninsula in western Cyprus and in the Makheras forest near the Makheras monastery. In some places in these areas, the species forms individual-rich populations with vivid purple-coloured flowers in the vast pine forests.

In the Pentadactylos Range and at the mountainous altitudes of the Karpasia peninsula, *Neotinea maculata* has other individual-rich occurrences, and it occurs also in this area in several different colourations. Outside the wooded areas, *Neotinea maculata* is rare and known at only a few locations.

Threats

Neotinea maculata is widespread at medium-high altitudes in the mountains and hardly threatened there. A strong decline can however be seen in the vast phrygana areas.

Hybrids

Unconfirmed.

Neo Chorio-Agios Minas (Akamas), 10.3.2002

Gerasa, 20.3.2002

Alevkaya (Pentadactylos Range), 18.3.2002

Alevkaya (Pentadactylos Range), 18.3.2002

Apsiou-Fasoulla, 20.3.2002

Neo Chorio-Agios Minas (Akamas), 10.3.2002

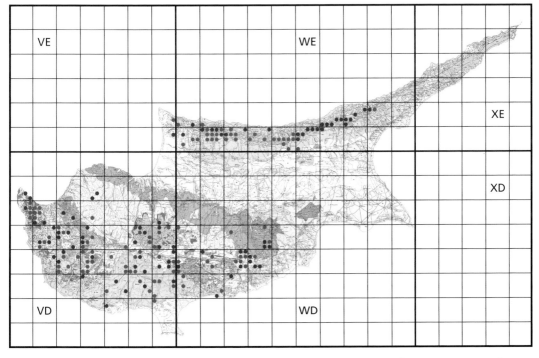

Neotinea maculata

12 Ophrys alasiatica
KREUTZ, SEGERS & H. WALRAVEN

Alasia-Ragwurz

Jour. Eur. Orch. 34 (3): 480 & 481 (2002)

Beschreibung

Schlanke, meist kräftige und hochwüchsige Pflanze, 30 bis 50 cm hoch. Laubblätter bläulichgrün, die unteren breit bis länglich-lanzettlich, am Grunde rosettig gehäuft, die oberen schmal-lanzettlich. Blütenstand verlängert und locker, mit 6 bis 12 mittelgroßen bis großen Blüten. Sepalen in der Grundfarbe hellgrün, selten weisslich, eiförmig-lanzettlich, abstehend bis nach vorne gebogen, das mittlere nach vorne gebogen. Seitliche Sepalen zweifarbig, im oberen Teil grünlich, im unteren Teil rötlich bis purpurn gefärbt, meist leicht nach vorne gerichtet. Petalen eiförmig-lanzettlich, olivgrün bis purpurn oder rosa, am Rande meist gewellt. Lippe eiförmig, rundlich bis oval, ungeteilt, schwach gewölbt, sehr selten schwach dreilappig, mit meist zurückgeschlagenen Rändern, im oberen Teil schwach gehöckert, hellbraun bis rötlichbraun gefärbt, am Rande meist sehr deutlich mit einem gelblichen Rand versehen. Mal aus zwei parallelen Streifen bestehend oder in der Form einer H-Zeichnung, meistens bläulich bis purpurn mit einem weissen Rand. Anhängsel sehr klein, gelb, leicht vorwärts gerichtet.

Standort

Lichte Nadelwälder, in und am Rande von Gebüschen, Waldränder, Straßengräben, grasiges Ödland, Magerrasen, Macchien und Phrygana; auf trockenen bis mäßig feuchten, kalkreichen Böden.

Blütezeit

Von Mitte Februar bis Mitte (Ende) März.

Höhenverbreitung

Von der Küste bis 700 m.

Gesamtverbreitung

Endemische Art von Zypern.

Verbreitung auf Zypern

Nur im mittleren Süden und südwestlicher Teil der Insel verbreitet.

Bemerkungen

Die früh blühende *Ophrys alasiatica* mit ihren mittelgroßen bis großen Blüten wurde 2002 von KREUTZ, SEGERS & WALRAVEN neu beschrieben. Davor wurden Pflanzen der Art mit verschiedenen Namen versehen (unter anderem mit *Ophrys aesculapiiformis* (Arbeitsname) in G. & K. MORSCHEK, 1996) oder verschiedenen anderen Arten wie *Ophrys sintenisii* (PAULUS & GACK, 1990a) bzw. *Ophrys aesculapii* (WOOD, 1980; DE LANGHE & D'HOSE, 1982) zugeordnet oder als Hybride zwischen *Ophrys mammosa* und *Ophrys transhyrcana* (*Ophrys morio*) angesehen (WOOD, 1985).

Ophrys alasiatica ist eine sehr stattliche Pflanze. Die Pflanzen sind meist hochwüchsig, kräftig und vielblütig. Die Blüten gleichen denen von *Ophrys aesculapii* RENZ, denn die Lippe hat fast immer einen deutlichen, ziemlich breiten gelben Rand. Pflanzen mit einem braunen Rand kommen jedoch auch vor. Die Malzeichnung besteht aus zwei parallelen, meistens bläulich bis purpurn gefärbten Streifen oder einer H-Zeichnung, die von einem weissen Rand umgeben ist.

An vielen Standorten, wie zum Beispiel in der weiteren Umgebung von Mathikoloni im mittleren Süden der Insel, bildet sie Anfang März größere Populationen blühender Pflanzen. Hier wird sie nicht selten von *Ophrys iricolor* und *Ophrys lapethica* begleitet. Auch in der Umgebung von Choulou, im Südwesten Zyperns, hat *Ophrys alasiatica* reich besetzte Fundorte. Viele stattliche Exemplare wachsen hier an vielen Stellen in den aufgelassenen Wein- und Olivenhainen, meist von *Ophrys morio* und *Ophrys mammosa* begleitet.

Gefährdung

Ophrys alasiatica ist auf Zypern vor allem im mittleren Süden weit verbreitet und nicht selten. Sie ist deshalb als nicht gefährdet einzustufen.

Hybriden

Mit *Ophrys sicula* und *Ophrys umbilicata* (*Ophrys xlefkarensis* SEGERS & H. WALRAVEN).

Bemerkungen zu der Verbreitungskarte

Die meisten bei HANSEN, KREUTZ & U. & D. RÜCKBRODT (1990) als *Ophrys sphegodes* s.l. angegeben Funde wurden in diesem Buch in die Verbreitungskarte von *Ophrys alasiatica* aufgenommen, weil aus der Pflanzenbeschreibung deutlich hervorgeht, dass es sich mit Sicherheit um Funde dieser Art handelt.

Mathikoloni-Apsiou, 5.3.2002

Mathikoloni-Apsiou, 5.3.2002

Ophrys alasiatica

KREUTZ, SEGERS & H. WALRAVEN

Alasian Ophrys

Jour. Eur. Orch. 34 (3): 480 & 481 (2002)

Description

Slender, mostly tall and vigorous plant, 30 to 50 cm tall. Foliage leaves bluish green, lower leaves broadly to oblong-lanceolate, forming a rosette at the base, upper leaves narrowly lanceolate. Inflorescence elongated and lax, with 6 to 12 medium-sized to large flowers. Base colour of sepals light green, rarely whitish, ovate-lanceolate, spreading to bent forwards, dorsal sepal bent forwards. Lateral sepals bi-coloured, greenish in upper part, reddish to purple in lower part, usually slightly directed forwards. Petals ovate-lanceolate, olive-green to purple or pink, mostly wavy at the edges. Labellum ovate, roundish to oval, undivided, slightly domed, very rarely slightly three-lobed, mostly with reflexed edges, slight protuberances in upper part, light brown to reddish brown, mostly very distinct yellow margin at edge. Marking consists of two parallel stripes or an H-shape, usually bluish to purple with a white margin. Appendage very small, yellow, slightly directed forwards.

Habitat

Light coniferous woods, in and at the margins of shrublands, edges of forests, roadside embankments, grassy wasteland, neglected grasslands, maquis and phrygana; on arid to moderately moist, calcareous soils.

Flowering time

From mid-February to mid- (late) March.

Altitude distribution

From sea level to 700 m.

Overall distribution

Endemic species of Cyprus.

Distribution on Cyprus

Only distributed in the central southern and western parts of the island.

Remarks

The early-flowering *Ophrys alasiatica* with its medium-sized to large flowers was redescribed in 2002 by KREUTZ, SEGERS & WALRAVEN. Earlier, the plants of this species had been given various names (such as *Ophrys aesculapiiformis* (preliminary name) in G. & K. MORSCHEK, 1996) or had been classified under widely varying species such as *Ophrys sintenisii* (PAULUS & GACK, 1990a) and *Ophrys aesculapii* (WOOD, 1980; DE LANGHE & D'HOSE, 1982) or regarded as hybrid between *Ophrys mammosa* and *Ophrys transhyrcana* (*Ophrys morio*) (WOOD, 1985).

Ophrys alasiatica is a very stately plant. The plants are mostly tall, vigorous and many-flowered. The flowers resemble those of *Ophrys aesculapii* RENZ, as the labellum almost always has a distinct, fairly wide yellow edge. Plants with a brown edge also occur however. The speculum marking consists of two parallel stripes or an H-shape, usually bluish to purple, surrounded by a white edge.

At many habitats, for example in the area around Mathikoloni in the central southern part of the island, it forms large populations of flowering plants in early March. On this sites *Ophrys alasiatica* is often accompanied by *Ophrys iricolor* und *Ophrys lapethica*. Also near Choulou, in the southwest of Cyprus, *Ophrys alasiatica* is very abundant. A lot of vigorous plants grow there on many places in abandoned vineyards and olive groves, there mostly accompanied by *Ophrys morio* and *Ophrys mammosa*.

Threats

Ophrys alasiatica is widely distributed and not rare on Cyprus, particularly in the central southern part of the island. It can therefore be categorized as not threatened.

Hybrids

With *Ophrys sicula* and *Ophrys umbilicata* (*Ophrys xlefkarensis* SEGERS & H. WALRAVEN).

Remarks concerning the distribution map

Most of the findings made by HANSEN, KREUTZ & U. & D. RÜCKBRODT (1990) concerning *Ophrys sphegodes* s.l., have been incorporated into the distribution map of *Ophrys alasiatica* in this book, as it is clear from the plant description that these findings undoubtedly concern this species.

Mathikoloni-Apsiou, 5.3.2002

Mathikoloni-Fasoulla, 20.3.2002

Kantou-Souni, 13.3.2002

Choulou, 12.3.2002

Vavla, 6.3.2002

Choulou, 12.3.2002

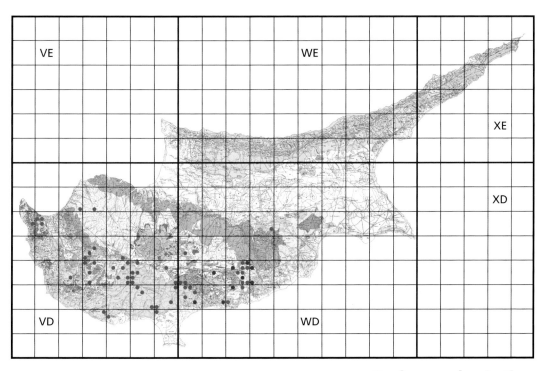

Ophrys alasiatica

13 Ophrys herae
Frühe Spinnen-Ragwurz

M. Hirth & H. Spaeth

Mitteilungsbl. Arbeitskr. Heim. Orch.
Baden-Württ. 24 (1): 6 (1992)

Synonyme

Ophrys pseudomammosa Renz (pro hybr.), Repert. Spec. Nov. Regni Veg. 25: 262 (1928); *Ophrys janrenzii* M. Hirth, Jahresber. Naturwiss. Vereins Wuppertal 55: 170 & 171 (2002); *Ophrys aranifera* forma *oodicheila* Renz, Repert. Spec. Nov. Regni Veg. 25: 248 (1928); *Ophrys sphegodes* subsp. *oodicheila* (Renz) A. Riechelmann, Jour. Eur. Orch. 36 (2): 533 (2004).

Beschreibung

Schlanke Pflanze, 20 bis 50 cm hoch, mit 3 bis 8 Blüten. Laubblätter bläulichgrün, die unteren breitlanzettlich, am Grunde rosettig gehäuft, die oberen linealisch-lanzettlich. Blüten klein bis mittelgroß. Sepalen länglich-eiförmig, (hell)grün bis gelblichgrün, die seitlichen leicht zurückgeschlagen, die untere Hälfte der Sepalen meist schwach rosa bis rötlich überlaufen oder rosa gefleckt. Mittleres Sepalblatt länglich, schmaler als die seitlichen Sepalen, aufgerichtet. Petalen lanzettlich, am Rande meist schwach gewellt, gelblichgrün, schwach purpurn überlaufen. Lippe klein bis mittelgroß, oval bis längsoval, ungeteilt, ganzrandig, gehöckert, gewölbt, an den Rändern stark behaart, rötlichbraun; Seitenränder bisweilen heller (gelblich bis gelblichbraun) gefärbt. Höcker an der Innenseite kahl, an der Aussenseite behaart. Mal H-förmig oder aus zwei parallelen Linien bestehend, stahlblau bis purpurviolett, mit hellem, weisslichem Rand. Anhängsel klein, gelblich, abwärts gerichtet.

Biotop

Aufgelassene Terrassen, Straßenränder, Ödland, Gebüschränder und lichte Kiefern- und Pinienwälder; auf trockenen bis wechselfeuchten, basenreichen bis kalkreichen Böden.

Blütezeit

Anfang Februar bis Mitte (Ende) März.

Höhenverbreitung

Von der Küste bis 700 m.

Gesamtverbreitung

Kreta, Korfu, Ionische und Ostägäische Inseln, Samos, Griechisches Festland und Zypern.

Verbreitung auf Zypern

Die seltene Art ist hauptsächlich im mittleren Süden der Insel verbreitet.

Bemerkungen

Auf Zypern wachsen Pflanzen, die *Ophrys herae* besonders nahe kommen. Es sind mittelgroße, schlanke und sehr früh blühende Pflanzen mit kleinen bis mittelgroßen Blüten, die zwischen der mitteleuropäischen *Ophrys sphegodes* und *Ophrys mammosa* vermitteln, und die früher meist zu *Ophrys sphegodes* subsp. *sphegodes* gestellt wurden (Gumprecht, 1964; Wood, 1985). Auf Zypern blühen diese Pflanzen schon ab Anfang Februar als erster Vertreter des *Ophrys sphegodes-mammosa* Komplexes. Aus diesem Grund wurden diese Pflanzen in diesem Buch zu *Ophrys herae* gestellt. Durch Bestäubungsversuche sollte aber untersucht werden, ob die zypriotischen Pflanzen mit der typischen *Ophrys herae* von Samos, die dort als Bestäuber *Andrena thoracica* hat, übereinstimmen.

Ophrys herae wurde 1992 von Hirth & Spaeth von Samos als eine endemische Art mit vermutlich hybridogenem Ursprung beschrieben. Diese Art ist wahrscheinlich identisch mit *Ophrys pseudomammosa*, die von Renz (1928) von der Insel Korfu als wahrscheinliche Hybride zwischen *Ophrys sphegodes* s.l. und *Ophrys mammosa* beschrieben wurde. Delforge (1992) ergänzte die Originalbeschreibung von *Ophrys herae* und erweiterte das Verbreitungsgebiet dieser Art mit Korfu, den anderen Ionischen Inseln, dem griechischen Festland, einigen weiteren Ostägäischen Inseln, Kreta und Zypern, wobei er *Ophrys pseudomammosa* als Hybride zwischen *Ophrys herae* und *Ophrys cephalonica* bewertete. Weil nicht mehr mit Sicherheit gesagt werden kann, was Renz seinerzeit unter *Ophrys pseudomammosa* verstanden und beschrieben hat, wurde der Name *Ophrys herae* (obwohl viel später beschrieben) beibehalten.

Vor allem entlang der Straße zwischen Pentalia und Kolineia südlich von Lefkosia und in der weiteren Umgebung von Kato Drys ist *Ophrys herae* relativ häufig. Wood (1985) hat *Ophrys herae* auch zwischen Vavla und Kato Drys beobachtet. Er merkte an, dass diese Pflanzen einige Merkmale von *Ophrys mammosa* aufwiesen und bestimmte diese Pflanzen damals als *Ophrys sphegodes* subsp. *sphegodes*.

Zusammenfassend kann gesagt werden, dass die zypriotischen Pflanzen *Ophrys herae* sehr nahe stehen, und dass aber weitere Untersuchungen erforderlich sind, um den Status dieser Pflanzen zu klären.

Gefährdung

Ophrys herae ist auf Zypern selten und fast ausschliesslich im mittleren Süden verbreitet. Weil viele Fundorte an Straßenböschungen liegen, ist sie durch Mahd und Verbreiterung der Straßen stark gefährdet.

Hybriden

Nicht mit Sicherheit nachgewiesen.

Ophrys herae
Early Flowering Spider Ophrys

M. Hirth & H. Spaeth

Mitteilungsbl. Arbeitskr. Heim. Orch.
Baden-Württ. 24 (1): 6 (1992)

Synonyms

Ophrys pseudomammosa Renz (pro hybr.) Repert. Spec. Nov. Regni Veg. 25: 262 (1928); *Ophrys janrenzii* M. Hirth, Jahresber. Naturwiss. Vereins Wuppertal 55: 170 & 171 (2002); *Ophrys aranifera* forma *oodicheila* Renz, Repert. Spec. Nov. Regni Veg. 25: 248 (1928); *Ophrys sphegodes* subsp. *oodicheila* (Renz) A. Riechelmann, Jour. Eur. Orch. 36 (2): 533 (2004).

Description

Slender plant, 20 to 50 cm tall, with 3 to 8 flowers. Foliage leaves bluish green, lower leaves broadly lanceolate, forming a basal rosette, upper leaves linear-lanceolate. Flowers small to medium-sized. Sepals oblong-ovate, (light) green to yellowish green, lateral sepals slightly reflexed, lower half of sepals mostly a faint pink to reddish tinged or with pink spots. Dorsal sepal oblong, narrower than lateral sepals, erect. Petals lanceolate, mostly slightly wavy at edges, yellowish green, with faint purple tinges. Labellum small to medium-sized, oval to oblong-oval, undivided, entire, with protuberances, convex, strongly pubescent at edges, reddish brown; margins sometimes lighter coloured (yellowish to yellowish brown). Interior of protuberances glabrous, exterior pubescent. Marking H-shaped or consisting of two parallel lines, steel-blue to purple-violet, with a light whitish edge. Appendage small, yellowish, directed downwards.

Habitat

Neglected terraces, roadside edges, wasteland, shrubland edges and light coniferous woods; on arid to sometimes moist, base-rich to calcareous soils.

Flowering time

Early February to mid- (late) March.

Altitude distribution

From sea level to 700 m.

Overall distribution

Crete, Corfu, the Ionian and Eastern Aegean islands, Samos, Greek mainland and Cyprus.

Distribution on Cyprus

This rare species is primarily distributed in the central southern part of the island.

Remarks

In Cyprus plants occur which strongly resemble *Ophrys herae*. They are medium-sized, slender and very early-flowering plants with small to medium-sized flowers, which resembles between the Central European *Ophrys sphegodes* and *Ophrys mammosa* and in the past was mostly identified as *Ophrys sphegodes* subsp. *sphegodes* (Gumprecht, 1964; Wood, 1985). On Cyprus it is already in flower in early February as the first representative of the *Ophrys* sphegodes-mammosa complex. For this reason these plants have been listed under *Ophrys herae* in this book. Investigation is necessary by a study of pollination, to determine whether the Cypriot plants correspond to the typical *Ophrys herae* of Samos, which has *Andrena thoracica* as pollinator there.

Hirth & Spaeth described *Ophrys herae* from Samos in 1992, as an endemic species of possible hybridogenic origin. This species is probably identical with *Ophrys pseudomammosa* a species that was described by Renz (1928) as a possible hybrid between *Ophrys mammosa* and *Ophrys sphegodes* s.l. on the island of Corfu. Delforge (1992) complemented the original description and enlarged the distribution area of this species to include Corfu, the other Ionian islands, the Greek mainland, some other Eastern Aegean islands, Crete and Cyprus, and he also rated *Ophrys pseudomammosa* as a hybrid between *Ophrys herae* and *Ophrys cephalonica*. As it is no longer possible to establish with certainty what Renz meant and described as *Ophrys pseudomammosa*, the name of *Ophrys herae* (although descibed much later) was therefore chosen for this species.

Along the road between Pentalia and Kolineia south of Lefkosia in particular, and in the area around Kato Drys, *Ophrys herae* is relatively abundant. Wood (1985) has also seen *Ophrys herae* between Vavla and Kato Drys. He notes that these plants show some characteristics of *Ophrys mammosa* and identified these plants as *Ophrys sphegodes* subsp. *sphegodes*.

Thus as described, the Cypriot plants have a lot in common with *Ophrys herae*, nevertheless further investigations are necessary to clear the taxonomical status of the Cypriot plants.

Threats

Ophrys herae is mainly distributed in the central south and rare. As many locations are situated on roadside embankments, it is heavily threatened by mowing and road-widening.

Hybrids

Not yet confirmed.

Kofinou, 10.3.2002

Kato Drys, 6.3.2002

Kofinou, 10.3.2002

Kayalar-Sadrazamköy, 14.3.2002

Karman-Kayalar, 14.3.2002

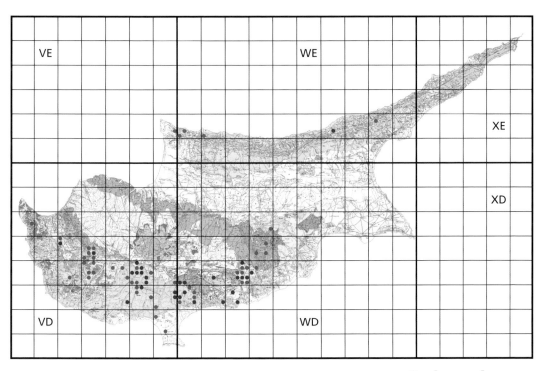

Ophrys herae

14 Ophrys hystera
Spätblühende Busen-Ragwurz

KREUTZ & R. PETER

Jour. Eur. Orch. 30 (1): 128 (1998).
(pre-print 1997)

Basionym

Ophrys mammosa subsp. *serotina* B. & E. WILLING, Mitteilungsbl. Arbeitskr. Heim. Orch. Baden-Württ. 17 (4): 525 (1985).

Beschreibung

Schlanke Pflanze, 30 bis 70 cm hoch. Untere Laubblätter lanzettlich, am Grunde rosettig gehäuft, die oberen schmal-lanzettlich. Blütenstand gestreckt und ziemlich locker, mit 2 bis 9 großen Blüten. Sepalen in der Grundfarbe olivgrün, untere Hälfte meist rotbraun überlaufen, aufrecht bis schwach abstehend, eiförmig-lanzettlich. Petalen eiförmig-lanzettlich, überwiegend gelblichgrün, selten purpurn angelaufen, am Rande meist schwach gewellt. Lippe eiförmig bis (länglich) oval, ungeteilt, stark gewölbt mit zurückgeschlagenen Rändern, im oberen Teil stark gehökkert (Höcker innen kahl, aussen behaart), hellbraun bis rötlichbraun gefärbt. Mal aus zwei parallelen Streifen bestehend oder in der Form einer H-Zeichnung, meist bläulich bis purpurn mit weissem Rand. Anhängsel sehr klein, meist gelblich, leicht vorwärts gerichtet.

Biotop

Lichte Kiefernwälder, Gebüsch- und Waldränder, Straßenböschungen, Phrygana und Macchien; auf trockenen bis mäßig feuchten, kalkreichen Böden.

Blütezeit

Von (Mitte) Ende März bis Ende April.

Höhenverbreitung

Von der Küste bis 600 m.

Gesamtverbreitung

Östliches Mittelmeergebiet (Griechenland, Südtürkei und Zypern).

Verbreitung auf Zypern

Die Art ist auf Zypern sehr selten, und wegen der späten Blütezeit wurde sie nur selten beobachtet. Vor allem in der weiteren Umgebung des Salzsees bei Larnaka und im Westen der Insel wurde die Art nachgewiesen. G. & K. MORSCHEK (1996) bilden in ihrem Buch auf Seite 133 eine *Ophrys hystera* ab.

Bemerkungen

Der Erstnachweis von *Ophrys hystera* auf Zypern stammt vermutlich von FORST (1995). In der ersten Aprilwoche fand er aufblühende Pflanzen an Standorten, wo Ende März *Ophrys morio* und *Ophrys mammosa* bereits im Abblühen waren. Diese Pflanzen waren eindeutig als *Ophrys hystera* anzusprechen, und sie wiesen keinerlei Merkmale von *Ophrys morio* auf. Nach FORST (1995) entsprachen diese Pflanzen *Ophrys mammosa*, wie sie aus Griechenland bekannt sind.

Ophrys hystera ist vor allem an ihrer späten Blütezeit, ihrem hohen Wuchs und ihren sehr großen, weit auseinander stehenden Blüten leicht zu erkennen. Ausserdem ist der Mittellappen der Blüte meist spitz. *Ophrys mammosa*, die auch auf Zypern vorkommt, blüht etwa einen Monat früher, hat aber einen viel gedrungeneren Wuchs und kleinere Blüten mit einer mehr rundlichen Lippe.

Besonders typische Pflanzen kommen am Salzsee bei Larnaka vor. Bereits Ende März öffnen sich hier die ersten Blüten. Das Gebiet um den Salzsee ist sehr weitläufig, und *Ophrys hystera* wächst in diesem Gebiet nur vereinzelt und sehr zerstreut im Schatten und am Rande einzelner Gebüsche. Jährlich kommen an diesem Standort etwa zwanzig bis fünfzig Pflanzen zur Blüte.

Gefährdung

Obwohl *Ophrys hystera* auf Zypern selten ist, ist sie kaum gefährdet. Nur am Fundort bei Larnaka sind die Pflanzen durch Pflücken, Waldrodung, intensivere Bewirtschaftung und durch Bebauung bedroht.

Hybriden

Nicht nachgewiesen.

Bemerkungen zu der Verbreitungskarte

Mit Sicherheit ist *Ophrys hystera* viel weiter verbreitet als aus der Verbreitungskarte hervorgeht, einerseits, weil sie auf Zypern erst vor kurzem als eigenständige Art identifiziert wurde, andererseits weil sie wegen ihrer späten Blütezeit nur selten beobachtet wurde. Ausserdem sind zur dieser Zeit meist nur wenig Orchideensucher auf Zypern.

Larnaka (Salt lake), 21.3.2002   Larnaka (Salt lake), 21.3.2002

Ophrys hystera
Late Flowering Mammose Ophrys

KREUTZ & R. PETER

Jour. Eur. Orch. 30 (1): 128 (1998).
(pre-print 1997)

Basionym

Ophrys mammosa subsp. *serotina* B. & E. WILLING, Mitteilungsbl. Arbeitskr. Heim. Orch. Baden-Württ. 17 (4): 525 (1985).

Description

Slender plant, 30 to 70 cm tall. Lower foliage leaves lanceolate, forming a rosette at the base, upper leaves narrowly lanceolate. Inflorescence elongated and fairly lax, with 2 to 9 large flowers. Base colour of sepals olive-green, lower half mostly with red-brown tinges, erect to slightly spreading, ovate-lanceolate. Petals ovate-lanceolate, predominantly yellowish green, rarely with purple tinges; mostly slightly wavy at edges. Labellum ovate to (oblong-) oval, undivided, strongly convex with reflexed margins, and large protuberances in the upper part (interior glabrous, exterior pubescent), light brown to reddish brown. Marking consists of two parallel stripes or an H-shape, mostly bluish to purple with a white margin. Appendage very small, mostly yellowish, slightly directed forwards.

Habitat

Light coniferous woods, shrubland and forest edges, roadside embankments, phrygana and maquis; on arid to moderately moist, calcareous soils.

Flowering time

From (mid-) late March to late April.

Altitude distribution

From sea level to 600 m.

Overall distribution

Eastern Mediterranean region (Greece, southern Turkey and Cyprus).

Distribution on Cyprus

The species is very rare on Cyprus and rarely seen because of its late flowering time. The species has been reported, particularly near Larnaka, around the salt lake, and in de western part of the island. G. & K. MORSCHEK (1996) show *Ophrys hystera* in their book on page 133.

Remarks

The first evidence of *Ophrys hystera* on Cyprus probably originates from FORST (1995). In the first week of April he found blossoming plants at locations where *Ophrys morio* and *Ophrys mammosa* were already starting to wither in late March. These plants could clearly be distinguished as *Ophrys hystera* and they had no characteristics whatsoever of *Ophrys morio*. According to FORST (1995), these plants corresponded with *Ophrys mammosa*, as it is known from Greece.

Ophrys hystera can particularly be recognized by its late flowering time, its tall growth and its very large, very laxly arranged flowers. Also, the dorsal sepal of the flowers is usually acuminate. *Ophrys mammosa*, which also occurs on Cyprus, flowers about a month earlier, has also a much more compact growth and smaller flowers with a rounder labellum.

Particularly typical plants occur at the Larnaka salt lake. In late March, the first flowers are already starting to open there. The area around the salt lake is immense, and *Ophrys hystera* grows sporadically and at intervals throughout this area, in the shade and at the edges of several shrubby areas. About twenty to fifty plants bloom at this site each year.

Threats

Although *Ophrys hystera* is rare on Cyprus, it is not really threatened. Only at the location near Larnaka are the plants threatened by culling, wood-clearance, intensified cultivation and building development.

Hybrids

Unconfirmed.

Remarks concerning the distribution map

Ophrys hystera is certainly much more widely distributed than the distribution map shows, partly because it has only recently been identified as an independent species for Cyprus, and also because it is rarely recorded due to its late flowering time, as few orchid observers visit Cyprus at that time.

Larnaka (Salt lake), 21.3.2002

Larnaka (Salt lake), 21.3.2002

Larnaka (Salt lake), 21.3.2002

Larnaka (Salt lake), 21.3.2002

Larnaka (Salt lake), 21.3.2002   Larnaka (Salt lake), 21.3.2002

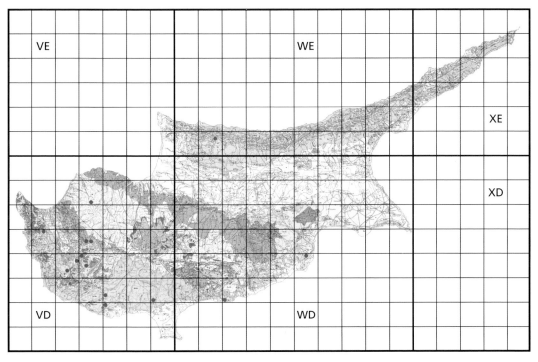

Ophrys hystera

15

Ophrys mammosa

DESFONTAINES

Frühblühende Busen-Ragwurz

Ann. Mus. Hist. Nat. 10: 222 (1807)

Synonyme

Ophrys aranifera subsp. *mammosa* (DESFONTAINES) Soó, Notizbl. Bot. Gart. Berlin-Dahlem 9 (88): 907 (1926); *Ophrys sphegodes* subsp. *mammosa* (DESFONTAINES) Soó, Acta Bot. Acad. Sci. Hung. 16 (3/4): 383 (1970, publ. 1971).

Beschreibung

Schlanke und hochwüchsige Pflanze, 20 bis 50 cm hoch. Laubblätter bläulichgrün, die unteren breit-lanzettlich, am Grunde rosettig gehäuft, die oberen schmal-lanzettlich. Blütenstand verlängert, ziemlich locker mit 4 bis 8 mittelgroßen Blüten. Sepalen in der Grundfarbe grün bis hellgrün, untere Hälfte rot überlaufen, aufrecht bis abstehend, eiförmig-lanzettlich. Petalen eiförmig-lanzettlich, gelblichgrün bis purpurn, am Rande meist schwach gewellt. Lippe eiförmig bis oval, ungeteilt, stark gewölbt, flach ausgebreitet, meist mit zurückgeschlagenen Rändern, im oberen Teil stark gehöckert (Höcker innen kahl, aussen behaart), hellbraun bis rötlichbraun gefärbt. Mal aus zwei parallelen Streifen bestehend oder H-förmig, meistens bläulich bis purpurn. Anhängsel sehr klein, gelb oder braun, leicht vorwärts gerichtet.

Standort

Lichte Nadelwälder, Gebüsch- und Waldränder, Straßengräben, grasiges Ödland, Magerrasen, aufgelassene Olivenhaine, Macchien und Phrygana; auf trokkenen bis mäßig feuchten, kalkreichen Böden.

Blütezeit

Von (Anfang) Mitte Februar bis Ende März.

Höhenverbreitung

Von der Küste bis 800 m.

Gesamtverbreitung

Das Areal von *Ophrys mammosa* umfasst das östliche Mittelmeergebiet, nämlich die Balkanhalbinsel (Montenegro, Mazedonien, Bulgarien, Albanien, Griechenland), die Ägäis, Kleinasien (Türkei, Nordsyrien, die Krim und Zypern) und Aserbaidschan (D. & U. RÜCKBRODT, GÜGEL, & ZAISS, 1997), wo sie ihre östliche Verbreitungsgrenze erreicht.

Verbreitung auf Zypern

Im Westen, Süden und Norden der Insel verbreitet. Schöne Bestände gibt es nordöstlich von Pafos und in der weiteren Umgebung von Kourdaka. Dort bildet die Art in den weitläufigen Phrygana-Gebieten stellenweise größere Populationen.

Bemerkungen

Ophrys mammosa ist eng mit *Ophrys hystera* verwandt, unterscheidet sich jedoch von dieser Art durch kleinere mehr rundliche Blüten, eine eiförmige bis ovale, ungeteilte, stark gewölbte Lippe, die im obe-ren Teil stark gehöckert (Höcker innen kahl, aussen stark behaart) ist, durch den viel kürzeren Konnektivfortsatz, eine frühere Blütezeit und einen gedrungeneren Wuchs.

WOOD (1985) bemerkte, dass die untere Hälfte der seitlichen Sepalen von *Ophrys mammosa* auf Zypern einen größeren Rotanteil aufweist, was auch bei *Ophrys morio* festgestellt wurde.

In der Umgebung von Choulou im Westen Zyperns, wo *Ophrys mammosa* an mehreren Stellen individuenreiche Populationen bildet, wachsen einige bemerkenswerte Pflanzen. Diese haben auf der Lippe kein H-förmiges Mal, sondern ein größeres hellblaues Feld. Sie sind unter dem Arbeitsnamen *Ophrys mammosa* var. 'planimaculata' bekannt. Diese Pflanzen wachsen in einem Straßengraben, der regelmäßig vom angrenzenden Acker aus gedüngt wird, was möglicherweise die abweichende Lippenfarbe verursacht hat.

WOOD (1985) bemerkte, dass die untere Hälfte der seitlichen Sepalen von *Ophrys mammosa* auf Zypern einen größeren Rotanteil aufweisen als in ihrem übrigen Verbreitungsgebiet.

Gefährdung

Ophrys mammosa ist auf Zypern relativ selten und daher gefährdet. Sie ist vor allem durch den zunehmenden Tourismus (Bebauung), Ausdehnung der Siedlungen und intensivere Bewirtschaftung stark zurückgegangen.

Hybriden

Mit *Ophrys kotschyi* (*Ophrys ×kreutziana* P. DELFORGE) und *Ophrys morio*.

176   Kofinou, 14.2.1995

Ophrys mammosa

DESFONTAINES

Early Flowering Mammose Ophrys

Ann. Mus. Hist. Nat. 10: 222 (1807)

Synonyms

Ophrys aranifera subsp. *mammosa* (DESFONTAINES) Soó, Notizbl. Bot. Gart. Berlin-Dahlem 9 (88): 907 (1926); *Ophrys sphegodes* subsp. *mammosa* (DESFONTAINES) Soó, Acta Bot. Acad. Sci. Hung. 16 (3/4): 383 (1970, publ. 1971).

Description

Slender and tall plant, 20 to 50 cm. Foliage leaves bluish green, lower leaves broadly lanceolate, forming a rosette at base, upper leaves narrowly lanceolate. Inflorescence elongated, fairly lax with 4 to 8 medium-sized to large flowers. Base colour of sepals light green, lower half tinged with red, erect to spreading, ovate-lanceolate. Petals ovate-lanceolate, yellowish green to purple, mostly faintly wavy at edges. Labellum ovate to oval, undivided, strongly convex, spreading, mostly with reflexed margins, with large protuberances in the upper part (interior glabrous, exterior pubescent), light brown to reddish-brown tinged. Marking consists of two parallel stripes or an H-shape, mostly bluish to purple. Appendage very small, yellow or brown, directed slightly forwards.

Habitat

Light coniferous woods, shrubland and forest edges, roadside embankments, grassy wasteland, neglected meadows and abandoned olive groves, maquis and phrygana; on arid to moderately moist, calcareous soils.

Flowering time

From early (mid-) February to late March.

Altitude distribution

From sea level to 800 m.

Overall distribution

The distribution area of *Ophrys mammosa* covers the Eastern Mediterranean region, namely the Balkan Peninsula (Montenegro, Macedonia, Bulgaria, Albania, Greece), the Aegean, Asia Minor (Turkey, northern Syria, the Crimea and Cyprus) and Azerbaidjan (D. & U. RÜCKBRODT, GÜGEL, & ZAISS, 1997), where it probably has its easternmost distribution boundary.

Distribution on Cyprus

Primarily distributed throughout the western, southern and northern parts of the island. Beautiful populations can be found northeast of Pafos and in the area around Kourdaka. The species forms large populations there in places, in the vast phrygana fields.

Remarks

Ophrys mammosa shows a strong relationship to *Ophrys hystera*, but can however be distinguished from this species by smaller, rounder flowers, an ovate to oval, undivided, strongly convex labellum, which has large protuberances in the upper part (interior glabrous, exterior strongly pubescent), by the much shorter connective extension, the earlier flowering time and more compact growth.

WOOD (1985) remarks that the lower half of the lateral sepals of *Ophrys mammosa* on Cyprus possess a much redder hue, which has also been established for *Ophrys morio*.

In the vicinity of Choulou in the west of Cyprus, where *Ophrys mammosa* forms individual-rich populations at several places, some remarkable plants grow. These plants have no H-shaped marking on the labellum, but instead, a large light blue panel. They are known under the preliminary name of *Ophrys mammosa* var. '*planimaculata*'. These plants grow on a roadside embankment, which receives regular fertilisation from a neighbouring field, which may have led to this aberrant labellum marking.

WOOD (1985) remarks that of the populations of *Ophrys mammosa*, the lower half of the sepals of these plants have a larger amount of red than in the rest of of distribution area of *Ophrys mammosa*.

Threats

Ophrys mammosa is relatively rare on Cyprus and is therefore threatened. It has declined considerably, mainly because of increasing tourism (building development), expansion of towns and intensified cultivation.

Hybrids

With *Ophrys kotschyi* (*Ophrys* ×*kreutziana* P. DELFORGE) and *Ophrys morio*.

Kofinou, 14.2.1995

Kayalar-Sadrazamköy, 14.3.2002

Kofinou, 14.2.1995

Choulou, 12.3.2002

Souni, 13.3.2002

Choulou, 12.3.2002

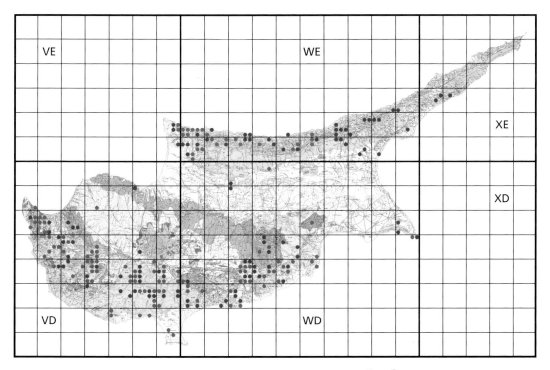

Ophrys mammosa

16

Ophrys morio
Dunkle Zypern-Ragwurz

H.F. Paulus & Kreutz

Orchid. Zyperns: 415 (2004)

Beschreibung

Kräftige und hochwüchsige Pflanze, 30 bis 70 cm hoch. Untere Laubblätter breit-lanzettlich, rosettig gehäuft, die oberen locker am Stängel verteilt und in tragblattartige Laubblätter übergehend. Blütenstand langgestreckt und sehr locker, 8- bis 20-blütig, die Blüten meist über eine Länge von zwei Dritteln am Stängel verteilt. Tragblätter lanzettlich, meist länger als der Fruchtknoten. Seitliche Sepalen meist kräftig zweifarbig, im oberen Teil grünlich, im unteren Teil rötlich bis dunkelpurpurn gefärbt, abstehend bis rückwärts gerichtet, lanzettlich. Petalen eiförmig-lanzettlich bis lang dreieckig, grünlich bis purpurn, am Rande leicht gewellt. Lippe ziemlich lang bis breit-eiförmig, meist stark dreilappig, konvex gewölbt, schwach oder selten ungehöckert, gelegentlich nach vorne allmählich schmaler werdend, dunkelbraun bis rötlichbraun mit einem in der Regel hellbraunen Basalfeld, das sich farblich von der dunkleren Lippe absetzt, am Rande dicht purpurn behaart. Mal aus zwei parallelen Streifen bestehend oder H-förmig, diese Streifen meistens bläulich bis purpurn. Konnektivfortsatz sehr lang und zugespitzt. Anhängsel klein und spitz, gelblich, abwärts gerichtet.

Standort

Lichte Nadelwälder, aufgelassene Terrassen, Macchien, Phrygana und Wiesenflächen; auf trockenen bis mäßig feuchten, kalkreichen Böden.

Blütezeit

Von (Anfang) Mitte Februar bis Ende März.

Höhenverbreitung

Von Meereshöhe bis 700 m Höhe.

Gesamtverbreitung

Nach dem heutigen Kenntnisstand nur auf Zypern und wahrscheinlich auch in der südlichen Türkei verbreitet.

Verbreitung auf Zypern

Weit verbreitet und stellenweise häufig. Vor allem in den mittleren Gebirgslagen im Norden (Umgebung von Alevkaya, Antiphonitis und Karpasia-Halbinsel) und Süden der Insel.

Bemerkungen

Ophrys morio wurde in diesem Buch neu beschrieben, weil die bisher von Zypern unter dem Namen *Ophrys transhyrcana* beschriebenen Pflanzen morphologisch nicht mit dieser Art übereinstimmen und mit *Andrena morio* auch einen anderen Bestäuber haben. In einem extra Artikel (in Vorbereitung) wird näher auf die morphologischen Unterschiede und die Gegenüberstellung mit den anderen Vertre-tern des *Ophrys sphegodes-mammosa* Komplexes näher und ausführlich eingegangen.

Ophrys morio unterscheidet sich von den anderen Vertretern des *Ophrys sphegodes-mammosa* Komplexes auf Zypern vor allem durch eine ziemlich lange, breit-eiförmige, konvex gewölbte, leicht gehökkerte und gelegentlich nach vorne allmählich schmaler werdende Lippe. Solche Blüten sind dann extrem dreilappig. Ausserdem hat *Ophrys morio* in der Regel ein hellbraunes Basalfeld, das sich farblich von der dunklen Lippe absetzt und die seitlichen Sepalen sind fast immer sehr kräftig zweifarbig.

Ophrys morio blüht etwa zur gleichen Zeit als *Ophrys mammosa* und *Ophrys alasiatica*. Ihre Blüten sind etwa so groß wie die von *Ophrys alasiatica* und *Ophrys mammosa*, aber kleiner als von *Ophrys hystera*. Sie ist im Februar/März in Zypern neben *Ophrys alasiatica* die dominierende und am weitesten verbreitete Art der *Ophrys sphegodes-mammosa* Gruppe und fällt vor allem durch ihre oft sehr hochwüchsige und kräftige Gestalt auf.

Während *Ophrys morio* nur auf Zypern und offenbar auch in der Südtürkei vorkommt, ist die nahe verwandte *Ophrys transhyrcana* von Nordisrael, über Libanon, Westjordanien, Westsyrien und die Süd- und Südosttürkei unt weiter ostwärts von den nördlichen Zagrosbergen (Iran) bis zu den Ufern des Kaspischen Meeres (Nordiran) und Süd-Turkmenistan (Kopeth-Dagh: locus typicus) verbreitet.

Gefährdung

Ophrys morio ist auf Zypern vor allem durch die Ausdehnung der Siedlungen und durch intensivere Bewirtschaftung ihrer Standorte zahlenmäßig stark zurückgegangen und deswegen ziemlich gefährdet.

Hybriden

Mit *Ophrys bornmuelleri* (*Ophrys* x*cailliauana* P. Delforge) und *Ophrys sicula* (*Ophrys* x*demangeana* P. Delforge). Ausserdem treten Individuen auf, die sehr an *Ophrys mammosa* erinnern und möglicherweise introgressiv beeinflusst sind.

Ophrys morio
Dark Cypriot Ophrys

H.F. Paulus & Kreutz

Orchid. Zyperns: 415 (2004)

Description

Tall vigorous plant, 30 to 70 cm in height. Lower foliage leaves broadly lanceolate, arranged in a rosette, upper leaves distributed laxly along stem and merging into bract-like foliage leaves. Inflorescence elongated and very lax, 8 to 20 flowers, which are often divided over two-thirds of the stem. Bracts lanceolate, mostly longer than ovary. Lateral sepals mostly strongly bi-coloured, upper part greenish, lower part reddish to dark purple, spreading to bending back, lanceolate. Petals ovate-lanceolate to oblong-triangular, greenish to purple, slightly wavy at edges. Labellum fairly long to broadly ovate, mostly strongly three-lobed, convexly arched, with slight or rarely no protuberances, occasionally gradually getting narrower towards apex, dark brown to reddish brown, reddish-brown with a generally light brown basal field, contrasting in colour with the dark labellum, covered in dense purple hairs at edges. Marking consisting of two parallel stripes or H-shaped, stripes mostly bluish to purple. Connective extension very long and pointed. Appendage small and acuminate, yellowish, directed downwards.

Habitat

Light pine woods, abandoned terraces, maquis, phrygana and meadows; on arid to moderately moist, calcareous soils.

Flowering time

From (early) mid-February to late March.

Altitude distribution

From sea level to 700 m.

Overall distribution

According to the current state of knowledge *Ophrys morio* occurs only on Cyprus and probably also in southern Turkey.

Distribution on Cyprus

Widespread, and here and there abundant. Especially distributed at medium-high mountainous altitudes (around Alevkaya, Antiphonitis and Karpasia peninsula) and in the south of the island.

Remarks

Ophrys morio was redescribed as the plants on Cyprus are not identical to the plants commonly described as *Ophrys transhyrcana* and moreover they have a different pollinator, namely *Andrena morio*. The morphologically differences and the comparison with the other representatives of the *Ophrys sphegodes-mammosa* species group will be discussed in an separate article (in prep.).

Ophrys morio can be distinguished from other representatives of the *Ophrys sphegodes-mammosa* species group on Cyprus primarily by a fairly long, wide-ovate, convexly rounded, slightly humped and occasionally gradually narrowing labellum. Such flowers are strongly three-lobed. *Ophrys morio* generally also has a light brown basal field, which contrasts in colour with the dark labellum and the lateral sepals are almost always very vigorously bi-coloured.

Ophrys morio flowers about the same time as *Ophrys mammosa* and *Ophrys alasiatica*. Its flowers are almost as large as those of *Ophrys alasiatica* and *Ophrys mammosa*, but smaller than those of *Ophrys hystera*. Besides *Ophrys alasiatica*, *Ophrys morio* is the dominant and most wide-spread species of the *Ophrys sphegodes-mammosa* group in February/March on Cyprus and usually stand out due to their often tall and vigorous form.

Whereas *Ophrys morio* only occurs on Cyprus and apparently also in southern Turkey, the closely related *Ophrys transhyrcana* is distributed from northern Israel, through Lebanon, western Jordan, western Syria and south and south-east Turkey, and more eastwards from the northern Zagros mountains (Iran) as far as the shores of the Caspian Sea (northern Iran) and southern Turkmenistan (Kopeth-Dagh: locus typicus).

Threats

The number of *Ophrys morio* plants has declined considerably on Cyprus due to the expansion of towns and intensifying cultivation of its habitats and is therefore fairly threatened.

Hybrids

With *Ophrys bornmuelleri* (*Ophrys* ×*cailliauana* P. Delforge) and *Ophrys sicula* (*Ophrys* ×*demangeana* P. Delforge). Individuals also occur which resemble *Ophrys mammosa* and are possibly introgressively influenced.

Choulou, 12.3.2002

Tochni, 13.3.2002

Souni, 13.3.2002

Alevkaya (Pentadactylos Range), 18.3.2002

Nata-Eledio, 12.3.2002

Kayalar-Karavas, 14.3.2002

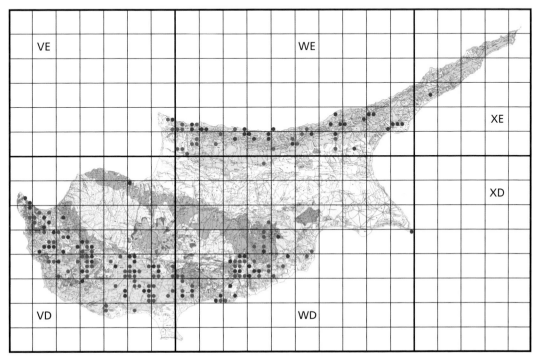

Ophrys morio

17

Ophrys apifera
Bienen-Ragwurz

Synonyme

Arachnitis apifera (HUDSON) HOFFMANN, Deutschl. Fl. ed. 2,2: 180 (1804); *Ophrys aquisgranensis* KALTENBACH, Fl. Aachen. Beckens: 519. tab. 7 (1845); *Ophrys austriaca* WIESBAUR ex DICHTL, Deutsche Bot. Monatsschr. 1: 148 (1883); *Ophrys apifera* var. *austriaca* (WIESBAUR ex DICHTL) BECK, Fl. Nieder-Österreich 1: 198 (1890); *Ophrys apifera* subsp. *austriaca* (WIESBAUR ex DICHTL) K. RICHTER, Pl. Eur. 1: 264 (1890); *Ophrys ripaensis* PORTA, Atti Acc. Rovereto, ser. 3 (11), fasc. 2: 7 (1905).

Beschreibung

Schlanke Pflanze, 15 bis 40 cm hoch. Stängel kräftig, aufrecht, hell- bis blassgrün. Laubblätter hell- bis dunkelgrün, die unteren in einer Rosette, lanzettlich und oft mit Frostschäden (treibt schon im Herbst die Grundblätter aus); die oberen länglich-lanzettlich, aufwärts gerichtet, stängelumfassend. Blütenstand locker und langgestreckt mit 3 bis 7 Blüten. Tragblätter hellgrün, lanzettlich, deutlich länger als der Fruchtknoten. Blüten mittelgross, schräg abstehend. Sepalen weiss, rosa bis dunkelrot, eiförmig-lanzettlich, abstehend bis zurückgeschlagen. Petalen sehr klein bis verlängert, meist grün, selten purpurn. Lippe am Grunde tief dreilappig. Mittellappen kastanienbraun, stark gewölbt, mit zurückgeschlagenen Rändern. Seitenlappen gehöckert, aussen dicht behaart. Malzeichnung fast das ganze Basalfeld umfassend, braun mit gelblichweisser Umrandung. Anhängsel gross, gelblichgrün, abwärts gerichtet. *Ophrys apifera* ist autogam.

Standort

Bevorzugt feuchte Wiesen mit Kopfbinsen in Meereshöhe (im Winter oft überschwemmt), weiter in Macchien, Phrygana, Ödland, ungedüngten Magerrasen, Weidearealen, Gebüsch- und Strassenrändern und in lichte Kiefern- und Pinienwäldern; auf trockenen bis wechselfeuchten, basenreichen Böden.

Blütezeit

Von (Mitte) Ende März bis Anfang Mai.

Höhenverbreitung

Von der Küste bis 900 m.

Gesamtverbreitung

Ophrys apifera ist in Europa von der meridionalen bis zur temperaten Zone verbreitet. Das Areal reicht von Irland bis Vorderasien (Türkei, Zypern, Syrien, Israel), nördlich bis Nordengland, die Niederlande und Norddeutschland und südlich bis Nordafrika; auch im Kaukasus, Nordirak und Nordiran.

Verbreitung auf Zypern

Die Art kommt auf Zypern sehr zerstreut vor und ist selten. Nur im Süden auf der Halbinsel Akrotiri ist sie relativ häufig. Dort wächst *Ophrys apifera* bevorzugt an feuchten Stellen, wie in Strassengräben und in binsenbewachsenen Wiesenflächen auf Meereshöhe. Leider werden diese Standorte immer weiter trockengelegt, wodurch die Anzahl der Pflanzen an vielen Stellen stark abnimmt. Im Norden ist *Ophrys apifera* sehr selten und bisher nur aus der Umgebung von Kyrenia und Yayla bekannt (VINEY, 1994).

Bemerkungen

Auf Zypern sind die Blüten von *Ophrys apifera* im Allgemeinen heller gefärbt als die der mitteleuropäischen Pflanzen. Bereits RENZ (1929) hat darauf hingewiesen. Im Mittelmeergebiet ist *Ophrys apifera* eher selten, und ihre Fundorte sind überwiegend schwächer besetzt. Mit Ausnahme der Akrotiri-Halbinsel bestehen die Populationen von *Ophrys apifera* auch auf Zypern meist nur aus wenigen Pflanzen. Weil *Ophrys apifera* autogam ist werden durch Inzucht Defekte vererbt, die zu Missbildungen führen können, wodurch Varianten in Blütenbau und Malzeichnung vorkommen. Auch auf Zypern gibt es zwei Varietäten, wobei *Ophrys apifera* var. *bicolor* (NAEGELI) E. NELSON und *Ophrys apifera* var. *chlorantha* (HEGETSCHW.) RICHTER im Westen der Insel bei Neo Chorio (Akamas), auf der Akrotiri-Halbinsel im Süden und bei Pafos vorkommen. Auch im Norden Zyperns wächst *Ophrys apifera* var. *chlorantha*, nämlich in mit Phrygana bewachsenen Berghängen bei Ceçitköy (VINEY, 1994).

Vor allem auf der Halbinsel Akrotiri, unweit der englischen Militärbasis, hat *Ophrys apifera* einige reich besetzte Fundorte. In Küstennähe blühen ab Ende März zwischen bewirtschafteten Feldern und Olivenhainen sowie in den spärlich bewachsenen, Salz beeinflussten Wiesenarealen, in Feuchtwiesen, binsenbewachsenen Wiesenflächen und Buschwerk viele hundert Pflanzen dieser Art. Sehr häufig wird *Ophrys apifera* hier von *Ophrys cinereophila* und *Ophrys kotschyi* begleitet. Wie schon gesagt wachsen hier auch viele Pflanzen von den beiden Varietäten *bicolor* und *chlorantha*. Reich besetzte Fundstellen beider Varietäten liegen sehr nahe der englischen Militärbasis, wodurch diese Standorte weitgehend geschützt sind.

Gefährdung

Nach den Kartierungsarbeiten zeigt sich, dass *Ophrys apifera* auf Zypern selten ist. Mit Sicherheit gibt es noch weitere Standorte, aber wegen ihrer späten Blütezeit sind in dieser Zeit meist nur wenige Orchideensucher auf Zypern unterwegs. Im Süden der Insel hat die Art relativ reich besetzte Standorte, die aber durch Entwässerung und Bebauung bedroht sind. Die Art ist somit als gefährdet einzustufen.

Hybriden

Nicht nachgewiesen.

Akrotiri (Asomatos), 22.3.2002

Ophrys apifera
Bee Orchid

HUDSON

Fl. Angl. ed. 1: 340 (1762)

Synonyms

Arachnitis apifera (HUDSON) HOFFMANN, Deutschl. Fl. ed. 2,2: 180 (1804); *Ophrys aquisgranensis* KALTENBACH, Fl. Aachen. Beckens: 519. tab. 7 (1845); *Ophrys austriaca* WIESBAUR ex DICHTL, Deutsche Bot. Monatsschr. 1: 148 (1883); *Ophrys apifera* var. *austriaca* (WIESBAUR ex DICHTL) BECK, Fl. Nieder-Österreich 1: 198 (1890); *Ophrys apifera* subsp. *austriaca* (WIESBAUR ex DICHTL) K. RICHTER, Pl. Eur. 1: 264 (1890); *Ophrys ripaensis* PORTA, Atti Acc. Rovereto, ser. 3 (11), fasc. 2: 7 (1905).

Description

Slender plant, 15 to 40 cm tall. Stem vigorous, erect, light to very light green. Foliage leaves light to dark green, lower leaves forming a rosette, lanceolate and often with frost damage (ground leaves emerge in autumn); upper leaves oblong-lanceolate, directed upwards, stem-sheathing. Inflorescence lax and elongated with 3 to 7 flowers. Bracts light green, lanceolate, clearly longer than ovary. Flowers medium-sized, spreading obliquely. Sepals white, pink to deep reddish, ovate-lanceolate, spreading to reflexed. Petals very small to elongated, often green, rarely purple. Labellum deeply three-lobed at base. Middle lobe chestnut-brown, strongly domed with recurved margins. Lateral lobes with protuberances, exterior densely pubescent. Speculum marking encircling almost entire basal area, brown with yellowish white border. Appendage large, yellowish green, directed downwards. *Ophrys apifera* is autogamous.

Habitat

Prefers wet reedy meadows at sea level (in winter often submerged), also in maquis, phrygana, wasteland, unfertilized neglected meadows, grassy pastures, shrubland and roadside edges and in light coniferous woods; on arid to variably moist, base-rich soils.

Flowering time

From (mid-) late March to early May.

Altitude distribution

From sea level to 900 m.

Overall distribution

Ophrys apifera is distributed from the meridional zone to the temperate zone. Its area stretches from Ireland to the Near East (Turkey, Syria, Israel), northwards as far as northern England, the Netherlands and northern Germany and southwards as far as North Africa. Also in the Caucasus, northern Iraq and northern Iran.

Distribution on Cyprus

This species occurs very sporadically on Cyprus and is rare. Only in the south on the Akrotiri peninsula is it relatively abundant. There, *Ophrys apifera* prefers moist localities, such as roadside embankments and reedbeds at sea level. These habitats are unfortunately being drained, causing the number of these plants to plummet. *Ophrys apifera* is very rare in the north and only known from the area around Kyrenia and Yayla (VINEY, 1994).

Remarks

The flowers on Cyprus are generally of a lighter colour than the Central European ones. RENZ (1929) noted this also at that time. *Ophrys apifera* is mostly rare in the Mediterranean region and its locations are predominantly sparsely populated. On Cyprus too, except on the Akrotiri peninsula, populations of *Ophrys apifera* mostly consist of just a few plants.

In the case of *Ophrys apifera,* autogamy occurs. Because of this, only its own genes are inherited, and therefore variations do not occur. But because of inbreeding, defects are also inherited, which can lead to abnormalities, giving rise to varieties in flower structure and speculum marking. This is the reason why there are so many varieties of *Ophrys apifera*. Two varieties can be found on Cyprus also, namely *Ophrys apifera* var. *bicolor* (NAEGELI) E. NELSON and *Ophrys apifera* var. *chlorantha* (HEGETSCHW.) RICHTER. Both varieties occur at several places in the west of the island, near Neo Chorio (Akamas), on the Akrotiri peninsula in the south and near Pafos. *Ophrys apifera* var. *chlorantha* also occurs in the north of the island, namely on the phrygana-covered mountain slopes near Ceçitköy (VINEY, 1994).

On the Akrotiri peninsula in particular, not very far from the British military base, *Ophrys apifera* has some densely populated locations. In these coastal areas, many hundreds of plants bloom from early March in cultivated fields and olive groves, in sparse growing meadows influenced by the sea, in marshes, in reedbeds and in the scrubland. *Ophrys apifera* is often accompanied there by *Ophrys cinereophila* and *Ophrys kotschyi*. As stated before, many plants of the varieties *bicolor* and *chlorantha* also grow here. Densely populated sites of both varieties are situated very close to the British military base and are therefore thoroughly protected.

Threats

Charting work has shown that *Ophrys apifera* is rare on Cyprus. There are certainly more habitats, but because its flowering time is late, only very few orchidologists visit Cyprus at its peak time. The species has densely populated habitats in the south of the island, which are however threatened by drainage and building development. The species can therefore be categorized as threatened.

Hybrids

Unconfirmed.

Akrotiri (Asomatos), 22.3.2002

Akrotiri (Asomatos), var. *bicolor*, 22.3.2002

Amargeti, 20.3.2002

Amargeti, 20.3.2002

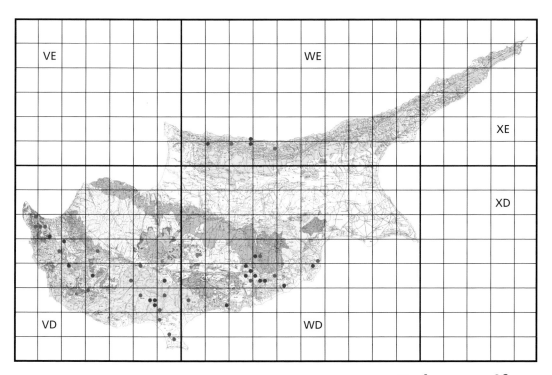

63 Meldungen / Reports

Ophrys apifera

192   Akrotiri (Asomatos), var. *bicolor*, 22.3.2002

Akrotiri (Asomatos), var. *flavescens*, 22.3.2002

Akrotiri (Asomatos), var. *flavescens*, 22.3.2002

Akrotiri (Asomatos), var. *flavescens*, 22.3.2002

Akrotiri (Asomatos), 22.3.2002

193

18 Ophrys attica (BOISSIER & ORPHANIDES) B.D. JACKSON
Attische Ragwurz

Index Kew. 2: 354 (1894)

Basionym

Ophrys arachnites var. *attica* BOISSIER & ORPHANIDES in P.E. BOISSIER, Diagn. Pl. Orient., ser. 2, 3 (4): 91 (1859).

Synonyme

Ophrys arachnites subsp. *attica* (BOISSIER & ORPHANIDES) K. RICHTER, Pl. Eur. 1: 262 (1890); *Ophrys carmeli* subsp. *attica* (BOISSIER & ORPHANIDES) RENZ in K.H. RECHINGER, Fl. Iran 126: 79 (1978); *Ophrys scolopax* subsp. *attica* (BOISSIER & ORPHANIDES) E. NELSON, Monogr. Ophrys: 156 (1962), nom. inval.; *Ophrys umbilicata* subsp. *attica* (BOISSIER & ORPHANIDES) J.J. WOOD, Kew Bull. 38: 136 (1983).

Beschreibung

Kräftige, gedrungene Pflanze, 10 bis 25 cm hoch. Untere Laubblätter breit-lanzettlich, rosettig gehäuft, die oberen länglich-lanzettlich, locker am Stängel verteilt, aufgerichtet bis abstehend. Blütenstand gedrängt, breit-zylindrisch, 3- bis 14-blütig. Blüten relativ klein, schräg vom Stängel abstehend. Perigonblätter grün, oft mit dunkelgrünen Mittelnerven. Sepalen breit-eiförmig bis eiförmig-lanzettlich, die beiden seitlichen abstehend, das mittlere Sepal stark nach vorne gekrümmt. Petalen dreieckig-lanzettlichbis lanzettlich, ziemlich kurz, spitz, am Rande schwach gewellt, meist intensiver als die Sepalen gefärbt, oft mit einem leichten Gelbton, oberseits und am Rande oft dicht behaart. Lippe klein bis mittelgroß, im oberen Teil tief dreilappig, rundlich, nach oben in Höcker verlängert, die aussen dicht behaart sind; Mittellappen längsoval bis rundlich, gewölbt, bräunlich bis rötlichbraun gefärbt. Lippenzeichnung großflächig und ringförmig, bräunlichlila bis gelblichbraun mit weissem oder gelblichem Rand. Anhängsel breit, gelblichgrün, aufwärts gerichtet.

Standort

Phrygana, lichte Kiefernwälder, Macchien, Gebüsche und grasigen Flächen; auf trockenen, kalkreichen Böden.

Blütezeit

Anfang Februar bis Ende März.

Höhenverbreitung

Von der Küste bis 300 m.

Gesamtverbreitung

Griechenland, Zypern und die Südtürkei.

Verbreitung auf Zypern

Diese Art kommt auf Zypern sehr zerstreut vor und ist relativ selten. Typische Pflanzen gibt es hauptsächlich in der Umgebung von Larnaka (Salzsee), bei Souni im Süden, und an mehreren Stellen im Patadactylos-Gebirge und auf der Karpasia-Halbinsel.

Bemerkungen

Die Bestimmung von *Ophrys attica* kann auf Zypern manchmal problematisch sein, weil die ihr nahe verwandten Taxa *Ophrys flavomarginata*, *Ophrys lapethica*, *Ophrys rhodia* und *Ophrys umbilicata* hier auch vorkommen. *Ophrys flavomarginata* ist deutlich an ihrer großen, breiten, elliptischen, gelb umrandeten Lippe zu erkennen. Ausserdem sind die Blüten von *Ophrys flavomarginata* etwa doppelt so groß wie die von *Ophrys attica*. *Ophrys rhodia* unterscheidet sich von *Ophrys attica* durch die nach unten gezogenen seitlichen Sepalen, die reich gegliederte, bis zum Lippenende reichende Malzeichnung, die dreieckigen, kurzen Petalen und das meist aufrechte mittlere Sepal. *Ophrys umbilicata* unterscheidet sich von *Ophrys attica* durch eine breitere Lippe und ihre bunten Perigonblätter. *Ophrys lapethica* unterscheidet sich von *Ophrys attica* durch ihre weiss bis intensiv rosaviolett gefärbten Perigonblätter, ihre dreilappige, braun bis rötlichbraun gefärbte und gehöckerte Lippe, einen langen und schmalen Mittellappen und eine blauschwarze oder schwarzviolette H- bis X-förmige Malzeichnung mit elfenbeinfarbiger Umrandung und meist schildförmigem Zentrum.

Das Vorkommen von *Ophrys attica* auf Zypern war lange Zeit umstritten, aber der Autor sowie andere Orchideenforscher, konnten sie an mehreren Stellen nachweisen. Wie in der Türkei handelt es sich auch auf Zypern meist um Einzelpflanzen. Trotzdem kommt *Ophrys attica* auf Zypern zweifelsfrei vor, und Hybriden zwischen den oben genannten Taxa wurden bisher nicht gefunden.

Gefährdung

Ophrys attica besitzt nur wenige aktuelle Fundorte auf Zypern, aber es sind viele potentielle Biotope vorhanden, wo diese Art sich weiter ansiedeln könnte. Trotzdem wurde sie wenig nachgewiesen. Sie ist deshalb als stark gefährdet einzustufen.

Hybriden

Mit *Ophrys kotschyi* und *Ophrys levantina*.

◀ Akrotiri (Salt lake), 8.3.2002

Kantou-Souni, 13.3.2002   Kantou-Souni, 13.3.2002

Ophrys attica (Boissier & Orphanides) B.D. Jackson
Carmel Ophrys

Index Kew. 2: 354 (1894)

Basionym
Ophrys arachnites var. *attica* Boissier & Orphanides in P.E. Boissier, Diagn. Pl. Orient., ser. 2, 3 (4): 91 (1859).

Synonyms
Ophrys arachnites subsp. *attica* (Boissier & Orphanides) K. Richter, Pl. Eur. 1: 262 (1890); *Ophrys carmeli* subsp. *attica* (Boissier & Orphanides) Renz in K.H. Rechinger, Fl. Iran 126: 79 (1978); *Ophrys scolopax* subsp. *attica* (Boissier & Orphanides) E. Nelson, Monogr. Ophrys: 156 (1962), nom. inval.; *Ophrys umbilicata* subsp. *attica* (Boissier & Orphanides) J.J. Wood, Kew Bull. 38: 136 (1983).

Description
Vigorous, compact plant, 10 to 25 cm tall. Lower foliage leaves broadly lanceolate, forming a rosette, upper leaves oblong-lanceolate, laxly distributed along stem, erect to spreading. Inflorescence compact, broadly cylindrical, 3 to 14 flowers. Flowers relatively small, spreading obliquely from stem. Perianth segments green, often with a dark green mid-vein. Sepals broadly ovate to ovate-lanceolate, both laterals spreading, dorsal sepal strongly bent forwards. Petals triangular-lanceolate to lanceolate, fairly short, acuminate, slightly wavy at edges, mostly with a more intense colouration than sepals, often with a light yellow tone, densely pubescent in upper part and at edges. Labellum small to medium-sized, deeply three-lobed in upper part, roundish, elongated into protuberances in upper part, these densely pubescent on exterior; central lobe oblong-oval to roundish, domed, brownish to reddish brown. Labellum marking covering a large area and ring-shaped, brownish lilac to yellowish brown with a white or yellowish border. Appendage wide, yellowish green, directed upwards.

Habitat
Phrygana, light coniferous woods, maquis, shrublands and grassy areas; on arid, calcareous soils.

Flowering time
Early February to late March.

Altitude distribution
From sea level to 300 m.

Overall distribution
Greece, Cyprus and southern Turkey.

Distribution on Cyprus
The species occurs sporadically on Cyprus and is relatively rare. Typical plants can mainly be found in the vicinity of Larnaka (salt lake) and near Souni in the south, and at several places in the Pentadactylos Range and on the Karpasia peninsula.

Remarks
The identification of *Ophrys attica* on Cyprus can often give rise to problems, as the closely related species *Ophrys flavomarginata*, *Ophrys lapethica*, *Ophrys rhodia* and *Ophrys umbilicata* also occur here. *Ophrys flavomarginata* can easily be recognized by its large, wide, elliptical labellum with a yellow border. The flowers of *Ophrys flavomarginata* are also about twice as large as those of *Ophrys attica*. *Ophrys rhodia* can be distinguished from *Ophrys attica* by the lateral sepals which are directed downwards, the richly branched marking which reaches as far as the apex of the labellum, the triangular, short petals and the mostly erect dorsal sepal. *Ophrys umbilicata* can be distinguished from *Ophrys attica* by a much wider labellum and by its colourful perianth segments. *Ophrys lapethica* can be distingushed from *Ophrys attica* by its white to intense pink-violet perianth segments, its three-lobed, brown to reddish brown labellum with protuberances, a long and narrow central lobe and a blue-black or black-violet H- to X-shaped marking with an ivory-coloured border and mostly with a shield-shaped centre.

The occurrence of *Ophrys attica* had been disputed for a long time, until the author and other orchid researchers, were able to identify the species at several places. Just as in Turkey, they usually occur as solitary plants. *Ophrys attica* does however undoubtedly occur on Cyprus, but hybrids with the species mentioned above were not yet found.

Threats
Ophrys attica possesses only a few habitats on Cyprus, but there are many potential habitats present where this species could establish itself. The species has however been identified only a few times. It can therefore be categorized as heavily threatened.

Hybrids
With *Ophrys kotschyi* and *Ophrys levantina*.

Kayalar, 14.3.2002

Hirsarköy, 14.3.2002

Alethriko, 6.3.2002

Akrotiri (Salt lake), 8.3.2002

Hirsarköy, 14.3.2002

Souni, 7.3.2002

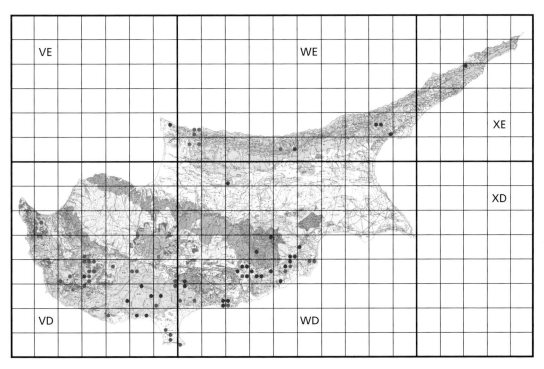

Ophrys attica

19

Ophrys flavomarginata
Gelbrandige Ragwurz

(Renz) H. Baumann & Künkele

Mitteilungsbl. Arbeitskr. Heim. Orch. Baden-Württ. 13 (3): 301 (1981)

Basionym

Ophrys attica forma *flavomarginata* Renz, Repert. Spec. Nov. Regni Veg. 27: 204 (1929). ('*flavo-marginata*')

Synonym

Ophrys umbilicata subsp. *flavomarginata* (Renz) Faurholdt, Jour. Eur. Orch. 35 (4): 745 (2003).

Beschreibung

Kräftige, mittelgroße Pflanze, 15 bis 30 cm hoch. Untere Laubblätter eiförmig-lanzettlich bis elliptisch, zugespitzt, am Grunde rosettig gehäuft, die oberen länglich-lanzettlich, locker am Stängel verteilt, aufgerichtet bis abstehend und in stängelumfassenden Hochblätter übergehend. Blütenstand gedrängt bis breit-zylindrisch, 2 bis 8-blütig. Blüten mittelgroß bis groß, schräg vom Stängel abstehend. Perigonblätter überwiegend grünlich- bis gelblichweiss, oft mit grünem Mittelnerv. Sepalen breit-eiförmig bis eiförmig, stumpf, die beiden seitlichen abstehend oder schräg nach unten gerichtet, das mittlere Sepal stark nach vorne gekrümmt. Petalen dreieckig, ziemlich kurz, spitz, meist gelblicher als die Sepalen gefärbt. Lippe groß, trapezförmig bis längsoval, im oberen Teil tief dreilappig, stark gewölbt; Seitenlappen dreieckig und im oberen Teil in stumpfe Höcker übergehend, am Rande dicht zottig behaart; Mittellappen längsoval bis rundlich, bräunlich bis rötlichbraun, mit breiten, tiefgelben Seitenrändern. Lippenzeichnung großflächig, aus Kreisen und gekrümmten Linien bestehend, gelblich bis gelblichweiss mit einem violetten Kern. Anhängsel ziemlich breit und kurz, gelblichgrün, aufwärts gerichtet.

Standort

Lichte Kiefernwälder, Ödland, Magerwiesen, grasiges Weideland, Phrygana und Macchien; auf trockenen bis mäßig feuchten, kalkreichen Böden. *Ophrys flavomarginata* wächst mit Vorliebe in Straßengräben, in relativ dichter Macchie oder an schattigen Stellen in und am Rande von Pinienwäldern.

Blütezeit

Ende Januar bis Ende März.

Höhenverbreitung

Von der Küste bis 600 m.

Gesamtverbreitung

Nur von Zypern und Israel bekannt.

Verbreitung auf Zypern

Die Art ist auf Zypern weit verbreitet und nicht selten. Vor allem im Norden und Süden ist die Art stellenweise häufig.

Bemerkungen

Ophrys flavomarginata ist gut an ihrer großen, elliptischen, gelb umrandeten Lippe und dem grünen Perigon zu erkennen. Sehr selten bildet die Art Hybriden mit *Ophrys umbilicata*, die dann schwer zuzuordnen sind. Nach Gölz & Reinhard (1985) besteht im qualitativen Bereich nur ein einziger auffälliger Unterschied zu *Ophrys umbilicata*: Bei *Ophrys flavomarginata* hat die Lippe eine breite gelbe und kahle Randzone, die im apikalen Teil oft stark aufgebogen ist, aber wie in der Beschreibung schon abgehandelt, ist *Ophrys flavomarginata* eine gut definierte und leicht zu erkennende Art, die deutlich an ihrer großen, elliptischen, gelb umrandeten Lippe und ihre großen Blüten zu erkennen ist. Im Vergleich zu Israel, wo *Ophrys flavomarginata* nur an wenigen Stellen vorkommt und dort viele Hybriden mit *Ophrys umbilicata* bildet, sind die Pflanzen auf Zypern meist problemlos zu bestimmen. Hybriden mit anderen *Ophrys*-Arten sind selten, auch mit ihr nahe verwandten Arten (*Ophrys attica*, *Ophrys lapethica*, *Ophrys rhodia* und *Ophrys umbilicata*) und wurden bisher sehr selten beobachtet.

Nach Kretzschmar (1995) ist *Ophrys flavomarginata* die zuerst aufblühende *Ophrys*-Art auf Zypern. Er fand schon in der zweiten Februarwoche voll aufgeblühte Pflanzen, woraus geschlossen werden kann, dass der Beginn der Blütezeit bereits im Januar liegt.

Gefährdung

Ophrys flavomarginata ist auf Zypern weit verbreitet und bildet stellenweise größere Populationen. Die Art ist kaum gefährdet.

Hybriden

Mit *Ophrys kotschyi* (*Ophrys* ×*lefkosiana* H. Baumann & Künkele), *Ophrys bornmuelleri*, *Ophrys levantina* und *Ophrys umbilicata*.

Choirokoitia (Kalavasos dam), 4.3.2002

Ophrys flavomarginata
Yellow-rimmed Ophrys

(RENZ) H. BAUMANN
& KÜNKELE

Mitteilungsbl. Arbeitskr. Heim. Orch.
Baden-Württ. 13 (3): 301 (1981)

Basionym

Ophrys attica forma *flavomarginata* RENZ, Repert. Spec. Nov. Regni Veg. 27: 204 (1929). ('*flavo-mar-ginata*')

Synonym

Ophrys umbilicata subsp. *flavomarginata* (RENZ) FAURHOLDT, Jour. Eur. Orch. 35 (4): 745 (2003).

Description

Vigorous, medium-sized plant, 15 to 30 cm tall. Lower foliage leaves ovate-lanceolate to elliptical, acuminate, forming a rosette at the base, upper leaves oblong-lanceolate, laxly distributed along the stem, erect to spreading and merging into stem-sheathing upper leaves. Inflorescence compact to broadly elliptical, 2 to 8 flowers. Flowers medium-sized to large, spreading obliquely from the stem. Perianth segments predominantly greenish to yellowish white, often with a green mid-vein. Sepals broadly ovate to ovate, obtuse, laterals spreading or obliquely directed downwards, dorsal sepal strongly bent forwards. Petals triangular, fairly short, acuminate, often yellower than sepals. Labellum large, trapezoid to oblong-oval, deeply three-lobed in the upper part, strongly domed; lateral lobes triangular and merging into blunt protuberances in the upper part, covered in dense velvety hairs at edges, middle lobe oblong-oval to roundish, brownish to reddish brown, with wide, deep yellow margins. Labellum marking large, consisting of circles and curved lines, yellowish to yellowish white with a violet centre. Appendage fairly wide and short, yellowish green, directed upwards.

Habitat

Light coniferous woods, wasteland, neglected meadows, grassy pastures, phrygana and maquis; on arid to moderately moist, calcareous soils. *Ophrys flavomarginata* favours roadside embankments, relatively dense maquis or shady places in and at the edges of pine forests.

Flowering time

Late January to late March.

Altitude distribution

From sea level to 600 m.

Overall distribution

Only known from Cyprus and Israel.

Distribution on Cyprus

The species is widely distributed on Cyprus and not rare. Especially in the north and in the south, the species is at times abundant.

Remarks

Ophrys flavomarginata can easily be recognized by its large, elliptical, yellow-bordered labellum and by its green perianth. Very rarely, it forms hybrids with *Ophrys umbilicata*, which are then very difficult to identify. According to GÖLZ & REINHARD (1985), there is only one clear qualitative difference from *Ophrys umbilicata*, which is that the labellum of *Ophrys flavomarginata* has a wide yellow and glabrous marginal zone, which is strongly bent upwards in the apical part. However, as already stated in the description, *Ophrys flavomarginata* is a well-defined and easily recognizable species, which can clearly be identified by its large, elliptical, yellow-bordered labellum and its large flowers.

In contrast with Israel, where *Ophrys flavomarginata* occurs at a few places and where it forms many hybrids with *Ophrys umbilicata*, the plants on Cyprus can usually be recognized without problems. Hybrids with other *Ophrys* species are rare, and hybrids with the closely related species (*Ophrys attica*, *Ophrys lapethica*, *Ophrys rhodia* and *Ophrys umbilicata*) have so far very rarely been seen.

According to KRETZSCHMAR (1995), *Ophrys flavomarginata* is the first *Ophrys* species to flower on Cyprus, as he found plants in full bloom in the second week of February, which led to the conclusion that its flowering time had already started in January.

Threats

Ophrys flavomarginata is widely distributed on Cyprus and occasionally forms large populations. The species is scarcely threatened.

Hybrids

With *Ophrys kotschyi* (*Ophrys ×lefkosiana* H. BAUMANN & KÜNKELE), *Ophrys bornmuelleri*, *Ophrys levantina* and *Ophrys umbilicata*.

Gerasa, 7.3.2002

Kato Drys-Vavla, 6.3.2002

Alethriko, 6.3.2002

Neo Chorio (Akamas), 10.3.2002

Choirokoitia (Kalavasos dam), 4.3.2002

Souni, 13.3.2002

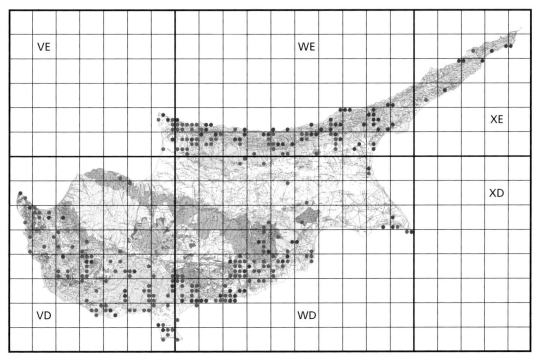

Ophrys flavomarginata

20

Ophrys lapethica
Lapethos-Ragwurz

GÖLZ & H.R. REINHARD

Mitteilungsbl. Arbeitskr. Heim. Orch.
Baden-Württ. 21 (4): 1052 (1989)

Synonyme

Ophrys scolopax subsp. *lapethica* (GÖLZ & H.R. REINHARD) G. & K. MORSCHEK, Orch. Cyprus: 128 (1996); *Ophrys umbilicata* subsp. *lapethica* (GÖLZ & H.R. REINHARD) FAURHOLDT, Jour. Eur. Orch. 35 (4): 745 (2003).

Beschreibung

Pflanze 20 bis 45 cm hoch. Blütenstand langgestreckt und lockerblütig, mit 4 bis 8 Blüten, diese oft mehr als die Hälfte der Pflanzenhöhe einnehmend. Laubblätter grün bis gelblichgrün, die unteren eiförmig-lanzettlich, gehäuft, die oberen länglich-lanzettlich, aufgerichtet bis abstehend. Blüten klein bis mittelgroß. Perigonblätter weisslich oder hellrosa, oft mit grünem Mittelnerv. Sepalen eiförmig-lanzettlich, mittleres Sepal weit über die Säule geneigt. Petalen dreieckig, behaart, gelegentlich schwach geöhrt. Lippe dreilappig mit stumpfen Höckern, braun bis rötlichbraun; Mittellappen lang und schmal, seitliche Ränder stark zurückgebogen (berühren sich auf der Rückseite). Seitenlappenhöcker sehr kurz, gerundet stumpf. Mal H- bis X-förmig, meist mit schildförmigem Zentrum, dunkel- bis schwarzviolett, mit elfenbeinfarbiger Umrandung. Anhängsel weit vorgezogen, gelblich bis gelblichgrün, vorwärts bis aufwärts gerichtet.

Standort

Grasige Phrygana, Macchien, lockere Kiefernwälder, Wiesenflächen und aufgelassene Wein- und Olivenhaine; auf trockenen bis mäßig feuchten, überwiegend kalkreichen Böden.

Blütezeit

Ende Februar bis Ende März.

Höhenverbreitung

Von Meereshöhe bis 800 m.

Gesamtverbreitung

Zypern und die mittlere Südtürkei.

Verbreitung auf Zypern

Hauptsächlich im Süden und mittleren Norden der Insel verbreitet, wo die Art zerstreut und an den meisten Standorten in nur wenigen Exemplaren vorkommt.

Bemerkungen

Ophrys lapethica ist schon seit Beginn des vorigen Jahrhunderts von Zypern bekannt. Sie wurde bis zur Neubeschreibung durch GÖLZ & REINHARD (1989) als *Ophrys scolopax* kartiert. Diese Funde wurden in diesem Buch zu *Ophrys lapethica* gestellt und auf der Verbreitungskarte eingezeichnet.

Ophrys lapethica wächst vor allem im Süden und mittleren Norden der Insel. Im Norden hat die Art ihren Verbreitungsschwerpunkt im Pentadactylos-Gebirge (unter anderem bei Esentepe). Sie wurde aus dieser Umgebung von GÖLZ & REINHARD (1989) beschrieben und nach dem Ort Lapta benannt.

Im Süden ist *Ophrys lapethica* vor allem im mittleren Teil verbreitet, wo sie vor allem in den niedrigen, südlichen Lagen des Troodos-Gebirges und in der weiteren Umgebung von Mathikoloni, Kato Drys und Vavla vorkommt.

Sie wächst dort bevorzugt in abgebrannten Hängen. Südlich von Vavla, im mittleren Süden, bildet sie dicht stehende Gruppen, und sie ist dort meist mit *Ophrys morio* und *Orchis italica* vergesellschaftet. Die Art ist auf Zypern meist klar von den anderen dort vorkommenden *Ophrys*-Arten abzugrenzen. Nur mit *Ophrys umbilicata* könnte sie verwechselt werden. Sie unterscheidet sich aber von dieser Art durch ihre weiss bis intensiv rosaviolett gefärbten Perigonblätter, ihre dreilappige, braun bis rötlichbraun gefärbte und gehöckerte Lippe, einen langen und schmalen Mittellappen und eine blauschwarze oder schwarzviolette H- bis X-förmige Malzeichnung mit elfenbeinfarbiger Umrandung und meist schildförmigem Zentrum.

Gefährdung

Ophrys lapethica ist auf Zypern relativ selten und sie ist damit als gefährdet einzustufen.

Hybriden

Mit *Ophrys kotschyi* (*Ophrys ×denglerensis* A. RIECHELMANN*), *Ophrys levantina* (*Ophrys ×liebischiana* R. KOHLMÜLLER) und *Ophrys umbilicata*.

Kato Drys-Vavla, 6.3.2002

Ophrys lapethica
Lapethos Ophrys

GÖLZ & H.R. REINHARD

Mitteilungsbl. Arbeitskr. Heim. Orch.
Baden-Württ. 21 (4): 1052 (1989)

Synonyms

Ophrys scolopax subsp. *lapethica* (GÖLZ & H.R. REINHARD) G. & K. MORSCHEK, Orch. Cyprus: 128 (1996); *Ophrys umbilicata* subsp. *lapethica* (GÖLZ & H.R. REINHARD) FAURHOLDT, Jour. Eur. Orch. 35 (4): 745 (2003).

Description

Plant 20 to 45 cm tall. Inflorescence elongated and lax-flowered, with 4 to 8 flowers, often taking up more than half the height of the plant. Foliage leaves green to yellowish green, lower leaves ovate-lanceolate, bunched, upper leaves oblong-lanceolate, erect to spreading. Flowers small to medium-sized. Perianth segments whitish or light pink, often with a green mid-vein. Sepals ovate-lanceolate, dorsal sepal bent over and extending past column. Petals triangular, pubescent, occasionally slightly auriculate. Labellum three-lobed with blunt protuberances, brown to reddish brown; middle lobe long and narrow, lateral edges strongly reflexed (touching behind). Protuberances on lateral lobes very short, rounded obtuse. Marking H- to X-shaped, mostly with a shield-shaped centre, dark to black-violet, with ivory-coloured border. Appendage drawn out, yellowish to yellowish green, directed forwards to upwards.

Habitat

Grassy phrygana, maquis, open coniferous woods, grasslands, abandoned vineyards and olive groves; on arid to moderately moist, predominantly calcareous soils.

Flowering time

Late February to late March.

Altitude distribution

From sea level to 800 m.

Overall distribution

Cyprus and central southern Turkey.

Distribution on Cyprus

Primarily distributed in the southern and central northern part of the island, where the species occurs sporadically and at most locations as only a few specimens.

Remarks

Ophrys lapethica was already known at the beginning of the last century. It was charted then as *Ophrys scolopax* until the description by GÖLZ & REINHARD (1989). These findings have been listed in this book under *Ophrys lapethica* and put into the distribution map.

Ophrys lapethica grows mainly in the south and central north of the island. In the north, the focal point of its distribution is situated in the Pentadacty-los Range (for example near Esentepe). It was described from this area by GÖLZ & REINHARD (1989) and named after the town of Lapta.

In the south, *Ophrys lapethica* is distributed in the central part in particular, where it mainly occurs at lower altitudes on the southern slopes of the Troodos Mountains and in the area around Mathikoloni, Kato Drys and Vavla. There it prefers slopes cleared by fires. South of Vavla in the central south, it forms dense groups and is mostly accompanied by *Ophrys morio* and *Orchis italica*.

On Cyprus, the species is mostly clearly distinguishable from other *Ophrys* species. It can only really be confused with *Ophrys umbilicata*. However, it differs from this species in its white to intense pink-violet perianth segments, its three-lobed, brown to reddish brown labellum with protuberances, and in its long and narrow middle lobe and blue-black or black-violet H- to X-shaped marking with an ivory-coloured border and usually shield-shaped centre.

Threats

Ophrys lapethica is relatively rare on Cyprus and can be categorized as threatened.

Hybrids

With *Ophrys kotschyi* (*Ophrys ×denglerensis* A. RIECHELMANN*), *Ophrys levantina* (*Ophrys ×liebischiana* R. KOHLMÜLLER) and *Ophrys umbilicata*.

Mathikoloni, 20.3.2002

Mathikoloni, 20.3.2002

Neo Chorio-Agios Minas (Akamas), 3.3.2002

Apsiou-Louvaras, 5.3.2002

Mathikoloni, 5.3.2002

Mathikoloni, 5.3.2002

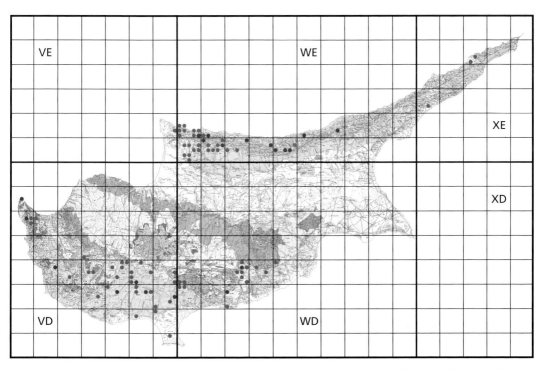

Ophrys lapethica

Basionym

Ophrys umbilicata subsp. *rhodia* H. Baumann & Künkele, Mitteilungsbl. Arbeitskr. Heim. Orch. Baden-Württ. 18 (3): 388 (1986).

Synonym

Ophrys scolopax subsp. *rhodia* (H. Baumann & Künkele) H.A. Pedersen & Faurholdt, Die Orchidee 48 (6): 235 (1997).

Beschreibung

Kräftige, mittelgroße Pflanze, 20 bis 35 cm hoch. Laubblätter grün bis gelblichgrün, am Grunde rosettig gehäuft, die unteren eiförmig-lanzettlich bis länglich-lanzettlich, nach oben in tragblattartige Laubblätter übergehend. Blütenstand dicht und reichblütig, mehr oder weniger gedrängt, 5 bis 12 Blüten. Sepalen hell- bis dunkelgrün, abgerundet, die beiden seitlichen nach unten gebogen, das mittlere Sepal leicht rückwärts gebogen bis vornübergeneigt. Petalen gelblichgrün, dreieckig und stark behaart. Lippe extrem bauchig, gewölbt, stark dreilappig, mit zwei stark behaarten, zugespitzten Höckern, hell- bis dunkelbraun, an der Basis stark behaart. Malzeichnung reich gegliedert, bis zum Lippenende reichend, marmoriert; die Malzeichnung schließt ein orangefarbenes Basalfeld ein, darunter umrahmt sie ein bläulich-metallisch gefärbtes Feld. Anhängsel relativ klein, grün bis gelblichgrün, waagerecht abstehend.

Standort

Grasige Hänge, Olivenhaine und Wiesenflächen; Affodillfluren, Straßenböschungen, Macchien und Phrygana; auf frischen, mäßig trockenen bis feuchten, basenreichen oder kalkhaltigen Böden.

Blütezeit

Mitte Februar bis Ende März.

Höhenverbreitung

Von der Küste bis 600 m.

Gesamtverbreitung

Auf einigen Ägäischen Inseln (Rhodos und Karpathos) und auf Zypern vorkommend. Sie wurde vermutlich auch in Israel gefunden (Kreutz, 1997).

Verbreitung auf Zypern

Eines der seltensten Taxa von Zypern. Vor allem im südlichen Teil der Insel am Larnaka Salzsee und auf der Halbinsel Akrotiri verbreitet. Nach Georgiades (1998ab) auch in der Umgebung von Mazotos, Maroni, Stavrovouni, Kornos, Delikipos, Kato Drys, Athalassa, Latsia, Protaras und Kap Greco. Im Norden der Insel ist *Ophrys rhodia* sehr selten. Aktuell gibt es nur wenige Fundstellen, zum Beispiel bei Hirsanköy.

Bemerkungen

Ophrys rhodia hat gewisse Ähnlichkeit mit *Ophrys attica* (grünes Perigon) und *Ophrys umbilicata* (buntes Perigon), unterscheidet sich aber von diesen beiden Taxa durch die nach unten gezogenen seitlichen Sepalen, die reich gegliederte, bis zum Lippenende reichende Malzeichnung, die dreieckigen, kurzen Petalen und das aufrechte mittlere Sepal (Baumann & Künkele, 1986). *Ophrys rhodia* blüht meist auch etwas später als ihre nahe verwandten Taxa *Ophrys attica*, *Ophrys lapethica* und *Ophrys umbilicata*.

Funde von *Ophrys rhodia* waren früher auf Zypern immer umstritten, weil sie nicht immer zweifelsfrei von *Ophrys attica* oder *Ophrys flavomarginata* zu unterscheiden ist. In den letzten Jahren wurden durch eingehende Kartierungsarbeiten, bei denen besonders auf diese Art geachtet wurde, viele neue Fundstellen von *Ophrys rhodia* entdeckt (unter anderem von Delforge, 1990). Bemerkenswert ist aber, dass die Populationen von *Ophrys rhodia* meist nur aus wenigen Exemplaren, an manchen Fundstellen sogar nur aus Einzelpflanzen bestehen. Nur in der Umgebung des Salzsees bei Larnaka ist sie relativ häufig.

Nach Faurholdt (2003) kommt *Ophrys rhodia* nicht auf Zypern vor. Seiner Meinung nach sind die Stellung des mittleren Sepals (leicht rückwärts gebogen), sowie die grüne Farbe der Sepalen die wichtigsten Merkmale dieser Art. Meiner Ansicht nach sind diese beiden Merkmale jedoch nicht die wichtigsten, sondern Form, Farbe und Zeichnung der Lippe zeigen die wichtigeren Unterscheidungsmerkmale. Auch auf Rhodos, wo *Ophrys rhodia* in der typischen Ausprägung vorkommt, wachsen Pflanzen, bei deren Blüten das mittlere Sepal stark vornübergeneigt ist (Kreutz, 2002: 226, 228). Ausserdem haben Pedersen & Faurholdt (1997) *Ophrys rhodia* nach meiner Meinung zu Unrecht als Unterart bei der westmediterranen *Ophrys scolopax* (*Ophrys scolopax* subsp. *rhodia*) eingegliedert.

Gefährdung

Ophrys rhodia ist vor allem in den küstennahen Gebieten durch Bebauung und intensivere Bewirtschaftung ihrer Standorte stark zurückgegangen und deswegen ziemlich gefährdet. Vor allem bei Larnaka, in der weiteren Umgebung des Salzsees, ist sie durch Trockenlegung und Trittschäden durch Urlauber und Wanderer bedroht. *Ophrys rhodia* ist deshalb als stark gefährdet einzustufen

Hybriden

Nicht nachgewiesen.

Ophrys rhodia (H. Baumann & Künkele) P. Delforge
Rhodian Ophrys

Natural. Belges 71: 124 & 125 (1990)

Basionym

Ophrys umbilicata subsp. *rhodia* H. Baumann & Künkele, Mitteilungsbl. Arbeitskr. Heim. Orch. Baden-Württ. 18 (3): 388 (1986).

Synonym

Ophrys scolopax subsp. *rhodia* (H. Baumann & Künkele) H.A. Pedersen & Faurholdt, Die Orchidee 48 (6): 235 (1997).

Description

Vigorous, medium-sized plant, 20 to 35 cm tall. Foliage leaves green to yellowish green, forming a rosette at the base, lower leaves ovate-lanceolate to oblong-lanceolate, merging upwards into bract-like foliage leaves. Inflorescence dense and many-flowered, more or less compact, 5 to 12 flowers. Sepals light to dark green, rounded, the two lateral sepals bent downwards, dorsal sepal slightly bent backwards or directed forwards. Petals yellowish green, triangular and densely pubescent. Labellum extremely arched, domed, deeply three-lobed, with two densely pubescent, pointed protuberances, light to dark brown, densely pubescent at base. Marking multi-branched, reaching apex, marbled; marking surrounds an orange basal area, and below that a metallic bluish field. Appendage relatively small, green to yellowish green, spreading horizontally.

Habitat

Grassy slopes, olive groves and grasslands; asphodel fields, on roadside embankments, maquis and phrygana; on fresh, semi-arid to moist, base-rich or calcareous soils.

Flowering time

Mid-February to late March.

Altitude distribution

From sea level to 600 m.

Overall distribution

On some Aegean islands (Rhodes and Karpathos) and on Cyprus. It was probably also found in Israel (Kreutz, 1997).

Distribution on Cyprus

One of the rarest species on Cyprus. Mainly distributed in the southern part of the island at the Larnaka salt lake and on the Akrotiri peninsula. According to Georgiades (1998ab), it is also in the vicinity of Mazotos, Maroni, Stavrovouni, Kornos, Delikipos, Kato Drys, Athalassa, Latsia, Protaras and Cape Greco. *Ophrys rhodia* is very rare in the northern part of the island. At the moment there are very few locations, for example near Hirsanköy.

Remarks

Ophrys rhodia has certain similarities with *Ophrys attica* (green perianth) and *Ophrys umbilicata* (colourful perianth), but can be distinguished from these species by the lateral sepals that are drawn downwards, the multi-branched marking reaching the apex of the labellum, the triangular, short petals and the erect dorsal sepal (Baumann & Künkele, 1986). The species blooms normally a little bit later than its closest related species *Ophrys attica*, *Ophrys lapethica* and *Ophrys umbilicata*.

In former times findings of *Ophrys rhodia* on Cyprus have always been controversial, as the species is not always easy to distinguish from either *Ophrys attica* or *Ophrys flavomarginata*. In recent years, extensive charting work, in which particular attention was paid to this species, has resulted in the discovery of new sites for *Ophrys rhodia* (such as Delforge, 1990). It is noteworthy, however, that populations of *Ophrys rhodia* only consist of a few specimens; some sites even have only a solitary plant. *Ophrys rhodia* is only relatively abundant in the vicinity of the salt lake near Larnaka.

According to Faurholdt (2003), *Ophrys rhodia* does not occur on Cyprus. In his opinion, the placement of the dorsal sepal (slightly bent backwards), as well as the green colour of the sepals are the most important characteristics of this species. I believe that aforementioned characteristics are not the most important. Shape, colour and markings on the labellum are other very important distinguishing features. Also on Rhodes, were *Ophrys rhodia* occurs in its typical appearance, there are plants where the dorsal sepal is directed forwards (Kreutz, 2002: 226, 228). I am also of the opinion that Pedersen & Faurholdt (1997) have placed *Ophrys rhodia* wrongly as subspecies of the Western Mediterranean *Ophrys scolopax* (*Ophrys scolopax* subsp. *rhodia*).

Threats

Ophrys rhodia has declined considerably in the coastal areas because of building development and intensifying cultivation of its habitats and is therefore fairly threatened. Especially near Larnaka, around the salt lake, the species is endangered by drainage and damage caused by trampling by tourists and hikers. The species can therefore be categorised as heavily threatened.

Hybrids

Unconfirmed.

Larnaka (Salt lake), 9.3.2002

Larnaka (Salt lake), 9.3.2002

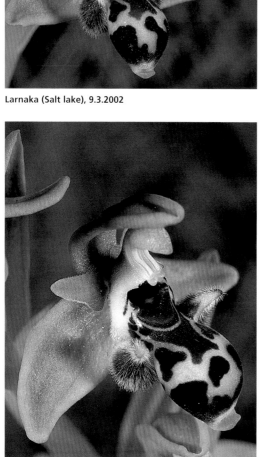

Larnaka (Salt lake), 9.3.2002

Larnaka (Salt lake), 9.3.2002

Choirokoitia (Kalavasos dam), 4.3.2002

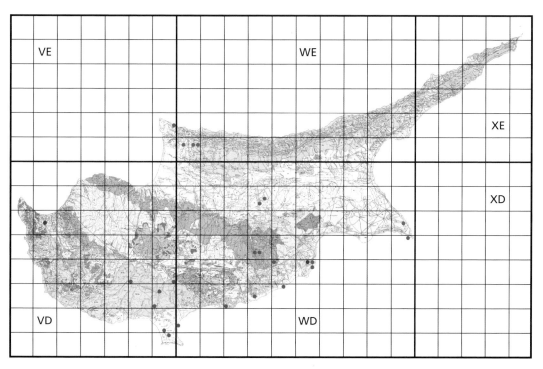

Ophrys rhodia

22

Ophrys umbilicata
Nabel-Ragwurz

DESFONTAINES

Ann. Mus. Hist. Nat. 10: 227 (1807)

Synonyme

Ophrys carmeli H. FLEISCHMANN & BORNMÜLLER, Ann. Naturhist. Mus. Wien 36: 7 (1923); *Ophrys umbilicata* subsp. *carmeli* (H. FLEISCHMANN & BORNMÜLLER) J.J. WOOD, Kew Bull. 38: 136 (1983); *Ophrys dinsmorei* SCHLECHTER, Repert. Spec. Nov. Regni Veg. 19: 46 (1923); *Ophrys scolopax* subsp. *dinsmorei* (SCHLECHTER) E.G. CAMUS & A. CAMUS, Iconogr. Orchid. Europe, Text (1): 315 (1928); *Ophrys cornuta* subsp. *orientalis* RENZ, Repert. Spec. Nov. Regni Veg. 27: 205 (1929); *Ophrys orientalis* (RENZ) SÓO in KELLER & SÓO, Monogr. Iconogr. Orchid. Eur. 2 (2/3): 65, 448 (1931); *Ophrys oestrifera* subsp. *orientalis* (RENZ) SÓO, Acta Bot. Acad. Sci. Hung. 5: 447 (1959); *Ophrys scolopax* subsp. *orientalis* (RENZ) E. NELSON, Monogr. Ophrys: 158 (1962), nom. inval.; *Ophrys carmeli* subsp. *orientalis* (RENZ) SÓO, Acta Bot. Acad. Sci. Hung. 16: 381 (1973); *Ophrys oestrifera* subsp. *umbilicata* (DESFONTAINES) HAYEK, Repert. Spec. Nov. Regni Veg., Sonderbeih. 30 (3): 378 (1933).

Beschreibung

Kräftige Pflanze, 15 bis 30 cm hoch. Untere Laubblätter eiförmig-lanzettlich, am Grunde rosettig gehäuft, die oberen länglich-lanzettlich, locker am Stängel verteilt, aufgerichtet bis abstehend, nach oben in tragblattartige Laubblätter übergehend. Blütenstand gedrängt, zylindrisch, 2- bis 8-blütig. Blüten relativ klein, schräg vom Stängel abstehend. Perigonblätter überwiegend rosa, rötlich- bis grünlichweiss gefärbt, oft mit grünem Mittelnerv. Sepalen eiförmig bis eiförmig-lanzettlich, die beiden seitlichen abstehend bis leicht zurückgeschlagen, das mittlere Sepal aufgerichtet bis stark nach vorne gekrümmt. Petalen dreieckig-lanzettlich, ziemlich kurz, spitz, meist dunkler als die Sepalen gefärbt. Lippe relativ klein, im oberen Teil tief dreilappig, rundlich und kurz gehöckert; Mittellappen längsoval bis rundlich, bräunlich bis rötlichbraun. Lippenzeichnung großflächig und ringförmig, bräunlichlila bis gelblichbraun, mit weissem oder gelblichem Rand. Anhängsel groß, gelblichgrün, vorwärts gerichtet.

Standort

Lichte Kiefernwälder, grasiges Ödland, Magerwiesen, feuchtes, grasiges Weideland, Phrygana und Macchien; auf trockenen bis mäßig feuchten, kalkreichen Böden.

Blütezeit

Anfang März bis Mitte April.

Höhenverbreitung

Von der Küste bis 800 m.

Gesamtverbreitung

Östlicher Mittelmeerraum: Ägäische Inseln, Türkei, Westsyrien, Libanon, Israel und Zypern. *Ophrys umbilicata* ist in Griechenland, auf den Ägäischen Inseln, in der Westtürkei und auf Zypern häufig. Nach Osten (Westsyrien, Libanon und Israel) wird sie immer seltener.

Verbreitung auf Zypern

Ophrys umbilicata ist auf Zypern weit verbreitet und nicht selten. Sie bildet auf den südlichen Hängen des Troodos-Gebirges und im Pentadactylos-Gebirge individuenreiche Populationen.

Bemerkungen

Ophrys umbilicata ist eine gut anzusprechende Art, die auf Zypern eigentlich nur mit *Ophrys attica* oder *Ophrys flavomarginata* verwechselt werden kann. Im Gegensatz zu diesen beiden Arten hat *Ophrys umbilicata* immer bunte Perigonblätter, wobei die Blüten von *Ophrys flavomarginata* ausserdem größer sind, und die Lippen fast immer einen gelben Rand besitzen.

Auf Zypern sind Hybriden mit anderen Vertretern dieser Gruppe (*Ophrys attica, Ophrys flavomarginata, Ophrys lapethica* und *Ophrys rhodia*) sehr selten und es wurden bisher nur Hybriden zwischen *Ophrys flavomarginata* und *Ophrys umbilicata* sowie zwischen *Ophrys lapethica* und *Ophrys umbilicata* beobachtet. Hauptsächlich in der Umgebung von Vavla, wo mehrere Arten von diesem Formenkreis zusammen vorkommen, sind diese Hybriden vorhanden und dann meist schwer zu identifizieren.

Gefährdung

Ophrys umbilicata kommt auf Zypern häufig vor. Sie ist daher nicht gefährdet.

Hybriden

Mit *Ophrys alasiatica* (*Ophrys* x*lefkarensis* SEGERS & H. WALRAVEN), *Ophrys elegans* und *Ophrys kotschyi* (*Ophrys* x*paphosiana* nsubsp. *paphosiana* H. BAUMANN & KÜNKELE). Sie bildet ausserdem an einigen Stellen Hybriden mit *Ophrys flavomarginata* und *Ophrys lapethica*.

220   Larnaka (Salt lake), 9.3.2002

Ophrys umbilicata

Woodcock Ophrys

DESFONTAINES

Ann. Mus. Hist. Nat. 10: 227 (1807)

Synonyms

Ophrys carmeli H. FLEISCHMANN & BORNMÜLLER, Ann. Naturhist. Mus. Wien 36: 7 (1923); *Ophrys umbilicata* subsp. *carmeli* (H. FLEISCHMANN & BORNMÜLLER) J.J. WOOD, Kew Bull. 38: 136 (1983); *Ophrys dinsmorei* SCHLECHTER, Repert. Spec. Nov. Regni Veg. 19: 46 (1923); *Ophrys scolopax* subsp. *dinsmorei* (SCHLECHTER) E.G. CAMUS & A. CAMUS, Iconogr. Orchid. Europe, Text (1): 315 (1928); *Ophrys cornuta* subsp. *orientalis* RENZ, Repert. Spec. Nov. Regni Veg. 27: 205 (1929); *Ophrys orientalis* (RENZ) SÓO in KELLER & SOÓ, Monogr. Iconogr. Orchid. Eur. 2 (2/3): 65, 448 (1931); *Ophrys oestrifera* subsp. *orientalis* (RENZ) SOÓ, Acta Bot. Acad. Sci. Hung. 5: 447 (1959); *Ophrys scolopax* subsp. *orientalis* (RENZ) E. NELSON, Monogr. Ophrys: 158 (1962), nom. inval.; *Ophrys carmeli* subsp. *orientalis* (RENZ) Soó, Acta Bot. Acad. Sci. Hung. 16: 381 (1973); *Ophrys oestrifera* subsp. *umbilicata* (DESFONTAINES) HAYEK, Repert. Spec. Nov. Regni Veg., Sonderbeih. 30 (3): 378 (1933).

Description

Vigorous plant, 15 to 30 cm tall. Lower foliage leaves ovate-lanceolate, forming a rosette at the base, upper leaves oblong-lanceolate, laxly distributed along stem, erect to spreading, merging into bract-like foliage leaves towards the top. Inflorescence compact, cylindrical, 2 to 8 flowers. Flowers relatively small, spreading obliquely from the axis. Perianth segments generally pink, reddish to greenish white, often with a green mid-vein. Sepals ovate to ovate-lanceolate, lateral sepals spreading to slightly reflexed, dorsal sepal erect to strongly curved forwards. Petals triangular-lanceolate, fairly short, acuminate, mostly darker than sepals. Labellum relatively small, deeply three-lobed in upper part, roundish and with short protuberances; middle lobe oblong-oval to roundish, brownish to reddish brown. Marking covering a large surface and ring-shaped, brownish lilac to yellowish brown with a white or yellow border. Appendage large, yellowish green, directed upwards.

Habitat

Light coniferous woods, grassy wasteland, neglected pastures, wet grasslands, phrygana and maquis; on arid to moderately moist, calcareous soils.

Flowering time

Early March to mid-April.

Altitude distribution

From sea level to 800 m.

Overall distribution

Eastern Mediterranean region: Aegean islands, Turkey, western Syria, Lebanon, Israel and Cyprus.

Ophrys umbilicata is abundant in Greece, on the Aegean islands, in western Turkey and on Cyprus. It gets rarer towards the east (western Syria, Lebanon and Israel).

Distribution on Cyprus

Ophrys umbilicata is widely distributed on Cyprus and not rare. It forms individual-rich populations on the southern slopes of the Troodos mountains and in the Pentadactylos Range.

Remarks

Ophrys umbilicata is an easily identifiable species, which can really only be confused with *Ophrys attica* and *Ophrys flavomarginata*. *Ophrys umbilicata* always has, in contrast to these other species, a colourful perianth, the flowers of *Ophrys flavomarginata* are larger and the labellum has almost always a yellow border.

Hybrids with other representatives of this group (*Ophrys attica, Ophrys flavomarginata, Ophrys lapethica* und *Ophrys rhodia*) are very rare on Cyprus and until now hybrids were only found between *Ophrys flavomarginata* and *Ophrys umbilicata* as well as between *Ophrys lapethica* and *Ophrys umbilicata*. These hybrids principally occur in the vicinity of Vavla, where several species of this complex occur together, and are mostly difficult to identify.

Threats

Ophrys umbilicata is abundant on Cyprus. It is therefore not threatened.

Hybrids

With *Ophrys alasiatica* (*Ophrys* x*lefkarensis* SEGERS & H. WALRAVEN), *Ophrys elegans* and *Ophrys kotschyi* (*Ophrys* x*paphosiana* nsubsp. *paphosiana* H. BAUMANN & KÜNKELE). It also forms hybrids with *Ophrys flavomarginata* and *Ophrys lapethica* in some places.

Choirokoitia (Kalavasos dam), 4.3.2002

Alethriko, 6.3.2002

Souni, 7.3.2002

Choirokoitia (Kalavasos dam), 4.3.2002

Larnaka (Salt lake), 9.3.2002

Neo Chorio (Akamas), 10.3.2002

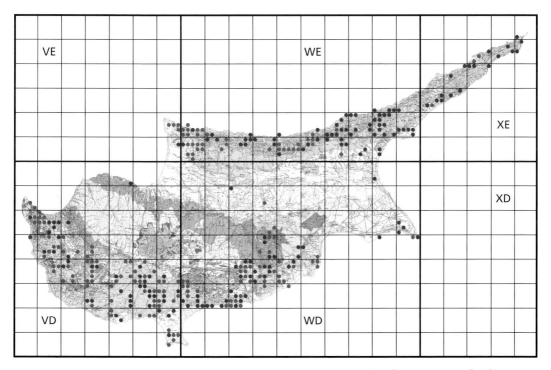

Ophrys umbilicata

23

Ophrys bornmuelleri
Bornmüllers Ragwurz

M. Schulze

Mitt. Thüring. Bot. Vereins, N.F. 13/14:
127 (1899). ('*bornmülleri*')

Synonyme

Ophrys fuciflora subsp. *bornmuelleri* (M. Schulze)
B. & E. Willing, Die Orchidee 26 (2): 78 (1975);
Ophrys holoserica subsp. *bornmuelleri* (M. Schulze) Sundermann, Taxon 24 (5/6): 625 (1975).

Beschreibung

Schlanke Pflanze, 15 bis 45 cm hoch mit gestrecktem, lockerem Blütenstand, mit 6 bis 9 ziemlich kleinen Blüten. Laubblätter dunkel- bis gelblichgrün, die unteren eiförmig-lanzettlich, rosettig gehäuft, die oberen länglich-lanzettlich, aufgerichtet bis abstehend, bisweilen stängelumfassend, kurz zugespitzt. Sepalen breit eiförmig, grünlich, rosa oder weisslich; die seitlichen abstehend, das mittlere etwas nach vorne geneigt, lang und zugespitzt. Petalen sehr klein, dreieckig, rosa bis rötlich gefärbt. Lippe relativ breit, trapezförmig, ungeteilt, fast horizontal vom Stängel abstehend, an den Rändern stark silbrig bis violett behaart und aufgewölbt (Mittelgrad der Höcker sehr spitz), kräftig gehöckert, bräunlich bis rötlichbraun. Malzeichnung besonders im oberen Teil der Lippe, meistens H-förmig mit Verzweigungen oder aus rundlichen Streifen bestehend, stahlblau bis blauviolett, nach aussen öfter gelblich gefärbt oder mit gelbem Rand. Anhängsel groß und breit, gelblich und nach vorne gerichtet.

Standort

Lichte Kiefern- und Pinienwälder, Phrygana, Macchien, Gebüsche, Böschungen und vor allem im Norden der Insel an grasigen Stellen unter Johannisbrotbäume; auf trockenen bis mäßig feuchten, basen- oder kalkreichen Böden.

Blütezeit

Mitte März bis Mitte April. Beginnt etwa zwei Wochen später als *Ophrys levantina* zu blühen.

Höhenverbreitung

Von der Küste bis 900 m.

Gesamtverbreitung

Östliches Mittelmeergebiet: Türkei, Westsyrien, Libanon, Israel, Nordirak und Zypern. Mit Ausnahme von Zypern und Israel ist die Art selten und tritt zerstreut auf.

Verbreitung auf Zypern

Auf Zypern hat *Ophrys bornmuelleri* ihre Hauptverbreitung, und sie ist im Süden sowie im Norden der Insel nicht selten. Vor allem in der Umgebung von Kyrenia und im Pentadactylos-Gebirge gehört die Art zu den häufiger vorkommenden Orchideen.

Bemerkungen

Ophrys bornmuelleri unterscheidet sich unter anderem von *Ophrys levantina* durch einen sehr langgestreckten Blütenstand und die kleineren Blüten, die fast horizontal vom Stängel abstehen, ausserdem durch eine andere Malzeichnung. Darüber hinaus ist die Lippe von *Ophrys levantina* ziemlich breit, rundlich oder abgerundet quadratisch bis leicht trapezförmig und vertikal abwärts gerichtet.

Nach Gölz und Reinhard (1985) ist *Ophrys bornmuelleri* ohne Probleme von *Ophrys levantina* zu unterscheiden und im Feld durch ihre Blütezeit, Blütengröße, Stellung der Lippe gegenüber dem Stängel, Lippenform und -behaarung, Höckerbildung und Malgestaltung schnell und zuverlässig anzusprechen. Nach Ansicht der meisten Autoren sind *Ophrys bornmuelleri* und *Ophrys levantina* nahe verwandte Arten. Diese Behauptung ist meiner Meinung nach nicht korrekt, weil *Ophrys bornmuelleri* mit *Ophrys carduchorum* und *Ophrys ziyaretiana* zu einem eigenen Formenkreis gehört, und *Ophrys levantina* ist eine separate Sippe auf der Rangstufe der Art.

Auf Zypern wächst die Art in ihrer meist typischen Ausprägung. Die Pflanzen sind durchschnittlich 30 cm hoch, und der Blütenstand ist besonders locker und langgestreckt. In der Türkei, wo *Ophrys bornmuelleri* nur im mittleren Süden des Landes vorkommt, sind die Pflanzen meist niedriger. Ausserdem wachsen in der Türkei die nahe verwandten Arten *Ophrys carduchorum* und *Ophrys ziyaretiana*, die manchmal Bestimmungsprobleme verursachen (Kreutz, 1998).

Gefährdung

Ophrys bornmuelleri ist auf Zypern nicht selten und weit verbreitet. Sie ist daher nicht besonders gefährdet.

Hybriden

Mit *Ophrys elegans*, *Ophrys flavomarginata*, *Ophrys levantina*, *Ophrys morio* (*Ophrys xcailliauana* P. Delforge) und *Ophrys sicula* (*Ophrys xjansenii* P. Delforge).

Souni-Pano Kivides, 20.3.2002

Ophrys bornmuelleri
Bornmueller's Ophrys

M. Schulze

Mitt. Thüring. Bot. Vereins, N.F. 13/14: 127 (1899). ('*bornmülleri*')

Synonyms

Ophrys fuciflora subsp. *bornmuelleri* (M. Schulze) B. & E. Willing, Die Orchidee 26 (2): 78 (1975); *Ophrys holoserica* subsp. *bornmuelleri* (M. Schulze) Sundermann, Taxon 24 (5/6): 625 (1975).

Description

Slender plant, 15 to 45 cm tall with an elongated, lax inflorescence, with 6 to 9 fairly small flowers. Foliage leaves dark green to yellowish green, lower leaves ovate-lanceolate, forming a rosette, upper leaves oblong-lanceolate, erect to spreading, sometimes stem-sheathing, shortly acuminate. Sepals broadly ovate, greenish, to pink or whitish; laterals spreading, dorsal sepal slightly directed forwards, long and acuminate. Petals very small, triangular, pink to reddish. Labellum relatively wide, trapezoid, undivided, spreading almost horizontally from axis, covered in silvery to violet-coloured hairs at the edges and domed (centres of protuberances very acuminate), protuberances prominent, brownish to reddish brown. Marking mainly in upper part of labellum, usually H-shaped with branches or consisting of rounded stripes, steel-blue to blue-violet, towards the edge often yellowish or with a yellow border. Appendage large and wide, yellowish and directed forwards.

Habitat

Light coniferous woods, phrygana, maquis, shrublands, roadside embankments and particularly in the north of the island, in grassy places under carob trees; on arid to moderately moist, base-rich of calcareous soils.

Flowering time

Mid-March to mid-April. Starts to bloom about two weeks later than *Ophrys levantina*.

Altitude distribution

From sea level to 900 m.

Overall distribution

Eastern Mediterranean region: Turkey, western Syria, Lebanon, Israel, northern Iraq and Cyprus. Except for Cyprus and Israel, the species is rare and occurs sporadically.

Distribution on Cyprus

Ophrys bornmuelleri has its main distribution on Cyprus and both in the north and in the south of the island it is not rare. Especially in the vicinity of Kyrenia and in the Pentadactylos mountains, the species belongs to the more abundantly occurring orchids.

Remarks

Ophrys bornmuelleri can be distinguished from, for example *Ophrys levantina,* by its very elongated inflorescence and smaller flowers, which spread almost horizontally from the stem, and also by a different marking. Above all, the labellum of *Ophrys levantina* is fairly wide, roundish or obtusely quadratic to slightly trapezoid and directed vertically downwards.

According to Gölz und Reinhard (1985), *Ophrys bornmuelleri* can be distinguished from *Ophrys levantina* without any problems and can be quickly and reliably identified in the field by its flowering time, flower size, placement of the labellum in relation to the stem, shape of the labellum and its pubescence, formation of the protuberances and composition of the marking. Most authors regarded *Ophrys bornmuelleri* and *Ophrys levantina* as closely related species. This is however not my opinion, *Ophrys bornmuelleri* belongs with *Ophrys carduchorum* and *Ophrys ziyaretiana* to a separate complex and *Ophrys levantina* is a clear independent species on species rank.

The species grows in its most typical appearance on Cyprus. The plants are on average 30 cm tall and the inflorescence is exceptionally lax and elongated. In Turkey, where *Ophrys bornmuelleri* only occurs in the central south of the country, the plants are mostly shorter. The closely related species *Ophrys carduchorum* and *Ophrys ziyaretiana* also occur in Turkey, which can give rise to identification problems (Kreutz, 1998).

Threats

Ophrys bornmuelleri is not rare and is widely distributed in Cyprus. It is therefore not particularly threatened.

Hybrids

With *Ophrys elegans, Ophrys flavomarginata, Ophrys morio* (*Ophrys* ×*cailliauana* P. Delforge), *Ophrys sicula* (*Ophrys* ×*jansenii* P. Delforge) and very rarely with *Ophrys levantina*.

Souni, 13.3.2002

Pegeia (Akamas), 19.3.2002

Kayalar-Sadrazamköy, 14.3.2002

Esentepe (Pentadactylos Range), 18.3.2002

Esentepe (Pentadactylos Range), 18.3.2002

Souni-Pano Kivides, 20.3.2002

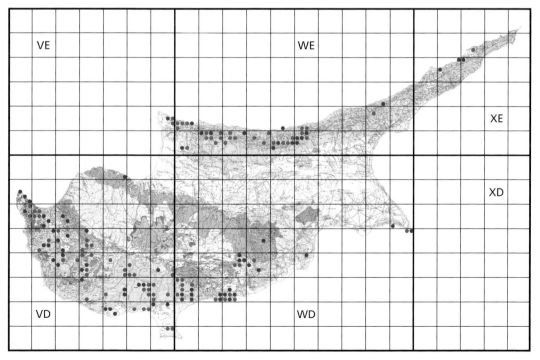

Ophrys bornmuelleri

24

Ophrys cinereophila
Kleinblütige Braune Ragwurz

H.F. Paulus & Gack

Jour. Eur. Orch. 30 (1): 170 (1998)

Synonym

Ophrys fusca subsp. *cinereophila* (H.F. Paulus & Gack) Faurholdt, Die Orchidee 53 (3): 345 (2002).

Beschreibung

Schlanke Pflanze, 10 bis 35 cm hoch. Laubblätter bläulich- bis gelblichgrün, die unteren eiförmig-lanzettlich, rosettig gehäuft, die oberen länglich-lanzettlich, aufgerichtet bis abstehend. Blütenstand locker, langgestreckt, mit 5 bis 7, manchmal bis zu 10 sehr kleinen Blüten. Sepalen breit-eiförmig bis lanzettlich, gelblich bis gelblichgrün gefärbt, das mittlere Sepal stark vornübergebeugt. Petalen länglich-lanzettlich, am Rande gewellt, gelblichgrün, selten am Rande bräunlich überlaufen; Petalen und Sepalen einen ziemlich lockeren Helm bildend. Lippe sehr klein, dunkelbraun bis schwarzviolett, waagerecht vom Stängel abstehend und stark gebogen, dreilappig, am Rande mit einem schmalen, hellgelben Saum umgeben, am Grunde V-förmig eingekerbt, dicht behaart und ungehöckert. Mal vom Grunde an aus zwei geteilten eiförmigen Flächen bestehend, (stahl)blau oder braun gefärbt, glänzend, selten im unteren Teil mit einem weisslichen Rand umgeben. Anhängsel fehlt.

Standort

Macchien, Phrygana, in lichten Kiefernwäldern und aufgelassenen Oliven- und Weinhainen; seltener in Affodillfluren und auf Ödland; auf kalkhaltigen Böden.

Blütezeit

Mitte Februar bis Ende März.

Höhenverbreitung

Von Meereshöhe bis 1.000 m.

Gesamtverbreitung

Im östlichen Mittelmeerraum weit verbreitet. Zumindest im Süden Griechenlands, vermutlich in der gesamten Ägäis (von Amorgos über Naxos, Lesbos, Rhodos, Karpathos und Kreta bis zu einigen Ionischen Inseln), in der West- und Südwesttürkei, auf Zypern und im Libanon.

Verbreitung auf Zypern

Ophrys cinereophila ist auf Zypern weit verbreitet und nicht selten. Besonders in küstennahen Gebieten, aber auch im Landesinneren bildet sie individuenreiche Bestände. *Ophrys cinereophila* wächst mit Vorliebe in *Pinus brutia*-Wäldern, wo sie meist von *Orchis syriaca* vergesellschaftet ist.

Bemerkungen

Im Gegensatz zu den Ägäischen Inseln und der Türkei sind die Vertreter der *Ophrys fusca*-Gruppe auf Zypern problemlos zu unterscheiden. Auf Zypern kommen nur drei Taxa aus diesem Formenkreis vor, nämlich *Ophrys cinereophila*, *Ophrys iricolor* und *Ophrys israelitica*.

Die charakteristischen Merkmale von *Ophrys cinereophila* sind ihre kleinen Blüten und ihre frühe Blütezeit. Darüber hinaus ist die Lippe von *Ophrys cinereophila* oft stark gebogen, und sie steht waagerecht vom Stängel ab. Ausserdem ist die Lippe mit einem kleinen, gelblichen Rand umgeben.

Die großblütige *Ophrys iricolor* ist mit ihrem leuchtend blauen Mal und intensiv roter oder rotbrauner Lippenunterseite nicht mit anderen Arten aus dem *Ophrys fusca*-Formenkreis zu verwechseln.

Ophrys israelitica unterscheidet sich von *Ophrys cinereophila* und *Ophrys iricolor* durch ihre flache Lippe, die im unteren Teil meist dunkelbraun bis violettbraun und im basalen Teil violettbläulich gefärbt ist und durch das Fehlen des V-förmigen Einschnittes an der Lippenbasis. *Ophrys cinereophila* wurde früher auf Zypern oft als Hybride zwischen *Ophrys fusca* und *Ophrys sicula* angesprochen (Dostmann & Stern, 1996).

Von einigen Autoren wurde für Zypern statt *Ophrys cinereophila* die nahe verwandte *Ophrys funerea* Viviani angegeben (vergleiche Georgiades, 1998ab und Christofides, 2001), und sie wurde bei G & K. Morschek (1996) unter *Ophrys fusca* geführt. Diese Art hat aber eine westliche Verbreitung (Korsika, Sardinien und Mt. Argentario) und unterscheidet sich von *Ophrys cinereophila* durch kleinere Blüten, eine dunklere Lippenfärbung, spätere Blütezeit und eine flache Lippe.

Gefährdung

Ophrys cinereophila hat auf Zypern viele Standorte (vor allem auf der Halbinsel Akrotiri im Süden) und bildet stellenweise sehr große Bestände. Die Art ist deshalb nicht gefährdet.

Hybriden

Nicht nachgewiesen.

◀ Akrotiri (Salt lake), 13.3.2002

Alevkaya (Pentadactylos Range), 18.3.2002

Ophrys cinereophila
Small-Flowered Brown Ophrys

H.F. Paulus & Gack

Jour. Eur. Orch. 30 (1): 170 (1998)

Synonym

Ophrys fusca subsp. *cinereophila* (H.F. Paulus & Gack) Faurholdt, Die Orchidee 53 (3): 345 (2002).

Description

Slender plant, 10 to 35 cm tall. Foliage leaves bluish to yellowish green, lower leaves ovate-lanceolate, arranged in a rosette, upper leaves oblong-lanceolate, erect to spreading. Inflorescence lax, elongated, with 5 to 7, sometimes up to 10 very small flowers. Sepals broadly ovate to lanceolate, yellowish to yellowish green, dorsal sepal strongly curved over forwards. Petals oblong-lanceolate, with wavy edges, yellowish green, rarely with a brownish tinge at margins; petals and sepals forming a fairly loose hood. Labellum very small, dark brown to black-violet, spreading horizontally from the axis and strongly curved, three-lobed, margins with a narrow light yellow border, V-shaped groove at the base, densely pubescent and without protuberances. Marking consisting of two separate ovate patches from the base, (steel-)blue or brown, shining, lower part rarely surrounded by a whitish border. Appendage absent.

Habitat

Maquis, phrygana, in light coniferous woods, abandoned olive groves and vineyards; more rarely in asphodel fields and wasteland; on calcareous soils.

Flowering time

Mid-February to late March.

Altitude distribution

From sea level to 1,000 m.

Overall distribution

Widely distributed in the eastern Mediterranean region. At least in southern Greece, and probably throughout the whole of the Aegean (from Amorgos to Naxos, Lesbos, Rhodes, Karpathos and Crete and as far as some Ionian islands), in western and southwestern Turkey, on Cyprus and in Lebanon.

Distribution on Cyprus

Ophrys cinereophila is well distributed in Cyprus and not rare. It forms individual-rich stands especially in coastal areas, but also in the interior. *Ophrys cinereophila* prefers *Pinus brutia* woods, where it is mostly accompanied by *Orchis syriaca*.

Remarks

The representatives of the *Ophrys fusca* group on Cyprus can be distinguished without difficulty, in contrast to those on the Aegean islands and in Turkey. Only three taxa of this complex occur on Cyprus, namely *Ophrys cinereophila, Ophrys iricolor* and *Ophrys israelitica*.

The distinguishing characteristics of *Ophrys cinereophila* are its small flowers and its early flowering time. Above all, the labellum of *Ophrys cinereophila* is often strongly curved, and spreads horizontally from the stem. Moreover, its labellum is surrounded by a small yellow border.

The large-flowered *Ophrys iricolor* cannot be confused with other species of the *Ophrys fusca* complex as its labellum has a bright blue marking and intense red to red-brown ventral side.

Ophrys israelitica can be distinguished from *Ophrys cinereophila* and *Ophrys iricolor* by its flat labellum, which is mostly dark brown to violet-brown in the lower part and violet-bluish in the basal part, and by the absence of a V-shaped groove at the base of the labellum. *Ophrys cinereophila* was often identified as a hybrid between *Ophrys fusca* and *Ophrys sicula* on Cyprus (Dostmann & Stern, 1996).

Some authors specified *Ophrys cinereophila* as the closely related *Ophrys funerea* Viviani (compare Georgiades, 1998ab and Christofides, 2001) for Cyprus and it was listed under *Ophrys fusca* by G & K. Morschek (1996). This species has however a western distribution (Corsica, Sardinia and Mt. Argentario) and differs from *Ophrys cinereophila* in smaller flowers, a darker labellum, later flowering time and a flat labellum.

Threats

Ophrys cinereophila has many habitats on Cyprus (mainly on the Akrotiri peninsula in the south) and in places forms very large stands. The species is therefore not threatened.

Hybrids

Unconfirmed.

Gerasa, 20.3.2002

Alevkaya (Pentadactylos Range), 18.3.2002

Neo Chorio-Agios Minas (Akamas), 3.3.2002

Choirokoitia, 4.3.2002

Tsada, 17.3.2002

Esentepe (Pentadactylos Range), 18.3.2002

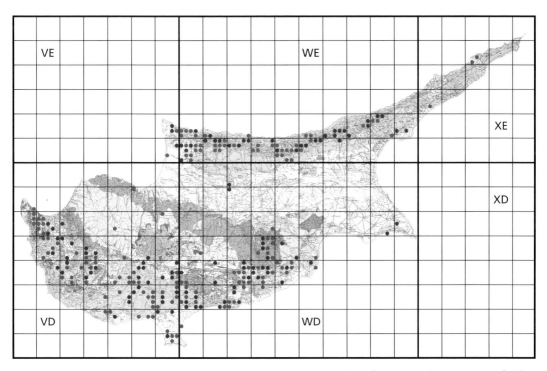

Ophrys cinereophila

25

Ophrys iricolor
Regenbogen-Ragwurz

Synonyme

Ophrys fusca subsp. *iricolor* (DESFONTAINES) K. RICHTER, Pl. Eur. 1: 261 (1890); *Arachnites iricolor* (DESFONTAINES) BUBANI, Fl. Pyrénées IV: 49 (1902). ('*incolor*')

Beschreibung

Pflanze kräftig, 15 bis 30 cm hoch. Laubblätter hell- bis gelblichgrün, die unteren eiförmig-lanzettlich bis oval, rosettig gehäuft, die oberen länglich-lanzettlich, aufgerichtet bis schräg abstehend. Blütenstand relativ kurz und mit 2 bis 6 Blüten; diese groß bis sehr groß, schräg abstehend. Sepalen breit eiförmig bis eiförmig-lanzettlich, die beiden seitlichen etwas nach vorne gebogen oder leicht zurückgeschlagen, das mittlere vornüber gebogen, hell- bis dunkelgrün gefärbt. Petalen schmal-lanzettlich, stumpf, braun bis rotbraun, an den Rändern leicht gewellt und meist grün oder bräunlich. Lippe groß, ziemlich lang, im apikalen Teil dreilappig, flach ausgebreitet, ohne Höcker, dunkelbraun bis schwarzviolett, die Seitenlappen stark dunkelbraun behaart. Lippenrückseite intensiv rötlich bis rötlichbraun gefärbt. Malzeichnung in der Form von zwei eiförmigen, leuchtend blauen Flächen ausgebildet, die oberen zwei Drittel der gesamten Lippe einnehmend. Anhängsel fehlt.

Standort

Macchien, Phrygana, Olivenhaine, Magerrasen, lichte Kiefernwälder und Ödland; auf steinigen, kalkhaltigen bis basischen Böden.

Blütezeit

(Anfang) Februar bis Mitte (Ende) März.

Höhenverbreitung

Von Meereshöhe bis 800 m.

Gesamtverbreitung

Im östlichen Mittelmeergebiet von Griechenland (Peloponnes, Ionische und Ägäische Inseln und Kreta) über die West- und Südtürkei bis nach Syrien, Libanon, Israel und Zypern.

Verbreitung auf Zypern

Ophrys iricolor ist auf Zypern relativ selten, doch ziemlich weit verbreitet, vor allem im Süden und im Pentadactylos-Gebirge im Norden der Insel.

Bemerkungen

Diese markante Art ist im östlichen Mittelmeerraum weit verbreitet, aber nur selten wirklich häufig (PAULUS, 2001b). *Ophrys iricolor* ist eine typische Art der Phrygana, wo die Pflanzen häufig im Schutz der Dornsträucher wachsen und ihre Blüten dann nach oben aus diesem Gestrüpp herausstrecken. Auch auf Zypern wächst sie mit Vorliebe in der Macchie unter *Calicotome villosa* und *Cistus*-Arten. Selten findet man diese Art in lichten Pinienwäldern, dort gerne mit *Neotinea maculata* vergesellschaftet.

Die Blütezeit von *Ophrys iricolor* fängt auf Zypern schon sehr früh an; sie blüht gleichzeitig mit *Ophrys elegans* auf. Wie KRETZSCHMAR berichtet (1995), der die Insel im Februar besuchte, weisen die früh blühenden Pflanzen von Zypern keinerlei Abweichung vom Typus auf, wie zum Beispiel auf Kreta, wo die frühblühende Sippe von PAULUS & ALIBERTIS als *Ophrys mesaritica* abgetrennt und neu beschrieben wurde. *Ophrys iricolor* hat auf Zypern eine lange Blütezeit, die frühblühenden Pflanzen sind ganz sicher identisch mit denen, die in März blühen.

Ophrys iricolor gehört als großblütige Art mit leuchtend blauem Mal und intensiv roter oder rotbrauner Lippenunterseite im Mittelmeerraum zu den schönsten und großblütigsten *Ophrys*-Arten. Sie ist nicht mit den anderen Arten aus dem *Ophrys fusca*-Formenkreis zu verwechseln. Ein sicheres Merkmal von *Ophrys iricolor* ist ihre immer rötlich bis rötlichbraun gefärbte Lippenrückseite.

Gefährdung

Ophrys iricolor ist auf Zypern zwar ziemlich selten, dafür aber weit verbreitet. Sie ist kaum gefährdet.

Hybriden

Nicht nachgewiesen.

238   Choirokoitia (Kalavasos dam), 4.3.2002

Ophrys iricolor
Rainbow Ophrys

DESFONTAINES

Ann. Mus. Hist. Nat. 10: 224 (1807)

Synonyms

Ophrys fusca subsp. *iricolor* (DESFONTAINES) K. RICHTER, Pl. Eur. 1: 261 (1890); *Arachnites iricolor* (DESFONTAINES) BUBANI, Fl. Pyrénées IV: 49 (1902). (*'incolor'*)

Description

Plant vigorous, 15 to 30 cm tall. Foliage leaves light to yellowish green, lower leaves ovate-lanceolate to oval, forming a rosette, upper leaves ovate-lanceolate, erect to spreading obliquely. Inflorescence relatively short, with 2 to 6 large to very large flowers, spreading obliquely. Sepals broadly ovate to ovate-lanceolate, the two lateral sepals slightly curved forwards or slightly reflexed, dorsal sepal curved over forwards, light to dark green. Petals narrowly lanceolate, with slightly wavy edges, obtuse, brown to red-brown, mostly green or brownish at edges. Labellum large, fairly long, three-lobed in apical part, spread out, without protuberances, dark brown to black-violet, lateral lobes covered with strong dark brown hairs. Ventral side of labellum intense reddish to reddish brown. Marking consisting of two ovate, bright blue patches, covering upper two-thirds of entire labellum. Appendage absent.

Habitat

Maquis, phrygana, olive groves, neglected grassland, light coniferous woods and wasteland; on rocky, calcareous to basic soils.

Flowering time

(Early) February to mid- (end) March.

Altitude distribution

From sea level to 800 m.

Overall distribution

In the eastern Mediterranean region from Greece (Peloponnese, Ionian and Aegean islands, Crete) through western and southern Turkey to Syria, Lebanon, Israel and Cyprus.

Distribution on Cyprus

Ophrys iricolor is relatively rare on Cyprus, but fairly widely distributed, especially in the south and in the Pentadactylos mountains in the north of the island.

Remarks

This remarkable species is widely distributed in the eastern Mediterranean region, but only seldom really abundant (PAULUS, 2001b). *Ophrys iricolor* is a typical species of the phrygana, where the plants grow abundantly under the protection of thorn bushes, and the flowers stand out above them. On Cyprus it also grows under *Calicotome villosa* and *Cistus* species in the maquis. Rarely, one can find this species in light pine woods, where it is often accompanied by *Neotinea maculata*.

The flowering time of *Ophrys iricolor* starts very early on Cyprus; it blooms at the same time as *Ophrys elegans*. As KRETZSCHMAR, who visited the island in February, reports (1995), these Cypriot early-flowering plants show no variation whatsoever from the normal type, as happened, for example on Crete, where the early-flowering taxon was separated and described by PAULUS & ALIBERTIS as *Ophrys mesaritica*. *Ophrys iricolor* has a long flowering time on Cyprus, and the early-flowering plants are almost certainly identical with those that bloom in March.

As a large-flowered species with a shiny blue speculum and intense red or red-brown ventral side, *Ophrys iricolor* belongs to the most beautiful and largest-flowered of the *Ophrys* species in the Mediterranean region. It can not be confused with other species of the *Ophrys fusca* species group. A distinctive characteristic of *Ophrys iricolor* is the ventral side of the labellum, which is always reddish or reddish brown.

Threats

Although *Ophrys iricolor* is fairly rare on Cyprus, it is however widely distributed. It is little threatened.

Hybrids

Unconfirmed.

Potamiou-Omodos, 15.3.2002

Choirokoitia (Kalavasos dam), 4.3.2002

Mathikoloni-Apsiou, 5.3.2002

Alevkaya (Pentadactylos Range), 18.3.2002

Apsiou, 5.3.2002

Mathikoloni-Apsiou, 5.3.2002

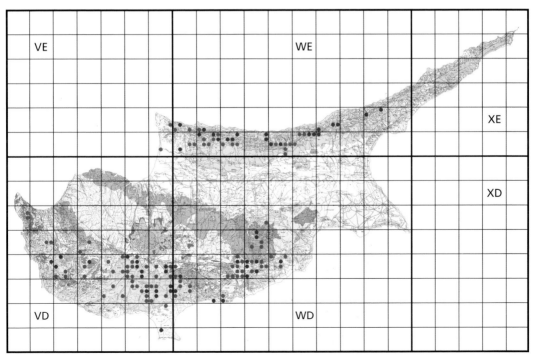

Ophrys iricolor

26 Ophrys israelitica

Israelische Ragwurz

H. Baumann & Künkele

Mitteilungsbl. Arbeitskr. Heim. Orch.
Baden-Württ. 20 (3): 613 & 614 (1988)

Synonym

Ophrys omegaifera subsp. *israelitica* (H. Baumann & Künkele) G. & K. Morschek, Orch. Cyprus: 126 (1996).

Beschreibung

Schlanke Pflanze, 10 bis 35 cm hoch, mit 2 bis 11 Blüten. Laubblätter bläulich- bis gelblichgrün, die unteren breit-eiförmig bis eiförmig-lanzettlich, rosettig gehäuft, die oberen länglich-lanzettlich, aufgerichtet bis schräg abstehend. Blüten mittelgroß und fast horizontal vom Stängel abstehend. Sepalen länglich-eiförmig, grünlichgelb bis hellgrün gefärbt, die beiden seitlichen abstehend, das mittlere stark nach vorne gebogen. Petalen lanzettlich, meist etwas dunkler als die Sepalen, gewellt und an den Rändern violett überlaufen. Lippe am Grunde schwach gewölbt, in der Mitte dreilappig, dunkelbraun, schwarzbraun bis violettbraun, im basalen Teil violettbläulich, selten mit gelbem Rand; Mittellappen am Grunde meist gekerbt, die beiden Seitenlappen flach und an der Aussenseite schwach violett behaart. Malzeichnung auf die basale und apikale Lippenhälfte beschränkt, 'Omega'-förmig und bleigrau bis weisslich. Anhängsel fehlt.

Standort

Ödland, lichte Kiefernwälder, Macchien, Phrygana und Gebüsch, häufig auch auf aufgelassenen Kulturflächen (ehemaligen Weinbergterrassen); auf kalkreichen bis basischen Böden.

Blütezeit

Von Anfang Februar bis Ende März.

Höhenverbreitung

Von 200 bis 900 m.

Gesamtverbreitung

Östliches Mittelmeergebiet, nämlich Südtürkei, Israel, Libanon, Jordanien und Zypern. Auch auf Naxos, Paros und Siros (Paulus & Gack, 1990a; Delforge, 1995b; Kretzschmar, 1996). Wahrscheinlich auch in Westsyrien. Mit Ausnahme von Zypern ist *Ophrys israelitica* im ganzen Verbreitungsgebiet selten. In Israel kommt diese Art als einziger Vertreter aus dem *Ophrys omegaifera*-Aggregat bzw. dem *Ophrys fusca*-Formenkreis vor (Baumann & Künkele, 1988b).

Verbreitung auf Zypern

Hauptsächlich im Süden, im Norden vor allem im Pentadactylos-Gebirge verbreitet. *Ophrys israelitica* ist auf Zypern häufig und vielgestaltig.

Bemerkungen

Ophrys israelitica wurde 1988 von Baumann & Künkele (1988b) beschrieben. Funde dieser Art wurden vor der Neubeschreibung meist zu *Ophrys fleischmannii* gestellt.

Ophrys israelitica ist auf Zypern, ihrem Hauptverbreitungsgebiet, ohne Probleme von den anderen Vertretern des *Ophrys fusca*-Formenkreises zu unterscheiden. Sie ähnelt vor allem *Ophrys omegaifera*, die aber auf Zypern nicht vorkommt, obwohl sie von mehreren Autoren für Zypern angegeben wurde (unter anderem Hansen, Kreutz & U. & D. Rückbrodt, 1990; Georgiades, 1998ab; Hubbard & Scraton, 2001). Sie unterscheidet sich von *Ophrys omegaifera* durch ihre flache Lippe, die im unteren Teil meist schwarzbraun bis violettbraun und im basalen Teil violettbläulich gefärbt ist. Von *Ophrys iricolor* unterscheidet die Art sich vor allem durch das Fehlen eines markanten, stahlblauen Mals und von *Ophrys cinereophila* durch ihre größeren Blüten. Darüber hinaus ist die Lippe von *Ophrys cinereophila* oft stark gebogen, steht waagerecht vom Stängel ab, und die Blüten sind mit einem kleinen, gelblichen Rand umgeben.

Von Wood (1985) wurde *Ophrys israelitica* unter *Ophrys fusca* subsp. *fleischmannii* (Hayek) Soó (*Ophrys fleischmannii* Hayek) geführt, weil *Ophrys israelitica* zu dieser Zeit noch nicht beschrieben war. *Ophrys fleischmannii* kommt nach dem heutigen Kenntnisstand nur auf Kreta und Hydra vor.

Gefährdung

Ophrys israelitica ist auf Zypern weit verbreitet und häufig. Sie ist deswegen als nicht gefährdet einzustufen.

Hybriden

Nicht nachgewiesen.

Agios Paraskevi-Kalo Chorio, 5.3.2002

Ophrys israelitica
Israeli Ophrys

H. Baumann & Künkele

Mitteilungsbl. Arbeitskr. Heim. Orch.
Baden-Württ. 20 (3): 613 & 614 (1988)

Synonym

Ophrys omegaifera subsp. *israelitica* (H. Baumann & Künkele) G. & K. Morschek, Orch. Cyprus: 126 (1996).

Description

Slender plant, 10 to 35 cm tall, with 2 to 11 flowers. Foliage leaves bluish to yellowish green, lower leaves broadly ovate to ovate-lanceolate, forming a rosette, upper leaves oblong-lanceolate, erect to spreading obliquely. Flowers medium-sized and spreading almost horizontally from the stem. Sepals oblong-ovate, greenish yellow to light green, both laterals spreading, dorsal sepal strongly bent forwards. Petals lanceolate, mostly somewhat darker than sepals, wavy and violet tinged at edges. Labellum slightly convex at base, three-lobed from the middle, dark brown, black-brown to violet-brown, violet-bluish in basal part, rarely with yellow border; middle lobe usually grooved at base, both lateral lobes flat and covered with faint violet hairs on exterior. Marking limited to basal and apical part of labellum, 'omega'-shaped and blue-grey to whitish. Appendage absent.

Habitat

Wasteland, light coniferous woods, maquis, phryga-na and shrubland, also abundant in neglected cultivated fields (former vineyard terraces); on calcareous to basic soils.

Flowering time

From early February to late March.

Altitude distribution

From 200 to 900 m.

Overall distribution

Eastern Mediterranean region, namely southern Turkey, Israel, Lebanon, Jordan and Cyprus. Also on Naxos, Paros and Siros (Paulus & Gack, 1990a; Delforge, 1995b; Kretzschmar, 1996). Probably also in western Syria. *Ophrys israelitica* is rare in its whole distibution area, except for Cyprus. This species occurs in Israel as the only representative of the *Ophrys omegaifera* sub-group in the *Ophrys fusca* group (Baumann & Künkele, 1988b).

Distribution on Cyprus

Predominantly in the south; in the north mainly found in the Pentadactylos mountains. *Ophrys israelitica* is abundant on Cyprus and polymorphic.

Remarks

Ophrys israelitica was described in 1988 by Baumann & Künkele (1988b). Findings of this species were mostly placed under *Ophrys fleischmannii* before the redescription.

Ophrys israelitica can be distinguished without difficulty from other representatives of the *Ophrys fus-ca* group on Cyprus, its main distribution area. It strongly resembles *Ophrys omegaifera*, which does not however occur on Cyprus, although it has been specified by several authors for Cyprus (such as Hansen, Kreutz & U. & D. Rückbrodt, 1990; Georgiades, 1998ab; Hubbard & Scraton, 2001). It can be distinguished from *Ophrys omegaifera* by its flat labellum, which is mostly black-brown to violet-brown in the lower part and violet-bluish in the basal part. The species mainly differs from *Ophrys iricolor* by the absence of a striking steel-blue marking and from *Ophrys cinereophila* by its larger flowers. Above all, the labellum of *Ophrys cinereophila* is often strongly bent, spreads horizontally from the stem and its flowers are surrounded by a small, yellow border.

Wood (1985) placed *Ophrys israelitica* under *Ophrys fusca* subsp. *fleischmannii* (Hayek) Soó (*Ophrys fleischmannii* Hayek), as *Ophrys israelitica* had not been described at the time. According to the current state of knowledge, *Ophrys fleischmannii* occurs only on Crete and Hydra.

Threats

Ophrys israelitica is widely distributed and abundant on Cyprus. It is therefore not threatened.

Hybrids

Unconfirmed.

Apsiou-Louvaras, 5.3.2002

Potamiou-Omodos, 15.3.2002

Choirokoitia, 11.3.2002

Apsiou-Louvaras, 5.3.2002

Alevkaya (Pentadactylos Range), 18.3.2002

Tsada, 17.3.2002

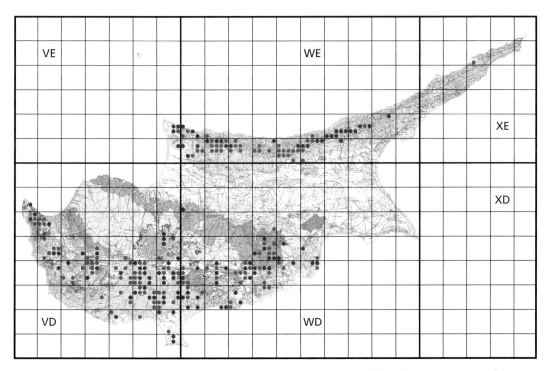

Ophrys israelitica

27

Ophrys elegans
Zierliche Ragwurz

(RENZ) H. BAUMANN & KÜNKELE

Mitteilungsbl. Arbeitskr. Heim. Orch.
Baden-Württ. 13 (3): 350 (1981)

Basionym

Ophrys gottfriediana subsp. *elegans* RENZ, Repert. Spec. Nov. Regni Veg. 27: 206 (1929).

Synonym

Ophrys argolica H. FLEISCHMANN subsp. *elegans* (RENZ) E. NELSON, Monogr. Ophrys: 153 (1962).

Beschreibung

Pflanze zierlich und schlank, 10 bis 20 cm hoch. Laubblätter grün bis gelblichgrün, die unteren eiförmig-lanzettlich, die oberen länglich-lanzettlich und in stängelumfassende Hochblätter übergehend. Blütenstand kurz und lockerblütig. Blüten klein, meist schräg vom Stängel abstehend. Sepalen weiss bis rosaviolett, oft mit grünem Mittelnerv, eiförmig-lanzettlich und zugespitzt, die seitlichen abstehend bis zurückgeschlagen, das mittlere Sepal schmal-lanzettlich, weit zurückgeschlagen. Petalen rosa bis violett gefärbt, dreieckig bis länglich-dreieckig, abstehend bis leicht zurückgeschlagen, meist dicht papillös behaart. Lippe dreieckig, dreilappig bis fast ganzrandig, mit stumpfen Höckern, braun bis rötlichbraun; Mittellappen länglich-dreieckig, seitliche Ränder stark zurückgebogen. Seitenlappenhöcker ausgesprochen kurz, gerundet, stumpf, stark zottig behaart. Mal über die Lippe verteilt, aus Flecken und Bögen bestehend, blauschwarz oder schwarzviolett. Anhängsel klein, vorgezogen, gelblich, vorwärts gerichtet.

Standort

Lichte Kiefern- und Zypressenwälder, Phrygana und Macchien, selten auf Ödland oder im Gebüsch; auf trockenen bis mäßig feuchten, überwiegend kalkreichen bis sandigen Böden.

Blütezeit

Von Mitte Februar bis Mitte (Ende) März.

Höhenverbreitung

Von Meereshöhe bis 500 m.

Gesamtverbreitung

Endemische Art von Zypern. Die Art wird von verschiedenen Autoren auch für Südanatolien angegeben (SUNDERMANN & TAUBENHEIM, 1978; VÖTH, 1967; BAUMANN & KÜNKELE, 1982a, 1988a; BUTTLER, 1986; DELFORGE, 1994). Von all diesen Angaben existieren aber keine Herbar- und Fotobelege. Auch später konnten niemals typische Exemplare dieser Art ausserhalb Zyperns nachgewiesen werden. Vermutlich handelt es sich hier um Angaben von *Ophrys lucis*, einer Art, die im mittleren Süden der Türkei und auf Rhodos vorkommt und gewisse Ähnlichkeiten mit *Ophrys elegans* aufweist.

Verbreitung auf Zypern

Auf der ganzen Insel verbreitet, aber zerstreut und an vielen Standorten meist in nur wenigen Exemplaren vorkommend.

Bemerkungen

Ophrys elegans ist auf Zypern vor allem in lichten Kiefernwäldern verbreitet und kommt dort oft zusammen mit *Orchis syriaca* und Arten des *Ophrys fusca*-Formenkreises vor. Auch kommt sie in niedrig gelegenen Bereichen vor. Dort wächst sie gerne in der Phrygana und in felsigen Biotopen auf kalkreichen bis basischen Böden. Kleinere Blüten zeigt *Ophrys elegans* an höher gelegenen Standorten, wo sie auf trockenen, meist spärlich bewachsenen Stellen vorkommt (WOOD, 1985).

Ihre Hauptvorkommen liegen im Norden (Pentadactylos-Gebirge), im mittleren Süden und im Akamas-Gebiet. Nach VINEY (1994) wächst *Ophrys elegans* im Norden der Insel im Bereich der Karpasia-Halbinsel von Kap Koruçam bis Khelones in Pinien-, Zypressen- und Wacholderwäldern und in Sanddünen. Besonders häufig ist die Art in den Pinienwäldern auf sandigen Böden in der Umgebung von Akdeniz.

Die Art ist auf Zypern ohne Probleme von den anderen dort vorkommenden *Ophrys*-Arten zu unterscheiden. Typische Merkmale dieser Art sind ihre mittelgroßen Blüten und ihre kleinen, dreieckigen bis länglich-dreieckigen, abstehenden bis leicht zurückgeschlagenen, braunen bis rötlichbraunen Lippen mit stumpfen Höckern.

HANSSON (2001) berichtet über das Vorkommen von *Ophrys aegaea* auf Zypern, einer Art aus dem Formenkreis von *Ophrys elegans*. Zwar sieht die Pflanze, die er auf Zypern gefunden hat *Ophrys aegaea* ähnlich, aber es handelt sich bei dieser Pflanze vermutlich um eine abweichende Form von *Ophrys elegans*, zumal das Verbreitungsgebiet von *Ophrys aegaea* auf Karpathos und Kasos doch sehr entfernt ist.

Gefährdung

Ophrys elegans ist auf Zypern zwar selten, aber weit verbreitet. Sie ist deshalb als nicht gefährdet einzustufen.

Hybriden

Mit *Ophrys bornmuelleri*, *Ophrys levantina* und *Ophrys umbilicata*.

250   **Kofinou, 10.3.2002**

Ophrys elegans
Elegant Ophrys

(Renz) H. Baumann & Künkele

Mitteilungsbl. Arbeitskr. Heim. Orch.
Baden-Württ. 13 (3): 350 (1981)

Basionym

Ophrys gottfriediana subsp. *elegans* Renz, Repert. Spec. Nov. Regni Veg. 27: 206 (1929).

Synonym

Ophrys argolica H. Fleischmann subsp. *elegans* (Renz) E. Nelson, Monogr. Ophrys: 153 (1962).

Description

Plant delicate and slender, 10 to 20 cm tall. Foliage leaves green to yellowish green, lower leaves ovate-lanceolate, upper leaves oblong-lanceolate and merging into stem-sheathing upper leaves. Inflorescence short and lax-flowered. Flowers small, mostly spreading obliquely from stem. Sepals white to pink-violet, often with a green mid-vein, ovate-lanceolate and acuminate, laterals spreading to reflexed, dorsal sepal narrowly lanceolate, widely reflexed. Petals pink to violet, triangular to oblong-triangular, spreading to slightly reflexed, usually densely papillose. Labellum three-lobed to almost entire, with blunt protuberances, brown to reddish brown; middle lobe oblong-triangular, lateral edges strongly bent backwards. Protuberances on lateral lobes markedly short, rounded, obtuse, densely villose. Marking covering labellum, consisting of patches and arches, blue-black or black-violet. Appendage small, drawn-out forwards, yellowish, directed forwards.

Habitat

Light coniferous and cypress woods, phrygana and maquis, rarely on wasteland or among shrubs; on arid to moderately moist, primarily calcareous to sandy soils.

Flowering time

From mid-February to mid- (end) March.

Altitude distribution

From sea level to 500 m.

Overall distribution

Endemic species of Cyprus. The species is also specified by various authors for southern Anatolia (Sundermann & Taubenheim, 1978; Vöth, 1967; Baumann & Künkele, 1982a, 1988a; Buttler, 1986; Delforge, 1994). There is however no botanical or photographic evidence for these reports. Recently, typical specimens of this species have not been found outside Cyprus. These reports probably concerned *Ophrys lucis*, a species which occurs in the central southern part of Turkey and on Rhodes and which shows certain similarities with *Ophrys elegans*.

Distribution on Cyprus

Distributed throughout the whole island, but occurring only sporadically and at many locations usually as only a few specimens.

Remarks

Ophrys elegans is mainly distributed in light coniferous woods and is often accompanied there by *Orchis syriaca* and by species of the *Ophrys fusca* group. It also occurs in low-lying areas, and there it prefers phrygana and rocky biotopes, on calcareous to basic soils. *Ophrys elegans* has smaller flowers at higher altitudes, where it occurs on arid, mainly sparsely vegetated locations (Wood, 1985).

Its main distribution is in the north of the island (Pentadaclylos-mountains), in the central southern part and in the Akamas area. According to Viney (1994) *Ophrys elegans* grows in the north of the island in the region of the Karpasia peninsula from Cape Koruçam to Khelones in pine, cypress and juniper woodlands and in sand dunes. The species is exceptionally abundant on the sandy soils of the pine woods near Akdeniz.

This species can easily be distinguished from other *Ophrys* species in Cyprus. Typical characteristics are its medium-sized flowers and its small triangular to oblong-triangular, spreading to slightly reflexed, brown to reddish brown labellum with obtuse protuberances.

Hansson (2001) reports on the occurrence of *Ophrys aegaea* on Cyprus, a species of the *Ophrys elegans* species group. The plant on Cyprus resembles *Ophrys aegaea*, but this plant is more probably an aberrant form of *Ophrys elegans*, and additionally, the distribution area of *Ophrys aegaea* on Karpathos and Kasos is far removed.

Threats

Although *Ophrys elegans* is very rare on Cyprus, it is widely distributed. It can therefore be categorized as not threatened.

Hybrids

With *Ophrys bornmuelleri*, *Ophrys levantina* and *Ophrys umbilicata*.

Kayalar-Sadrazamköy, 14.3.2002

Kofinou, 10.3.2002

Neo Chorio-Agios Minas (Akamas), 10.3.2002

Agios Paraskevi-Gerasa, 5.3.2002

Neo Chorio-Agios Minas (Akamas), 10.3.2002

Agios Paraskevi-Gerasa, 5.3.2002

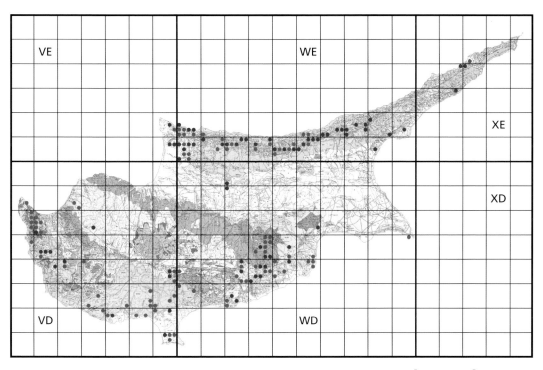

265 Meldungen / Reports

Ophrys elegans

28

Ophrys kotschyi
Kotschys Ragwurz

H. Fleischmann & Soó emend. Soó

Repert. Spec. Nov. Regni Veg. 24: 27 (1927)

Synonyme

Ophrys sintenisii subsp. *kotschyi* (H. Fleischmann & Soó) Soó, Bot. Arch. 23: 31 (1929); *Ophrys cypria* Renz, Repert. Spec. Nov. Regni Veg. 27: 202 (1929).

Beschreibung

Relativ kräftige Pflanze, 15 bis 30 cm hoch. Laubblätter grün bis bläulichgrün, am Grunde rosettig gehäuft, die unteren breit-lanzettlich bis elliptisch, die oberen stängelumfassend. Blütenstand meist gedrängt, 2- bis 7-blütig, selten bis zu 12 Blüten. Blüten groß, abstehend. Sepalen länglich-eiförmig bis elliptisch, stumpf; mittleres Sepal stark nach vorne gebogen und lanzettlicher als die beiden seitlichen Sepalen, hellgrün bis grün gefärbt. Petalen dreieckig bis lanzettlich, kurz papillös behaart, olivgrün oder braun bis braungrün. Lippe groß, elliptisch bis oval, im oberen Teil stark dreilappig, meist bauchig erweitert, stumpf gehökkert, schwarzpurpurn bis schwarzviolett, Seitenlappen stark zurückgekrümmt, dicht und kurz behaart. Höcker an der Innenseite leicht behaart, an der Aussenseite stark weisslich behaart. Mal über die ganze Lippe verteilt, Kernzonen auberginenfarbig mit silbriger Umrandung. Anhängsel sehr klein und spitz, gelblichgrün, leicht aufwärts gebogen.

Standort

Phrygana, Gebüsche, Magerrasen, grasiges Ödland, lichte Kiefernwälder, in Karuben- und Olivenhainen, unter Zypressen und Eukalyptusbäumen. Ausserdem in küstennahen, feuchten, spärlich bewachsenen, Salz beeinflussten Wiesenarealen; auf trockenen bis mäßig feuchten, besonders kalkreichen bis sandigen Böden.

Blütezeit

Von Mitte Februar bis Ende März, manchmal auch noch bis Mitte April.

Höhenverbreitung

Von der Meereshöhe bis 800 m.

Gesamtverbreitung

Endemische Art von Zypern.

Verbreitung auf Zypern

Ophrys kotschyi ist eine seltene Art, die hauptsächlich im Norden (vor allem im Pentadactylos-Gebirge), auf der Akrotiri-Halbinsel im Süden und auf mehreren Kalkhügeln im Osten der Insel vorkommt. Ausserdem, aber selten, im Akamas-Gebiet.

Bemerkungen

Die endemische *Ophrys kotschyi* gehört zu den schönsten Ragwurzarten Europas. Mit ihren ziemlich großen, schwarz bis dunkelviolett gefärbten Blüten ist sie im Gelände eine prachtvolle Erscheinung. Mit Ausnahme der Vorkommen auf der Halbinsel Akrotiri bestehen die Populationen von *Ophrys kotschyi* meist nur aus wenigen Exemplaren. Nach

Viney (1994) variiert die Art jährlich stark in der Anzahl blühender Pflanzen.

Nach Baumann & Künkele (1994) wächst die Art in zwei Teilarealen, in denen etwa die gleiche Anzahl von Populationen und Pflanzen vorkommen. In Nordzypern konzentrieren sich die Vorkommen auf die aus Kalkstein aufgebaute Nordkette (Pentadactylos-Gebirge), die sich von Kap Kormakiti im Westen parallel zur Küste bis zum Kap Andreas im Osten erstreckt. Ab der Mitte dieses Gebirgszuges tritt nach Osten eine Ausdünnung der Vorkommen ein. Das Verbreitungsgebiet in Südzypern liegt in der schmalen Zone aus tertiären Kalken und kalkreichem Mergel, die die Abdachungen des Troodos-Gebirges im Norden, Osten und Süden hufeisenförmig umfasst.

Im Süden Zyperns hat die Art eine Vorliebe für feuchte, küstennahe Standorte. So wächst sie auf der Halbinsel Akrotiri zu Tausenden in den weitläufigen, feuchten, sandigen, mehr oder weniger Salz beeinflussten Wiesenarealen. Hier ist *Ophrys kotschyi* oft mit *Ophrys umbilicata* und *Ophrys attica* vergesellschaftet und bildet mit ihnen viele Hybriden.

In letzter Zeit wurde *Ophrys kotschyi* auch an mehreren Standorten auf der Akamas Halbinsel nachgewiesen (Singer, 1996; Dostmann & Stern, 1996). Die Standorte sind in diesem Gebiet aber bei weitem nicht so stark besetzt wie im Norden oder Süden der Insel, und an einigen Fundorten wachsen nur Einzelpflanzen, wobei Dostmann & Stern (1996) vier Wuchsorte mit insgesamt 33 Pflanzen notierten. Die Phrygana-Biotope im Akamas sind aber durch Beweidung und Bebauung stark gefährdet.

Gefährdung

Aus dem aktuellen Kartierungsstand geht hervor, dass *Ophrys kotschyi* auf Zypern selten ist. An den Arealrändern der Karpasia-Halbinsel, der Mesaoria-Ebene, der Umgebung von Lefkosia und Dhekelia sowie der Bucht von Akrotiri ist *Ophrys kotschyi* stark rückläufig oder sogar bereits erloschen (Baumann & Künkele, 1994). An einigen Standorten gibt es aber immer noch recht individuenreiche Populationen. Die Art ist deshalb weniger gefährdet als von Baumann & Künkele (1994) angegeben.

Hybriden

Mit *Ophrys attica*, *Ophrys flavomarginata* (*Ophrys* x*lefkosiana* H. Baumann & Künkele), *Ophrys lapethica* (*Ophrys* x*denglerensis* A. Riechelmann), *Ophrys levantina*, *Ophrys mammosa* (*Ophrys* x*kreutziana* P. Delforge) und *Ophrys umbilicata* (*Ophrys* x*paphosiana* nsubsp. *paphosiana* H. Baumann & Künkele) nachgewiesen.

Akrotiri (Moni Agios Nikolaos), 8.3.2002

Ophrys kotschyi
Kotschy's Ophrys

H. Fleischmann & Soó emend. Soó

Repert. Spec. Nov. Regni Veg. 24: 27 (1927)

Synonyms

Ophrys sintenisii subsp. *kotschyi* (H. Fleischmann & Soó) Soó, Bot. Arch. 23: 31 (1929); *Ophrys cypria* Renz, Repert. Spec. Nov. Regni Veg. 27: 202 (1929).

Description

Relatively vigorous plant, 15 to 30 cm tall. Foliage leaves green to bluish green, forming a rosette at the base, lower leaves broadly lanceolate to elliptical, upper leaves stem-sheathing. Inflorescence mostly compact, 2 to 7 flowers, rarely up to 12 flowers. Flowers large, spreading. Sepals oblong-ovate to elliptical, obtuse; dorsal sepal strongly bent forwards and more lanceolate than lateral sepals, light green to green. Petals triangular to lanceolate, velvety, olivegreen or brown to brown-green. Labellum large, elliptical to oval, deeply three-lobed in upper part, usually convexly arched, protuberances blunt, black-purple to black-violet, lateral lobes strongly reflexed, covered in dense short hairs. Interior of protuberances slightly hairy, exterior covered in dense white hairs. Marking covering entire labellum, central areas aubergine with a silvery border. Appendage very small and acuminate, yellowish green, slightly bent upwards.

Habitat

Phrygana, shrublands, neglected grassland, grassy wasteland, light coniferous woods, in carob and olive groves, under cypresses and eucalyptus trees. Also in coastal, moist, sparsely overgrown meadows with saline influence; on arid to moderately moist, particularly calcareous to sandy soils.

Flowering time

From mid-February to late March, sometimes even until mid-April.

Altitude distribution

From sea level to 800 m.

Overall distribution

Endemic species of Cyprus.

Distribution on Cyprus

Ophrys kotschyi is a rare species, which primarily occurs in the north (especially in the Pentadactylos mountains), on the Akrotiri peninsula in the south and on several limestone-hills in the east. Also, but very rare in the Akamas area.

Remarks

The endemic *Ophrys kotschyi* is one of the most beautiful *Ophrys* species in Europe. Its fairly large, black to dark violet flowers give it a splendid appearance in open terrain. Populations of *Ophrys kotschyi* mostly consist of a few specimens, except in the Akrotiri peninsula. According to Viney (1994), the number of flowering plants varies widely from year to year.

According to Baumann & Künkele (1994), the species grows in two separate zones, in which a similar number of populations and plants occur. In northern Cyprus, the occurrences are centred around the limestone mountain chain (Pentadactylos mountains), which stretches from Cape Kormakiti in the west, and runs parallel with the coast to Cape Andreas in the east. The number of occurrences tapers off from the middle of this mountain chain towards the east. The distribution area in southern Cyprus consists of a narrow band of tertiary limestone and calcareous marl, which encloses the slopes of the Troodos mountains in a horseshoe-shape.

In southern Cyprus, the species prefers moist, coastal habitats. Thousands of *Ophrys kotschyi* grow for example on the Akrotiri peninsula in the vast, moist, more or less saline-influenced sandy meadows. *Ophrys kotschyi* is often accompanied there by *Ophrys umbilicata* and *Ophrys attica* and forms many hybrids with it.

Ophrys kotschyi has also recently been identified at several locations on the Akamas peninsula (Singer, 1996; Dostmann & Stern, 1996). The locations in this area however are not by far as densely populated as in the north or south of the island, and in some localities only solitary plants have been found. Dostmann & Stern (1996) have reported that these locations involve four sites with a total of 33 specimens. However, the phrygana biotopes on the Akamas peninsula are heavily threatened by fertilisation and building development.

Threats

According to the current state of charting, *Ophrys kotschyi* is rare on Cyprus. At the edges of its habitats on the Karpasia peninsula, in the Mesaoria plains, in the vicinity of Lefkosia and Dhekelia, and Akrotiri Bay, *Ophrys kotschyi* has declined considerably or is even now extinct. (Baumann & Künkele, 1994). At some locations however, there are still relatively individual-rich populations. The species is therefore less threatened than reported by Baumann & Künkele (1994).

Hybrids

Confirmed with *Ophrys attica, Ophrys flavomarginata* (*Ophrys* ×*lefkosiana* H. Baumann & Künkele), *Ophrys lapethica* (*Ophrys* ×*denglerensis* A. Riechelmann), *Ophrys levantina, Ophrys mammosa* (*Ophrys* ×*kreutziana* P. Delforge) and *Ophrys umbilicata* (*Ophrys* ×*paphosiana* nsubsp. *paphosiana* H. Baumann & Künkele).

Hirsarköy, 14.3.2002

Hirsarköy, 14.3.2002

Akrotiri (Moni Agios Nikolaos), 8.3.2002

Akrotiri (Salt lake), 8.3.2002

Kayalar, 14.3.2002   Alethriko, 6.3.2002

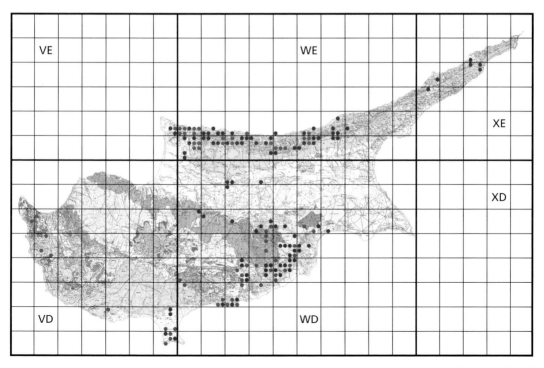

Ophrys kotschyi

29 Ophrys levantina

Levante-Ragwurz

GÖLZ & H.R. REINHARD

Mitteilungsbl. Arbeitskr. Heim. Orch.
Baden-Württ. 17 (3): 461 & 462 (1985)

Synonyme

Ophrys fuciflora subsp. *bornmuelleri* var. *grandiflora* (H. FLEISCHMANN & SOÓ) B. & E. WILLING, Die Orchidee 26 (2): 78 (1975); *Ophrys holoserica* subsp. *bornmuelleri* var. *grandiflora* (H. FLEISCHMANN & SOÓ) LANDWEHR, Wilde Orch. Eur. 2: 472 (1977). nom. nud.; *Ophrys bornmuelleri* subsp. *grandiflora* (H. FLEISCHMANN & SOÓ) RENZ & TAUBENHEIM, Notes Roy. Bot. Gard. Edinburgh 41: 276 (1983).

Beschreibung

Kräftige Pflanze mit lockerem Blütenstand, 20 bis 30 cm hoch, der 5 bis 10 Blüten trägt. Laubblätter hell- bis gelblichgrün, die unteren eiförmig-lanzettlich, rosettig gehäuft, die oberen länglich-lanzettlich, aufgerichtet bis abstehend, bisweilen stängelumfassend. Blüten mittelgroß bis groß, ziemlich locker angeordnet. Sepalen breit eiförmig, kurz, abgerundet, grünlichweiss gefärbt mit grünen Adern, die seitlichen abstehend, das mittlere aufrecht. Petalen sehr klein, dreieckig, weisslichgrün oder rosa bis rötlich. Lippe ziemlich breit, rundlich oder abgerundet quadratisch bis leicht trapezförmig, ungeteilt, vertikal abwärts gerichtet, schwach gewölbt, kräftig gehöckert (Höcker groß und stumpf), hell bis dunkelbraun oder olivbraun gefärbt, an den Rändern stark bräunlich, grau bis violett behaart. Malzeichnung isoliert, das Basalfeld nicht umfassend, meist H-förmig oder reduziert, dunkelbraun, und hell umrandet. Anhängsel groß, gelblich, nach vorne gerichtet.

Standort

Macchien, Phrygana, mäßig feuchte Wiesenflächen, Straßenböschungen und in lichten Kiefernwäldern; auf kalkreichen Böden.

Blütezeit

Mitte Februar bis Mitte März. Blüht etwa zwei Wochen früher als *Ophrys bornmuelleri*.

Höhenverbreitung

Von der Küste bis 700 m.

Gesamtverbreitung

Zypern und sehr selten in der mittlerer Südtürkei. Die Funde von *Ophrys levantina* aus dem westlichen Teil von Syrien, Libanon, Israel und der Osttürkei beziehen sich auf *Ophrys holoserica* subsp. *grandiflora* (H. FLEISCHMANN & SOÓ) FAURHOLDT. Diese Pflanzen sind viel hochwüchsiger, die Blüten viel größer, grauer gefärbt und mehr rechteckig (KREUTZ, 1998).

Verbreitung auf Zypern

Hauptsächlich im Süden, Westen und Norden der Insel verbreitet.

Bemerkungen

Ophrys levantina kommt fast ausschließlich in Zypern vor und ist stellenweise häufig. Die Pflanzen sind durchschnittlich zwischen 20 und 30 cm hoch, der Blütenstand mit den relativ großen Blüten ist ziemlich gedrungen.

Die Art wurde lange Zeit als eine Unterart von *Ophrys bornmuelleri* angesehen, mit der sie eigentlich nichts gemein hat. GÖLZ & REINHARD (1985) haben diese Sippe dann auch zurecht als eine eigene Art beschrieben. *Ophrys levantina* ist gegen *Ophrys bornmuelleri* sehr gut abgegrenzt. Ein gutes Merkmal von *Ophrys levantina* ist der Stand der Blütenlippe zum Stängel, der bei *Ophrys levantina* schräg zurück geneigt ist, während er bei *Ophrys bornmuelleri* mehr oder weniger horizontal vom Stängel absteht. Ausserdem ist die Lippe von *Ophrys levantina* stark behaart und rundlich bis leicht trapezförmig, während sie bei *Ophrys bornmuelleri* mehr trapezförmig gestaltet ist.

Beide Arten wachsen oft zusammen am gleichen Standort. Sie sind jedoch immer ohne Schwierigkeiten von einander zu unterscheiden. Ausserdem sind sie durch den um zwei bis drei Wochen unterschiedlichen Beginn der Blütezeit deutlich voneinander getrennt. Nach WOOD (1985) wurden bisher keine Hybriden zwischen *Ophrys levantina* und *Ophrys bornmuelleri* beobachtet. Vom Autor wurde jedoch bei Esentepe im nördlichen Teil Zyperns eine Pflanze mit deutlich intermediären Merkmalen gefunden.

Gefährdung

Ophrys levantina ist auf Zypern nicht selten, und sie besitzt noch viele Fundstellen. Sie ist daher als nicht besonders gefährdet einzustufen.

Hybriden

Mit *Ophrys attica*, *Ophrys bornmuelleri*, *Ophrys elegans*, *Ophrys flavomarginata*, *Ophrys lapethica* (*Ophrys* ×*liebischiana* R. KOHLMÜLLER), *Ophrys kotschyi* und *Ophrys mammosa*.

Kato Drys-Vavla, 6.3.2002

Ophrys levantina

Levant Ophrys

GÖLZ & H.R. REINHARD

Mitteilungsbl. Arbeitskr. Heim. Orch.
Baden-Württ. 17 (3): 461 & 462 (1985)

Synonyms

Ophrys fuciflora subsp. *bornmuelleri* var. *grandiflora* (H. FLEISCHMANN & SOÓ) B. & E. WILLING, Die Orchidee 26 (2): 78 (1975); *Ophrys holoserica* subsp. *bornmuelleri* var. *grandiflora* (H. FLEISCHMANN & SOÓ) LANDWEHR, Wilde Orch. Eur. 2: 472 (1977). nom. nud.; *Ophrys bornmuelleri* subsp. *grandiflora* (H. FLEISCHMANN & SOÓ) RENZ & TAUBENHEIM, Notes Roy. Bot. Gard. Edinburgh 41: 276 (1983).

Description

Vigorous plant with a lax inflorescence, 20 to 30 cm tall, bearing 5 to 10 flowers. Foliage leaves light to yellowish green, lower leaves ovate-lanceolate, arranged in a rosette, upper leaves oblong-lanceolate, erect to spreading, at times stem-sheathing. Flowers medium-sized to large, fairly laxly arranged. Sepals broadly ovate, short, obtuse, greenish white with green veins, the lateral lobes spreading, dorsal sepal erect. Petals very small, triangular, whitish green or pink to reddish. Labellum fairly wide, roundish or obtusely quadratic to slightly trapezoid, undivided, directed vertically downwards, slightly convex, vigorous protuberances (large and obtuse), light to dark brown or olive-brown, deep brownish at edges, grey to violet hairs. Marking isolated, not enclosing basal field, mostly H-shaped or reduced, dark brown, with a light-coloured border. Appendage large, yellowish, directed forwards.

Habitat

Maquis, phrygana, moderately moist grasslands, roadside embankments and in light coniferous woods; on calcareous soils.

Flowering time

Mid-February to mid-March. Blooms about two weeks earlier than *Ophrys bornmuelleri*.

Altitude distribution

From sea level to 700 m.

Overall distribution

Cyprus and very rare in central southern Turkey. Findings of *Ophrys levantina* from the western part of Syria, Lebanon, Israel and Eastern Turkey refer to *Ophrys holoserica* subsp. *grandiflora* (H. FLEISCHMANN & SOÓ) FAURHOLDT. These plants are much taller and the flowers are much bigger, greyer and more rectangular (KREUTZ, 1998).

Distribution on Cyprus

Primarily distributed in the south, west and north of the island.

Remarks

Ophrys levantina ist allmost only on Cyprus distributed and very abundant at some places. The plants are on average between 20 to 30 cm tall, the inflorescence is fairly compact with relatively large flowers.

The species was regarded for a long time as a subspecies of *Ophrys bornmuelleri*, with which it does not have much in common. GÖLZ & REINHARD (1985) have therefore rightly described this taxon as an independent species. *Ophrys levantina* is plainly distinguishable from *Ophrys bornmuelleri*. A clear characteristic of *Ophrys levantina* is the somewhat reflexed position of the labellum; thus it is directed obliquely backwards, while that of *Ophrys bornmuelleri* more or less spreads horizontally. Moreover, the labellum of *Ophrys levantina* is densely pubescent and roundish to slightly trapezoid while that of *Ophrys bornmuelleri* is more trapezoid.

The two species often grow together in the same habitats. They can however be distinguished from one another without any problems, and are also clearly separated from each other by their starting flowering times, which differ by two to three weeks. According to WOOD (1985), so far no hybrids between *Ophrys levantina* and *Ophrys bornmuelleri* have been found. However, the author found one plant with definite intermediary characteristics near Esentepe in the northern part of Cyprus.

Threats

Although *Ophrys levantina* is not rare on Cyprus and there are many places where it can be found. It can therefore be catergorized as not particularly threatened.

Hybrids

With *Ophrys attica*, *Ophrys elegans*, *Ophrys flavomarginata*, *Ophrys lapethica* (*Ophrys ×liebischiana* R. KOHLMÜLLER), *Ophrys kotschyi* and *Ophrys mammosa*, very rarely also with *Ophrys bornmuelleri*.

Choirokoitia (Kalavasos dam), 4.3.2002

Kayalar, 14.3.2002

Apsiou-Louvaras, 5.3.2002

Kayalar-Sadrazamköy, 14.3.2002

Gerasa, 7.3.2002

Choirokoitia (Kalavasos dam), 4.3.2002

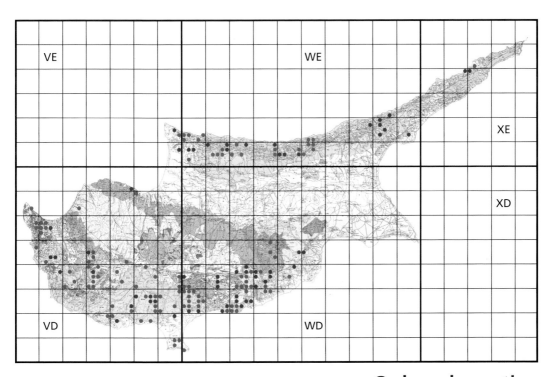

Ophrys levantina

30 Ophrys melena
Dunkellippige Ragwurz

(Renz) H.F. Paulus & Gack (pro hybr.)

Israel J. Bot. 39: 79 (1990)

Basionym

Ophrys lutea subsp. *melena*, Renz, Repert. Spec. Nov. Regni Veg. 25: 264 (1928).

Synonyme

Ophrys murbeckii subsp. *melena* (Renz) Soó, Acta Bot. Acad. Sci. Hung. 5: 440 (1959); *Ophrys lutea* var. *melena* (Renz) E. Nelson, Monogr. Ophrys: 216 (1962), nom. inval.; *Ophrys galilaea* subsp. *melena* (Renz) Del Prete, Webbia 38: 213 (1984).

Beschreibung

Schlanke, kleine bis mittelgroße Pflanze, 10 bis 20 cm hoch mit 3 bis 6 Blüten. Laubblätter hell- bis gelblichgrün, die unteren eiförmig-lanzettlich, rosettig gehäuft, die oberen länglich-lanzettlich, aufgerichtet bis abstehend, bisweilen als stängelumfassende Hochblätter. Blüten mittelgroß, locker am Stängel angeordnet und fast waagerecht abstehend. Sepalen breit-eiförmig bis lanzettlich, stumpf, olivgrün bis grünlichgelb gefärbt, das mittlere stark vornübergeneigt. Petalen kleiner, länglich-lanzettlich, gelblichgrün bis gelblich, stumpf, an den Rändern meist gewellt. Petalen und das mittlere Sepal einen offenen Helm bildend. Lippe mittelgroß, rundlich eiförmig bis oval, im unteren Teil dreilappig, flach, bisweilen leicht gewölbt, nicht oder kaum nach unten geknickt, dunkelbraun bis gelblichbraun, ohne oder mit einem schmalen, gelben Rand; Seitenlappen meist etwas nach oben gebogen. Malzeichnung auf die obere Hälfte der Lippe beschränkt, schildförmig, bläulich oder dunkelviolett. Anhängsel fehlt.

Standort

Magerrasen, Olivenhaine, Affodillfluren, lichte Kiefernwälder, Ödland, Phrygana und Macchien; auf basischen oder kalkhaltigen Böden.

Blütezeit

Anfang bis Ende März.

Höhenverbreitung

Von Meereshöhe bis 200 m.

Gesamtverbreitung

Hauptsächlich in Griechenland, dort im Südosten (Euböa, Attika und Nordost-Peloponnes) und im Nordwesten, sowie auf Korfu. Ausserdem auf Zypern.

Verbreitung auf Zypern

Sehr selten, nur von wenigen Fundstellen bekannt.

Bemerkungen

Lange Zeit waren die taxonomische Rangstufe und das Verbreitungsgebiet von *Ophrys melena*, eine Sippe, die zwischen dem *Ophrys lutea*- und dem *Ophrys fusca*-Formenkreis vermittelt, umstritten. Sie wurde oft als Hybride zwischen *Ophrys fusca* und *Ophrys lutea* betrachtet. Nach eingehenden Studien von Delforge (2000) und Devillers & Devillers-Ter-schuren (2000ab) hat sich gezeigt, dass vor allem im westlichen Mittelmeerraum (Sardinien, Sizilien und Tunesien) mehrere Sippen aus dem *Ophrys fusca-lutea* Formenkreis vorkommen, und einige davon wurden deshalb als neue Arten beschrieben (*Ophrys archimedea* P. Delforge & M. Walraven, *Ophrys aspea* J. Devillers-Terschuren & P. Devillers, *Ophrys battandieri* E.G. Camus (pro hybr.), *Ophrys flammeola* P. Delforge, *Ophrys numida* J. Devillers-Terschuren & P. Devillers und *Ophrys subfusca* (Reichenbach fil.) Hausknecht). Diese Pflanzen, die vor allem in Tunesien, Sardinien und Sizilien vorkommen, sind wegen ihrer gelblich-orangen Lippenfarbe besonders attraktiv, und *Ophrys melena* gehört sicherlich auch zu diesem Formenkreis.

In typischer Ausprägung kommt *Ophrys melena* hauptsächlich auf der Peloponnes (Griechenland) vor. Die Pflanzen von Zypern stimmen morphologisch mit denen der Peloponnes fast überein. Nur die Blüten der zypriotischen Pflanzen sind durchschnittlich etwas kleiner als die der Pflanzen auf der Peloponnes.

Wie *Ophrys attica* und *Ophrys rhodia* ist auch *Ophrys melena* auf Zypern sehr selten. Im Gebiet sind nur einzelne Pflanzen zu finden, da *Ophrys melena* auf Zypern die Ostgrenze ihres Areals erreicht.

Gefährdung

Ophrys melena ist auf Zypern sehr selten und wurde bis heute nur an wenigen Standorten nachgewiesen. Diese liegen z.B. bei Larnaka am Salzsee, wo sie durch Trockenlegung und Trittschäden durch Urlauber und Wanderer bedroht sind. Die Art ist deshalb als stark gefährdet einzustufen.

Hybriden

Nicht nachgewiesen. Bildet vermutlich Hybriden mit *Ophrys sicula*.

Larnaka (Salt lake), 9.3.2002

Ophrys melena (Renz) H.F. Paulus & Gack (pro hybr.)
Melanic Ophrys

Israel J. Bot. 39: 79 (1990)

Basionym

Ophrys lutea subsp. *melena*, Renz, Repert. Spec. Nov. Regni Veg. 25: 264 (1928).

Synonyms

Ophrys murbeckii subsp. *melena* (Renz) Soó, Acta Bot. Acad. Sci. Hung. 5: 440 (1959); *Ophrys lutea* var. *melena* (Renz) E. Nelson, Monogr. Ophrys: 216 (1962), nom. inval.; *Ophrys galilaea* subsp. *melena* (Renz) Del Prete, Webbia 38: 213 (1984).

Description

Slender, small to medium-sized plant, 10 to 20 cm tall with 3 to 6 flowers. Foliage leaves light green to yellowish green, lower leaves ovate-lanceolate, forming a rosette, upper leaves oblong-lanceolate, erect to spreading, sometimes stem-sheathing. Flowers medium-sized, arranged laxly along stem and spreading almost horizontally. Sepals broadly ovate to lanceolate, obtuse, olive-green to yellowish green, dorsal sepal strongly directed forwards. Petals smaller, oblong-lanceolate, yellowish green to yellowish, obtuse, mostly wavy at edges. Petals and dorsal sepal forming a loose hood. Labellum fairly large, roundish ovate to oval, three-lobed in lower part, flat, or sometimes slightly arched, not or hardly bent downwards, dark brown to yellowish brown, without or with narrow yellow border; lateral lobes mostly slightly bent upwards. Marking limited to upper half of labellum, shield-shaped, bluish or dark violet. Appendage absent.

Habitat

Neglected grassland, olive groves, asphodel fields, light coniferous woods, wasteland, phrygana and maquis; on basic or calcareous soils.

Flowering time

Early to late March.

Altitude distribution

From sea level to 200 m.

Overall distribution

Primarily in Greece, in the southeast (Euboea, Attica and northeastern Peloponnese) and in the northwest. Also on Corfu and Cyprus.

Distribution on Cyprus

Very rare, known from only a few sites.

Remarks

For a long time the taxonomical status and distribution area of *Ophrys melena*, a species belonging between the *Ophrys lutea* and *Ophrys fusca* species groups, were debated. The plants were often regarded as a hybrid between *Ophrys fusca* and *Ophrys lutea*. Extensive research by Delforge (2000) and Devillers & Devillers-Terschuren (2000ab) has shown that several taxa of this *Ophrys fusca-lutea* species group occur especially in the western Mediterranean region (Sardinia, Sicily and Tunisia) and therefore some of them have been described as new species (*Ophrys archimedea* P. Delforge & M. Walraven, *Ophrys aspea* J. Devillers-Terschuren & P. Devillers, *Ophrys battandieri* E.G. Camus (pro hybr.), *Ophrys flammeola* P. Delforge, *Ophrys numida* J. Devillers-Terschuren & P. Devillers and *Ophrys subfusca* (Reichenbach fil.) Hausknecht). These plants, which mainly occur in Tunisia, on Sardinia and Sicily, are exceptionally attractive because of the yellowish orange labellum and *Ophrys melena* certainly belongs to this complex.

Ophrys melena occurs in its typical appearance primarily on the Peloponnese (Greece). The Cypriot plants morphologically match those of the Peloponnese, except for flower size. The flowers on Cyprus are on average slightly smaller than those on the Peloponnese.

Ophrys melena is very rare on Cyprus, just like *Ophrys attica* and *Ophrys rhodia*. Only a few plants are to be found as *Ophrys melena* reaches its easternmost distribution boundary on Cyprus.

Threats

Ophrys melena is very rare on Cyprus and has been confirmed at only a few sites until now. These are situated for example at the salt lake near Larnaka, where the species is threatened by drainage and trampling by tourists and walkers. It can therefore be categorized as heavily threatened.

Hybrids

Unconfirmed. Probably forms hybrids with *Ophrys sicula*.

Larnaka (Salt lake), 9.3.2002

Larnaka (Salt lake), 9.3.2002

Larnaka (Salt lake), 9.3.2002

Larnaka (Salt lake), 9.3.2002

Larnaka (Salt lake), (mit/with *Orchis italica*), 9.3.2002

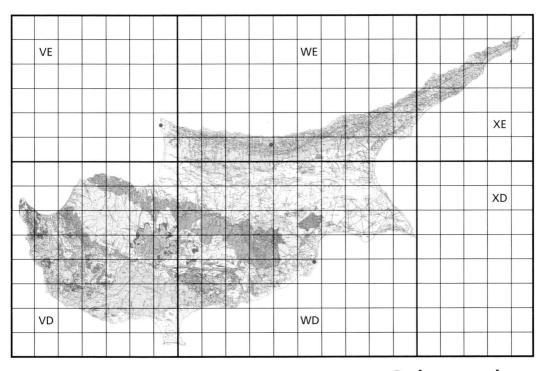

VE

WE

XE

XD

VD

WD

Ophrys melena

Basionym

Arachnites lutea var. *minor* TODARO, Orchid. Sicul.: 97, tab. 2, fig. 9 &10 (1842).

Synonyme

Ophrys lutea var. *minor* (TODARO) GUSSONE, Fl. Sicul. Syn. 2 (2): 550 (1844); *Ophrys insectifera* var. *lutea* GOUAN, Fl. Monsp.: 299 (1765); *Ophrys lutea* subsp. *sicula* (TINEO) A. SALDANO, Atti Soc. Ital. Sci. Nat. Mus. Civ. Stor. Nat. Milano 133 (10): 115 (1992, publ. 1993); *Ophrys galilaea* H. FLEISCHMANN & BORNMÜLLER, Ann. Naturhist. Mus. Wien 36: 12 (1923); *Ophrys lutea* subsp. *galilaea* (H. FLEISCHMANN & BORNMÜLLER) SOÓ, Notizbl. Bot. Gart. Berlin-Dahlem 9 (89): 906 (1926); *Ophrys lutea* CAVANILLES subsp. *minor* (TODARO) O. & E. DANESCH, Pl. Syst. Evol. 124: 82 (1975); *Ophrys minor* subsp. *galilaea* (H. FLEISCHMANN & BORNMÜLLER) H.F. PAULUS & GACK, Jahresber. Naturwiss. Vereins Wuppertal 39: 66 (1986); *Ophrys sicula* subsp. *galilaea* (H. FLEISCHMANN & BORNMÜLLER) H.F. PAULUS & GACK, Jahresber. Naturwiss. Vereins Wuppertal 43: 106 (1990); *Ophrys corsica* SOLEIROL ex G. & W. FOELSCHE, Jour. Eur. Orch. 34 (4): 845 (2002).

Beschreibung

Schlanke Pflanze, 10 bis 25 cm hoch, mit 3 bis 7 Blüten. Laubblätter hell- bis gelblichgrün, die unteren eiförmig-lanzettlich, rosettig gehäuft, die oberen länglich-lanzettlich, aufgerichtet bis abstehend, bisweilen mit stängelumfassenden Hochblättern. Blüten locker am Stängel angeordnet und fast waagerecht abstehend, klein. Sepalen eiförmig-lanzettlich, stumpf, grünlich, grünlichgelb bis bräunlichgrün gefärbt, das mittlere vornübergeneigt. Petalen kleiner, länglich-lanzettlich, gelblichgrün bis gelblich, an den Rändern meist gewellt. Petalen und das mittlere Sepal einen lockeren Helm bildend. Lippe sehr klein, eiförmig-lanzettlich bis oval, im unteren Teil dreilappig mit einem kleinen Einschnitt, flach, nicht oder kaum nach unten geknickt, dunkelbraun bis schwarzviolett mit einem schmalen gelben Rand; Seitenlappen etwas nach oben gebogen. Malzeichnung auf dem oberen und mittleren Teil der Lippe beschränkt, braun bis bläulich oder dunkelviolett. Typisch sind die braunen Ausläufer des Lippenmittellappens. Anhängsel fehlt.

Standort

Magerrasen, Olivenhaine, Affodillfluren, lichte Kiefernwälder, ehemaliges Kulturland, Ödland, Phrygana und Macchien; auf basischen oder kalkhaltigen Böden.

Blütezeit

Mitte Februar bis Ende März.

Höhenverbreitung

Von Meereshöhe bis 1.100 m.

Gesamtverbreitung

Von Korsika und Sardinien, Süditalien und Sizilien über die Balkanhalbinsel, die Ägäischen Inseln, Zypern, die Türkei bis in den Libanon und nach Israel verbreitet. Die Pflanzen von Südkorsika und Sardinien wurden 2002 als *Ophrys corsica* SOLEIROL ex G. & W. FOELSCHE abgetrennt (G. & W. FOELSCHE, 2002). Nach meiner Einschätzung wurde diese Art aber zu Unrecht von *Ophrys sicula* abgetrennt. Während eines Besuches 2003 auf Korsika und Sardinien konnte ich keine wesentlichen Merkmale feststellen, die eine Abtrennung rechtfertigen.

Verbreitung auf Zypern

Mit Ausnahme des Ostens ist *Ophrys sicula* auf der ganzen Insel weit verbreitet.

Bemerkungen

Ophrys lutea s.l. ist im Mittelmeerraum durch viele Arten und Unterarten vertreten. Vor allem im östlichen Mittelmeerbereich bereiten einige Sippen aus diesem Formenkreis Schwierigkeiten mit der Bestimmung, und es war lange Zeit nicht geklärt, welche Sippen aus dem *Ophrys lutea*-Formenkreis hier vorkamen, da die Autoren der gängigen Bestimmungswerke sowie diverse Veröffentlichungen der letzten Jahre taxonomisch unterschiedlicher Auffassung waren. Einige dieser Probleme wurden gelöst, indem die Pflanzen, die früher als Hybriden zwischen dem *Ophrys fusca*- und dem *Ophrys lutea*-Formenkreis angesehen wurden, als neue Arten beschrieben wurden. Vor allem von Tunesien, Sardinien und Sizilien wurden einige neue Arten aus diesem Formenkreis mit ihren gelblich bis gelblich-orangen Farben neu beschrieben (*Ophrys archimedea* P. DELFORGE & M. WALRAVEN, *Ophrys aspea* J. DEVILLERS-TERSCHUREN & P. DEVILLERS, *Ophrys battandieri* E.G. CAMUS (pro hybr.), *Ophrys flammeola* P. DELFORGE, *Ophrys numida* J. DEVILLERS-TERSCHUREN & P. DEVILLERS und *Ophrys subfusca* (REICHENBACH fil.) HAUSKNECHT). Bestimmungsprobleme mit anderen Vertretern aus der *Ophrys lutea*-Gruppe gibt es auf Zypern nicht, da hier nur *Ophrys melena* und *Ophrys sicula* vorkommen, zwei Taxa, die leicht von einander getrennt werden können.

Gefährdung

Ophrys sicula ist auf Zypern nicht selten und weit verbreitet und deshalb kaum gefährdet.

Hybriden

Mit *Ophrys alasiatica, Ophrys bornmuelleri* (*Ophrys* x*jansenii* P. DELFORGE) und *Ophrys morio* (*Ophrys* x*demangeana* P. DELFORGE).

Larnaka (Salt lake), 9.3.2002

Ophrys sicula
Sicilian Ophrys

Basionym

Arachnites lutea var. *minor* TODARO, Orchid. Sicul.: 97, tab. 2, fig. 9 &10 (1842).

Synonyms

Ophrys lutea var. *minor* (TODARO) GUSSONE, Fl. Sicul. Syn. 2 (2): 550 (1844); *Ophrys insectifera* var. *lutea* GOUAN, Fl. Monsp.: 299 (1765); *Ophrys lutea* subsp. *sicula* (TINEO) A. SALDANO, Atti Soc. Ital. Sci. Nat. Mus. Civ. Stor. Nat. Milano 133 (10): 115 (1992, publ. 1993); *Ophrys galilaea* H. FLEISCHMANN & BORNMÜLLER, Ann. Naturhist. Mus. Wien 36: 12 (1923); *Ophrys lutea* subsp. *galilaea* (H. FLEISCHMANN & BORNMÜLLER) SOÓ, Notizbl. Bot. Gart. Berlin-Dahlem 9 (89): 906 (1926); *Ophrys lutea* CAVANILLES subsp. *minor* (TODARO) O. & E. DANESCH, Pl. Syst. Evol. 124: 82 (1975); *Ophrys minor* subsp. *galilaea* (H. FLEISCHMANN & BORNMÜLLER) H.F. PAULUS & GACK, Jahresber. Naturwiss. Vereins Wuppertal 39: 66 (1986); *Ophrys sicula* subsp. *galilaea* (H. FLEISCHMANN & BORNMÜLLER) H.F. PAULUS & GACK, Jahresber. Naturwiss. Vereins Wuppertal 43: 106 (1990); *Ophrys corsica* SOLEIROL ex G. & W. FOELSCHE, Jour. Eur. Orch. 34 (4): 845 (2002).

Description

Slender plant, 10 to 25 cm tall, with 3 to 7 flowers. Foliage leaves light green to yellowish green, lower leaves ovate-lanceolate, forming a rosette, upper leaves oblong-lanceolate, erect to spreading, sometimes with stem-sheathing spathaceous bracts. Flowers laxly arranged on stem and spreading almost horizontally, small. Sepals ovate-lanceolate, obtuse, greenish, greenish yellow to brownish yellow, dorsal sepal curved over forwards. Petals smaller, oblong-lanceolate, yellowish green to yellowish, often wavy at edges. Petals and dorsal sepal forming a fairly loose hood. Labellum very small, ovate-lanceolate to oval, three-lobed in lower part with a small incision, flat, not or slightly bent downwards, dark brown to black-violet with a narrow yellow border; lateral lobes slightly bent upwards. Marking restricted to upper and central parts of labellum, brown to bluish or dark violet. Brown specks on the middle lobe of the labellum are typical. Appendage absent.

Habitat

Neglected grasslands, olive groves, asphodel fields, light coniferous woods, formerly cultivated acreage, wasteland, phrygana and maquis; on basic or calcareous soils.

Flowering time

Mid-February to late March.

Altitude distribution

From sea level to 1,100 m.

Overall distribution

From Corsica and Sardinia, southern Italy and Sicily through the Balkan Peninsula, the Aegean islands, Turkey to Lebanon and Israel. The plants of southern Corsica and Sardinia were separated in 2002 as *Ophrys corsica* SOLEIROL ex G. & W. FOELSCHE (G. & W. FOELSCHE, 2002). According to my findings, this species was unjustifiably separated from *Ophrys sicula*. During a visit to Corsica and Sardinia in 2003, I could not determine any fundamental characteristic to justify a separation.

Distribution on Cyprus

Widely distributed throughout the whole island, except in the east where *Ophrys sicula* is rare.

Remarks

Ophrys lutea s.l. is represented by many species and subspecies in the Mediterranean region. Several taxa of this group give rise to identification problems, especially in the eastern Mediterranean region and it was uncertain for a long time which taxa of the *Ophrys lutea* complex occur in the Eastern Mediterranean region, as authors of most identification works and publications in recent years were of different taxonomic opinions. Some of these problems were solved when plants that were at first classified as hybrids between the *Ophrys fusca* and *Ophrys lutea* species groups were described as new species. Several new species from this group with its yellowish or yellowish-orange colours were redescribed, especially from Tunisia, Sardinia and Sicily (*Ophrys archimedea* P. DELFORGE & M. WALRAVEN, *Ophrys aspea* J. DEVILLERS-TERSCHUREN & P. DEVILLERS, *Ophrys battandieri* E.G. CAMUS (pro hybr.), *Ophrys flammeola* P. DELFORGE, *Ophrys numida* J. DEVILLERS-TERSCHUREN & P. DEVILLERS and *Ophrys subfusca* (REICHENBACH fil.) HAUSKNECHT).

There are no identification problems with other representatives of the *Ophrys lutea* group on Cyprus, as only *Ophrys melena* and *Ophrys sicula* are found here, two taxa which can easily be distinguished from one another.

Threats

Ophrys sicula is on Cyprus abundant and widespread and therefore hardly threatened.

Hybrids

With *Ophrys alasiatica*, *Ophrys bornmuelleri* (*Ophrys* ×*jansenii* P. DELFORGE) and *Ophrys morio* (*Ophrys* ×*demangeana* P. DELFORGE).

Larnaka (Salt lake), 9.3.2002

Alethriko, 6.3.2002

Choirokoitia (Kalavasos dam), 4.3.2002

Kayalar-Sadrazamköy, 14.3.2002

Alethriko, 6.3.2002

Hirsarköy, 14.3.2002

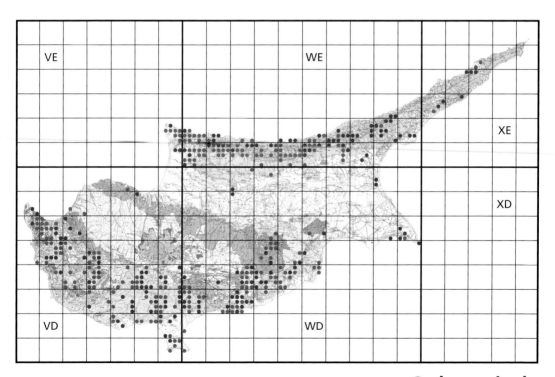

32 Ophrys tenthredinifera
Wespen-Ragwurz

WILLDENOW

Sp. Pl. ed. 4, 4 (1): 67 (1805)

Synonyme

Ophrys limbata LINK, Handbuch 1: 247 (1829); *Arachnitis tenthredinifera* (WILLDENOW) TODARO, Orchid. Sicul.: 85 (1842), nom. illeg

Beschreibung

Niedrige, kräftige Pflanze, 10 bis 30 cm hoch. Laubblätter hell- bis gelblichgrün, die unteren eiförmig-lanzettlich, rosettig gehäuft, die oberen länglich-lanzettlich, aufgerichtet bis abstehend, bisweilen als stängelumfassende Hochblätter. Blütenstand locker, mit 2 bis 6 Blüten. Blüten mittelgross bis gross, schräg abstehend. Sepalen breit-eiförmig bis eiförmig, stumpf, aufrecht oder schwach rückwärts gerichtet, hell- bis dunkelrosa oder hellviolett. Petalen dreieckig-eiförmig, kurz, oft dunkler als die Sepalen gefärbt. Lippe rechteckig, trapezförmig, konvex, am Grunde schwach gehöckert, im Zentrum dunkelbraun bis rötlichbraun, an den Rändern von einer breiten, hellbraunen Zone umgeben; in der Mitte der Lippe schwach und an den Rändern dicht gelblichweiss behaart. Malzeichnung auf den basalen Teil der Lippe beschränkt, klein, graulila bis stahlblau mit weisslichem Rand. Anhängsel ziemlich gross, gelblich, aufwärts gerichtet.

Standort

Lichte Kiefernwälder, Macchien, Phrygana, Ödland, Olivenhaine, Affodillfluren, Ruderalstellen und Magerrasen; auf basischen oder kalkhaltigen Böden.

Blütezeit

Von Anfang Februar bis Anfang (Mitte) März.

Höhenverbreitung

Aktuell nur von einem Fundort in etwa 300 m Höhe bekannt.

Gesamtverbreitung

Ophrys tenthredinifera s.l. weist ein grosses Verbreitungsgebiet auf, nämlich von Portugal bis Kleinasien. Ausserdem in Nordafrika und auf Zypern.

Verbreitung auf Zypern

Die seltenste Orchidee Zyperns. Aktuell nur von einem Fundort auf der Akamas-Halbinsel bekannt.

Bemerkungen

Vor allem im westlichen und mittleren mediterranen Gebiet ist *Ophrys tenthredinifera* durch mehrere Unterarten vertreten. DEVILLERS, DEVILLERS-TERSCHUREN & TYTECA (2003) haben in einem ausführlichen Beitrag alle Unterarten von *Ophrys tenthredinifera* neu gegliedert und diese alle als Art bewertet. Der Artrang dieser neuen Arten ist zu hoch bewertet, weil die Taxa zu wenig von einander abgegrenzt sind. Im östlichen Mittelmeergebiet wird *Ophrys tenthredinifera* (mit Ausnahme von der Türkei) durch *Ophrys tenthredinifera* subsp. *villosa* (DESFONTAINES) H. BAUMANN & KÜNKELE vertreten. Diese Unterart unterscheidet sich von der Nominatform durch eine frühere Blütezeit und eine schmalere und längere, rechteckige Lippe. Weiter ist die Färbung der Lippe im Zentrum dunkelbraun und an den Rändern hellbraun (BAUMANN & KÜNKELE, 1988a) und sind die Blüten kleiner als die der Nominatsippe.

Im Jahre 1992 wurden von BEDFORD auf Zypern zwei blühende Pflanzen nachgewiesen und in dem Buch von G. & K. MORSCHEK (1996) abgebildet. Der Fundort befindet sich bei Agios Minas auf der Akamas-Halbinsel. Fast jedes Jahr kommen dort zwei Exemplare zur Blüte. Der Standort ist wegen intensiver Beweidung durch Schafe und Ziegen und starken Zulaufs von Touristen und Einheimischen zu der Kapelle Agios Minas stark gefährdet. Von einheimischen Orchideenkennern wird aber behauptet, dass diese beiden Pflanzen angesalbt wurden!

Die zypriotischen Pflanzen sind kräftiger und ihre Blüten grösser und dunkler gefärbt als bei *Ophrys tenthredinifera* subsp. *villosa*. Diese Pflanzen sind also eher mit denen der Türkei zu vergleichen, die Merkmale der westeuropäischen Pflanzen zeigen. Deswegen wurden die zypriotischen Pflanzen vorläufig zu der Nominatform gestellt. Der Habitus, Lippenform und -farbe der beiden Pflanzen könnte die Erklärung dafür sein, dass die Pflanzen vermutlich aus der Türkei oder aus dem westlichen Mittelmeergebiet stammen und hier angesalbt wurden.

In früherer Zeit wurden mehrmals Funde von *Ophrys tenthredinifera* für Zypern angegeben. So wurde sie erstmals 1787 von SIBTHORP gefunden, weiter 1860 in der Umgebung von Lefkara und von UNGER und KOTSCHY (HOLMBOE, 1914) im östlichen Teil des Troodos-Massivs (DEVILLERS, DEVILLERS-TERSCHUREN & TYTECA, 2003). Diese Funde wurden bei STUART THOMPSON, (1906), HOLMBOE (1914), Soó (1929), B. & E. WILLING (1975) und auch bei SUNDERMANN (1980) aufgelistet. Die Art konnte aber niemals zweifelsfrei für Zypern bestätigt werden, da keine Herbar- oder Fotobelege existieren. Die Möglichkeit besteht aber, dass diese historischen Funde von *Ophrys tenthredinifera* Verwechselungen mit *Ophrys levantina* sind, die einige gemeinsame habituelle Merkmale (gedrungener Habitus und Lippenform) mit *Ophrys tenthredinifera* aufweist. Auch B. & E. WILLING (1975) kommen zu dieser Schlussfolgerung. Aus diesem Grund wurden diese Funde nicht auf der Verbreitungskarte eingezeichnet, ausserdem ist die genaue Lage der Standorte nicht bekannt.

Gefährdung

Ophrys tenthredinifera ist nur von einem Standort bekannt. Sie ist damit als stark gefährdet einzustufen.

Hybriden

Nicht nachgewiesen.

Neo Chorio-Agios Minas (Akamas), 3.3.2002

Ophrys tenthredinifera

Sawfly Ophrys

WILLDENOW

Sp. Pl. ed. 4, 4 (1): 67 (1805)

Synonyms

Ophrys limbata LINK, Handbuch 1: 247 (1829); *Arachnitis tenthredinifera* (WILLDENOW) TODARO, Orchid. Sicul.: 85 (1842), nom. illeg

Description

Short, vigorous plant, 10 to 30 cm tall. Foliage leaves light to yellowish green, lower leaves ovate-lanceolate, forming a rosette, upper leaves oblong-lanceolate, erect to spreading, sometimes as stem-sheathing spathaceous bracts. Inflorescence lax, bearing 2 to 6 flowers. Flowers medium-sized to large, spreading obliquely. Sepals broadly ovate to ovate, obtuse, erect or slightly directed backwards, pale to deep pink or pale violet. Petals triangular-ovate, short, often darker than sepals. Labellum rectangular, trapezoid, convex, with weak protuberances at the base, dark brown to reddish brown in the centre, surrounded by a wide light brown zone at the edges; middle of labellum weakly and edges densely pubescent with yellowish white hairs. Marking restricted to basal part of labellum, small, grey-lilac to steel-blue with a whitish margin. Appendage fairly large, yellowish and directed upwards.

Habitat

Light coniferous woods, maquis, phrygana, wasteland, olive groves, asphodel fields, uncultivated ground and neglected grasslands; on basic or calcareous soils.

Flowering time

From early February to early (mid-) March.

Altitude distribution

Currently known from one location at 300 m height.

Overall distribution

Ophrys tenthredinifera s.l. has a large distribution area, namely from Portugal to Asia Minor; also in North Africa and on Cyprus.

Distribution on Cyprus

The rarest species on Cyprus. Currently only known from one location on the Akamas peninsula.

Remarks

Ophrys tenthredinifera is represented by several subspecies, especially in the western and central Mediterranean region. In an extensive contribution, DEVILLERS, DEVILLERS-TERSCHUREN & TYTECA (2003) reorganized all subspecies of *Ophrys tenthredinifera* and assessed them all as species. The species ranking of these new taxa is too high, because these taxa are not clearly distinguished from one another.

In the Eastern Mediterranean region (except for Turkey), *Ophrys tenthredinifera* is replaced by *Ophrys tenthredinifera* subsp. *villosa* (DESFONTAINES) H. BAUMANN & KÜNKELE. This subspecies differs from the nominate form by an earlier flowering time and a narrower and longer, rectangular labellum. Further-more, the colouration of the labellum is dark brown in the centre and light brown at the edges (BAUMANN & KÜNKELE, 1988a). The flowers of *Ophrys tenthredinifera* subsp. *villosa* are also smaller than the nominate taxon.

In 1992, BEDFORD confirmed the existence of two plants in flower, depicted in the book from G. & K. MORSCHEK (1996). The site is located near Agios Minas on the Akamas peninsula. Almost every year, two specimens bloom there. The location is heavily threatened by extensive grazing by sheep and goats and by the marked increase in tourists and locals visiting the chapel of Agios Minas. Local orchidologists, however, are of the opinion that the two individuals were planted there!

Compared to *Ophrys tenthredinifera* subsp. *villosa* the Cypriot plants are much vigorous, the flowers much more bigger and darker coloured. The Cypriot plants share thus more characteristics with the Turkish or the Western Mediterranean plants. Therefore the Cypriot plants have been preliminary placed under the nominate form. The Western Mediterranean habitus, the labellum shape and colour could be the explanation that both plants are native from the Western Mediterranean area or from Turkey, as they were probably planted there.

In the past, several findings of *Ophrys tenthredinifera* were reported for Cyprus. The species was for example found for the first time in 1787 by SIBTHORP, later again in 1860 in the vicinity of Lefkara and by UNGER and KOTSCHY (HOLMBOE, 1914) in the eastern part of the Troodos massif (DEVILLERS, DEVILLERS-TERSCHUREN & TYTECA, 2003). These findings were listed by STUART THOMPSON, (1906), HOLMBOE (1914), SOÓ (1929), B. & E. WILLING (1975) and also by SUNDERMANN (1980). However the species could never be confirmed without doubt for Cyprus, as there is no botanical or photographic evidence in existence. There is a possibility that these historical findings of *Ophrys tenthredinifera* were confusions with *Ophrys levantina*, a species which shares some equal characteristics (compact habitus and labellum shape) with *Ophrys tenthredinifera*. B. & E. WILLING (1975) also come to this conclusion. Therefore these sites are not indicated on the distribution map, and moreover the exact sites are unknown.

Threats

Ophrys tenthredinifera is only known from one location on Cyprus. The species can therefore be categorized as heavily threatened.

Hybrids

Unconfirmed.

Neo Chorio-Agios Minas (Akamas), 3.3.2002

Neo Chorio-Agios Minas (Akamas), 3.3.2002   Neo Chorio-Agios Minas (Akamas), 3.3.2002

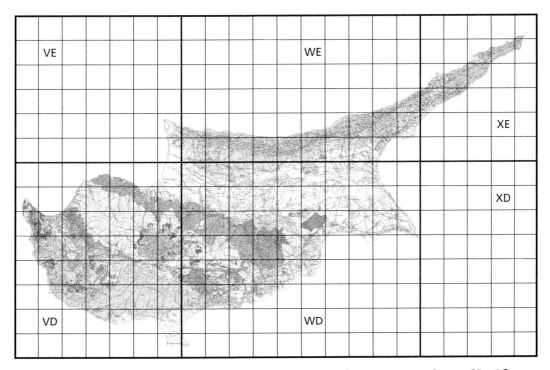

1 Meldung / Report

Ophrys tenthredinifera

33 Orchis anatolica

Anatolisches Knabenkraut

Boissier

Diagn. Pl. Orient., ser. 1, 1 (5): 56 (1844)

Synonyme

Orchis rariflora C. Koch, Linnaea 19: 13 (1847); *Orchis anatolica* var. *kochii* Boissier, Fl. Orient. 5 (1): 70 (1884).

Beschreibung

Schlanke, hochwüchsige Pflanze, 15 bis 30 cm hoch. Stängel leicht hin und her gebogen, vor allem im oberen Teil kräftig rötlich überlaufen. Laubblätter lanzettlich, zugespitzt, leicht bis stark gefleckt, die unteren in einer Rosette angeordnet, die oberen in scheidige Stängelblätter übergehend. Blütenstand locker und langgestreckt. Tragblätter zugespitzt, kürzer als der Fruchtknoten. Blüten ziemlich groß, hellrosa bis rosa (selten purpurrot) gefärbt. Sepalen oft mit deutlichen grünen Nerven, seitliche Sepalen eiförmig-lanzettlich, abstehend bis leicht zurückgeschlagen, das mittlere über die beiden Petalen gebogen. Petalen schmal-lanzettlich, spitz. Lippe breiter als lang, dreilappig, die beiden Seitenlappen mehr oder weniger stark zurückgeschlagen, (hell)rosa bis purpurrot, an der Basis weisslich. Die hellere Lippenbasis ist mit dunkelroten Streifen oder purpurnen Punkten besetzt. Sporn gerade oder schwach nach unten gebogen und fast doppelt so lang wie der Fruchtknoten.

Standort

Schattige Stellen in lichten Kiefernwäldern, auf steinigen Hängen, Ödland, Gebüsch, felsigem Gelände und Macchien; meist auf trockenen, basischen oder schwach sauren Böden.

Blütezeit

Von Mitte Februar bis Ende März.

Höhenverbreitung

Von 100 bis 800 m.

Gesamtverbreitung

Das Areal von *Orchis anatolica* reicht von Kreta über die Ägäischen Inseln, die Türkei bis nach Iran, Syrien, Libanon und Nordisrael (Kreutz, 1993). Auch auf Zypern.

Verbreitung auf Zypern

Orchis anatolica ist auf Zypern sehr selten. Typische Exemplare wachsen nur im Norden der Insel im Pentadactylos-Gebirge (Kerynia Range) und in der weiteren Umgebung der mittleren und nordöstlichen Regionen des Troodos-Gebirges. Vor allem im Makheras Wald, in der weiteren Umgebung des Makheras Klosters im Südosten Zyperns, kommen sehr typische Exemplare vor.

Bemerkungen

Lange Zeit war unklar, welche Arten aus dem *Orchis anatolica* Formenkreis auf Zypern vorkommen, weil neben typischen Exemplaren von *Orchis ana-tolica* auch eine sehr weit verbreitete Form vorhanden ist, die weder zu *Orchis anatolica* noch zu *Orchis quadripunctata* Cyrillo ex Tenore gestellt werden konnte. Nach eingehenden Untersuchungen von B. & H. Baumann (1991) wurde dann die vermutlich hybridogen entstandene *Orchis*-Sippe zwischen *Orchis anatolica* und *Orchis quadripunctata* 1991 als *Orchis sezikiana* B. & H. Baumann (pro hybr.) beschrieben. Vor der Neubeschreibung wurden diese Pflanzen als *Orchis quadripunctata* Tenore geführt (unter anderem von Hansen, Kreutz & U. & D. Rückbrodt, 1990 und G. & K. Morschek, 1996).

Auf Zypern wächst auch die endemische *Orchis troodi*, eine großblütige und zierliche Verwandte von *Orchis anatolica*. *Orchis anatolica* unterscheidet sich von dieser Art durch kleinere Blüten, einen meist horizontal gerichteten Sporn und die blassere Farbe der Blüten.

Die Fundortangaben in Hansen, Kreutz & U. & D. Rückbrodt (1990) wurden nicht alle auf die Verbreitungskarte übertragen, weil in dieser Arbeit *Orchis anatolica* und *Orchis troodi* wegen der geringen morphologischen Unterschiede nicht separat unterschieden wurden. Ausserdem wurden in dieser Arbeit *Orchis anatolica* und *Orchis troodi* wegen des Vorkommens zahlreicher Übergangsformen zusammengefasst, und in den Fundmeldungen verschiedener Orchideenforscher vor 1990 meist nur als lokale Varietät gewertet, und deshalb als *Orchis anatolica* bestimmt.

Gefährdung

Orchis anatolica ist von zwei größeren Gebieten auf Zypern bekannt. Beide Areale sind ausgedehnte Kiefernwälder. Trotzdem ist die Art hier selten. Sie ist damit als gefährdet einzustufen.

Hybriden

Eindeutige Hybriden wurden nicht nachgewiesen.

Bemerkungen zu der Verbreitungskarte

Auf der Verbreitungskarte stellen viele Angaben im Süden und Südwesten von vor 1990 mit Sicherheit *Orchis troodi* dar, weil diese Art damals in den Fundmeldungen verschiedener Orchideenforscher meist nur als lokale Varietät bewertet und unter *Orchis anatolica* erfasst wurden.

Lythrodontas (Makheras Forest), 9.3.2002   Alevkaya (Pentadactylos Range), 18.3.2002

Orchis anatolica

BOISSIER

Anatolian Orchid

Diagn. Pl. Orient., ser. 1, 1 (5): 56 (1844)

Synonyms

Orchis rariflora C. KOCH, Linnaea 19: 13 (1847); *Orchis anatolica* var. *kochii* BOISSIER, Fl. Orient. 5 (1): 70 (1884).

Description

Tall slender plant, 15 to 30 cm in height. Stem slightly flexuose, strongly red tinged, especially in the upper part. Foliage leaves lanceolate, acuminate, faintly to strongly speckled, lower leaves forming a rosette, upper leaves merging into sheathing stem leaves. Inflorescence lax and elongated. Bracts acuminate, shorter than ovary. Flowers fairly large, pale pink to pink (rarely purple-red). Sepals often with distinct green veins, lateral sepals ovate-lanceolate, spreading to slightly reflexed, dorsal sepal curved over the two petals. Petals narrowly lanceolate, acuminate. Labellum is wider than it is long, three-lobed, the two lateral lobes more or less strongly reflexed, (pale) pink to purple-red, whitish at the base. The lighter-coloured base of labellum is covered with dark red dashes or purple dots. Spur straight or slighty curved downwards and almost twice as long as ovary.

Habitat

Shady spots in light coniferous woods, on rocky slopes, wasteland, among shrubs, in rocky fields and maquis; mostly on arid, basic or slightly acidic soils.

Flowering time

From mid-February to late March.

Altitude distribution

From 100 to 800 m.

Overall distribution

The habitat of *Orchis anatolica* stretches from Crete through the Aegean islands, Turkey into Iran, Syria, Lebanon and northern Israel (KREUTZ, 1993). Also on Cyprus.

Distribution on Cyprus

Orchis anatolica is very rare on Cyprus. Typical specimens only grow in the Pentadactylos mountains (Kerynia Range) in the north of the island and in the area around the central and north-eastern parts of the Troodos mountains. Very typical specimens occur in Makheras Forest around the Makheras monastery in southeastern Cyprus.

Remarks

Alongside typical specimens of *Orchis anatolica*, there also exists a very widely distributed variety which could not be placed under *Orchis anatolica* or *Orchis quadripunctata* CYRILLO ex TENORE, and it was therefore uncertain for a long time which species of the *Orchis anatolica* complex occur on Cyprus. After extensive research by B. & H. BAUMANN (1991) this *Orchis* taxon between *Orchis anatolica* and *Orchis quadripunctata* of possible hybridogenous origin was described as *Orchis sezikiana* B. & H. BAUMANN (pro hybr.) in 1991. Before this new description, these plants were placed under *Orchis quadripunctata* TENORE (for example by HANSEN, KREUTZ & U. & D. RÜCKBRODT, 1990 and G. & K. MORSCHEK, 1996).

The endemic *Orchis troodi*, a large-flowered and elegant relative of *Orchis anatolica* also grows on Cyprus. *Orchis anatolica* can be distinguished from this species by smaller flowers, a mostly horizontal spur and by the lighter colour of the flowers.

The location reports in HANSEN, KREUTZ & U. & D. RÜCKBRODT (1990) have not all been transferred to the distribution map, as *Orchis anatolica* and *Orchis troodi* were not separated in this work because of their small morphological difference. Furthermore, *Orchis anatolica* and *Orchis troodi* were combined in this work because of the occurrence of numerous transitional forms which had been classed as local varieties in the location reports of various orchid researchers before 1990, and therefore specified as *Orchis anatolica*.

Threats

Orchis anatolica is known from two large areas in Cyprus. Both habitats are vast coniferous forests. Nonetheless, the species is rare there. It can therefore be categorized as threatened.

Hybrids

Distinct hybrids have not been confirmed.

Remarks concerning the distribution map

On the distribution map, many reports from before 1990 in the south and south-west certainly represent *Orchis troodi*, as this species had mostly only been classed as local variety in the location reports of various orchid researchers, and therefore specified as *Orchis anatolica*.

Lythrodontas (Makheras Forest), 9.3.2002

Lythrodontas (Makheras Forest), 9.3.2002

Lythrodontas (Makheras Forest), 9.3.2002

Alevkaya (Pentadactylos Range), 18.3.2002

Alevkaya (Pentadactylos Range), 18.3.2002

Alevkaya (Pentadactylos Range), 18.3.2002

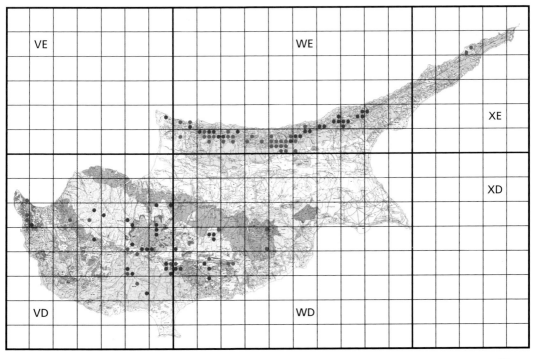

Orchis anatolica

B. & H. Baumann (pro hybr.)

Mitteilungsbl. Arbeitskr. Heim. Orch.
Baden-Württ. 23 (1): 215 & 216 (1991)

Beschreibung

Zierliche, schlanke Pflanze, 15 bis 40 cm hoch. Stängel dünn, rötlich überlaufen. Laubblätter lanzettlich bis breit-lanzettlich, die unteren in einer grundständigen Rosette angeordnet, die oberen in scheidige Stängelblätter übergehend, ungefleckt oder gefleckt. Blütenstand zylindrisch, locker- und meist armblütig. Tragblätter schmal-lanzettlich, kürzer als der Fruchtknoten. Blüten mittelgroß, rosa, hell- bis dunkelrot gefärbt, die Perigonblätter mit grünen Nerven. Sepalen eiförmig-lanzettlich bis lanzettlich, seitlich abstehend, das mittlere über die beiden Petalen gebogen. Petalen lanzettlich bis eiförmig-lanzettlich, helmförmig zusammenneigend. Lippe tief dreilappig, der Mittellappen vom Sporneingang bis zum unteren Teil weisslich, mit vielen dunkelpurpurnen Punkten in zwei Reihen besetzt; Seitenlappen flach ausgebreitet bis zurückgeschlagen. Sporn dünn und lang, waagerecht abstehend bis aufwärts gerichtet, länger als der Fruchtknoten.

Standort

Offene und sonnige Stellen; lichte Wälder, Phrygana und Macchien; an steinigen und felsigen Stellen, auf kalkhaltigen Böden.

Blütezeit

Ende Februar bis Ende März.

Höhenverbreitung

Von Meereshöhe bis 900 m.

Gesamtverbreitung

Das aktuelle Areal von *Orchis sezikiana* umfasst die West- und Südwesttürkei, die Ägäischen Inseln Ikaria, Samos und Kreta. Auch auf Zypern.

Verbreitung auf Zypern

Im Süden relativ weit verbreitet und stellenweise häufig. Vor allem in den niedrigen Lagen vom Troodos-Gebirge. Fehlt im Norden und Osten fast völlig.

Bemerkungen

In vielen Fundortangaben verschiedener Orchideenforscher und in der Literatur verschiedener Orchideenforscher wurde immer wieder von *Orchis quadripunctata* Cyrillo ex Tenore oder von Hybriden zwischen *Orchis anatolica* und *Orchis quadripunctata* auf Zypern und in der Südwesttürkei berichtet (siehe unter anderem B. & E. Willing, 1976; Wood, 1985 und Christofides, 2001). Diese Pflanzen haben im Gegensatz zu *Orchis quadripunctata* größere, meist hellere Blüten und mehr als vier Punkte auf der Lippe. B. & H. Baumann haben diese hybridogen entstandene *Orchis*-Sippe zwischen *Orchis anatolica* und *Orchis quadripunctata* 1991 als *Orchis sezi-kiana* beschrieben. Mit dieser Neubeschreibung wurden die taxonomischen Probleme in soweit geklärt, dass *Orchis quadripunctata* nach diesen Erkenntnissen auf Zypern nicht vorkommt!

Orchis sezikiana ist eine sehr variable Art. Nach B. & H. Baumann (1991) kann die Variationsbreite innerhalb einer Population beträchtlich sein, und je nach den am Standort herrschenden Bedingungen fast das gesamte Spektrum zwischen den beiden Elternarten abdecken.

Individuenreiche Populationen wachsen in der Umgebung von Gerasa und in dem Gebiet zwischen Pafos und Polis. In diesem Gebiet ist *Orchis sezikiana* in und am Rande von Pinienwäldern aber auch an grasigen, offenen Stellen in der Macchie nicht selten und weit verbreitet. Im Norden und Osten Zyperns fehlt *Orchis sezikiana* fast völlig, weil in diesem Gebiet weite Teile der Böden basisch bis schwach sauer sind. Hier kommt hauptsächlich die nahe verwandte *Orchis anatolica* vor.

G. & K. Morschek (1996) beschreiben in ihrem Buch von der Akamas-Halbinsel auffallend zierliche und frühblühende Pflanzen, die selten eine Höhe von zehn Zentimetern erreichen und rein weisse Blüten haben. Sie haben diese Pflanzen mit den Arbeitsnamen *Orchis quadripunctata* var. *akamasica* versehen.

Gefährdung

Die Art ist auf Zypern ziemlich häufig und verbreitet und deshalb kaum gefährdet.

Hybriden

Nicht nachgewiesen.

292   Gerasa, 7.3.2002

Orchis sezikiana
Sezik's Orchid

B. & H. BAUMANN (pro hybr.)

Mitteilungsbl. Arbeitskr. Heim. Orch.
Baden-Württ. 23 (1): 215 & 216 (1991)

Description

Elegant, slender plant, 15 to 40 cm tall. Stem thin, with reddish tinges. Foliage leaves lanceolate to broadly lanceolate, lower leaves arranged in a rosette at the base, upper leaves merging into sheathing stem leaves, spotted or unspotted. Inflorescence cylindrical, lax and mostly few-flowered. Bracts narrowly lanceolate, shorter than ovary. Flowers medium-sized, pink, light to dark red, perianth segments with green veins. Sepals ovate-lanceolate to lanceolate, laterals spreading, dorsal sepal bent over the petals. Petals lanceolate to ovate-lanceolate, connivent to forming a hood. Labellum deeply three-lobed, middle lobe whitish from spur entrance to lower part, with many deep purple dots arranged in two rows; lateral lobes spread out flat to reflexed. Spur thin and long, horizontal to erect, longer than ovary.

Habitat

Open and sunny places; light woods, phrygana and maquis; in stony and rocky places, on calcareous soils.

Flowering time

Late February to late March.

Altitude distribution

From sea level to 900 m.

Overall distribution

The current range of *Orchis sezikiana* stretches from western and southwestern Turkey to the Aegean islands of Icaria, Samos and Crete. Also on Cyprus.

Distribution on Cyprus

In the south relatively widely distributed and abundant at some places. Found particularly in the lower altitudes of the Troodos mountains. Almost absent in the northern and eastern part.

Remarks

Accounts of various orchid researchers of *Orchis quadripunctata* CYRILLO ex TENORE or of hybrids between *Orchis anatolica* and *Orchis quadripunctata* for Cyprus and southwestern Turkey were given time and again in many location reports and in literature from various orchid researchers (see for example B. & E. WILLING, 1976; WOOD, 1985 and CHRISTOFIDES, 2001). These plants have, in contrast to *Orchis quadripunctata*, larger, mostly lighter coloured flowers and more than four dots on the labellum. B. & H. BAUMANN described this *Orchis* taxon of hybridogenous origin between *Orchis anatolica* and *Orchis quadripunctata* as *Orchis sezikiana* in 1991. Taxonomic problems were solved to such an extent with this new description that, according to these findings, *Orchis quadripunctata* does not occur on Cyprus!

Orchis sezikiana is a very variable species. According to B. & H. BAUMANN (1991) the degree of variation within a single population can be considerable, and depending on the conditions at the site, can encompass the entire spectrum between the two parent species.

Individual-rich populations grow around Gerasa and in the area between Pafos and Polis. *Orchis sezikiana* is not rare and is widely distributed there, in and at the edges of pine forests, and also on grassy open places in the maquis. *Orchis sezikiana* is almost absent from northern and eastern Cyprus, as large areas there are basic or slightly acidic. The closely related *Orchis anatolica* primarily occurs there.

G. & K. MORSCHEK (1996) describe exceptionally elegant and early-flowering plants from the Akamas peninsula in their book, which rarely reach to a height of ten centimeters and have pure white flowers. They have given these plants the preliminary name of *Orchis quadripunctata* var. *akamasica*.

Threats

The species is relatively abundant and widespread and therefore hardly threatened.

Hybrids

Unconfirmed.

Gerasa, 7.3.2002

Drouseia (Akamas), 3.3.2002

Gerasa, 7.3.2002

Gerasa, 7.3.2002

Gerasa, 7.3.2002

Gerasa, 7.3.2002

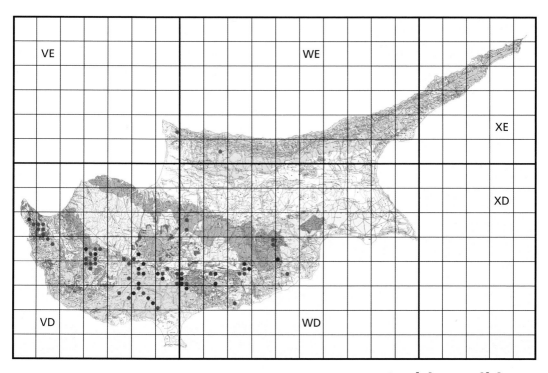

Orchis sezikiana

35 Orchis troodi
Troodos Knabenkraut

(Renz) P. Delforge

Natural. Belges 71: 107 (1990)

Basionym

Orchis anatolica var. *troodi* Renz, Repert. Spec. Nov. Regni Veg. 27: 209 (1929).

Synonym

Orchis anatolica subsp. *troodi* (Renz) Renz, Repert. Spec. Nov. Regni Veg. 30: 100 (1932)

Beschreibung

Schlanke, mittelgroße, zierliche bis hochwüchsige Pflanze, 15 bis 50 cm hoch. Stängel leicht hin und her gebogen, vor allem im oberen Teil besonders rötlich überlaufen. Laubblätter lanzettlich, zugespitzt, meist stark gefleckt, die unteren in einer Rosette angeordnet, die oberen in scheidige Stängelblätter übergehend. Blütenstand sehr locker und langgestreckt. Tragblätter zugespitzt, kürzer als der Fruchtknoten. Blüten groß, rosa bis purpurrot gefärbt. Sepalen oft mit deutlichen grünen Nerven, seitliche Sepalen eiförmig-lanzettlich, nach oben gerichtet bis leicht zurückgeschlagen, das mittlere über die beiden Petalen gebogen. Petalen schmal-lanzettlich, spitz, meist nach vorne gerichtet. Lippe ziemlich breit, deutlich dreilappig, die beiden Seitenlappen mehr oder weniger stark zurückgeschlagen, (hell)-rosa bis purpurrot, an der Basis weisslich. Die hellere Lippenbasis ist deutlich mit dunkelroten Streifen oder purpurnen Punkten besetzt. Sporn konisch, steil aufwärts gerichtet und fast doppelt so lang wie der Fruchtknoten.

Standort

In lichten und meist unterwuchsfreien Kiefernwäldern, auf steinigen Hängen, Ödland, im Gebüsch, an Waldrändern und Macchien; meist auf trockenen, basischen bis kalkhaltigen Böden.

Blütezeit

Von Anfang März bis etwa Mitte April.

Höhenverbreitung

Von 100 bis 1.500 m.

Gesamtverbreitung

Endemische Art von Zypern.

Verbreitung auf Zypern

Die attraktive Art wächst vor allem auf Waldlichtungen in den höheren Lagen des Troodos-Gebirges unter *Pinus brutia*, *Pinus nigra* subsp. *pallasiana* und *Quercus alnifolia* zusammen mit *Thymus integer* und *Cistus salviifolius* (Wood, 1985; Georgiades, 1998ab). Ausserdem kommt sie in größeren Beständen auf der Akamas-Halbinsel und in der Zedernschlucht vor. Sie fehlt im Norden Zyperns.

Bemerkungen

An den Südhängen des Troodos-Gebirges wächst *Orchis troodi* oft zusammen mit *Dactylorhiza romana*, *Neotinea maculata* und *Ophrys israelitica*.

Westlich von Gerasa, wo *Orchis troodi* in den weitläufigen Pinien- und Kiefernwäldern größere Populationen bildet, wird sie oft von *Ophrys elegans* begleitet. Schöne, kräftige und besonders typische Pflanzen wachsen auch an den südexponierten Hanglagen in der Umgebung des Kykko Klosters. Zur Blütezeit ist *Orchis troodi* hier meist mit austreibenden Exemplaren von *Limodorum abortivum* vergesellschaftet.

Orchis troodi unterscheidet sich von *Orchis anatolica* durch ihre sehr großen Blüten (fast doppelt so groß wie die der Nominatform), ihren steil aufwärts gerichteten, konischen Sporn und die Farbe der Blüten, die entgegen der hellrosa *Orchis anatolica* meist purpurrot gefärbt sind. Ausserdem sind die Pflanzen von *Orchis troodi* viel schlanker, zierlicher und hochwüchsiger und der Blütenstand lockerer und langgestreckter als bei *Orchis anatolica*.

Gefährdung

Orchis troodi ist in den ausgedehnten Kiefernwäldern im Troodos-Gebirge und dessen Randgebieten, sowie im Akamas-Gebiet weit verbreitet. Sie ist daher als nicht gefährdet einzustufen.

Hybriden

Mit *Orchis syriaca*.

Bemerkungen zu der Verbreitungskarte

Die Fundortangaben in Hansen, Kreutz & U. & D. Rückbrodt (1990) wurden nicht alle auf die Verbreitungskarte übertragen, weil in dieser Arbeit *Orchis anatolica* und *Orchis troodi* wegen der geringen morphologische Unterschiede nicht separat unterschieden wurden. Ausserdem wurden in dieser Arbeit *Orchis anatolica* und *Orchis troodi* wegen des Vorkommens zahlreicher Übergangsformen zusammengefasst und in den Fundmeldungen verschiedener Orchideenforscher von vor 1990 meist nur als lokale Varietät gewertet und deshalb als *Orchis anatolica* bestimmt.

Neo Chorio (Akamas), 10.3.2002   Kykkos-Pano Panagia, 16.3.2002

Orchis troodi
Troodos Orchid

(RENZ) P. DELFORGE

Natural. Belges 71: 107 (1990)

Basionym

Orchis anatolica var. *troodi* RENZ, Repert. Spec. Nov. Regni Veg. 27: 209 (1929).

Synonym

Orchis anatolica subsp. *troodi* (RENZ) RENZ, Repert. Spec. Nov. Regni Veg. 30: 100 (1932)

Description

Slender, medium-sized, elegant to tall plant, 15 to 50 cm in height. Stem lightly flexuose, tinged red, especially in the upper part. Foliage leaves lanceolate, acuminate, mostly strongly flecked, lower leaves forming a rosette, upper leaves merging into sheathing stem leaves. Inflorescence very lax and elongated. Bracts acuminate, shorter than ovary. Flowers large, pink to purple-red. Sepals often with distinct green veins, lateral sepals ovate-lanceolate, directed upwards to slightly reflexed, dorsal sepal bent over the petals. Petals narrowly lanceolate, acuminate, usually directed forwards. Labellum fairly wide, distinctly three-lobed, the two lateral lobes more or less strongly reflexed, (light) pink to purple-red, whitish at the base. The lighter-coloured base of the labellum is clearly marked with dark red dashes or purple dots. Spur conical, directed upwards and almost twice as long as ovary.

Habitat

In light coniferous woods free of undergrowth, on stony slopes, wasteland, among shrubs, at forest edges and in maquis; mostly on arid, basic to calcareous soils.

Flowering time

From early March until mid-April.

Altitude distribution

From 100 to 1,500 m.

Overall distribution

Endemic species of Cyprus.

Distribution on Cyprus

This attractive species mainly grows in forest clearings in the higher altitudes of the Troodos mountains under *Pinus brutia, Pinus nigra* subsp. *pallasiana* and *Quercus alnifolia* together with *Thymus integer* and *Cistus salviifolius* (WOOD, 1985; GEORGIADES, 1998ab). *Orchis troodi* also occurs in larger stands on the Akamas peninsula and in the Cedar Valley. Absent in the northern part of Cyprus.

Remarks

Orchis troodi often grows together with *Dactylorhiza romana, Neotinea maculata* and *Ophrys israelitica* on the southern slopes of the Troodos mountains. Westwards from Gerasa, where *Orchis troodi* forms large stands in the vast pine forests, the species is often accompanied by *Ophrys elegans*. Beautiful, vigorous and exceptionally typical plants also grow on the south-facing slopes near the Kykkos monastery. During its flowering time, *Orchis troodi* is often accompanied by emerging specimens of *Limodorum abortivum*.

Orchis troodi differs from *Orchis anatolica* by its very large flowers (almost twice as large as the nominate form), its upwardly directed conical spur and by the colour of its flowers, which are mostly purple-red as against the pale pink flowers of *Orchis anatolica*. Furthermore, the plants of *Orchis troodi* are much more slender, more elegant and taller, and the inflorescence is more lax and more elongated than that of *Orchis anatolica*.

Threats

The species is widely distributed in the vast coniferous forests of the Troodos mountains and its outskirts as in the Akamas area. It is therefore not threatened.

Hybrids

With *Orchis syriaca*.

Remarks concerning the distribution map

The location reports in HANSEN, KREUTZ & U. & D. RÜCKBRODT (1990) have not all been transferred to the distribution map, as *Orchis anatolica* and *Orchis troodi* were not separated in this work because of their small morphological difference. Furthermore, *Orchis anatolica* and *Orchis troodi* were combined in this work because of the occurrence of numerous transitional forms which had been classed as local varieties in the location reports of various orchid researchers before 1990, and therefore specified as *Orchis anatolica*.

Gerasa-Agios Paraskevi, 5.3.2002

Kykkos-Pano Panagia, 16.3.2002

Gerasa-Agios Paraskevi, 5.3.2002

Gerasa-Agios Paraskevi, 5.3.2002

Gerasa-Agios Paraskevi, 5.3.2002

Gerasa-Agios Paraskevi, 5.3.2002

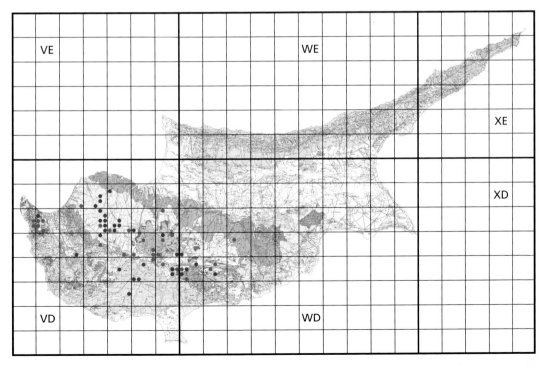

Orchis troodi

36 Orchis caspia
Kaspisches Schmetterlings-Knabenkraut

TRAUTVETTER

Acta Horti Petrop.
2: 484 (1873)

Synonyme

Orchis papilionacea var. bruhnsiana GRUNER, Bull. Soc. Imp. Naturalistes Moscou 4: 463 (1867); *Orchis bruhnsiana* (GRUNER) MAJOROV ex GROSSHEIM, Fl. Kavk. 1: 263 (1928); *Orchis papilionacea* subsp. *bruhnsiana* (GRUNER) SOÓ in KELLER & SOÓ, Monogr. Iconogr. Orchid. Eur. 2 (4/5): 136 (1932); *Orchis schirwanica* WORONOW, Izv. Kavkazsk. Muz. 4 (3): 265 (1909); *Orchis papilionacea* susbp. *schirwanica* (WORONOW) SOÓ, Repert. Spec. Nov. Regni Veg. 24: 28 (1927).

Beschreibung

Kräftige, schlanke Pflanze, 15 bis 25 cm hoch. Stängel, hellgrün, im oberen Teil rötlich überlaufen. Laubblätter eiförmig-lanzettlich bis schmal-lanzettlich, am Grunde rosettig gehäuft, ungefleckt, nach oben in lineal-lanzettliche, scheidenartige Laubblätter übergehend. Blütenstand länglich bis zylindrisch und reichblütig. Tragblätter sehr breit und zugespitzt, etwa so lang wie der Fruchtknoten. Blüten ziemlich dicht angeordnet, mittelgroß, rötlich bis rötlichviolett gefärbt. Sepalen und Petalen einen lockeren, geöffneten Helm bildend mit dunkler gefärbten, deutlich hervortretenden Nerven. Sepalen länglich-lanzettlich, das mittlere etwas kürzer. Petalen kürzer als die Sepalen und zugespitzt. Lippe ziemlich klein, ungeteilt und flach, die Ränder schwach gezähnelt, länglich-eiförmig, im Zentrum hellrosa bis weiss, am Rande mit rötlichen bis purpurnen Strichen oder Punkten gezeichnet, vor allem im unteren Teil und an den Seitenrändern. Sporn gebogen und leicht abwärts gerichtet, kürzer als der Fruchtknoten.

Standort

Lichte Kiefernwälder, Macchien, Phrygana und Gebüschränder; auf trockenen bis mäßig feuchten, kalkreichen Böden.

Blütezeit

Mitte bis Ende März.

Höhenverbreitung

Nur von einem Fundort in 300 m Höhe bekannt.

Gesamtverbreitung

Ostmediterrane Art: Südtürkei, Rhodos (?), Zypern, Westsyrien, Libanon, Israel, Aserbaidschan und im Nordiran.

Verbreitung auf Zypern

Nur von einem Fundort bei Choirokoitia im Südosten bekannt.

Bemerkungen

Die erste Angabe von *Orchis caspia* stammt von SPARROW (WOOD, 1985), gefunden 1960 auf der Halbinsel Akrotiri (nördlich vom Salzsee). WOOD (1985) gibt an, dass der Fund von SPARROW später nicht mehr bestätigt werden konnte, und dass weitere Funde dieser Art auf Zypern nicht mehr gemacht wurden.

Dann, mehr als 40 Jahre nach dem Erstfund, wurde die Art 2001 erneut gefunden und zwar zwischen Lemesos und Larnaka, nahe Choirokoitia (SCRATON 2001; KREUTZ & SCRATON, 2002). An dieser Fundstelle wurde die Art unter anderem zusammen mit vielen Pflanzen von *Orchis syriaca* beobachtet, die aber zur Blütezeit von *Orchis caspia* bereits im Abblühen waren. Ausserdem wurden einige Hybriden zwischen *Orchis caspia* und *Orchis syriaca* gefunden.

Orchis caspia wächst in einem ehemals landwirtschaftlich genutzten Gebiet mit einzelnen Pinien nahe einem großen Stausee (Kalavasos dam). Der Standort weist eine typische Phrygana-Vegetation mit Arten wie *Thymus capitatus*, *Sarcopoterium spinosum* und *Asphodelus aestivus* auf. Weiterhin kommen hier *Ophrys flavomarginata*, *Ophrys kotschyi*, *Ophrys lapethica*, *Ophrys levantina*, *Orchis punctulata* und *Orchis syriaca* vor. An diesem Standort wachsen nur wenige Pflanzen von *Orchis caspia*, durchschnittlich etwa 15 Exemplare jährlich, und trotz intensiver Suche in der weiteren Umgebung wurden keine weiteren Pflanzen mehr gefunden.

Gefährdung

Orchis caspia ist auf Zypern nur von einer Fundstelle bei Choirokoitia im Osten der Insel bekannt. Der Standort grenzt unmittelbar an einem Acker. Die Möglichkeit besteht, dass dieser in absehbarer Zeit als Ackerland genutzt wird. Damit ist sie als besonders gefährdet einzustufen.

Hybriden

Mit *Orchis syriaca* (*Orchis xchoirokitiana* KREUTZ & P. SCRATON).

Choirokoitia (Kalavasos dam), 10.3.2002

Orchis caspia
Caspian Butterfly Orchid

TRAUTVETTER

Acta Horti Petrop. 2: 484 (1873)

Synonyms

Orchis papilionacea var. bruhnsiana GRUNER, Bull. Soc. Imp. Naturalistes Moscou 4: 463 (1867); *Orchis bruhnsiana* (GRUNER) MAJOROV ex GROSSHEIM, Fl. Kavk. 1: 263 (1928); *Orchis papilionacea* subsp. *bruhnsiana* (GRUNER) SOÓ in KELLER & SOÓ, Monogr. Iconogr. Orchid. Eur. 2 (4/5): 136 (1932); *Orchis schirwanica* WORONOW, Izv. Kavkazsk. Muz. 4 (3): 265 (1909); *Orchis papilionacea* susbp. *schirwanica* (WORONOW) SOÓ, Repert. Spec. Nov. Regni Veg. 24: 28 (1927).

Description

Vigorous, slender plant, 15 to 25 cm tall. Stem light green, with reddish tinges in upper part. Foliage leaves ovate-lanceolate to narrowly lanceolate, forming a rosette at base, unspotted, merging into linear-lanceolate, stem-sheathing foliage leaves towards the top. Inflorescence oblong to cylindrical and many-flowered. Bracts very wide and acuminate, about as long as ovary. Flowers fairly densely arranged, medium-sized, reddish to reddish violet. Sepals and petals forming a loose, open hood with distinct, dark veins. Sepals oblong-lanceolate, dorsal sepal somewhat shorter. Petals shorter than sepals and acuminate. Labellum fairly small, undivided and flat, edges faintly toothed, oblong-ovate, light pink to white in centre, reddish to purple streaks or dots at edges, especially in lower part and on lateral edges. Spur curved and slightly directed downwards, shorter than ovary.

Habitat

Light coniferous woods, maquis, phrygana and shrubland edges, on arid to moderately moist, calcareous soils.

Flowering time

Mid- to late March.

Altitude distribution

Only known from one location at 300 m height.

Overall distribution

Eastern Mediterranean species: southern Turkey, Rhodes (?), Cyprus, western Syria, Lebanon, Israel, Azerbaidjan and in northern Iraq.

Distribution on Cyprus

Known from only one location near Choirokoitia in the southeast.

Remarks

The first report of *Orchis caspia* originates from SPARROW (WOOD, 1985), found in 1960 on the Akrotiri peninsula (north of the salt lake). WOOD (1985) reports that the find made by SPARROW could not be verified in later years and that other findings of this species had not been made again on Cyprus.

Then, in 2001, more than 40 years after the initial find, the species was found again between Lemesos and Larnaka, near Choirokoitia (SCRATON 2001; KREUTZ & SCRATON, 2002). This species was seen accompanied by many plants of *Orchis syriaca,* which had however wilted during the flowering time of *Orchis caspia.* Some hybrids between *Orchis caspia* and *Orchis syriaca* were also found.

Orchis caspia grows in a former agricultural area with occasional pine trees near a large reservoir (Kalavasos dam). The habitat exhibits typical phrygana vegetation with species such as *Thymus capitatus, Sarcopoterium spinosum* and *Asphodelus aestivus. Ophrys flavomarginata, Ophrys kotschyi, Ophrys lapethica, Ophrys levantina, Orchis punctulata* and *Orchis syriaca* also occur here. Only a few plants of *Orchis caspia,* on average about 15 specimens each year, grow at this site and despite intensive research in the surrounding area, no other plants were found.

Threats

Orchis caspia is only known at one location near Choirokoitia in eastern Cyprus. The site borders directly on a field. There is a possibility that this field will be used as farmland. The species can therefore be categorised as especially threatened.

Hybrids

With *Orchis syriaca* (*Orchis ×choirokitiana* KREUTZ & P. SCRATON).

Choirokoitia (Kalavasos dam), 10.3.2002

Choirokoitia (Kalavasos dam), 10.3.2002

Choirokoitia (Kalavasos dam), 10.3.2002

Choirokoitia (Kalavasos dam), 10.3.2002

Choirokoitia (Kalavasos dam), 10.3.2002

Choirokoitia (Kalavasos dam), 10.3.2002

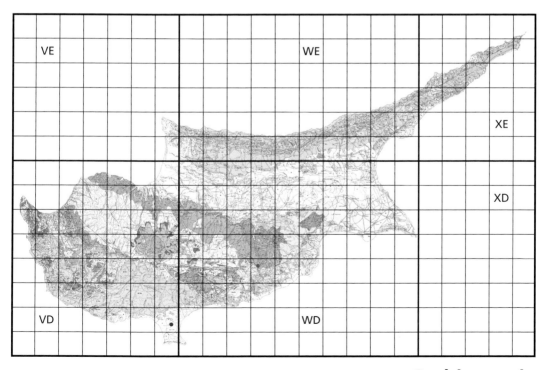

Orchis caspia

37 Orchis collina

Hügel-Knabenkraut

Banks & Solander ex A. Russell

Nat. Hist. Aleppo ed. 2, 2: 264 (1798)

Synonyme

Anacamptis collina (Banks & Solander ex A. Russel) R.M. Bateman, Pridgeon & M.W. Chase, Lindleyana 12 (3): 120 (1997); *Orchis saccata* Tenore, Fl. Napol. 1: 53 (1813); *Orchis sparsiflora* Spruner ex. Reichenbach fil., Icon. Fl. Germ. Helv. 13/14: 37 (1851); *Orchis chlorotica* Woronow, Izv. Kavkazsk. Muz. 4 (3): 265 (1909); *Orchis collina* subsp. *chlorotica* (Woronow) Averyanov, Bot. Zhurn. 79 (10): 118 (1994); *Orchis papilionacea* subsp. *chlorotica* (Woronow) Soó, Repert. Spec. Nov. Regni Veg. 24: 28 (1927); *Orchis fedtschenkoi* Czerniakowska, Notul. Syst. Herb. Horti Bot. Petrop. 3: 147 (1922); *Orchis saccata* subsp. *fedtschenkoi* (Czerniakowska) Soó, Bot. Arch. 23: 50 (1929); *Orchis saccata* var. *fedtschenkoi* (Czerniakowska) Hautzinger, Ann. Naturhist. Mus. Wien 81: 49 (1978); *Orchis collina* subsp. *fedtschenkoi* (Czerniakowska) Averyanov, Bot. Zhurn. 79 (10): 119 (1994); *Orchis leucoglossa* O. Schwarz, Repert. Spec. Nov. Regni Veg. 36: 76 (1934); *Barlia collina* (Banks & Solander ex A. Russel) Szlachetko, Polish Bot. J. 46 (2): 127 (2001).

Beschreibung

Kräftige Pflanze, 15 bis 40 cm hoch, mit relativ dickem, steifem, aufrechtem Stängel. Untere Laubblätter eine Rosette bildend, die oberen den Stängel scheidig umhüllend, ungefleckt. Blütenstand eiförmig bis zylindrisch, arm- bis vielblütig. Tragblätter groß, lanzettlich, dunkelbraun bis rötlichbraun gefärbt, die unteren länger als der Fruchtknoten, die oberen etwa so lang wie der Fruchtknoten. Blüten mittelgroß und locker am Stängel angeordnet. Perigonblätter bräunlich bis rötlichbraun gefärbt, länglich-lanzettlich bis eiförmig-lanzettlich, die beiden seitlichen abstehend bis zurückgeschlagen, das mittlere mit den Petalen helmförmig zusammenneigend. Lippe trapezförmig, ungeteilt, an den Rändern zurückgeschlagen und kaum gewellt, rot bis rotbraun, selten auch grünlich bis grünlichweiss, an der Lippenbasis weisslich. Sporn kurz und dick, schräg abwärts gebogen, halb so lang wie der Fruchtknoten.

Standort

Wächst bevorzugt an trockenen, grasigen und steinigen Stellen in Ödland, Magerrasen, Wiesen, Ackerrändern, Macchien und Phrygana, selten an offenen Stellen in lichten Kiefernwäldern; auf kalkreichen Böden.

Blütezeit

Von Mitte Januar bis Ende Februar, manchmal noch bis Anfang März.

Höhenverbreitung

Von der Küste bis 900 m.

Gesamtverbreitung

Mittelmeergebiet. Von Portugal im Südwesten bis zur Levante im Osten. Ausserdem in Kleinasien, den Kaukasusländern, Turkmenistan bis in den Iran. Im ganzen mediterranen Raum ist die Art selten. Nur auf Kreta, Rhodos und Zypern ist sie relativ häufig.

Verbreitung auf Zypern

Orchis collina ist vor allem im südlichen und westlichen Teil der Insel verbreitet. Im Norden ist die Art viel seltener, und sie blüht dort auch meistens etwas später.

Bemerkungen

Orchis collina ist die am frühesten blühende Art auf Zypern. Sie blüht wenige Wochen nach der zuletzt blühenden Orchidee, nämlich *Spiranthes spiralis*, die je nach Witterung von Mitte Oktober bis Mitte Dezember blüht. Die Blütezeit von *Orchis collina* beginnt bereits Mitte Januar.

Ende Januar blüht *Orchis collina* in größeren Beständen in tief gelegenen, meeresnahen Standorten, wie zum Beispiel in der Umgebung der Moni Power Station, am Salzsee bei Larnaka und auf der Halbinsel Akrotiri. Kretzschmar (1995) fand die Art in bereits verblühtem Zustand oder in Hochblüte in der zweiten Februarwoche. Nach seinen Beobachtungen ist *Orchis collina* auf Zypern nicht selten und allgemein verbreitet, oft ist sie sogar in Massen anzutreffen. Nach Georgiades (1998ab) ist die Art vor allem in der Umgebung von Lefkosia, Athalassa, Latsia, Dali, Lymbia, Tseri, Koshy, Aradippou und Athienou weit verbreitet. Sie ist zwar wenig variabel in der Gestalt, in der Blütenfarbe variiert *Orchis collina* allerdings von purpur, olivgrün oder weisslichgelb bis weiss.

Gefährdung

Orchis collina ist auf Zypern nicht selten. Sie ist durch Ausdehnung der Wohngebiete und intensivere landwirtschaftliche Nutzung ihrer Biotope bereits an vielen Stellen verschwunden. Ausserdem ist die Art besonders empfindlich gegenüber Düngung und Verbuschung ihrer Standorte. Sie ist damit als gefährdet einzustufen.

Hybriden

Nicht nachgewiesen.

310   Kolossi (Akrotiri), 16.2.1995

Orchis collina
Fan-Lipped Orchid

BANKS & SOLANDER EX A. RUSSELL

Nat. Hist. Aleppo ed. 2, 2: 264 (1798)

Synonyms

Anacamptis collina (BANKS & SOLANDER ex A. RUSSEL) R.M. BATEMAN, PRIDGEON & M.W. CHASE, Lindleyana 12 (3): 120 (1997); *Orchis saccata* TENORE, Fl. Napol. 1: 53 (1813); *Orchis sparsiflora* SPRUNER ex. REICHENBACH fil., Icon. Fl. Germ. Helv. 13/14: 37 (1851); *Orchis chlorotica* WORONOW, Izv. Kavkazsk. Muz. 4 (3): 265 (1909); *Orchis collina* subsp. *chlorotica* (WORONOW) AVERYANOV, Bot. Zhurn. 79 (10): 118 (1994); *Orchis papilionacea* subsp. *chlorotica* (WORONOW) SOÓ, Repert. Spec. Nov. Regni Veg. 24: 28 (1927); *Orchis fedtschenkoi* CZERNIAKOWSKA, Notul. Syst. Herb. Horti Bot. Petrop. 3: 147 (1922); *Orchis saccata* subsp. *fedtschenkoi* (CZERNIAKOWSKA) SOÓ, Bot. Arch. 23: 50 (1929); *Orchis saccata* var. *fedtschenkoi* (CZERNIAKOWSKA) HAUTZINGER, Ann. Naturhist. Mus. Wien 81: 49 (1978); *Orchis collina* subsp. *fedtschenkoi* (CZERNIAKOWSKA) AVERYANOV, Bot. Zhurn. 79 (10): 119 (1994); *Orchis leucoglossa* O. SCHWARZ, Repert. Spec. Nov. Regni Veg. 36: 76 (1934); *Barlia collina* (BANKS & SOLANDER ex A. RUSSEL) SZLACHETKO, Polish Bot. J. 46 (2): 127 (2001).

Description

Vigorous plant, 15 to 40 cm tall, with a relatively thick, rigid, erect stem. Lower foliage leaves form a rosette, upper leaves sheathing the stem, unspotted. Inflorescence ovate to cylindrical, few- to many-flowered. Bracts large, lanceolate, dark brown to reddish brown, lower leaves longer than ovary, upper leaves about as long as ovary. Flowers medium-sized and laxly arranged on stem. Perianth segments brownish to reddish brown, oblong-lanceolate to ovate-lanceolate, lateral sepals spreading to reflexed, the dorsal forming a hood with petals. Labellum trapeziform, undivided, reflexed at edges and slightly wavy, red to red-brown, rarely also greenish to greenish white, whitish at base. Spur short and thick, bent obliquely downwards, half as long as ovary.

Habitat

Favours arid, grassy and rocky places in wasteland, neglected grasslands, meadows, field edges, maquis and phrygana, growing rarely in open places in light coniferous woods; on calcareous soils.

Flowering time

From mid-January to late February, sometimes until early March.

Altitude distribution

From sea level to 900 m.

Overall distribution

Mediterranean region, from Portugal in the southwest to the Levant in the east. Also in Asia Minor, the Caucasian countries, Turkmenistan as far as Iran. The species is rare in the whole of the Mediterranean region; only relatively abundant on Crete, Rhodes and Cyprus.

Distribution on Cyprus

Orchis collina is mainly distributed in the southern and western parts of the island. The species is much rarer in the north, and mostly blooms there slightly later.

Remarks

Orchis collina is the earliest flowering species on Cyprus. It blooms just a few weeks later than the last of the late-flowering orchids, namely *Spiranthes spiralis*, which blooms, depending on the weather, from mid-October to mid-December. The flowering time of *Orchis collina* starts in mid-January.

Orchis collina blooms in late-January in large stands in low-lying locations directly next to the sea, as for example in the vicinity of the Moni Power Station, at the salt lake near Larnaka and on the Akrotiri peninsula. KRETZSCHMAR (1995) found the species in a withered state or in full bloom in the second week of February. According to his observations, *Orchis collina* is not rare on Cyprus but widely distributed and can sometimes even be found in huge quantities. According to GEORGIADES (1998ab), the species is mainly widely distributed near Lefkosia, Athalassa, Latsia, Dali, Lymbia, Tseri, Koshy, Aradippou and Athienou. Although it is hardly variable in shape, the flower colour of *Orchis collina* does vary from purple, olive-green or whitish yellow to white.

Threats

Orchis collina is not rare on Cyprus. It has, however, already disappeared from many places due to the expansion of residential areas and intensive agricultural use of its biotopes. Furthermore, the species is highly sensitive to fertilisation and shrub encroachment. It can therefore be categorized as threatened.

Hybrids

Unconfirmed.

Kato Polemidia, 20.1.1998

Drouseia (Akamas), 3.3.2002

Kolossi (Akrotiri), 16.2.1995

Kolossi (Akrotiri), 16.2.1995

Trimiklini, 21.3.2002

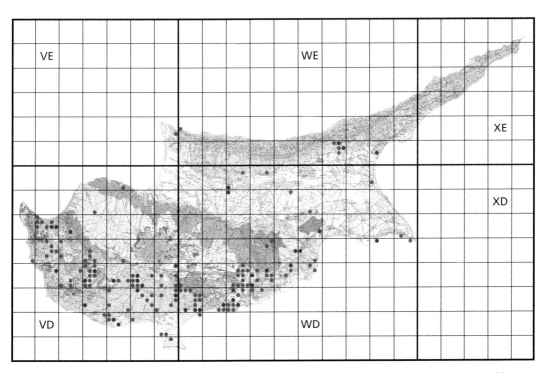

Orchis collina

38 Orchis fragrans

Wohlriechendes Wanzen-Knabenkraut

POLLINI

Elem. Bot. 2: 155 (1811)

Synonyme

Orchis coriophora var. *fragrans* (POLLINI) BOISSIER, Voy. Bot. Espagne 2 (19): 593 (1842); *Orchis coriophora* subsp. *fragrans* (POLLINI) K. RICHTER, Pl. Eur. 1: 268 (1890); *Anteriorchis coriophora* subsp. *fragrans* (POLLINI) P. JACQUET, l'Orchidophile (Asnières) 28 (125): III (1997), comb. inval.; *Anteriorchis coriophora* subsp. *fragrans* (POLLINI) P. JACQUET, l'Orchidophile (Asnières) 28 (127): 134 (1997); *Anteriorchis fragrans* (POLLINI) SZLACHETKO, Polish Bot. J. 46 (2): 127 (2001); *Anacamptis coriophora* subsp. *fragrans* (POLLINI) R.M. BATEMAN, PRIDGEON & M.W. CHASE, Lindleyana 12 (3): 120 (1997); *Anacamptis fragrans* (POLLINI) R.M. BATEMAN, Bot. J. Linn. Soc. 142 (1): 12 (2003); *Orchis cassidea* F.A.M. VON BIEBERSTEIN, Fl. Taur.-Caucas. 3: 600 (1819).

Beschreibung

Schlanke, meist zierliche Pflanze, 20 bis 45 cm hoch. Stängel aufrecht, dünn, grün. Laubblätter linealisch bis lanzettlich, aufrecht, ungefleckt, am Grunde rosettig angeordnet, die oberen in scheidige Stängelblätter übergehend, zugespitzt. Blütenstand zylindrisch, ziemlich dicht- bis lockerblütig, vielblütig. Tragblätter linealisch-lanzettlich, zugespitzt, etwa so lang wie der Fruchtknoten. Blüten relativ klein bis mittelgroß, grünlich bis grünlichweiss gefärbt, nach Vanille duftend. Sepalen und Petalen helmförmig zusammenneigend. Sepalen eiförmig-lanzettlich, zugespitzt, die seitlichen etwas länger als das mittlere. Petalen linealisch und kürzer als die Sepalen. Lippe dreilappig, die beiden Seitenlappen kürzer als der Mittellappen, breit eiförmig, im unteren Teil meist stark zurückgebogen, (hell)grün bis grünlichweiss, Lippenbasis weisslich, mit rosa Punkten oder Strichen besetzt. Sporn kurz, kegelförmig, abwärts gerichtet, etwa so lang wie der Fruchtknoten.

Standort

Lichte Kiefernwälder, Straßenböschungen, Trockenwiesen, Macchien, Phrygana und Gebüsch; auf trockenen bis mäßig feuchten, basischen Böden.

Blütezeit

Von (Mitte) Ende März im Süden bis Ende April.

Höhenverbreitung

Von der Küste bis 1.400 m.

Gesamtverbreitung

Fast im ganzen Mittelmeergebiet und Vorderasien verbreitet. Die nördlichsten Standorte liegen am Gardasee in Italien; östlich bis in den Kaukasus, Nordirak und Iran. Auch in Nordafrika.

Verbreitung auf Zypern

Nicht selten und stellenweise häufig auf den unbewaldeten Nordhängen der Akamas- und Akrotiri-Halbinsel und am Salzsee bei Larnaka. Im Norden häufig in Macchien und in trockenen, grasigen Arealen von Lapta bis Kyrenia und auf der Karpasia-Halbinsel (VINEY, 1994).

Bemerkungen

Orchis fragrans ist auf Zypern nicht selten. Hauptsächlich auf in Meereshöhe gelegenen Standorten bildet sie Massenbestände. Im Norden der Insel und in den weitläufigen, Salz beeinflussten, ufernahen Sanddünen der Akrotiri-Halbinsel bildet sie mit der nahe verwandter *Orchis sancta* Hybridschwärme.

Orchis fragrans hat mehrere gemeinsame Merkmale mit *Orchis sancta*, die auf Zypern zwei bis drei Wochen später blüht. *Orchis fragrans* unterscheidet sich von *Orchis sancta* durch einen dichteren und kürzeren Blütenstand, eine im unteren Teil meist zurückgeschlagene Lippe, wobei die Lippenbasis weisslich und mit rosa Punkten oder Strichen besetzt ist. Die Lippe von *Orchis sancta* ist immer einheitlich (hell)rosa gefärbt und im unteren Teil nach vorne gebogen. *Orchis fragrans* variiert auf Zypern in der Blütenfarbe, von (hell)grün bis dunkelrot.

Früher wurden *Orchis fragrans* und *Orchis coriophora* als eine Art bewertet. Heute sind sie aber in die mitteleuropäische *Orchis coriophora* und die mediterrane *Orchis fragrans* aufgegliedert. Im Gegensatz zu *Orchis coriophora* besiedelt *Orchis fragrans* hauptsächlich trockene Standorte in Macchien und Phrygana. Ausserdem ist der Blütenstand von *Orchis coriophora* meist eiförmig, der von *Orchis fragrans* zylindrisch, bisweilen langgestreckt, und die Blütenfarbe von *Orchis coriophora* ist dunkelbraun, die von *Orchis fragrans* grünlich bis grünlichweiss.

Auf Grund der Ergebnisse chemischer Untersuchungen der Blütenfarbstoffe haben STRACK, BUSCH & KLEIN (1989) die Abtrennung von *Orchis coriophora* und *Orchis sancta* von der Gattung *Orchis* vorgenommen und diese als *Anteriorchis coriophora* (L.) KLEIN & STRACK und *Anteriorchis sancta* (L.) KLEIN & STRACK (1989) beschrieben, und später wurde *Orchis fragrans* von JACQUET (ENGEL, JACQUET & QUENTIN, 1997) in *Anteriorchis coriophora* (L.) KLEIN & STRACK subsp. *fragrans* (POLLINI) JACQUET umkombiniert. Andere Autoren (vergleiche U. & D. RÜCKBRODT & K. & R.-B. HANSEN, 1992; DELFORGE, 1994) haben die Abtrennung der neuen Gattung nicht übernommen. Auch im vorliegenden Buch wurde der altbekannte Name *Orchis fragrans* beibehalten.

Gefährdung

Orchis fragrans ist auf Zypern häufig und daher kaum gefährdet.

Hybriden

Mit *Orchis sancta* (*Orchis* x*kallithea* KLEIN) nachgewiesen. Ausserdem mit *Anacamtis pyramidalis*.

◄ Akrotiri (Moni Agios Nikolaos), 22.3.2002

Akrotiri (Moni Agios Nikolaos), 22.3.2002

Orchis fragrans
Fragrant Bug Orchid

POLLINI

Elem. Bot. 2: 155 (1811)

Synonyms

Orchis coriophora var. *fragrans* (POLLINI) BOISSIER, Voy. Bot. Espagne 2 (19): 593 (1842); *Orchis coriophora* subsp. *fragrans* (POLLINI) K. RICHTER, Pl. Eur. 1: 268 (1890); *Anteriorchis coriophora* subsp. *fragrans* (POLLINI) P. JACQUET, l'Orchidophile (Asnières) 28 (125): III (1997), comb. inval.; *Anteriorchis coriophora* subsp. *fragrans* (POLLINI) P. JACQUET, l'Orchidophile (Asnières) 28 (127): 134 (1997); *Anteriorchis fragrans* (POLLINI) SZLACHETKO, Polish Bot. J. 46 (2): 127 (2001); *Anacamptis coriophora* subsp. *fragrans* (POLLINI) R.M. BATEMAN, PRIDGEON & M.W. CHASE, Lindleyana 12 (3): 120 (1997); *Anacamptis fragrans* (POLLINI) R.M. BATEMAN, Bot. J. Linn. Soc. 142 (1): 12 (2003); *Orchis cassidea* F.A.M. VON BIEBERSTEIN, Fl. Taur.-Caucas. 3: 600 (1819).

Description

Slender, usually elegant plant, 20 to 45 cm tall. Stem erect, thin, green. Foliage leaves linear to lanceolate, erect, unspotted, forming a rosette at ground level, upper leaves merging into sheathing stem leaves, acuminate. Inflorescence cylindrical, flowers fairly dense to laxly arranged, and numerous. Bracts linear-lanceolate, acuminate, about as long as ovary. Flowers relatively small to medium-sized, greenish to greenish white, vanilla scented. Sepals and petals connivent to forming a hood. Sepals ovate-lanceolate, acuminate, lateral sepals slightly longer than dorsal sepal. Petals linear and shorter than sepals. Labellum three-lobed, the two lateral lobes shorter than middle lobe, broadly ovate, mostly strongly bent backwards in lower part, (light) green to greenish white, base of labellum whitish, with pink dots or dashes. Spur short, conical, directed downwards, about as long as ovary.

Habitat

Light coniferous woods, roadside embankments, dry meadows, maquis, phrygana, shrublands; on arid to moderately moist, basic soils.

Flowering time

From (mid-) late March in the south to late April.

Altitude distribution

From sea level to 1,400 m.

Overall distribution

Distributed throughout almost the whole of the Mediterranean region and the Near East. The northernmost habitats are situated at Lake Garda in Italy; spreading eastwards as far as the Caucasus, northern Iraq and Iran. Also in North Africa.

Distribution on Cyprus

Not rare and abundant at some places on the unwooded northern slopes of the Akamas and Akrotiri peninsula and at the salt lake near Larnaka. Abundant in maquis and arid, grassy areas in the north from Lapta to Kyrenia and on the Karpasia Peninsula (VINEY, 1994).

Remarks

Orchis fragrans can be found at many places in Cyprus. It forms mass populations, primarily in habitats at sea level. In the north of the island and in the vast coastal sand dunes influenced by the sea on the Akrotiri peninsula, it forms hybrid swarms with its close relative *Orchis sancta*.

Orchis fragrans has several characteristics in common with *Orchis sancta*, which blooms about two to three weeks later on Cyprus. *Orchis fragrans* can be distinguished from *Orchis sancta* by a denser and shorter inflorescence, a labellum reflexed in the lower part, with the base whitish with pink dots or dashes. The labellum of *Orchis sancta* is always uniformly (light) pink and bent forwards in the lower part. *Orchis fragrans* varies greatly on Cyprus in flower colouration, from (light) green to dark red.

Orchis fragrans and *Orchis coriophora* were once specified as one and the same species but are now divided into the Central European *Orchis coriophora* and the Mediterranean *Orchis fragrans*. *Orchis coriophora* occurs in moist to fresh meadows, *Orchis fragrans* mainly populates arid habitats in maquis and phrygana. The inflorescence of *Orchis coriophora* is mostly ovate, by contrast with that of *Orchis fragrans* which is cylindrical, sometimes elongated. Furthermore, the flower colour of *Orchis coriophora* is dark brown, and that of *Orchis fragrans* greenish to greenish white.

Based on the results of chemical research into the flower pigments, STRACK, BUSCH & KLEIN (1989) have separated *Orchis coriophora* and *Orchis sancta* from the *Orchis* genus and described these as *Anteriorchis coriophora* (L.) KLEIN & STRACK and *Anteriorchis sancta* (L.) KLEIN & STRACK (1989). Lastly, JACQUET (ENGEL, JACQUET & QUENTIN, 1997) has recombined *Orchis fragrans* as *Anteriorchis coriophora* (L.) KLEIN & STRACK subsp. *fragrans* (POLLINI) JACQUET. Other authors, like U. & D. RÜCKBRODT & K. & R.-B. HANSEN (1992) and DELFORGE (1994) have not adopted the separation of this genus. In this book also, the old well-known name of *Orchis fragrans* has been maintained.

Threats

Orchis fragrans is abundant on Cyprus and therefore hardly threatened.

Hybrids

Confirmed with the close relative *Orchis sancta* (*Orchis* x*kallithea* KLEIN). Also with *Anacamptis pyramidalis*.

Akrotiri (Moni Agios Nikolaos), 22.3.2002

Akrotiri (Moni Agios Nikolaos), 22.3.2002

Akrotiri (Salt lake), 22.3.2002

Akrotiri (Salt lake), 22.3.2002

Akrotiri (Salt lake), 22.3.2002

Akrotiri (Moni Agios Nikolaos), 22.3.2002

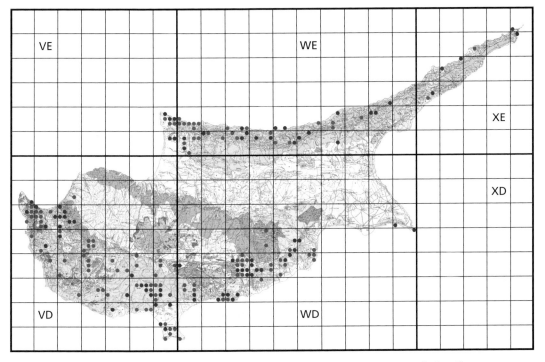

Orchis fragrans

Orchis sancta
Heiliges Knabenkraut

L.

Syst. nat. ed. 10, 2: 1242 (1759)

Synonyme

Orchis coriophora var. *sancta* (L.) REICHENBACH fil., Icon. Fl. Germ. Helv. 13/14: 173 (1851); *Orchis coriophora* subsp. *sancta* (L.) HAYEK, Repert. Spec. Nov. Regni Veg. 30: 386 (1933); *Anteriorchis sancta* (L.) E. KLEIN & STRACK, Phytochemistry 28 (8): 2137 (1989); *Anacamptis sancta* (L.) R.M. BATEMAN, PRIDGEON & M.W. CHASE, Lindleyana 12 (3): 120 (1997).

Beschreibung

Zierliche Pflanze, 15 bis 30 cm hoch. Stängel hellgrün, aufrecht und relativ kräftig. Laubblätter linealisch bis lanzettlich, aufrecht bis abstehend, die oberen in scheidige Stängelblätter übergehend, ungefleckt, zur Blütezeit verwelkt. Blütenstand zylindrisch, ziemlich locker- und vielblütig, langgestreckt. Tragblätter lanzettlich, etwa so lang wie der Fruchtknoten. Blüten klein bis mittelgroß, rosa bis dunkelrot gefärbt. Sepalen und Petalen bilden einen lang geschnäbelten, verklebten bis verwachsenen Helm. Sepalen eiförmig-lanzettlich, zugespitzt, die seitlichen etwas länger als das mittlere, an der Aussenseite oft grünlich überlaufen. Petalen lanzettlich und kürzer als die Sepalen. Lippe rosa bis dunkelrot, dreilappig (der Mittellappen länger als die beiden breiteren, grob gezähnten Seitenlappen), länglich-eiförmig, im unteren Teil meist etwas nach vorne gebogen. Sporn etwa so lang wie der Fruchtknoten, abwärts gerichtet und im unteren Teil nach vorne gekrümmt.

Standort

Mager- und Trockenwiesen, aufgelassene Oliventerrassen, Affodillfluren, in küstennahen Sanddünen, trockenen Flussbetten, Macchien und Phrygana; auf trockenen, kalkreichen oder sandigen Böden.

Blütezeit

Mitte April bis Mitte Mai. *Orchis sancta* blüht auf Zypern etwa zwei bis drei Wochen später als *Orchis fragrans*. In höheren Lagen überlappen sich die Blütezeiten der beiden Taxa.

Höhenverbreitung

Von der Küste bis 900 m.

Gesamtverbreitung

Östliches Mittelmeergebiet, Ägäische Inseln, Türkei, bis nach Israel. Auch auf Zypern und im Kaukasusgebiet. Westlich bis Kreta. *Orchis sancta* hat auf Rhodos ihr Hauptverbreitungsgebiet. Von dieser Insel strahlt sie südwestlich über Karpathos bis nach Kreta aus und östlich über die Südtürkei, Zypern, Israel bis in den Kaukasus.

Verbreitung auf Zypern

Orchis sancta ist auf Zypern selten. Stellenweise häufig ist sie nur auf der Halbinsel Akrotiri in der weiteren Umgebung des Salzsees und in küstennahen Gebieten im Nordosten. Im Norden findet man die Art in Macchien, auf trockenen Berghängen, in Wacholdergebüschen und in küstennahen Sanddünen (VINEY, 1994).

Bemerkungen

Orchis sancta stellt auf Zypern keine hohen Ansprüche an Boden und Bodenfeuchtigkeit; sie wächst oft an den gleichen Standorten wie *Orchis fragrans*, wobei Hybriden zwischen beiden Arten nicht selten sind. Auf Zypern zeigt *Orchis sancta* eine starke, von hellrosa bis dunkelrot reichende Variabilität in der Blütenfarbe.

Schöne Bestände von *Orchis sancta* gibt es im Westen der Insel und auf der Akrotiri Halbinsel. Vor allem auf der Halbinsel Akrotiri wachsen in der direkten Umgebung des Salzsees in guten Jahren mehrere hundert Exemplare auf dem sandigen, spärlich bewachsenen Boden,.

Orchis sancta zeigt morphologisch gewisse Merkmale von *Orchis fragrans*, unterscheidet sich von dieser Art durch einen lockereren und langgestreckten Blütenstand, die im unteren Teil nach vorne gebogen Lippe, den nach vorne gebogenen Sporn und die rosa Lippenbasis, die keine Punkte oder Striche besitzt. Ferner blüht *Orchis sancta* auf Zypern zwei bis drei Wochen später. Weiterhin duftet *Orchis sancta* nicht, und sie ist in nicht blühendem Zustand an ihren welkenden Laubblättern und ihrem hellgrünen Stängel relativ einfach von *Orchis fragrans* zu unterscheiden.

Gefährdung

Orchis sancta ist auf Zypern selten und fast ausschließlich in küstennahen Gebieten verbreitet. Sie ist dort durch die sich immer weiter ausbreitenden Hotelanlagen und die starke landwirtschaftliche Nutzung relativ stark gefährdet.

Hybriden

Mit *Orchis fragrans* bildet sie Hybridschwärme (*Orchis* x*kallithea* KLEIN), die stark in der Form und Blütenfarbe variieren.

Bemerkungen zu der Verbreitungskarte

Die Art ist sicherlich weiter verbreitet als auf der Verbreitungskarte zu sehen ist. Wegen der späten Blütezeit, in der nur wenige Orchideensucher auf Zypern unterwegs sind, wurde sie bisher nur wenig beobachtet.

◄ Akrotiri (Salt lake), 15.4.2002

Akrotiri (Salt lake), 15.4.2002

Akrotiri (Salt lake), (mit/with *Orchis fragrans*), 22.3.2002

Orchis sancta

Holy Orchid

L.

Syst. nat. ed. 10, 2: 1242 (1759)

Synonyms

Orchis coriophora var. *sancta* (L.) Reichenbach fil., Icon. Fl. Germ. Helv. 13/14: 173 (1851); *Orchis coriophora* subsp. *sancta* (L.) Hayek, Repert. Spec. Nov. Regni Veg. 30: 386 (1933); *Anteriorchis sancta* (L.) E. Klein & Strack, Phytochemistry 28 (8): 2137 (1989); *Anacamptis sancta* (L.) R.M. Bateman, Pridgeon & M.W. Chase, Lindleyana 12 (3): 120 (1997).

Description

Elegant plant, 15 to 30 cm tall. Stem light green, erect and relatively vigorous. Foliage leaves linear to lanceolate, erect to spreading, upper leaves merging into sheathing stem leaves, unspotted, usually wilted during the flowering period. Inflorescence cylindrical, fairly lax and many-flowered, elongate. Bracts lanceolate, about as long as ovary. Flowers small to medium-sized, pink to dark red. Sepals and petals form a long bill-shaped, coalesced to fused, hood. Sepals ovate-lanceolate, acuminate, lateral sepals slightly longer than dorsal sepal, often tinged greenish on the outside. Petals lanceolate and shorter than sepals. Labellum pink to dark red, three-lobed (middle lobe longer than the two wide, roughly toothed lateral lobes), oblong-ovate, lower part mostly slightly bent forwards. Spur about as long as ovary, directed downwards and curved forwards in lower part.

Habitat

Neglected and dry hay meadows, abandoned olive terraces, asphodel fields, in coastal sand dunes, arid river beds, maquis and phrygana; on arid, calcareous or sandy soils.

Flowering time

Mid-April to mid-May. *Orchis sancta* blooms about two to three weeks later than *Orchis fragrans* on Cyprus. In higher altitudes the flowering times of the two species overlap.

Altitude distribution

From sea level to 900 m.

Overall distribution

Eastern Mediterranean region, Aegean islands, Turkey, as far as Israel. Also on Cyprus and in the Caucasian region; westwards as far as Crete. *Orchis sancta* has its main distribution area on Rhodes. It spreads from this island southwestwards through Karpathos as far as Crete, and eastwards through southern Turkey, Cyprus, Israel as far as the Caucasus.

Distribution on Cyprus

Orchis sancta is rare on Cyprus. It is only abundant at some places on the Akrotiri peninsula area around the salt lake and in the coastal areas of the northeast. In the north, one can find the species in maquis, on arid slopes, among juniper shrubs and in coastal sand dunes (Viney, 1994).

Remarks

Orchis sancta does not place high requirements on soil and soil humidity on Cyprus; it often grows in the same habitats as *Orchis fragrans*, where hybrids between the two species are not rare. *Orchis sancta* displays a strong variability in its flower colour on Cyprus, ranging from light pink to deep red.

Beautiful stands of *Orchis sancta* can be found in the western part of the island and on the Akrotiri peninsula. On Akrotiri peninsula particularly, in favourable years, several hundred specimens grow in the direct vicinity of the salt lake on the sandy, sparsely overgrown soils.

Orchis sancta shares certain morphological characteristics with *Orchis fragrans*, but can be distinguished from this species by a lax and elongated inflorescence, by the labellum which is bent forwards in the lower part, by the spur which is bent forwards and by the pink base of the labellum which has no dots or dashes. Furthermore, *Orchis sancta* blooms two to three weeks later on Cyprus. Furthermore, *Orchis sancta* has no scent, and in its nonflowering state can be distinguished relatively easily from *Orchis fragrans* by its wilting foliage leaves and its light green stem.

Threats

Orchis sancta is rare on Cyprus and almost only distributed throughout the coastal areas. It is relatively heavily threatened there by the ever-expanding construction of hotel complexes and intensive agricultural use of the area.

Hybrids

It forms hybrid swarms with *Orchis fragrans* (*Orchis* x*kallithea* Klein), which can vary widely in shape and flower colour.

Remarks concerning the distribution map

The species is certainly more widely distributed than the distribution map shows. Due to its late flowering time, during which few orchidologists visit Cyprus, it is seen only seldom.

Akrotiri (Salt lake), 15.4.2002

Akrotiri (Salt lake), 15.4.2002

Akrotiri (Salt lake), 15.4.2002

Akrotiri (Salt lake), 15.4.2002

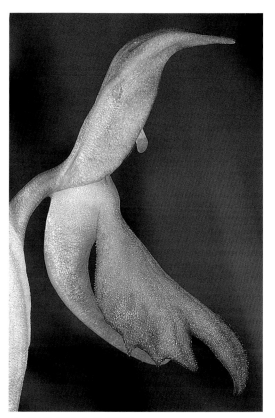

Akrotiri (Salt lake), 15.4.2002

Akrotiri (Salt lake), 15.4.2002

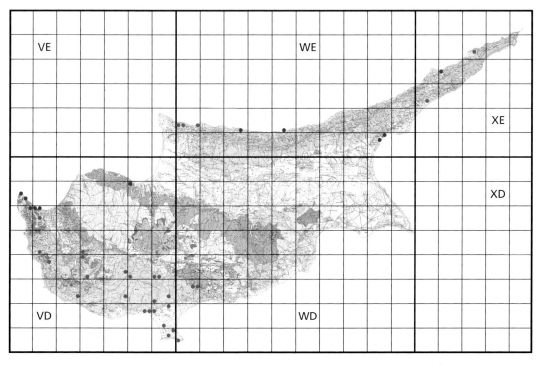

Orchis sancta

40 Orchis italica

Italienisches Knabenkraut

POIRET

J.B.A.P. Lamarck, Encycl. 4 (2): 600 (1798)

Synonyme

Orchis longicruris LINK in J. Bot. (SCHRADER) 2 (2): 323 (1800, publ. 1799); *Orchis undulatifolia* BIVONA-BERNARDI, Sicul. Pl. Cent. 2: 44 & 45 (1806); *Orchis welwitschii* REICHENBACH fil., Icon. Fl. Germ. Helv. 13/14: 183 (1851); *Orchis longicruris* subsp. *longipenis* FONT QUER & PALAU, Collect. Bot. (Barcelona) 4 (2): 209 (1954).

Beschreibung

Kräftige Pflanze, 20 bis 40 cm hoch. Stängel aufrecht, ziemlich dick, hell- bis gelblichgrün. Laubblätter elliptisch-lanzettlich, ungefleckt oder gefleckt, am Rande stark gewellt, die unteren in eine Grundrosette, die oberen in scheidige Stängelblätter übergehend. Blütenstand halbkugelig bis zylindrisch, dicht- und vielblütig. Tragblätter lanzettlich und klein, etwa ein Drittel so lang wie der Fruchtknoten. Blüten ziemlich groß, schräg abstehend. Perigonblätter einen dichten bis lockeren Helm bildend, (hell)rosa bis purpurn mit dunkel purpurroten Nerven. Sepalen eiförmig-lanzettlich und lang zugespitzt. Petalen lanzettlich und kurz. Lippe tief dreilappig, der Mittellappen nochmals zweigeteilt mit einem spitzen Mittelzahn; Seitenlappen und die beiden Zipfel des Mittellappens schwach nach oben gebogen, (hell)rosa bis purpurn oder rötlich, an der Basis weisslich mit dunkelpurpurnen Flecken. Sporn zylindrisch, abwärts gebogen, etwa halb so lang wie der Fruchtknoten.

Standort

Ödland, lichte Pinienwälder, Magerrasen, Macchien, Phrygana, steinige Hänge, aufgelassene Terrassen und Gebüschränder; auf basischen bis kalkreichen Böden.

Blütezeit

(Anfang) Mitte März bis Mitte April.

Höhenverbreitung

Von der Küste bis 800 m.

Gesamtverbreitung

Mittelmeergebiet, von Portugal bis zur Levante. Auch in Nordafrika.

Verbreitung auf Zypern

Vor allem im südlichen und westlichen Teil der Insel verbreitet. Im Norden hauptsächlich in den Pinienwäldern des Pentadactylos-Gebirges.

Bemerkungen

Orchis italica ist auf Zypern weit verbreitet und eine der häufigsten Orchideenarten. Viele reich besetzte Standorte hat die Art in den südlichen Hängen des Troodos-Gebirges, in der weiteren Umgebung von Larnaka (Salzsee) und bei Kato Drys und Gerasa im Süden der Insel. Sehr schöne Populationen finden sich auch bei Choulou im Westen Zyperns. Hier stehen die Pflanzen an vielen Fundorten so dicht beieinander, dass die Landschaft von weitem gesehen von einem rosa bis roten Schimmer überzogen ist.

Im nördlichen Teil Zyperns ist die Art seltener als im südlichen Teil. Nach VINEY (1994) wächst *Orchis italica* dort in Macchien, Phrygana und lockeren Pinienwäldern in den zentral-nördlichen Gebieten von Alsançak bis Mersinlik und lokal auch auf der Karpasia-Halbinsel.

Orchis italica wächst bevorzugt in der Phrygana auf steinigen, offenen Stellen, meist zusammen mit vielen anderen Orchideenarten. Sie ist häufig mit *Asphodelus aestivus*, *Arisarum vulgare* und *Ranunculus asiaticus* vergesellschaftet. Ausserdem steht *Orchis italica* gerne auf abgebrannten Flächen (GEORGIADES, 1998ab), wie zum Beispiel bei Kato Drys, wo sie nach einem Brand der Macchie in mehreren tausend Exemplaren zur Blüte kam.

Auf Zypern variiert die Art ziemlich stark in der Blütenfarbe. Neben dunkelpurpurnen Exemplaren, die hauptsächlich an den Südhängen des Troodos-Gebirges bei Moniatis wachsen, kommen auch ganz weissblütige Pflanzen vor.

Gefährdung

Orchis italica kommt auf Zypern häufig vor. Im Süden ist die Art nicht gefährdet. Im Norden Zyperns gehört sie aber zu den gefährdeten Orchideenarten, weil ihre Knollen zur Herstellung von Salep ausgegraben, getrocknet und gemahlen werden (VINEY, 1994).

Hybriden

Mit *Orchis punctulata* (*Orchis* ×*tochniana* KREUTZ & P. SCRATON). WOOD (1985) gibt an, dass im Pentadactylos-Gebirge und südlich des Troodos-Gebirges auch Hybriden zwischen *Orchis italica* und *Orchis simia* gefunden wurden. Hybriden dieser zwei Arten sind ausserordentlich selten und wurden bisher niemals mit Sicherheit nachgewiesen. Vermutlich handelt es sich bei diesen Pflanzen um armblütige Exemplare von *Orchis italica*.

Larnaka (Salt lake), 9.3.2002

Orchis italica

Naked Man Orchid

POIRET

J.B.A.P. Lamarck, Encycl. 4 (2): 600 (1798)

Synonyms

Orchis longicruris Link in J. Bot. (Schrader) 2 (2): 323 (1800, publ. 1799); *Orchis undulatifolia* Bivona-Bernardi, Sicul. Pl. Cent. 2: 44 & 45 (1806); *Orchis welwitschii* Reichenbach fil., Icon. Fl. Germ. Helv. 13/14: 183 (1851); *Orchis longicruris* subsp. *longipenis* Font Quer & Palau, Collect. Bot. (Barcelona) 4 (2): 209 (1954).

Description

Vigorous plant, 20 to 40 cm tall. Stem erect, fairly thick, light to yellowish green. Foliage leaves elliptic-lanceolate, spotted or unspotted, very wavy at edges, lower leaves forming a rosette at base, upper leaves merging into sheathing stem leaves. Inflorescence semi-spherical to cylindrical, dense and many-flowered. Bracts lanceolate and small, about one third of ovary. Flowers fairly large, spreading o-bliquely. Perianth segments form a closed to loose hood, (light) pink to purple with dark purple-red veins. Sepals ovate-lanceolate and long acuminate. Petals lanceolate and short. Labellum deeply three-lobed, middle lobe divided into two, and with a pointed middle tooth; lateral lobes and both parts of middle lobe slightly bent upwards, (light) pink to purple or reddish, whitish at base dappled with deep purple. Spur cylindrical, bent downwards, about half as long as ovary.

Habitat

Wasteland, light pine woods, neglected grasslands, maquis, phrygana, rocky slopes, abandoned terraces and shrubland margins; on basic to calcareous soils.

Flowering time

(Early) Mid-March to mid-April.

Altitude distribution

From sea level to 800 m.

Overall distribution

Mediterranean region, from Portugal to the Levant. Also in North Africa.

Distribution on Cyprus

Mainly distributed in the southern and western parts of the island. In the north primarily in the pine woods of the Pentadactylos mountains.

Remarks

Orchis italica is widely distributed on Cyprus and one of the most abundant orchid species. The species has many densely populated habitats on the southern slopes of the Troodos mountains, in the area around Larnaka (salt lake) and near Kato Drys and Gerasa in the south of the island. Very beautiful populations can be found near Choulou in the west of Cyprus. The plants here stand so close together that it seems, from a distance, as if the landscape has been covered by a pink/red carpet. The species is rarer in the northern part of Cyprus than in the south. According to Viney (1994), *Orchis italica* grows there in maquis, phrygana and light pine woods in the central northern areas from Alsançak to Mersinlik and locally also on the Karpasia peninsula.

Orchis italica favours phrygana and rocky, open places, usually growing with a number of other orchid species. The species is accompanied abundantly by *Asphodelus aestivus, Arisarum vulgare* and *Ranunculus asiaticus. Orchis italica* also likes to grow in burnt fields (Georgiades, 1998ab), as for example near Kato Drys, where several thousand specimens blossomed in the maquis after a fire.

The species varies fairly widely in flower colour on Cyprus. Besides deep purple specimens, which primarily grow on the southern slopes of the Troodos mountains near Moniatis, one can also find plants with completely white flowers.

Threats

Orchis italica is abundant on Cyprus. The species is not threatened in the south. In the north however it belongs with the threatened orchid species of Cyprus, as its bulbs are digged out, dried and ground for the manufacture of salep (Viney, 1994).

Hybrids

With *Orchis punctulata* (*Orchis* ×*tochniana* Kreutz & P. Scraton). Wood (1985) reports that hybrids have also been found between *Orchis italica* and *Orchis simia* in the Pentadactylos mountains and south of the Troodos mountains. Hybrids of these two species are extraordinarily rare and have never been confirmed with certainty so far. These plants are probably few-flowered specimens of *Orchis italica*.

Tsada-Pitargou, 17.3.2002

Kayalar-Sadrazamköy, 18.3.2002

Larnaka (Salt lake), 9.3.2002

Alevkaya (Pentadactylos Range), 18.3.2002

Tsada-Pitargou, 17.3.2002

Tsada-Pitargou, 17.3.2002

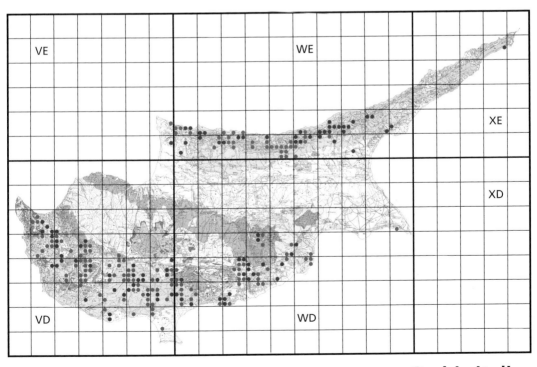

Orchis italica

41

Orchis laxiflora
Lockerblütiges Knabenkraut

LAMARCK

Fl. Franc. (ed. 1), 3: 504 (1779)

Synonyme

Orchis ensifolia VILLARS, Hist. Pl. Dauph. 2: 29 (1787); *Orchis palustris* subsp. *laxiflora* (LAMARCK) BATTANDIER & TRABUT, Fl. Alger.: 30 (1895); *Orchis laxiflora* subsp. *ensifolia* (VILLARS) ASCHERSON & GRÄBNER, Syn. Mitteleur. Fl. 3: 711 (1907); *Anacamptis laxiflora* (LAMARCK) R.M. BATEMAN, PRIDGEON & M.W. CHASE, Lindleyana 12 (3): 120 (1997).

Beschreibung

Schlanke, meist hochwüchsige Pflanze, 30 bis 50 cm hoch. Stängel aufrecht, steif und etwas hin und her gebogen, im oberen Teil purpurn überlaufen. Laubblätter schmal-lanzettlich bis lanzettlich, ungefleckt, schräg aufwärts gerichtet, stark gefaltet. Blütenstand lockerblütig und langgestreckt, vielblütig. Tragblätter lang zugespitzt, die unteren etwas länger, die oberen so lang wie der Fruchtknoten. Blüten mittelgross, dunkelviolett bis rötlichviolett gefärbt, an der Lippenbasis weiss. Sepalen eiförmig bis eiförmig-lanzettlich, die beiden seitlichen aufgerichtet bis zurückgeschlagen, das mittlere Sepal über die beiden Petalen gebogen. Petalen schmal-lanzettlich bis eiförmig, zusammenneigend. Lippe undeutlich dreilappig, die Seitenlappen stark zurückgeschlagen und länger als der Mittellappen, purpurrot bis rotviolett, mit weisslicher Lippenbasis und ohne Malzeichnung. Sporn zylindrisch, aufwärts gerichtet, etwas kürzer als der Fruchtknoten.

Standort

Feucht- und Sumpfwiesen, entlang von Fluss- und Bachufern und in Quellgebieten; auf kalkhaltigen, lehmigen Böden.

Blütezeit

(Anfang) Mitte März bis Mitte April.

Höhenverbreitung

Die wenigen bekannten Fundorte liegen zwischen 200 und 800 m Höhe.

Gesamtverbreitung

Fast das ganze Mittelmeergebiet umfassend, nördlich bis Nordwestfrankreich und die Kanalinseln und östlich bis in den mittleren Teil der Türkei, Zypern, Nordisrael und die Kaukasusländer.

Verbreitung auf Zypern

Die Art ist auf Zypern sehr selten und nur von wenigen Fundstellen bekannt, wie nordöstlich von Pafos bei Nata, zwischen Polis und Drouseia (Akamas) und zwischen Mandria und Omodos (Troodos).

Bemerkungen

Orchis laxiflora gehört auf Zypern zu den seltensten und am meisten gefährdeten Orchideen und ist aktuell nur noch an sehr wenigen Fundstellen vorhanden. B. & E. WILLING (1976) konnten *Orchis laxiflora* im Gebiet zwischen Pafos und Polis (zwischen den Orten Loukrounou und Skoulli) nachweisen. WOOD (1985) nennt Fundstellen zwischen Khrysokhou und Polis, zwischen Lachi und Neo Chorio, bei Mandria, Perapedhi und Lefkosia. Die meisten dieser Standorte sind inzwischen erloschen. Nach WOOD (1985) hatte die Art vor allem im Westen Zyperns in den küstennahen Sumpfgebieten viele Vorkommen. Diese Standorte sind heute durch Trockenlegung fast ganz verschwunden. Vermutlich aber handelte es sich hier um Standorte von *Orchis palustris*, denn *Orchis laxiflora* findet man nur selten in küstennahen Sumpfgebieten, weil diese Feuchtgebiete meist relativ stark Salz beeinflusst sind. Standorte, an denen *Orchis laxiflora* und *Orchis palustris* zusammen vorkommen, sind sehr selten. Der Hybrid zwischen beiden Arten, *Orchis* xlloydiana ROUY, mit einem dichten Blütenstand und einer stark dreilappigen Lippe, der bei WOOD (1985) für Zypern erwähnt wird, wurde auch ausserhalb von Zypern wenig beobachtet.

Die aktuellen Standorte zeigen heute nur noch kleine Restbestände. Der Standort nordöstlich von Pafos zwischen Nata und Choletria entlang des Xeros Potamos ist durch Trockenlegung sehr stark bedroht. Es ist zu erwarten, dass dieser Standort innerhalb den nächsten Jahren verschwunden sein wird. Weitere aktuelle Angaben stammen von ERHARDT, HILLER & KALTEISEN (Standortangaben 2002) und von SCRATON (Standortangaben 2004). ERHARDT, HILLER & KALTEISEN (l.s.) fanden in einer feuchten Senke zwischen Polis und Drouseia (Akamas) etwa 80 blühenden Exemplare, ausserdem einige Hybriden mit *Orchis syriaca*. In dieser Umgebung wachsen weitere Pflanzen zwischen Feldern am Rande kleiner Flüsse. Dieser Standort und eine weitere Angabe in der Umgebung von Kritou-Tera, etwa 2 km östlich von Drouseia (Akamas), werden auch von SCRATON (l.s.) angegeben. Eine weitere aktuelle Fundstelle wurde erst vor wenigen Jahren im Troodos-Gebirge entdeckt. Sie liegt an der alten Straße zwischen Omodos und Mandria. Die Pflanzen wachsen dort in einer Feuchtwiese am Rande einer alten Weinbergterrasse. Es ist zu hoffen, dass wenigstens einige dieser Standorte für die Zukunft erhalten bleiben.

Gefährdung

Die ohnehin sehr seltene *Orchis laxiflora* ist durch Trockenlegung, Düngung und Intensivierung der Landwirtschaft stark zurückgegangen. Sie ist daher besonders stark gefährdet.

Hybriden

Mit *Orchis syriaca*. Hybriden mit *Orchis palustris*, die von WOOD (1985) für Zypern angegeben wurden, sind sehr schwierig zu identifizieren und beruhen vermutlich auf einer Fehlbestimmung.

◀ Nata-Choletria (Xeros Potamos), 12.3.2002

333

Nata-Choletria (Xeros Potamos), 12.3.2002

Orchis laxiflora

Loose-Flowered Orchid

LAMARCK

Fl. Franc. (ed. 1), 3: 504 (1779)

Synonyms

Orchis ensifolia VILLARS, Hist. Pl. Dauph. 2: 29 (1787); *Orchis palustris* subsp. *laxiflora* (LAMARCK) BATTANDIER & TRABUT, Fl. Alger.: 30 (1895); *Orchis laxiflora* subsp. *ensifolia* (VILLARS) ASCHERSON & GRÄB-NER, Syn. Mitteleur. Fl. 3: 711 (1907); *Anacamptis laxiflora* (LAMARCK) R.M. BATEMAN, PRIDGEON & M.W. CHASE, Lindleyana 12 (3): 120 (1997).

Description

Slender, mostly tall plant, 30 to 50 cm in height. Stem erect, stiff and slightly flexuose, purple tinged in upper part. Foliage leaves narrowly lanceolate to lanceolate, unspotted, obliquely erect, keeled. Inflorescence lax and elongated, many-flowered. Bracts long and acuminate, lower leaves slightly longer, upper leaves as long as ovary. Flowers medium-sized, deep violet to reddish violet, white at base of labellum. Sepals ovate to ovate-lanceolate, the two lateral sepals erect to reflexed, dorsal sepal bent over the two petals. Petals narrowly lanceolate to ovate, connivent. Labellum indistinctly three-lobed, lateral lobes strongly folded backwards and longer than middle lobe, purple-red to red-violet, with whitish labellum base and without marking. Spur cylindrical, directed upwards, slightly shorter than ovary.

Habitat

Marshes and wet areas, alongside rivers and streams and near springs; on calcareous, clay soils

Flowering time

(Early) Mid-March to mid-April.

Altitude distribution

The known few sites are situated between 200 and 800 m height.

Overall distribution

Covering almost the entire Mediterranean region, northwards as far as northwestern France and the Channel Islands and eastwards as far as the central part of Turkey, Cyprus, northern Israel and the Caucasian countries.

Distribution on Cyprus

The species is very rare on Cyprus and known from only a few sites; for example northeast of Pafos near Nata, between Polis and Drouseia (Akamas) and in the Troodos mountains between Mandria and Omodos.

Remarks

Orchis laxiflora is among the rarest and most threatened orchids of Cyprus and is currently only known from just a few sites. B. & E. WILLING (1976) could confirm *Orchis laxiflora* in the area between Pafos and Polis (between the towns of Loukrounou and Skoulli). WOOD (1985) mentions sites between Khrysokhou and Polis, between Lachi and Neo Chorio, near Mandria, Perapedhi and Lefkosia. Most of these habitats have disappeared since then.

According to WOOD (1985), the species had many sites, mainly in western Cyprus in the coastal marshes. These habitats have almost completely disappeared today because of drainage. The sites probably involve *Orchis palustris* however, as *Orchis laxiflora* rarely occurs in coastal marshes, because of their relatively strong salinity. Habitats where *Orchis laxiflora* and *Orchis palustris* occur together are rare. The hybrid between the two species, *Orchis* x*lloydiana* ROUY, with a dense inflorescence and a deeply three-lobed labellum, was recorded by WOOD (1985) for Cyprus, but has been seen only a few times outside Cyprus.

Current habitats possess only small residual stands. The habitat northeast of Pafos between Nata and Choletria along the Xeros Potamos is heavily threatened by drainage. It is to be expected that this habitat will have disappeared in the next few years. Further recent sites were found by ERHARDT, HILLER & KALTEISEN (site descriptions 2002) and SCRATON (site descriptions 2004). ERHARDT, HILLER & KALTEISEN (l.s.) found over 80 flowering plants in a wet ditch between Polis and Drouseia (Akamas), and some hybrids with *Orchis syriaca*. In this neighbourhood more plants are situated amidst fields bordering several small streams. This site and another habitat in the neighbourhood of Kritou-Tera, about 2 km east of Drouseia (Akamas) has also been reported by SCRATON (l.s.). A new location has recently been discovered in the Troodos mountains. This site is located along the old road between Omodos and Mandria. The plants grow there in a wet meadow at the back of old vines. One hopes that at least some of these locations will be preserved for the future.

Threats

The already very rare *Orchis laxiflora* has declined considerably due to drainage, fertilisation and ever intensifying agriculture. It is therefore especially threatened.

Hybrids

With *Orchis syriaca*. Hybrids with *Orchis palustris*, which were reported by WOOD (1985) for Cyprus, are exceptionally difficult to identify and were probably based upon a false idenitification.

Nata-Choletria (Xeros Potamos), 12.3.2002

Nata-Choletria (Xeros Potamos), 12.3.2002

Nata-Choletria (Xeros Potamos), 12.3.2002

Nata-Choletria (Xeros Potamos), 12.3.2002

Nata-Choletria (Xeros Potamos), 12.3.2002

Nata-Choletria (Xeros Potamos), 12.3.2002

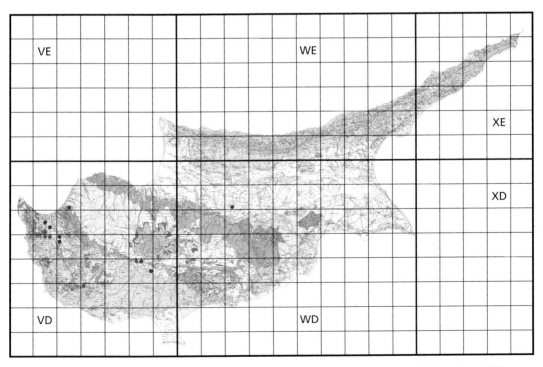

Orchis laxiflora

42

Orchis palustris
Sumpf-Knabenkraut

JACQUIN

Collectanea 1: 75 & 76, no. CX (1786)

Synonyme

Orchis laxiflora var. *palustris* (JACQUIN) W.D.J. KOCH, Syn. Fl. Germ. Helv. ed. 2, 2: 792 (1844); *Orchis laxiflora* subsp. *palustris* (JACQUIN) BONNIER & LAYENS, Tabl. Syn. Pl. Vasc. France 1: 311 (1894); *Anacamptis palustris* (JACQUIN) R.M. BATEMAN, PRIDGEON & M.W. CHASE, Lindleyana 12 (3): 120 (1997); *Orchis mediterranea* GUSSONE, Pl. Rar.: 365 & 366 (1826); *Orchis palustris* var. *mediterranea* (GUSSONE) SCHLECHTER, Monogr. Iconogr. Orchid. Eur. 1 (5/6): 192 (1927); *Orchis palustris* subsp. *mediterranea* (GUSSONE) MALAGARRIGA, Acta Phytotax. Barcinon. 1: 64 (1968); *Orchis laxiflora* var. *mediterranea* (GUSSONE) RIVERA NUÑEZ & LÓPES VÉLEZ, Orq. Prov. Albacete: 140 (1987).

Beschreibung

Zierliche, schlanke Pflanze, 50 bis 60 cm hoch. Stängel aufrecht, ziemlich dünn, grasgrün, im oberen Teil purpurn überlaufen. Laubblätter grasartig, schmallanzettlich, rinnig gefaltet, spitz, schräg aufgerichtet, ungefleckt. Blütenstand zylindrisch bis langgestreckt, ziemlich locker- und vielblütig, selten armblütig. Tragblätter linealisch, meist so lang wie der Fruchtknoten. Blüten mittelgroß bis groß, schräg abstehend, rotviolett, rötlich bis rosa, selten weiss. Sepalen eiförmig-lanzettlich, die beiden seitlichen schräg seitwärts gerichtet oder zurückgeschlagen, das mittlere über beide Petalen gebogen, stumpf. Petalen lanzettlich, zusammengeneigt. Lippe violett oder rötlich bis rosa, im unteren Teil leicht dreilappig, die Seitenlappen flach ausgebreitet oder leicht zurückgeschlagen und etwas kürzer als der ausgerandete Mittellappen; Lippenbasis weisslich, mit purpurnen Strichen oder kurzen Linien besetzt. Sporn zylindrisch, waagerecht oder aufwärts gebogen, etwa so lang wie der Fruchtknoten.

Standort

Sumpfwiesen und Seeufer (dort meist zwischen lockerem Schilf); auf sehr feuchten, basenreichen bis kalkhaltigen, humosen Böden.

Blütezeit

Mitte April bis Ende Mai.

Höhenverbreitung

Nur in Meereshöhe.

Gesamtverbreitung

Mittlerer Teil Europas, mit einzelnen Vorkommen in Spanien und Gotland (Schweden). Ausserdem in der Türkei, Zypern und den Kaukasusländern.

Verbreitung auf Zypern

Die Art ist auf Zypern äusserst selten und nur von einer Fundstelle auf der Halbinsel Akrotiri bekannt.

Bemerkungen

Orchis palustris gehört mit *Ophrys tenthredinifera* zu den seltensten und am meisten gefährdeten Orchideenarten Zyperns.

UNGER & KOTSCHY (1865) und HOLMBOE (1914) geben *Orchis palustris* für die Umgebung von Lefkosia an. Auch RENZ (1929) erwähnt diese Standorte, kommt aber zum Ergebnis, dass diese Pflanzen zu *Orchis laxiflora* gehören. WOOD (1985) gibt auch nur sehr wenige Fundstellen an, nämlich bei Phini (KOTSCHY, 1862) und Dhikomo (UNGER & KOTSCHY, 1865), weitere in der Umgebung von Lemesos und auf der Halbinsel Akrotiri.

Die letzte aktuelle Fundstelle der schon immer sehr seltenen Art liegt in den weitläufigen Schilfbeständen der Halbinsel Akrotiri. In diesem Gebiet hatte *Orchis palustris* früher mehrere Fundstellen. Sie ist aber durch Trockenlegung, verursacht 1985 durch den Bau des Kouris Staudammes nördlich von Lemesos, an vielen Stellen verschwunden und zeigt aktuell nur noch einen Fundort mit einem kleinen Restbestand. Die letzten Pflanzen, weniger als zehn, wachsen in einem trockenen Bachbett und sind zur Blütezeit im Mai von einer Ruderalflora völlig überwuchert. An der zweiten Fundstelle, auch ein trockenes Bachbett etwa ein Kilometer von der erstgenannten Stelle entfernt, wurde *Orchis palustris* in den letzten Jahren nicht mehr gefunden. Ergiebige Regenfälle im Jahre 2004 haben dazu geführt, dass der Kouris Staudamm geflutet wurde, wodurch die (ehemaligen) Sumpfgebiete nach 20 Jahren wieder reichlich mit Wasser versorgt wurden. Es ist zu hoffen, dass sich der Bestand von *Orchis palustris* hierdurch wieder etwas erholen kann.

Genau wie auf Kreta und Mallorca wurden die Küstensümpfe mit ihren *Orchis palustris*-Populationen auch auf Zypern fast vollständig trockengelegt. Werden hier nicht umgehend effektive Schutzmaßnahmen getroffen, dann wird *Orchis palustris* auf Zypern in einigen Jahren verschwunden sein.

Gefährdung

Die besonders seltene *Orchis palustris* ist durch Trockenlegung und fehlende Schutzmaßnahmen so stark zurückgegangen, dass sie akut vom Aussterben bedroht ist.

Hybriden

Nicht nachgewiesen

Bemerkungen zu der Verbreitungskarte

Der Standort bei Phini wurde auf der Verbreitungskarte nicht berücksichtigt, weil es sich hier schon wegen der Höhenlage höchstwahrscheinlich um einen Fundort von *Orchis laxiflora* handelt, die aktuell in dieser Gegend vorkommt.

340   Akrotiri (Salt lake), 11.5.2002

Orchis palustris
Bog Orchid

JACQUIN

Collectanea 1: 75 & 76, no. CX (1786)

Synonyms

Orchis laxiflora var. *palustris* (JACQUIN) W.D.J. KOCH, Syn. Fl. Germ. Helv. ed. 2, 2: 792 (1844); *Orchis laxiflora* subsp. *palustris* (JACQUIN) BONNIER & LAYENS, Tabl. Syn. Pl. Vasc. France 1: 311 (1894); *Anacamptis palustris* (JACQUIN) R.M. BATEMAN, PRIDGEON & M.W. CHASE, Lindleyana 12 (3): 120 (1997); *Orchis mediterranea* GUSSONE, Pl. Rar.: 365 & 366 (1826); *Orchis palustris* var. *mediterranea* (GUSSONE) SCHLECHTER, Monogr. Iconogr. Orchid. Eur. 1 (5/6): 192 (1927); *Orchis palustris* subsp. *mediterranea* (GUSSONE) MALAGARRIGA, Acta Phytotax. Barcinon. 1: 64 (1968); *Orchis laxiflora* var. *mediterranea* (GUSSONE) RIVERA NUÑEZ & LÓPES VÉLEZ, Orq. Prov. Albacete: 140 (1987).

Description

Elegant, slender plant, 50 to 60 cm tall. Stem erect, fairly thin, grass-green with purple tinges in upper part. Foliage leaves grass-like, narrowly lanceolate, grooved, acuminate, obliquely erect, unspotted. Inflorescence cylindrical to elongated, fairly lax and many-flowered, rarely few-flowered. Bracts linear, usually as long as ovary. Flowers medium-sized to large, spreading obliquely, red-violet, reddish to pink, rarely white. Sepals ovate-lanceolate, both laterals directed obliquely sideways or reflexed, dorsal sepal bent over petals, obtuse. Petals lanceolate, connivent. Labellum violet or reddish to pink, slightly three-lobed in lower part, lateral lobes spread out flat or slightly reflexed and somewhat shorter than the emarginate middle lobe; base of labellum whitish, with purple streaks or dashes. Spur cylindrical, horizontal or curving upwards, about as long as ovary.

Habitat

Marshes and lakesides (usually between open reeds); on very moist, base-rich to calcareous, humous soils.

Flowering time

Mid-April until late May.

Altitude distribution

Only at sea level.

Overall distribution

Central part of Europe, with sporadic occurrences in Spain and Gotland (Sweden). Also in Turkey, Cyprus and the Caucasian countries.

Distribution on Cyprus

The species is extremely rare on Cyprus and known at only one location on the Akrotiri peninsula.

Remarks

Together with *Ophrys tenthredinifera*, *Orchis palustris* is one of the rarest and most threatened orchis species of Cyprus.

UNGER & KOTSCHY (1865) and HOLMBOE (1914) specify *Orchis palustris* for the area around Lefkosia.

RENZ (1929) also reports this location, but comes to the conclusion that these plants are actually *Orchis laxiflora*. WOOD (1985) also indicates only a few locations, namely near Phini (KOTSCHY, 1862) and Dhikomo (UNGER & KOTSCHY, 1865), others are in the area around Lemesos and on the Akrotiri peninsula. The last current location of this already very rare species is sited in the vast reed stands of the Akrotiri peninsula. *Orchis palustris* had several locations in this area but due to drying out, because of the building in 1985 of the Kouris dam, the huge water reservoir north of Lemesos, *Orchis palustris* has disappeared from most habitats and current habitats have only small remaining populations. Especially in recent years the species has disappeared from several places due to drainage and only a residual stand remains at one location. The last plants, less than ten, grow in a dry stream bed and are completely overgrown by weeds during their flowering time. At the second location, *Orchis palustris* has not been found at all in recent years. Because of extreme rainfalls in 2004 the Kouris dam was overflowing. This means that for the first time in 20 years there was a lot of water in the (former) marshlands and hopefully this will benefit the remaining population of *Orchis palustris* and reestablish the decent population.

The coastal swamps of Cyprus with their *Orchis palustris* populations have been almost completely drained of water just as those on Crete and Mallorca have. If immediate precautionary measures are not taken, *Orchis palustris* will have disappeared from Cyprus in a few years.

Threats

Numbers of the exceptionally rare *Orchis palustris* have declined considerably due to drainage and the absence of precautionary measures, to such an extent that it is acutely threatened.

Hybrids

Unconfirmed

Remarks concerning the distribution map

The site near Phini has not been included on the distribution map as it is highly likely given the altitude, that this involves a finding of *Orchis laxiflora*; also *Orchis laxiflora* currently occurs in this vicinity.

Akrotiri (Salt lake), 10.5.1993

Akrotiri (Salt lake), 4.5.2002

Akrotiri (Salt lake), 4.5.2002

Akrotiri (Salt lake), 4.5.2002

Akrotiri (Salt lake), 4.5.2002

Akrotiri (Salt lake), 15.4.2002

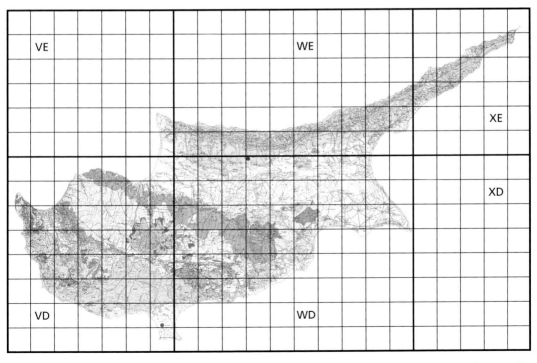

Orchis palustris

43 Orchis punctulata
Punktiertes Knabenkraut

STEVEN ex LINDLEY

Gen. Sp. Orchid. Pl. (4): 273 (1835)

Beschreibung

Kräftige, stattliche Pflanze, 20 bis 70 cm hoch. Stängel aufrecht. Laubblätter am Grunde rosettig angeordnet, die oberen in scheidige Stängelblätter übergehend, breit-lanzettlich bis lanzettlich, grün, glänzend, ungefleckt. Blütenstand zylindrisch bis verlängert, reich- und dichtblütig. Tragblätter klein, etwa halb so lang wie der Fruchtknoten. Blüten mittelgroß, intensiv gelb bis grünlichgelb gefärbt. Sepalen eiförmig bis eiförmig-lanzettlich. Petalen lanzettlich, kürzer als die Sepalen. Perigonblätter helmförmig zusammenneigend, auf der Aussenseite grünlichgelb, auf der Innenseite heller, mit bräunlichen Nerven. Lippe tief dreiteilig; die beiden Seitenlappen abstehend bis nach unten gerichtet; Mittellappen zweispaltig, ziemlich breit, in der Einbuchtung mit einem kleinen Zähnchen, zitronengelb bis grünlichgelb, bisweilen rotbraun gerandet, und mit bräunlichen Haarbüscheln besetzt; Ränder des Mittellappens und der Seitenlappen manchmal braunrot überlaufen. Sporn zylindrisch, abwärts gebogen, halb so lang wie der Fruchtknoten.

Standort

Lockere Kiefernwälder, Phrygana, Macchien, Wiesenflächen und Ödland; auf trockenen oder feuchten, kalkhaltigen Böden.

Blütezeit

Von Anfang Februar bis Mitte März.

Höhenverbreitung

Von Meereshöhe bis 500 m.

Gesamtverbreitung

Orchis punctulata ist im östlichen Mittelmeer (Thrakien, Türkei, Rhodos, Zypern, Westsyrien, Libanon, Israel), sowie im Kaukasus und der Krim verbreitet.

Verbreitung auf Zypern

Eine der seltenen Arten von Zypern, hauptsächlich im mittleren Süden der Insel und im Akamas-Gebiet verbreitet. Im Norden sehr selten und stark rückgängig.

Bemerkungen

Orchis punctulata gehört zweifellos zu den schönsten und stattlichsten Orchideenarten Europas. Im Habitus gleicht sie der mitteleuropäischen *Orchis purpurea*, weicht aber deutlich durch die intensiv gelb bis grünlichgelb gefärbten und bräunlich punktierten Blüten von ihr ab, die zudem nur etwa halb so groß wie die von *Orchis purpurea* sind. Vor allem in Israel und auf Zypern kommen Pflanzen vor, deren Blütenstand aussergewöhnlich langgestreckt und sehr reichblütig ist (manchmal zwei Drittel der Länge der gesamten Pflanze). Auch DAVIES, DAVIES & HUXLEY (1983) berichten von besonders robusten und hochwüchsigen Pflanzen mit verlängertem Blütenstand auch von Zypern.

Auf Zypern gibt es schöne Bestände auf der Akamas-Halbinsel im Westen, bei Hirsarköy im Norden, bei Kato Drys und bei Tochni im Südosten. Am letztgenannten Standort, der wahrscheinlich der individuenreichste Standort von Zypern ist, wächst *Orchis punctulata* zusammen mit *Orchis italica* in der dichten Macchie, die sich dort aus Pflanzenarten wie *Pistacia terebinthus*, *Calicotome villosa*, *Ceratonia siliqua*, *Thymus capitatus*, *Sarcopoterium spinosum*, *Stachys cretica*, *Eryngium creticum* und wenigen *Pinus brutia* zusammensetzt.

Im Norden Zyperns ist *Orchis punctulata* viel seltener als im Süden. Die Art war lange Zeit nur von einem Standort, einem Nordhang im Pentadactylos-Gebirge bei Kayalar bekannt, bis 1993 zahlreiche Pflanzen in abgebrannten Waldhängen auf der Südseite des Mt. Kornos bei Hirsarköy gefunden wurden. *Orchis punctulata* steht an einigen diesen Fundorte bereits Mitte Februar in Hochblüte. Obwohl die Art in diesem Gebiet durch Beweidung rückgängig ist, wurden 2002 an mehreren Stellen noch etwa fünfzig blühende Exemplare gezählt.

Nach KRETZSCHMAR (1995) kommen auf Zypern an einem Standort manchmal gleichzeitig fast voll erblühte Exemplare neben noch knospigen Pflanzen vor, was auf eine insgesamt recht lange Blütezeit hindeutet. Die in der Blütenfarbe sehr variablen Pflanzen (völlig zitronengelb bis rotbraun gerandet) zeigen dabei keine Unterschiede hinsichtlich des Beginns der Blütezeit.

Gefährdung

Durch Ausdehnung der Wohngebiete und intensivere landwirtschaftliche Nutzung ihrer Biotope ist *Orchis punctulata* in ständigem Rückgang begriffen. Die Anzahl blühender Pflanzen ist in den letzten zwanzig Jahren rapide gesunken, und viele ihrer Standorte sind bereits erloschen. Die Art ist damit als hochgradig gefährdet einzustufen.

Hybriden

Mit *Orchis italica* (*Orchis ×tochniana* KREUTZ & P. SCRATON).

Choirokoitia, 10.3.2002

Neo Chorio (Akamas), 10.3.2002

Orchis punctulata
Punctate Orchid

STEVEN ex LINDLEY

Gen. Sp. Orchid. Pl. (4): 273 (1835)

Description

Vigorous, stately plant, 20 to 70 cm tall. Stem erect. Foliage leaves forming a rosette at base, upper leaves merging into sheathing stem leaves, broadly lanceolate to lanceolate, green, shiny, unspotted. Inflorescence cylindrical to elongated, dense- and many-flowered. Bracts small, about half as long as ovary. Flowers medium-sized, intense yellow to greenish yellow. Sepals ovate to ovate-lanceolate. Petals lanceolate, shorter than sepals. Perianth segments connivent to forming a hood, exterior greenish yellow, interior of a light colour, with brownish veins. Labellum deeply three-lobed; both lateral lobes spreading to directed downwards; middle lobe two-pointed, fairly wide, with a small tooth in the indentation; lemon-yellow to greenish yellow, at times with red-brown edges, with small brownish clumps of hair, and sometimes tinges of brown-red on edges of middle lobe and both lateral lobes. Spur cylindrical, curving downwards, half as long as ovary.

Habitat

Open coniferous woods, phrygana, maquis, meadows and wasteland; on arid to moist, calcareous soils.

Flowering time

From early February to mid-March.

Altitude distribution

From sea level to 500 m.

Overall distribution

Orchis punctulata is distributed throughout the eastern Mediterranean region (Thrace, Turkey, Rhodes, Cyprus, western Syria, Lebanon, Israel), as well in the Caucasus and the Crimea.

Distribution on Cyprus

One of the rare species of Cyprus, primarily distributed in the central south of the island and in the Akamas region. In the north very rare and heavily declining.

Remarks

Orchis punctulata is undoubtedly one of the most beautiful and stately orchid species in Europe. With the habitat taken into consideration, it corresponds with the Central European *Orchis purpurea*, but clearly differs from it in its intense yellow to greenish yellow coloured and brownish dotted flowers, which are about half the size of those of *Orchis purpurea*. Plants with extraordinarily elongated and very dense inflorescences (at times two-thirds of the whole plant) also occur, especially in Israel and on Cyprus. DAVIES, DAVIES & HUXLEY (1983) also report on exceptionally robust and tall plants with an elongated inflorescence also from Cyprus.

There are beautiful stands on Cyprus, on the Akamas penisula in the west, near Hirsarköy in the north, near Kato Drys and near Tochni in the southeast. At the last-mentioned location, which is probably the most individual-rich location of Cyprus, *Orchis punctulata* grows together with *Orchis italica* in the dense maquis, which consists there of plant species such as *Pistacia terebinthus, Calicotome villosa, Ceratonia siliqua, Thymus capitatus, Sarcopoterium spinosum, Stachys cretica, Eryngium creticum* and some *Pinus brutia*.

Orchis punctulata is much rarer in the north than in the south. The species was known for a long time from only one location, on a northern slope in the Pentadactylos mountains near Kayalar, until numerous plants were found in 1993 on burnt slopes on the southern side of Mt. Kornos near Hirsarköy. *Orchis punctulata* is already at its prime here in mid-February. Although the numbers of this species in this area are plummeting due to grazing, about fifty flowering specimens were still found in 2002. According to KRETZSCHMAR (1995), fully flowering specimens often occur next to plants in bud on Cyprus at the same location, which suggests an exceptionally long flowering time. These plants, which vary widely in flower colour (from completely lemon-yellow to red-brown edges) apparently show no differences at the beginning of their flowering time.

Threats

Orchis punctulata is caught in a continual decline due to the expansion of residential areas and intensifying agricultural use of its biotopes. The number of flowering plants has fallen rapidly in the last twenty years, and many of its locations have already disappeared. The species can therefore be categorised as profoundly threatened.

Hybrids

With *Orchis italica* (*Orchis xtochniana* KREUTZ & P. SCRATON).

Kato Drys, 6.3.2002

Kato Drys, 6.3.2002

Kato Drys, 6.3.2002

Neo Chorio (Akamas), 10.3.2002

Kato Drys, 6.3.2002

Choirokoitia, 10.3.2002

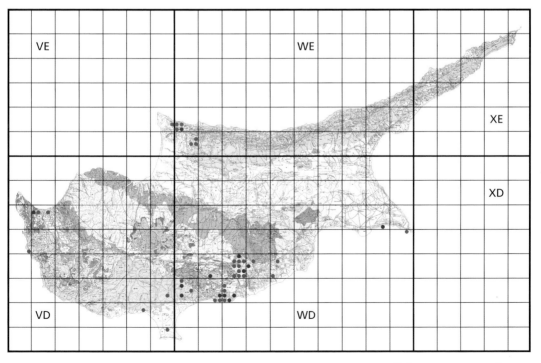

Orchis punctulata

Synonyme

Orchis militaris subsp. *simia* (J.B.A.P. LAMARCK) BONNIER & LAYENS, Tabl. Syn. Pl. Vasc. France 1: 310 (1894); *Orchis macra* LINDLEY in BABINGT, Man. Brit. Bot.: 290 (1843).

Beschreibung

Meist kräftige Pflanze, 20 bis 45 cm hoch. Stängel kräftig, hellgrün. Laubblätter eiförmig-lanzettlich bis lanzettlich, glänzend, ungefleckt, hellgrün bis grün, am Grunde rosettig angeordnet, die oberen in scheidige Stängelblätter übergehend. Blütenstand eiförmig bis zylindrisch, dicht- und reichblütig, von oben nach unten aufblühend. Tragblätter klein und zugespitzt, etwa halb so lang wie der Fruchtknoten. Blüten mittelgroß. Perigonblätter einen lockeren bis geschlossenen Helm bildend, die Spitzen nach aussen umgebogen, an der Aussenseite weisslich bis (hell)rosa, an der Innenseite mit lila Nerven. Sepalen eiförmig-lanzettlich. Petalen schmal-lanzettlich, kürzer als die Sepalen. Lippe dunkelrot bis purpurn, an der Basis tief dreilappig mit zweispaltigem, breiterem Mittellappen. Mittellappen weisslich bis hellrosa, mit dunkelroten Papillen besetzt. Seitenlappen und Zipfel der Mittellappen aufwärts gebogen und leicht gedreht. Sporn zylindrisch, abwärts gerichtet, halb so lang wie der Fruchtknoten.

Biotop

Macchien, Phrygana, Böschungen, Gebüschränder und offene Stellen in Kiefernwäldern; auf kalkhaltigen, meist leicht feuchten, humosen Böden.

Blütezeit

Von Mitte März bis Mitte April.

Höhenverbreitung

Von 600 bis 800 m.

Gesamtverbreitung

Das Verbreitungsgebiet erstreckt sich von Südengland über Frankreich, Italien, den Balkan, Kleinasien, Kaukasus, Nordirak, Iran bis Turkmenistan. Unter anderem auch auf Kreta, Rhodos, Karpathos, Zypern und in Nordafrika. Die Vorkommen von *Orchis simia* im Mittelmeerraum sind zerstreut, aber sie ist an ihren Standorten meist reichlich vertreten.

Verbreitung auf Zypern

Sehr selten und nur von wenigen aktuellen Standorten bekannt. Die Art wächst hauptsächlich in einer schmalen Zone von dem kalkreichen Gebiet nördlich von Lemesos bis in die Umgebung des Larnaka Salzsees. Im Norden kommt *Orchis simia* meist zusammen mit *Orchis italica* vor (VINEY, 1994), wie unter anderem in den lichten Pinienwäldern und Macchien des Pentadactylos-Gebirges und der Karpasia-Halbinsel, vor allem zwischen Mersinlik und Kantara.

Bemerkungen

Im Gegensatz zu Mitteleuropa, wo *Orchis simia* auf Kalkmagerrasen wächst, kommt diese Art im südlichen Mittelmeerraum in lichten Pinienwäldern oder im Gebüsch vor. Ein gleiches Erscheinungsbild zeigt *Orchis purpurea*, die auch sehr weit südlich im Mittelmeergebiet vorkommt, die dort zum Teil durch *Orchis lokiana* H. BAUMANN und *Orchis caucasica* REGEL vertreten ist. Mittlerweile wurde auch in Libyen eine neue Art von *Orchis simia* abgetrennt und von B. & H. BAUMANN (2001) als *Orchis taubertiana* neu beschrieben. Nur *Orchis caucasica* unterscheidet sich wesentlich von der Nominatform, die beiden anderen Arten, *Orchis lokiana* und *Orchis taubertiana* zeigen keine wesentlichen Unterschiede zu *Orchis purpurea* beziehungsweise zu *Orchis simia*.

Orchis simia ist im Süden Zyperns sehr selten und wurde dort nur an wenigen Standorten nachgewiesen. Der individuenreichste Standort befindet sich in der Umgebung von Gerasa im mittleren Süden. Am Rande einer dichten Gebüschreihe und in der angrenzenden Phrygana wachsen an diesem Fundort jährlich etwa fünfzig bis hundert Pflanzen. Es ist ein besonders individuenreicher Standort, wo neben *Orchis simia* unter anderem auch noch *Ophrys levantina* und *Orchis sezikiana* vorkommen. Das Vorkommen von *Orchis simia* ist an diesem Standort schon lange bekannt. Die Pflanzen sind hier durch Verbuschung und intensive Beweidung stark gefährdet.

Im Norden ist die ehemals ziemlich verbreitete Art seltener als im Süden geworden. RENZ berichtete 1929 in seinem Beitrag über 'Neue Orchideen von Rhodos, Cypern und Syrien', dass das häufige Auftreten von *Orchis simia* im Nordgebirge Zyperns auffallend ist, und dass sie in diesem Gebiet bevorzugt auf Bergkämmen und meist in Begleitung von *Orchis italica* wächst.

Gefährdung

Orchis simia ist auf Zypern selten und durch übermäßige Beweidung zurückgehend. Die Art ist damit als gefährdet einzustufen.

Hybriden

Nicht bekannt.

352 Gerasa, 5.3.2002

Orchis simia

Monkey Orchid

LAMARCK

Fl. Franc. (ed. 1), 3: 507 (1779)

Synonyms

Orchis militaris subsp. *simia* (J.B.A.P. LAMARCK) BONNIER & LAYENS, Tabl. Syn. Pl. Vasc. France 1: 310 (1894); *Orchis macra* LINDLEY in BABINGT, Man. Brit. Bot.: 290 (1843).

Description

Usually vigorous plant, 20 to 45 cm tall. Stem sturdy, light green. Foliage leaves ovate-lanceolate to lanceolate, shiny, unspotted, light green to green, forming a rosette at base, upper leaves merging into sheathing stem leaves. Inflorescence ovate to cylindrical, dense and many-flowered, flowering from the top towards the bottom. Bracts small and acuminate, about half as long as ovary. Flowers medium-sized. Perianth segments forming a loose to closed hood, the ends curving outwards, exterior whitish to (light) pink, interior with lilac veins. Sepals ovate-lanceolate. Petals narrowly lanceolate, shorter then sepals. Labellum dark red to purple, deeply three-lobed at the base with two-pointed, wide middle lobe. Middle lobe whitish to light pink, with red papillae. Lateral lobes and tip of middle lobe bent upwards and slightly rotated. Spur cylindrical, directed downwards, half as long as ovary.

Habitat

Maquis, phrygana, slopes, shrubland edges and open places in coniferous woods; on calcareous, mostly slightly moist, humous soils.

Flowering time

From mid-March to mid-April.

Altitude distribution

From 600 to 800 m.

Overall distribution

The distribution area stretches from southern England through France, Italy, the Balkans, Asia Minor, Caucasus, northern Iraq, Iran to Turkmenistan. Also on Crete, Rhodes, Karpathos, Cyprus and in North Africa. The occurrences of *Orchis simia* in the Mediterranean region are sporadic, but its locations are mostly densely populated.

Distribution on Cyprus

Very rare and known at only a few recent sites. The species primarily grows in a narrow zone from the calcareous area north of Lemesos to the area around the Larnaka salt lake. In the north *Orchis simia* mostly occurs together with *Orchis italica* (VINEY, 1994), for example in the light pine woods and maquis of the Pentadactylos mountains and Karpasia peninsula, especially between Mersinlik and Kantara.

Remarks

In contrast to Central Europe, where *Orchis simia* grows on chalky neglected meadows, this species occurs in light pine woods or in shrublands in the southern Mediterranean region. The same is true of *Orchis purpurea*, which also occurs far to the south in the Mediterranean region, but where it is partly represented by *Orchis lokiana* H. BAUMANN and *Orchis caucasica* REGEL. In the meantime a new species from Libya was separated from *Orchis simia* and newly described by B. & H. BAUMANN (2001) as *Orchis taubertiana*. Only *Orchis caucasica* differs considerably from the normal type, but the two other species, *Orchis lokiana* and *Orchis taubertiana*, show no significant differences from *Orchis purpurea* or *Orchis simia*.

Orchis simia is very rare in southern Cyprus and has been confirmed at only a few sites there. The most individual-rich site is near Gerasa in the central south. At this site, about fifty to a hundred plants grow each year at the edge of a dense row of shrubs and in the neighbouring phrygana. It is an exceptionally individual-rich site, where besides *Orchis simia* other orchids such as *Ophrys levantina* and *Orchis sezikiana* also occur. It has been known for a long time now that *Orchis simia* occurs at this site. The plants are heavily threatened by expansion of shrubs and intensive grazing.

In the north, the former relatively widely distributed *Orchis simia* has now become much more rare than in the south. RENZ reported in 1929 in his contribution on 'New orchids of Rhodes, Cyprus and Syria', that the abundant occurrence of *Orchis simia* in the northern mountains of Cyprus is remarkable, and that it favours mountain ridges and is usually accompanied by *Orchis italica*.

Threats

Orchis simia is rare on Cyprus and its numbers are also declining due to excessive grazing. The species can therefore be categorised as threatened.

Hybrids

Unknown.

Gerasa, 20.3.2002

Gerasa, 20.3.2002

Pano Kivides, 20.3.2002

Pano Kivides, 20.3.2002

Gerasa, 20.3.2002

Pano Kivides, 20.3.2002

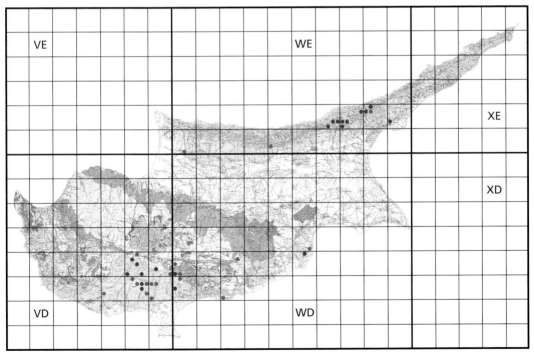

Orchis simia

45 Orchis syriaca
Syrisches Knabenkraut

Boissier ex H. Baumann & Künkele

Mitteilungsbl. Arbeitskr. Heim. Orch.
Baden-Württ. 13 (3): 351 (1981)

Synonyme

Orchis morio subsp. *syriaca* E.G. Camus, P. Bergon & A. Camus, Monogr. orchid.: 106 (1908); *Orchis morio* subsp. *libani* Renz, Repert. Spec. Nov. Regni Veg. 27: 209 (1930); *Orchis morio* subsp. *picta* var. *syriaca* (E.G. Camus) Soó, Repert. Spec. Nov. Regni Veg., Sonderbeih. A, 2: 139 (1932), nom. illeg.; *Anacamptis syriaca* (Boissier ex H. Baumann & Künkele) R.M. Bateman, Pridgeon & M.W. Chase, Lindleyana 12 (3): 120 (1997).

Beschreibung

Schlanke, niedrige Pflanze, 15 bis 25 cm hoch. Stängel aufrecht, hell bis dunkelgrün, im oberen Teil oft purpurn angelaufen. Laubblätter am Grunde rosettig angeordnet, die oberen in scheidige Stängelblätter übergehend, schmal-lanzettlich bis linealisch-lanzettlich, grün, ungefleckt. Blütenstand kurz, ziemlich locker- und armblütig. Tragblätter breit-lanzettlich, etwa dreiviertel so lang wie der Fruchtknoten. Blüten klein bis mittelgroß, locker am Stängel angeordnet. Perigonblätter einen lockeren Helm bildend, rosa bis violett gefärbt; Nerven der Perigonblätter grün. Sepalen eiförmig bis eiförmig-lanzettlich. Petalen lanzettlich. Lippe schwach dreilappig, die beiden Seitenlappen etwas kürzer und größer als der Mittellappen und zurückgeschlagen, meist weiss, (hell)gelb bis rosa gefärbt. Lippenbasis oft weisslich, ohne jede Malzeichnung. Sporn zylindrisch, waagerecht, schwach aufwärts gebogen, etwa so lang wie der Fruchtknoten.

Standort

Lichte Kiefernwälder, Affodillfluren, Macchien und Phrygana; auf kalkhaltigen bis basenreichen Böden.

Blütezeit

Mitte Februar bis Mitte März.

Höhenverbreitung

Von Meereshöhe bis 1.000 m.

Gesamtverbreitung

Orientalische Art. Ihr kleines Areal reicht von der Südwest- und Südtürkei über Zypern und Westsyrien bis nach Libanon. Auch auf Rhodos.

Verbreitung auf Zypern

Weit verbreitet und nicht selten. *Orchis syriaca* ist eine der häufigsten Orchideenarten Zyperns.

Bemerkungen

Orchis syriaca löst *Orchis morio* L. subsp. *morio* und *Orchis morio* L. subsp. *picta* (Loiseleur) K. Richter nach Südosten hin ab und kommt dort hauptsächlich in den küstennahen Bereiche des Mittelmeerraumes vor. Auf Zypern hat sie ihr Hauptverbreitungsgebiet, und sie wächst dort auch im Landesinneren und in den mittleren montanen Lagen.

Im Troodos-Gebirge wächst sie mit Vorliebe unter *Pinus brutia* zusammen mit *Thymus integer*, und sie ist in diesem Gebiet meist mit *Dactylorhiza romana* und *Orchis troodi* vergesellschaftet.

Renz (1929) bemerkte, dass *Orchis syriaca* (damals noch *Orchis picta* Loiseleur subsp. *libani* Renz) wenig variabel ist. Soó (1932) schreibt, dass *Orchis syriaca Orchis morio* subsp. *picta* nach Südosten (z.B. auf Zypern und in Syrien) hin ersetzt. Sundermann (1975) und Landwehr (1977) bewerten die Sippe als Unterart von *Orchis morio* (*Orchis morio* L. subsp. *libani* (Renz) Sundermann) und geben an, dass diese Unterart *Orchis morio* subsp. *picta* nach Osten hin ersetzt. Nach dem Studium der zahlreichen Herbarbelege und anhand lebender Pflanzen kommt Wood (1985) zu der Schlussfolgerung, dass *Orchis syriaca* auf Zypern nicht vorkommt, sondern nur *Orchis morio* subsp. *picta*. Er gibt *Orchis morio* subsp. *picta* für viele Bereiche von Zypern an und schreibt weiter, dass sie weit verbreitet ist und hauptsächlich in den montanen Lagen aber auch lokal in der Ebene vorkommt. Nach Viney (1994) kommen in der Macchie, Phrygana und in den lichten Pinienwäldern in der schmalen Zone von Tepebaşı bis Karpas im Norden Zyperns beide Arten vor, nämlich *Orchis syriaca* mit weisslicher bis schwach rosa Lippe und *Orchis morio* subsp. *picta* mit purpurn gepunkteter Lippe.

Nach den heutigen Erkenntnisse kommt auf Zypern nur *Orchis syriaca* vor. Pflanzen mit purpurn gepunkteter Lippe (Viney, 1994) gehören vermutlich zu hyperchromen Pflanzen dieser Art, die auf Zypern auch bei *Orchis italica* vorkommen.

Im Gegensatz zu Renz (1929) aber übereinstimmend mit Hansen, Kreutz & U. & D. Rückbrodt (1990) ist *Orchis syriaca* sehr variabel in der Lippenform, -größe und -färbung. Das ist sicherlich der Grund dafür, dass von einigen Autoren (Wood, 1985; Viney, 1994) das Vorkommen von *Orchis morio* subsp. *picta* für Zypern angegeben wurde.

Gefährdung

Orchis syriaca ist auf Zypern weit verbreitet und häufig. Die Art ist nicht gefährdet.

Hybriden

Mit *Orchis caspia* (*Orchis xchoirokitiana* Kreutz & P. Scraton), *Orchis laxiflora*, *Orchis troodi* und *Serapias levantina* (als X*Orchiserapias dhiorii* M. & M. Ackermann zwischen *Orchis syriaca* und *Serapias orientalis* beschrieben).

358   **Neo Chorio-Agios Minas (Akamas), 3.3.2002**

Alevkaya (Pentadactylos Range), 18.3.2002

Alevkaya (Pentadactylos Range), 18.3.2002

Neo Chorio-Agios Minas (Akamas), 3.3.2002

Drouseia (Akamas), 3.3.2002

Neo Chorio-Agios Minas (Akamas), 3.3.2002   Gerasa-Kalo Chorio, 5.3.2002

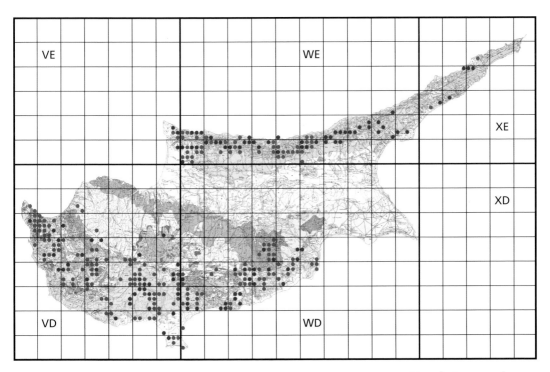

Orchis syriaca

Orchis syriaca
Syrian Orchid

Boissier ex H. Baumann & Künkele

Mitteilungsbl. Arbeitskr. Heim. Orch.
Baden-Württ. 13 (3): 351 (1981)

Synonyms

Orchis morio subsp. *syriaca* E.G. Camus, P. Bergon & A. Camus, Monogr. orchid.: 106 (1908); *Orchis morio* subsp. *libani* Renz, Repert. Spec. Nov. Regni Veg. 27: 209 (1930); *Orchis morio* subsp. *picta* var. *syriaca* (E.G. Camus) Soó, Repert. Spec. Nov. Regni Veg., Sonderbeih. A, 2: 139 (1932), nom. illeg.; *Anacamptis syriaca* (Boissier ex H. Baumann & Künkele) R.M. Bateman, Pridgeon & M.W. Chase, Lindleyana 12 (3): 120 (1997).

Description

Slender, short plant, 15 to 25 cm tall. Stem erect, light to dark green, often with purple tinges in upper part. Foliage leaves forming a rosette at base, upper leaves merging into sheathing stem leaves, narrowly lanceolate to linear-lanceolate, green, unspotted. Inflorescence short, fairly lax and few-flowered. Bracts broadly lanceolate, about three-quarters of the length of the ovary. Flowers small to medium-sized, laxly arranged on stem. Perianth segments form a loose hood, pink to violet; with green veins. Sepals ovate to ovate-lanceolate. Petals lanceolate. Labellum weakly three-lobed, lateral lobes slightly shorter and larger than middle lobe and reflexed, usually white, (pale) yellow to pink. Base of labellum often whitish, without any marking. Spur cylindrical, horizontal, slightly bent upwards, about as long as ovary.

Habitat

Light coniferous woods, asphodel fields, maquis and phrygana; on calcareous to base-rich soils.

Flowering time

Mid-February to mid-March.

Altitude distribution

From sea level to 1,000 m.

Overall distribution

Oriental species. Its small habitat stretches from southwestern and southern Turkey through Cyprus and western Syria to Lebanon. Also on Rhodes.

Distribution on Cyprus

Widely distributed and not rare. *Orchis syriaca* is one of the most abundant orchid species on Cyprus.

Remarks

Orchis syriaca replaces *Orchis morio* L. subsp. *morio* and *Orchis morio* L. subsp. *picta* (Loiseleur) K. Richter towards the southeast and primarily occurs in the coastal areas of the Mediterranean region. Its main distribution area is found on Cyprus and it also grows there in the interior and at medium-high mountainous altitudes.

It favours growing beneath *Pinus brutia* together with *Thymus integer* in the Troodos mountains, and it is usually accompanied by *Dactylorhiza romana* and *Orchis troodi* in this area.

Renz (1929) remarked that *Orchis syriaca* (then known as *Orchis picta* Loiseleur subsp. *libani* Renz) is scarcely variable. Soó (1932) writes that *Orchis syriaca* replaces *Orchis morio* subsp. *picta* towards the southeast (e.g. Cyprus and in Syria). Sundermann (1975) and Landwehr (1977) assessed the taxon as a subspecies of *Orchis morio* (*Orchis morio* L. subsp. *libani* (Renz) Sundermann) and indicated that this subspecies replaces *Orchis morio* subsp. *picta* towards the east. After studying considerable botanical evidence and living plants, Wood (1985) comes to the conclusion that *Orchis syriaca* does not occur on Cyprus, but rather only *Orchis morio* subsp. *picta*. He specifies *Orchis morio* subsp. *picta* for many areas on Cyprus and also writes that it is widely distributed and primarily occurs in mountainous altitudes but also locally on the plains. According to Viney (1994), both species, namely *Orchis syriaca* with whitish to pale pink labellum and *Orchis morio* subsp. *picta* with purple-dotted labellum, occur in the maquis, phrygana and in the light pine woods of the narrow zone from Tepebaşi to Karpas in northern Cyprus.

According to the current state of knowledge, only *Orchis syriaca* occurs on Cyprus. Plants with a purple-dotted labellum (Viney, 1994) are presumably attributable to hyperchromy, which also occurs amongst *Orchis italica*.

In contradiction to Renz (1929), but in accordance with Hansen, Kreutz & U. & D. Rückbrodt (1990), *Orchis syriaca* is very variable in its labellum shape, size, and colouration. This is certainly the reason why some authors (Wood, 1985; Viney, 1994) specified the occurrence of *Orchis morio* subsp. *picta* for Cyprus.

Threats

Orchis syriaca is widely distributed and abundant on Cyprus. The species is not threatened.

Hybrids

With *Orchis caspia* (*Orchis xchoirokitiana* Kreutz & P. Scraton), *Orchis laxiflora*, *Orchis troodi* and *Serapias levantina* (described as X*Orchiserapias dhiorii* M. & M. Ackermann between *Orchis syriaca* and *Serapias orientalis*).

46

Orchis tridentata
Dreizähniges Knabenkraut

Synonyme

Neotinea tridentata (SCOPOLI) R.M. BATEMAN, PRIDGEON & M.W. CHASE, Lindleyana 12 (3): 122 (1997); *Orchis variegata* ALLIONI, Fl. Pedem. 2: 147 (1785); *Orchis tridentata* var. *variegata* (ALLIONI) REICHENBACH fil., Icon. Fl. Germ. Helv. 13/14: 23 (1851); *Orchis tridentata* SCOPOLI var. *commutata* (TODARO) REICHENBACH fil., Icon. Fl. Germ. Helv. 13/14: 24 (1851); *Orchis commutata* TODARO, Orchid. Sicul.: 24 (1842), nom. illeg.; *Orchis tridentata* SCOPOLI subsp. *commutata* (TODARO) NYMAN, Consp. Fl. Eur. 4: 691 (1882); *Neotinea tridentata* subsp. *commutata* (TODARO) R.M. BATEMAN, PRIDGEON & M.W. CHASE, Lindleyana 12 (3): 122 (1997).

Beschreibung

Zierliche Pflanze, 20 bis 40 cm hoch. Stängel aufrecht, relativ kräftig, hellgrün. Laubblätter lanzettlich bis schmal-lanzettlich, bläulichgrün, ungefleckt, die unteren eine Grundrosette bildend, die oberen in scheidige Stängelblätter übergehend. Blütenstand kugelig, selten zylindrisch, dicht- und vielblütig. Tragblätter linealisch, zugespitzt, etwa so lang wie der Fruchtknoten. Blüten klein, rosa bis hellviolett. Perigonblätter einen lockeren Helm bildend, die lang zugespitzten Enden zurückgebogen, (hell)rosa bis weiss oder hellviolett. Sepalen eiförmig-lanzettlich, meist mit violetten Nerven. Petalen schmal-lanzettlich, kürzer als die Sepalen. Lippe flach ausgebreitet, an den Rändern leicht aufwärts gebogen, tief dreilappig mit zweispaltigem, vorgestrecktem Mittellappen, der zusätzlich mit einem kleinen Zähnchen versehen ist, weisslich bis hellrosa und rot gepunktet. Sporn zylindrisch, abwärts gebogen, etwa halb so lang wie der Fruchtknoten.

Standort

Macchien, Phrygana, Wiesenflächen, Ödland, Kiefernwälder, Gebüschränder, Olivenhaine; auf basenreichen oder kalkhaltigen Böden.

Blütezeit

Mitte März bis Mitte April.

Höhenverbreitung

Von Meereshöhe bis 500 m.

Gesamtverbreitung

Vor allem im mittleren und östlichen Mittelmeerraum. In Mitteleuropa inselartig in Hessen und Thüringen; ausserdem in der Türkei, im Kaukasus, Nordsyrien, Nordirak und Nordiran, und auf Zypern.

Verbreitung auf Zypern

Sehr selten, und nur von drei Fundstellen bekannt.

Bemerkungen

Orchis tridentata wurde auf Zypern drei Mal gefunden. Im März 1983 wurde von ERRULAT und JANSEN (mündl. Mittlg. JANSEN, 2004) in der Umgebung von Souni bei Pano Kivides in einem aufgelassenen Gartengelände etwa 50 Pflanzen gefunden (eine Pflanze aufblühend, die anderen knospend). Von dieser blühenden Pflanze ist in G. & K. MORSCHEK (1996) und in diesem Buch ein fotografischer Beleg vorhanden. Beide Bilder zeigen eine Pflanze von *Orchis tridentata*, die in Form und Farbe Pflanzen gleicht, die auf Kreta vorkommen. Die kretischen Pflanzen zeichnen sich durch eine dunklere Blütenfarbe und eine besonders dreilappige Lippe aus, wobei die Ränder der Lippe und der Seitenlappen stark gezähnelt sind. Ausserdem sind die Spitzen der Sepalen lang ausgezogen. Damit wären sowohl die kretischen als auch die zypriotischen Pflanzen als *Orchis tridentata* var. *commutata* (TODARO) REICHENBACH fil. zu bewerten.

Im März 1991 fanden A. & H. ARBIRK ein weiteres blühendes Exemplar dieser Art in der Phrygana in der Umgebung von Pano Lefkara im südlichen Teil Zyperns. Fotografische Belege (PEDERSEN & FAURHOLDT, 1997) zeigen deutlich, dass es sich auch hier um *Orchis tridentata* var. *commutata* handelt. Auch die Dias, die mir von H. ARBIRK zur Verfügung gestellt wurden, zeigen deutlich die wesentlichen Merkmale dieser Varietät.

Ein dritter Fund wurde im März 1996 im nördlichen, türkischen Teil der Insel von KOCH gemacht (PEDERSEN & FAURHOLDT, 1997). Hier wurde die Art etwa hundert Meter westlich der Hauptverkehrsstraße zwischen Girne und Güzelyurt (etwa 2 km nördlich von Geçitköy) gefunden, und zwar in einer Gruppe von drei blühenden Pflanzen, vergesellschaftet von *Ophrys bornmuelleri*. Diese Angaben wurden mittels Farbaufnahmen von D.E. VINEY und von K. & R.-B. HANSEN (PEDERSEN & FAURHOLDT, 1997) bestätigt. Bei dieser Angabe handelt es sich auch um *Orchis tridentata* var. *commutata*. Weitere Funde von *Orchis tridentata* auf Zypern gibt es bis heute nicht.

WOOD (1985) berichtet von einem Herbarbeleg, der mit *Orchis tridentata* beschriftet war, der aber *Anacamptis pyramidalis* darstellte. Weiterhin existieren einigen Fundortberichte (z. B. bei ESSINK, 1997) mit weiteren Angaben von *Orchis tridentata* auf Zypern. Einige dieser Angaben wurden vom Autor überprüft, es wurde dort immer nur *Orchis italica* gefunden. Also liegen hier höchstwahrscheinlich Verwechslungen mit armblütigen Exemplaren von *Orchis italica* vor. Weitere Vorkommen dieser Art sind auf Zypern nicht auszuschließen, weil Zypern im Areal dieser Art liegt.

Gefährdung

Orchis tridentata ist auf Zypern sehr selten und Funde wurden in den letzten Jahren nicht mehr bestätigt. *Orchis tridentata* ist auf Zypern verschollen.

Hybriden

Nicht nachgewiesen.

◀ Pano Lefkara, 24.3.1991

Pano Kivides (ehemaliger Standort von/Former site of *Orchis tridentata*), 20.3.2002

Orchis tridentata
Toothed Orchid

SCOPOLI

Fl. Carniol. ed. 2, 2: 190 (1772)

Synonyms

Neotinea tridentata (SCOPOLI) R.M. BATEMAN, PRIDGEON & M.W. CHASE, Lindleyana 12 (3): 122 (1997); *Orchis variegata* ALLIONI, Fl. Pedem. 2: 147 (1785); *Orchis tridentata* var. *variegata* (ALLIONI) REICHENBACH fil., Icon. Fl. Germ. Helv. 13/14: 23 (1851); *Orchis tridentata* SCOPOLI var. *commutata* (TODARO) REICHENBACH fil., Icon. Fl. Germ. Helv. 13/14: 24 (1851); *Orchis commutata* TODARO, Orchid. Sicul.: 24 (1842), nom. illeg.; *Orchis tridentata* SCOPOLI subsp. *commutata* (TODARO) NYMAN, Consp. Fl. Eur. 4: 691 (1882); *Neotinea tridentata* subsp. *commutata* (TODARO) R.M. BATEMAN, PRIDGEON & M.W. CHASE, Lindleyana 12 (3): 122 (1997).

Description

Elegant plant, 20 to 40 cm tall. Stem erect, relatively vigorous, light green. Foliage leaves lanceolate to narrowly lanceolate, bluish green, unspotted, lower leaves forming a rosette at base, upper leaves merging into sheathing stem leaves. Inflorescence spherical, rarely cylindrical, dense- and many-flowered. Bracts linear, acuminate, about as long as ovary. Flowers small, pink to light violet. Perianth segments forming a loose hood, long acuminate, ends reflexed, (pale) pink to white or light violet. Sepals ovate-lanceolate, mostly with violet veins. Petals narrowly lanceolate, shorter than sepals. Labellum spread out flat, slightly bent upwards at edges, deeply three-lobed with a two-pronged elongated middle lobe, also having a small tooth, whitish to light pink, with scattered red dots. Spur cylindrical, curving downwards, about half as long as ovary.

Habitat

Maquis, phrygana, meadows, wasteland, light coniferous woods, shrubland margins, olive groves; on base-rich or calcareous soils.

Flowering time

Mid-March to mid-April.

Altitude distribution

From sea level to 500 m.

Overall distribution

Mainly distributed in the central and eastern Mediterranean regions, where it occurs in small pockets in Hessen and Thüringen in Central Europe; furthermore in Turkey, Caucasus, northern Syria, northern Iraq and northern Iran, also on Cyprus.

Distribution on Cyprus

Very rare, and up to now known from three locations.

Remarks

Orchis tridentata has been found three times on Cyprus. ERRULAT and JANSEN (oral correspondence JANSEN, 2004) found about 50 plants (one plant in flower, the others in bud) in the Souni area near Pano Kivides, in an abandoned garden in March 1983. There is photographic evidence of the flowering plant in G. & K. MORSCHEK (1996) and in this book. Both pictures show a plant of *Orchis tridentata*, which, in shape and colour, resembles plants found on Crete. The Cretan plants are characterised by a darker flower colouration and by a remarkable three-lobed labellum, of which the edges and those of the lateral lobes are deeply toothed. Furthermore, the ends of the sepals are very elongated. For this reason, both the Cretan plants and the Cypriot plants can be evaluated as *Orchis tridentata* var. *commutata* (TODARO) REICHENBACH fil.

In March 1991, A. & H. ARBIRK found another flowering specimen of this species in the phrygana in the area of Pano Lefkara in the southern part of Cyprus. Photographic evidence (PEDERSEN & FAURHOLDT, 1997) clearly shows that this also involves *Orchis tridentata* var. *commutata*. The photographs, which were made available to me by H. ARBIRK, clearly show the main characteristics of this variety.

A third find was made in March 1996 in the northern, turkisch part of the island by KOCH (PEDERSEN & FAURHOLDT, 1997). The species was found there about one hundred metres west of the main road between Girne and Güzelyurt (about 2 km north of Geçitköy), in a group of three flowering plants, accompanied by *Ophrys bornmuelleri*. These reports were confirmed by colour photographs by D. E. VINEY and by K. & R.-B HANSEN (PEDERSEN & FAURHOLDT, 1997). This report also involves *Orchis tridentata* var. *commutata*. Other findings of *Orchis tridentata* have not been made on Cyprus so far.

WOOD (1985) reports on botanical evidence that was tagged with the name *Orchis tridentata*, but which was of *Anacamptis pyramidalis*. There are also some reports (e.g. from ESSINK, 1997) with further claims of *Orchis tridentata* on Cyprus. Some of these claims have been checked by the author, but each time *Orchis italica* was found there. It is therefore highly probable that they are confusions with few-flowered specimens of *Orchis italica*. Other occurrences of this species on Cyprus can not be ruled out. Moreover, the distribution area of *Orchis tridentata* almost completely covers the central and eastern Mediterranean regions, including Crete and southern Turkey, and Cyprus is therefore situated in its area.

Threats

Orchis tridentata is very rare on Cyprus and findings in recent years have not been confirmed. *Orchis tridentata* is extinct on Cyprus.

Hybrids

Unconfirmed.

Pano Lefkara, 24.3.1991

Pano Kivides, 28.3.1983

366   Geçitköy, 29.3.1996

Pano Lefkara, 22.3.2002

Kayalar-Kyrenia, 14.3.2002

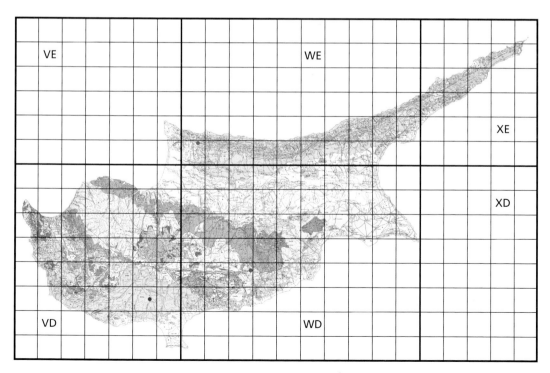

VE

WE

XE

XD

VD

WD

3 Meldungen / Reports

Orchis tridentata

47

Platanthera holmboei
Holmboes Waldhyazinthe

H. LINDBERG

Arsbok-Vuosik. Soc. Sci. Fenn. 20B,
Nr. 7: 4 (1942)

Synonyme

Platanthera chlorantha subsp. *holmboei* (H. LINDBERG) J.J. WOOD, Orchid Rev. 88: 122 (1980); *Platanthera montana* subsp. *holmboei* (H. LINDBERG) STRÖHLE, Jour. Eur. Orch. 35 (4): 834 (2003).

Beschreibung

Kräftige, stattliche Pflanze, 30 bis 50 cm hoch. Stängel aufrecht, steif, dunkelgrün. Untere Laubblätter sehr groß, elliptisch bis eiförmig-lanzettlich, grundständig, dunkelgrün, mit zahlreichen Längsnerven; die oberen in Tragblätter übergehend. Blütenstand zylindrisch und meist reichblütig, manchmal aber auch armblütig. Tragblätter lanzettlich bis schmal-lanzettlich, lang zugespitzt, dunkelgrün, schräg aufwärts gerichtet, die unteren etwas länger, die oberen kürzer als der Fruchtknoten. Blüten locker am Stängel angeordnet, klein bis mittelgroß, grün bis grünlichgelb gefärbt. Seitliche Sepalen schief abstehend. Petalen schmal-lanzettlich. Die beiden Petalen und das mittlere Sepal helmförmig zusammenneigend. Lippe zungenförmig, zurückgebogen oder herabhängend und zur Spitze hin nicht verschmälert, grün. Staubbeutelfächer trapezförmig auseinanderspreizend. Sporn dünn, fadenförmig, waagerecht abstehend, viel länger als der Fruchtknoten.

Standort

Lockere Kiefernwälder, Waldlichtungen und Ufersäume zeitweise ausgetrockneter Bachläufe, manchmal in der Nähe fließender Gewässer; auf trockenen bis wechselfeuchten, basenreichen Böden.

Blütezeit

Mitte Mai bis Ende Juni (Anfang Juli).

Höhenverbreitung

Von 800 bis 1.600 m.

Gesamtverbreitung

Östliches Mittelmeergebiet, Lesbos, Türkei, Israel, Libanon, Westsyrien und Zypern. Lange Zeit galt diese Art als endemisch für Zypern.

Verbreitung auf Zypern

Im Troodos-Gebirge weit verbreitet, dort stellenweise nicht selten. Im Zederntal sehr selten.

Bemerkungen

Platanthera holmboei, die 1946 von LINDBERG aus Zypern beschrieben wurde, hat im Troodos-Gebirge ihr Hauptverbreitungsgebiet und ist im Juni vor allem in den Südhängen eine häufige Erscheinung. In diesen Berglagen wächst *Platanthera holmboei* bevorzugt im Schatten der Kiefern und an Waldrändern, sowie in Schluchten unter *Pinus brutia, Platanus orientalis, Quercus alnifolia* und *Alnus orientalis*; in den höheren Lagen dagegen bevorzugt unter *Pinus nigra* subsp. *pallasiana* und an schattigen Stellen entlang von Bergbächen (WOOD, 1985; GEORGIADES, 1998ab). Vor allem in der direkten Umgebung der englischen Militärbasis nahe dem Gipfel des Troodos-Gebirges ist sie häufig zu finden.

WOOD (1985) gibt für Zypern auch *Platanthera chlorantha* an. In den niedrigen Lagen gibt es tatsächlich Pflanzen, die von *Platanthera chlorantha* schwierig zu unterscheiden sind. Auch in der Türkei, zum Beispiel am Uludağ bei Bursa, gibt es in den niedrigen Lagen Pflanzen, die sowohl Merkmale von *Platanthera chlorantha* als auch von *Platanthera holmboei* aufweisen (KREUTZ, 1998). Mit zunehmender Höhenlage gehen die Pflanzen in die typische *Platanthera holmboei* über (HANSEN, KREUTZ & U. & D. RÜCKBRODT, 1990). In diesem Buch wurden alle Angaben zur Gattung *Platanthera* unter *Platanthera holmboei* zusammengefasst, weil es sich bei den vermeintlichen Funden von *Platanthera chlorantha* mit Sicherheit um heller gefärbte Exemplare von *Platanthera holmboei* handelt.

Platanthera holmboei ähnelt *Platanthera chlorantha*, unterscheidet sich aber von dieser Art durch den lockereren Blütenstand, die hell- bis dunkelgrün gefärbten, bedeutend kleineren Blüten und einen fadenförmigen, nicht keulig verdickten und waagerecht abstehenden Sporn.

Gefährdung

Platanthera holmboei ist im Troodos-Gebirge weit verbreitet und nicht selten. Durch die Einstellung der Bergweidewirtschaft während der englischen Besatzung hat sich die Art im Gebirge stark verbreitet (ROBATSCH, 1980). Sie ist damit als nicht gefährdet einzustufen.

Hybriden

Nicht nachgewiesen.

Pano Platres, 20.6.2002

Platanthera holmboei
Holmboe's Butterfly Orchid

H. Lindberg

Arsbok-Vuosik. Soc. Sci. Fenn. 20B,
Nr. 7: 4 (1942)

Synonyms

Platanthera chlorantha subsp. *holmboei* (H. LIND-BERG) J.J. WOOD, Orchid Rev. 88: 122 (1980); *Platanthera montana* subsp. *holmboei* (H. LINDBERG) STRÖHLE, Jour. Eur. Orch. 35 (4): 834 (2003).

Description

Vigorous, stately plant, 30 to 50 cm tall. Stem erect, stiff, dark green. Lower foliage leaves very large, elliptical to ovate-lanceolate, spreading at ground level, dark green, with numerous longitudinal veins; upper leaves merging into bracts. Inflorescence cylindrical and usually dense-flowered, but often few-flowered. Bracts lanceolate to narrowly lanceolate, acuminate, dark green, obliquely directed upwards, lower bracts somewhat longer, upper bracts shorter than ovary. Flowers arranged laxly along stem, small to medium-sized, green to greenish yellow. Lateral sepals spreading obliquely. Petals narrowly lanceolate. Both petals and dorsal sepal connivent to forming a hood. Labellum tongue-shaped, bending backwards or pendant and not narrowly elongated towards apex. Anther trapeziform, spread out. Spur thin, filiform, horizontal, much longer than ovary.

Habitat

Light coniferous woods, forest clearings and riverbanks, at times in dry stream beds, sometimes near flowing water; on arid to variably moist, base-rich soils.

Flowering time

Mid-May to late June (early July).

Altitude distribution

From 800 to 1,600 m.

Overall distribution

Eastern Mediterranean region, Lesbos, Turkey, Israel, Lebanon, western Syria and Cyprus. Considered for a long time as endemic to Cyprus.

Distribution on Cyprus

Widely distributed in the Troodos mountains, not rare there in some places. Very rare in the Cedar Valley.

Remarks

Described from Cyprus by LINDBERG in 1946, this species has its main distribution area in the Troodos mountains and makes an abundant appearance in June, especially on the southern slopes. At these altitudes *Platanthera holmboei* favours the shade of conifers and the edges of woods, as well as gullies under *Pinus brutia, Platanus orientalis, Quercus alnifolia* and *Alnus orientalis*; at higher altitudes it favours growing beneath *Pinus nigra* subsp. *pallasiana* and in shady places along mountain streams (WOOD, 1985; GEORGIADES, 1998ab). The species can be found in abundance in the immediate vicinity of the British military station near the top of the Troodos mountains.

WOOD (1985) also reports *Platanthera chlorantha* for Cyprus. There are indeed plants at the lower altitudes which are difficult to differentiate from *Platanthera chlorantha*. There are plants at lower altitudes in Turkey, e.g. at Uludağ near Bursa, which share characterics both of *Platanthera chlorantha* and also *Platanthera holmboei* (KREUTZ, 1998). The plants are replaced by typical *Platanthera holmboei* at higher altitudes (HANSEN, KREUTZ & U. & D. RÜCKBRODT,1990). All reports for the genus *Platanthera* have been placed in this book under *Platanthera holmboei*, as the probably findings of *Platanthera chlorantha* certainly involve lighter coloured specimens of *Platanthera holmboei*.

Platanthera holmboei resembles *Platanthera chlorantha*, but can be distinguished from this species by a lax inflorescence, by distinctly smaller light to dark green flowers and by a thread-like, not clubbed, horizontally directed spur.

Threats

Platanthera holmboei is widely distributed and not rare in the Troodos mountains. The species has spread considerably in the mountains after cultivation of the mountain pastures stopped during the British occupation (ROBATSCH, 1980). It can therefore be categorized as not threatened.

Hybrids

No known.

Troodos (Troodos), 20.6.2002

Pano Platres, 20.6.2002

Pano Platres, 20.6.2002

Troodos (Troodos), 26.6.2002

Pano Platres, 20.6.2002

Pano Platres, 26.6.2002

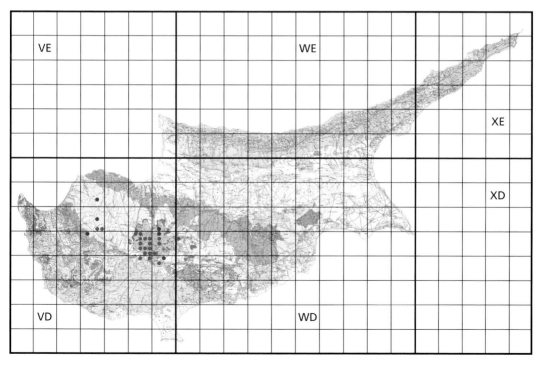

Platanthera holmboei

Beschreibung

Sehr schlanke, meist hochwüchsige, zierliche Pflanze, 15 bis 30 cm hoch. Stängel schlank mit wenigen Schuppenblättern, grün, im Bereich des Blütenstandes rötlich überlaufen. Laubblätter linealisch, grün bis gelblichgrün, schräg aufrecht bis gebogen, rinnig, gekielt, die oberen in tragblattartige Laubblätter übergehend und violett überlaufen. Blütenstand sehr locker- und armblütig, gewöhnlich eine bis zu 10 bis 15 cm lange Ähre mit 3 bis 6 Blüten. Tragblätter lanzettlich und zugespitzt, bei den unteren Blüten den Sepalhelm erreichend, bei den oberen Blüten genau so lang wie dieser oder etwas kürzer, meist purpurn überlaufen. Blüten klein, schräg aufgerichtet. Perigonblätter lanzettlich, zugespitzt, helmförmig zusammenneigend, aussen grauviolett und purpurn geädert, innen purpurviolett, schräg aufwärts gerichtet. Lippe zweigliedrig, mit 2 fast parallelen Schwielen. Hypochil halbkreisförmig, Seitenlappen aufrecht und völlig im Helm verborgen, am Rande dunkelrot, im Zentrum heller purpurn. Epichil sehr klein, spitz, purpurn, rückwärts gegen das Hypochil gebogen oder vertikal herabhängend.

Standort

Trockene bis feuchte Stellen in grasigen Wiesenflächen, manchmal auch an Bachufern, in Macchien, aufgelassenen Oliven- und Weinhainen, Phrygana, Ödland, Trockenwiesen, in lichten Kiefern- und Pinienwäldern, an Gebüschrändern, und in küstennahen Feucht- und Magerwiesen; auf kalkhaltigen bis schwach sauren Böden.

Blütezeit

(Anfang) Mitte März bis Anfang April.

Höhenverbreitung

Von der Küste bis 500 m.

Gesamtverbreitung

Endemische Art von Zypern.

Verbreitung auf Zypern

Die Art ist vor allem auf der Akamas-Halbinsel verbreitet, in anderen Teilen Zyperns sehr selten und zerstreut vorkommend.

Bemerkungen

Auf Zypern gibt es an einigen Stellen Serapias Populationen, deren Pflanzen sich durch einen viel schlankeren und zierlicheren Wuchs, einen sehr lockerblütigen und gestreckten Blütenstand, viel kleinere Blüten und ein schmal-lanzettliches, sehr spitzes, verlängertes und zurückgebogenes, beziehungsweise vertikal abwärts gerichtetes Epichil deutlich von Serapias bergonii unterscheiden. Sie erinnern auf den ersten Blick an Hybridschwärme zwischen Serapias bergonii und Serapias parviflora. Diese Pflanzen, die im Gelände etwa zwei bis drei Wochen früher als Serapias parviflora blühen, sind problemlos als eigenständige Art zu unterscheiden. Delforge (1990) hat diese Pflanzen als eine neue Art unter dem Namen Serapias aphroditae abgetrennt. Nach Berücksichtigung der quantitativen Kriterien und der Unmöglichkeit einer klaren Sippendiskriminanz kommen Gölz & Reinhard (1994) aber zu der Schlussfolgerung, dass die zypriotischen Populationen (Serapias aphroditae im Sinne von Delforge) und die korfiotischen Populationen (Serapias bergonii im Sinne von Baumann & Künkele) als identisch betrachtet werden müssen. Serapias aphroditae ist aber eine gute und klar definierte Art, die deutlich und problemlos als eigenständige Art zu bestimmen ist.

Serapias aphroditae gehört mit Serapias parviflora zu den seltensten Serapias-Arten Zyperns. Vor der Neubeschreibung von Serapias aphroditae wurden Pflanzen dieser neuen Art oft als Serapias parviflora (unter anderem bei Vaslet, 1984) oder als Hybridschwärme zwischen Serapias bergonii und Serapias parviflora bestimmt.

Gefährdung

Serapias aphroditae ist selten. Sie ist durch Beweidung und Mahd gefährdet.

Hybriden

Mit Serapias bergonii. Wurde von Delforge (1990) als Hybride Serapias xmastiana zwischen Serapias aphroditae und Serapias hellenica (= Serapias bergonii) beschrieben.

Bemerkungen zu der Verbreitungskarte

Auf der Verbreitungskarte sind möglicherweise Funde von Serapias parviflora enthalten, weil Serapias aphroditae erst 1990 von Delforge neu beschrieben und von Serapias parviflora, beziehungsweise von Serapias bergonii abgetrennt wurde.

Neo Chorio (Akamas), 10.3.2002

Neo Chorio (Akamas), 10.3.2002

Serapias aphroditae
Aphrodite's Serapias

P. DELFORGE

Natural. Belges 71: 113 (1990)

Description

Very slender, usually tall, elegant plant, 15 to 30 cm tall. Stem slender with few scale leaves, green, with reddish tinges near the inflorescence. Foliage leaves linear, green to yellowish green, obliquely erect to bending, grooved, keeled, upper leaves merging into bract-like foliage leaves with violet tinges. Inflorescence very lax and few-flowered, usually one long spike, 10 to 15 cm tall, with 3 to 6 flowers. Bracts lanceolate and acuminate, near the lower flowers reaching the hood formed by the sepals, near upper flowers as long as or slightly shorter than the hood, usually with purple tinges. Flowers small, obliquely erect. Perianth segments lanceolate, acuminate, connivent to forming a hood, exterior grey-violet with purple veins, interior purple-violet, obliquely directed upwards. Labellum bipartite, with 2 almost parallel ridges. Hypochile semi-spherical, lateral lobes erect and completely hidden in the hood, dark red at edges, light purple in the centre. Epichile very small, acuminate, purple, bent backwards towards the hypochile or vertically pendant.

Habitat

Arid to moist places in grassy meadows, often also along streams, in maquis, neglected olive groves and vineyards, phrygana, wasteland, dry meadows, light coniferous woods, shrubland edges, and in coastal marshes and grasslands; on calcareous to slightly acidic soils.

Flowering time

(Early) mid-March to early April.

Altitude distribution

From sea level to 500 m.

Overall distribution

Endemic species of Cyprus.

Distribution on Cyprus

The species is mainly distributed in the Akamas peninsula, elsewhere on Cyprus very rare and scattered.

Remarks

There are some places on Cyprus where *Serapias* populations grow of which the plants can clearly be distinguished from *Serapias bergonii* by a much more slender and elegant growth, a very lax and elongated inflorescence, much smaller flowers and a narrowly lanceolate, very acuminate, elongated and reflexed, or vertically pendant epichile. At first glance, they resemble a hybrid swarm between *Serapias bergonii* and *Serapias parviflora*. These plants which bloom about two or three weeks earlier than *Serapias parviflora* in the field, can be distinguished without problem as an independent species. DELFORGE (1990) separated these plants into a new species and named them *Serapias aphroditae*. After considering the quantitative criteria and due to the impossibility of clear discrimination between the taxa, GÖLZ & REINHARD (1994) however come to the conclusion that the Cypriot populations (*Serapias aphroditae* according to DELFORGE) and the Corfiot populations (*Serapias bergonii* according to BAUMANN & KÜNKELE) should be regarded as identical. *Serapias aphroditae* is however a clear and well defined taxa and can be distinguished without problems as an independent species. Together with *Serapias parviflora*, *Serapias aphroditae* is one of the rarest *Serapias* species of Cyprus. Before the new description of *Serapias aphroditae*, plants of this new species were often identified as *Serapias parviflora* (amongst others by VASLET, 1984) or as hybrid swarms between *Serapias bergonii* and *Serapias parviflora*.

Threats

Serapias aphroditae is rare. It is threatened by grazing and mowing.

Hybrids

With *Serapias bergonii*. Was described by DELFORGE (1990) as the hybrid *Serapias* x*mastiana* between *Serapias aphroditae* and *Serapias hellenica* (= *Serapias bergonii*).

Remarks concerning the distribution map

Locations of *Serapias parviflora* may have possibly been included on the distribution map, as *Serapias aphroditae* was only recently described by Delforge in 1990 and separated from *Serapias parviflora* and *Serapias bergonii*.

Neo Chorio (Akamas), 10.3.2002

Pegeia (Akamas), 19.3.2002

Neo Chorio (Akamas), 10.3.2002

Akrotiri (Salt lake), 8.3.2002

Pegeia (Akamas), 19.3.2002 Neo Chorio (Akamas), 10.3.2002

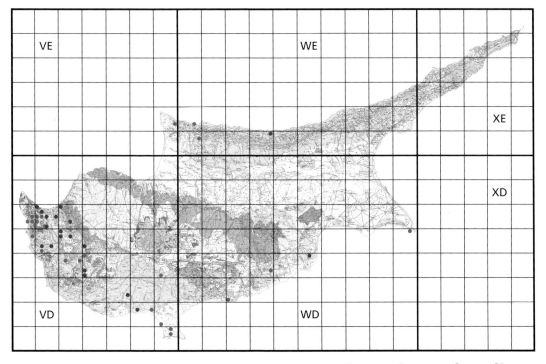

Serapias aphroditae

49 Serapias bergonii
Bergons Zungenständel

E.G. CAMUS, P. BERGON
& A. CAMUS (pro hybr.)

Monogr. Orchid.: 61 (1908) ('bergoni')

Synonyme

Serapias laxiflora CHAUBARD, Nouv. Fl. Pélop.: 62 (1838), nom. illeg.; *Serapias parviflora* subsp. *laxiflora* Soó, Repert. Spec. Nov. Regni Veg. 24: 33 (1927); *Serapias vomeracea* subsp. *laxiflora* (Soó) GÖLZ & H.R. REINHARD, Die Orchidee 28 (3): 114 (1977); *Serapias cordigera* subsp. *laxiflora* (Soó) SUNDERMANN, Eur. Medit. Orch. ed. 3: 39 (1980); *Serapias columnae* AUNIER ex REICHENBACH fil., Icon. Fl. Germ. Helv. 13/14: 13 (1851); *Serapias laxiflora* var. *columnae* REICHENBACH fil., Icon. Fl. Germ. Helv. 13/14: 13 (1851); *Serapias parviflora* subsp. *columnae* (REICHENBACH fil.) Soó in KELLER & Soó, Monogr. Iconogr. Orchid. Eur. 2: 91 (1931); *Serapias vomeracea* subsp. *columnae* (AUNIER ex REICHENBACH fil.) SUNDERMANN in J. LANDWEHR, Wilde Orch. Eur. 2: 360 (1977), nom. nud.; *Serapias wettsteinii* H. FLEISCHMANN, Österr. Bot. Zeitschr. 74: 190 (1925); *Serapias hellenica* RENZ, Repert. Spec. Nov. Regni Veg. 25: 230 (1928); *Serapias laxiflora* subsp. *hellenica* (RENZ) RENZ, Repert. Spec. Nov. Regni Veg. 27: 210 (1929).

Beschreibung

Schlanke, meist hochwüchsige, zierliche Pflanze, 25 bis 50 cm hoch. Stängel kräftig, mit wenigen Schuppenblättern, grün, im Bereich des Blütenstandes rötlich überlaufen. Laubblätter lanzettlich, grün bis bläulichgrün, schräg aufrecht gerichtet bis abwärts gebogen, rinnig, die oberen violett überlaufen und in tragblattartige Laubblätter übergehend. Blütenstand locker- und vielblütig, gewöhnlich eine bis zu 20 cm lange Ähre mit 5 bis 10 Blüten. Tragblätter lanzettlich, den Sepalhelm meist überragend, purpurn überlaufen. Blüten mittelgroß, schräg aufgerichtet. Perigonblätter lanzettlich, zugespitzt, genervt, helmförmig zusammenneigend, aussen graulila, innen purpurviolett, steil bis schräg aufwärts gerichtet. Lippe zweigliedrig, mit 2 bräunlichen, parallelen Schwielen. Hypochil am Grunde keilförmig, Seitenlappen aufrecht und im Helm verborgen, schwarzpurpurn bis purpurn. Epichil länglich-lanzettlich, rötlichbraun, an der Basis schwach behaart (selten kahl), etwa 1,5-mal so lang wie das Hypochil, herabhängend bis rückwärts gegen das Hypochil gebogen.

Standort

Grasige Wiesenflächen, Macchien, Phrygana, Ödland, Felsfluren, Trockenwiesen, Straßenböschungen, Olivenhaine, lichte Kiefernwälder und Feuchtwiesen; auf kalkhaltigen bis schwach sauren, meist feuchten Böden.

Blütezeit

(Anfang) Mitte März bis Ende April.

Höhenverbreitung

Von der Küste bis 900 m.

Gesamtverbreitung

Das Areal reicht von Italien (von Parma im Norden bis Süditalien und Sizilien) über die griechische Insel Korfu, das griechische Festland und Kreta, die Ägäischen Inseln bis in die südöstliche Provinz Hatay in der Türkei und Zypern.

Verbreitung auf Zypern

Vor allem im südlichen Teil der Insel verbreitet.

Bemerkungen

Serapias bergonii ist eine im ostmediterranen Raum häufige und weit verbreitete Sippe. Von mehreren Autoren wird diese Art unter *Serapias laxiflora* geführt. Von BAUMANN & KÜNKELE (1988b) wurde begründet, warum *Serapias bergonii* vor *Serapias laxiflora* prioritätsberechtigt ist.

Zuweilen kann die Bestimmung Schwierigkeiten bereiten, da *Serapias bergonii* Hybriden mit anderen *Serapias*-Arten bildet. Auf Zypern sind diese Hybridschwärme jedoch selten, und *Serapias bergonii* ist meist leicht zu identifizieren. Nur die Abgrenzung zu *Serapias aphroditae* macht gelegentlich Probleme, mit der *Serapias bergonii* manchmal am gleichen Standort vorkommt. In typischer Ausprägung ist *Serapias bergonii* kaum verwechselbar. Diese Art ist an ihrem sehr langen, lockerblütigen Blütenstand zu erkennen. Das Epichil ist etwa doppelt so groß und nicht wie bei *Serapias aphroditae* rückwärts gegen das Hypochil gebogen. *Serapias aphroditae* hat einen viel schlankeren und zierlicheren Wuchs, einen sehr lockerblütigen und gestreckten Blütenstand, viel kleinere Blüten und ein schmal-lanzettliches, vertikal herabhängendes oder stark rückwärts gebogenes Epichil. Pflanzen dieser Art erinnern auf den ersten Blick an Hybridschwärme zwischen *Serapias bergonii* und *Serapias parviflora*.

Gefährdung

Serapias bergonii ist auf Zypern zwar die häufigste *Serapias*-Art, aber trotzdem nicht so allgemein wie zum Beispiel auf den Ägäischen Inseln. Sie ist aber kaum gefährdet.

Hybriden

Mit *Serapias aphroditae*. Wurde von DELFORGE (1990) als Hybride *Serapias* ×*mastiana* zwischen *Serapias hellenica* (= *Serapias bergonii*) und *Serapias aphroditae* beschrieben.

Serapias bergonii
Bergon's Serapias

E.G. Camus, P. Bergon
& A. Camus (pro hybr.)

Monogr. Orchid.: 61 (1908) ('bergoni')

Synonyms

Serapias laxiflora Chaubard, Nouv. Fl. Pélop.: 62 (1838), nom. illeg.; *Serapias parviflora* subsp. *laxiflora* Soó, Repert. Spec. Nov. Regni Veg. 24: 33 (1927); *Serapias vomeracea* subsp. *laxiflora* (Soó) Gölz & H.R. Reinhard, Die Orchidee 28 (3): 114 (1977); *Serapias cordigera* subsp. *laxiflora* (Soó) Sundermann, Eur. Medit. Orch. ed. 3: 39 (1980); *Serapias columnae* Aunier ex Reichenbach fil., Icon. Fl. Germ. Helv. 13/14: 13 (1851); *Serapias laxiflora* var. *columnae* Reichenbach fil., Icon. Fl. Germ. Helv. 13/14: 13 (1851); *Serapias parviflora* subsp. *columnae* (Reichenbach fil.) Soó in Keller & Soó, Monogr. Iconogr. Orchid. Eur. 2: 91 (1931); *Serapias vomeracea* subsp. *columnae* (Aunier ex Reichenbach fil.) Sundermann in J. Landwehr, Wilde Orch. Eur. 2: 360 (1977), nom. nud.; *Serapias wettsteinii* H. Fleischmann, Österr. Bot. Zeitschr. 74: 190 (1925); *Serapias hellenica* Renz, Repert. Spec. Nov. Regni Veg. 25: 230 (1928); *Serapias laxiflora* subsp. *hellenica* (Renz) Renz, Repert. Spec. Nov. Regni Veg. 27: 210 (1929).

Description

Slender, usually tall, delicate plant, 25 to 50 cm tall. Stem vigorous, with few scale leaves, green, with reddish tinges near the spike. Foliage leaves lanceolate, green to bluish green, obliquely erect to bent downwards, grooved, upper leaves merging into bract-like foliage leaves and tinged violet. Inflorescence lax and many-flowered, normally one spike up to 20 cm long, with 5 to 10 flowers. Bracts lanceolate, usually exceeding hood, tinged purple. Flowers medium-sized, obliquely erect. Perianth segments lanceolate, acuminate, veined, connivent to forming a hood, exterior grey-lilac, interior purple-violet, erect to obliquely directed upwards. Labellum bipartite, with two brownish, parallel ridges. Hypochile wedge-shaped at base, lateral lobes erect and hidden inside hood, blackish purple to purple. Epichile oblong-lanceolate, reddish brown, weakly hairy at base (rarely glabrous), about 1.5 times longer than hypochile, pendent to bent backwards towards hypochile.

Habitat

Grassy meadows, maquis, phrygana, wasteland, rocky fields, arid meadows, roadside slopes, olive groves, light coniferous woods and marshy areas; on calcareous to slightly acidic, usually moist soils.

Flowering time

(Early) Mid-March to late April.

Altitude distribution

From sea level to 900 m.

Overall distribution

Its habitat stretches from Italy (from Parma in the north as far as southern Italy and Sicily) through the Greek island of Corfu, the Greek mainland and Crete, the Aegean islands to the southeastern province of Hatay in Turkey, and on Cyprus.

Distibution on Cyprus

Mainly distributed in the southern part of the island.

Remarks

Serapias bergonii is an abundant and widespread taxon in the eastern Mediterranean region. Several authors have listed this species under *Serapias laxiflora*. Baumann & Künkele (1988b) have explained why the name *Serapias bergonii* has priority over *Serapias laxiflora*.

At times the identification can cause difficulties, as *Serapias bergonii* forms hybrids with other *Serapias* species. These hybrid swarms are however rare on Cyprus, and *Serapias bergonii* can usually be identified easily. The differentiation from *Serapias aphroditae* however can cause occasional problems, as it often occurs together with *Serapias bergonii* at the same site. In its typical appearance *Serapias bergonii* can hardly be confused. This species can be recognized by its very long, laxly flowered inflorescence. The epichile is almost twice as large as that of *Serapias aphroditae* and is not reflexed towards the hypochile. *Serapias aphroditae* has a more slender and elegant growth, a very lax-flowered and elongated inflorescence, much smaller flowers and a narrowly lanceolate, vertically pendant or strongly reflexed epichile. Plants of this species at first glance resemble hybrid swarms between *Serapias bergonii* and *Serapias parviflora*.

Threats

Although *Serapias bergonii* is the most abundant *Serapias* species on Cyprus, it is not as common as for example on the Aegean islands. It is however hardly threatened.

Hybrids

With *Serapias aphroditae*. Described by Delforge (1990) as the hybrid *Serapias* ×*mastiana* between *Serapias hellenica* (= *Serapias bergonii*) and *Serapias aphroditae*.

Nata-Choletria (Xeros Potamos), 12.3.2002

Kayalar-Sadrazamköy, 14.3.2002

Gerasa, 20.3.2002

Gerasa, 20.3.2002

Nata-Choletria (Xeros Potamos), 12.3.2002

Gerasa, 20.3.2002

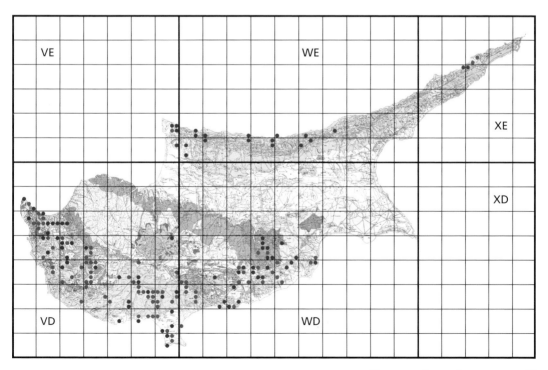

Serapias bergonii

50 Serapias levantina
Levante-Zungenständel

H. Baumann & Künkele

Mitteilungsbl. Arbeitskr. Heim. Orch.
Baden-Württ. 21 (3): 766 & 767 (1989)

Beschreibung

Kräftige Pflanze, 20 bis 40 cm hoch. Stängel hellgrün, im Bereich des Blütenstandes rötlich überlaufen. Laubblätter hell- bis gelblichgrün, lanzettlich bis breit-lanzettlich, lang zugespitzt, am Grunde rosettig gehäuft, schräg aufrecht gerichtet bis abstehend; die oberen Laubblätter scheidenförmig und den Blütenstand nicht erreichend. Blütenstand kurz oder verlängert, bis zu 15 cm lang, arm- bis reichblütig, mit 3 bis 10 locker angeordneten Blüten. Tragblätter lanzettlich bis breit-lanzettlich, vielnervig, rötlichbraun, die unteren Tragblätter deutlich die Blüten überragend. Blüten groß, dunkelbraun bis rötlichbraun. Perigonblätter lanzettlich, zugespitzt, genervt, helmförmig zusammenneigend, aussen hellviolett, entlang den Nerven dunkelviolett, waagerecht oder schräg aufwärts gerichtet. Lippe zweigliedrig, am Grunde mit zwei Schwielen, deren Ränder nach unten divergieren. Hypochil herzförmig, die Seitenlappen kaum aus dem Sepalhelm hervortretend, braunrot gefärbt. Epichil schmal-lanzettlich bis eiförmig, dunkelrot, im Zentrum mit zahlreichen violetten Haaren besetzt.

Standort

Lichte Kiefernwälder, offene Stellen in Macchien und Phrygana, Magerrasen, Olivenhaine, mäßig feuchte Wiesen, Straßenböschungen und an Bachufern; auf basischen oder kalkhaltigen Böden.

Blütezeit

Anfang März bis Mitte April.

Höhenverbreitung

Von Meereshöhe bis 400 m.

Gesamtverbreitung

Von der mittleren Südtürkei über Syrien und Libanon bis nach Israel und Zypern.

Verbreitung auf Zypern

Die Art ist im Süden besonders selten; im Norden der Insel allgemeiner und weiter verbreitet.

Bemerkungen

Serapias levantina gehört auf Zypern zu den seltenen Orchideenarten. Größere Populationen finden sich im Süden unter anderem bei Larnaka in der Umgebung des Salzsees. Die Art wächst in diesem Gebiet in der Phrygana und im Schatten der Gebüschzonen. Im Norden Zyperns ist Serapias levantina häufiger als im Süden. Sie bildet hier mehrere kleinere Populationen in und am Rande lichter Pinienwälder.

In der umfangreichen Publikation 'Die Gattung Serapias L. – eine taxonomische Übersicht' (1989) von Baumann & Künkele wurden die Populationen aus der Südtürkei, Syrien, Libanon, Israel und Zypern von Serapias orientalis abgetrennt und zur neu beschriebenen Serapias levantina gestellt. Die neue Serapias levantina weist Merkmale einer Übergangsform zwischen Serapias vomeracea (N.L. Burman) Briquet subsp. vomeracea und Serapias orientalis subsp. carica H. Baumann & Künkele auf. Auch nach Delforge (1994) ist Serapias levantina wahrscheinlich eine intermediäre Sippe zwischen Serapias orientalis und Serapias vomeracea.

Durch ihren gedrungenen Wuchs und ihre relativ wenigen und sehr großen Blüten ist Serapias levantina zumindest auf Zypern recht gut von den anderen dort vorkommenden Serapias-Arten zu unterscheiden.

Bei einigen Autoren (zum Beispiel bei Wood, 1985; bei Georgiades, 1998ab und Christofides, 2001) werden auch Serapias orientalis subsp. orientalis und Serapias vomeracea subsp. vomeracea für Zypern angegeben. Beide Sippen, Serapias vomeracea subsp. vomeracea und Serapias orientalis subsp. orientalis, sowie die nahe verwandte Serapias orientalis subsp. carica kommen aber im Verbreitungsgebiet von Serapias levantina nicht vor.

Gefährdung

Serapias levantina ist auf Zypern zwar weit verbreitet, ist aber überall selten und schon deshalb gefährdet. Im Norden Zyperns gehört sie zu den am meisten gefährdeten Orchideenarten, weil die Knollen dieser Art zur Bereitung von Salep ausgegraben, getrocknet und gemahlen werden (Viney, 1994).

Hybriden

Mit Serapias bergonii und Orchis syriaca (als XOrchiserapias dhiorii M. & M. Ackermann zwischen Orchis syriaca und Serapias orientalis beschrieben).

Larnaka (Salt lake), 9.3.2002

Serapias levantina
Levant Serapias

H. Baumann & Künkele

Mitteilungsbl. Arbeitskr. Heim. Orch.
Baden-Württ. 21 (3): 766 & 767 (1989)

Description

Vigorous plant, 20 to 40 cm tall. Stem light green, with reddish tinges near the inflorescence. Foliage leaves light to yellowish green, lanceolate to broadly lanceolate, oblong acuminate, forming a rosette at the base, directed obliquely upwards to spreading; upper leaves stem-sheathing and not exceeding inflorescence. Inflorescence short or elongated, up to 15 cm long, sparsely to densely flowered, with 3 to 10 laxly arranged flowers. Bracts lanceolate to broadly lanceolate, densely veined, reddish brown, lower bracts clearly exceeding the flowers. Flowers medium-sized, dark brown to reddish brown. Perianth segments lanceolate, acuminate, veined, connivent to forming a hood, exterior light violet, dark violet along veins, horizontal to obliquely directed upwards. Labellum bipartite, with two ridges at base, the edges of which diverge downwards. Hypochile cordate, lateral lobes scarcely protruding from hood, brown red. Epichile narrowly lanceolate to ovate, dark red, with numerous violet hairs at the centre.

Habitat

Light coniferous woods, open spots in maquis and phrygana, neglected grasslands, olive groves, moderately moist meadows, roadside slopes and by streams; on basic to calcareous soils.

Flowering time

Early March to mid-April.

Altitude distribution

From sea level to 400 m.

Overall distribution

From central southern Turkey through Syria and Lebanon to Israel and Cyprus.

Distribution on Cyprus

The species is very rare in the south; more widely distributed and common in the north.

Remarks

Serapias levantina must be counted among the rare orchid species of Cyprus. Larger populations can be found in the south, such as near Larnaka around both salt lakes. The species grows there in the phrygana and in the shade of the shrubland zones. *Serapias levantina* is more abundant in northern Cyprus than in the south. It forms several smaller populations there in and at the edges of light pine forests.

In the extensive publication 'Die Gattung *Serapias* L. – eine taxonomische Übersicht' (1989) by Baumann & Künkele, the populations in southern Turkey, Syria, Lebanon, Israel and Cyprus were separated from *Serapias orientalis* and listed under the newly described *Serapias levantina*. The new *Serapias levantina* exhibits the characteristics of a transitional form between *Serapias vomeracea* (N.L. Burman) Briquet subsp. *vomeracea* and *Serapias orientalis* subsp. *carica* H. Baumann & Künkele. According to Delforge (1994) also, *Serapias levantina* is probably an intermediate taxon between *Serapias orientalis* and *Serapias vomeracea*.

Because of its compact growth and its relatively few and very large flowers, *Serapias levantina* can very easily be distinguished from other *Serapias* species which occur there, at least on Cyprus.

Some authors (for example Wood, 1985; Georgiades, 1998ab and Christofides, 2001) have also reported *Serapias orientalis* subsp. *orientalis* and *Serapias vomeracea* subsp. *vomeracea* for Cyprus. Both taxa, *Serapias vomeracea* subsp. *vomeracea* and *Serapias orientalis* subsp. *orientalis*, as well as the closely related *Serapias orientalis* subsp. *carica* do not, however, occur in the distribution area of *Serapias levantina*.

Threats

Although *Serapias levantina* is widely distributed on Cyprus, it is rare everywhere and therefore threatened. In northern Cyprus it is among the most threatened orchid species, as its bulbs are digged out, dried and ground for the production of salep (Viney, 1994).

Hybrids

With *Serapias bergonii* and *Orchis syriaca* (described as X*Orchiserapias dhiorii* M. & M. Ackermann between *Orchis syriaca* and *Serapias orientalis*).

Larnaka (Salt lake), 9.3.2002

Kayalar-Sadrazamköy, 14.3.2002

Kayalar-Kyrenia, 14.3.2002

Larnaka (Salt lake), 9.3.2002

Kayalar-Kyrenia, 14.3.2002

Larnaka (Salt lake), 9.3.2002

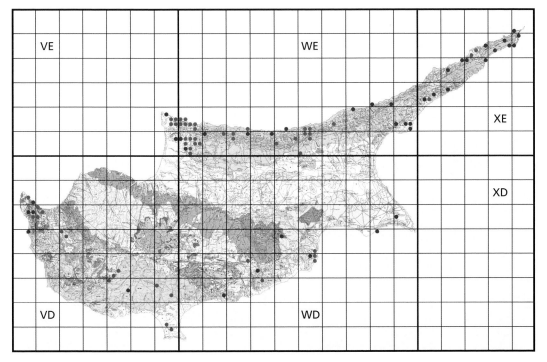

Serapias levantina

Serapias parviflora
Kleinblütiger Zungenständel

PARLATORE

Giorn. Sci. Sicilia 59 (175): 66 (1837)

Synonyme

Serapias occultata GAY ex CAVALIER, Note sur 2 Pl. de France (1848); *Serapias occultata* GAY ex WILLKOMM in WILLKOMM & LANGE, Prodr. Fl. Hispan. 1: 163 (1861), nom. illeg.; *Serapias parviflora* subsp. *occultata* (GAY ex CAVALIER) MAIRE & A. WEILLER, Fl. Afr. Nord 6: 322 (1959), comb. illeg.; *Serapias laxiflora* var. *parviflora* (PARLATORE) REICHENBACH fil., Icon. Fl. Germ. Helv. 13/14: 13 (1851); *Serapias elongata* TODARO, Hort. bot. panorm. 2: 25 (1879).

Beschreibung

Schlanke, mittelgroße, zierliche Pflanze, bis 30 cm hoch. Stängel relativ kräftig, hellgrün, im unteren Teil purpurn gestrichelt, im Bereich des Blütenstandes purpurn überlaufen. Laubblätter linealisch-lanzettlich bis lanzettlich, grün bis bläulichgrün, die unteren abstehend bis überhängend, die mittleren schräg aufrecht, häufig die Basis des Blütenstandes erreichend und violett überlaufen. Blütenstand locker- und armblütig, gewöhnlich eine bis zu 10 cm lange Ähre mit 3 bis 8 Blüten; Blüten sehr klein, schräg abstehend bis steil aufgerichtet. Brakteen breit-lanzettlich, kürzer als oder so lang wie der Sepalhelm, purpurn überlaufen. Perigonblätter lanzettlich, zugespitzt, genervt, helmförmig zusammenneigend, aussen rötlich bis graulila, innen purpurviolett, schräg aufwärts gerichtet. Lippe sehr kurz, stark zurückgeschlagen, zweigliedrig, mit 2 roten, parallelen Schwielen. Hypochil am Grund breit keilförmig, Seitenlappen aufrecht und kaum aus dem Sepalhelm hervortretend, braunrot. Epichil schmallanzettlich, braunrötlich bis gelblich, an der Basis nur schwach behaart bis kahl, herabhängend, zumeist stark nach unten oder rückwärts gerichtet. *Serapias parviflora* ist autogam, bereits im Knospenstadium ist der Fruchtknoten deutlich angeschwollen.

Standort

Ödland, lichte Pinienwälder und Straßenränder, seltener in grasiger, lockerer Phrygana; auf alkalischen bis sauren Böden.

Blütezeit

Von Mitte März bis Mitte (Ende) April.

Höhenverbreitung

Von der Küste bis 300 m.

Gesamtverbreitung

Das Verbreitungsgebiet von *Serapias parviflora* umfasst fast das ganze Mittelmeergebiet, nämlich von der Iberischen Halbinsel bis zu den Ägäischen Inseln. Die Art ist im Küstenbereich Kretas häufig, aber auf Rhodos selten. Erst in jüngerer Zeit wurde sie auch für Zypern nachgewiesen. Nach BIEL (1998) kommt *Serapias parviflora* auch auf Lesbos an zwei Standorten vor.

Verbreitung auf Zypern

Serapias parviflora ist auf Zypern sehr selten. Aktuelle Standorte der Art befinden sich vor allem auf der Halbinsel Akrotiri im Süden, wo sie bevorzugt in lichten Kiefernwäldern und in mäßig feuchten Wiesenflächen wächst. Im Norden wurde die Art 1992 in einem Pinienwald in der Umgebung von Çatalköy gefunden. Nachdem dieser Fundort vernichtet worden war, wurde *Serapias parviflora* in einer Feuchtwiese am Berg Kornos beobachtet (VINEY, 1994).

Bemerkungen

Vermutlich erbrachte NAGEL den Erstnachweis von *Serapias parviflora* für Zypern (HERTEL, 1984). 1984 fand er auf der Halbinsel Akrotiri *Serapias* Pflanzen, die dann von HERTEL (1984) zweifelsfrei als *Serapias parviflora* bestimmt wurden. Damals war dieser Fund insofern überraschend, als diese Art bisher niemals so weit östlich gefunden worden war, und sie erreicht damit noch heute auf Zypern ihre östliche Verbreitungsgrenze. KOHLMÜLLER (1990) und anderen Orchideenforscher berichten in ihren Standortangaben mehrfach über Funde von *Serapias parviflora* im Westen (Akamas) der Insel. Aus dieser Umgebung wurde 1990 von DELFORGE *Serapias aphroditae* beschrieben, eine Art die, auf den ersten Blick an *Serapias parviflora* erinnert (Blütengröße, spätere Blütezeit). Die von KOHLMÜLLER (l.s.) und von den anderen Orchideenforschern gefundenen Pflanzen sind höchstwahrscheinlich zu dieser neuen Sippe zu stellen. Auf Zypern erreicht die Art ihre östliche Verbreitungsgrenze. Dies wird wahrscheinlich der Grund dafür sein, dass die Pflanzen hier etwas vom Typus abweichen, wie zum Beispiel auch auf Rhodos oder Kreta. Die zypriotischen Pflanzen sind niederwüchsiger, haben weniger Blüten, und ihre Lippe ist meist etwas größer als bei der Nominatform. Auch NELSON (1968) weist darauf hin, dass *Serapias parviflora* im östlichen Teilareal relativ selten vorkommt und zwar "kaum in einer den westlichen Typus vollkommen erreichenden Form" (HANSEN, KREUTZ & U. & D. RÜCKBRODT, 1990).

Serapias parviflora gehört zu den später blühenden Orchideenarten Zyperns. Weil zu dieser Zeit wenig Orchideensucher auf Zypern unterwegs sind, wurde sie deswegen nur wenig beobachtet.

Gefährdung

Serapias parviflora ist auf Zypern sehr selten und wurde bis heute nur an wenigen Standorten nachgewiesen. Die Art ist deshalb als stark gefährdet einzustufen.

Hybriden

Keine Nachweise bekannt.

◀ Akrotiri (Moni Agios Nikolaos), 22.3.2002

Akrotiri (Moni Agios Nikolaos), 22.3.2002

Serapias parviflora

Small-Flowered Serapias

PARLATORE

Giorn. Sci. Sicilia 59 (175): 66 (1837)

Synonyms

Serapias occultata GAY ex CAVALIER, Note sur 2 Pl. de France (1848); *Serapias occultata* GAY ex WILLKOMM in WILLKOMM & LANGE, Prodr. Fl. Hispan. 1: 163 (1861), nom. illeg.; *Serapias parviflora* subsp. *occultata* (GAY ex CAVALIER) MAIRE & A. WEILLER, Fl. Afr. Nord 6: 322 (1959), comb. illeg.; *Serapias laxiflora* var. *parviflora* (PARLATORE) REICHENBACH fil., Icon. Fl. Germ. Helv. 13/14: 13 (1851); *Serapias elongata* TODARO, Hort. bot. panorm. 2: 25 (1879).

Description

Slender, medium-sized, delicate plant, up to 30 cm tall. Stem relatively vigorous, light green, with purple streaks in lower part, purple tinged near inflorescence. Foliage leaves linear-lanceolate to lanceolate, green to bluish green, lower leaves spreading to pendant, the central leaves obliquely erect, often reaching base of spike and with violet tinges. Inflorescence lax and few-flowered, normally one, up to a 10 cm long spike with 3 to 8 flowers; flowers very small, spreading obliquely. Bracts broadly lanceolate, shorter than or as long as hood, with purple tinges. Perianth segments lanceolate, acuminate, veined, connivent to forming a hood, exterior reddish to grey-lilac, interior purple-violet, sharply to obliquely directed upwards. Labellum very short, strongly reflexed, two-lobed, with two red, parallel ridges. Hypochile widely wedge-shaped at base, lateral lobes erect and hardly projecting from hood, brown-red. Epichile narrowly lanceolate, brown-reddish to yellowish, weakly hairy to almost glabrous at base, pendant, usually pointing strongly downwards or backwards. *Serapias parviflora* is autogamous, the ovary already clearly swollen at the bud stage.

Habitat

Wasteland, pine woods and roadside margins, rarely in grassy, light phrygana; on alkaline to acidic soils.

Flowering time

From mid-March to mid- (late) April.

Altitude distribution

From sea level to 300 m.

Overall distribution

The distribution area of *Serapias parviflora* covers almost the entire Mediterranean region, namely from the Iberian Peninsula to the Aegean islands. The species is abundant in the coastal areas of Crete, but rare on Rhodes, and only recently identified on Cyprus. According to BIEL (1998), *Serapias parviflora* also occurs in two habitats on Lesbos.

Distribution on Cyprus

Serapias parviflora is very rare on Cyprus. Recent sites for the species can mainly be found on the Akrotiri peninsula in the south, where it favours light coniferous woods and moderately moist meadows. The species was found in 1992 in a pine forest near Çatalköy in the north. After this site was destroyed, *Serapias parviflora* was found in a marsh at Mount Kornos (VINEY, 1994).

Remarks

NAGEL was probably the first person who brought forward evidence for *Serapias parviflora* on Cyprus (HERTEL, 1984). NAGEL found *Serapias* plants in 1984 on the Akrotiri peninsula, which were identified by HERTEL (1984) without a doubt as *Serapias parviflora*. At the time this finding was surprising in that this species had never been found this far east, and it now has its easternmost distribution boundary on Cyprus. KOHLMÜLLER (1990) and other orchid searchers reported in their site descriptions several findings of *Serapias parviflora* in the western part of the island (Akamas). DELFORGE described *Serapias aphroditae* in 1990 from this area, a species which resembles *Serapias parviflora* at first glance (flower size, later flowering time). The plants found by KOHLMÜLLER (l.s.) and from the other orchid searchers can surely be listed under this new taxon.

Serapias parviflora can be recognized by its short and lax-flowered inflorescence, of which the flowers are very small, arranged more or less closely to the axis and directed upwards. Other typical characteristics are the very short, strongly reflexed epichile, and the purple streaks on the base of the stem. The most important characteristic of *Serapias parviflora* is however the autogamy of the species. At the bud stage, the ovary is already clearly swollen.

The species reaches its easternmost distribution boundary on Cyprus. This is probably the reason why these plants differ little from the normal type, as for example on Rhodes or Crete. Compared with the nominate species the Cypriot plants are more compact, have fewer flowers, and the labellum is usually slightly larger. NELSON (1968) notes that *Serapias parviflora* is relatively rare in its eastern distribution area and "hardly in a shape that conforms with the western normal type" (HANSEN, KREUTZ & U. & D. RÜCKBRODT, 1990).

Serapias parviflora is among the later flowering orchid species of Cyprus. As there are few orchid seekers on Cyprus at that time, it has been found only a few times.

Threats

Serapias parviflora is very rare on Cyprus and has been found at only a few sites up to now. The species can therefore be categorized as heavily threatened.

Hybrids

No known proof.

Akrotiri (Moni Agios Nikolaos), 22.3.2002

Akrotiri (Moni Agios Nikolaos), 22.3.2002

Akrotiri (Moni Agios Nikolaos), 22.3.2002

Akrotiri (Moni Agios Nikolaos), 22.3.2002

Akrotiri (Moni Agios Nikolaos), 22.3.2002   Akrotiri (Moni Agios Nikolaos), 22.3.2002

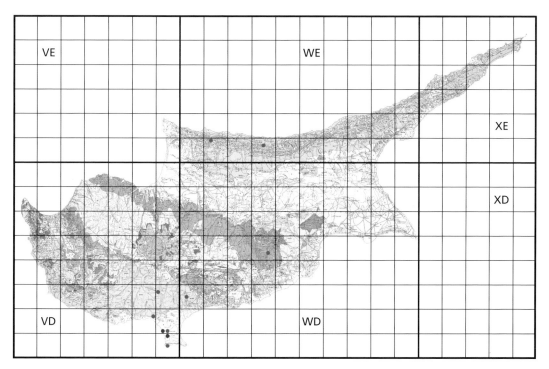

10 Meldungen / Reports

Serapias parviflora

52 Spiranthes spiralis
Herbst-Drehwurz

(L.) CHEVALLIER

Fl. Gén. Env. Paris ed. 1, 2 (1): 330 (1827)

Basionym

Ophrys spiralis L., Sp. Pl. 2: 945 (1753).

Synonyme

Neottia spiralis (L.) WILLDENOW, Sp. Pl. ed. 4, 4 (1): 73 (1805); *Ophrys autumnalis* BALBIS, Elenco: 96 (1801); *Spiranthes autumnalis* L.C.M. RICHARD, De Orchid. Eur.: 37 (1817), nom. illeg.

Beschreibung

Sehr schlanke Pflanze, 10 bis 30 cm hoch. Stängel aufrecht, hell- bis dunkelgrün, stark weisslich drüsig behaart. Laubblätter in einer Grundrosette, eiförmig bis elliptisch, bläulich- bis dunkelgrün, ungefleckt. Die Rosette des nächsten Jahres wird während der Blütezeit direkt neben der diesjährigen Pflanze entwickelt und überwintert. Blütenstand lang, dicht- und reichblütig. Tragblätter schmal-lanzettlich, lang zugespitzt, grün, schräg aufwärts gerichtet, länger als der Fruchtknoten. Blüten sehr klein, spiralförmig bis einseitswendig am Stängel angeordnet, horizontal abstehend, überwiegend grünlichweiss bis weiss. Perigonblätter aussen drüsig behaart. Sepalen länglich-lanzettlich bis eiförmig-lanzettlich, die beiden seitlichen meist waagerecht abstehend, das mittlere mit den Petalen röhrig zusammenneigend. Petalen länglich-lanzettlich. Lippe grünlichweiss bis gelblichgrün, innen (hell)grün, der Vorderteil an den Rändern gekerbt und nach unten gebogen. Sporn fehlt.

Standort

Lichte Kiefernwälder (bevorzugt grasige Stellen in *Pinus brutia*-Wälder), Macchien, offene Phrygana und beweidetes Ödland; auf basischen bis leicht sauren, frischen, etwas feuchten, lehmigen Böden.

Blütezeit

Mitte Oktober bis Mitte Dezember.

Höhenverbreitung

Von Meereshöhe bis 800 m.

Gesamtverbreitung

Mit Ausnahme des Nordens fast in ganz Europa verbreitet. Nördlich bis Nordirland, Zentral-England, Dänemark und Nordpolen. Auch in Nordafrika und Kleinasien; östlich bis zum Kaukasus und bis zum Nordiran. Auch auf Zypern.

Verbreitung auf Zypern

Im Norden schwerpunktmäßig bei Tepebaşi, Alsançak, Kyrenia und Karaağac, Im Süden vor allem bei Polis, Akrotiri-Halbinsel, in den Wäldern bei Pegeia, Larnaka-Salzsee und Akamas-Halbinsel.

Bemerkungen

Die am Boden angedrückten, glänzenden Blattrosetten sind im Gelände auch im Frühjahr eindeutig und leicht zu erkennen. Die Rosetten sind meist leicht zu finden, weil sie viel größer sind als bei den mitteleuropäischen Pflanzen und, weil sie fast immer ohne Konkurrenz anderer Pflanzen im nackten Boden wachsen. Sie bevorzugen dabei mäßig feuchte Stellen in der Phrygana oder in lichten Kiefernwäldern.

Die Art ist in Südeuropa weit verbreitet und stellenweise häufig. Im Mittelmeerraum sind die Pflanzen überwiegend deutlich höher und die Blüten meist zierlicher als die mitteleuropäischen Pflanzen. Die Blütenstände erreichen oft eine Länge von 15 cm mit mehreren Dutzend Blüten. Ausserdem sind die Blüten größer, und die beiden seitlichen Sepalen stehen meist (auf Zypern eher selten) waagerecht ab (KREUTZ, 1994).

Spiranthes spiralis blüht im Mittelmeerraum deutlich später als in Mitteleuropa. KRETZSCHMAR (1995) konnte die spätere Blütezeit bestätigen. Er fand auf Zypern Anfang bis Mitte Februar kräftige Rosetten mit Fruchtständen, die noch völlig grün waren. Nach Angaben von KULYEV (schriftl. Mittlg, 2002) und Bildmaterial verschiedener Orchideenfreunde blüht die Art tatsächlich sehr spät, nämlich von Ende Oktober bis Mitte Dezember. Es ist bemerkenswert, dass die Blütentriebe von *Spiranthes spiralis* auf Zypern meist vor der Regenperiode im Winter erscheinen. Mit der Blüte von *Spiranthes spiralis* schließt das Orchideenjahr auf Zypern ab. Etwas später, Mitte Januar fängt das Orchideenjahr mit der Blüte von *Orchis collina* wieder an!

Mit Sicherheit ist *Spiranthes spiralis* weiter verbreitet als auf der Verbreitungskarte angegeben. Obwohl die Rosetten von *Spiranthes spiralis* schon im Frühjahr deutlich im Gelände zu erkennen sind, sind sie doch weit schwieriger zu finden als blühende Pflanzen. Zur Vervollständigung der Kartierung wären Besuche zur Blütezeit im Winter angebracht.

Gefährdung

Spiranthes spiralis ist auf Zypern nicht besonders selten und bildet an einigen Standorten Massenpopulationen. Die Art ist daher nicht gefährdet.

Hybriden

Nicht nachgewiesen.

400   Akrotiri (Salt lake), 23.10.1995   Akrotiri (Salt lake), 12.11.2002

Spiranthes spiralis

(L.) CHEVALLIER

Autumn Lady's-Tresses

Fl. Gén. Env. Paris ed. 1, 2 (1): 330 (1827)

Basionym

Ophrys spiralis L., Sp. Pl. 2: 945 (1753).

Synonyms

Neottia spiralis (L.) WILLDENOW, Sp. Pl. ed. 4, 4 (1): 73 (1805); *Ophrys autumnalis* BALBIS, Elenco: 96 (1801); *Spiranthes autumnalis* L.C.M. RICHARD, De Orchid. Eur.: 37 (1817), nom. illeg.

Description

Very delicate plant, 10 to 30 cm tall. Stem erect, light to dark green, covered in whitish pubescence. Foliage leaves forming a rosette at base, ovate to elliptical, bluish to dark green, unspotted. The rosette for the following year is formed during the flowering period directly adjacent to this year's plant, and is then dormant. Inflorescence long, dense and many-flowered. Bracts narrowly lanceolate, oblong acuminate, green, directed obliquely upwards, longer than ovary. Flowers very small, arranged spirally to secund along stem, spreading horizontally, mainly greenish white to white. Perianth segments covered with pubescence on the exterior. Sepals oblong-lanceolate to ovate-lanceolate, both lateral sepals usually spreading horizontally, dorsal sepal connivent to forming a tube with petals. Petals oblong-lanceolate. Labellum greenish white to yellowish white, interior (light) green, margins of epichile grooved and bent downwards. Spur absent.

Habitat

Light coniferous woods (favours grassy places in *Pinus brutia* woods), maquis, open phrygana and cultivated wasteland; on basic to slightly acidic, fresh, slightly moist, loamy soils.

Flowering time

Mid-October mid-December.

Altitude distribution

From sea level to 800 m.

Overall distribution

Distributed through almost the whole of Europe, with the exception of the North. Northwards as far as Northern Ireland, central England, Denmark and northern Poland. Also in North Africa and Asia Minor; eastwards as far as the Caucasus and northern Iran. Also on Cyprus.

Distribution on Cyprus

In the north it has its focal point near Tepebaşi, Alsançak, Kyrenia and Karaağac. In the south, mainly near Polis, the Akrotiri peninsula, in the woods near Pegeia, the Larnaka salt lake and the Akamas peninsula.

Remarks

Its shiny foliage rosettes, which are close to the ground in the fields, can clearly and easily be identified, in spring also. The rosettes are easy to find, as they are much larger than Central European plants and because the species almost always grows without any competition from other plants in bare soil. It favours moderately moist places in phrygana or light coniferous woods.

The species is widely distributed and in some places abundant in southern Europe. In the Mediterranean region its plants are generally distinctly taller and its flowers mostly more delicate than the Central European plants. The spike often reaches a height of 15 cm with several dozen flowers. Furthermore, the flowers are larger and both lateral sepals usually (on Cyprus rather rare) spread horizontally (KREUTZ, 1994).

Spiranthes spiralis clearly blossoms later in the Mediterranean region than in Central Europe. KRETZSCHMAR (1995) could confirm the late flowering period. He found on Cyprus vigorous rosettes with stands of buds, which were still completely green in early to mid-February. According to reports made by KULYEV (written correspondence, 2002) and according to photographic material from various orchid friends, the species does indeed bloom very late, namely from late October to mid-December. It is remarkable that the buds of *Spiranthes spiralis* on Cyprus usually appear before the rainy season in winter. The orchid year on Cyprus is concluded with the flowers of *Spiranthes spiralis*. A little bit later, the next orchid year commences with the flowers of *Orchis collina* in mid-January!

Spiranthes spiralis is almost certainly more widely distributed than indicated on the distribution map. Although the rosettes of *Spiranthes spiralis* can easily be recognized in the field in spring, they are still more difficult to find than plants in flower. To be able to chart it accurately, a visit during its flowering time in winter is advisable.

Threats

Spiranthes spiralis is not rare on Cyprus and at some sites it creates mass populations. The species is therefore not particularly threatened.

Hybrids

Unidentified.

Akrotiri (Salt lake), 12.11.2002

Pegeia (Akamas), 28.10.2002

Pegeia (Akamas), 28.10.2002

Pegeia (Akamas), 28.10.2002

Akrotiri (Salt lake), 12.11.2002   Akrotiri (Salt lake), 12.11.2002

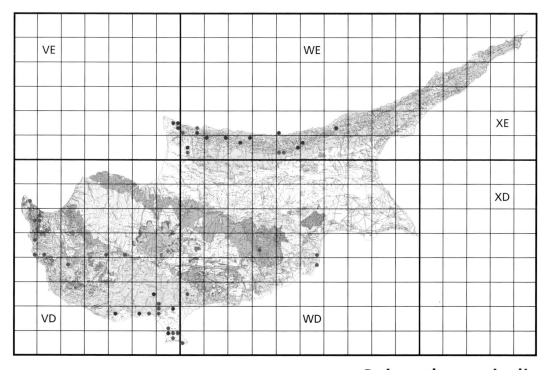

VE   WE

XE

XD

VD   WD

64 Meldungen / Reports

Spiranthes spiralis

Orchis italica x *Orchis punctulata* (*Orchis xtochniana* KREUTZ & P. SCRATON), Tochni, 13.3.2002

Hybriden

Wo immer Arten der selben Gattung oder Arten nahe verwandter Gattungen eng benachbart vorkommen, die nicht durch ihre Blütezeit getrennt sind, kann man mit Hybriden rechnen. Bevor man die Diagnose einer Hybridbildung stellt, sollte man stets überprüfen, ob man nicht statt eines Hybrids nur eine stark abweichende Variante einer Art vor sich hat (BUTTLER, 1986).

Hybriden treten meist als Einzelpflanzen auf und sind dann von den anderen Orchideenarten meist gut zu unterscheiden. In wenigen Fällen gibt es völlig stabilisierte Hybridpopulationen, die einen eigenständigen Eindruck erwecken und ein relativ großes Areal besiedeln, wobei eine oder sogar beide Elternarten völlig verschwunden sein können (BAUMANN & KÜNKELE, 1982a). Derartige Hybridpopulationen wurden manchmal als neue Art (pro hybr.) beschrieben.

Im Gegensatz etwa zu Rhodos oder zur Türkei ist die Bestimmung der meisten Arten auf Zypern unproblematisch, ja sogar einfach. Das ist auch der Grund dafür, dass viele zypriotischen Hybriden meist problemlos zu bestimmen sind. Nur bei den Hybriden der Arten des *Ophrys sphegodes-mammosa* Formenkreises und bei der Gattung *Serapias* gibt es manchmal Bestimmungsprobleme.

Es ist unmöglich, alle von Zypern gemeldeten Hybriden vorzustellen. Daher werden in diesem Buch beispielhaft nur einige besonders schöne und seltene Hybriden abgebildet.

Hybrids

Wherever species of the same complex or species of closely related taxa occur together, and are not separated by their flowering periods, one can count on hybrids. Before hybridization can be diagnosed, one should always verify whether the specimen considered is a hybrid and not a greatly differing variety (BUTTLER, 1986).

Hybrids usually occur as solitary plants and can therefore easily be distinguished from other orchid species. Sometimes totally stabilized hybrid populations can be found that populate a relatively large habitat and give the impression of being an independent species, where one of the parent species has completely disappeared, or even both of them (BAUMANN & KÜNKELE, 1982a). These hybrid populations have often been described as a new species (pro hybr.).

In contrast to, for instance Rhodes or Turkey, the identification of most species on Cyprus is without problem, or even easy. This is also the reason that many Cypriot hybrids can easily be identified. Only with hybrids of the species from the *Ophrys sphegodes-mammosa* group and the *Serapias* genus there are often problems with identification.

It is impossible to include all the hybrids that have been reported from Cyprus in this book. Therefore only a few exceptionally beautiful and rare hybrids have been illustrated here.

Ophrys bornmuelleri x *Ophrys levantina*; Esentepe, 18.3.2002

Ophrys attica x *Ophrys kotschyi,*
Akrotiri, 22.3.2002

Ophrys bornmuelleri x *Ophrys morio*
(*Ophrys* x*cailliauana* P. Delforge), Pegeia, 6.4.1989

Ophrys bornmuelleri x *Ophrys sicula*
(*Ophrys* x*jansenii* P. Delforge), Prastio, 4.4.1989

Ophrys kotschyi x *Ophrys mammosa*
(*Ophrys* x*kreutziana* P. Delforge), Pano Lefkara, 29.3.1989

Ophrys morio x *Ophrys sicula*
(*Ophrys xdemangeana* P. Delforge), Vavla, 29.3.1989

Orchis caspia x *Orchis syriaca* (*Orchis xchoirokitiana* Kreutz
& P. Scraton), Choirokoitia (Kalavasos dam), 14.3.2002

Orchis fragrans x *Orchis sancta* (*Orchis xkallithea* Klein),
Akrotiri, 25.3.2002

Serapias aphroditae x *Serapias bergonii*
(*Serapias xmastiana* P. Delforge), Polis, 5.4.1989

407

Literaturverzeichnis / Literature

ACKERMANN, M. & M. (1990): Fund der Gattungshybride *Orchis syriaca* x *Serapias orientalis* auf Nordzypern. Mitt. Bl. Arbeitskr. Heim. Orch. Baden-Württ. 22 (2): 332-336.

ASCHERSON, P.F. & K.O. GRAEBNER (1907): Synopsis der mitteleuropäischen Flora 3: 612-925.

BAEDEKER, K. (1999): Allianz Reiseführer Rhodos (GALENSCHOVSKI). Verlag K. Baedeker.

BAEDEKER, K. (2001): Allianz Reiseführer Zypern (FELTES-PETER). Verlag K. Baedeker.

BALTZINGER, E. (1982): Zypern und seine Orchideen, Bull. Assoc. Philom. Alsace Loraine 19: 65-70.

BARTOLO, G. & S. PULVIRENTI (1999). *Limodorum rubriflorum* (*Orchidaceae*): specie nuova del Mediterraneo orientale. Caesiana 12: 1-10.

BATEMAN, R. M. (2001): Evolution and classification of European orchids: insights from molecular and morphological characters. Jour. Eur. Orch. 33 (1): 33-119.

BATEMAN, R. M., A. M. PRIDGEON & M. W. CHASE (1997): Polygenetics of subtribe Orchidinae (Orchidoiceae, Orchidaceae) based on nuclear ITS sequences. 2. Infrageneric relationships and reclassification to achieve monophyly of *Orchis sensu stricto*. Lindleyana 12 (3): 113-141.

BAUMANN, H. (1986): Zur Polymorphie von *Orchis papilionacea* L. Jahresb. Naturwiss. Ver. Wuppertal 39: 87-97.

BAUMANN, H. (1987): Zur Taxonomie einiger orientalischer Orchideen. Mitt. Bl. Arbeitskr. Heim. Orch. Baden-Württ. 19 (1): 119-130.

BAUMANN, B. & H. (1991): Hybridogene Populationen zwischen *Orchis anatolica* BOISS. und *Orchis quadripunctata* CYR. ex TEN. in der Ostmediterraneis. Mitt. Bl. Arbeitskr. Heim. Orch. Baden-Württ. 23 (1): 203-242.

BAUMANN, B. & H. (2001): Zur Kenntnis der Orchideenflora der Cyrenaika (Libyen). Jour. Eur. Orch. 33 (2): 691-725.

BAUMANN, H & A. DAFNI (1981): Differenzierung und Arealform des *Ophrys omegaifera*-Komplexes im Mittelmeergebiet. Beih. Veröff. Naturschutz Landschaftspfl. Baden-Württemberg 19: 129-153.

BAUMANN, H. & G. HALX (1972): *Ophrys* – die Pflanze mit 'Sex'. Kosmos 68: 78-80.

BAUMANN, H. & S. KÜNKELE (1979): Das Optima-Projekt zur Kartierung mediterraner Orchideen. Mitt. Bl. Arbeitskr. Heim. Orch. Baden-Württ. 11 (1): 12-53.

BAUMANN, H. & S. KÜNKELE (1981a): *Ophrys umbilicata* DESF. – eine gute, aber falsch interpretierte *Ophrys*-Art aus dem östlichen Mittelmeergebiet. Mitt. Bl. Arbeitskr. Heim. Orch. Baden-Württ. 13 (3): 285-310.

BAUMANN, H. & S. KÜNKELE (1981b): Beiträge zur Taxonomie europäischer Orchideenarten. Mitt. Bl. Arbeitskr. Heim. Orch. Baden-Württ. 13 (3): 337-373.

BAUMANN, H. & S. KÜNKELE (1982a): Die wildwachsenden Orchideen Europas. Kosmos Naturführer, Franckh'sche Verlagshandlung, Stuttgart.

BAUMANN, H. & S. KÜNKELE (1982b): Beiträge zur Taxonomie von *Ophrys oestrifera* M.-BIEB und *Ophrys scolopax* Cav. Mitt. Bl. Arbeitskr. Heim. Orch. Baden-Württ. 14 (2): 204-240.

BAUMANN, H. & S. KÜNKELE (1983): Beiträge zur Taxonomie europäischer und orientalischer Orchideen. Jahresb. Naturwiss. Ver. Wuppertal 36: 12-16.

BAUMANN, H. & S. KÜNKELE (1986): Die Gattung *Ophrys* L. eine taxonomische Übersicht. Mitt. Bl. Arbeitskr. Heim. Orch. Baden-Württ. 18 (3): 305-688.

BAUMANN, H. & S. KÜNKELE (1988a): Die Orchideen Europas. Kosmos Naturführer, Franckh'sche Verlagshandlung, Stuttgart.

BAUMANN, H. & S. KÜNKELE (1988b): Neue Beiträge zur Taxonomie europäischer und mediterraner Orchideen. Mitt. Bl. Arbeitskr. Heim. Orch. Baden-Württ. 20 (3): 610-651.

BAUMANN, H. & S. KÜNKELE (1989): Die Gattung *Serapias* L. – eine taxonomische Übersicht. Mitt. Bl. Arbeitskr. Heim. Orch. Baden-Württ. 21 (3): 701-946.

BAUMANN, H. & S. KÜNKELE (1994): *Ophrys kotschyi* H. FLEISCHMANN & SOÓ, eine gefährdete und endemische Orchidee von Zypern. Jour. Eur. Orch. 26 (3/4): 317-364.

BAUMANN, H., S. KÜNKELE & R. LORENZ (2002): Taxonomische Liste der Orchideen Deutschlands. – Jour. Eur. Orch. 34 (1): 129-206.

BAUMBACH, N. (2003): Orchideen auf der Akamas-Halbinsel in Zypern – ein Osterspaziergang. Die Orchidee 54 (2): 189-192.

BAYER, M. (1982): Anleitung zur Praxis der Orchideen-Kartierung. Mitt. Bl. Arbeitskr. Heim. Orch. Baden-Württ. 14 (1): 125-137.

BECHTEL, H. (1980). Wie wär's mit Rhodos im April? Kosmos 76 (12): 927-935.

BERGEL, G. (1987): Transkaukasische Ragwurzbeobachtungen. Die Orchidee 38: 187-191.

BIEL, B (1998): Die Orchideenflora der Insel Lesvos (Griechenland). Jour. Eur. Orch. 30 (2): 251-443.

BOG, E. (2002): Atavistische *Ophrys fusca* in Nordzypern. Ber. Arbeitskr. Heim. Orch. 18 (2): 126.

BOISSIER, E. (1884): Flora Orientalis 5: 51-94 (Orchidaceae). Genevae & Basileae.

BORNMÜLLER, J. F. N. (1898): Ein Beitrag zur Kenntnis der Flora von Syrien und Palästina. Verh. Zool.-bot. Ges. Wien 48: 635.

BORNMÜLLER, J. F. N. (1917): Zur Flora des nördlichen Syriens. Notizbl. Königl. Bot. Gart. Mus. Berlin-Dahlem 63: 1-44.

BOURNÉRIAS, M. *et al.* (2002): Les Orchidées de France, Belgique et Luxembourg. Societé Française d'Orchidophilie, Paris.

BREINER, E. & R. BREINER (1979a): Beiträge zur Orchideenflora von Zypern. Ber. Naturwiss. Ver. Schwaben, 83 (3/4): 52-63.

BREINER, R. (1979b): pH-Messungen an Orchideen-Standorten auf Kreta und Zypern. Mitt. Bl. Arbeitskr. Heim. Orch. Baden-Württ. 11 (3): 54-58.

BREINER, E. & R. (1982): Orchidées de Chypre. Orchidées d'Europe, 5. Colloque d'automne, Paris 28 et 29 novembre 1981. Société Française d'Orchidophile, Paris.

BREINER, E. & R. (1989): Beiträge zur Orchideenflora von Zypern-Nordzypern. Ber. Naturwiss. Ver. Schwaben 93 (4): 82-91.

BRUMMITT, R.K. & C. E. POWELL (1992): Authors of Plant Names. Royal Botanic Gardens, Kew.

BUTTLER, K.P. (1983): Die *Ophrys-ciliata* (*speculum*)-Gruppe, eine Neubewertung (Orchidaceae: Orchideae). Jahresb. Naturwiss. Ver. Wuppertal 36: 37-57.

BUTTLER, K.P. (1986): Orchideen. Die wildwachsenden Arten und Unterarten Europas, Vorderasiens und Nordafrikas. Steinbachs Naturführer, Mosaik Verlag München.

BUTTLER, K.P. (1991): Field Guide to Orchids of Britain and Europe. The species and subspecies growing wild in Europe, the Near East and North Africa with drawings by the author. The Crowood Press, Swindon.

CAMUS, E.G. (1894): Monographie des Orchidées de France. Journal de Botanique, Paris.

CAMUS, E.G., P. BERGON & A. CAMUS (1908): Monographie des Orchidées de l'Europe, de l'Afrique septentrionale, de l'Asie Mineure et des provinces russes transcaspiennes. Paris.

CAMUS, E.G. & A. CAMUS (1921-1928): Iconographie des Orchidées d'Europe et du Bassin Méditerranéen. Paris.

CHRISTOFIDES, Y. (2001): The Orchids of Cyprus. Platres, Cyprus.

CINGEL, N.A., VAN DER (1997): *Ophrys reinholdii* (ssp. *straussii*) op Cyprus, een uitbreiding van het bekende areaal. Eurorchis 9: 81-82.

CZERNIAKOWSKA, E.G. (1923): Fragmenta florae Transcaspiae II. De generis Ophrydis specie nova ex Turkestania. Not. Syst. Herb. Horti Bot. Petrop. 4 (1): 1-4.

DAFNI, A. (1973): Analytical key to the Orchids of Israel. Teva Váaretz 16.

DAFNI, A. (1979): Orchids of Israel: Notes on distribution, local variation and ecology. Mitt. Bl. Arbeitskr. Heim. Orch. Baden-Württ. 11 (2): 206-222.

DAFNI, A. (1981): Orchids of Israel. Massada LTD. Israel.

DAFNI, A., TALMOM, Y. & Y. GERTMAN (1987): Updated list of the orchids of Israel. Israel J. Bot., 36: 145-157.

DANDY, J.E. (1967): Index of generic names of Vascular Plants: 1753-1774, British Museum (Natural History), Utrecht.

DAVIES, P.H. (1965): Cyprus and its orchids. Orchid Rev. 103: 116-123, 203-205.

DAVIES, P.H., J.A. DAVIES & A. HUXLEY (1983): Wild Orchids of Britain and Europe. Chatto & Windus, The Hogarth Press, London.

DAVIS, S. (1951). Orchids of Cyprus. Amer. Orchid Soc. Bull. 20: 33-34.

DAVIS, S. (1959). Orchids of Cyprus. Orchid Journal 3: 161-164.

DAVIS, P.H. (1965): Introduction. In: P.H. DAVIS: Flora of Turkey and the East Aegean Islands 1: 1-28. Edinburgh.

DAVIS, P.H., R.R. MILL & K. TAN (1988): Supplement. In: P.H. DAVIS: Flora of Turkey and the East Aegean Islands 10: 288-289. University Press, Edinburgh.

DE LANGHE, J.E. & R. D'HOSE (1982): Les orchidées de Chypre. Prospections faites en 1980 et 1981 dans la partie sud-ouest de l'île. Bull. Soc. Roy. Bot. Belg. 115: 297-311.

DELFORGE, P. (1990): Contribution à la connaissance des orchidées du sud-ouest de Chypre et remarques sur quelques espèces méditerranéennes. Les Naturalistes Belges 71 (3): 103-144.

DELFORGE, P. (1992): Contribution à l'étude de trois espèces d'Ophrys récemment décrites: Ophrys cephalonica, Ophrys herae et Ophrys minoa (Orchidaceae). Les Naturalistes Belges 73 (6): 71-105.

DELFORGE, P. (1993): Nouvelles observations sur Ophrys herae (Orchidaceae). Les Naturalistes Belges 74 (6): 107-112.

DELFORGE, P. (1994): Guide des Orchidées d'Europe, d'Afrique du Nord et du Proche-Orient. Delachaux et Niestlé S. A. Lausanne (Switzerland).

DELFORGE, P. (1995a): Orchids of Britain & Europe. Collins Guide. Harper Collins Publishers. London.

DELFORGE, P. (1995b): Les Orchidées des îles de Paros et Antiparos (Cyclades, Grèce). Observations, cartographie et description d'Ophrys parosica, une nouvelle espèce du sous-groupe d'Ophrys fusca. Les Naturalistes Belges (Orchidées 8) 76 (3): 144-221.

DELFORGE, P. (2000): Contribution a la connaissance des Ophrys apparemment intermédiaires entre Ophrys fusca et O. lutea en Sicile. Les Naturalistes Belges (Orchidées 13) 81 (3): 237-256.

DELFORGE, P. (2001): Guide des Orchidées d'Europe, d'Afrique du Nord et du Proche-Orient. 2e édition, entierement revue et corrigée. Delachaux et Niestlé S. A. Lausanne (Switzerland).

DELFORGE, P., J. DEVILLERS-TERSCHUREN & P. DEVILLERS (1991): Contributions taxonomiques et nomenclaturales aux Orchidées d'Europe (Orchidaceae). Les Naturalistes Belges 72 (3): 99-101.

DESFONTAINES, R.L. (1807): Ann. Mus. Hist. Nat. Paris 10: 222.

DEVILLERS, P. & J. DEVILLERS-TERSCHUREN (1994): Essai d'analyse systématique du genre Ophrys. Les Naturalistes Belges 75, hors-série special 'Orchidées' 7, supplement: 273-400.

DEVILLERS, P. & J. DEVILLERS-TERSCHUREN (2000a): Observation sur les Ophrys du groupe d'Ophrys subfusca en Tunisie. Les Naturalistes Belges (Orchidées 13) 81 (3): 283-297.

DEVILLERS, P. & J. DEVILLERS-TERSCHUREN (2000b): Notes phylogénétiques sur quelques Ophrys du complexe d'Ophrys fusca s.l. en Méditerranée centrale. Les Naturalistes Belges (Orchidées 13) 81 (3): 298-322.

DEVILLERS, P., J. DEVILLERS-TERSCHUREN & D. TYTECA (2003): Notes on some of the taxa comprising the group of Ophrys tenthredinifera WILLDENOW. Jour. Eur. Orch. 35 (1): 109-162.

DOSTMANN, H. & W. STERN (1996): Neufunde von Ophrys kotschyi im Akamas (Zypern). Ber. Arbeitskr. Heim. Orch. 13 (2): 28-30.

ENGEL, R., P. JACQUET & P. QUENTIN (1997): Combinaisons nouvelles pour les Orchidaceae de la Flore de France. l'Orchidophile 28 (127): 133-134.

FAURHOLDT, N. (2003): Notes on the genus Ophrys in Cyprus and Israel. Jour. Eur. Orch. 35 (4): 739-749.

FEINBRUN, N. (1944/1945): Materials for a rivised flora of Palestine. Proc. Linn. Soc. London 157 (1): 48-53.

FEINBRUN-DOTHAN, N. (1986): In Flora Palaestina 4: 375-396; plates 497-525. Jerusalem.

FLEISCHMANN, H. (1923): Neue Ophrys-Arten aus Asien. Ann. Naturhist. Museum Wien 36: 7-14.

FOELSCHE. G. & W. (2002): Ophrys corsica und Orchis corsica, zwei zu Unrecht vergessene Namen. Jour. Eur. Orch. 34 (4): 823-885.

FORST, H. & U. (1995): Beobachtungen zu Ophrys mammosa und Ophrys transbyrcana auf Nordzypern. Ber. Arbeitskr. Heim. Orch. 12 (1): 63-64.

GALAN CELA, P. & R. GAMARRA (2002): Checklist of the Iberian and Balearic Orchids-1. Aceras R. BR. – Nigritella RICH. Anales Jard. Bot. Madrid 59 (2): 187-208, 2002.

GALAN CELA, P. & R. GAMARRA (2002): Checklist of the Iberian and Balearic Orchids-2. Ophrys L. – Spiranthes RICH. Anales Jard. Bot. Madrid 60 (2): 309-329, 2003.

GEORGIADES, C. (1998a): Orchids of Cyprus (Fieldguide). Lefkosia – Cyprus.

GEORGIADES, C. (1998b): Orchids of Cyprus (Reference book). Lefkosia – Cyprus.

GODFERY, M.J. (1917): The genus Ophrys. Jour. Bot. 55: 329-332. London.

GÖLZ, P. & H.R. REINHARD (1977): Statistische Untersuchungen über einige Arten der Gattung Serapias. Die Orchidee 28 (3): 108-116.

GÖLZ, P. & H.R. REINHARD (1980): Serapias (Orchidaceae). Ergebnisse statistischer und chorologischer Untersuchungen. Mitt. Bl. Arbeitskr. Heim. Orch. Baden-Württ. 12 (3): 123-189.

GÖLZ, P. & H.R. REINHARD (1985): Statistische Untersuchungen an Ophrys bornmuelleri M. Schulze und Ophrys kotschyi H. Fleischmann & Soó. Mitt. Bl. Arbeitskr. Heim. Orch. Baden-Württ. 17 (3): 446-491.

GÖLZ, P. & H.R. REINHARD (1989): Über einige Besonderheiten im ostmediterranen Ophrys scolopax-Komplex. Mitt. Bl. Arbeitskr. Heim. Orch. Baden-Württ. 21 (4): 1040-1067.

GÖLZ, P. & H.R. REINHARD (1993): Serapias-Probleme unter besonderer Berücksichtigung der Serapias-Flora der Insel Kerkira (Korfu) 1. Mitt. Bl. Arbeitskr. Heim. Orch. Baden-Württ. 25 (1): 1-58.

GÖLZ, P. & H.R. REINHARD (1994): Serapias-Probleme unter besonderer Berücksichtigung der Serapias-Flora der Insel Kerkira (Korfu), ergänzt durch Untersuchungen an der Serapias-Flora Zyperns 2. Jour. Eur. Orch. 26 (3/4): 365-425.

GUMPRECHT, R. (1964): Ophrys-Studien auf Cypern. Jahresber. Naturwiss. Ver. Wuppertal 19: 36-38.

HÁGSATER, E & V. DUMONT (1996): Orchids. Status Survey and Conservation Action Plan. IUCN/SSC Orchid Specialist Group. Gland, Switzerland & Cambridge, UK.

HANSEN, R.-B., C.A.J. KREUTZ & U. & D. RÜCKBRODT (1990): Beitrag zur Kenntnis und Verbreitung der Orchideenflora von Zypern mit Interims-Verbreitungskarten. Mitt. Bl. Arbeitskr. Heim. Orch. Baden-Württ. 22 (1): 73-171.

HANSSON, S. (2001): *Ophrys aegaea* auf Zypern. Jour. Eur. Orch. 33 (3): 925.

HAUTZINGER, L. (1978): Genus *Orchis* L. (Orchidaceae); Sectio *Robustocalcare* Hautz. Ann. Naturhist. Mus. Wien 81: 1-73. Wien.

HENNECKE, G. & M. (2002): Orchideen in Israel. Jour. Eur. Orch. 34 (1): 97-114.

HERMJACOB, G. (1969): Orchideen-Urlaub auf Cypern. Kosmos 65: 195-198.

HERMJACOB, G. (1974): Orchids of Greece and Cyprus. Goulandris Museum Kiffisia.

HERTEL, H. (1984): *Serapias parviflora* auf Zypern. Ber. Arbeitskr. Heim. Orch. 1(2): 166.

HERVOUET, J.-M. (1984): *Ophrys bornmuelleri* à Rhodos. l'Orchidophile 15 (64): 710.

HIRTH, M. (2002): Zur Systematik einiger *Ophrys*-Arten aus dem *sphegodes-mammosa*-Kompex von Kerkira (Korfu) und NW Griechenland. Jahresber. Naturwiss. Ver. Wuppertal 55: 163-188.

HIRTH, M. & H. SPAETH (1992): Zur Orchideenflora von Samos. Mitt. Bl. Arbeitskr. Heim. Orch. Baden-Württ. 24(1): 1-51.

HOLMBOE, J. (1914): Studies on the vegetation of Cyprus: 56-57. Bergens Museums Skrifter, Bergen.

HUBBARD, J. & SCRATON, P. (2001): The Orchids of Cyprus and where to find them. Published by the authors.

JANSEN, H. (1985). Zwei neue Ophrys-Bastarde aus Cypern. Ber. Arbeitskrs. Heim. Orch. 2 (2): 101-105.

JARVIS, J.E., F.R. BARRIE, D.M. ALLEN & J.L. REVEAL (1993): A List of Linnaean Generic Names and their Types. Koeltz Scientific Books, Königstein.

JOUANDOUDET, F. (2004): A la découverté des Orchidées sauvages d'Aquitane. Parthénope Collection Biotope.

KAJAN, E. (1984): Zypern – Insel der Orchideen. Ber. Arbeitskr. Heim. Orch. 1 (2): 161-163.

KALTEISEN, M. & H.R. REINHARD (1987): Zwei neue *Ophrys*-Taxa (Orchidaceae) aus dem Ägäischen Archipel. Mitt. Bl. Arbeitskr. Heim. Orch. Baden-Württ. 19 (4): 895-938.

KELLER, G. & R. SCHLECHTER (1928): Monographie und Iconographie der Orchideen Europas und des Mittelmeergebietes. Bd. 1: Monographie der Gattungen und Arten (mit Blüten-analysen). Repert. Spec. Nov. Regni Veg., Sonderbeiheft A. Dahlem bei Berlin.

KELLER, G., R. SCHLECHTER & R. VON SOÓ (1930-1940): Monographie und Iconographie der Orchideen Europas und des Mittelmeergebietes. Bd. 2: Kritische Monographie, enthaltend die Beschreibung der Arten und Unterarten, Rassen, Varietäten, Formen und Bastarde, nebst Literaturangaben und biologischen Anmerkungen. Repert. Spec. Nov. Regni Veg., Sonderbeiheft A. Dahlem bei Berlin.

KLEIN, E. (1973): *Orchis sancta* x *Orchis coriophora* L. ssp. *fragrans* (Poll.) Camus, die erste intragenerische Hybride der Sektion *Coriophora* Parlet. Die Orchidee 24 (5): 209-211.

KOHLMÜLLER, R. (1990): Interessante Entdeckungen während einer Zypernreise Ostern 1989. Mitt. Bl. Arbeitskr. Heim. Orch. Baden-Württ. 22 (4): 808-817.

KRETZSCHMAR, G. & H. (1995): Zum Beginn der Blütezeit von Orchideen auf Zypern. Ber. Arbeitskrs. Heim. Orch. 12 (1): 65-68.

KRETZSCHMAR, G. & H. (1996): Orchideen der Insel Naxos. Ber. Arbeitskrs. Heim. Orch. 13 (1): 4-30.

KRETZSCHMAR, H. & G. & W. ECCARIUS (2004): Orchideen Kreta & Dodekanes. Die Orchideenflora der Inseln Kreta, Kasos, Karpathos und Rhodos. Mediterraneo Editions, Rythmno Crete.

KREUTZ, C.A.J. (1985a): Bijdrage tot de kennis van de verspreiding en beschrijving van de orchideeën op Cyprus (Griekse gedeelte) 1. Orchideeën 47 (2): 42-48.

KREUTZ, C.A.J. (1985b): Bijdrage tot de kennis van de verspreiding en beschrijving van de orchideeën op Cyprus (Griekse gedeelte) 2. Orchideeën 47 (4): 127-132.

KREUTZ, C.A.J. (1993): Orchideeën in Israël. Eurorchis 5: 7-36.

KREUTZ, C.A.J. (1994): Sierlijke bloeiwijzen bij mediterrane exemplaren van *Spiranthes spiralis* Chevall. Eurorchis 6: 79-80.

KREUTZ, C.A.J. (1997): *Ophrys rhodia* (H. Baumann & Künkele) P. Delforge in Israel?! Ber. Arbeitskrs. Heim. Orch. 14 (1): 69-74.

KREUTZ, C.A.J. (1998): Die Orchideen der Türkei. Selbstverlag. Landgraaf & Raalte.

KREUTZ, C.A.J. (2001): Orchidaceae. In: A. GÜBER, N. ÖZHATAY & T. BASER, Flora of Turkey and the East Aegean Islands – Volume 11. Edinburgh University Press.

KREUTZ, C.A.J. (2002): Die Orchideen von Rhodos und Karpathos/The orchids of Rhodes and Karpathos. Selbstverlag B.J. Seckel & C.A.J. Kreutz.

KREUTZ, C.A.J. & R. PETER (1998): Untersuchungen an *Ophrys*-Arten der Süd- und Osttürkei, Teil 2. Jour. Eur. Orch. 30: 81-156.

KREUTZ, C.A.J. & P. SCRATON (2002): Contributions to the Orchids of Cyprus. Journ. Eur. Orch. 34 (4): 813-822.

KREUTZ, C.A.J. & P. SCRATON (2003): Contributions to the Orchids of Cyprus. The Hardy Orchid Society Newsletter 28: 11-15.

KREUTZ, C.A.J., M. SEGERS & H. WALRAVEN (2002): Contributions to the *Ophrys mammosa*-Group of Cyprus, *Ophrys alasiatica* C.A.J. KREUTZ, SEGERS & H. WALRAVEN spec. nov. Journ. Eur. Orch. 34 (3): 463-492.

LANDWEHR, J. (1977): Wilde Orchideeën van Europa 1 & 2. Vereniging tot Behoud van Natuurmonumenten in Nederland, 's-Graveland.

LIEBISCH, W., PIEPER, R., RYSY, W. & H.W. ZAISS (1984): Fundmeldungen aus Zypern – Ergebnisse einer Orchideen-Exkursion in den südlichen Teil Zyperns vom 14.03.-28.03.1980. Ber. Arbeitskr. Heim. Orch. 1 (2): 164-166.

LINDBERG, H. (1942): En Botanisk Resa Till Cypern 1939. Societatis Scientiarum Fennicae, Arsbok-XX, Helsingfors.

LINDBERG, H. (1946): Iter Cyprium. Acta Societatis Scientiarum Fennicae, N.S.B. Tom. II, Helsingfors.

MAURIÈRES, A. (1983): Hypothese sur les origines de l'*Ophrys attica*. l'Orchidophile 14 (57): 410-411.

MEGAW, E & R.D. MEIKLE (1973): Wild flowers of Cyprus. London

MEIKLE, R.D. (1977): Flora of Cyprus 1. Edinburgh, London, Melbourne.

MEIKLE, R.D. (1985): Flora of Cyprus 2. Edinburgh, London, Melbourne.

MILLOT, H. & P. (1984): Voyage de la S.F.O. à Chypre du 24 mars au 6 avril 1984. l'Orchidophile, 15 (64): 715-727.

MORSCHEK, K. (1989): Ist Nord-Zypern eine Reise wert? Ber. Arbeitskr. Heim. Orch. 6 (2): 37-40.

MORSCHEK, G. & K. (1996): Orchids of Cyprus/Zyperns Orchideen. Selbstverlag, Moers.

MOUTERDE, P. (1966a): Nouvelle Flore de Liban et de la Syrie, tome 1, LII-LXXXII. Beyrouth.

MOUTERDE, P. (1966b): Nouvelle Flore de Liban et de la Syrie, tome 1, 322-346. Beyrouth.

MOYSICH, F. & I. (1984): Beitrag zur Kenntnis der Orchideenverbreitung im südlichen Zypern. Ber. Arbeitskr. Heim. Orch. 1 (2): 147-160.

NANNFELDT, I.A. (1946): Tre för Norden nya Epipactis-arter, *E. persica* HAUSSKN. *E. leptochila* (GODF.) GODF. och *E. purpurata* SM. Bot. Not.: 1-28. Lund.

NELSON, E. (1962): Gestaltwandel und Artbildung, erörtert am Beispiel der Orchidaceen Europas und der Mittelmeerländer insbesondere der Gattung *Ophrys* mit einer Monographie und Iconographie der Gattung *Ophrys*. Verlag E. Nelson, Chernex-Montreux.

NELSON, E. (1968): Monographie und Iconographie der Orchidaceen-Gattungen *Serapias, Aceras, Loroglossum, Barlia*. Verlag E. Nelson, Chernex-Montreux.

NELSON, E. (1976): Monographie und Ikonographie der Orchidaceen-Gattung *Dactylorhiza*. Verlag E. Nelson, Chernex-Montreux.

NELSON, E. (2001): Die Gattung *Orchis*. Stiftung Dr. h.c. ERICH NELSON, Zürich.

NEVSKI, S.A. (1968), *Orchidaceae* In: V.L. KOMAROV, ed., Flora USSR, volume 4, 589-730, 751-754; English translation, volume 4, 448-554, 571-575.

OSORIO-TAFALL, B.F. & G.M. SERAPHIM (1973): List of the Vascular Plants of Cyprus. Ministry of Agriculture and Natural Resources, Lefkosia.

PANTELAS, V., T. PARACHRISTOPHOROU & P. CHRISTODOULOU (1983): Cyprus flora in colour: The endemics. Zypern.

PAULUS, H.F. (1994): Untersuchungen am *Ophrys cretica*-Komplex mit Beschreibung von *Ophrys ariadnae* H.F. Paulus spec. nov (Orchidaceae). Jour. Eur. Orch. 26 (3/4): 629-643.

PAULUS, H.F. (1998): Der *Ophrys fusca* s. str. Komplex auf Kreta und anderer Ägäisinseln mit Beschreibungen von *O. blitopertha, O. creberrima, O. cinereophila, O. cressa, O. thriptiensis* und *O. creticola* ssp. nov. (Orchidaceae). Jour. Eur. Orch. 30 (1): 157-201.

PAULUS, H.F. (2001a): Material zu einer Revision des *Ophrys fusca* s.str Artenkreises. 1. – *Ophrys nigroaenea-fusca, O. colletes-fusca, O. flavipes-fusca, O. funerea, O. forestieri* oder was ist die typische *Ophrys fusca* Link 1799 (Orchidaceae). Jour. Eur. Orch. 33 (1): 121-177.

PAULUS, H.F. (2001b): Daten zur Bestäubungsbiologie und Systematik der Gattung *Ophrys* in Rhodos (Griechenland) mit Beschreibung von *Ophrys parvula, Ophrys persephonae, Ophrys lindia, Ophrys eptapigiensis* spec. nov. aus der *Ophrys fusca* s.str. Gruppe und *Ophrys cornutula* spec. nov. aus der *Ophrys oestrifera*-Gruppe (Orchidaceae und Insecta, Apoidea). Ber. Arbeitskrs. Heim. Orch. 18 (1): 38-81.

PAULUS, H.F. (2001c). *Andrena paucisquama*-Männchen als Bestäuber der Sexualtäuschblume *Ophrys aesculapii* Renz 1928 (Orchidaceae; Insecta, Apoidea: Andrenidae). Ber. Arbeitskr. Heim. Orch. 18: 4-10.

PAULUS, H. F. & C. A. ALIBERTIS (1990): *Ophrys mesaritica* H. F. PAULUS und C. & A. ALIBERTIS spec. nov. aus Kreta, eine neue Art aus dem *Ophrys fusca-iricolor*-Artenkreis. Mitt. Bl. Arbeitskr. Heim. Orch. Baden-Württ. 22 (4): 772-787.

PAULUS, H.F. & C. GACK (1986): Neue Befunde zur Pseudokopulation und Bestäuberspezifität in der Orchideengattung *Ophrys* – Untersuchungen in Kreta, Süditalien und Israel. Jahresber. Naturw. Verein Wuppertal 39: 48-86.

PAULUS, H.F. & C. GACK (1990a): Pollination of *Ophrys* (Orchidaceae) in Cyprus. Plant Syst. Evol. 169: 177-207.

PAULUS, H.F. & C. GACK (1990b): Pollinators as prepollinating isolation factors: Evolution and speciation in *Ophrys* (Orchidaceae). Israel Journal of Botany 39: 43-79.

PAULUS, H.F. & C. GACK (1990c): Untersuchungen zur Pseudokopulation und Bestäuberspezifität in der Gattung *Ophrys* im östlichen Mittelmeergebiet (Orchidaceae, Hymenoptera, Apoidea). Jahresb. Naturwiss. Ver. Wuppertal 43: 80-118.

PEDERSEN, H.A. & N. FAURHOLDT (1997). Beiträge zur Orchideenflora der ostmediterranen Inseln Rhodos und Zypern. Die Orchidee 48 (6): 232-236.

PEDERSEN, H.A. & N. FAURHOLDT (2002). *Ophrys* – Versuchsweise Definitionen der Kategorien Art, Unterart und Varietät in der Gattung und einige daraus resultierende taxonomische Änderungen. Die Orchidee 53 (3): 341-346.

PERKO, M.L. (2004): Die Orchideen Kärntens. Kärntner Druck- und Verlagsgesellschaft m.b.H.

PETER, R. (1989): Ergänzungen zur Orchideenflora von Rhodos. Mitt. Bl. Arbeitskr. Heim. Orch. Baden-Württ. 21 (2): 279-350.

PLITMANN, U., HEYN, C.C., DANIN, A., SHMIDA, A. & D. DAROM (1982): Pictural flora of Israel: 267

POST, G.E. (1896): Flora of Syria, Palestine and Sinai, 753-766. The American Press, Beirut, Syria.

POST, G.E. (1900): Plantae Postianae, Fasciculus X. Mémoires de l'Herbier Boissier 18: 100.

POST, G.E. & J.E. DINSMORE (1933): Flora of Syria, Palestine and Sinai, 2nd edition, volume 2: 559-582. American Press, Beirut.

PRIDGEON, A. M, R. M. BATEMAN, A. V. COX, J. R. HAPEMAN & M. W. CHASE (1997): Polygenetics of subtribe Orchidinae (*Orchidoiceae, Orchidaceae*) based on nuclear ITS sequences. 1. Intergeneric relationships and polyphyly of *Orchis sensu lato*. Lindleyana 12 (2): 89-109.

QUENTIN, P. (1995): Synopsis des Orchidées Européennes. Edition no. 2 revue et corrigée. Cahiers de la Société Française d'Orchidophile 2: 1-141.

RECHINGER, K.H. (1929): Beitrag zur Kenntnis der Flora der Ägäischen Inseln und Ostgriechenland. Ann. Naturhist. Mus. Wien 43: 269-340.

REICHENBACH, H.G. fil., (1851): Deutschlands Flora als Beleg für die Flora Germanica Excursoria, Die Orchideen 13, Leipzig.

REICHENBACH H.G. fil., (1851): Orchidae in Flora Germanica Recensitae-Tentamen Orchidiographie Europaeae. Lipsiae.

RENZ, J. (1928): Zur Kenntnis der griechischen Orchideen. Repert. Spec. Nov. Regni Veg. 25 (19-26): 225-270.

RENZ, J. (1929): Über neue Orchideen von Rhodos, Cypern und Syrien. Repert. Spec. Nov. Regni Veg. 27 (1-3): 193-222.

RENZ, J. (1943): Orchidaceae. In: K.H. RECHINGER, Flora Aegaea, Denkschr. Akad. Wiss. Wien, Math.-Nat. Kl. 105 (1): 809-845.

RENZ, J. (1976): Die Gattung *Ophrys* an der Ostgrenze ihres Areals. Jahresber. des Naturwiss. Ver. Wuppertal 29: 70-77.

RENZ, J. (1978): Orchidaceae. – In: RECHINGER (ed.), K. H., Flora Iranica: 126. Flora des iranischen Hochlandes und der umrahmenden Gebirge Persiens, Afghanistans, Teile von West-Pakistan, Nord-Irak, Azerbaidjan, Turkmenistan. Akademische Druck- und Verlagsanstalt Graz-Austria.

RENZ, J. & G. TAUBENHEIM (1983): Materials for a flora of Turkey XXXIX: *Orchidaceae*. Notes Roy. Bot. Garden 41 (2): 269-277. Edinburgh.

RENZ, J. & G. TAUBENHEIM (1984): Orchidaceae. In: P.H. DAVIS, Flora of Turkey and the East Aegean Islands 8: 450-552, 587-599. Edinburgh.

RIECHELMANN, A. (1998): *Ophrys* x*denglerensis* – eine neue *Ophrys*-Hybride von Nord-Zypern. Ber. Arbeitskr. Heim. Orch. 15 (1): 57-61.

ROBATSCH, K. (1980): Beiträge zur Verbreitung und Taxonomie der zyprischen Bergorchideen. Die Orchidee 31 (5): 195-200.

RÜCKBRODT, D. & U. (1990): *Ophrys transhyrcana* CZERNIAK., Neufund für Rhodos. Mitt. Bl. Arbeitskr. Heim. Orch. Baden-Württ. 22 (4): 736-739.

RÜCKBRODT, D. & U. (1998): Bemerkungen zur Verbreitung der Orchideen im südlichen Kaukasus. Jahresber. Naturw. Ver. Wuppertal 51: 13-22.

RÜCKBRODT, D. & U. (2001): Über einige Typusexemplare im Herbarium des Botanischen Instituts der Akademie der Wissenschaften von Russland in St. Petersburg aus dem Kaukasus und angrenzenden Gebieten (Gattung *Ophrys*). Ber. Arbeitskr. Heim. Orch. 18 (2): 107-123.

RÜCKBRODT, D. & U., GÜGEL, E. & H.W. ZAISS (1997): Orchideen-Exkursionen in die Kaukasusländer Aserbaidschan und Georgien. Ber. Arbeitskr. Heim. Orch. 14 (1): 4-40.

RÜCKBRODT, U. & D. und K. & R.-B. HANSEN (1992): Bemerkungen zu den in der Türkei vorkommenden Orchideenarten und ihrer Verbreitung. Ber. Arbeitskrs. Heim. Orch. 9 (1): 4-103, 161-176 (66 Abb.).

SCHÄFER, P.A. (1971): Vorläufiger Beitrag zur Orchis laxiflora-Gruppe. Die Orchidee 22 (5): 200-205.

SCHLECHTER, R. (1918): Mitteilungen über einige europäische und mediterrane Orchideen 1 (Die Gattungen Aceras, Himantoglossum und Anacamptis). Repert. Spec. Nov. Regni Veg. 15 (18/19): 273-290. Berlin.

SCHÖNFELDER, M. & H. (2001): Orchideen im Libanon. Ber. Arbeitskr. Heim. Orch. 18 (2): 64-88.

SCRATON, P. (2001): Re-discovery of Orchis papilionacea in The Republic of Cyprus. Journ. Eur. Orch. 33 (3): 926.

SCRATON, P. (2002): Re-discovery of Anacamptis papilionacea in the Republic of Cyprus 2001. The Hardy Orchid Society Newsletter 24: 14.

SEEGERS, M. & H. WALRAVEN (2002): Ophrys xlefkarensis SEGERS & WALRAVEN nothosp. nat. nov.; a new hybrid of Ophrys alasiatica C.A.J. KREUTZ, SEGERS & WALRAVEN and Ophrys umbilicata Desf. Journ. Eur. Orch. 34 (4): 807-812.

SENGHAS, K.-H. (1968): Taxonomische Übersicht der Gattung Dactylorhiza NECKER ex NEVSKI. Jahresb. Naturwiss. Ver. Wuppertal 21/22: 32-67.

SHIFMAN, A. (1989): The Wild Orchids of Israel. Jerusalem.

SINGER, R. (1996): Ophrys kotschyi auch im Westen von Zypern? Jour. Eur. Orch. 28 (1): i.

SINTENIS, P. (1881-1882): Cypern und seine Flora. Österr. Bot. Zeitschr. 31-32. Wien.

SOÓ, R. v. (1927): Orchideae novae europeae et mediterraneae. Repert. Spec. Nov. Regni Veg. 24: 25-37.

SOÓ, R. v. (1929): Revision der Orchideen Südosteuropas und Südwestasiens. Bot. Arch. 23: 1-196. Leipzig.

SOÓ, R. v. (1932): Die Orchideen Europas und des Mittelmeergebietes. Die Pflanzenareale 3 (7): 73-81. Jena.

SOÓ, R. v. (1959): Ophrys-Studien, Acta Bot. Acad. Sci. Hung. 5: 437-471.

SOÓ, R. v. (1969): Nomina Nova Generis Dactylorhiza. 1-11. Budapest.

SOÓ, R. v. (1970): Species and subspecies of the genus Ophrys, Acta Bot. Acad. Sci. Hung. 16: 373-392.

SOÓ, R. v. (1972): Die Arten und Unterarten der Gattung Orchis s. str. Jahresb. Naturwiss. Ver. Wuppertal 25: 37-48.

SOUCHE, R. (2004): Les Orchidées sauvages de France. Grandeur Nature des Créations du Pélican, Editions VILO.

STEWART, J. (1992): The conservation of European orchids. Nature and environment 57: 1-64. Council of Europe Press.

STRACK, D., E. BUSCH & E. KLEIN (1989): Anthocyanin patterns in European orchids and their taxonomic and phylogenetic relevance. Phytochemistry 28 (8): 2127-2139.

STRÖHLE, W. (2003): Nomenklatorische Liste der europäischen Orchideentaxa – Arten und Unterarten. Jour. Eur. Orch. 35 (4): 771-860.

SUNDERMANN, H. (1964): Zum Problem der Artabgrenzung innerhalb der Gattung Ophrys. Jahresb. Naturwiss. Ver. Wuppertal 19: 9-17.

SUNDERMANN, H. (1969a): Über einige ostmediterrane Orchideen. Die Orchidee 20 (2): 79-83.

SUNDERMANN, H. (1969b): Die Orchideen im südwestlichen Kleinasien. Die Orchidee 20 (6): 309-317.

SUNDERMANN, H. (1972a): Ergänzungen zum Verbreitungsgebiet einiger Orchideenarten. Die Orchidee 23 (5): 211.

SUNDERMANN, H. (1972b): Die spezifisch ostmediterranen Arten der Gattung Orchis. Jahresb. Naturwiss. Ver. Wuppertal 25: 59-60.

SUNDERMANN, H. (1975): Europäische und mediterrane Orchideen. Eine Bestimmungsflora. ed. 2. Hildesheim.

SUNDERMANN, H. (1980): Europäische und mediterrane Orchideen. Eine Bestimmungsflora mit Berücksichtigung der Ökologie, 3. Auflage. Brücke Verlag Kurt Schmersow, Hildesheim.

SUNDERMANN, H. & G. TAUBENHEIM (1978): Die Verbreitung der Orchideen in der Türkei I. Die Orchidee 29: 172-179.

SUNDERMANN, H. & G. TAUBENHEIM (1981a): Die Verbreitung der Orchideen in der Türkei II/1. Ein Beitrag zur 'Flora of Turkey': 2. Die Gattung Serapias L. Die Orchidee 32 (5): 202-207.

SUNDERMANN, H. & G. TAUBENHEIM (1981b): Die Verbreitung der Orchideen in der Türkei II/1. Ein Beitrag zur 'Flora of Turkey': 2. Die Gattung Serapias L. Die Orchidee 32 (6): 214-219.

TAUBENHEIM, G. (1977): Die Verbreitung der Gattung Epipactis in der Türkei. Sonderheft Die Orchidee.

TAUBENHEIM, G. & H. SUNDERMANN (1974): Epipactis-Arten in Kleinasien. Die Orchidee 25 (1): 7-13.

THOMPSON, H.S. (1906): The flora of Cyprus. Journal of Botany 44: 338-339.

TUTIN, T.G., V.H. HEYWOOD, N.A. BURGES, D.M. MOORE, D.H. VALENTINE, S.M. WALTERS & D.A. WEBB (1980): Flora Europaea 5: 325-350. Cambridge University Press, Cambridge.

UNGER, F. & TH. KOTSCHY (1865): Die Insel Zypern, ihrer physischen und organischen Natur nach, mit Rücksicht auf ihre frühere Gestalt. Braumüller, Wien.

VASLET, D. (1984): Serapias parviflora Parl. à Chypre. l'Orchidophile 15 (63): 668.

VERMEULEN, P. (1972): Übersicht zur Systematik und Taxonomie der Gattung Orchis s. str. Jahresb. Naturwiss. Ver. Wuppertal 25: 22-36.

VINEY, D.E. (1994, 1996): An illustrated flora of North Cyprus. Koeltz Scientific Books, Königstein, Germany.

VÖTH, W. (1967): Ophrys bombyliflora auf Rhodos. Die Orchidee 18 (2): 58-60.

VÖTH, W. (1980): Können Serapiasblüten Nesttäuschblumen sein? Die Orchidee 31 (2): 159-162.

WALTMANN, H. (2003): Orchideen auf Zypern, auf der Insel der Aphrodite. Die Orchidee 54 (5): 542-544.

WILDHABER, J. W. (1976): Samenstruktur von Epipactis condensata, E. persica und E. pontica. Jahresb. Naturwiss. Ver. Wuppertal 29: 153-154.

WILLING, B. & E. (1975): Diskussionsbeiträge zur Orchideenflora Zyperns 1. Die Orchidee 26 (2): 74-79.

WILLING, B. & E. (1976): Diskussionsbeiträge zur Orchideenflora Zyperns 2. Die Orchidee 27 (3): 112-116.

WILLING, B. & E. (1979): Optima-Projekt 'Kartierung der mediterranen Orchideen'. Beih. Veröff. Naturschutz Landschaftspflege Baden-Württemberg 14: 1-163.

WOOD, J.J. (1980): Beitrag zur Orchideenflora von Zypern: Die Unterarten von Ophrys sphegodes Mill. in Zypern und dem östlichen Mittelmeerraum. Die Orchidee 31 (2): 228-235.

WOOD, J.J. (1980): Contributions to the orchid flora of Cyprus. Orchid Review 88: 121-122.

WOOD, J.J. (1981): Contributions to the orchid flora of Cyprus, The Subspecies of Ophrys sphegodes Mill. in Cyprus and the Eastern Mediterranean. Orchid Review 89: 292-299.

WOOD, J.J. (1985): Orchidaceae In: R.D. MEIKLE, Flora of Cyprus, volume 2, 1511-1535.

YOUNG, D.P. (1970): Notizen über einige südwestasiatische Epipactis-Arten. – Jahresb. Naturwiss. Ver. Wuppertal 23: 106-108.

ZIER, L. (1973): Ragwurzblüte und Vogelzug auf Zypern. In: Streifzüge durch Naturparadiese in Europa: 144-153. DRW Verlag Stuttgart.

Danksagung

Herzlich danken möchte ich:

– Herrn Dr. CHR. F. GEMBARDT (Weinheim-Hohensachsen, D) und Herrn H.W.E. VAN BRUGGEN (Amersfoort, NL) für die kritische Durchsicht des Manuskriptes,

– Herrn Dr. H. KRETZSCHMAR (Bad Hersfeld, D) für die Hilfe bei der Herstellung der UTM-Rasterverbreitungskarten von Zypern und seine Unterstützung beim EDV-Kartierungsprogramm INKA,

– Herrn Dr. Y. CHRISTOFIDES (Platres, Cy), Herrn N.A. VAN DER CINGEL (Paterswolde, NL), Herrn R. CONSTANTINIDES (Lefkosia, Cy), Herrn P. DELFORGE (Rhode St.-Genèse, B), Herrn W. ERRULAT (Solingen, D), Frau A. GÖTHGEN (Kirke Hyllinge, DK), Frau J. HUBBARD (Pafos, Cy), Herrn C. KOCH (Vordingborg, DK), Herrn Dr. H. KRETZSCHMAR (Bad Hersfeld, D), Herrn Prof. Dr. H.F. PAULUS (Wien) und Herrn Y. KULYEV (Lemesos, Cy) für das zur Verfügungstellen von Bildmaterial,

– Herrn R. SINNEMA (Sittard, NL) für die Übersetzung ins Englische und Frau P. SCRATON (Akrounta, Cy) für die Korrekturlesung des englischen Textes,

– der ARBEITSGRUPPE NIEDERLÄNDISCHER ORCHIDEEN (W.E.O., Vogelenzang, NL), Herrn. P. BREDEROO (Leiden, NL), Herrn N.A. VAN DER CINGEL (Paterswolde, NL), Herrn E. VAN DOMMELEN (Rijswijk, NL),), Herrn Dr. CHR. F. GEMBARDT (Weinheim-Hohensachsen, D), Herrn und Frau J. & L. ESSINK (Elp, NL), Herrn J. JONKER (Lippenhuizen, NL), Herrn J. REUVERS (Schiedam, NL), Herrn R. SCHOT (Amersfoort), Herrn J. VAN DER STRAATEN (Tilburg, NL) und Herrn J. VERBURGH (Deventer, NL) für ihre finanzielle Unterstützung um dieses Buch zu publizieren.

Die Herausgabe dieses Buches wäre nicht möglich gewesen, ohne die Verwendung einer großen Anzahl von bisher unveröffentlichten Fundlisten und Reiseberichten, die ich von vielen Orchideenfreunden persönlich erhalten habe. Durch ihre Mitwirkung konnte ich viele Standorte auf Zypern untersuchen und die Verbreitungskarten dementsprechend erweitern. Folgenden Orchideenfreunden bin ich deshalb zu besonderem Dank verpflichtet:

M. & M. Ackermann (Wuppertal, D), B. Apitz (Ehingen, D), R. Baudisch (Coburg, D), H. Baum (Endersbach, D), H. Baumgartner (Kehl-Kork, D), Prof. M. Bayer (Stuttgart, D), C.J. van den Berg (Wijhe, NL), M. van den Berg (NL), Dr. H. & B. Binder (Kulmbach, D), Dr. F. Blaschke (Witten, D), J. Bol (Enschede, NL), P. Brederoo (Leiden, NL), Dr. R. & E. Breiner (Neusäss, D), Dr. Y. Christofides (Platres, Cy), N.A. van der Cingel (Paterswolde, NL), R. Constantinides (Lefkosia, Cy), J. & P. Davies (Bath, UK), H. Dekker (Hoogeveen, NL), P. Delforge (Rhode St.-Genèse, B), H. Dengler (Ebermannstadt, D), H. Dostmann (Seelze), T. Dübendorfer (Bassersdorf, CH), Prof. Dr. W. Eccarius (Eisenach, D), M. Engeli-Strasser (Meisterschwanden, CH), S. Erhardt (Illertissen, D), W. Errulat (Solingen, D), J. & L. Essink (Elp, NL), D.M.T. Ettlinger (Dorking, UK), U. Forst (D), H. Fredriks (Haarlem, NL), Dr. Chr. F. Gembardt (Weinheim-Hohensachsen, D), E. Gügel (München, D), Dr. R. Gumprecht (Freiburg, D), G. Halx (Wörth/Donau, D), K. & R.-B. Hansen (Mössingen, D), K. Heise (Bebra ,D), H. Hertel (D), S. Hertel (Haag, D), K. Heubel (D), W. Hiller (Göppingen, D), H.-F. Hoffmann (München, D), J. Hubbard (Pafos, Cy), H. Jansen (Essen, D), W.D. Jansen (Amsterdam, NL), Dr. J. Jersakova (Çeske Budejovice, CZ), E. Kajan (Duisburg, D), M. Kalteisen (Ulm, D), C. Keitel (Ellwangen, D), J. Ketelaar (Bussum, NL), Dr. W. & O. Kleinlein (Fürth, D), J. Kleynen

Weiterhin möchte ich nicht versäumen, allen Personen und Institutionen, die in irgendeiner Form zum Gelingen dieses Buches beigetragen haben, für ihre Unterstützung zu danken.

Acknowledgements

I would like to thank:

– Mr Dr. CHR. F. GEMBARDT (Weinheim-Hohensachsen, D) and Mr H.W.E. VAN BRUGGEN (Amersfoort, NL) for meticulously looking over the manuscripts,

– Mr Dr. H. KRETZSCHMAR (Bad Hersfeld, D) for his help in making the UTM-grid distribution maps of Cyprus and for his support with the EDV-charting program INKA,

– Mr Dr. Y. CHRISTOFIDES (Platres, Cy), Mr N.A. VAN DER CINGEL (Paterswolde, NL), Mr R. CONSTANTINIDES (Lefkosia, Cy), Mr P. DELFORGE (Rhode St.-Genèse, B), Mr W. ERRULAT (Solingen, D), Mrs A. GÖTHGEN (Kirke Hyllinge, DK), Ms J. HUBBARD (Pafos, Cy), Mr C. KOCH (Vordingborg, DK), Mr Dr. H. KRETZSCHMAR (Bad Hersfeld, D), Mr Prof. Dr. H.F. PAULUS (Vienna) and Mr Y. KULYEV (Lemesos, Cy) for providing photographic images,

– Mr R. SINNEMA (Sittard, NL) for translating the German manuscript into English and Mrs P. SCRATON (Akrounta, Cy) for meticulously checking the English translation,

– The ARBEITSGRUPPE NIEDERLÄNDISCHER ORCHIDEEN (W.E.O., Vogelenzang, NL), Mr P. BREDEROO (Leiden, NL), Mr N.A. VAN DER CINGEL (Paterswolde, NL), Mr E. VAN DOMMELEN (Rijswijk, NL),), Mr Dr. CHR. F. GEMBARDT (Weinheim-Hohensachsen, D), Mr J. & Mrs L. ESSINK (Elp, NL), Mr J. JONKER (Lippenhuizen, NL), Mr J. REUVERS (Schiedam, NL), Mr R. SCHOT (Amersfoort), Mr J. VAN DER STRAATEN (Tilburg, NL) and Mr J. VERBURGH (Deventer, NL) for their financial support, without which this book would not have been possible.

The publication of this book would also not have been possible without the use of a large number of until now unpublished location lists and travel accounts, which I received personally from many orchidophiles. With their contributions I was able to examine many habitats on Cyprus, and was therefore able to complement the distribution maps accordingly. I therefore owe my special thanks to the following orchidophiles:

(Bunde, NL), C. KOCH (Vordingborg, DK), E. Kongshaug (Tiller, N), Dr. M. Kraft (D), Dr. H. Kretzschmar (Bad Hersfeld, D), Dr. D. Krey (Neumünster, D), H. Läpple (Rastatt, D), W. Liebisch (Erlangen, D), M.R. Lowe (Durham, UK), W. Lüders (Hersberg, D), W. Matterne (Nürtingen-Reudern, D), H. Mayer (Wien, A), A. Michel (Bern, CH), P. & H. Millot (F), P. Molenaar (Amersfoort, NL), G. & K. Morschek (Moers, D), H. Neumann (Koblenz, D), L. & U. Ney (Wiesbaden, D), M. Perko (Klagenfurt, AU), R. Peter (Olten, CH), M. Peterek (Hameln, D), R. Pieper (D), R. Poot (Vlaardingen, NL), H. Rauschenberger (Ulm, D), H.R. Reinhard (Zürich, CH), W. Remm (Niederstotzingen, D), A. & A. Riechelmann (Forchheim, D), K. Robatsch (Klagenfurt, AU), A. & E. Robertz (Viersen, D), D. & U. Rückbrodt (Lampertheim, D), Dr. W. Rysy (Erlangen-Bruck, D), H.-E. Salkowski (Vallendar, D), K. U. Sarg (Selm, D), M. Schmidt (Wuppertal, D), W. Schmidt (Reutlingen, D), P. Scraton (Akrounta, Cy), W. Seiz (Zierenberg, D), N. Sischka (Germersheim, D), J. Smitak (Brno, CZ), Dr. W. Stern (Hannover, D), Prof. Dr. H. Sundermann (Wuppertal, D), M.-L. Taubald (Wuppertal, D), D. Vaslet (Argentan, F), W. Vöth (Wien, A), K. Wagner (Braunschweig, D), M. & R. Wagner (Niederhausen-Reisbach, D), H. Walraven (Rijswijk, NL), Dr. W. Werner (Darmstadt, D), Prof. Dr. B. & E. Willing (Berlin, D) und H.-W. Zaiss (Marloffstein, D).

Furthermore, I would like to thank all institutes and people who have participated in any way in the making of this book, for their support.

413

Werkgroep Europese Orchideeën v.d. KNNV (W.E.O.)

Der niederländische Arbeitskreis Europäische Orchideen ist einer der spezialisierten Arbeitskreise des 'Königlichen Niederländischen Naturhistorischen Vereins' (KNNV). Der KNNV ist der allgemeine Naturhistorische Verein in den Niederlanden.

Mitglied des Arbeitskreises kann werden, wer über gute Kenntnisse der europäischen Orchideen verfügt und bereit ist, sich aktiv für die Ziele des Arbeitskreises – Erforschung und Schutz der europäischen Orchideen und deren Biotope – einzusetzen. Im Augenblick zählt der Arbeitskreis etwa 110 Mitglieder. Von allen Mitgliedern wird erwartet, dass sie sich auf irgendeine Weise aktiv mit den europäischen Orchideen beschäftigen: Kartierung oder Inventarisierung, Arten- und Biotopforschung, Pflegemaßnahmen oder ein Beitrag zu den Veranstaltungen. Die Daten, die die Mitglieder bei ihren Tätigkeiten sammeln, werden den in Frage kommenden Instanzen zur Verfügung gestellt.

Zweimal im Jahr findet eine ganztägige Versammlung statt. Es gibt Vorträge und allerlei, was sich auf die europäischen Orchideen bezieht, kann zur Sprache kommen; neu erschienene Literatur wird besprochen und liegt oft zur Einsicht vor. Die meisten Vorträge werden von den eigenen Mitgliedern gehalten (wir bilden einen *Arbeits*kreis), aber gelegentlich gibt es auch Gastredner. Von allen Vorträgen werden Berichte abgefasst, die die Mitglieder nach einiger Zeit per Post oder E-Mail zugeschickt bekommen.

Der Arbeitskreis hat im September 1992 das internationale Symposium Eurorchis 92 in Nijmegen veranstaltet. Das Symposium wurde von 123 Teilnehmern aus 7 Ländern besucht.

Der Arbeitskreis verfügt über eine kleine Bibliothek, aus der sich die Mitglieder gegen Zahlung der Versandkosten Bücher und Zeitschriften leihen oder Kopien von Artikeln anfertigen lassen können. Der Arbeitskreis unterhält einen Schriftentausch, u.a. mit deutschen und belgischen Zeitschriften.

Seit Februar 1989 gibt der Arbeitskreis die eigene Zeitschrift Eurorchis heraus, die einmal im Jahr in einem Umfang von etwa 120 Seiten erscheint. Auch Nichtmitglieder können Eurorchis bestellen.

Auf der Internetseite des Arbeitskreises findet man mehr Informationen und die Mitgliedschaft, über Eurorchis und die Bezugsmöglichkeiten (auch auf Deutsch) und über europäische Orchideen. Die Internet-Adresse lautet: www.knnv.nl/europorchidwg/ index.html.

Anschrift/Address:
Werkgroep Europese Orchideeën v.d. KNNV
Gravin Adahof 1
NL-2114 DW Vogelenzang
europorchidwg@knnv.nl

Research group European Orchids of the KNNV (W.E.O.)

The Dutch research group European Orchids is one of the most specialized of the 'Royal Dutch Society for Study of Wildlife' (KNNV). The KNNV is the general natural history society of the Netherlands.

Those who would like to be a member of the research group, need a well-rounded knowledge of European orchids, and should be willing to commit themselves actively to the goals of the research group-research and conservation of European orchids and their biotopes. At the moment the group has 110 members. It is expected of all members that they occupy themselves actively in any manner possible with European orchids: charting or inventory, species and biotope research, support or participation in activities. Dates on which members gather for these activities are supplied to eligible institutions.

Twice a year, a full-time meeting takes place. Lectures are held, and all issues concerning European orchids can be brought up; newly published literature is discussed and is often available for viewing. Most lectures are given by members, but occassionally guest speakers are invited. Reports are written of all lectures, and sent to members by mail or e-mail.

The research group held the International Symposium Eurorchis 92 in Nijmegen in September 1992. This symposium was attended by 123 participants from 7 countries.

The group also possesses a small library, from which members can borrow books and magazines, against payment of shipping and handling, or have copies made of articles. The research group also maintains an exchange of periodicals, amongst others of German and Belgian magazines.

The research group has published its own magazine Eurorchis since February 1989, which is issued once a year and contains 120 pages. Non-members can also order Eurorchis.

More information on the research group European Orchids and membership, on Eurorchis and methods of obtaining it (also in German), and information on European orchids can be found on the internet page of the research group. The internet adress is www.knnv.nl/europorchidwg/index.html

Ophrys morio H.F. Paulus & Kreutz, spec nov.

Diagnosis

Planta robusta 25-70 cm alta. Inflorescence laxus, 8-20 flores, distributio praeter duae partes racemi; Sepala laterales pallide viridia parte dimidio inferiore pauci usque ad rubro-brunea-rubida. Labellum integrum (rarum) vel trilobatum vel ad crassum trilobatum, Ø 14,2 mm longum, Ø 12,5 mm latum, in locus tuberculi mammae. Labellum forma rotundum vel ovatum; mammae brevis, latae elongatus acutus. Color labelli fuscus vel rubro-bruneum, area basalis flavo-bruneo. Columna rostrata (0,9-4 mm). Floret ab initium Februarii usque ad finis Martii. Pollinator *Andrena morio*.

Holotypus

Cyprus meridianus, regio Pafos-Larnaka, ad occidentem vergens Malia via Dora, ca. 600 m altitudine, 9.3.1986, leg. H.F. Paulus, una flora in temetum, in coll. Biozentrum Vindobona.

Beschreibung

Kräftige und hochwüchsige Pflanze, 30 bis 70 cm hoch. Blütenstand langgestreckt und sehr locker, 8- bis 20-blütig, die Blüten meist über eine Länge von zwei Dritteln am Stängel verteilt. Tragblätter lanzettlich, meist länger als der Fruchtknoten. Seitliche **Sepalen** meist auffällig kräftig zweifarbig, im oberen Teil grünlich, im unteren Teil rötlich bis dunkelpurpurn gefärbt, abstehend bis rückwärts gerichtet, lanzettlich, 12,2-15,6 (Ø 13,6 σ = 0,43) mm lang, 4,7-7,7 (Ø 5,6 σ = 0,29) mm breit. **Petalen** eiförmig-lanzettlich bis meist lang dreieckig, grünlich bis meist purpurn, am Rande leicht gewellt, 8,2-11,5 (Ø 9,7 σ = 0,28) mm lang, 2,5-3,4 (Ø 2,9 σ = 0,21) mm breit. **Lippe** rundlich, breit oder ziemlich lang bis breit-eiförmig, ganzrandig (selten) oder häufiger leicht dreilappig oder sogar stark dreilappig, konvex gewölbt, schwach oder selten ungehöckert, die Höcker breit, fast länglich-brettförmig verrundet. dunkelbraun bis rötlichbraun, am Rande dicht purpurn behaart. Labellumlänge 13,6-15,2 (Ø 14,2 σ = 1,47) mm, Labellumbreite im Bereich der Höcker 11,2-13,8 (Ø 12,5 σ = 0,98) mm; Ähnlich wie bei *Ophrys alasiatica* Lippe mit einem in der Regel hellbraunen Basalfeld, das sich farblich von der dunkleren Lippe absetzt; bei *Ophrys mammosa* und *Ophrys transhyrcana* ist dies stets ganz dunkel bis schwarz. Mal aus zwei parallelen Streifen bestehend oder H-förmig, diese Streifen meistens bläulich bis purpurn. Narbenkopf ähnlich wie bei *Ophrys mammosa* eingeschnürt, von der Lippe abgesetzt, rundlich, max. Außenbreite 5,7-6,6 (Ø 6,1 σ = 0,57) mm, basale Breite am Labellum 4,2-4,7 (Ø 4,3 σ = 0,49) mm. Konnektivfortsatz lang bis sehr lang (1,1-3,9 mm) und zugespitzt. Anhängsel klein und spitz, gelblich, abwärts gerichtet.

Bestäuber

Andrena morio [(*Apoidea, Andrenidae*) (Paulus & Gack 1990ab)].

Holotypus (Foto)

Süd-Zypern, östlich Pafos, 3 km westlich Malia Richtung Dora 9.3.1986, 1 Blüte in 70% Alkohol, leg. H.F. Paulus, in coll. Paulus, Biozentrum Wien.

Blütezeit

Von Anfang Februar bis Ende März, in höheren Lagen länger.

Name

Benannt nach ihrem Bestäuber, der schwarzen Sandbiene *Andrena morio*; morio = Narr.

Gesamtverbreitung

Nach dem heutigen Kenntnisstand nur auf Zypern, vermutlich aber auch in der südlichen Türkei verbreitet. Die Pflanzen der Südtürkei (westlich Antalya und im Raum Adana-Karatepe) blühen allerdings später als *Ophrys mammosa*, so daß die Identität überprüft werden muss.

Ophrys morio (Holotypus), Malia-Dora, 9.3.1986

Verzeichnis der wissenschaftlichen Orchideennamen / Index of scientific orchid names